EXISTENTIAL
METAPHYSICS

EXISTENTIAL METAPHYSICS

by *Alvin Thalheimer*

Copyright, 1960, by
Philosophical Library, Inc.
15 East 40th Street, New York, N.Y.

All rights reserved

Library of Congress Catalog Card Number: 60-15047

Printed in the United States of America

PHILOSOPHICAL LIBRARY
New York

Copyright, 1960, by
Philosophical Library, Inc.
15 East 40th Street, New York, N. Y.

Library of Congress Catalog Card Number: 60-15963

Printed in the United States of America

TABLE OF CONTENTS

PREFACE

Probably every book reaches the reader before it is completely satisfactory to its author. For, despite the changes that suggest themselves at each reading of the manuscript, the point is reached at which it seems probable that further emendations and additions will not warrant the delay in publication which they would involve.

The book before you is, however, in a less finished state than most. Eight of the projected twenty-five chapters appear only as titles in the table of contents. Nevertheless, the guiding principle —the method—has been rather fully developed. And it has been applied to a sufficient number of problems to indicate to the reader what my attitude would in general be with respect to those subjects which I have not had an opportunity to discuss. The listing by titles of the unwritten chapters serves the purpose of pointing to those subjects which in my opinion should have been discussed to make this treatise a well-rounded system of metaphysics.

A second mark of the incompleteness of this treatise is the place left open at the end of Chapter Three, for an enumeration of certain existent and certain non-existent entities. It will be obvious that lists of this sort could only have been developed as the treatise developed. Whereas for purposes of exposition, to give the treatise a deductive form, such lists belong in the place left open for them, I have not intended the reader to believe that these lists were fully developed in my thought before I had considered specific metaphysical problems. Deduction is after all a method of exposition rather than a complete account of the processes of cogitation. And the omission of the lists, no matter how essential they are for deductive purposes, emphasizes their *ad hoc* character.

Further study of the manuscript, I may also point out, may well have resulted in a more consistent use of such terms as "same," "many," "cause" and the like. In the course of this treatise various terms are assigned technical and rather exact meanings. And yet there are passages, I am sure, where these very terms, occurring incidentally, do not have the exact meanings elsewhere assigned them. Such inconsistencies can, to be sure, point to a serious confusion in thinking. But they can, on the other hand, be quite trivial. They can—and in most cases, I hope, do—permit us to express in simpler language what, to be accurately expressed, would require sentences more complicated and less easily understood.

These are the misgivings that I have in submitting this book to the reader in its present state. The flaws in it are, I am sure, much more serious than those to which I have alluded. But these I leave to my readers—if I have any readers—to point out.

Chapter 1

THE EXISTENTIAL METHOD

"Philosophy . . . has been cultivated for many years by the best minds that have ever lived"; nevertheless, says Descartes,[1] "no single thing is to be found in it which is not subject of dispute and in consequence which is not dubious." In the period which begins with Descartes, metaphysics was cultivated perhaps more assiduously and more intelligently than ever before. Yet, a century and a half later, Kant finds differences of opinion just as profound and the goal just as elusive. "In metaphysics," he writes,[2] "reason . . . is constantly brought to a standstill, and we are obliged again and again to retrace our steps . . .; while as to any unanimity among those who are engaged in the same work, there is so little of it in metaphysics that it has rather become an arena specially destined, it would seem, for those who wish to exercise themselves in mock fights, and where no combatant has, as yet, succeeded in gaining an inch of ground that he could permanently call his own." Nor is the situation different today. Metaphysical problems still attract able thinkers both because of their intrinsic charm and because of their fundamental character. And yet the remarkable progress that has been made in other fields of human endeavor contrasts more vividly than ever before with the instability and uncertainty of our writings on metaphysics.

If then we are to attempt once more to discuss the problems of metaphysics in a thorough and encyclopedic fashion, it is necessary that we approach our task with a befitting humility and circumspection. We must realize that we have here a labyrinth similar to that in which the Minotaur held sway, a maze which it will require our most vigilant skill to penetrate. Instead, then,

1

of rushing confidently into the midst of things, it seems that we should first devote painstaking consideration to the selection of a fruitful plan of attack. Instead of beginning with a discussion of specific problems of metaphysics, it seems that we should first select with great care a method which may perchance furnish the correct approach to these problems and for want of which so many eminent minds may have failed. "He who enters the labyrinth," says Descartes,[3] "must follow the thread which guided Theseus." And he who hopes successfully to penetrate the maze of metaphysical problems must come prepared with a method which will enable him to cope with the perplexities he is to encounter.

It is perhaps to the great thinkers of the seventeenth and eighteenth centuries that we are most indebted for what depth and clarity there is in our metaphysics today. It is therefore highly significant that many of these philosophers felt the selection of a fruitful method to be among the most important tasks confronting them. "It were far better," says Descartes,[4] "never to think of investigating truth at all than to do so without a method. ... As well might a man burning with an unintelligent desire to find treasure continuously roam the streets seeking to find something that a passer-by might have chanced to drop." "I do not deny," he continues, "that sometimes in these wanderings" those who philosophize in this manner "are lucky enough to find something true . . . But I do not allow that this argues greater industry on their part, but only greater luck." The beginning of metaphysical wisdom, for Descartes as well as for many of his contemporaries and successors, comes with the choice of a correct method. To succeed, they hold, one must proceed along the proper path; an advance in some other direction, with some other method, is really no advance at all. Indeed, as Bacon puts it, "the lame . . . in the path outstrip the swift who wander from it, and it is clear that the very skill and swiftness of him who runs not in the right direction must increase his aberration." [5]

Bacon's own contribution to the selection of a proper method is chiefly a word of caution. We must avoid all hasty generalizations; only after prolonged and intimate acquaintance with particulars through sense-experience and experiment may we permit ourselves gradually to consider universals of wider and

2

wider significance.[6] Among the English philosophers of the period, Bacon is undoubtedly the better known. Thomas Hobbes of Malmesbury is however a more acute thinker whose excellent style fittingly indicates the clarity and profundity of his thought. Hobbes too felt the need to rebuild our metaphysics upon the basis of a new method. He emphasizes the importance of a precise terminology. Like many thinkers as far back as Leonardo da Vinci and possibly further, he feels that metaphysicians may learn much from a consideration of the method used so successfully in mathematics. Leonardo had written:[7] "There is no certainty where one can neither apply any of the mathematical sciences nor any of those which are based on the mathematical sciences." And Hobbes, selecting one feature for emulation in metaphysics, writes: "A man that seeketh precise truth hath need to remember what every name he uses stands for, and to place it accordingly . . . And therefore in geometry, which is the only science that it hath pleased God hitherto to bestow on mankind, men begin at settling the significations of their words." [8] Propositions explaining words that represent our fundamental concepts are, Hobbes holds, of indubitable truth. With these as a basis, he holds, we should in teaching philosophy demonstrate those things "which immediately succeed to universal definitions";[9] and so on down to less general propositions, affirming nothing "which hath not good coherence" [10] with the definitions previously set forth.

Descartes' contributions to the methodology of metaphysics are likewise traceable to a desire to emulate the successes of mathematics. "Archimedes, in order that he might draw the terrestrial globe out of its plane and transport it elsewhere, demanded only that one point should be fixed and immovable; in the same way," writes Descartes,[11] "I shall have the right to conceive high hopes if I am happy enough to discover one thing only which is certain and indubitable." It is not sufficient, however, to have a fundamental proposition which is free from all doubt. We must at all times, Descartes insists, eschew vague thinking and doubtful ideas. In following out the implications of our fundamental proposition, we must use scrupulous care to assure ourselves that our ideas are at all stages "clear and distinct." To reach our goal, we must make use of the deductive method so success-

3

ful in mathematics; and we must continually guard ourselves against vague and indistinct ideas. Moreover, we must not discuss metaphysical problems in whatever sequence they happen to come to our attention. On the contrary, we must pay careful attention to the order in which various subjects are considered, not attempting to resolve complex problems before we have the answers to the simpler problems which logically precede them. "Those long chains of reasoning," says Descartes,[12] "simple and easy as they are, of which geometricians make use in order to arrive at the most difficult demonstrations, had caused me to imagine that all those things which fall under the cognizance of man might very likely be mutually related in the same fashion; and that, provided only that we abstain from receiving anything as true which is not so, and always retain the order which is necessary in order to deduce the one conclusion from the other, there can be nothing so remote that we can not reach to it, nor so recondite that we can not discover it."

In the "Essay concerning Human Understanding," Locke, like many of his predecessors, stresses the importance of a carefully examined terminology. "I must confess," he says,[13] "that when I first began this discourse of the understanding, and a good while after, I had not the least thought that any consideration of words was at all necessary to it. But when, having passed over the original and composition of our ideas, I began to examine the extent and certainty of our knowledge, I found it had so near a connexion with words, that unless their force and manner of signification were first well observed, there could be very little said clearly and pertinently concerning knowledge." "I am apt to imagine," he continues, "that, were the imperfections of language . . . more thoroughly weighed, a great many of the controversies that make such a noise in the world would of themselves cease; and the way to knowledge, and perhaps peace too, lie a great deal opener than it does." "Some gross and confused conceptions men indeed ordinarily have, to which they apply the common words of their language; and such a loose use of their words serves them well enough in their ordinary discourses or affairs. But this is not sufficient for philosophical inquiries." Besides stressing the importance of clarity in thought and language, Locke calls our attention to the desirability of determining the

4

limits beyond which our minds can not engage in fruitful discussions. "If we can find out how far the understanding can extend its view, how far it has faculties to attain certainty, and in what cases it can only judge and guess, we may learn to content ourselves with what is attainable by us in this state." [14]

The need to determine the limits within which the human understanding must operate is emphasized more strongly by Immanuel Kant. Beyond the limits of possible experience, Kant holds, no knowledge is possible. "I had to remove *knowledge*," he writes,[15] "in order to make room for *belief*." Yet in marking such a frontier, Kant was also motivated by a desire to determine a region within which there can be developed a metaphysics and a science having absolute certainty. Within the limits of possible experience we can develop a metaphysics that will not be problematical but apodictic. We can develop such a metaphysics, Kant holds, if we allow reason to "move forward with the principles of her judgments according to fixed law" and allow her to "compel nature to answer her questions." [16] These principles with which the mind operates are not, to be sure, divorced from experience, since they are discovered only through attending to the mind in action. Yet, with them as a basis, we must make use of the deductive method that has already been so successfully employed in mathematics and in physics.

These references to certain philosophers of the seventeenth and eighteenth centuries constitute of course only a small portion of the voluminous material on the subject of method. Incomplete as they are, however, they recall to us certain suggestions that have been made time and again, suggestions as to what is needed for the development of a successful metaphysics. Time and again our attention is called to the necessity of clear thinking and an unambiguous terminology. One writer urges us to cling to clear and distinct ideas, another insists on determinate ideas, and a third advises determining the significations of our terms. In one form or another we are told that a successful metaphysics can be developed only if we know exactly what we are thinking about and just what our terms represent. We also find ourselves urged to confine our thinking to subjects with which the human intellect is competent to cope. For it is felt that, unless we know what kind of problem can be handled with a prospect of successful solution, much effort will be wasted in unprofitable discussion. Finally, we meet repeatedly with the warning that we must proceed slowly and cautiously. At each stage in the development of our thought we must guard against the temptation to jump to the consideration of problems for which we are not yet sufficiently prepared.

Let us seek to adhere in this treatise to the methodological prescriptions which we have just discussed. Let us endeavor, that is to say, (1) to make our thinking and the terminology through which we express ourselves clear and precise, (2) to take up the philosophical problems with which we shall deal in an orderly manner and (3) to limit our attention to those matters which are within the limits of human knowledge.

First, then, how are we to make our thinking and the terminology through which we express ourselves clear and precise? The two, it would appear, are so interrelated that clear thinking is well-nigh impossible without a carefully chosen terminology. It seems to be the fate of words that, like machines, they are capable of doing only a certain amount of work before they are in need of repair and rehabilitation. In the course of an extensive use, words acquire secondary significations and collateral meanings. They come to refer to no definite and precise entity, but rather to a composite something composed of various concepts not clearly distinguished from one another. If then we are to restrict ourselves to words that have definite significations, such words as have, in the course of an extensive use, come to have vague and indefinite meanings must either be banned or rehabilitated.

Consider, for example, the word "idea." If we use the word "idea" without first asking ourselves what definite entity we are using it to represent, we shall almost unavoidably be using this word to represent now one and now another portion of a vaguely demarcated field of more or less related entities. Such an uncritical use of the word "idea" on the part of others will make it well-nigh impossible for us to understand and to evaluate their pronouncements. If an author who uses "idea" without explanation puts before us an argument whose pretended conclusion is that ideas are necessarily involved in our thinking, or that ideas are the sole objects of our thought, we shall find ourselves unable to determine whether or not his argument is sound and his conclusion true. For before a proposition may be accepted or rejected, it must first be understood. And a proposition in which the word "idea" has the vague meaning that this word commonly has is so lacking in exact reference as to be almost unintelligible.

The situation which obtains with respect to the word "idea" obtains also, we hold, with respect to the word "existence." The word "existence" has been held to represent what is permanent and independent of our thought; and it has also been held to represent what is given in sense-perception and is inseparable from our thought. In the course of an extensive use, the significations of the word "existence" have become so various, so ramified and so vague that the word as it comes to us out of the vocabulary of current usage seems to have hardly any meaning at all. It follows then that we can not use this word as it is commonly used without becoming involved in vagueness and obscurity. If we are to make a determined effort to keep our metaphysics free from vagueness and ambiguity, we must in our constructive efforts avoid the use of the word "existence" unless we explain it. How, moreover, are we to understand the writings of others in which the word "existence" occurs? The realist who is an epistemological monist tells us that ideas do not exist; the atheist tells us that God does not exist; some behaviorists tell us that consciousness does not exist. But if, when such assertions are made, we are not able to understand the word "existence" as it is used, we shall be unable to determine whether what is being considered with respect to ideas, God and consciousness is their intelligibility, their perceptibility, their inclusion in a systematic whole, or some vague combination of all of these characteristics. We shall gather that something is being denied of ideas, God or consciousness; but we shall be unable to determine precisely what it is that is being denied of them.

When we meet with the sentence: "Ideas exist," we are frequently unable to determine whether existence is being predicated of mental content or of universals. And, in view of the various senses in which *"existence"* has been used, we are frequently unable to determine whether what is being predicated of ideas is membership in some organic whole or perceptibility or freedom from dependence on any conscious subject. The

7

situation is similar when we meet with the sentence: "Conscious-ness exists." On the one hand, we may be unable to determine whether existence is being predicated of a certain sort of mental activity or whether it is being predicated of the field of objects. And, on the other hand, it may be one of several characteristics that the author is attributing to the entity he calls "consciousness." There is the sentence: "Ideas exist" (or do not exist) and the sentence: "Consciousness exists" (or does not exist). But we also meet with the sentences: "Evil exists" and "Electrons exist" and "Centaurs exist." Existence or non-existence may be predicated of anything. If, then, the signification of "existence" is left vague and indeterminate, we have on our hands, as it were, a general and blanket ambiguity which overspreads the more limited ambiguities arising from the indeterminate use of one or another of such words as "evil" or "consciousness" or "idea." We have on our hands this all-pervasive ambiguity, that is to say, unless either we use "existence" more sparingly than it is used or implied in ordinary speech, or unless we select for this word a determinate meaning.

It may be said, however, that the use of "existence" is by no means so widespread as we have suggested. It may be said that common speech uses "existence" but sparingly and that we can well forego any detailed consideration of the meaning of this term. Is not the term "existence" after all a scholastic and aca-demic one and the question whether an entity *exists* an artificial one? In the ordinary business of life, it is said, we are not confronted with the problem whether an alleged entity exists but only with the practical problem: what entities are we con-fronted by to which we must give consideration?[17] Yet when we ask what entities are we confronted by that deserve consideration, we are asking a question which might in common speech be ex-pressed as: "What entities are real?" And to ask what entities are real is to ask whether this or that apparent, alleged, subsistent entity is really existent or merely illusory and specious.[18] Ques-tions involving "existence" seem thus to be not merely artificial and academic, but to be deeply imbedded in our practical life and in our customary conversation. Indeed when a sentence used in our ordinary discourse does not explicitly contain the term "existence," it may frequently be replaced by a sentence synony-

8

mous with it in which some grammatical form of this term occurs, —a sentence synonymous with it in the sense that we would ordinarily take the two sentences to have the same meaning.[19] The "Some men are bald" of common speech is synonymous in this sense with: "Some bald men exist." The "Some men are not patriotic" of common speech is synonymous in this sense with: "Some unpatriotic men exist." And since these are typical particular categorical propositions, it would seem that all propositions of this form occurring in common speech are synonymous with existential propositions. It would seem, that is to say, that no particular categorical proposition of common speech is free from vagueness so long as "existence" has but an indeterminate meaning. With respect to this class of propositions, at any rate, it would seem that ordinary discourse is tainted by vagueness and points up the need for a renewed consideration of the meaning of "existence."

The existential import of universal categorical propositions used in common speech is not so obvious. Yet if "All men are mortal" is not synonymous with "Mortal men exist," it would seem that, keeping upon the level of ordinary discourse, a considerable part of what is expressed in "All men are mortal" may likewise be expressed in the sentence: "Immortal men do not exist." Similarly, the "No stone is alive" of common speech seems to be synonymous with "Living stones do not exist." [20] Thus those categorical propositions of common speech that are universal seem, like those that are particular, to be not wholly free from vagueness so long as "existence" is ambiguous. To the extent to which common speech is made up of categorical propositions, it would seem that even when "existence" does not occur explicitly, it may be said to occur implicitly, resulting in a vagueness and inaccuracy that can only be remedied by a careful determination of the meaning of this term.

It may be argued that common speech is not a reliable guide for the metaphysician in search of terminological exactitude. Though it may be agreed that common speech is thoroughly infected with a reference to "existence," it may be maintained that this fact points to the desirability, not of re-examining the meaning of "existence," but rather of developing a terminology in which the word "existence" has no place. In the development of such a terminology, modern mathematics, it may be felt, points out the way for us to follow. For, it may be held, the modern mathematician makes no legitimate and essential use of "existence." If perchance he speaks of the existence of certain roots, he is making an unfortunate and inappropriate use of the word. Generally speaking, he does not begin his task, it is held, by predicating existence of a certain space or of certain numbers. On the contrary, he takes this space and these numbers as subsistents, as postulated entities. And he proceeds to develop their implications while remaining entirely within the realm of subsistents. The mathematician, on this view, is not concerned whether, for example, Euclidean space exists or not. It is his task merely to point out that Euclidean space determines the sum of the interior angles of a plane triangle to a certain particular total.

So, it may be felt, we can develop a metaphysics in which the term "existence" has no place. The metaphysician too, it may be held, can begin with entities which are merely presented as *subsistents*. And he too can limit himself to developing the implications obtaining among these subsistents. His results, that is to say, may all take the form: "A implies B." Does A exist? Does B exist? Such questions, he may say, do not concern him as a metaphysician. Rather, he may hold, it is for practical experience and common usage to determine which entities are to be called "existent"; and it is for the theologian to determine which entities are worthy of being called "real."

Let us consider however the results that may be arrived at in a metaphysics of this type. We conclude, let us suppose, that the subsistent A implies the subsistent B. We assert: "A implies B"; and we do not assert that A implies the absence of B, do not assert: "A implies non-B." Yet when we have before us the two propositions: "A implies B" and "A implies non-B," on what basis can the metaphysician reject the latter and assert the former? Must he not hold that A and B are *really* linked together in a way in which A and non-B are not? Must he not be tacitly assuming that some such entity as is generally called "reality" is so constituted as to require the connection between A and B and to reject that between A and non-B? For if we make no such tacit assumption, if, on the contrary, we constantly remind ourselves that we are dealing with all subsistents, we must realize that the A that implies non-B

10

is a subsistent as well as the A that implies B. Without some limitation based upon some distinction between the real and the unreal, Euclidean space will be a subsistent and the Euclidean space which involves 180° as the sum of the interior angles of a plane triangle will be a subsistent. However, the Euclidean space which involves a total of 90° for such a sum will be a subsistent also. If we are merely discussing subsistents, in short, we may be justified in stating: "A implies B." But we would be equally justified in stating: "A implies non-B." We have no greater justification for making the one statement than for making the other; for all positive subsistential statements are on the same footing.

The metaphysician who would avoid "existence" holds at times that he is dealing only with what, for his purposes, may be mere subsistents. And he holds at times that he is dealing only with what, so far as he is concerned, may be mere postulates. It may not be inappropriate, consequently, to point out two senses in which the term "postulate" is used. In one sense an entity is postulated when its existence is neither asserted nor denied, when we seem to have it before us as a mere subsistent to be discussed. In another sense a *proposition*, one which we should hold to be explicitly or implicitly existential, will be said to be a postulate. Such a proposition is a postulate in the sense that it functions as a premise although unproved, although, that is to say, there are no other propositions from which it has been deduced. In the former sense God is a postulated entity in so far as God is regarded merely as a subsistent. In the latter sense the proposition: "God exists" may be regarded as a postulate; for this proposition may be held to be one which is not deduced from other propositions which are its premises.

The classic geometry brings before us the so-called postulate of parallels: through a given point there is only one line parallel to a given line. The assertion here can hardly be that there is only one such line that subsists. For every thing that appears to be presented to us as an object subsists. And unless a second parallel through the given point did at least appear to be presented to us, non-Euclidean geometry would be inconceivable and there would be no occasion for the postulate. The so-called postulate of parallels must therefore be the existential

11

proposition: Through a given point there *exists* but one line having certain characteristics. This proposition, it is obvious, is a postulate in the second of the two senses we have distinguished and not in the first. Since we are talking about an allegedly existing line, we are not holding this line before us merely as a subsistent. One may, to be sure, use an existential proposition as a postulate without accepting it. But to make use of an existential proposition is to concern one's self with 'existence.' It is likely then that the metaphysician who would avoid the term "existence," and who takes the works of geometers as his guide, has misread his mathematics. Generally speaking, mathematicians put before us existential propositions of which they make use in spite of the fact that these propositions are unproved. But they do not put before us entities whose existential status is left entirely out of consideration. They do not put before us the mere subsistents to which the metaphysicians whose views we are considering assign so important a role.

There is a further comment to be made on the doctrine that metaphysics should avoid "existence" and should deal largely with the relations obtaining among subsistents. As we have seen, a considerable part of what is ordinarily meant by: "All men are mortal" may be expressed in the sentence: "Immortal men do not exist." By analogy, it would seem that much of what is commonly expressed in "A implies B" might instead be expressed in the sentence: "The A does not imply B does not exist." If then a writer, believing that he is avoiding "existence" and that he is merely discussing subsistents, writes: "The subsistent A implies the subsistent B," it would seem that he is implicitly saying that a certain sort of A—the A, namely, that does not imply B— does not exist. It would seem, that is to say, that he is referring to 'existence' after all.

"To the extent to which common speech is made up of categorical propositions," we have seen,[21] it would seem that even when "existence" does not occur explicitly, it may be said to occur implicitly, resulting in a vagueness and inaccuracy that can only be remedied by a careful determination of the meaning of this term. And to the extent to which mathematical logicians fall back upon implication and hypothetical propositions, a redetermination of the meaning of "existence" is, it would seem, likewise indicated. It is true, that, when we assert: "If A is B, C is D," we do not assert that A is B. But we are not justified in disregarding the fact that we are asserting a connection between A being B and C being D, a connection that in some sense we are asserting to exist.

It would seem then that the ambiguities of "existence" as commonly used can not be avoided merely by the use of some alternative term, merely by concerning ourselves, for example, with "implication" instead. For he who would develop a metaphysics concerned merely with implications, must, if possible, describe "implication" so that no reference to existence is involved; and he must find a basis for rejecting: "A implies non-B" while he asserts: "A implies B."

It appears then to be no easy task to develop a metaphysics from which the term "existence" is excluded. Let us therefore acquiesce in the continued use of "existence." Let us indeed bring into the open the reference to existence that is so often implicit in our assertions. And in the development of a metaphysics in which "existence" has a prominent place, let us agree to make the effort involved in a reconsideration of the meaning of this term. Indeed, by continuing to use "existence," we shall be using a term extensively employed in common parlance. And we shall be employing a term which common parlance seems to regard as peculiarly appropriate in metaphysics. For what, after all, is commonly regarded as the proper field for metaphysical speculations? Is it not commonly felt that the task of the metaphysician is to determine in a general way the nature of existence, the nature of reality? And if this be the case, if, roughly speaking, the metaphysician has the task of determining the general characteristics of existence so far as they may be determined without experiment, surely it is inappropriate for him to avoid all mention of the term "existence."

Words that in the course of an extensive use have "come to have vague and indefinite meanings must," we have said,[22] "either be banned or rehabilitated." It has been our decision not to avoid all mention of "existence." And so it remains for us to set about rehabilitating this term. To assign "existence" a definite signification is however to assign it a meaning which does not coincide with the vague something to which "existence" commonly refers. A determinate signification can not be interchangeable with an indeterminate signification. Our task then will not be to arrive at some statement: "This is what 'existence' usually means"; but rather to arrive at some statement: "This is what 'existence' means for us."

Is it however permissible to assign a meaning to "existence" as we might assign a meaning to "piety" or to "school"? It may be agreed that I may assign "piety" whatever meaning I please so long as I am consistent in my use of that word. But existence, it may be held, is what it is. The word "existence," it may be held, can be used to represent nothing else.

An objection of this sort seems to stem from the belief that directly or indirectly we are aware of various entities, but not of existence which somehow attaches itself to some of our objects without being an object itself. If, however, existence characterized certain objects without itself being an object, then the distinction between existence and non-existence would be unintelligible to us. This however seems not to be the case. We *do* seem to be aware of certain entities which in some sense of the word we take to be existent and of certain entities which we take to be non-existent. Directly or indirectly, therefore, existence must be presented to us as a characteristic of certain objects. This characteristic, some modification of it, or, indeed, any entity among those of which we seem to be aware may, it would seem, be represented by the word: "existence." "Existence," it follows, may be used to represent a vague characteristic or a definite characteristic among the entities of which we are somehow aware. "Existence" *may* be given a definite meaning. And if "existence" is to occur in our vocabulary at all, to express ourselves understandably we *must* give it a rather definite meaning.

The motive impelling us to redetermine the significations of various words is the desire to establish for these words precise and unambiguous meanings. If then we were to vary the senses in which we use these words or were to shift from one signification to another, our purpose would be thwarted and our redetermination of the meanings of these words would be in vain. Let us bear such considerations in mind in redetermining the signification of "existence." Although we can not accept the suggestion that we leave all concern with existence out of our terminological discussions, there is a sense in which we can not play fast and loose with "existence." When once the meaning of "existence" has been even partially determined, all future use of that term must agree with the signification previously chosen. We can not continue to attach "existence" at random to whatever entities we please. On the contrary, we are required to adhere in all strictness to the meaning already selected. But before "existence" has had its signification redetermined, existence is by no means a concept that is sacred and untouchable. At such a stage it is not only possible but highly desirable that we give "existence" a determinate meaning.

Our initial discussion of method led us to three resolves, the first of which was to make our thinking and the terminology through which we express ourselves clear and precise.[23] This clarity and precision we shall attempt to attain by giving precise and determinate meanings to all important terms, the term "existence" being first in importance. A second conclusion to which we were led by our discussion of method is that we must consider metaphysical problems in their proper order, lest we attempt to discuss matters for which we are not yet sufficiently prepared. What, however, are these matters that we are called upon to discuss? The various questions which require resolution are for the most part existential questions. We are called upon to decide, for example, whether consciousness exists, whether a soul exists that is able to outlive the death of the body, whether unperceived entities exist, whether infinite collections exist, whether mental content exists mediating between the subject and the object. The resolution of each of these questions, it would appear, will be affected by the decision we make as to the meaning of "existence." For, the specific entities which exist and which together constitute the world of existent entities will vary with the signification given the term "existence." Not only may the determination of the meaning of this term put before us the distinguishing characteristics of existence as we are to use "existence"; it will also determine in large part the particular entities which exist. Only after the signification of "existence" has been determined are we in a position to resolve such questions as whether or not consciousness exists, whether or not unperceived entities exist, whether or not infinite collections exist. It behooves us, then, first to determine the signification of "existence"; and only after the meaning of "existence" has been determined, to concern ourselves with particular existential problems in the solution of which our decisions as to the meaning of "existence" may be applied.

The writers whose discussions of method we have examined have in the main emphasized three points.[24] They have urged clear thinking and an accurate terminology; they have urged an orderly procedure; and they have urged recognition of the limits beyond which there can be no fruitful thinking. Clarity of thought and accuracy in expression we shall attempt to attain through a close regard for the significations of our important terms. Indeed we shall seek a greater precision than has usually been attained through a very careful attention to the signification of the almost ubiquitous term: "existence." The order of procedure indicated for us to follow is, first, the determination of the meaning of "existence" and, second, the consideration of those existential problems which this determined signification can aid us in solving. What remains to be asked is how we can avoid the consideration of questions which in view of our equipment and resources must be unanswerable.

As has already been pointed out, "the various questions which require resolution are for the most part existential questions."[25] And so it would seem that when once "existence" has been given a definite meaning that can readily be applied, most questions put before us will be questions that we are prepared to attack. An entity whose existence is in question may not be clearly and unambiguously described. Or we may not be supplied with all of the data necessary to determine whether or not a given entity exists in our sense of "existence." But there will be no existential questions in the face of which we shall be unable to proceed, no entities to which the distinction between the real and the unreal will not apply. When, however, "existence" has no definite and unambiguous signification, then, to be sure, an existential problem may well be unanswerable.[26] To determine whether God exists, using "existence" in its usual indefinite sense, that indeed may be beyond our powers. But when once the signification of "existence" has been determined, it is not unexperienced entities that we shall avoid and not Kantian things-in-themselves. Rather it is questions involving an indefinite and

16

unexplained "existence" that we shall neglect in order to avoid the wasted effort that the consideration of an unanswerable question involves.

In accordance with the procedure which we have outlined, the determination of the signification of "existence" is to be the foundation stone in our metaphysical structure. What then, we ask ourselves, is the precise and definite entity which we should use the term "existence" to represent? What is the clear and unambiguous meaning which we should assign this most important of terms? As we have already had occasion to observe, current usage is, with respect to it, most indefinite.[27] So much so that, when we assert that an entity exists, we may seem to be doing no more than calling that entity to our hearer's attention. A hundred real dollars, it has been said, contain not a penny more than a hundred imaginary dollars. The assertion that the hundred dollars exist, it may seem, tells us nothing about the hundred dollars, joins no meaningful predicate to the subject term with which it is linked.

Nevertheless, the term "existence," as ordinarily used, seems to have *some* meaning. The assertion, for example, that God does not exist is commonly regarded as quite different from the assertion that God does exist, sufficiently different, in fact, to warrant the most extreme measures. And if there *is* a difference, if, rather, there is a difference of which we seem to be *aware,* that difference must be between the object apparently presented to us that seems to exist and the object apparently presented to us that seems not to exist. Seeming to have as an object a hundred real dollars is not identical with seeming to have as an object a hundred imaginary dollars. What in the former case seems to be added to the hundred dollars that is our object is not an additional quantity of pennies but some vague quality of being important. It is to be our task to substitute for this vague referend something more precise that our term "existence" is to mean.

We are at liberty, of course, to determine upon *one* definite and unambiguous meaning for our term "existence." Or we may determine upon two or more distinct meanings, each of them being definite and free from ambiguity. In the latter case, for example, we may give "existence" a certain meaning when "existence" is predicated of mathematical entities. And we may give it a different meaning when it is predicated of characters occurring in a novel. We may determine the signification of "existence" so that one definite sense of this term is in question when the existence of the number two is being considered; and so that a different sense of this term is in question when the existence of Hamlet or of Ivanhoe is being considered. We likewise are free to give "existence" and "reality" either the same or different meanings. Ordinary usage is equivocal in this respect, the terms often being used interchangeably, but sometimes not.

Common usage being indecisive, let us make the choice that will make our task simplest and our procedure the most direct. Let us agree to treat "existence" and "reality" as synonymous terms. In this way, we shall be concentrating our attention upon but a single task. Moreover, we shall find our language less monotonous in that we shall be able to refer to the entity that exists now by one of these terms and now by the other. Similarly let us determine for our term "existence" but a single unambiguous meaning. Let us agree to use "existence" in but one sense, no matter what the context and no matter what the entities are whose existence is being considered. By so doing, we shall be able to concentrate our attention upon the determination of a single definite and precise meaning. And we shall be spared the necessity of explaining in each context just which sense of "existence" is in question.

To be sure, we may commonly say of a lunatic that his million dollars exist in his head. We may commonly say that Zeus exists in Greek mythology but not in the physical world. And it may not be altogether at variance with common usage to say that the number two exists in the world of abstractions but not in the world of concrete entities.[28]

Yet in our ordinary speech we also recognize an existence that is absolute existence. If we ask the man in the street whether the lunatic's million dollars exist, he will answer immediately that they do not exist. He will not ask us to specify which realm of existence we are discussing. It appears then that when we commonly ask whether an entity exists, we are for the most part asking whether it exists in the universe of real objects; existence that is merely existence in thought or in the world of abstractions does not concern us. And it is to be noticed that when we insist upon

18

taking into account various realms of existence, upon utilizing various significations of "existence," the task of rendering the meaning of "existence" precise has not been accomplished, but has instead been replaced by a host of new and equally arduous tasks. We have now to ask what "existence" means when it is predicated of physical entities, what when it is predicated of mathematical entities, what when predicated of mental entities, and what when predicated of the entities of science. Let us consequently concentrate our attention upon the task of determining a single signification. For if we do otherwise, we disperse our attention and are likely to content ourselves with specious distinctions which do not make for real clarity but merely cover up the difficulty.[29]

We shall then select a definite signification which is to be the signification of "existence," no matter what the context, and which is likewise to be the signification of "reality." The proposition or group of propositions with which we shall conclude this part of our task will, let us suppose, be of the form: "An existent is an entity which is such and such." Our proposition obviously will not be one that we arrive at as a result of formal argument and strict proof. It will, on the contrary, be a postulate, an unproved assertion to be used as a premise in later discussion. It is however one thing to postulate the Euclidean character of perceptual space or the uniformity of nature; and it is another thing to start with the premise: "An existent, in the sense in which we use the term 'existence,' is an entity which is such and such." In the former case the reader may feel that he is in possession of some reason or of some experience which warrants his rejection of the postulate. But in the case of "the existent is the such and such," since we are merely presenting the meaning which the term "existence" is to have in our writings, the reader can have no reason for refusing us this terminological liberty.

We shall thus begin the construction of our metaphysical system by attempting to assign to "existence" a precise and unambiguous meaning. The propositions in which this meaning is set forth will be a postulate, a postulate, so to speak, which the reader can have no reason for not granting. And with this postulate as a basis, we shall, it is to be hoped, find ourselves in possession of a premise from which we can determine the existence or non-

19

existence—in our sense of the term "existence"—of God, of consciousness, and of unperceived entities.

When we come to consider particular existential problems, it is desirable, we have agreed, that we take them up in the proper order. In dealing with certain of these problems, to be sure, order may be a matter of indifference. It may be, for example, that the existence of individual substances can be considered as readily after the existence of universals as before. However, we must be on the watch for existential problems so related that the solution of one may reasonably be expected to aid us in the solution of the other. Moreover, in dealing with the particular existential problems which are subsequent to the determination of the meaning of "existence," order is not the sole consideration to which our discussion of method commits us. It is desirable that we assign a definite and unambiguous signification, not only to the term "existence," but also to the other important terms of which we are to make use. "Consciousness," "idea," "infinity,"—if these terms are to be used, they too must represent definite entities if our thinking is to be clear, and if, consequently, our metaphysical speculations are to result in sound conclusions. When then we come to consider the existence or non-existence of consciousness, it is not sufficient that we come to the task with an already determined definite signification for "existence." We must now distinguish the various concepts which the term "consciousness" has been used to represent. We must bring out one or more definite and unambiguous meanings which have been, or may be, assigned to this term. Only then shall we find ourselves in a position to determine whether consciousness in this sense, or in these senses, may be said to exist. Having determined upon a definite meaning for "existence," we must bring into play whatever inventiveness and circumspection we are capable of in order to bring before us the entities whose existence it is the task of the metaphysician to consider. We must clarify the concepts thus brought before us so that in all cases our thinking is clear, so that in all cases our important terms have definite and unambiguous meanings. Finally, we must bring the definite entities with which our analyses furnish us into relation with our propositions determining the signification of "existence." We must make use of our fundamental proposition

20

or group of propositions in determining the existence or non existence—in our sense of the term "existence"—of these definite entities.

A metaphysics which is developed in the manner which we have outlined we shall take the liberty of calling an *existential* metaphysics. And the method which we have outlined and determined upon is, we shall say, the existential method as applied to the solution of metaphysical problems.[30] A metaphysics that is existential will be based upon the realization that the term "existence" is of fundamental importance. It will be based upon the realization that this term needs a precise and unambiguous signification; and upon the conviction that common usage furnishes us with no signification of this sort. The metaphysician who makes use of the existential method will consequently begin his constructive labors by assigning to "existence" a definite, though to some extent an arbitrary, meaning. His first important propositions will be those which, taken together, render explicit the signification that this term has for him. And these propositions, taken together, will constitute the unfounded but unquestionable premise, the *pou sto*, of his metaphysical system. It is this existential method which we shall attempt to apply in the present treatise.

We shall consequently determine upon a precise signification which is to be the meaning that "existence" is to have in our writings. What we are calling the "existential" method does not however require the choice of the particular signification which we shall select for "existence." The existential method does not require us to replace the indefinite and general predicate in the group of propositions which we may for the present summarize as: "the existent is the such and such" with one particular and unambiguous group of words rather than with another. Yet, however the predicate of this primary proposition is filled in, expanded, or revised, the metaphysician who makes use of the method which we are calling "existential" will regard the propositions in which the signification of "existence" is determined the foundation stone of his metaphysical structure. He will utilize this primary proposition as a premise from which he may partially determine the existence or non-existence of various entities. The content of the world of existents will vary, we have seen, with the meaning that is chosen for the term: "existence."[31] Two metaphysicians starting from different meanings may arrive at different conclusions with respect to the existence or non-existence of some particular entity. Since however they may both be following the method which we are calling "existential," it follows that existential metaphysics does not involve any particular set of conclusions with respect to the content of the world of reality. Existential metaphysics, in short, derives its name from the existential method; and the system which is to be built up in the following pages is but one of the ways in which that method may be applied, is but one of the forms that an existential metaphysics may take.

Descartes begins his "Meditations" by calling into question practically all of our usual beliefs. He feels that in order to develop a metaphysical structure that is firmly established, it is first necessary to clear the ground. He resolves to "reject as absolutely false everything as to which" he can "imagine the least ground of doubt."[32] And so he concedes to the admirers of Montaigne the invalidity of almost every proposition that has been accepted as true. This task accomplished, Descartes undertakes to find an indubitable proposition which will serve as a foundation stone for a truly valid metaphysical structure. "Archimedes, in order that he might draw the terrestrial globe out of its plane and transport it elsewhere, demanded only that one point should be fixed and immovable; in the same way," says Descartes, "I shall have the right to conceive high hopes if I am happy enough to discover one thing only which is certain and indubitable."[33] The proposition: "I exist as a being who is now thinking" is for Descartes an indubitable truth of this sort. It is a proposition which is shown to be true by the fact that its denial is a self-contradiction. Not only, however, is this proposition indubitably true and in this sense clear; it also has, according to Descartes, the second characteristic which is essential in a first principle. "First, . . . the principles must be very clear, and . . . second" they must be such "that from them we may deduce all other things."[34] Paying close attention to order, Descartes proceeds, consequently, to deduce some of the implications of his fundamental proposition. And so he arrives at the existence of God, and, subsequently, at certain propositions "pertaining to corporeal nature in so far as it is the object of pure mathematics."[35]

Obviously, this procedure which Descartes employs has some resemblance to that which we have determined upon. Just as the Cartesian method begins by endeavoring to clear the ground, so does the method which we are calling "existential." Whereas Descartes holds that almost all pre-Cartesian assertions lack validity and a firm foundation, in a corresponding fashion it has been our thesis that almost all previous assertions explicitly or implicitly make use of a term which is vague and ambiguous. It is our contention that in view of their overt or implied use of "existence," these assertions, if not false, are vague and unintelligible. And, like Descartes, we too hold that they lack foundation. For they make use of a term for which no precise signification has as yet been established. In the matter of the foundation stone upon which the metaphysical structure is to be based, here too there is a resemblance between the Cartesian method and that which we are calling "existential." In the one method the structure is erected upon the "Cogito ergo sum," in the other upon a proposition or group of propositions in which the determinate signification to be assigned "existence" is laid down. There is a profound difference however in the grounds on which these propositions are found valid. The fundamental proposition of an existential metaphysics is in the nature of a postulate; its validity lies neither in self-evidence nor yet in proof, but rather in the liberty we have to develop a terminology which is in some sense our own. Yet when the fundamental proposition is once granted, an existential metaphysics develops in a manner similar to that in which Descartes intended his metaphysics to develop.

Let us however consider the possibility of arriving at a fundamental proposition in the Cartesian manner. Suppose I refuse to accept the existence of all those entities whose existence is usually granted. I am now doubting the existence of trees, of stones, of men and of God. From this it follows, according to Descartes, that I exist as an entity who is doubting these things. Such a conclusion follows, however, only because of the implicit use of "existence" in the proposition which is made to serve as a premise. Just as, using the language of common parlance, "some men are bald" appears to be equivalent to "some bald men exist,"[36] so the proposition: "I am doubting various things" appears to be

23

equivalent to the proposition: "I, as a doubter of various things, exist." It is this latter proposition which must then be regarded as the foundation stone in the Cartesian system. And yet, on what basis, we may ask, can the validity of this proposition be asserted? Must we not say that the only justification this proposition can have lies in the fact that in it the term "existence" is assigned a signification in accordance with which "existence" denotes, among other things, me the doubter? Descartes' fundamental proposition, it would seem, turns out to be a sentence partially describing in a denotative fashion the signification which "existence" has in his writings.

Perhaps, however, we have misinterpreted Descartes. Perhaps no reference to existence is to be read into the description of his doubtings. Perhaps instead of asserting the existence of his doubting, he is merely refraining from attributing existence to the various entities which appear to be his objects. Trees and men and God, let us assume, are now merely subsistent entities. And his doubting which also comes before him as an entity to be considered, this too, let us suppose, is to be regarded as a subsistent whose existence is neither asserted nor denied. But then the absence of doubting in his mind seems also to come before him as a subsistent. Yet in this situation, if we may so interpret Descartes, he finds himself perforce considering the former object, namely, the presence of doubting in his mind. He finds himself in short considering two contradictory entities, the presence of doubting and the absence of doubting, both of which, however, are to be regarded merely as appearances, as subsistents. But surely from this situation involving merely two subsistents, no conclusion can be drawn with respect to *reality*. It is a matter of common agreement that we can not find a term in our conclusion which does not occur in any of our premises. If then we are to conclude that one of these mutually contradictory subsistents is real, we must be tacitly assuming as a premise some proposition which contains the term "real." We must be tacitly making use as a premise of some such proposition as this: "If an entity insists on coming before us when its contradictory comes before us, then the former is a subsistent which is real." Again we find ourselves brought back to a fundamental proposition in which there is an assertion of existence. And here too, it appears, the validity

24

of our fundamental proposition must lie in the fact that it gives existence a certain character, that in it the term "existence" is being assigned a meaning.

An existential metaphysics, like the Cartesian philosophy, makes use of a fundamental proposition from which subsequent truths are deduced. With respect, however, to the *justification* of this fundamental proposition, we find ourselves in accord, not so much with Descartes, as with his English contemporary Hobbes. "Primary propositions," writes Hobbes,[37] "are nothing but definitions or parts of definitions, and these only are the principles of demonstration, being truths constituted arbitrarily by the inventors of speech, and therefore not to be demonstrated."

Descartes and Hobbes were in a sense innovators who set optimistically to work to rebuild philosophy upon a new and firmer basis. With the erudition and circumspection of Leibniz comes a more sympathetic appreciation of the past. Formal logic and the syllogism, Leibniz holds, deserve a respectful place in our philosophizing. Merely by developing the implications of certain premises in strict logical form, we can, Leibniz holds, uncover the self-contradictory character of certain propositions and of certain notions. Thus 'swiftest motion,' he maintains, must be unreal since logical analysis shows it to be self-contradictory. And the eternal truths of mathematics and logic are known to be true once it is shown that their contradictories involve self-contradiction. According to Leibniz, then, mere logical analysis reveals to us the non-existence of certain entities and the truth or falsity of many propositions. There remain, however, many propositions whose truth or falsity can not be determined by logical analysis. These are the propositions with respect to which logical analysis can uncover no self-contradiction either in them or in their contradictories. If then we are to determine, for example, whether there is ever a vacuum or whether, on the contrary, each place contains some body, we need, Leibniz holds, some other tool in addition to logical analysis, some other principle in addition to the principle of contradiction. "This simple principle (the principle of contradiction) is sufficient to demonstrate every part of arithmetic and geometry" . . . But, Leibniz holds,[38] "in order to proceed from mathematics to natural philosophy, another principle is requisite."

It is from a consideration of God's nature that Leibniz discovers the second principle needed to distinguish reality from unreality in those situations in which two contradictories are each free from self-contradiction. God in the act of creation could not have brought self-contradictory entities into existence. But in so far as he was confronted by alternative systems of entities, each free from internal contradiction, His nature, Leibniz holds, must have impelled Him to bring into being that system—and those entities compatible with it—that would result in the maximum of reality. If we are confronted by two contradictory entities each free from self-contradiction, we know, says Leibniz, that that one must have been brought into existence which accords with God's plan to bring into being the greatest possible number of compatible entities. We also know, he holds, that it would be inconsistent with God's nature for the act of creation to be in any particular the exercise of an arbitrary and irrational choice. And so if one of two contradictory propositions, each of which is free from self-contradiction, points back to an irrational choice in creation, we know that proposition to be false and its contradictory true. It is these deductions from our knowledge of God which, according to Leibniz, permit us to distinguish the real from the unreal in certain cases in which logical analysis fails to reveal any self-contradiction. A vacuum is not self-contradictory; but since it does not accord with the fullness of being which follows from God's nature, it is unreal. A situation in which two identically constituted substances are located at different places is not self-contradictory; but since such a situation points back to an irrational act in placing one here and one there rather than vice versa, this situation too is unreal.

This distinction made by Leibniz between the principle of contradiction and the principle of sufficient reason bears no resemblance to anything in Descartes' procedure. Yet here too there is a resemblance to the existential method. The meaning of "existence" as developed in an existential metaphysics, may be regarded as having two components. First, there is the vague and indeterminate signification of common usage. And, second, there is the definite but uncommon signification into which the former is transmuted through the terminological labors of the existential metaphysician. The former, the rough diamond furnished by common usage, may be regarded as supplying us with the principle of contradiction. And the more definite form added by the existential metaphysician may be regarded as supplying us with what may be called a principle of sufficient reason. Vague and conflicting as are the significations generally attached to "existence," it is generally agreed that the world of existent entities contains no contradictions within itself, that the term "existent" is not to be used to point to self-contradictory entities. This characteristic of existence, however, which may be regarded as implicit in the vague current meaning of "existence," does not by itself furnish us with a complete and definite signification. Whereas a law of contradiction may enable us to call certain self-contradictory entities "unreal," we must make use of some second principle if we are to be able more closely to delimit the real. The proposition in which a definite but perhaps uncommon signification is assigned "existence" is, it follows, that element in an existential metaphysics which is analogous to Leibniz's law of sufficient reason. For it is this further, more precise element in the signification of "existence" that must be brought into play if we are to determine whether or not the term "existent" is properly to be applied to given entities which, without it, do not appear self-contradictory.

Our discussion of the "Cogito ergo sum" of Descartes has shown us that the "Cogito" taken as the foundation stone of a metaphysical structure is in fact merely a proposition in which a signification is being assigned "existence." [39] In short, the Cartesian method turns out to be but a halting, partial, and unintended use of the method which we are calling "existential." In a similar fashion it is not difficult to show that Leibniz's principle of sufficient reason is but an unfounded determination of the meaning of "existence." What proof, for example, can be offered for the proposition that God has chosen the maximum of existence? Does not the validity of this proposition really lie in the fact that we are, in laying down this proposition, giving "existence" a signification in accordance with which it denotes the members of that system which contains the maximum of compatible entities?

It turns out then that the validity of the law of sufficient reason lies neither in self-evidence nor in proof. Like the "Cogito ergo sum," and indeed like any proposition determining the

27

meaning of "existence," its validity, we hold, lies merely in the freedom we have to develop a terminology which is in some sense our own. The justification which Leibniz had given for the law of sufficient reason was clearly unsatisfactory. And so some of his immediate successors in Germany set themselves to the task of establishing this law on what seemed to them a firmer basis. These eighteenth-century philosophers whose erudition and subtlety have not always been sufficiently appreciated, have left us with arguments purporting to show that a denial of the law of sufficient reason involves us in self-contradictions. Yet when Kant begins his labors, the gap between the two principles is still unbridged. On the one hand there is the law of contradiction, marking self-contradictory entities as unreal. And on the other hand, there is a second and independent principle which must be invoked, if we are not to accept all non-self-contradictory entities as real.

In the "Critique of Pure Reason" the distinction between these two principles is crystallized in the distinction between analytic judgments and synthetic judgments. "All analytic judgments," according to Kant,[40] "depend wholly on the law of contradiction." Synthetic judgments, whether a posteriori or a priori, agree, he holds, in this: "that they can not possibly spring solely from the principle of analysis, the law of contradiction." [41] "They require a quite different principle. From whatever they may be deduced, the deduction must, it is true, always be in accordance with the principle of contradiction. For this principle must never be violated. But at the same time everything can not be deduced from it." To be sure, the body of knowledge we may acquire solely through the use of the law of contradiction is for Kant more meagre than it is for Leibniz.[42] For Leibniz all mathematical propositions derive their truth solely from the principle of contradiction, whereas for Kant "seven plus five equals twelve" is a synthetic proposition.[43] Nevertheless, in the writings of both philosophers there is a distinction between two groups of truths; and it is recognized that we need some principle other than that of contradiction to give validity to what Kant calls our synthetic judgments.

One of the most important judgments which Kant holds to be synthetic is the judgment that all of our experience forms a unified whole. "Without . . . a unity which rests on a rule a priori and subjects all phenomena to itself, no permanent and general and therefore necessary unity of consciousness would be formed in the manifold of our perceptions. Such perceptions would then belong to no experience at all, they would be without an object, a blind play of representations,—less even than a dream." [44] Kant however seems determined that our perceptions shall not lack objective reference, that they shall not be a blind play of representations. And in order that they may be said to constitute "knowledge" and that the entities to which they refer may be said to be "real," Kant lays down the synthetic judgment upon which, he holds, this consequence depends. The validity of the proposition that our experience forms a unified whole seems thus to be based merely upon the fact that this proposition enables us to call the objects of our perceptions "real." This proposition, which, in Kant's terminology, is not analytic, seems thus to be merely an implicit determination of the content of reality and hence of the meaning of the term "real." We advance beyond the knowledge furnished us by the law of contradiction only by adding a proposition which is in the nature of an explanation further determining the signification of "reality."

The situation is very similar when we consider the synthetic proposition advanced by Kant that each event has a cause. "If we supposed that nothing precedes an event upon which such event must follow according to rule, all succession of perception would then exist in apprehension only, that is, subjectively . . . I could not say of the *object* that it followed, because the following in my apprehension only, without being determined by rule in reference to what precedes, would not justify us in admitting an objective following." [45] Kant however seems determined that reality shall include objective and necessary sequences. He seems to call such sequences "real" and to accept the causal law for the sole reason that it justifies us in giving these sequences such a designation. The proposition that each event has a cause seems thus to be valid merely in the sense that it determines the sequences we experience to be properly called "real." In laying down the causal law, Kant is in effect determining the meaning of "existence" in such a way that this term will be applied to these sequences. The validity which Kant finds for the causal law, that is to say, is only the validity which attaches to a proposition determining the meaning of a term. And so we add to the knowledge furnished us by the law of contradiction by making use of a proposition which implicitly determines somewhat further the meaning of "existence." [46]

The proposition that each event has a cause is not what Kant terms analytic. For, analyze as much as we like, "we shall never arrive from one object and its existence at the existence of another." [47] "There remained," Kant writes, "the possibility of experience as that knowledge in which all objects must in the end be capable of being given to us if their representation is to have any objective reality for us." There remained, he should have said, the promulgation of propositions determining the signification of "reality" in such a way that our possible experience would perforce be designated "real." "It was," quoting again from Kant, "because people were ignorant of this method and imagined that they could prove dogmatically synthetical propositions which the empirical use of the understanding follows as its principles that so many and always unsuccessful attempts have been made to prove the proposition of the 'sufficient reason.'"

In the foregoing discussion of Kant, we have been considering the reality of possible experience and the validity of the synthetic propositions which Kant holds apply to possible experience. Possible experience, however, Kant holds, is not the realm in which lie all of the entities to which our thought is directed. Beyond the "Herculean columns which nature herself has erected" lies "a boundless ocean which, after deceiving us again and again, makes us in the end cease all our laborious and tedious endeavors as perfectly hopeless." [48] This is the realm of "rationalizing or sophistical propositions which can neither hope for confirmation nor need fear refutation from experience." [49] This is the realm of vain, dogmatic metaphysics, and yet, to some extent also, of justifiable faith. It was the denial of metaphysics, the denial of knowledge of things-in-themselves that particularly impressed Kant's early critics. [50] And Kant was subsequently much concerned to refute the imputation that he had reduced everything to illusion.

Without following Kant in his specific replies, let us consider how such a criticism might well have been answered. "I confess

30

most humbly," Kant might have repeated,[51] that it "is entirely beyond my power . . . to extend human knowledge beyond the limits of all possible experience." "My denial of a transcendent metaphysics," he might have continued, "is based on the obvious absurdity in attempting to go beyond experience with concepts bound up with experience, and, more especially, on the various absurdities into which, as I have shown in my Antinomies, an attempt at transcendent metaphysics leads us. I also call your attention," he might have continued, "to other sections of my Dialectic in which I point out the invalidity of the principal arguments of rational theology and of the major propositions with which rational psychology is held to furnish us. If now you are not going to content yourself with the remark that my negative conclusions are displeasing to you, you must point out specific errors in these passages of mine."

"Moreover," Kant might have reminded his critics, "I have not contented myself with denying transcendent metaphysics. Having shown that there is 'no rational psychology as a doctrine furnishing any addition to our self-knowledge,' let me remark that 'this refusal of our reason to give a satisfactory answer to such curious questions which reach beyond the limits of this life' should be taken 'as a hint to turn our self-knowledge away from fruitless speculations to a fruitful practical use—a use which' . . . is 'directed always to objects of experience only.' "[52] And, he might have continued, "Before we venture beyond possible experience, let us ask ourselves first whether we might not be content with what possible experience contains."[53] "I suggest therefore," he might have replied, "that you turn your attention away from a transcendent metaphysics which I have shown to be impossible to an immanent metaphysics, accepting my new point of view that 'only in experience is there truth.' [54] I offer this suggestion without misgivings," he might have said, "for what things may be by themselves we know not, nor need we care to know, because after all a thing can never come before me otherwise than as a phenomenon."[55] "You may say," he might have added, "that you are not interested in experience-for-us, that you are concerned only about things in themselves. If, however, the arguments of my Antinomies are sound, you must be convinced that this hankering after transcendent metaphysics is but baying at the moon. And I am hopeful that a careful study of my Analytic will persuade you that the theses and problems of immanent metaphysics which I there discuss will worthily replace in your attention the transcendent metaphysics which you must in any case forego."

Our doctrine that the correct method for metaphysics is to develop the implications of propositions determining the signification that the term "existence" has for *us* seems naturally to evoke a criticism analogous to that which met Kant's "Critique of Pure Reason." "What we are interested in," our critic will tell us, "is the nature of reality as it objectively is in itself, not the nature of what you happen to choose to call 'real.' What we want to know is whether or not God, consciousness and ideas are objectively real. It will not satisfy us to be told that you have defined reality in such a way that in your terminology the word 'real' is properly to be linked with one or two of these entities but not with the third. For all we care, you may tell us that mermaids are real in the sense in which you choose to use the word 'real,' and that, as you use this word, the King of England is unreal." "Our interest," we shall be told, "lies in a realm beyond mere terminology. Our concern is not with the word 'real' but with the world of reality itself which is independent of any choice of words."

Just as this criticism is in some way analogous to that which met the Critique of Pure Reason, so it points to a reply analogous to the reply which, we have suggested, Kant might have made. Just as Kant might have referred his critic to passages in which he had in his opinion disproved the possibility of transcendent metaphysics, so we may recall what has been said on the unintelligibility of any discussion of reality which is divorced from a consideration of the signification of the term "real."[56] If what we have said is sound, then must our critic realize what nonsense it is to ask for a reality which is independent of any choice of words.

Moreover, we follow Kant further in not contenting ourselves with negative conclusions. We invite our critic to engage with us in a metaphysics which limits itself to the development of the implications which may be drawn from propositions determining the signification of our term "existence." And we are hopeful that a closer contact with such a metaphysics will show it to be a richer and more enticing field than it may at first appear to be. We are hopeful that, after our critic has been convinced of the absurdity of baying at the moon, a closer acquaintance with a metaphysics which applies the method which we call "existential" will persuade him to shift his attention and his endeavors to this more modest field. The inconclusiveness of a discussion of reality which is divorced from a consideration of the signification of the term "real",—this is a matter for argument and conviction. But just as Kant could not by logic have forced his reader to become interested in what is merely experience-for-us, so we can only *hope* to evoke an interest in a metaphysics which is founded upon an explanation of a term. Such a happy outcome, we are confident, will result from a careful study of the theses and problems of an existential metaphysics. And, to quote Descartes,[57] "it appears to me that I can not do better than cause this to be established by experience, that is to say, by inviting my readers to peruse this book."

Summary

In philosophy—and indeed in most of our statements—we are —implicitly, if not explicitly—asserting or denying the *existence* of some entity or other. The propositions through which we do this can not be understood or evaluated unless the meaning of our term "existence" is clear. Since "existence" has been used in various senses, our meaning will not be clear unless we make it so, unless we point out the specific sense in which we are using this term.

The propositions in which we *do* point out how we are using the term "existence" can not be overthrown by argument. Nevertheless, they are not trivial propositions. On the contrary, they will serve as a major premise in a syllogism leading to the determination of what exists and what does not exist in our sense of "existence."

Even this may seem trivial. But whether it seems so or no, it is as far as any one can go. If the proposition "X exists" attempts to make some assertion beyond "X exists in the sense in which I am using the term 'existence,'" it is meaningless.

The program of this treatise will be to point out the meaning our term "existence" has; to identify various entities whose existence or non-existence customarily concerns philosophers (distinguishing these entities in certain cases from others with which they may be confused); and then to determine whether or not these entities exist in our sense of "existence."

Chapter 11

TOWARDS DETERMINING THE MEANING
OF "EXISTENCE"

If a proposition is to be a definition, its subject-term and its predicate-term must, let us agree, represent co-extensive entities. If, for example, 'man' is to be defined as 'rational animal,' it must be true that there is no man who is not a rational animal; and it must be true that there is no rational animal who is not a man.

Now our task is to determine the meaning of our term "existence," to define, if possible, the entity that our term "existence" is to represent. What we seek is some proposition of the form: "The existent is the such and such" or of the form: "To exist is equivalent to being an A." And to accept as a *definition* a proposition of the form: "To exist is to be an A," we must be willing to accept both the proposition: "No entity exists which is not an A" and the proposition: "There is no A which does not exist."

But what about: "There is no A which does not exist?" If there is no A which does not exist, then all A's exist, and if "All A's exist" is true, then there is at least one universal affirmative existential proposition which is true. Thus in order that our term "existence" may be explained by means of a definition having the form: "the existent is the such and such," there must be some universal affirmative existential proposition which is true.

We have already had occasion to refer to certain existential propositions which are extensively used or implied in ordinary discourse.[1] We have found that the categorical propositions of common speech are to a considerable extent synonymous with existential propositions similar in form to: "Some bald men

exist" or similar in form to: "Immortal men do not exist." Of
the two existential propositions just stated, one, it is to be noted,
is a particular affirmative proposition and the other a universal
negative proposition. We have not found ordinary discourse
making use of, or implying, existential propositions which are
both universal and affirmative. We have not found ordinary discourse making use of that species of existential proposition of
which one instance must be true if our term "existence" is to be
explained by means of a definition having the form: "The existent is the such and such."

"All men exist" is a typical universal affirmative existential
proposition. But in what sense is it true that all men exist? All
real men, such as Socrates, Napoleon, you and I, do, let us agree,
exist. But if, in asserting that all men exist, we are asserting
merely that all existing men exist, our assertion conveys little
information. If the universal affirmative existential proposition:
"All A's exist" is synonymous with: "All existing A's exist,"
then the universal affirmative existential proposition is of little
use.

Let us see then what the situation is when our subject-term intends to denote, not merely existing A's, but also A's which may
be *alleged* to exist. Let us suppose that, when we say "All men
exist," our subject-term intends to denote every individual, real
or fictitious, who may be alleged to be a man. The subject-term of
our existential proposition now seems to denote, not only Socrates and Napoleon, but also Ivanhoe and the man whom I
imagine walking on my ceiling. But if our proposition is understood in this sense, it is a proposition which, using "existence" in
any usual sense, is false.

We run into a similar difficulty whatever term we choose as
the subject of our universal affirmative existential proposition. If
we say that all spatial entities exist, intending to assert that all real
entities having spatial position exist, our proposition is not very
informative. And if, on the other hand, we are intending to assert
that all entities which may be alleged to have spatial position are
real, then we are apparently asserting the existence of the gods
on Mount Olympus and of the dragons who roam the woods.

When I assert that all A's exist, my predicament, to put it
briefly, is this. If I am discussing all conceivable, imaginable,

subsistent A's, my proposition, using "existence" in any usual sense, is false. To be sure, since we may give "existence" any meaning we please, "All subsistent A's exist" might be held to be true. But if it is to be true that all subsistent A's exist, if it is to be true that any A which I choose to imagine is an existent entity, the world of existent entities must be regarded as a world that can be populated at will. If, for example, all subsistent spatial entities exist, I have merely to think of an entity as occurring somewhere and, presto, it becomes real. Either then all universal affirmative existential propositions are either false or of little value. Or, if we insist upon holding that there is some universal affirmative existential proposition which is both true and useful as a definition, then we must be willing to use "existence" in a sense from which it will follow that the world of existent entities can be populated at will.

Although "existence" as commonly used has a signification which is extremely vague and inchoate, there are nevertheless two or three propositions that may be laid down with respect to existence even before we refine upon the signification of this term. "Existent," as commonly used, seems to be predicable only of entities which are free from self-contradiction.[2] And "existence," as commonly used, seems to refer to a realm of entities which can not be populated at will. Whereas we have agreed to redetermine the signification of "existence," we also find it desirable to retain whatever is definite and clear in the signification of this term as it comes to us out of common speech. The rough diamond with which ordinary discourse furnishes us is not to be cast aside; it is to be treasured and cut and polished. If then "existence" as commonly used seems to refer to a realm of entities which can not be populated at will, let us agree to give *our* term "existence" a signification from which a similar consequence will follow.

If we admit universal affirmative existential propositions that are both true and useful as definitions, the world of existent entities will be one that can be populated at will. Since however we have agreed to determine for our term "existence" a signification such that the world of existent entities will not be one that can be populated at will, we must hold that there are no universal affirmative existential propositions that are both true and useful as definitions. We must hold, that is to say, that, using "existence" in the sense in which we are to use it, any proposition of the form: "All A's exist" is either false or of little value in describing existence.

Our methodological discussions in the preceding chapter have led us to determine to give to the term "existence" a signification which is in some sense our own. We have supposed that we would be able to assign a precise signification to "existence" by laying down some proposition reading: "The existent is the such and such." [3] We have supposed that we would be able to say that the existent, in the sense in which we are to use the term "existence," has such and such a characteristic; and that the entity having this characteristic exists in our sense of "existence." We have, in short, anticipated being able to say that all entities that are such and such, and that no entities that are not such and such, exist; and we have supposed that such a statement would make clear the signification we are assigning the term "existence." Since, however, we have agreed that the world of existent entities, in our sense of "existence," shall not be one that can be populated at will, we can not lay down a truly universal proposition of the form: "All subsistent entities having such and such a characteristic exist." If we are to make use of a universal affirmative existential proposition that is to be true at all, we must assert merely that all *existing* entities having such and such a characteristic exist. Yet, if our purpose is to make clear the signification which we are assigning "existence," a proposition of this latter form will be of little service.

It appears then that we can not very well explain our term "existence" by stating that all entities having such and such a characteristic exist—in our sense of "existence." And so we are left with but one-half of the statement which we had supposed would explain our term "existence." We are left, that is to say, with the proposition: "All *existents* have such and such a characteristic," or with the proposition which follows from it, the proposition: "No entity lacking such and such a characteristic exists."

If we lay down the proposition: "No non-spatial entities exist," we give the reader considerable information as to the meaning which we are assigning to our term "existence." We are inform-

38

ing him that "existence," in our sense of that term, is not a characteristic of a non-spatial God, of ideas that are presented as being in no place, or of universals regarded as not *in* their instances. Thus propositions of the form: "No entities with such and such a characteristic are real" are not to be disdained as a means of conveying information as to the meaning which is being assigned the term "real." If we say that no A's exist, the reader is informed that each subsistent A is a non-existent entity. Furthermore, the proposition which we thus put before the reader has what may be called deductive power. There may subsist X, Y and Z, entities whose existence is in question. But if X and Z appear with the quality A, the non-existence of X and Z is to be deduced directly from our initial proposition.

Whereas the proposition: "No subsisting such and such exists" can, as we have just seen, be of much service to us, nevertheless we can not be entirely satisfied with this proposition alone. If we wish to explain the word "man," we can hardly content ourselves with the proposition: "No finny creatures are men." The reader is informed that to be a man is to be lacking fins; but he does not have put before him other qualitites which belong to man. The logical intension of 'man' is only partially revealed. The logical extension of 'man' is less than that of 'non-finny creature.' We come closer to our objective when we add the proposition: "No invertebrates are men" or the proposition: "No quadrupeds are men." Similarly, when "existence" is the term to be explained. If we merely say that no subsisting A's exist, we leave the intension of 'existence' too meagre and its extension too large. But our failure is less marked when we add the proposition: "No B's exist" and the proposition: "No C's exist." In general, the more entities A, B, C . . . we refer to in this fashion in attempting to explain our word "existence," the more fully we describe existence and the more numerous the entities which are definitely marked out as non-existent.

With all this, however, we do not fully succeed in describing the signification which we are assigning the term "existence." Even when we say that no existent, as we use the term "existence," is either an A, a B, a C, or a D, our task has not been satisfactorily completed. For I may, it seems, imagine a man under my chair; and I may imagine this man as being a sense-datum, independent of my thinking, causally related to other entities, and so on. We can not rule out this man—who is to be ruled out, since we have agreed that the world of existents, in our sense of "existence," is not to be one that can be populated at will—merely by specifying some additional characteristic that an entity must lack if it is to be an existent. No matter how comprehensive and how varied the characteristics we make use of in our proposition: "No existent is an A or a B or a C . . ." we shall still fail to distinguish the subsistent non-A's, non-B's and non-C's which are unreal, and which merely appear to be non-A's, non-B's, and non-C's, from the subsistent non-A's, non-B's and non-C's which *are* non-A's and non-B's and non-C's and which consequently are real.

The proposition: "All existents are non-A's" or "No A's exist" assigns certain entities to the realm of non-existence. But in order that we may more fully describe the signification which we are assigning the term "existence," we need some proposition of another type. We can not complete our task by using only negative existential propositions. We have seen moreover that universal affirmative existential propositions can be of little service. And so we are forced to make use of singular or particular existential propositions. We can not fully explain the signification which we are assigning "existence" merely by laying down the proposition: "No A's exist." We can not make use of the additional proposition: "All X's exist." And so we must supplement our proposition: "No A's or B's or C's exist" with the proposition: "Some X's exist" or "X_1 and X_2 exist" and possibly with the proposition: "Some Y's do not exist" or "Y_1 and Y_2 are non-existents."

It appears then that the task of explaining "existence" will not be so simple as we had supposed. We shall be able to tell the reader that the subsistents that are real are neither A's nor B's nor C's nor D's. The more characteristics we make use of in this fashion, the more fully will we be describing the signification which we are assigning "existence." At the same time by making use of more and more such characteristics, we increase the deductive power of our explanation of "existence" with respect to subsequent metaphysical discussions. For with each additional characteristic, we may be assumed definitely to be assigning additional

40

entities to the realm of non-existence. To make our explanation still more complete, however, we shall also have to make use of propositions having the form: "X_1 and X_2 exist" and of propositions having the form: "Y_1 and Y_2 do not exist." We shall have to state that this particular entity and that particular entity are to be called "existent" in our sense of "existence" and that this particular entity and that particular entity are to be called "non-existent" in our sense of "existence." In short, our explanation of the term "existence" will have to fall into two parts. On the one hand, we shall be making use of universal negative existential propositions, marking out classes of entities that are unreal and characteristics which definitely determine their possessors to be non-existent. And on the other hand we shall be making use of singular or particular existential propositions, pointing out definite entities to be included in the denotation of "existence" and definite entities to be excluded from the denotation of "existence."

We shall thus attempt to explain our term "existence" through the combined use of some such propositions as: "No non-spatial entities exist," "The King of England exists" and "The immortal Barbarossa does not exist." But it is necessary to point out some of the results that propositions of these three types will, and some of the results that they will not, accomplish. Let me suppose a subsistent King of England alleged to be non-spatial. Since my subsistent appears with the characteristic of non-spatiality, it will follow, it may be said, that the King of England does not exist. In determining non-spatial subsistents to be unreal, I rule out of existence, it may be held, not merely unreal subsistents, but along with them certain subsistents which are real. It may seem that I have only in thought to give an existent the characteristic of non-spatiality and, presto, it becomes unreal. Let us however consider the singular negative proposition: "The immortal Barbarossa does not exist." From this proposition we can not conclude that there was no Barbarossa at all. We must, it would appear, distinguish between two different subsistents—on the one hand, Barbarossa with the qualities assigned him by the historian; on the other hand, Barbarossa with the qualities assigned him by legend. "The immortal Barbarossa does not exist" marks out one clearly described and readily identified subsistent as unreal.

It is not to be understood as carrying over into the realm of the non-existent other subsistent Barbarossas, among them the subsistent Barbarossa discussed by the historian. Similarly with the King of England. We must distinguish between the King of England thought of as residing in Buckingham Palace and the King of England thought of as non-spatial. "No non-spatial subsistents are real" marks out the latter as unreal. But it leaves the King of England residing in Buckingham Palace untouched. "No subsistent A's are real" marks out as non-existent all entities appearing with the quality A. But there may be some similar subsistent appearing without the quality A which is real. In short our singular affirmative existential propositions and our singular negative existential propositions determine the existential status of only those definitely described and readily identified subsistents which are represented by the subject terms of our singular propositions.

The narrow limits within which our existential propositions operate are also to be borne in mind when our propositions are universal and negative. "No non-spatial subsistents are real" disposes of subsistents appearing as non-spatial. But the world of subsistents also, let us suppose, contains subsistents appearing as extra-spatial and subsistents appearing as supra-spatial. It is as fecund as the Hydra which Hercules had to encounter. Just as Hercules struck off one head only to see two others appear, so we assign one characteristic to the world of non-existence only to have left confronting us other characteristics closely resembling what we have just disposed of. When we dispose of non-spatial subsistents, we dispose at the same time of extra-spatial subsistents *appearing* as non-spatial. After elaborating a description of extra-spatial subsistents, some of these subsistents no doubt *appear* as non-spatial. But there is a residue which does not. Extra-spatial subsistents, we may say, "resemble" or "are implied by" non-spatial subsistents. But it is conceivable for them not to *appear* to resemble, not to *appear* to be implied by, non-spatial subsistents. We may eliminate whatever *appears* to resemble non-spatiality. And by specifically eliminating, for example, supra-spatial subsistents, we may dispose of some particular group of subsistents whether they appear to resemble non-spatial entities or not. But there is a residue of resembling or implied subsistents which no

42

negative existential proposition, either universal or singular, can reach.

Not every subsistent is real, however, that a negative existential proposition does not mark out as unreal. It is the entities represented by the subjects of our singular or particular affirmative existential propositions that alone are definite members of the world of existents. An extra-spatial subsistent that does not appear as non-spatial is not unreal as a consequence of the proposition: "No non-spatial subsistents are real." But it is not definitely marked out as real unless it is enumerated among our X_1, X_2, X_3, . . . We can then determine not to enumerate among our existents any subsistent which appears as extra-spatial but not as non-spatial. Having made use of the proposition: "No subsistent A's are real," we shall not list as real any subsistent which "ought" to appear as resembling A or implied by A, but does not.

Whatever existential proposition we make use of in determining the signification of "existence," whether it be singular or universal, affirmative or negative, it determines the existential status of those subsistents only which it definitely describes and identifies. Unless we adopt this attitude with respect to negative existential propositions, the world of unreality has no obvious limits. And unless we adopt this attitude with respect to singular affirmative existential propositions, the world of reality can be populated at will. If "The King of England exists" has the consequence that the King of England thought of with whatever characteristics we please exists, then the King of England who died at St. Helena is real and the King of England who wrote the "Critique of Pure Reason." We hold consequently that the subject of our singular affirmative existential proposition is not the King of England with whatever qualities he might be assigned. The subject of our proposition is the King of England with his qualities—those which do in fact belong to him—fully noted. Or rather, since this is impossible, it is the King of England so described as to leave no doubt as to which subsistent our term "existence" is being used to denote. If then I am presented with the King of England thought of with various characteristics, I must distinguish between the various Kings of England presented to me. The subsistent King of England who lives in Buckingham Palace is represented by the subject of my affirmative existential proposition. This King of England, consequently, exists. The non-spatial King of England on the other hand, and the philosophical King of England, are not represented by the subject of my affirmative existential proposition. Consequently this proposition of mine does not imply the existence of these merely imaginary Kings of England.

There is a difference between the singular affirmative existential proposition and the universal affirmative existential proposition. If we say: "All subsisting non-A's exist," the world of existent entities comes to be one that may be populated at will. If we say: "X_1, thought of with whatever characteristics we please, exists," the world of existent entities is again one that may be populated at will. But in order that the universal proposition may be true, it must be emasculated to: "All existent non-A's exist." On the other hand, in order that the singular proposition may be true, it need merely be reduced to: "X_1, described as such and such a subsistent, appearing with this and that characteristic, exists." The singular proposition, thus reduced, is not tautological. We are not saying that the existing X_1 exists. We are pointing out an individual in such a manner that there is no doubt which subsistent individual we are pointing to; and we are saying that this subsistent individual is included in the denotation of "existence." The universal proposition, on the other hand, can not fail to be tautological so long as it remains universal. If we are to describe the existing non-A's without using the term "existence," our only recourse is to enumerate them, that is to say, to replace our universal proposition with a collection of singular propositions.

In order to describe the signification which we are assigning "existence," it appears then that we are to lay down the universal negative existential propositions: "No A's or B's or C's exist," and the singular or particular existential propositions: "X_1 and X_2 and X_3 exist" and "Y_1 and Y_2 and Y_3 do not exist." If we mention various characteristics—A, B, C,—and point to a sufficient number of individuals X_1, X_2, X_3, . . . Y_1, Y_2, Y_3, . . . the signification of our term "existence" will, it is to be hoped, be clear. And we shall, it is to be hoped, find ourselves in possession of a premise that will be of service in the solution of particular existential problems. In order to determine whether a given entity that

44

comes up for discussion is real or unreal, we shall have to apply our propositions determining the signification of "existence." We shall first have to ask ourselves if the given entity subsists with the characteristics A, B, or C. And if it appears that this entity *is* presented to us as an A or as a B or as a C, then our task is completed. The given entity, presented to us in this manner, is unreal. If, on the other hand, the given entity whose existence or non-existence is to be determined does not subsist as an A or as a B or as a C, then is our task not yet completed. We have still to bring into play the singular or particular existential propositions in which certain entities denoted by our term "existence" and certain entities denoted by our term "non-existence" are pointed out. If the entity under consideration is enumerated in the list of entities which are specifically excluded from the denotation of "existence," then, even though this entity lacks the characteristics A, B and C, it is unreal. And, on the other hand, if, in addition to lacking the characteristics A, B and C, it is listed among the entities which are specifically included in the denotation of "existence," then it is real.

We have agreed to lay down the universal negative existential propositions: "No A's exist" and "No B's exist" and "No C's exist." From these propositions, we have seen, it will follow that any subsistent presented with characteristics A, B, or C is unreal. There subsist, however, many subsistents lacking the characteristics: A, B, C. Some of these entities will be enumerated in the list which we are to draw up of entities specifically included in the denotation of "existence." Others of them will be enumerated in the list which we are to draw up of entities specifically *excluded* from the denotation of "existence." But no matter how lengthy we make these two lists, many subsistents lacking characteristics A, B and C will appear on neither list. Our propositions: "X_1 exists" and "X_2 exists" and "X_3 exists" and our propositions: "Y_1 does not exist" and "Y_2 does not exist" and "Y_3 does not exist" will by no means account for all of the subsistents appearing without characteristics A, B and C. With respect to the entities thus unaccounted for, we can not determine from the sort of explanation of "existence" that we have decided to give, whether in our sense of "existence" they are existent or non-existent. The sort of explanation of "existence" that we have decided to give is thus not a complete definition.

Our interest in this treatise, it is to be remembered, is primarily in the problems that are regarded as metaphysical. Were our interest in some other field, our list of entities included in the denotation of "existence" and our list of entities excluded from the denotation of "existence" would both of them have to mention entities that our lists will pass by. And were we attempting in this treatise to deduce a complete system of knowledge and not merely a system of metaphysics, our lists would have to be much more encyclopedic, or, what is saying the same thing, our singular affirmative existential propositions and our singular negative existential propositions would have to be much more numerous. Since, however, our interest in this treatise is primarily in metaphysics, our lists will not have to mention the North Star or the bee on yonder flower or the city of Bangkok. For we shall not be called upon in this treatise to determine the existence or non-existence of individual stars or bees or cities. We shall attempt to draw up our lists so that our explanation of "existence" will be available as a premise from which to deduce the existence or non-existence of those entities whose ontological status is generally regarded as a matter of concern to the metaphysician. If we succeed in doing this, then, for the limited subject-matter discussed in this treatise, our explanation of "existence" will be the touchstone we require.

We have rejected the universal affirmative existential proposition: All men exist. We have agreed to make use of the singular affirmative existential proposition: X_1 exists or Socrates exists. But what about the proposition: "The universal 'man' described in such and such a manner, exists"? In asserting such a proposition, it is to be noted, we are not asserting that any entity that is thought of as being a man exists. We are saying that the universal 'man,' considered as an idea in the mind of God, exists. Or we are saying that the universal 'man,' considered as an entity that is exemplified in certain individuals, such as Socrates and Plato, exists. The proposition: "The universal 'man,' described in such and such a manner, exists" does not, it seems, suffer from the disabilities which affect the proposition: "All men exist." For we are attributing 'existence' not to each real man nor to each subsisting man, but to a certain subsistent that we describe and call

46

the universal: 'man.' We can not, we hold, make effective use of the proposition: "All universals exist." But "The universal 'man,' described in such and such a manner, exists," is a proposition that may be both true and informative. The universal 'man' may consequently be given a place on our list of entities denoted by "existence" along with Socrates and Plato. So far as our present discussion has carried us, our list may mention individual substances and individual qualities and individual relations. And it may mention universal substances and universal qualities and universal relations, whenever there is a *suppositio individualis*.

It is to be one of our tasks to draw up a list of entities, each of which is denoted by our term "existence." And it is to be another of our tasks to draw up a list of entities, each of which is excluded from the denotation of our term "existence." For the drawing up of these two lists we require no further discussion. A place is reserved for these two lists at the end of the following chapter.[4] Taken together, they will, as we have said, partially describe the signification we are assigning "existence."

When we partially determine the meaning of "existence" by means of a singular existential proposition, we fix the existential status of one particular entity. We do this, at least, provided the subject-term of our singular existential proposition is so phrased that there is no doubt as to which the entity is to which it refers. When we partially determine the meaning of "existence" by means of a universal negative existential proposition, we assign to the realm of non-existents an entire class of entities. Here, too, however, it is necessary that the subject-term of our proposition be so phrased that there is not a complete uncertainty as to what entities are apparently denoted by it. For if we say that all A's are non-existents, and if the reader can not at all tell which entities are presented as A's, then there are no entities that are definitely being assigned to the realm of non-existents and our universal negative existential proposition is not explaining, even partially, our term: "existence." A universal negative existential proposition asserts that no entities having such and such a characteristic exist. It asserts that to exist is to be free from this or that characteristic. Yet if this characteristic is vague and indefinite, if in learning that existence is free from this characteristic we learn little about existence, then our universal negative existential proposition will scarcely help one to understand our term "existence." It follows, consequently, that our universal negative existential propositions should be so chosen that they mark out fairly definite groups of entities that are being assigned to the realm of non-existence.

Our task is to assign to the term "existence" a signification more precise than that which this term ordinarily bears. The "existence" of common speech is quite vague and ambiguous; nevertheless, we have seen, it has, even as commonly used, *some* meaning. To the extent to which the "existence" of common speech has a precise signification, we have agreed that it will be desirable to attach that signification to *our* term "existence." And where the "existence" of common speech is vague, we want our term "existence" to be more precise. If the "existence" of common speech is precise in so far as it makes freedom from self-contradiction a characteristic of existence, we want to explain our term "existence" also so that all self-contradictory subsistents will fall within the realm of the non-existent. We have agreed to explain our term "existence" in part by means of universal negative existential propositions. Each such proposition, it is expected, will assign to existence the property of being free from a certain characteristic; and it will assign a group of subsistent entities to the realm of the non-existent. We want to choose our universal negative existential propositions, consequently, in such a manner that we do not assign to the realm of non-existence entities which common speech definitely marks out as existent; and we do not want to leave out of the realm of non-existence entities which common speech definitely marks out as unreal.

We are at liberty to assign to our term "existence" any signification we please. And so, as a partial explanation of the signification we are assigning "existence," we are as much at liberty to lay down one universal negative existential proposition as we are to lay down another. One universal negative existential proposition, however, will assign to existence freedom from a richer, a more definite, characteristic than another. One will assign to the realm of the non-existent a more definite group of entities than another. And one will assign to our term "existence" a signification more in accord than another with the ordinary signification of "existence" in so far as that signification is precise. Whereas then any universal negative existential proposition that is to be used in assigning a signification to "existence" is in the nature of a postulate without premises from which it can be deduced, one universal negative existential proposition will enable us to carry out our purpose more readily than another. Whereas there are no logical grounds that force us to select one universal negative existential proposition and to reject another, there are grounds of expediency that permit us to prefer one universal negative existential proposition to another. Thus we are left with certain criticisms that we may bring, albeit no logical criticisms, against some of the universal negative existential propositions which may suggest themselves to us as propositions to be used in partially describing the signification to be assigned to the term "existence."

For the remainder of this chapter then, let us call to mind some of the universal negative existential propositions that might be used in partially describing the meaning to be assigned "existence." And, in view of the discussion of the preceding pages, let us see which of these propositions it will, without more detailed consideration later, be inexpedient to accept. In order to obtain the material to which our considerations of expediency are to be applied, let us review some of the philosophical writings of the past. We must remember however that the philosophers whom we are about to consider did not lay down universal negative existential propositions with the overt purpose of explaining the term "existence." They may have mentioned "existence" only casually; or they may have given assent to some universal affirmative existential proposition. It is not our primary purpose at this point to make an historical survey of the use of the term "existence" in the writings of various philosophers. Our task is to glance through the history of philosophy in order to put before us universal negative existential propositions from which to choose.

No question in Occidental philosophy, so far as we know, is older than the question: What is it to be real? When the Milesians found themselves confronted by a world of great variety and ceaseless change, they asked themselves what the "nature" of things is. "As Anaximandros and most of the physicists say," writes Aristotle,[5] the fundamental reality is something which "is immortal and indestructible." And so we may elicit the doctrine that only the permanent is real. This proposition, namely, that whatever is impermanent is non-existent, is not to be extracted merely from what has come down to us from the Milesians. From Parmenides to Anaxagoras the real is that which persists unchanged, unaffected by the lapse of time. There is disagreement as to the number of such permanent entities and the qualities that these entities possess, but among many Greek philosophers there seems to be agreement that whatever is impermanent is unreal. Indeed we find echoes of this doctrine as recent as Herbert Spencer. "The most conspicuous contrast," writes Spencer,[6] "is the contrast between that which perpetually changes and that which does not change, between each ever-varying cluster of vivid states and their unvarying *nexus*. This transcendent distinction needs a name. I must use some mark to imply this duration as distinguished from this transitoriness—this permanence in the midst of that which has no permanence. And the word 'existence,' as applied to the unknown nexus, has no other meaning. It expresses nothing beyond this primordial fact in my experience."

Shall we partially describe the meaning which we are to assign the term "existence" by means of the proposition: impermanent subsistents are unreal? If we take the term "permanence" as it comes to us out of our everyday discourse, the typical subsistents appearing as impermanent are such entities as flashes of lightning. We choose, however, not to make use, unless there are special considerations, of a universal negative existential proposition that will assign to the realm of non-existence entities which common speech unhesitatingly marks out as existent. Surely, there is no tendency in common speech to call mountains "real" rather than sunsets, and Gothic cathedrals "real" rather than soap bubbles. Common speech seems definitely to assign some sunsets and some flashes of lightning to the realm of existent entities. And so, unless permanence is used in some special sense, the proposition: "Impermanent subsistents are unreal" would give our term "reality" a meaning out of accord with common usage.

Fairly early in Greek thought the conviction developed that the material things with which we commonly deal in our everyday life are unimportant and unreal. Emphasis was shifted to numbers, to forms, to universals, to ideals, and to scientific generalizations as the only realities. It is reason, the eyes of the mind, that, it was said, puts us in touch with reality, not the senses which are the eyes of the body. Among the Pythagoreans, then by Socrates and by Plato, the world of intelligible entities was more and more intensively explored, became richer and richer in content. And the conviction grew that whatever is merely mundane, whatever is altogether a part of the spatial world, whatever is given to us in sense perception only, is unworthy, unstable and unreal. The Platonic dialogues are the great source of inspiration for this identification of the real with the intelligible. There we find in abundance passages in which the objects of the intellect, the Ideas, are eulogized and called "real," and in which entities which are merely objects for the senses are called "unreal." [7]

With the intensification of religious interest and the spread of Christianity, the conviction remains that only that is real which is intelligible and not essentially sensible. The world of intelligible entities is regarded somewhat differently. It is now not so much the realm of secular generalizations and of moral ideals that are independent of religious import as it is the realm of spiritual truths, the realm of God, His Word, and His ideas. The mind, says St. Augustine,[8] "is disabled by besotting and inveterate vices not merely from delighting and abiding in, but even from tolerating, His unchangeable light, until it has been gradually healed, and renewed, and made capable of such felicity." Man is naturally sinful; he usually is occupied with material things, with the world of sense which is the world of illusion and unreality. The world of sense, it is felt, has no existence *per se*. It has only a shadowy and reflected importance in so far as it is connected with, and derived from, the spiritual Word of God. Material things "are known in one way by the angels in the Word of God, in which are seen the eternally abiding causes and reasons according to which these things are made; and in another way in which these things are seen as they are in themselves. In the former way, they are known with a clearer knowledge; in the latter they are known with a dimmer knowledge, a knowledge rather of the bare works than of the design." [9] Scattered through the Middle Ages we find marks of this other-worldliness. That "in which there is any mutable element," says St. Anselm,[10] "is not altogether what it is. . . . And what has a past existence which is no longer or a future existence which is not yet,—this does not properly and absolutely exist."

With the great scientific generalizations formulated in the sixteenth and seventeenth centuries, the world of intelligible entities finds new inhabitants. The world of intelligible entities is still a world of spiritual truths. But the ideas of God are clear and distinct ideas, truths of reason, in a word, mathematical formulae. The world of mere sense is still unimportant and unreal. Material things have no reality except in so far as they exemplify mathematical formulae. And we have no real knowledge of mundane things except in so far as we can subject them to number and see their behavior as the fulfillment of some mathematical law.

A tremendously important line of philosophers thus presents us with a doctrine from which we may derive the proposition: Subsistents appearing as merely sensible are unreal. We have agreed not to make use, unless there are special considerations, of a universal negative existential proposition that would assign to our term "existence" a signification out of accord with common usage where common usage is precise and definite. If now we were partially to explain the meaning of our term "existence" by means of the proposition: "All sensible subsistents are unreal," we should be assigning to the realm of the non-existent, not merely sunsets and soap bubbles as these subsistents are commonly presented to us, but also ancient trees and Gothic cathedrals. If, then, we found the proposition: "Whatever subsists as impermanent is unreal" unacceptable because of its divergence from common usage, there is all the more reason for us to reject the proposition which we are now considering.

However, "All sensible subsistents are unreal" is to be distinguished from "all *merely* sensible subsistents are unreal." Sunsets and soap bubbles and Gothic cathedrals may be subsistents appearing as sensible; but they may not appear as *merely* sensible. Consequently in assigning the merely sensible to the realm of the non-existent, we may be leaving the door open for sunsets, soap bubbles and cathedrals, appearing with the characteristics with which they normally appear. Is there any respect, however, in which a subsisting Gothic cathedral appears to be connected with the eternal truths and some other subsisting sensible entity not connected? The cathedral appears with the characteristic of having been built in accordance with the formulae of physics;

its behavior exemplifies the law of gravitation. Yet, unless we are told just what the eternal truths are and what sort of connection with them is demanded, we have no basis upon which to distinguish the ontological status of a Gothic cathedral from that of any other alleged sensible entity. Practically every sensible entity appears connected, in some sense of the word "connection," with the realm of intelligible truths. The proposition: "Merely sensible subsistents are unreal" is ostensibly assigning to the realm of the non-existent certain sensible subsistents. Yet without a more detailed description of the intelligible and of the nature of the connection that is demanded, none of the sensible subsistents normally considered is indicated as falling within the class of the *merely* sensible. A universal negative existential proposition is effective in explaining the signification being assigned "existence" in so far as it assigns a definite characteristic to 'existence' and in so far as it assigns entities to the realm of the non-existent. It is hardly informative to be told that existence has the characteristic of being somehow intelligible. And in assigning the merely sensible to the realm of the non-existent, it turns out that we are, in the absence of further propositions, leaving the realm of the non-existent without any obvious inhabitants. It appears then that: "All sensible subsistents are unreal" will not assign to "existence" the sort of signification we seek to give it. And it appears that: "All merely sensible subsistents are unreal" will not, taken by itself, give "existence" a definite meaning.

At the beginning of Greek philosophy we meet with the doctrine that the impermanent is unreal. For many writers it is the world of sense which is impermanent. And so we have arrived at the doctrine that the sensible, or the merely sensible, is unreal. Instead, however, of opposing to the merely sensible that which is intelligible, there may be opposed to the merely sensible that which is independent of sense-perception, that which persists either unsensed or regardless of whether it is sensed or not. Independence of sense perception has grown into independence of any mental activity. We come thus to the doctrine known as realism, the doctrine that whatever is merely or essentially mental content is unreal, the doctrine that whatever is real is independent of any mind. A realism of this sort does not find very definite expression in writings prior to the eighteenth century. It was probably accepted by earlier writers. But the explicit statement of it seems first to have been called forth by the exposition of epistemological idealism. It has during the past century been advocated by many eminent writers. And there is no doubt but that the proposition: "Essentially mental subsistents are unreal" establishes a partial signification for the term "existence" which accords very well with current popular usage.

When we partially explain the signification being assigned "existence" by means of the universal negative existential proposition: "All essentially mental subsistents are unreal," we are definitely assigning to the realm of the non-existent subsistents appearing as dream objects, and we are definitely assigning to the realm of the non-existent subsistents appearing as members of a Berkeleian or Kantian world of experience. Moreover, we are definitely assigning to the realm of the non-existent the *ideas* which certain epistemological dualists hold are in all cases the immediate objects of our consciousness. For these ideas, as contrasted with the ulterior realities to which they refer, are normally thought of as having no life outside of the conscious states whose immediate objects they are. It follows then, if we may indulge in a digression, that one can hardly be an epistemological dualist proclaiming the existence of such ideas, if one is partially to explain the signification of "existence" by means of the proposition: "All essentially mental subsistents are unreal."

If, in partially explaining the signification which we are assigning to "existence," we make use of the proposition: "Whatever is essentially mental is unreal," we shall not be running counter to common usage. And we shall not be failing to give our term "existence" any definite meaning at all. We have already committed ourselves however to the acceptance of the proposition: "Self-contradictory subsistents are unreal." And we shall discover later that the entity that is in no sense an object of consciousness is self-contradictory.[11] If then we may assume that our later finding will be correct, the entity that is in no sense an object of consciousness is an entity that we shall find presented to us as self-contradictory. It is an entity, consequently, which our propositions setting forth the meaning of "existence" definitely will assign to the realm of the non-existent. If, then, in partially determining the signification of "existence," we were to make

54

use of the proposition: "All essentially mental subsistents are un-real," we should find assigned to the world of non-existence both the subsistent that is in no sense an object of consciousness and the subsistent that is essentially mental. We should be placing practically all subsistents among the unreals and should have nothing for the term "existent" to denote.

Whereas we have found many writers holding that the merely sensible is unimportant and unreal, there is a distinguished group of philosophers who take what is, generally speaking, an opposite point of view. "Reality and the evidence of sensation," [12] says Diogenes Laertius in expounding the Epicurean philosophy, "establish the certainty of the senses; for the impressions of the sight and hearing are just as real, just as evident, as pain." It is the entities with which we become acquainted through sense per-ception which are for these writers most certainly known to be real. Entities which are merely entities of thought are known less directly, less surely. In becoming acquainted with them the mind follows a more tortuous path and is more likely to be led astray. "Let men please themselves as they will," says Francis Bacon,[13] "in admiring and almost adoring the human mind, this is certain: that as an uneven mirror distorts the rays of objects according to its own figure and section, so the mind, when it receives impres-sions of objects through the sense, can not be trusted to report them truly, but in forming its notions mixes up its own nature with the nature of things." And so Bacon arrives at the position: "The evidence of the sense, helped and guarded by a certain process of correction, I retain. But the mental operation which follows the act of sense I for the most part reject." [14]

This acceptance of the reality of entities given to us in sense perception and this sceptical attitude towards entities not di-rectly bound up with sense perception finds expression in many passages in Locke, Berkeley and Hume. "The ideas of sense," says Berkeley [15] for example, "are allowed to have more reality in them . . . than the creatures of the mind." A similar attitude is frequently expressed by Kant. "What is real in external phe-nomena," says Kant,[16] "is real in perception only, and can not be given in any other way." "From such perceptions, whether by mere play of fancy or by experience, knowledge of objects can be produced, and here no doubt deceptive representations may arise without truly corresponding objects". . . "In order to escape from these false appearances, one has to follow the rule that *whatever is connected according to empirical laws with a perception is real.*"

"The postulate concerning our knowledge of the *reality* of things requires *perception,* therefore sensation and the consciousness of it, not, indeed, immediately of the object itself, the existence of which is to be known, but yet of a connection between it and some real perception according to the analogies of experience which determine in general all real combinations in experience. . . . But if we do not begin with experience or do not *proceed according to the laws of the empirical connection of phenomena,* we are only making a vain display as if we could guess and discover the existence of anything." [17]

It is unnecessary to trace this doctrine, which may be called "empiricism," down to our own day. It is the doctrine with so many recent exponents, the doctrine that entities given to us in sense perception are real, that entities connected with the objects of perception, objects of possible but not of actual experience, are less directly and less surely known to be real, and that entities not properly connected with sense experiences are unreal. In view of our discussion of the universal affirmative existential proposition, we are not interested in the proposition: "All objects of possible experience are real." But the proposition: "Subsistents appearing as not properly connected with sense experience are unreal" is a proposition of which we are at liberty to make use in partially explaining the signification to be attached to our terms: "reality" and "existence."

A universal negative existential proposition, let us remind ourselves again, will be effective in assigning a meaning to "existence" to the extent to which it definitely assigns entities to the realm of the non-existent. Which, then, are the entities that appear as not properly connected with sense experience? Unless the universal negative existential proposition with which we are dealing is expanded and the nature of a proper connection defined, there are no entities which will obviously fall within the realm of the unreal. Universals generally appear as the archetypes of the objects of sense experience. God appears with the characteristic of being implied by the objects of sense experience.

Even dream objects when recognized as dream objects frequently appear as caused by something in the world of sense-experience. Almost all entities, in short, are subsistents which appear as having *some* sort of connection with the objects of sense-experience. We can give the world of the non-existent some definite content and thus more effectively explain "existence" if we disregard the notion of a proper connection. If we lay down the proposition: "All subsistents not appearing as percepts are unreal," God, and the law of gravitation, and the other side of the moon, are at once marked out as subsistents that, as they usually appear, do not exist. Such a proposition, however, would assign to the term "existence" a signification out of accord both with common usage and with philosophical precedent.

Let us consider, then, the possibility of limiting reality to entities given to us as having a certain definite kind of connection with sense experience. The entity that seems merely to be implied by sense experience is not, we may say, properly connected with it. The only entities that are properly connected with the actual objects of sense experience, we may say, are those that are possible objects of sense experience, those entities that would be perceived if we were at a different place or had senses sufficiently acute. We thus arrive at the universal negative existential proposition: Whatever appears with the characteristic of being non-spatial is unreal. And we may in a similar fashion arrive at the proposition: All timeless subsistents are unreal.

At least as far back as Plato we meet with the doctrine that whatever is real must have a date. Against the timeless Being of Parmenides, the objection is raised that such an alleged being is unreal because it is not in time as an entity must be if it is to be real.[18] An entity that does not participate in time, it is held, does not participate in being. When we come down to Hobbes, we find a similar attitude clearly expressed with respect to spatial position. "If the triangle exists nowhere at all," Hobbes writes,[19] "I do not understand how it can have any nature; for that which exists nowhere does not exist." Sometimes it is required of a real entity only that it have a date, sometimes only that it have spatial position. But quite frequently the two requirements are joined. Reality is regarded as something that is limited to those subsistents appearing with *both* a date *and* a spatial position. As Crusius, one of the philosophers who wrote shortly before Kant, puts it, to give an entity that is merely thought—that is, an entity that in his terminology is merely possible—a date and a spatial position is to give it existence.[20] "If a substance is to exist, it must exist immediately in some place and at some time."[21] For Kant, space and time are transcendentally ideal but empirically real. Every external entity that is empirically real—that is to say, real as a phenomenon—must be in time and in space. And all real phenomena without exception must be in time. Only events, some recent writers seem to hold, are real. And an event, it is indicated, is an entity that has a date and a position in a four-dimensional spatio-temporal continuum.

If we partially explain "existence" by means of the proposition: "Whatever appears as lacking a date or a spatial position is unreal," there are various subsistents that our proposition definitely assigns to the realm of the non-existent. Such a proposition classifies as unreal mental processes and mental content presented as occurring nowhere, universals and scientific generalizations appearing as eternal, God appearing as a supra-spatial Deity. Moreover with such a proposition we assign to existence the character of being free from utter non-spatiality and the character of being free from utter timelessness. Thus it can not be objected that the proposition which we are considering gives no meaning to "existence." Nor does this proposition definitely assign to the realm of non-existence entities which common usage unhesitatingly calls "real." A preliminary and somewhat casual discussion, in short, fails to eliminate from further consideration: "Whatever appears as lacking a date or a spatial position is unreal." To be sure, there are such questions as: date with respect to what? and spatial position with respect to what? In order to determine which subsistents are unreal because of their lack of spatio-temporal characteristics, a further discussion of space, time, and of time-space is indicated. If the signification of "existence" is to be as precise as possible, the realm of non-existence must contain more entities than merely those which appear as totally undated and existence must have a more definite characteristic than freedom from utter timelessness. In order to make the meaning of our term "existence" as precise as possible, we shall later mark out as unreal all subsistents appearing as undated, or as lacking

58

a spatial position, with respect to a certain type of entity.[22] And we shall mark out as unreal subsistents appearing as not having a certain kind of date and position with respect to such an entity. But in view of this preliminary discussion and pending such modifications as our search for precision may later lead us to make, we may at this point agree in explaining "existence" to make use of the proposition: "Whatever appears as lacking a date or as having no spatial position is unreal."

It is frequently felt that existent entities are related to one another in that each of them is in some place and each of them at some time. It is felt that existent entities taken together form a system of entities that is bound up with a system of places or Space and with a system of dates or Time. The non-existent, it may be felt, is what does not belong to this system, what does not fit into this one Space and this one Time. With some writers, however, membership in this one Space and this one Time does not seem to be the outstanding determinant of membership in the system of existent entities. To exist is to be a member of a system of related entities; but membership in this system is not primarily a matter of place and time. Existence is evidenced by a wealth of relations of all sorts with various other entities. The non-existent is that which subsists disjoined from most other entities and unconnected with them.

It is the consideration of fables and dream objects that is likely to lead us to distinguish the existent from the non-existent in this fashion. "And I ought," says Descartes at the end of his "Meditations," "to set aside all the doubts of these past few days as hyperbolical and ridiculous, especially that very common uncertainty respecting sleep, which I could not distinguish from the waking state; for at present I find a very notable difference between the two, inasmuch as our memory can never connect our dreams one with the other, or with the whole course of our lives, as it unites events which happen to us while we are awake. And, as a matter of fact, if some one, while I was awake, quite suddenly appeared to me and disappeared as fast as do the images which I see in sleep, so that I could not know from whence the form came nor whither it went, it would not be without reason that I should deem it a spectre or a phantom formed by my brain (and similar to those which I form in sleep) rather than a real man." Similarly, Christian Wolff [23] holds that "in a dream while you look at some one, he suddenly changes into some one else or he vanishes straight-way and no one comes back to take his place." Things behave in a strange, haphazard, and unreasonable manner. And it is this that distinguishes them from real entities and marks them as dreams. There is thus suggested to us another manner in which we might partially describe the signification of our term "existence." We can not make effective use of a universal affirmative existential proposition. And so we may pass by the proposition: Whatever has many points of contact with our usual experience is real. But perhaps in partially explaining the signification of "existence" it will be well for us to make use of the proposition: Whatever appears as out of accord with our usual experience, as having few points of contact with the entities of which we are normally aware, is unreal.

Our usual experience reveals to us stones that are mute. A subsistent stone that talks of its own accord differs from most of its fellow subsisting stones. It appears as something surprising and unusual, as something that could not be predicted or accounted for, as a phenomenon having few points of contact with our normal experience. If then in explaining "existence" we were to make use of the proposition: "Subsistents having few points of contact with our normal experience are unreal," it would be the unusual and extraordinary phenomenon,—the *rara avis*, as it were,—that we would be assigning to the realm of the non-existent. What, however, is usual, and what is unusual? Conversations with the Virgin Mary were not at all unusual in the Middle Ages; nor were witches unusual in the New England of Cotton Mather. The universal negative existential proposition which we are considering would not definitely and unambiguously assign to the realm of the non-existent either visions of the Virgin Mary or women riding on broom-sticks. Again, substances that give off emanations are unusual in our experience, though pieces of radium that give off such emanations are not rare. Consequently, if we start from the consideration of all substances rather than from the consideration merely of radium, our proposition seems to assign to the realm of non-existence all substances alleged to give off emanations. In general, we may say that the instances of any species are few in number, and that this species is rare, if we start with a genus that is sufficiently extensive. Rarity in short is a relative thing. And so if mere rarity implies unreality, membership in the realm of non-existence becomes relative and indeterminate.

The proposition: "Subsistents having few points of contact with our normal experience are unreal" does not definitely and unambiguously point out a limited group of entities as unreal. Nearly every phenomena is usual, if we take into consideration the experience of some special group of subjects. And nearly every phenomenon is rare, when we consider it an instance of an extremely extensive genus. If we describe more closely the notion of having many points of contact with normal experience, perhaps we can arrive at a proposition that will definitely and unambiguously assign a limited group of entities to the realm of the unreal. Perhaps this can be accomplished by identifying the phenomenon that is unusual with the phenomenon whose behavior is unpredictable. Perhaps it can be accomplished by identifying the phenomenon that is unusual with the phenomenon that is observed by but a single subject. If we partially explain "existence" by limiting reality to entities presented as having been perceived by more than one subject, we rule out of existence the fall of the tree of which I am the sole observer. We mark out as "non-existent," in our sense of the word "existence," an entity that common usage obviously calls "real." And if we say that the unpredictable is unreal, we meet with a problem akin to that into which we run when we limit reality, not to what is experienced, but merely to objects of possible experience. When is an entity that is not actually experienced an object of possible experience? We found this a question to be answered only through the introduction of other concepts than that of experience, through the introduction, for example, of the concepts of time and place. So it is with the question: When is a phenomenon that is not actually predicted one that might have been predicted? If we limit reality to what is actually predicted, we mark out as unreal many entities that common usage calls "real." And if we limit reality merely to what might be predicted, we are forced to examine other concepts if we would have our universal negative existential proposition one that definitely and unambiguously assigns a limited group of entities to the realm of non-existence.

A phenomenon is out of accord with our usual experience when it is rare, exceptional, and surprising. In a more special sense, however, a phenomenon may be held to be out of accord with our usual experience when it fails to conform with the various scientific generalizations that are valid for the objects of our normal experience. There are, it may be held, various laws which all real phenomena obey. There are, it may be held, various truths of reason which constitute the form of reality. A phenomenon is real, it may be said, when it conforms with these intelligible laws, when its behavior presents material for which these truths of reason can furnish a supplementing form. And a phenomenon is unreal, it may be held, when it appears inconsistent with these intelligible truths. A phenomenon is out of accord with our usual experience, has few points of contact with the system of existent entities, it may be said, when it disobeys the laws which constitute the form of reality.

Leibniz is an outstanding advocate of the doctrine that all existent entities are intimately bound up with one another through membership in a systematic network of relations. Each monad, to be sure, is its own cause; but the monads, taken together, form an organic system in which each bit is essential. The world of real entities is, he holds, a system of interrelated compossible entities. An entity is real if it belongs in the system, if it sustains the relations that all real entities do sustain towards one another. And a phenomenon is unreal if it appears to us as coming without antecedents and as going without consequents, as a stranger that has no connection with the interrelated world formed by most subsistents. In passages in which he alludes to the difference between the real and the unreal, Leibniz suggests some of the doctrines that we have just been discussing. An entity is real and belongs in the system of interrelated entities only if it harmonizes with our normal experiences. He uses such phrases as "agreement with the whole course of life" [24] and alludes to the phenomenon of "future things" being "in a certain degree . . . foreseen from past things." [25] There also appears however the more special doctrine that real entities are those which conform with certain truths of reason, with certain intelligible laws. "The basis of the truth of contingent and singular things," [26] he writes, "is in the succession which causes these phenomena of

62

the senses to be rightly united as the intelligible truths demand."

We thus elicit the universal negative existential proposition: Subsistents appearing as inconsistent with this, or with that, intelligible law are unreal. If we accept as an intelligible law the proposition that every event has a cause, then any subsistent appearing as an uncaused event is, in accordance with the proposition which we are considering, marked out forthwith as unreal. Our proposition does not fail to assign a definite group of entities to the realm of the non-existent. It marks out as unreal a group of entities that will be definite in proportion as our intelligible laws are expressed with precision; and it marks out as unreal a group of subsistents that will vary with the particular propositions that are accepted and laid down as intelligible laws. Nor, if our intelligible laws are carefully chosen, does it appear that the universal negative existential proposition which we are considering will assign to the realm of the non-existent any entities which common usage unhesitatingly calls "real." The problem we run into, however, is the problem: Which propositions are to be regarded as together constituting the intelligible laws? The proposition: "Every entity has a date and a spatial position" may be regarded as an intelligible law. And the proposition: "Every entity is self-consistent" may be regarded as an intelligible law. To the extent to which these propositions constitute the system of intelligible laws, we have already committed ourselves to the acceptance of the proposition: "Whatever is inconsistent with the intelligible laws is unreal." For this proposition now reduces to the proposition: "Whatever appears as lacking date or spatial position is unreal" and to the proposition: "Whatever subsists as self-contradictory is unreal."

When, in partially describing the signification to be attached to the term "existence," we choose to make use of the proposition: "Whatever subsists as inconsistent with the intelligible laws is unreal," there is one consequence which ensues which I should like to point out. The entity which subsists as inconsistent with some intelligible law is by our proposition forthwith assigned to the realm of the non-existent. If the proposition: "The quantity of matter is always constant" is regarded as an intelligible law, then any phenomenon involving an increase or a decrease in the quantity of matter is forthwith marked out as an unreal and illusory phenomenon. Our intelligible laws, consequently, turn out to be immune to overthrow by what are known as negative instances. For the negative instance, instead of weakening or destroying the validity of the intelligible law, is itself immediately ruled out as an illusory and unreal phenomenon.

These remarks apply with especial force to Kant, in whose writings the intelligible truths are developed in some detail. The most important of what we may call the intelligible laws seem for Kant to be the propositions discussed in the Analogies of Experience. In order to be real, a phenomenon must be given to us as consistent with the intelligible laws; and we are not left entirely in the dark as to what these intelligible laws are. For one thing, in order that a given phenomenon may be real, it must not in its behavior contradict the proposition that the quantity of substance is constant. For another thing, it must not contradict the proposition that every event has a cause. And for still another thing, it must not contradict the proposition that there is dynamical interaction between contemporaneous entities. These three propositions discussed in the Analogies of Experience constitute for Kant a part, though not the whole, of what we may call the intelligible laws. And if we have these propositions in mind when, in partially explaining "existence," we make use of the proposition: "Whatever subsists as inconsistent with the intelligible laws is unreal," then the phenomenon that appears, for example, as uncaused is immediately marked out as a phenomenon that is unreal. The proposition that every event has a cause comes to be a proposition whose validity does not rest upon experience. It comes to be a proposition which can not be over-thrown by any experience; for any phenomenon seeming to contradict it that might be presented to us would immediately be marked out as illusory and unreal. The causal law, in a word, comes to be a presupposition of experience. But it comes to be a presupposition of valid experience only in the sense that it is being taken as one of the intelligible laws to which we refer when, in partially explaining "existence," we say that whatever is given to us as inconsistent with the intelligible laws is unreal. We come thus, by a somewhat different route, to a position that has already been expressed in the previous chapter. "In laying down the causal law, Kant is implicitly determining the signification of 'existence.'"

And so it appears "that the validity which Kant finds for the causal law . . . is only the validity which attaches to a proposition determining the meaning of a term." [27]

We might go on to consider a number of universal negative existential propositions that we have not yet discussed in detail. With respect to each of them, we might ask whether it assigns a definite group of entities to the realm of the unreal and attaches to existence freedom from some clearly described characteristic. With respect to each of them we might also ask whether it definitely assigns to the realm of the non-existent entities which common usage unhesitatingly calls "real." In short, we might bring up for consideration universal negative existential propositions *ad nauseam.* And with respect to each of them we might ask whether it is the sort of proposition of which we can well make use in partially describing what we are to call "existence." We have however already met with some positive results. We have agreed to make use of the proposition: "Self-contradictory subsistents are unreal." And we have agreed to make use of the proposition: "Subsistents appearing as lacking a date or as lacking a spatial position are unreal." Perhaps then we can forego a more extended survey of the writings of the past. Perhaps we can fill out for ourselves the group of universal negative existential propositions of which we are to make use in partially explaining our term "existence."

With respect to logical self-consistency, one universal negative existential proposition is as suitable as another to the task of explaining "existence." Our selection of one universal negative existential proposition in preference to another is a matter of choice and not a matter of logical compulsion. We have stated however the considerations on which our choice will be based.[28] And, on the basis of these considerations, there are certain propositions of which we have already agreed to make use.

Universal negative existential propositions, we have seen, can not by themselves completely determine for the term "existence" a meaning that will be sufficiently precise. We must in addition make use of individual affirmative existential propositions and of individual negative existential propositions. However, other things being equal, the greater the number of universal negative existential propositions of which we make use, the more precise does the meaning of our term "existence" become. We have consequently the task of joining additional universal negative existential propositions to the proposition: "Self-contradictory subsistents are unreal" and to the proposition: "Subsistents appearing as lacking all date or all position are unreal."

Moreover, we have the task of assuring ourselves that the universal negative existential propositions of which we have already agreed to make use are sufficiently unambiguous and clear.

In a general way, however, we are at this point ready to enumerate the propositions which taken together will explain the meaning which "existence" is to have in the constructive parts of this treatise. We are ready to set ourselves to the task of laying down a number of universal negative existential propositions, each as clear in its expression and as unambiguous in its reference as possible; and to the task of supplementing these propositions with singular or particular existential propositions both affirmative and negative, with lists, that is to say, both of some of the entities that are included in, and of some of the entities that are excluded from, the denotation of "existence" in our sense of that term. We are ready in short to address ourselves in earnest to the task of laying down the group of existential propositions, which, taken together, are to occupy in our metaphysics a position similar to that which Descartes intended for his: "Cogito ergo sum."

Summary

We are at liberty to determine what meaning we are going to attach to our term "existence." Still we want the meaning we choose to conform with the common meaning of "existence" in so far as the latter can be determined and applied in such a way as to mark out definite groups of entities as existent and definite groups as non-existent.

One feature of the common meaning of "existence" is the 'hardness' of facts, the imperviousness of reality to expansion or contraction through mere thinking. In order that what *we* call "existence" may have this characteristic, our propositions explaining our term "existence" must be limited to universal negative ones, supplemented by individual or particular propositions.

Which universal negative propositions shall we use in our explanation? Various possibilities are considered from two angles: (1) would they determine for our term "existence" a meaning somewhat in accord with what "existence" commonly means— realizing of course that the common meaning is hazy; and (2) would they determine for our term "existence" a meaning from which it will follow that certain entities, but not all entities, are definitely marked out as unreal.

None of these considerations are binding. They merely incline us to give our term "existence" one meaning rather than another.

Chapter III

HOW WE SHALL USE THE TERMS: EXISTENCE
AND REALITY

There is no entity that is not what we are calling a "subsistent." The world of subsistents includes the man walking on my ceiling, God, everything, goodness, greater-than, mathematics. It includes everything that can be mentioned and everything that can not be mentioned,—my alleged objects, your alleged objects, and entities alleged to be objects for no one. It is this unlimited field, including all entities that may be held to be real and all entities that may be held to be unreal, that forms our universe of discourse and is to be dichotomized into the real and the unreal. It is difficult to refer to this unlimited field of subsistents without appearing to hold that its members exist. If we say that the man walking on my ceiling is a subsistent, the use of the word "is" may create the impression that this subsisting man exists. And a similar impression may be created by the remark that this man has the characteristic of walking on my ceiling. This danger of misinterpretation can not be completely overcome. We shall refer to the man on my ceiling as a subsistent or an appearance. And instead of saying that he *has* a certain characteristic, we shall, for the most part, say that he appears with this characteristic or is presented with this characteristic. But it is not to be assumed that a subsistent which appears is an appearance *of* something which is real. Nor is it at this point to be assumed that to appear is to appear to some conscious subject. Entities appearing with the characteristic of being objects for no one are subsistents. They too will be called "appearances." They too are included in the unlimited field which it is our task to dichotomize into the real and the unreal.

Some of the subsistents that are to be called "real" and some of the subsistents that we are to call "unreal" may be dismissed from our attention until we come to the end of this chapter. There we shall enumerate certain real subsistents and certain unreal subsistents. For we have planned to deal with certain members of our universe of discourse individually. The existential status of these subsistents will be determined, and our term "existence" explained in so far as it applies to them, by means of singular or particular existential propositions, some positive and some negative.

In determining the meaning of our term "existence," we have agreed to make use of such propositions as "X_1 exists" and "X_2 exists": and we have agreed to make use of such propositions as "Y_1 does not exist" and "Y_2 does not exist." But we have also agreed to make use of universal negative existential propositions, of propositions of the type: "No A's exist." Indeed, proposition for proposition, our universal negative existential propositions will describe the signification we are assigning "existence" more fully than will our singular existential propositions. And so it is to the selection of certain universal negative existential propositions that we turn.

There is one such proposition that we have already agreed to use, namely, "No self-contradictory subsistents are real." Self-contradictory subsistents, however, are subsistents which *appear* as self-contradictory. The King of England who resides in Buckingham Palace is a self-contradictory subsistent in so far as I think of him as self-contradictory. And a square circle is not a self-contradictory subsistent when its alleged squareness and its alleged circularity do not *appear* as mutually contradictory. The proposition: "No self-contradictory subsistents are real" marks out as unreal the King of England who appears as self-contradictory and the square circle which appears as self-contradictory. But it does not determine the existential status of either the subsisting King of England who does not appear as self-contradictory or of the subsisting square circle which does not appear as self-contradictory. Whatever appears as self-contradictory is, however, we say, unreal. Existence, as we describe it, is characterized by freedom from explicit self-contradiction.

There is the subsistent which appears as round and not-round. And there is the subsistent which appears as real and unreal. If we partially determine the signification of "existence" by means of the singular proposition: "X_1 exists," then X_1, let us suppose, appears as real. But X_1 may have been presented as, and may appear as, a self-contradictory or unreal subsistent. One might choose to use "real" in such a way that entities enumerated as real are in all cases real. One might hold, that is to say, that singular affirmative existential propositions used in determining the signification of "existence" are a court of final authority, that unreal appearances and self-contradictory appearances are real if they are enumerated as real. Let us however choose the opposite path. Let us hold that self-contradictory appearances and unreal appearances are unreal even though they are enumerated as real. Or, rather, let us agree to enumerate as real no subsistents which appear as unreal and no subsistents which appear as self-contradictory. If we partially determine the signification of "existence" by means of the proposition: "No A's exist," let us agree to limit the entities represented by the subject-terms of our singular affirmative existential propositions to "X_1 not appearing as an A," "X_2 not appearing as an A," etc.[1]

Self-contradictory appearances are in all cases unreal. Whatever appears as round and not-round, and hence as self-contradictory, does not exist. But what about the subsistent which appears as round and square? Round and not-round are explicitly A and non-A, round and square less explicitly so. To be sure, each square subsistent that I consider readily takes on the appearance of not-roundness. As soon as the quality of being not-round is suggested to me, I recognize this quality as being an additional characteristic with which my subsistent is appearing. The subsistent under discussion is a subsistent appearing as square which enlarges itself to be a subsistent appearing as square and appearing as not-round. With respect to subsistents which thus enlarge themselves, we may say that there are implicit characteristics with which they appear. The subsistent which I am considering appears explicitly, let us suppose, as round and as square; and it appears implicitly as not-round and as self-contradictory. Such subsistents which appear implicitly as self-contradictory are, let us say, unreal. Whereas we have already assigned to the realm of non-existence the subsistent appearing explicitly as round and as not-round and as self-contradictory, let us also assign to this realm the subsistent appearing explicitly as round and as square and only implicitly as self-contradictory. Let us, that is to say, lay down the additional proposition: "Whatever appears implicitly self-contradictory is unreal." Or, to put it another way, no subsistent is real whose explicit and implicit appearances appear to contradict one another.

This disposes of the round square subsistent which enlarges itself to become a round, square, not-round, self-contradictory subsistent. But, whereas the subsistent which we have been discussing grows from a subsistent appearing as square to a subsistent appearing as not-round, the unlimited world of subsistents contains round square subsistents which do not thus enlarge themselves. It is conceivable, for example, for some one to hold that round squares are not self-contradictory. The subsistent which he considers, or can be imagined to consider, does not grow. As we have already in effect noticed, there is no universal negative existential proposition that will eliminate from reality the round square subsistents which neither explicitly nor implicitly appear as self-contradictory.[2] But we can agree not to enumerate as real any of these non-growing round squares which do not, even implicitly, appear as self-contradictory. Our procedure must be to trace the growth of *a* subsistent from round and square to round, square, not-round and self-contradictory; and then to determine to enumerate as real *no other* subsistent which appears as round and as square. No A's, we may say, are real; and no subsistents implicitly appearing as A's. We may trace some subsistent S to the point where it appears as an A. We may, that is to say, point out some S which implicitly appears as an A. But all S's are unreal only in so far as we thereupon resolve to enumerate no S's among the entities we call existents. Subsistents which implicitly appear as self-contradictory are unreal. And when we[3] show one subsistent to appear as implicitly self-contradictory, all subsistents differing from it merely in that they do not appear as self-contradictory are likewise unreal. For we have resolved not to enumerate such resembling subsistents among the entities we call "real." We may point out some S which implicitly appears as an A. Therefore, we may say, no S is real. But this will be but a short-hand and condensed way of assuming that our resolve to enumerate no S's among our existents will be carried out.

Some subsistent appearing as round and square appears with explicit and implicit characteristics which appear to contradict one another. So too with the Cretan who appears as truly asserting that no Cretan ever speaks the truth. My subsistent is a Cretan making a certain true assertion. As an outgrowth of my original object, I am led to consider an alleged situation in which no Cretan ever speaks the truth. I come to consider various alleged mendacious Cretans, among them my Cretan informant. Indeed I come to consider my Cretan informant in the act of falsely asserting that no Cretan ever speaks truly. My subsistent is a Cretan appearing explicitly with the characteristic of having just made a certain true assertion. And this subsistent has grown to be a Cretan appearing with the characteristic of having just made a certain untrue assertion. It implicitly appears as self-contradictory. The Cretan that I am discussing is consequently unreal. And all subsisting Cretans who appear to be truly asserting that no Cretan ever speaks the truth, all such Cretans, whether they appear as self-contradictory or not, will be eliminated from our lists of real entities.

Obviously veracious Cretan does not enlarge itself to become mendacious Cretan and self-contradictory Cretan as readily as round square enlarges itself to become round, not-round, self-contradictory square. There are intermediate subsistents to be presented and these intermediate subsistents may not spontaneously offer themselves for discussion. Veracious Cretan not appearing as implicitly self-contradictory is a more common subsistent than round square not appearing as implicitly self-contradictory. But it is all subsistents, whether they be common or uncommon, that are to be dichotomized into the real and the unreal. It is *a* veracious Cretan asserting that no Cretan ever speaks the truth who implicitly appears as self-contradictory. Remaining in the unlimited universe of subsistents which is prior to the distinction between the real and the unreal, one may perhaps describe *this* Cretan as developing into a self-contradictory Cretan. But if "veracious Cretan is implicitly self-contradictory Cretan" is to apply to the veracious Cretan who does not appear self-contradictory as well as to the Cretan who does so appear, it will not suffice to trace the growth or enlargement of a given subsistent.[4] In this treatise the growth or development of certain subsistents is traced and the implicit appearances of these subsistents revealed. Similar subsistents which do not so develop—the opinions, we may say, of those who do not agree with the developments we trace—are disposed of through our determination not to list as real any subsistents similar to those which, as we develop them, are implicitly unreal.

We have so determined the signification of our term "existence" that all round, not-round subsistents are unreal. We have so determined the signification of "existence" that round squares are unreal. And we have so determined the signification of "existence" that any Cretan appearing as truly asserting that no Cretan ever speaks the truth is also unreal. No entity will be called "real" that, except for its development, is indistinguishable from a subsistent which *our* discussion reveals to us as self-contradictory.

How is it now, we may ask, with respect to the subsistent appearing as in no sense an object of consciousness? The thesis that only ideas exist is frequently regarded as the doctrine on which modern idealism is founded. Many idealists assert that only ideas exist, holding that entities not ideas and entities not objects of consciousness are self-contradictory. Let us then examine this alleged contradiction at this point. Let us see if 'entity appearing as in no sense an object of consciousness' develops into 'entity appearing as self-contradictory.'

"How say you, Hylas," asks Philonous,[5] "can you see a thing which is at the same time unseen?" "No," answers Hylas, "that were a contradiction." "Is it not as great a contradiction to talk of conceiving a thing which is unconceived?" "It is," admits Hylas. And he continues: "As I was thinking of a tree in a solitary place where no one was present to see it, methought that was to conceive a tree as existing unperceived or unthought of: not considering that I myself conceived it all the while." As Berkeley[6] explains it, "the mind, taking no notice of itself, is deluded to think it can and does conceive bodies existing unthought of, . . .

though at the same time they are apprehended by . . . itself."

During the present century as realism has renewed its vigor in Great Britain and in America, the fundamental doctrines of idealism have been re-examined. "No thinker to whom one may appeal," admits Perry,[7] "is able to mention a thing that is not idea for the obvious and simple reason that in mentioning it he makes it an idea." Consequently, we are unable to discover what things are as unknown. "In order to discover if possible exactly how a thing is modified by the cognitive relationship, I look for instances of things *out* of this relationship in order that I may compare them with instances of things *in* this relationship. But I can find no such instances, because 'finding' is a variety of the very relationship that I am trying to eliminate."[8] There is this barrier, which Perry calls the "ego-centric predicament," which prevents me from using ordinary methods to discover what difference knowing makes to objects. But this predicament, Perry holds, does not justify me in concluding that knowing makes all the difference between existing and not existing. "Every mentioned thing is an idea . . . But what the idealist requires is a proposition to the effect that everything is an idea or that only ideas exist."[9]

"We can not be aware of an entity that is not in some sense an object. Therefore the entity that is not in some sense an object does not exist." Here there is an obvious *non-sequitur*. If this were the best argument the idealist could put forth, Perry would be justified in regarding the ego-centric predicament as a methodological difficulty without ontological implications. But the real point of the idealist's proper argument is not that the entity that is in no sense an object of consciousness is undiscoverable. His real point is that this entity appears self-contradictory. Indeed, in some sense, the entity that is in no sense an object of consciousness *can* be discovered, *can* be mentioned, *can* be thought of. For we seem in the present paragraph to be discussing, mentioning and considering: 'the entity that is in no sense an object of consciousness.' If this entity were not a subsistent at all, we indeed could not conclude that this entity is non-existent. We would be in the predicament of not being able to assert that this entity exists or that it does not exist. But the idealist asserts that it does not exist; and the realist asserts that it may exist. In making such assertions they claim to be discussing the entity that is

74

in no sense an object of consciousness. Their assertions exemplify the fact that the entity that is in no sense an object of consciousness can to some degree be discussed and considered.[10]

There seems to be given to me, as a subsistent whose ontological status is to be discussed, 'the entity that is in no sense an object of consciousness.' Indeed at the present moment it is this subsistent that I am considering. This entity appears as in no sense an object of consciousness. And yet, as soon as the characteristic of being in some sense an object suggests itself, I recognize this characteristic as an additional appearance of the subsistent that I am considering. *Implicitly* my subsistent appears as an entity that I am considering, as in some sense an object of consciousness. The entity that is in no sense an object of consciousness explicitly appears with the characteristic of being in no sense an object of consciousness. And implicitly it appears with the characteristic of being in some sense an object of consciousness and hence with the characteristic of being self-contradictory. However, "whatever appears implicitly self-contradictory is unreal." [11] We hold, therefore, that the subsistent which we have been considering, the entity that appears as in no sense an object of consciousness, is unreal. And we resolve to list as real no 'entity that is in no sense an object of consciousness' even if it does not *appear* as self-contradictory.

The subsistent which we have been considering develops, it may be agreed, into a subsistent which appears as self-contradictory. But, it may be held, there are subsistents which no one considers. The subsistent which no one considers is, however, the very subsistent whose development we have just traced. The subsistent which no one considers is the entity which is in no sense an object of consciousness. I may refer to each member of the world of subsistents. And when I talk about all subsistents, there is no subsistent that—as I trace its development—does not take on the characteristic of being in some sense an object of consciousness. It is no ego-centric predicament which makes non-objects unreal. If non-objects could not be discussed, they could not be asserted to be unreal. Rather, neither their reality nor their unreality could be discussed. But the very fact that the realist holds that some of these non-objects may be real is evidence that these non-objects are not outside what we call the world of subsistents. Non-objects appear both as non-objects and as objects. And they are unreal because self-contradictory subsistents are unreal. The self-contradictory subsistent which appears self-contradictory is unreal because of the universal negative existential proposition which partially determines the signification of our term "existence." And the self-contradictory subsistent which does not appear self-contradictory, the entity in no sense an object of consciousness, for example, which, as it was apparently presented to Perry, does not develop the appearance of self-contradictoriness, this entity is unreal because of our resolve not to list it as real.

Whatever appears implicitly contradictory is unreal. And, we may add, whatever appears, explicitly or implicitly, as in no sense an object is unreal. The world of reality is free of subsistents appearing as non-objects. It contains no entities precluded from appearing as objects. It is by no means to be concluded however that each real entity is an immediate datum or object for some conscious subject. The proposition that no subsistents are real which appear as in no sense objects does not imply the non-existence of indirect objects or of entities referred to but not immediately given. For the entity that is in some fashion referred to is not an entity that is in no sense an object. The entity that is in some fashion referred to can develop the appearance of being in some sense an object without developing the appearance of self-contradictoriness. Likewise it is not to be concluded that each real entity is definitely and fully presented. Perhaps no one knows whether Descartes' great-great-grandfather was tall or short. Perhaps Descartes' great-great-grandfather is a subsistent which appears with few characteristics. It is a subsistent, let us suppose, which appears with the characteristic of being one of Descartes' ancestors, but without name, nationality or size. Nevertheless this subsistent can develop the appearance of being in some sense an object without developing the appearance of self-contradictoriness. I may refer to each member of the unlimited world of subsistents. But this is very different from cataloging and describing each subsistent. Subsistents appearing as in no sense objects are unreal. But, so far as we have yet seen, subsistents appearing with vague and barren characteristics may or may not be real.

"I know that there are Chinamen, but I know no individual Chinamen. . . . I may be able to think the universe, but may

76

know little of its details. It is therefore evident," says Spaulding,[12] "that there are two kinds of knowing." There is the full, detailed and explicit manner in which the pen with which I am writing appears as a subsistent. There is the vague indefinite and undetailed manner in which 'everything' appears. Indeed there are shades of definiteness, of fulness of content, between and at either end. A centaur is a subsistent which I consider when I seem to think of an animal with the body of a horse and the head of a man. The same subsistent appears more vaguely when I seem to think of a certain fabulous creature; and still more vaguely when I seem to think of a given subsistent. Whatever appears with the characteristic of being in no sense an object of consciousness is unreal. But up to this point we have not excluded from the world of existents,—as we are to use the term "existence,"—either 'a certain fabulous creature' or 'a given subsistent.'

There is the subsistent which appears simply as a fabulous creature. And there is the subsistent which is less vague, which appears with more detailed characteristics, the subsistent which appears as the centaur who attempted to carry off Dejanira, the wife of Hercules. It is no doubt possible for these subsistents to be distinguished from one another and to be regarded as two. Nevertheless as there suggest themselves the characteristic of having the head of a man, the characteristic of having the body of a horse and the characteristic of having attempted to carry off Dejanira, I recognize these characteristics as implicit appearances of the 'certain fabulous creature' that I was already considering. 'A certain fabulous creature' has developed into 'the centaur who attempted to carry off Dejanira' just as 'round square' may develop into 'round, not-round, self-contradictory square.'[13] We have, to be sure, distinguished the Barbarossa who appears to have died in Asia Minor from the Barbarossa who appears to be now asleep in a cave.[14] When I begin by considering a Barbarossa who died in Asia Minor and then come to consider a Barbarossa now asleep in a cave, I find that a characteristic of my former subsistent has been wiped out; I find that my subsistent has not developed but has, on the contrary, been displaced by another subsistent. A Barbarossa dead in Asia Minor which develops into, which implicitly appears as, Barbarossa now asleep in a cave is, let us suppose, unreal. But a Barbarossa dead in Asia Minor which does not so develop is, let us suppose, real, and is to be distinguished from Barbarossa appearing as asleep in a cave.

The fabulous creature which develops into the centaur who attempted to carry off Dejanira is not unreal because of any lack of definite characteristics. But what shall we say with respect to a subsistent described as 'a fabulous creature' which does not so develop? It too the universal negative existential propositions thus far adopted do not determine to be unreal. For, whereas this fabulous creature appears neither explicitly nor implicitly with definite characteristics, it does not develop the characteristic of being in no sense an object of consciousness and does not implicitly appear as self-contradictory. There is the fabulous creature which implicitly appears as the centaur who attempted to carry off Dejanira. And there is the fabulous creature which does not have any explicit definite appearances. But creatures which do not have any explicit definite appearances may again be divided. There is the fabulous creature of this sort which has, or develops, the characteristic of being definitely presented to no conscious subject. And there is the fabulous creature which, whereas it does not develop any definite characteristics as we continue to consider it, develops the appearance of appearing with definite characteristics to some one. When I think of paleontology, for example, I think of nothing definite. And, since I know no paleontology, as I continue to consider paleontology my subsistent continues without definite appearances. But my subsistent takes on the characteristic of appearing with more details to paleontologists. On the other hand, as I consider the millionth digit in the square root of two, not only does my subsistent not take on the characteristic of being, let us say, an eight or a nine, but, since it seems to me that no one will carry the square root of two out to a million places, my subsistent takes on the characteristic of appearing to no one as a definite number.

In holding self-contradictory subsistents to be unreal and in holding subsistents appearing as non-objects to be unreal, we do not mark those subsistents as unreal which appear with the characteristic of being definite appearances for no one. We are at liberty to determine the signification of "existence" in any manner that we find convenient. But to permit those subsistents to be real which appear to be definite appearances for no one is to make no attempt to exclude from the world of reality those 'given entities' and 'certain subsistents' which seem to be thoroughly useless. Let us then determine the signification of "existence" in such a manner that it will follow that subsistents with merely vague and undetailed appearances may in some cases be real. But let us hold that subsistents appearing with the characteristic of appearing to no one in a detailed manner are unreal. Indeed, let us rule out of existence, not merely those subsistents which originally appear as detailed appearances for no one, but also those subsistents which take on this characteristic when it suggests itself. Let us partially determine the signification of "existence," that is to say, by laying down the universal negative existential proposition: "Subsistents explicitly or implicitly appearing as definite appearances for no one are unreal." And let us resolve to list as real no subsistent which, except for its development, is indistinguishable from a subsistent which we find taking on the characteristic of being a definite appearance for no one.

We have in the preceding chapter adopted the rule that "our universal negative existential propositions should be so chosen that they mark out fairly definite groups of entities that are being assigned to the realm of non-existence." [15] In view of the fact, however, that there are so many shades of vagueness with which a subsistent may appear, the universal negative existential proposition which we have just laid down does not seem entirely satisfactory. Is the subsistent that is unreal the subsistent which appears with the characteristic of appearing to no one with as many as four details or is it the subsistent which appears with the characteristic of appearing to no one with as many as forty-four details? I believe that, without attempting at this point further to refine the distinction between vague appearances and detailed appearances, the universal negative existential proposition just laid down will be found to mark out some subsistents as unreal and to give some characteristic to 'reality.' We shall to some extent determine what is vague and what detailed as various subsistents are considered in the course of this treatise. We shall, that is to say, point out certain subsistents that appear with the characteristic of appearing to no one in a sufficiently detailed manner, subsistents that, we shall hold, the proposition just laid down marks out as unreal.

Appearing with the characteristic of appearing definitely to no one is to be distinguished from appearing without the characteristic of appearing definitely to some one. A subsistent is not unreal because it appears without a given characteristic. A subsistent is unreal when explicitly or implicitly it appears *with* the characteristic of being in no sense an object, *with* the characteristic, that is to say, of appearing to no one. And a subsistent is unreal when explicitly or implicitly it appears *with* the characteristic of appearing definitely to no one. But the subsistent which does not have or develop such an appearance, or the appearance of being self-contradictory, this subsistent, considering the implications that may be deduced from the universal negative existential propositions thus far adopted, need not be unreal. Likewise the subsistents which do not resemble one that we find developing the appearance of self-contradictoriness or the appearance of being no one's definite object, these too, so far as our present resolutions carry us, may be listed among existing entities.

The universal negative existential propositions that we have thus far laid down in partially determining the meaning of our term "existence" have in one way or another suggested themselves to us as a consequence of our interest in the self-contradictory. In the previous chapter we agreed to take as one starting point the proposition: "Self-contradictory subsistents are unreal." We also agreed, however, to make use of the proposition: "Whatever appears as lacking a date or as having no spatial position is unreal." From this latter proposition it follows that subsistents appearing as lacking any date or position are unreal along with subsistents appearing as self-contradictory, subsistents appearing as non-objects, and subsistents appearing as definite appearances for no one. Let us also lay down the proposition that subsistents developing the appearance of utter non-spatiality or the appearance of utter non-temporality are non-existent. And let us resolve to list as real no subsistents, which, except for their development, are indistinguishable from those which in this treatise we find taking on the appearance of utter non-temporality or the appearance of utter non-spatiality.

No subsistents are real that explicitly or implicitly appear as lacking all spatial position. No subsistents are real that explicitly or implicitly appear as utterly undated. What shall we say, however, with respect to the entity that explicitly or implicitly appears dated with respect to one entity but not with respect to another? Cinderella left for the ball before she lost her slipper. The loss of the slipper is presented as occurring after the departure for the ball. But it is presented, let us assume, as having neither preceded nor followed the fall of Constantinople. The fall of Constantinople, we likewise suppose, appears as having neither preceded nor followed the loss of the slipper. But whereas the fall of Constantinople appearing as not temporally related to the loss of the slipper appears without the claim that the loss of the slipper is nevertheless real, the loss of the slipper, appearing as not temporally related to the fall of Constantinople, does, we suppose, appear with the claim that the fall of Constantinople is nevertheless real. The fall of Constantinople presented in this fashion may, we hold, be real. The loss of the slipper we hold to be unreal. We mark out as unreal that entity which explicitly or implicitly appears as utterly undated, as undated with respect to any entity. And we also mark out as unreal that entity which explicitly or implicitly appears as undated with respect to some other entity while appearing explicitly or implicitly with the claim that that other entity is nevertheless real.

It is one thing to appear with the characteristic of lacking any date. It is another thing to appear without the characteristic of having a date. As we use the term "existence," an entity is not unreal in so far as it appears without a given characteristic. It is unreal if it appears, explicitly or implicitly, *with* a given characteristic, with, for example, the characteristic of having no date with respect to any entity, or with the characteristic of having no date with respect to some other entity and with the claim that this other entity is real. The entity that appears without the characteristic of having a date and without the characteristic of having no date may be real just as may the entity that appears with the characteristic of having a date. It is the entity that appears with the characteristic of having no date that is unreal; and the entity that appears with the characteristic of having no date with respect to an entity that appears real.

Without forgetting that the subsistent may be real that appears without the characteristic of having a date and without the characteristic of having no date, let us consider a subsistent that appears with the characteristic of *having* a date. A subsisting Socrates, let us suppose, appears with the characteristic of having a date with respect to Plato. And a phase of Socrates' life appears with the characteristic of being present, rather than past or future, with respect to a phase of Plato's life. The phase of Socrates' life which appears with the characteristic of being present with respect to a phase of Plato's life may appear with the characteristic of having a spatial position with respect to that phase of Plato's life or with the characteristic of having no spatial position with respect to that phase of Plato's life; or it may appear without either characteristic. But if it appears with the characteristic of having no spatial position with respect to an entity which appears real and with respect to which it appears to be present, then, let us say, it is unreal. As we use the term "reality," if we may be permitted to sum up the connections that have up to this point been brought out between existence, time and space, a subsistent is unreal if it appears with the characteristic of having no position with respect to any entity or with the characteristic of having no date with respect to any entity. Moreover it is unreal if it appears with the characteristic of having no date with respect to an entity that appears real; or if it appears with the characteristic of having no position with respect to an entity which appears real and with respect to which it appears present.

An entity is unreal if it appears both real and unreal and hence as implicitly self-contradictory, or if it appears temporally unrelated to an entity that appears real. It would of course be mere tautology to say that an entity is unreal if it *is* unreal. And it would be circular to say that an entity is unreal if it appears temporally unrelated to an entity that *is* real. But the world of subsistence which we are attempting to dichotomize includes, among other subsistents, some subsistents appearing as real and some subsistents appearing as unreal. It is, I believe, not tautological to eliminate those appearing as unreal; and not circular to eliminate those appearing temporally unrelated to subsistents appearing as real.

We are attempting to attach a signification to "existence" that will definitely assign certain subsistents to the realm of unreality. And we are attempting to attach a signification to "existence" that will not assign to the realm of unreality subsistents which common usage seems to be agreed in calling "real." These are resolves which we have adopted,—although it is not logical considerations which have compelled us to adopt them. We are, I believe, carrying out these resolves in marking out as unreal the loss of Cinderella's slipper which appears undatable with respect to the fall of Constantinople that appears real; and the castles which some novelist may present to us as being present with respect to allegedly real events, with respect, let us say, to the wars of Charlemagne, and yet as lacking spatial position with respect to them.

If, however, we were to mark out as unreal subsistents appearing to lack position with respect to entities alleged to be real and earlier, or if we were to mark out as unreal subsistents appearing to lack position with respect to entities alleged to be real and later, we might be assigning to the realm of unreality certain subsistents which are commonly called "real." The phase of Socrates' life in which he was about to drink the cup of hemlock appears real, let us suppose; and it appears earlier than my present writing. I may consider however that at different times the earth has different positions with respect to the sun and that whereas, taking the earth as at rest, I am a certain distance from the place where Socrates was, taking the sun as at rest I am a much greater distance from the place where the hemlock drinking occurred. I may consider, that is to say, that Socrates' position may be projected into the present in various ways and that it is only by taking one of these present positions as the "same" as Socrates' that I have position with respect to the hemlock drinking. I may hold that I have position primarily only with respect to present entities and that my position with respect to past entities is at the best ambiguous and is a position at all only in the sense that it is a position with respect to some present entity held to be in the "same" place. To hold then that my present writing has no unambiguous position and no direct position with respect to the hemlock drinking which appears both real and past might be to have my present writing appear as lacking position with respect to an entity appearing as real and with respect to which my present writing appears to be temporally related. And so, whereas we are, logically speaking, as much at liberty to mark out as unreal the subsistent appearing as lacking position with respect to an entity that appears real as we are to mark out as unreal the subsistent appearing as lacking date with respect to an entity that appears real, we choose in this connection to mark out as unreal merely that subsistent which appears as lacking position with respect to an entity that appears real *and with respect to which it also appears present.*

Certain subsistents, we say, are unreal that appear with the characteristic of being temporally unrelated to certain other sub-sistents. And certain subsistents, we say, are unreal that appear with the characteristic of being spatially unrelated to certain still other subsistents. The fall of Constantinople that appears tempo-rally unrelated to the loss of Cinderella's slipper that appears real is itself unreal. But the fall of Constantinople that appears tempo-rally unrelated to the loss of Cinderella's slipper that appears un-real, this is a different subsistent which, so far as we have yet seen, may be an existent entity.

It is then certain subsistents appearing with the characteristic of being temporally unrelated to certain other subsistents that are unreal; and certain subsistents appearing with the character-istic of being spatially unrelated to certain still other subsistents. What is it however to appear temporally or spatially unrelated to a given entity? The entity that appears as having several dates or several positions with respect to a given entity does not, we hold, appear spatially or temporally unrelated to that entity. If Julius Caesar appears real and the universal 'man' appears both with the past date with respect to Caesar that is commonly attributed to Alexander the Great and the future date with respect to Caesar that is commonly attributed to Napoleon, then the universal 'man' is not appearing temporally unrelated to an entity that appears real. To appear temporally unrelated to a given entity is not the same as appearing with the characteristic of having several dates, or with the characteristic of having no single date, with respect to that entity. A universal may be real if it appears as having several dates and not a single date with respect to a subsistent that appears real; or if it appears as having several positions and not a single position with respect to a subsistent that appears real and with respect to which some of its instances appear to be present. But the universal that appears to have no one date and no several dates, no one position and no several positions, such a

84

universal is unreal in the sense in which we choose to use the term "real."

A subsistent is unreal if it appears with the characteristic of having no date with respect to any entity or with the characteristic of having no date with respect to an entity that appears real. Also a subsistent is unreal if it appears with the characteristic of having no position with respect to any entity or with the characteristic of having no position with respect to an entity that appears real and with respect to which it appears present. What appears nowhere appears with the characteristic of having no position with respect to any entity. What appears everywhere appears, taken distributively, with the characteristic of having many positions and, taken collectively, with the characteristic of having one very vague position with respect to any entity with respect to which it appears present. The subsistent appearing to be everywhere, taken distributively, may, it would seem, be real. The subsistent appearing to be nowhere is, as we use "existence," unreal. But what shall we say with respect to the subsistent appearing to be everywhere, taken collectively? Shall we say that the cosmos, Space, Time, etc., appearing as each having a single indefinite date with respect to each entity that appears real may themselves be real? Or shall we mark out as unreal not only those entities appearing as having no date but also those appearing as having only an indefinite date?

A subsistent, we have seen, may appear with many or with few characteristics.[16] There are various degrees of accuracy or of vagueness with which it may be described and with which it may appear. Similarly there are degrees of accuracy, we may say, with which a subsistent may appear dated. With respect to the death of Napoleon, the Roman republic, the life of Cicero and the delivery of the first oration against Catiline all appear earlier. But the delivery of the first oration against Catiline appears with a more definite date with respect to the death of Napoleon than does the Roman republic. With respect to Napoleon's death, one subsistent may appear much earlier, another slightly earlier. But one may also appear as rather definitely dated, another as not so definitely dated. In determining the signification of our term "existence," we choose to make no use of the distinction between the subsistent appearing as much earlier and the subsistent appearing as slightly earlier, or the distinction between the subsistent appearing as earlier, the subsistent appearing as present and the subsistent appearing as later. But in order to eliminate from the world of reality subsistents that seem to be vague and unmanageable,[17] let us mark out as unreal certain subsistents appearing with indefinite dates. A subsistent is unreal, we have said, if it appears with the characteristic of having no date with respect to any entity or with the characteristic of having no date with respect to an entity that appears real. A subsistent is also unreal, let us add, if it appears with the characteristic of having only a very indefinite date with respect to an entity that appears real. If, that is to say, the death of Napoleon appears real and the Cosmos or the time continuum as a whole appears with the characteristic of having only a very indefinite date with respect to Napoleon's death, then, as we use the term "existence," the subsisting Cosmos or the subsisting time continuum, appearing in this fashion, is unreal.

Similarly with position. A subsistent is unreal, we have said, if it appears with the characteristic of having no position with respect to any entity or with the characteristic of having no position with respect to an entity which appears real and with respect to which it appears present. A subsistent is also unreal, let us add, if it appears with the characteristic of having only a very indefinite position with respect to an entity which appears real and with respect to which it appears present. We may again take the Cosmos as our example, or, better, that instantaneous phase of the Cosmos which may be alleged to have been the state of the Cosmos when Napoleon died. If Napoleon dying at St. Helena appears real and this state of the Cosmos appears both with the characteristic of being present with respect to the dying Napoleon and with the characteristic of having only a very indefinite position with respect to him, then this state of the Cosmos is appearing with characteristics which, as we use "existence," mark it as unreal.

An everlasting subsistent, taken collectively, is unreal in so far as it appears, explicitly or implicitly, with the characteristic of having only a very indefinite date with respect to an entity that appears real. An instantaneous but unlimited Space, as distinguished from limited portions of it, is unreal in so far as it appears, explicitly or implicitly, with the characteristic of having only a very indefinite position with respect to an entity which

86

appears real and with respect to which it appears present. An ever-lasting subsistent or an unlimited Space that appears without these characteristics is not ruled out of existence by the universal negative existential propositions which we have thus far adopted. It is ruled out only in so far as we take up for consideration some individual subsistent alleged to be everlasting or some individual subsistent described as an unlimited Space, find it unreal in accordance witth the universal negative existential proposition just accepted, and thereupon resolve to list no similar subsistents among those we call "real." [18]

What is it, however, to appear with the characteristic of having only a very indefinite date? The time continuum taken as a whole appears, we say, at least implicitly, with the characteristic of having only a very indefinite date with respect to the death of Napoleon that appears real. The delivery of the first oration against Catiline appears with a rather definite date, the Roman republic with a less definite date, with respect to the same entity. But just how vaguely, it may be asked, must an entity be dated for it to appear with the characteristic of having only a very indefinite date? In discussing the proposition that whatever appears with the characteristic of being a definite appearance for no one is unreal, we made no attempt to mark out any clear line of separation between the vague and the detailed, between definite appearances and indefinite appearances.[19] Similarly at this point we shall not attempt accurately to determine which dates are fairly definite and which are so indefinite that subsistents appearing to have them are unreal. The subsisting Cosmos that I am now considering appears with the characteristic of having only a very indefinite date with respect to the death of Napoleon that appears real. The Roman republic that I am now considering appears with the characteristic of having a not very definite date with respect to the death of Napoleon that appears real. But neither explicitly nor implicitly does it appear with the characteristic of having a date of such indefiniteness that our existential proposition marks it out as unreal. In short, somewhere between the Cosmos on the one hand and the Roman republic or the Middle Ages on the other, there is a line to be drawn between the subsistent appearing with a characteristic that marks it out as unreal and the subsistent with a characteristic that does not mark it out as unreal.

Since however we are determining the meaning of "existence" only in order that we may determine the ontological status of such entities as are to be considered in this treatise, we shall not attempt to place this line more accurately until occasion, if ever, requires it.

Whatever explicitly or implicitly appears as self-contradictory or as not an object or as a definite appearance for no one is unreal. Whatever explicitly or implicitly appears as lacking any date or as having no date with respect to an entity that appears real or as having only a very indefinite date with respect to an entity that appears real, that too is unreal. And so is the subsistent that explicitly or implicitly appears as lacking any position; the subsistent that explicitly or implicitly appears as having no position with respect to an entity which appears real and with respect to which it appears present; and the subsistent that explicitly or implicitly appears as having only a very indefinite position with respect to an entity which appears real and with respect to which it appears present. These are propositions which partially determine the meaning being assigned our term "existence." Together they assign to the realm of the non-existent many subsistents and they attribute to 'existence' the characteristic of freedom from self-contradiction, freedom from utter non-spatiality, freedom from this, and freedom from that. Our studies in the preceding chapter left us with the resolve to examine and to utilize in our propositions explaining "existence" the notions of self-contradiction, of time, and of space. The propositions with which this paragraph begins are the result.

We already know that the propositions thus far accepted will not suffice to give our term "existence" a precise meaning. We already know that in the end our universal negative existential propositions will have to be supplemented by singular or particular existential propositions, both affirmative and negative. But before we resort to singular existential propositions, let us attempt to develop additional universal negative propositions. Leaving self-contradiction and space and time behind, let us attempt to mark out some additional subsisting entities as unreal. The unlimited space which appears as having only an indefinite position with respect to the dying Napoleon who appears real and with respect to whom this unlimited space appears present, the eternal verity which appears utterly timeless and the square circle which appears self-contradictory, these subsistents are already marked out as unreal. But before we resort to individual existential propositions, let us attempt to eliminate the phlogiston that does not appear self-contradictory, the present King of France who does not appear to lack position with respect to me, and the sleeping Barbarossa who does not appear undated.

When I think of the King of England I seem to have a feeling of acceptance or assent or belief. No feeling of hesitation or of disbelief seems to intervene. But when I press my eyeball and seem to see a second rose in the vase on my desk, or when I try to imagine a man walking upside down on my ceiling, I may become aware of a feeling of hesitation, a feeling of dissent or rejection or disbelief. The King of England that I am now considering appears with the characteristic of being in some sense an object. And it appears with the characteristic of being an object such that the apparent awareness of it is generally accompanied by a feeling of belief. The man on my ceiling that I am now considering also appears with the characteristic of being in some sense an object. But it appears with the characteristic of being an object such that the apparent awareness of it is generally accompanied by a feeling of disbelief. The subsisting man on my ceiling and the subsisting second rose in the vase on my desk, unlike the King of England whom I am considering, appear with the characteristic of being generally discredited. They are therefore, let us say, unreal. Let us lay down the universal negative existential proposition that whatever explicitly or implicitly appears as generally discredited is unreal. And when a subsistent, as we develop it, takes on the characteristic of appearing generally discredited, let us resolve to list as real no subsistent which, except for its development, is indistinguishable from it.

The man on my ceiling, the second rose in the vase on my desk, phlogiston, and the sleeping Barbarossa, all of these subsistents, as we develop them, implicitly appear with the characteristic of being generally discredited. These subsistents are therefore unreal. And no other subsisting men on my ceiling, phlogistons, or sleeping Barbarossas will be listed among the entities we are to enumerate as real. Some subsisting King of England does, we may suppose, develop the appearance of being generally discredited, and is likewise unreal. But since the subsisting King of England which we are considering does not develop this appearance, this subsisting King of England, and other subsisting Kings of England which, like it, do not develop the appearance of being generally discredited, may very well be real.

No subsistent is real which appears with the characteristic of being generally discredited, with the characteristic of lacking all position, or with any one of various other characteristics. Representing that which appears with the characteristic of being self-contradictory by the letter A, that which appears with the characteristic of being generally discredited by the letter J, and so on, we may say that no subsisting A's or B's or . . . or J's are real. To exist is at the least to be free from A-ness and B-ness . . . and J-ness. But the subsistents that do not appears as A's or B's or as J's, the subsistents that neither explicitly nor implicitly appear with the characteristic of being self-contradictory or with the characteristic of being generally discredited are some of them real and some of them unreal. To exist is not merely to be free from A-ness, from B-ness, from . . . and from J-ness. To exist is in addition to be enumerated as real in one of our individual affirmative existential propositions. Some of the subsistents which do not appear as A's or B's or . . . or J's we have agreed not so to enumerate. We have agreed not to enumerate as real any subsistent, which, except for its development, is indistinguishable from one which, as we develop it, implicitly appears as an A or a B or . . . or a J. Since the subsisting phlogiston which we are now considering appears with the characteristic of being generally discredited, we resolve not to enumerate as real *any* subsisting phlogiston. But 'the fiftieth President of the United States, a Socialist named Jones' appears neither self-contradictory nor generally discredited; and, considering this subsistent as an individual subsistent, we have no rule to guide us and to determine us to list this subsistent as real rather than as unreal. It is not all subsistents not appearing as self-contradictory, etc., which are real; not even all subsistents not appearing to resemble one which, as we develop it, appears as self-contradictory. Reality is limited to those subsistents *really* free from self-contradictoriness. And those entities that are *really* free from self-contradictoriness can be further described only by enumerating some of them.

No subsistent is real which explicitly or implicitly appears as an A, a B, or . . . or a J. With respect to the subsistent which neither explicitly nor implicitly appears as an A, a B, or . . . or a J, it is real if listed below as X_1, X_2, or . . . or X_n, unreal if listed below as Y_1, Y_2, or . . . or Y_n. To exist is to appear free from A-ness, B-ness, . . . J--ness and to be enumerated as an X. To be unreal is to appear explicitly or implicitly as an A, a B, or . . . or a J; or to be enumerated as a Y. In so far as a subsistent does not appear as an A or . . . or a J and is not enumerated as an X or as a Y, its existential status is left undetermined and the significations of our terms "existence" and "non-existence" are left with some vagueness. It will be found however that our universal negative existential propositions: "No subsistent appearing as an A exists," etc., taken in conjunction with our existential propositions: "X_1, etc. exists," "Y_1, etc. does not exist," determine with reasonable precision the characteristics of 'existence' and 'non-existence' and will enable us to determine the existential status of most of the subsistents presented to us in the course of this treatise. When we have with a similar precision determined what it is to be true, we shall, I believe, be in a position to investigate various problems of concern to the metaphysician with a well-founded hope of being able to determine which of the entities discussed in these problems are real, and with a well-founded hope of being able to determine which of the propositions in which attitudes towards these problems may be expressed are true.

And so, before we turn from the distinction between the real and the unreal to the distinction between the true and the false, we have only to give the following recapitulation of the characteristics for which A, B, etc. stand and the following lists of X's and Y's.

        A—Self-contradictory.

        B—In no sense an object of consciousness.

        C—A definite appearance for no subject.

        D—Lacking all date.

        E—Having no date with respect to an entity that appears real.

        F—Having only a very indefinite date with respect to an entity that appears real.

        G—Lacking all position.

H—Having no position with respect to an entity which appears real and with respect to which it appears present.

I—Having only a very indefinite position with respect to an entity which appears real and with respect to which it appears present.

J—Generally discredited.

APPENDIX

A List of Certain Subsistents which, appearing neither explicitly nor implicitly as self-contradictory, undated, etc., are real.

X_1 —
X_2 —
X_3 —
X_4 —

A List of Certain Subsistents which, even when they appear neither explicitly nor implicitly as self-contradictory, undated, etc., are nevertheless unreal.

Y_1 —
Y_2 —
Y_3 —
Y_4 —

(I ask the reader to assume that there have just been enumerated each of the entities that will later be referred to as having been listed in this appendix)

Summary

We explain our term "existence" fairly adequately through singular existential propositions and the following universal propositions:

1. No entity is real which is presented as self-contradictory.
2. No entity is real which is presented as in no sense an object of consciousness.
3. No entity is real which is presented as a definite appearance for no subject.
4. No entity is real which is presented as lacking all date.

5. No entity is real which is presented as having no date with respect to an entity that appears real.
6. No entity is real which is presented as having only a very indefinite date with respect to an entity that appears real.
7. No entity is real which is presented as lacking all position.
8. No entity is real which is presented as having no position with respect to an entity which appears real and contemporaneous with it.
9. No entity is real which is presented as having only a very indefinite position with respect to an entity which appears real and contemporaneous with it.
10. No entity is real which is presented as generally discredited.

Propositions 1, 4 and 7 seem to give our term "existence" a meaning in accord with common usage. But they leave the existential status of various subsistents undetermined to a greater extent than is desirable. By considering 1, 4 and 7 in turn, we are led to choose to supplement them with 2 and then with 3, with 5 and 6, and with 8 and 9. Proposition 10 is added in an effort to enlarge the content of the world of non-existing entities in our sense of "existence" and to reduce the reliance that has to be placed on individual existential propositions.

The discussion of proposition 2 is probably of greatest general interest. The position taken is that the entity in no sense an object of consciousness appears with the characteristic of being implicitly self-contradictory and hence is unreal.

Chapter IV

TOWARDS DETERMINING THE MEANING OF "TRUTH"

At this point in our story the meaning of our term "existence" has been more or less determined. At this point we have agreed that certain entities Y_1, Y_2, Y_3, even when appearing neither explicitly nor implicitly as self-contradictory, as undated, etc., are unreal. And we have agreed that certain entities X_1, X_2, X_3, when appearing neither explicitly nor implicitly as self-contradictory or as undated, etc., are real in the sense in which we are using the term "reality." Now, among the entities which are real in our sense of "reality," among the entities X_1, X_2, X_3, are certain *words*. The word "Socrates," occurring in the copy of Plato's "Republic" that is in my library and appearing neither explicitly nor implicitly as self-contradictory, etc., is a real entity. And the word "Ivanhoe" appearing with the characteristic of being in my copy of Scott's novel is likewise a real entity.

Each entity that can be discussed is a subsistent. Some of these subsistents, as, for example, the words "Socrates" and "Ivanhoe" to which we have just pointed, are real entities. And some of these subsistents are entities which, in our sense of the term "existence," are unreal entities. Without stopping to enquire whether they are real or unreal, let us note that within the world of subsistents there appear the entities: 'Socrates, the Athenian philosopher' and 'Ivanhoe, the medieval knight.' Thus we seem to have before us the subsistent 'Socrates, the Athenian philosopher' whose ontological status we may for the present leave undetermined, and an instance of the word "Socrates" which is real; the subsistent 'Ivanhoe, the medieval knight', whose ontological status we may for the present leave undetermined, and an instance of the word "Ivanhoe" which

94

is real. Obviously there is a certain connection or a certain pseudo-connection between the real word "Socrates" and the subsistent: 'Socrates, the Athenian philosopher,' between the real word "Ivanhoe" and the subsistent: 'Ivanhoe, the medieval knight.' To put it briefly, the word "Socrates" represents or intends to represent the Athenian philosopher and the word "Ivanhoe" represents or intends to represent the medieval knight. It would carry us too far afield to attempt at this stage in our exposition to analyze what this representation or this intention to represent consists in.[1] Let us note simply that certain words are real and that by virtue of their being words they seem to intend, to point to, or to represent, certain other subsistents which may or may not be real.

The word "Socrates," occurring in my copy of Plato's "Republic" is real; and the word "Ivanhoe" occurring in my copy of Scott's novel is real. In a similar fashion the words "man" and "large" appearing with the characteristic of occurring on this page are each of them subsistents which are real. Whereas, however, the words "Socrates" and "Ivanhoe" represent or intend to represent subsistents which, if real, are individual substances, "man" and "large" represent or intend to represent subsistents which, if real, are in the one case a universal substance and in the other case a universal quality. Nonetheless, the instances of "man" and "large" to which reference has just been made are words which are real, words which are to be kept in view along with "Socrates" and "Ivanhoe." Indeed, we may enlarge the domain of real entities to which we are attending by pointing to the words: "walking quickly down the street" and to the words: "President of the United States." Each of these word groups subsisting with the characteristic of occurring on this page is real and each of them represents or intends to represent a subsistent which if real is a quality or substance outside of this page. There is then one instance of the word "Socrates" which is real, one instance of "Ivanhoe," one instance of "man," one instance of "large," one instance of "walking quickly down the street" and one instance of "President of the United States." Without further ado we may say at once that many words and word groups are real, and that many sentences are real. We may agree, for example, that each of the preceding sentences in your copy of this book, appearing

95

neither explicitly nor implicitly as undated, etc. is a real sentence. And we may agree that each of these sentences contains words, word groups and phrases which severally represent, or intend to represent, subsistents which may or may not be real.

We are working in this chapter towards the determination of the significations to be assigned the terms "truth" and "falsity." And we have come to have before us for our consideration various real sentences, as, for example, the preceding sentences in your copy of this book, in order that we may apply the distinction between the true and the false somewhere within the realm of real sentences. It may be well therefore at this point to note that the adjectives "true" and "false" as they occur in common speech are by no means exclusively associated with such entities as sentences. We commonly speak of true sentences, true propositions, true judgments, true pictures, true ideas, true beliefs and true friends. And so we ask ourselves whether, when we attempt to determine the signification of "truth" by applying the distinction between the true and the false somewhere within the realm of real sentences, we are maintaining the contact with ordinary usage that we wish to maintain. In so far as truth is commonly predicated of such entities as propositions and judgments, we need not be disturbed. For our concern with words, terms and sentences will guide our attention to propositions and to judgments and will enable us to point out certain entities to be called true propositions, certain entities to be called true judgments and certain entities to be called false propositions. But the signification of "truth" which we are developing will not enable us to apply the distinction between the true and the false to friends or to pictures, to beliefs or to ideas.

What we commonly call a true friend is, I suppose, a devoted friend, a real friend; what we commonly call a false friend an apparent friend who is not a friend. The distinction between the real on the one hand and the unreal on the other is, it appears, involved in the distinction between the so-called true friend and the so-called false friend. Let us not use "true" and "false" to point to the very distinction to which the contrast between the real and the unreal points. And so let us not determine the signification of our term "truth" in such a way that there will be true friends and false friends.

Just as it is the distinction between the real and the unreal rather than the distinction between the true and the false that, we shall say, applies to friends, so it is the distinction between knowledge and error rather than the distinction between the true and the false that applies, in our terminology, to such psychological or epistemological entities as may be called ideas, opinions, or beliefs. In a later chapter we shall deal at some length with the distinction between knowledge and error.[2] And so we are not permanently neglecting this important distinction when we leave beliefs, ideas and opinions out of consideration in concerning ourselves with the notion of truth and with the distinction between the true and the false.

The words, word groups and phrases that occur in sentences represent, as we have seen,[3] or intend to represent, subsistent entities other than themselves. And the truth or falsity of these sentences depends, we shall hold, upon the ontological status of these subsistent entities that are intended to be represented. There is a sense then in which sentences look beyond themselves and in which their truth or falsity depends upon their correspondence with entities beyond themselves. What more natural, then, than that pictures should be called true or false and that their truth or falsity should be held to depend upon their correspondence or lack of correspondence with the objects they intend to portray? Despite the similarity between words and pictures, however, I believe we are not violating the ordinary usage of words in distinguishing between words and pictures, and in making the distinction between truth and falsity one which does not apply to pictures but, rather, applies exclusively to words and their derivatives, to sentences, propositions and judgments.

It is within the realm of real sentences that we shall first attempt to apply the distinction between the true and the false. And yet it is not each real sentence that we shall hold is either true or false. There is the real sentence: "Where are you going?" and the real sentence: "Shut the door"; but "Where are you going?" is not true and "Shut the door" not false. It is: "You seem to be going some place" that may be true, "I desire you to shut the door" that may be false. The distinction between the true and the false, in short, is to be applied only to real sentences that are declarative, not to real sentences that are interrogations or

97

commands.

Just as "Shut the door" is neither true nor false, so it is, as we shall use the terms "truth" and "falsity," with the sentence: "Take as your alleged object a subsisting Socrates." A subsisting Socrates is presented as a datum; but the mere presentation involves no assertion to be concurred in or denied. Similarly with the sentence: 'Socrates is (i.e., appears as) a subsistent." "Socrates subsists" expresses no real assertion, adds nothing to the datum that "Subsisting Socrates" seems to present. Nor have we arrived at a real assertion when the subsisting Socrates as a subsistent is said to appear with various characteristics. For "Socrates appears or subsists as a Greek and as a philosopher" still merely presents an alleged datum and expresses no attitude with respect to this datum that can be concurred in or denied. It is, one might say, synonymous with: "Let Socrates be a Greek philosopher." Only declarative sentences, we have said, are true or false. But sentences of the type: "X subsists" or "X does not subsist" or "X subsists with characteristic A," although declarative in form, are rather to be classed with interrogations and commands than with the declarative sentences to which we shall apply the distinction between the true and the false.

The only sentences that we shall call true or false are declarative sentences, declarative sentences which are real and which contain words, word groups or phrases which severally represent or intend to represent subsistent entities. Among these declarative sentences which we have before us, however, there are some which do not conform to the grammar of the language in which they are expressed. The English sentence "Green is or" is ungrammatical and so is "We am here." It is desirable that we put such sentences aside in working towards the determination of the signification of "truth"; for without such an elimination we have the task of applying the distinction between the true and the false to many sentences which are incomprehensible or ambiguous. The rules of grammar are many and vary from language to language. They are however rather definite and are fairly generally understood. With respect to any given sentence it is usually obvious that it does, or that it does not, conform to the grammar of the language in which it is expressed. It is generally agreed, for example, that each English declarative sentence must

98

have a verb and a subject. And so it is clear that a given sentence which contains no subject is a sentence to which, in the sense in which we are using the terms "truth" and "falsity," the distinction between the true and the false does not apply. It may likewise be said to be a rule of English grammar that the subject must be a noun or pronoun. And so, if "Green is a color" is to be held to be a sentence to which the distinction between the true and the false applies, the word "green" as it occurs in this sentence must be held to be a noun. Let us hold that in our sentence "Green is a color" the word "green" is indeed a noun. Let us hold that this instance of the word "green" represents a substance whose important and outstanding quality is its greenness. Let us, consequently, agree to use "truth" and "falsity" in such a manner that the distinction between the true and the false applies to our sentence: "Green is a color." It is only with respect to some few sentences—"Green is a color" is one of them—that their conformity or lack of conformity to the rules of grammar is disputable. And so it is only a few sentences and a few grammatical rules that we need discuss in order to make clear which sentences we are eliminating from further consideration in working towards the determination of the signification of "truth."

The subject of a grammatical English declarative sentence must be a noun or a pronoun. Our sentence: "Green is a color" is grammatically correct in that "green" is in this instance a noun. Our sentence: "White is always serviceable" is grammatically correct in that "white" in this instance modifies some such noun as "clothing" which has been elided. Not only, however, must the subject of a grammatical English declarative sentence be a noun or pronoun; with certain predicates, abstract nouns are ruled out as possible subjects of grammatical English declarative sentences. "Brightness is fire" is not grammatically correct. It is a sentence to which, as we employ "truth," the distinction between truth and falsity does not apply. There is, to be sure, the grammatically correct sentence: "Brightness is cheerful" and the grammatically correct sentence: "Charity is godliness." [4] But a sentence whose subject-term is an abstract noun is never grammatically correct, we hold, when this subject-term is copulated with a concrete noun or when the predicate-term is a cognate verb. "Brightness is fire" is, we hold, ungrammatical; and so is "Motion moves." "Brightness is fire" and "Motion moves" are both sentences, we hold, that lie outside the distinction between the true and the false. They are sentences to be eliminated from our further consideration along with "Green is or" and "We am here" in so far as we are working towards the determination of the signification of "truth."

At this point we have before us sentences which are real, sentences containing words, word-groups and phrases which severally represent, or intend to represent, subsistents, sentences which are declarative, which do not merely predicate subsistence, and which conform to the grammatical rules of the language in which they are expressed. These sentences which we have before us are, let us say, propositions. And so we may say that sentences which are not propositions are neither true nor false; and we may say that, with respect to sentences, it is within the realm of propositions that the distinction between the true and the false is to be applied.

Among the propositions which we have before us, let us pick out for special consideration those sentences of ours which are singular affirmative existential propositions. There is, for example, the proposition: "Socrates, the Athenian philosopher, exists" and there is the proposition: "Ivanhoe, the medieval knight, exists." It is with respect to propositions having this form that we shall find it simplest to apply the distinction between the true and the false and thus partially to explain our term "truth." Our sentence: "Socrates exists" is a true proposition, we shall say, if, and only if, in our sense of "existence," the entity exists which the word "Socrates" as it occurs in this sentence intends to represent. And our sentence: "Ivanhoe exists" is a true proposition as we use the term "truth" if, and only if, in our sense of "existence," the entity exists which the word "Ivanhoe" as it occurs in this sentence intends to represent. Since Socrates, the Athenian philosopher, appearing neither explicitly nor implicitly as self-contradictory or as undated, etc., is real in the sense in which we are using the term "reality," the real proposition: "Socrates exists" which occurs on this page is true in the sense in which we are using the term "truth." And since Ivanhoe the medieval knight, even when he appears neither explicitly nor implicitly as contradictory or as undated, is unreal, our sentence: "Ivanhoe

100

exists" is in our terminology an untrue or false proposition. We have thus certain real propositions definitely marked out as true in our sense of "truth" and certain real propositions definitely marked out as false in our sense of "falsity." We have thus made a beginning in determining the meaning of our term "truth."

It is a simple matter to go on to determine the truth or falsity of our negative singular existential propositions. Our sentence: "Socrates does not exist" is false, let us say, if the entity exists that the word "Socrates" as used in this sentence intends to represent; true if this entity does not exist. We are in a position, it follows, to determine the truth or falsity of any singular existential proposition of ours. If the individual exists that our word X intends to represent, "X exists" is true and "X does not exist" false. And if the individual that our word X intends to represent does not exist, "X exists" is false and "X does not exist" true. In their application to singular existential propositions of ours, the significations which we are assigning to the terms "truth" and "falsity" have thus been determined.

To the extent to which we have thus far determined the significations of "truth" and "falsity," we have done so by referring back to the distinction between the real and the unreal. Roughly speaking, we have made the distinction between the real and the unreal prior to the distinction between the true and the false; and we have explained "truth" in terms of "reality." There are those however who would object to the treatment of reality and truth in this order. Truth, according to Bertrand Russell,[5] is prior to reality, not reality prior to truth. When we discuss reality, we do so by means of propositions. And our discussion of reality has validity, it is held, only in so far as our propositions referring to reality are true. "When I say: this paper exists, I must," says Moore,[6] "require that this proposition be true." If I am to make valid remarks about reality, I must, it is held, already know what constitutes validity, I must already understand the term "truth." Do we however avoid such objections when we begin with a discussion of truth and proceed thence to a discussion of reality? The distinction between truth and falsity, after it has once been put before us, applies to all propositions including those in which "reality" is explained. Similarly, however, the distinction between the real and the unreal, after it has once been put before us, applies to all entities including the sentences in which the meaning of "truth" is discussed. Unless these sentences are real, they can neither *be* true nor determine for us the meaning of "truth." A discussion of truth presupposes the reality of the sentences in which truth is discussed just as a discussion of reality presupposes the truth of the propositions in which reality is discusssed. In a sense, then, truth presupposes reality; and reality presupposes truth. Wherever we begin we find ourselves in a circle rather than at the beginning of a linear chain. Indeed this circle is even narrower than we have yet indicated. Not only does truth in a sense presuppose reality, and reality truth; but reality in a sense presupposes reality and truth presupposes truth. Just as the sentences are real in which we determine the meaning of "truth," so the sentences are real in which we determine the meaning of "reality." And just as some of the propositions are true in which we discuss reality, so some of the propositions are true in which we discuss truth. In a sense we can not discuss reality unless we make use of real sentences and we can not make valid propositions referring to truth unless these propositions are themselves valid and true, unless, it may be said, we already know what validity and truth are.

It would be absurd to hold that such observations prevent us from ever properly discussing either truth or reality. When we attend to a concept with the purpose of discussing, analyzing and defining it, we are not always introducing a term which has no relevance to anything that has gone before. Rather we clarify a concept so that as a result of the discussion the application of the concept will be clear both with respect to what has preceded and with respect to what is to follow. The sentences in the first chapter of your copy of this book are real, but we did not know them to be real until we had determined the signification of "reality." The propositions in which we determine the significations of "truth" and "falsity" are true; but we do not know them to be true until we shall have determined the signification of "truth." Without knowing a given sentence to be real or true we can gather from it the signification that is being assigned "truth" or "reality." And so a valid discussion of either truth or reality takes place through the medium of propositions which are true and of entities which are real, although these propositions are not revealed as true and these entities are not revealed as real until the discussion has been completed. Obviously the distinction between the real and the unreal applies to all entities and, limiting our attention to propositions occurring in this treatise, the distinction between the true and the false applies, we shall hold,[7] to all propositions. If this is the case, then we can not discuss either 'truth' or 'reality' by means of propositions without making use of entities to which these distinctions which are in the course of being elucidated already apply. But we can, we hold, and in many cases must, analyze and define concepts whose application is not limited to what is to follow. With both 'truth' and 'reality,' this is the case; and it is as much the case with the one as with the other. In exposition, we hold, we are at liberty to begin with either concept and then to proceed to the other. Our difficulties are just as great, or, we should hold, just as unimportant, whether we begin with reality and proceed to a discussion of truth or whether we begin with truth and proceed to a discussion of reality.

It has been our decision to begin with a discussion of "reality" and to explain "truth" in terms of 'reality.' If the argument of the preceding paragraph is sound, there is no logical reason to compel us to alter this decision and to begin instead with a discussion of "truth." But, we may ask, are there not motives of expediency that may determine us to alter our decision? Before we proceed to explain "truth" in terms of reality, will it not be well for us to consider the possibility of explaining "reality" in terms of 'truth' or at least of explaining "truth" without referring back to a previous discussion of 'reality'? To explain "truth" in terms of reality is not logically unsound, but it may be inexpedient. And explaining "truth" without referring back to a previous discussion of reality, whereas it is not logically necessary, may make for greater simplicity in exposition.

There are those, we have seen,[8] who hold that truth is prior to reality. A proposition or judgment is true or false, it may be said, not according as the entities intended to be represented by its terms are real or unreal, but rather according as it has or lacks intrinsic marks which directly determine it to be true. Certain judgments, it may be said, come before our minds with an insistence and a claim that forces us to recognize them as true; and certain judgments come before our minds, it may be said, with a weakness and a logical unattractiveness that forces us to reject them as false. Thus "two and two are four," it may be said, is true, not because of anything concerning the ontological status of 'two' and 'four,' but because "two and two are four" has an intrinsic vitality and claim which we are bound to recognize. "The recognition of the claim of a judgment," says Rickert,[9] "constitutes its truth." In no other way, he holds, is truth to be defined. For, he continues, "truth can only be defined as the peculiar value that judgments have." There is here an attempt to discuss truth without reference to reality. And since we may begin with either concept, since, moreover, we are at liberty to assign to terms whatever significations we please, there is no logical objection that can be raised against this procedure. We may introduce the term "truth" without referring to a previous discussion of "reality." And we may subsequently introduce the term "reality" by saying that an entity is real when the judgment that it is real has the validity, the claim upon us, that characterizes true judgments. But whereas there are no logical objections that can be raised against this procedure, we may question whether a procedure of this sort explains with any success either "truth" or "reality." And we may question whether a procedure of this sort assists us in any way in applying the distinction between the true and the false to individual propositions and judgments. If we are in doubt as to the truth of an instance of "Ivanhoe exists," it will not help us to be told that "Ivanhoe exists" is true if it has a claim upon us. For, we may ask with James,[10] "What do you mean by 'claim' here?" But it *will* help us to be told that our sentence "Ivanhoe exists" is true if Ivanhoe the medieval knight is a real entity; and then to be referred back to the rather full discussion of reality in chapter three.

Just as it may be said that a judgment is true if intrinsically it has a claim upon us, so it may be said that a judgment is true if intrinsically it is clear and distinct. "I am certain that I am a thing which thinks," says Descartes;[11] "but do I not then likewise know what is requisite to render me certain of a truth? Certainly in this first knowledge there is nothing that assures me of its truth, excepting the clear and distinct perception of that which I state." This clear and distinct perception would not "assure

104

me that what I say is true, if it could ever happen that a thing which I conceived so clearly and distinctly could be false; and accordingly it seems to me that already I can establish as a general rule that all things which I perceive very clearly and very distinctly are true." In this passage, to be sure, Descartes is not holding that only those judgments are true which are clear and distinct. But just as it may be held that a true judgment is one which has validity and a logical claim upon us, so it may be held that a true judgment is one which is clear and distinct. With either explanation of "truth," however, we have little to guide us in applying the distinction between the true and the false to individual propositions and judgments. To make either explanation serviceable, there would be required a rather complete account in the one case of 'claim' or 'validity' and in the other case of 'clear and distinct.' There would be required indeed something of an enumeration of the propositions or judgments that have a claim or are clear and distinct. And so we should explain "truth" prior to "reality" only by putting something analogous to the appendix to our third chapter into our explanation of "truth" instead of into our explanation of "reality."

Let us then proceed in the direction in which we have started. Let us work towards determining the meaning of "truth" by continuing to refer back to our explanation of "reality." If the individual exists that our term X intends to represent, then our real sentence: "X exists," let us continue to say,[12] is true and our real sentence: "X does not exist" false. And if the individual that our term X intends to represent does not exist, then our real sentence: "X exists," let us continue to say, is false and our real sentence: "X does not exist" true. We are proceeding thus from reality to truth, from reality to truth in so far as truth is a characteristic of the real sentences that we call propositions.

But although it may be acceptable to proceed from reality to truth rather than vice versa, it may seem strange that we leap at one bound from reality to that aspect of the notion of truth in which truth is considered a characteristic of the sentences that we call propositions. "Just one moment!", we may be told; "Truth is primarily a characteristic of judgments. It has application to the sentences that you call propositions, sentences occurring on this page and on that page, only secondarily, only in so far as these sentences represent or express or symbolize true judgments." Indeed there are those who hold that the distinction between the true and the false is never properly applied to sentences occurring on this page and on that page, that it applies only to judgments which are outside of the printed or spoken word. It is from this point of view that Leibniz finds fault with Locke's discussion of truth. "What I find least to my taste in your definition of truth," says Leibniz,[13] "is that you seek truth in words. Thus the same sense expressed in Latin, German, English, French, will not be the same truth. . . . We shall then have also literal truths which may be distinguished as truths upon paper or parchment, of ordinary black ink or of printer's ink." Is there however any *reductio ad absurdam* in this conclusion? Sentences exist that are on this page or on that page. Some of them are of ordinary black ink and some of them are of printer's ink; some of them in Latin and some in French. Among these real sentences which are here and there, of various kinds of ink and in various languages, there are some which, in the sense in which we are using the terms "truth" and "falsity," are true and some which are false. We are at liberty to determine the meaning of "truth" in such a manner that the distinction between the true and the false applies to certain real sentences. And we are exercising this liberty in a manner not altogether at variance with common usage when we call certain sentences propositions and call some propositions true and some false.

It is obvious however that certain sentences which are true in our sense of "truth" have a common point of reference. There is the sentence: "Socrates exists" which occurs on one page of my copy of this book; and there is the sentence: "Socrates exists" which occurs on a corresponding page in your copy of this book. There is the sentence: "Socrates exists" which occurs on another page of my copy of this book; there is the sentence: "Socrates exists" which occurs in my manuscript; and there is the sentence: "Socrates est" which occurs, let us suppose, in some Latin manuscript. Each of these sentences is true and each of them, we may suppose, refers to the same fact. Ought we not then seek truth in this fact, in this common point of reference? In concentrating our attention upon sentences made by ink or by pencil, we are dealing, it would seem, with mere shadows, with entities whose

106

truth or falsity is merely a reflection of the truth or falsity of some objective situation outside these sentences.

What however is the fact which several sentences, each reading: "Socrates exists," have as their common point of reference? When I write the word "Socrates," there is something in my mind. And so the word "Socrates" is somehow related to some act of cognition or to some idea of mine. At the same time, however, the word "Socrates" is somehow related, directly or indirectly, to an objective subsistent which is alleged to be outside of me and outside of the word "Socrates." As we have seen,[14] the word "Socrates" represents or intends to represent Socrates the Athenian philosopher who scorned the Sophists and died in jail. In the case of the word "Socrates" there is thus what we may roughly contrast as a subjective reference and an objective reference. When we turn from the word "Socrates" to the sentence: "Socrates exists," there is, it would seem, a similar dual reference. There is on the one hand an act of judgment, or an asserting, taking place in my mind; or the copulation of mental ideas that we may call a mental judgment. And, on the other hand, there may be some objective fact, some situation involving Socrates himself, to which the sentence: "Socrates exists" may be said to refer. Now the former of these entities, the act of judgment taking place in my mind, or the copulation of mental ideas that we may call a mental judgment, belongs within the realm of psychological or epistemological entities to which we have agreed to apply the distinction between knowledge and error rather than the distinction between the true and the false.[15] It may be a common reference to some such mental judgment that links together an instance of the sentence: "Socrates exists" and an instance of the sentence "Socrates est." Nevertheless let us turn our attention to the investigation of the possibility of these two sentences being linked together, not by a common subjective reference, but by a common objective reference, by a common reference, that is to say, to some objective situation involving Socrates himself.

What, however, is the objective fact which we may call a judgment and to which we may say that the sentence: "Socrates exists" intends to refer? It is not the substance Socrates himself, for this substance the simple word "Socrates" represents or intends to represent. Nor, we shall say, is the objective fact which might be called a judgment some non-temporal fact having its habitat in a world of objective but disembodied entities. For we choose to deal primarily with real entities; and, in the sense in which we are using the term "reality," any entity that appears as utterly non-spatial is unreal.[16] The entity related to the sentence "Socrates exists" that we shall call a judgment or fact is some situation involving Socrates himself; and yet it is not the substance Socrates. It is, let us say, the existence of Socrates; that is to say, existence appearing as an alleged quality of the subsistent Socrates. When I utter the word "Socrates" or the word "Ivanhoe," I am apparently making no assertion. My expression intends to refer to a subsistent which may or may not be real. But if I say "Socrates exists," there seems to be something that I am asserting, namely, the existence of Socrates. If then we call such entities as 'the existence of Socrates' judgments, our use of the word "judgment" will permit us to say that a judgment is something that may be asserted. Let us then call the existence of Socrates a fact or judgment; and, since Socrates exists, let us furthermore call it a true judgment. In the 'existence of Socrates,' we hold, we have an instance of a judgment which is an objective situation, a situation to which various sentences each reading: "Socrates exists" may be said to refer. Not only, however, is the existence of Socrates an objective judgment to which various propositions each reading: "Socrates exists" may be said to refer. It is likewise a true judgment; and its truth may be thought of as determining the truth of the propositions which refer to it. Truth may be thought of, in short, as belonging primarily to the judgment: 'the existence of Socrates' and as belonging secondarily and by reflection, as it were, to the proposition: "Socrates exists" which occurs on this page and to the proposition: "Socrates est" which occurs in some Latin manuscript.

Socrates the Athenian philosopher is a subsistent. Appearing neither as self-contradictory nor as undated, etc., this subsistent is real. Likewise the quality of being an Athenian is a subsistent, a subsistent which, appearing as a quality of Socrates, is real. Similarly with the quality of existence, appearing as a quality of Socrates. The existence of Socrates is a real subsistent, or, what is the same thing, the true judgment 'the existence of Socrates' is a real entity. How is it however with respect to non-existence

108

subsisting as a quality of Socrates? If Socrates appears as unreal, both this subsistent and its alleged quality of non-existence are unreal. Even the Socrates that appears both as real and as unreal is unreal; and the non-existence of Socrates alleged to inhere in it unreal. For the subsistent which I am considering appears as self-contradictory.[17] There is, we conclude, no real objective situation different from, but analogous to, the existence of Socrates to which the proposition: "Socrates does not exist" refers. There is no real non-existence of Socrates that might be called a judgment. And so, whereas we have been successful in identifying a real objective situation that is a true judgment and to which various true propositions reading: "Socrates exists" may be said to refer, we have been unsuccessful in our search for another real objective situation that might be called a judgment and to which various false propositions reading: "Socrates does not exist" might similarly be said to refer.

The judgment 'the existence of Socrates,' appearing neither as self-contradictory nor as undated, etc., is real. And 'the non-existence of Socrates' is unreal. What, however, about the reality or unreality of 'the existence of Ivanhoe'? If Ivanhoe appears with the characteristic of being generally discredited, Ivanhoe is unreal and the qualities that are alleged to inhere in such an Ivanhoe are unreal. It would seem that if my subsistent is an existing Ivanhoe, I am apparently thinking about an Ivanhoe that, by hypothesis, is real and about the real judgment: the existence of Ivanhoe. But if I appear to be thinking about an Ivanhoe that subsists both as real and as generally discredited, my subsistent appears as implicitly self-contradictory and, in the sense in which we are using the term "reality," is unreal.[18] If Ivanhoe appears as generally discredited, this Ivanhoe is unreal and each of the qualities inhering in this Ivanhoe is unreal. 'The existence of Ivanhoe' is unreal; and 'the non-existence of Ivanhoe' is unreal. Just as there is no real 'non-existence of Socrates' that might be called a judgment, so there is no real 'existence of Ivanhoe' and no real 'non-existence of Ivanhoe' that might serve as real judgments.

It appears then that the only real objective judgment involved in a singular existential proposition is that directly referred to by a true affirmative singular existential proposition, namely, existence appearing as a quality of some real entity. The proposition: "Socrates exists" which appears on this page and the proposition: "Socrates est" which appears in some Latin manuscript both refer to a common judgment which is real and true. Both of these propositions may be regarded as deriving their truth from the truth of the judgment: the existence of Socrates. But the 'existence of Ivanhoe' to which two sentences each reading: "Ivanhoe exists" might be held to refer is not a real judgment at all. And so there is no real objective judgment which these two sentences have as their common reference, no real objective judgment whose falsity determines the falsity of these two propositions, no fact to which these two false propositions are directly related.

Our desire then to determine the truth or falsity of groups of propositions by first determining the truth or falsity of objective judgments to which they refer has been only partially carried out. If various false propositions reading: "Socrates does not exist" are to be regarded as having a common reference to a real objective situation, the reference which they may be regarded as having in common is what we might call a contra-reference to the true judgment: 'the existence of Socrates.' And even this sort of common contra-reference is lacking as a common characteristic of various true propositions each reading: "Ivanhoe does not exist."

It appears then that we can not describe truth and falsity merely with respect to objective judgments or facts and expect the distinction between truth and falsity thus determined within the domain of judgments to indicate to us where falsity ends and where truth begins within the entire domain of propositions, or even within the entire domain of singular categorical existential propositions. The truth of our sentence: "X exists" and the falsity of our sentence: "X does not exist" may be said to be corollaries of the truth of the judgment: the existence of X. But the truth of our sentence: "Y does not exist" and the falsity of our sentence: "Y exists" are laid down as partial explanations of "truth" applied directly to the domain of sentences or propositions.

At this point we have behind us the determination of the signification of "truth" with respect to certain entities that we call "judgments." And we have behind us the determination of the significations of both "truth" and "falsity" with respect to singu-

110

lar categorical existential propositions of ours. How is it, however, with respect to categorical existential propositions that are not singular? How is it with respect to our sentences: "All men exist," "Some men exist," "No men exist" and "Some men do not exist"? The universal 'man' it will be remembered,[19] "may . . . be given a place on our list of entities denoted by 'existence' along with Socrates and Plato." Just as the alleged individual Socrates may be real and the alleged individual Ivanhoe unreal, so the alleged universal 'man' may be real and the alleged universal 'centaur' unreal. Just as we hold that, when the alleged individual X is real, our proposition: "X exists" is true and our proposition: "X does not exist" false, so let us hold that, when the alleged universal U is real, our proposition: "Some U's exist" is true and our proposition: "No U's exist" false. And just as we hold that when the alleged individual X is unreal, our proposition: "X exists" is false and our proposition: "X does not exist" true, so let us hold that, when the alleged universal U is unreal, our proposition: "Some U's exist" is false and our proposition: "No U's exist" true. If, then, the alleged universal 'centaur' is unreal in our sense of "reality," our sentence: "Some centaurs exist" is false as we explain our term "falsity" and our sentence: "No centaurs exist" true as we explain our term "truth." And if the alleged universal 'man' is real in our sense of "reality," our sentence: "Some men exist" is true and our sentence: "No men exist" false.

There is, to be sure, the proposition: "Some men do not exist" as well as the proposition: "Some men exist," the proposition: "All men exist" as well as the proposition: "No men exist." As has already been pointed out, however, "all men" as it occurs in an existential proposition, is synonymous either with "All existing men" or with "All subsisting men."[20] But: "All subsisting men exist" is, let us say, false. And I can think of no assertion expressed in: "All existing men exist" that is not expressed in: "Some men exist." As "All men exist" is synonymous either with: "All existing men exist" or with: "All subsisting men exist," so: "Some centaurs do not exist" is, it would seem, synonymous either with: "Some subsisting centaurs do not exist" or with: "Some existing centaurs do not exist." But our sentence: "Some subsisting centaurs do not exist" is, let us say, true. And if: "Some existing centaurs do not exist" is to be considered at all, I can think of no assertion expressed in it that is not expressed in: "No centaurs exist." Since our sentences: "Some men exist" and: "No centaurs exist" have both been determined to be true in our sense of "truth," our sentence: "All existing men exist" is, we hold, true; and our sentence: "Some existing centaurs do not exist" true. And since our sentences: "No men exist" and: "Some centaurs exist" have both been determined to be false in our sense of "falsity," "Some existing men do not exist," which seems to be synonymous with the former, is, we hold, false, and: "All existing centaurs exist," which seems to be synonymous with the latter, likewise false.

We may then formalize as follows our explanations of "truth" and "falsity" with respect to such categorical existential propositions of ours as: "Some U's do not exist" and: "All U's exist." If the alleged universal U is real, "All subsisting U's exist" is false and "All existing U's exist" true, "Some subsisting U's do not exist" true and "Some existing U's do not exist" false. And if the alleged universal U is unreal, then "All subsisting U's exist" and "All existing U's exist" are both false, "Some subsisting U's do not exist" and "Some existing U's do not exist" both true.

A categorical existential proposition of ours may express an assertion with respect to alleged existing entities or with respect to alleged subsisting entities; it may be affirmative or negative; it may be a singular proposition, a particular proposition or a universal proposition. In any case it is true or false according as the individual or universal whose existence is asserted is real or unreal; true or false according as the individual or universal whose non-existence is asserted is unreal or real. It is thus some entity's reality or unreality in our sense of "reality" that determines the truth or falsity—as we explain "truth" and "falsity"—of each categorical existential proposition of ours.

But what about the categorical existential propositions of others? Since "existence" as used by others may not have the meaning we have assigned that term, the: "Socrates exists" of some other writer may not express an assertion with respect to Socrates which is identical with the assertion expressed in our: "Socrates exists." Shall we say that his: "Socrates exists" is true if Socrates exists in the sense in which *he* is using "existence," in a sense of "existence" which is perhaps vague and indefinite? Or shall we say that his: "Socrates exists" is true if Socrates exists in the sense in which *we* have explained "existence"? The former course leads to as many meanings of "truth" as there are meanings of "reality." For, taking such a course, the: "Socrates exists" of one writer would be true, if the Socrates presented complied with one set of qualifications; the: "Socrates exists" of another writer true, if the Socrates presented complied with another set of qualifications. No author's: "Socrates exists" is true, let us say, unless Socrates exists in the sense in which we have explained "existence." But no author's: "Socrates exists" is true, let us also say, if it is a statement that we should express in "Socrates subsists."[21] Since our sentence: "Socrates subsists" expresses no assertion[22] and is, we hold, neither true nor false, the: "Socrates exists" of some other writer that is synonymous with it likewise expresses no assertion and is likewise, let us hold, neither true nor false. The proposition that is true is our: "Socrates exists." And the proposition that is true is the proposition of some other writer that is synonymous with it, whatever form it may take. The: "Socrates exists" of some other author is true, let us say, if it is synonymous with a proposition which, in the form in which it would be expressed by us, is true. The: "Socrates exists" of some other author is false, let us say, if it is synonymous with a proposition which, in the form in which it would be expressed by us, is false. And the: "Socrates exists" of some other author which is synonymous with no proposition as it would be used by us is, let us say, neither true nor false.

Our terms "truth" and "falsity" have been explained with respect to categorical existential propositions of ours and with respect to propositions of others that are synonymous with them. Each such proposition is true or false according as some entity is real or unreal. Indeed it is the reality or unreality of some entity or of some entities—using "reality" in our sense of that word—that, we hold, determines the truth or falsity of each sentence of ours that is a proposition. For each real declarative sentence of ours which does not merely predicate subsistence, which conforms to the grammatical rules of the language in which it is expressed, and which contains words, word-groups and phrases representing or intending to represent subsistents,[23] each such sentence of ours is, we hold, synonymous with one or more of our categorical exist-

113

ential propositions. The explanation of our terms "truth" and "falsity" in their application to propositions of ours which are not categorical existential propositions is thus to be accomplished through the reduction of such propositions to the categorical existential propositions of ours with which, we hold, they are synonymous.

To say that proposition B as it occurs in this treatise is synonymous with our existential proposition A is to say that A and B express similar mental attitudes of mine. Since A, being a categorical existential proposition, is true or false according as some alleged entity is real or unreal in our sense of "reality," the reader is enabled to determine the alleged entity upon whose reality the truth or falsity of our proposition B depends. It would seem to require only patience and circumspection to designate categorical existential propositions of ours synonymous-for-me with each proposition as it might be used by me; and thus to support the assertion that each proposition as it might be used by me is synonymous with one or more of our categorical existential propositions. Moreover, the designation of synonymous propositions sufficient to enable our terms "truth" and "falsity" to be applied to each of the propositions in this treatise will be a fairly adequate explanation of our terms "truth" and "falsity."

Let us however not lose sight of those sentences outside of this treatise that do not have the form of categorical existential propositions. There are sentences outside of this treatise which do not express an assertion either of existence or of non-existence in our sense of "existence" and which consequently are neither true nor false as we use "truth" and "falsity." But there is the sentence A of some other writer which has the form of a categorical existential proposition and which expresses an assertion of existence or of non-existence in some other sense of "existence." And there is that writer's sentence B which, whereas it does not have the form of a categorical existential proposition, expresses a mental attitude of its author's identical with that expressed by his proposition A. From the point of view of its author, B, that is to say, is synonymous with A. From the point of view of its author, there is expressed in B an assertion of existence in the very sense of "existence" in which there is an assertion of existence expressed in A. The proposition B occurring in *this* treatise and the existential proposition A of ours to which it will be reduced, they both, we assume, express an assertion of existence in a sense of "existence" different from his. But in choosing the categorical existential proposition A of ours to which our proposition B is to be reduced, let us not lose sight of the A of some other author with which that author's B seems to be synonymous. If some other author's: "There is no Socrates" seems to be synonymous with his: "Socrates does not exist," then, even though it is another sense of "existence" that is involved, let us say that our: "There is no Socrates" and our: "Socrates does not exist" are synonymous with one other, that our: "There is no Socrates" expresses an assertion of existence identical with that expressed in our: "Socrates does not exist," that our: "There is no Socrates" is true or false according as Socrates is unreal or real in our sense of "reality." Let us in short attempt to conform with general usage in reducing to categorical existential propositions those propositions of ours which are not categorical existential propositions, even though in our case "existence" is used in one sense and in the case of general usage in some other sense.

There is moreover, let us suppose, the categorical existential proposition A outside of this treatise which expresses an assertion of existence or of non-existence in our sense of "existence." And there is the proposition B outside of this treatise which does not have the form of a categorical existential proposition, but which likewise expresses an assertion of existence or of non-existence in our sense of "existence." The sentence outside of this treatise which expresses no assertion of existence or of non-existence in our sense of "existence" is, we have said,[24] as we use "truth" and "falsity," neither true nor false. But our terms "truth" and "falsity" are to be applied to propositions in which there are expressed assertions of existence or of non-existence in our sense of "existence," whether these propositions be propositions of ours or propositions of others. And yet in order that our terms "truth" and "falsity" may be applied to these propositions of others that do not have the form of categorical existential propositions, we must determine the categorical existential propositions of ours with which these propositions, as used by their authors, are synonymous.

The reduction of propositions that are not existential in form to the categorical existential propositions of ours with which they are synonymous is thus to be considered from two points of view. On the one hand, we have the task of explaining our terms "truth" and "falsity" in their application to propositions,—not categorical existential propositions,—as they occur in this treatise or as they might be used by me. And on the other hand, we have the task of explaining our terms "truth" and "falsity" in their application to those propositions of others which are not categorical existential propositions but which may perhaps be synonymous with categorical existential propositions of ours. With respect to the former task we can speak with assurance. For, although we choose to be guided by general usage in determining the existential propositions with which a proposition of a given form as used by us is to be synonymous, it is *our* usage that is being set forth, it is what is synonymous for *me* that is being stated. With respect to the latter task, however, we can not speak with assurance. For even though it should be existence in our sense of "existence" that is asserted in categorical existential propositions of others, one writer's proposition that is not a categorical existential proposition may be synonymous with a certain categorical existential proposition of ours, another writer's synonymous with another of our categorical existential propositions, a third writer's synonymous with none of our categorical existential propositions at all. We can but point out the existential proposition of ours with which some such writer's proposition, not explicitly existential, may be presumed to be synonymous, point out the entity or entities whose existence or non-existence in our sense of "existence" may be presumed to determine the truth or falsity of his proposition. And we can on occasion point out alternative categorical existential propositions of ours with which his proposition may be synonymous, point out alternative entities whose existence or non-existence in our sense of "existence" may determine the truth or falsity of his proposition. The meaning of our terms "truth" and "falsity" in their application to propositions of various forms as they might be used by me can, in short, be adequately set forth. But even where "existence" has the meaning that it has in our writings, the application of our terms "truth" and "falsity" to propositions of others will vary with the assertions of existence or of non-existence that a proposition of a given

116

form is used to express.

There is our singular affirmative categorical existential proposition: "This large house exists"; and there is the proposition: "This house is large," which is synonymous with it. Similarly, it would seem that,—as generally used, and certainly as it occurs in this treatise,—"Socrates, the author of the Critique of Pure Reason, exists" is synonymous with: "Socrates is the author of the Critique of Pure Reason." So with: "The man Socrates exists" and: "Socrates is a man." And so with: "A prince named Orion who had seven daughters and lived at some past date exists" and: "Once upon a time there lived a prince named Orion who had seven daughters." Both in the sense of being synonymous-for-me and in the sense of being synonymous as generally used, the singular affirmative proposition: "S_1 is P" is, we hold, synonymous with some singular existential proposition: "S_1P exists." This large house is, we assume, a real entity, the man Socrates a real entity. Our proposition: "This large house exists" is, then, true and: "The man Socrates exists" true. And so our proposition: "This house is large" is true and our proposition: "Socrates is a man" true. On the other hand, Socrates, the author of the Critique of Pure Reason, is, we assume, an unreal entity and Prince Orion with seven daughters an unreal entity. And so it follows that, as we explain "falsity," "Socrates, the author of the Critique of Pure Reason, exists" is false and "A prince named Orion who had seven daughters and lived at some past date exists" false; hence "Socrates is the author of the Critique of Pure Reason" false and "Once upon a time there lived a prince named Orion who had seven daughters" false.

"This house is large" is, we assume, a true proposition. We assume, that is to say, that this large house is a real entity, that this house, considered as a unit enduring from its construction to its demolition, has the quality of largeness inhering in it. But what about: "Caesar crossed the Rubicon"? The quality of crossing the Rubicon was not a quality of that phase of Caesar's life in which he was combatting Vercingetorix or of that phase of his life in which he was consorting with Catiline. Strictly speaking, the quality of crossing the Rubicon does not inhere in Caesar taken as a substance enduring from birth to death; rather, it may be held to inhere in a brief phase of Caesar's life, in the transitory

117

substance which is Caesar at a momentous instant in his career.[25] If: "Caesar crossed the Rubicon" is synonymous with: "A Caesar crossing the Rubicon throughout his career exists," then our: "Caesar crossed the Rubicon" is false. It is our existential proposition: "Caesar-at-moment-M, having the quality of crossing the Rubicon, exists" that is, we may say, true. And it is only if it is synonymous with this latter proposition that: "Caesar crossed the Rubicon" is true. Generalizing from the example: "This house is large," it may seem that any proposition: "S_1 is P" is to be reduced to a corresponding existential proposition of the form: "S_1P exists." But, both generally and perhaps in this treatise too, we on occasion refer to some part or related substance by using words which, if used out of context, would refer to the whole. We may use the term "France" to refer to the government of France, may say: "Virgil is difficult to translate" in place of: "The poems of Virgil are difficult to translate." "S_1 is P" is, we hold, both generally and in this treatise, synonymous with some existential proposition of the form "S_1P exists." But the S_1 occurring in "S_1P exists" may not refer exactly to the entity which our original subject-term, taken out of context, would normally represent. "Caesar crossed the Rubicon" is, it would seem, synonymous with the existential proposition: "Caesar-at-moment-M, having the quality of crossing the Rubicon, exists," not with the existential proposition: "A Caesar crossing the Rubicon throughout his career exists." And "Washington crossed the Hellespont" is, it would seem, synonymous with the existential proposition: "Washington-at-some-moment-M, having the quality of crossing the Hellespont, exists," not with the existential proposition: "A Washington crossing the Hellespont throughout his career exists." It is because the former proposition of ours is false, not because the latter is false, that our: "Washington crossed the Hellespont" is false.

The question has been asked how the entity represented by the subject-term of a proposition can *be* the entity represented by the predicate-term.[26] It may seem that for S to be P, for "S is P" to be true, "S" and "P" must refer to the same entity and express identical mental attitudes. For S, it may be held, can only be S; it cannot be P in addition. And P, it may be held, can only be P. As we explain "truth," however, it is not necessary, in order for: "This house is large" to be true, that this house be identical with largeness. "This house" may express one mental attitude, "large" another. "This house" may represent a substance and "large" a quality of that substance. What is necessary, in order that: "This house is large" may be true as we explain "truth," is that this large house exist in our sense of "existence." And this large house can exist only if there are instances of a quality inhering in a substance. Similarly, since: "Socrates is a man" is synonymous with: "The man Socrates exists," "Socrates is a man" can be true only if there are individuals that are instances of universals. Problems concerning substance and quality and problems concerning the universal and its individual instances will, however, engage our attention further on in this treatise.[27] It is in later sections of this treatise that we shall arrive at conclusions from which it will follow that the S P that is an alleged substance with its quality, or an alleged universal instanced in an individual, may be real. And it is our explanation of "truth" in the present chapter that determines that, when S_1P is real in our sense of "reality," our "S_1 is P" is true; and that, when S_1P is unreal in our sense of "unreality," our "S_1 is P" is false.

The singular affirmative proposition: "Socrates is mortal" reduces, we hold, to the existential proposition: "Mortal Socrates exists"; the singular affirmative proposition: "Socrates is immortal" to the existential proposition: "Immortal Socrates exists." But what shall we say with respect to the singular negative proposition: "Socrates is not mortal"? Let us assume that a mortal Socrates exists and that a non-mortal—or immortal—Socrates does not exist. Whether, then, "Socrates is not mortal" reduces to the existential proposition: "Mortal Socrates does not exist" or to the existential proposition: "non-mortal Socrates exists," it is, when our sense of reality is involved, a proposition which, as we explain "falsity," is false. But if: "The present King of France is not bald" is synonymous with our: "The not-bald present King of France exists," it is a proposition which is false; whereas if it is synonymous with our: "The bald present King of France does not exist," it is a proposition which is true. In either case, "The present King of France is not bald" seems to be synonymous with an existential proposition, seems to be true according as *some* alleged entity is real or unreal, false according as *some* alleged

119

entity is unreal or real. In the field in which we can speak with certainty, in the field of what is synonymous-for-me, "The present King of France is not bald," let us say, reduces to: "The present non-bald King of France exists"; and "S_1 is not P" reduces to: "S_1: not-P exists." Whether the: "S_1 is not P" of some other writer reduces to one existential proposition of ours or another or to no existential proposition of ours at all, the: "S_1 is not P" that occurs in this treatise is true or false, as we explain "truth" and "falsity," according as S_1: not-P is real or unreal.

As we explain "truth" and "falsity," "Socrates is not mortal," as it occurs in this treatise, is true or false according as a not-mortal Socrates is real or unreal, "Socrates is not a man" true or false according as a Socrates who is not a man is real or unreal. But "A Socrates who is not a man" is not synonymous with "A man who is not Socrates." As we explain "truth" and "falsity," "S_1 is not P," as it occurs in this treatise, is true or false, that is to say, not as P_1: not-S is real or unreal, but as S_1: not-P is real or unreal.

Both in the sense of being synonymous-for-me and in the sense of being synonymous as generally used, the singular affirmative proposition: "S_1 is P" is, we hold, synonymous with some singular existential proposition: "S_1P exists." [28] And both in the sense of being synonymous-for-me and in the sense of being synonymous as generally used, the particular affirmative proposition: "Some S is P" is, it would seem, synonymous with some particular existential proposition: "Some SP's exist." Our: "Some men are mortal" reduces to: "Some mortal men exist" and is, let us say, true or false according as 'mortal man' is real or unreal. Our: "Some men are black" reduces to: "Some black men exist" and is, let us say, true or false according as 'black man' is real or unreal. But just as some instances of: "The present King of France is not bald" express the assertion that there is no bald present King of France rather than the assertion that a not-bald present King of France exists, so some instance of: "Some centaurs are not intelligent" may express the assertion that some alleged intelligent centaurs do not exist rather than the assertion that unintelligent centaurs exist. However uncertain the existential import of some instance of: "Some centaurs are not intelligent," the instance that is an expression of ours reduces to: "Some unintelligent centaurs exist" and is, let us say, true or false according as 'unintelligent centaur' is real or unreal. Just as our "S_1 is not P" reduces to: "S_1: not-P exists" and is true or false according as the alleged individual S_1: not P is real or unreal in our sense of "reality," so our: "Some S is not P," let us say, reduces to: "Some S: not-P's exist" and is true or false according as the alleged universal S: not-P is real or unreal.

"This house is large" reduces to, and is synonymous with, the existential proposition: "This large house exists." "Some men are mortal" reduces to, and is synonymous with: "Some mortal men exist." And at least in a sense of synonymity lacking universality in its application, "This house is not large" reduces to: "This not-large house exists" and: "Some men are not mortal" to: "Some immortal men exist." It may be one or another existential proposition with which some singular negative proposition is synonymous. It may be one or another existential proposition with which some particular negative proposition is synonymous. But there appears to be no similar ambiguity with respect to the universal negative proposition. The universal negative proposition: "No men are immortal" seems to reduce to the existential proposition: "No immortal men exist," the universal negative proposition: "No stone is alive" to the existential proposition: "Living stones do not exist." [29] There may, to be sure, be instances of "No stone is alive" in which more is asserted than the non-existence of 'living stone.' Some one may use the sentence: "No stone is. alive" to assert in addition the existence of 'stone,' the existence of lifeless stones. In the uncertain field of general usage, "No S is P" may be synonymous with the single existential proposition: "No SP exists" or with the two existential propositions: "No SP exists" and "S exists," asserted jointly. In the more limited but more certain field where we explain our terms "truth" and "falsity" with respect to propositions as they would be used by me, "No stone is alive" is, let us say, synonymous with the single existential proposition: "Living stones do not exist" and is true or false according as the alleged universal 'living stone' is unreal or real in our sense of "reality." There are propositions —singular, particular and universal—in which the predicate-term is not "mortal" or "immortal" or "alive," but, rather, "real" or "unreal" or "true" or "false." Propositions with predicate-terms of the latter group require special consideration. But with these terms excepted, using "P"—here and indeed throughout this chapter—to stand for any predicate-term other than "real," "unreal," "true" or "false," the universal negative proposition: "No S is P," as it occurs in this treatise, reduces to "No SP exists" and is true or false according as the alleged universal SP is unreal or real in our sense of "reality."

There is the universal negative proposition: "No stone is alive." And there is the universal affirmative proposition: "All men are mortal." Some instances of "No stone is alive" are synonymous with instances of the existential proposition: "Living stones do not exist," some instances of "All men are mortal" synonymous with instances of the existential proposition: "Immortal men do not exist." [30] There may, we have seen,[31] be instances of "No stone is alive" in which more is asserted than the non-existence of 'living stone.' And there may be instances of "All men are mortal" in which more is asserted than the non-existence of 'immortal man.' It is probable that the land-owner whose sign reads: "All trespassers will be punished" is merely asserting the non-existence of unpunished trespassers.[32] It is not probable that he is asserting in addition that there will be trespassers. But just as "No stone is alive" may be synonymous, not merely with "Living stones do not exist," but may in addition express a belief in the existence of 'stone,' of lifeless stones; so "All men are mortal" may be synonymous, not merely with "Immortal men do not exist," but may in addition express a belief in the .existence of 'man,' in the existence of men who are mortal. "In the uncertain field of general usage, "No S is P" may be synonymous with the single existential proposition: "No SP exists" or with the two existential propositions: "No SP exists" and "S exists," asserted jointly." [33] And in the uncertain field of general usage, "All S is P" may be synonymous with the single existential proposition: "No S: not-P exists" or with the two existential propositions: "No S: not-P exists" and "S exists," asserted jointly. We have partially explained our terms "truth" and "falsity" in their application to propositions occurring in this treatise by reducing "No S is P" as it occurs in this treatise to: "No SP exists" and by calling it "true" or "false" according as SP is unreal or real in our sense of "reality." Let us further explain our terms "truth" and "falsity" in their application to propositions occurring in this treatise by

122

holding "All men are mortal" synonymous-for-me with "Immortal men do not exist" and with "Some mortal men exist," asserted jointly. The proposition: "All S is P" that occurs in this treatise is true, that is to say, if SP is real and S: not-P unreal; the proposition: "All S is P" that occurs in this treatise is false if SP is unreal or if S: not-P is real.

"All men are mortal," as it occurs in this treatise, is synonymous with "Immortal men do not exist" and "Some mortal men exist," asserted jointly. Our universal affirmative proposition: "All S is P," that is to say, reduces to a universal negative existential proposition plus a particular affirmative existential proposition. But our: "All existing men exist" has not been described as synonymous with a corresponding pair of existential propositions. Our "All existing men exist" has been described as synonymous with "Some men exist," [34] not with: "Non-existing existing men do not exist" plus "Some existing men exist." It reduces, that is to say, to a particular affirmative existential proposition and thus is no instance of our universal affirmative proposition: "All S is P."

Just as in our "All men exist" the word "all" is not the mark of what we call a universal affirmative proposition, so in the uncertain field of general usage the word "all" may occur in propositions which are not universal propositions. "All the books in the British Museum would fit into Westminster Abbey" is, it would seem, a singular proposition.[35] And so is the nursery rhyme: "All the King's horses and all the King's men could not put Humpty Dumpty together again." For the latter proposition, despite its use of "all," appears synonymous with a singular existential proposition of the form: "The individual army exists which is made up of such and such members and which has the quality: inability to perform such and such a feat."

Just as the word "all" may occur in a proposition which is singular rather than universal, so the word "all" may occur in what seems to be an enumerative proposition rather than a universal proposition. Unlike the instance of the universal proposition: "All men are mortal" which, as it occurs in this treatise, expresses a belief in the existence of the universal 'mortal man,' there are propositions of the form: "All S is P" which seem to express a belief in the existence of various individual SP's. Various instances of "All of the pieces of furniture in this room are

123

old" for example, seem not so much to express belief in the reality of the universal: 'piece of furniture in this room that is old' and belief in the unreality of the universal: 'piece of furniture in this room that is not old'; they seem rather to express belief in the existence of various individuals each of which is presented as an old piece of furniture in this room. There is, in short, the instance of "All S is P" which is an enumerative proposition and which may be read: "Each S is P." And whereas the universal affirmative proposition as it occurs in this treatise is true if the *universal* S: not P is unreal, and the *universal* SP real, the enumerative proposition: "Each S is P" is, let us say, synonymous with a group of singular propositions, being true if each of them is true, false if one of them is false. "Each S is P" is true, that is to say, only if the *individuals* S_1P, S_2P, S_3P, . . . exist; "Each S is not P" true only if the individuals S_1: not-P, S_2: not-P, S_3: not-P, . . . exist.

There is then the universal proposition: "All S is P" and the enumerative proposition which, whereas it on occasion may also have the form: "All S is P," is less ambiguous in the form: "Each S is P." The distinction between them, it is often held, is based, not so much upon the use of the word "each" in the one case and the use of the word "all" in the other, as upon the fact that in the one case each S could be enumerated by the author of the proposition, in the other case not. As it occurs in this treatise, "All men are mortal" is a universal proposition, not merely because it makes use of the word "all," but because it expresses an assertion with respect to the universal 'mortal man' rather than an assertion with respect to individual men. Can it not be, however, that an author who writes: "All men are mortal" is making an assertion with respect to each individual man? Admittedly, he is not definitely aware of each individual man. But may he not primarily be holding, not that there are *some* mortal men, not that 'mortal man' exists, but rather that each individual man is mortal? "A true proposition," says Hobbes,[36] "is that whose predicate contains or comprehends its subject or whose predicate is the name of every thing of which the subject is the name. As, *man is a living creature* is therefore a true proposition because whatever is called *man,* the same is also called "living creature." To think of the subject as being included in the predicate is,

124

however, to think of one group of entities as being included within another group of entities. It is to think of groups, of classes; in short, it involves taking what is represented by the subject-term distributively. The fact that the truth of "All S is P" is held by some writers to be a matter of inclusion, of classes within classes, evidences the fact that "All S is P" is sometimes taken distributively, that "All S is P" is sometimes the expression of an assertion that might have been expressed as "Each S is P."

There are, to be sure, propositions occurring in this treatise which conform with no one of the categorical forms thus far discussed. We have still to point out the entities upon whose reality or unreality the truth or falsity of hypothetical and disjunctive propositions occurring in this treatise depends. And since "P" as it occurs in this chapter does not cover the predicate-terms "real," "unreal," "true" and "false," [37] we have not yet discussed the truth or falsity of such propositions as: "This proposition is false" and "Each of the propositions in this book is true." With these exceptions, however, our terms "truth" and "falsity," in their application to propositions occurring in this treatise or as they might be used by me, have at this point, we hold, been explained. Propositions are true or false, as we explain our terms "truth" and "falsity," according as some entity or entities are real or unreal in our sense of "reality." And each proposition as it occurs in this treatise or as it might be used by me expresses an assertion of the reality or unreality—in our sense of "reality"—of some entity or entities.

We have moreover explained our terms "truth" and "falsity" in their application to various propositions of others who use the term "existence" as we do. To be sure, the conditions under which such a writer's: "All S is P" is true may not be the conditions under which our: "All S is P" is true. His "All S is P" may be true whenever S:not P is unreal, whereas our "All S is P" is true only if S:not-P is unreal and S P real.[38] And his "S_1 is not P" may be true when S_1 P is unreal, whereas our "S_1 is not P" is true when S_1: not-P is real.[39] "Even though it should be existence in our sense of "existence" that is asserted in categorical existential propositions of others, one writer's proposition that is not a categorical existential proposition may be synonymous with a certain categorical existential proposition of ours, another writer's synonymous with another of our categorical existential propositions, a third writer's synonymous with none of our categorical existential propositions at all." [40] Our "Ivanhoe is Ivanhoe" is a proposition of the form "S_1 is P" and, as "truth" and "falsity" have been explained in their application to propositions of ours, is true only if S_1 P is real, only if an Ivanhoe who is an Ivanhoe is real. But the "Ivanhoe is Ivanhoe" of some other writer, even if he uses "existence" as we do, may be synonymous with no existential proposition at all, may express no assertion of existence in our sense of "existence" and may consequently, as we explain "truth" and "falsity," be neither true nor false.

Since Ivanhoe does not exist, our proposition: "Ivanhoe is Ivanhoe" is false. And since the alleged universal 'centaur' does not exist, our proposition: "All centaurs are centaurs" is false. Our proposition : "A is A" is true if A exists, false if A does not exist. As we explain "truth" and "falsity" and as we reduce propositions to categorical existential propositions, it follows that "A is A" is not always true. " 'A is A' is always true" is, it may be held, a formulation of the law of identity. But "A is A' is always true" has as its predicate-term the word "true." And whether or not "A is A" is true depends upon the meaning of "truth." The word "truth" may be assigned a meaning such that it will follow that "A is A" is always true. Or, as in this chapter, the word "truth" may be assigned a meaning such that it will not follow that "A is A" is always true. The law of identity, in short,—at least, the law of identity that may be formulated as: " 'A is A' is always true"—is thus dependent upon, and not independent of, the meaning of "truth." Apart from whatever meaning may be assigned "truth," it is neither a law of thought nor a law of things. It is within the framework of our explanation of "reality" that there is the law of things: A real A is real. And it is within the framework of our explanation of "truth" that, when A is real, our proposition "A is A" is true.

Of any pair of propositions: "S_1 is P" and S_1 is not P," at least one is false. Of any pair of propositions: "All S is P" and "Some S is not P," at least one is false. Of any pair of propositions: "No S is P" and "Some S is P," at least one is false. These three sentences taken together may be said to constitute the law of contradiction. But since the word "false" is the predicate-term in:

126

"One of a given pair of propositions is false," whether or not one of a given pair of propositions is false will depend upon the meaning of "falsity." What, then, is the situation with respect to our propositions, let us ask, when "falsity" has the meaning assigned it in this chapter? Can we say that, in our sense of "falsity," of any pair of our propositions: "S_1 is P" and "S_1 is not P," at least one is false; that of any pair of our propositions: "All S is P" and "Some S is not P," at least one is false; that of any pair of our propositions: "No S is P" and "Some S is P," at least one is false?

In order that our "S_1 is P" may be true in our sense of "truth," S_1 P must be a real entity. And in order that our "S_1 is not P" may be true in our sense of "truth," S_1: not-P must be a real entity. S_1 P and S_1: not-P can not both, however, be real entities. For S_1 P and S_1: not-P could both be real only if the self-contradictory entity S_1: P-and-not-P were real, only if an entity were real that, in the course of our explanation of "reality," was marked out as unreal.[41] Again, in order that our "All S is P" may be true in our sense of "truth," S: not-P must be unreal. And in order that our "Some S is not P" may be true in our sense of "truth," S: not P must be real. But S: not-P can not be real when it appears unreal. For as we have explained "reality," the entity that appears both real and unreal has been marked out as unreal. Similarly with our: "No S is P" and our: "Some S is P." Our "No S is P" is true in our sense of "truth" only if SP is unreal, our "Some S is P" only if SP is real. It follows then that as we explain "truth" and "falsity" at least one of our corresponding propositions: "S_1 is P" and "S_1 is not P" must be false, at least one of our corresponding propositions: "All S is P" and "Some S is not P" false, at least one of our corresponding propositions: "No S is P" and "Some S is P" false. For each new meaning of the term "falsity," a new validation of the law of contradiction is, it would appear, required. What has just been shown is that, in our sense of "falsity" and with respect to propositions of ours, at least one of each pair of what are commonly called contradictory propositions is false.

There are the contradictory propositions: "All S is P" and "Some S is not P," the contradictory propositions: "No S is P" and "Some S is P." And there subsists the self-contradictory entity A: not-A and the self-contradictory entity S: P-and-not-P. As words are commonly used, "contradictory propositions" is no doubt a more familiar and a less awkward expression than "self-contradictory entities." An object that appears round and not round is unreal, it may appear, because "This object is round" and "This object is not "round" are contradictory; not "This object is round" and "This object is not round" contradictory because a round, not-round object is a self-contradictory entity. There are those, we have seen, who regard truth as prior to reality.[42] And a discussion of truth and reality that permits "reality" to be explained by a reference back to 'truth' has the advantage of permitting the more familiar expression: "contradictory propositions" to be introduced before the more awkward expression: "self-contradictory entities." It has been our choice, however, to discuss reality before discussing truth, hence to introduce the expression: "self-contradictory entity" before introducing the expression: "contradictory propositions."[43] But the introduction of our term: "self-contradictory entity" prior to a discussion of contradictory propositions does not, I hope, detract from the understanding of our expression: "self-contradictory entity." There subsists the alleged entity which appears both straight and not-straight, the alleged entity which appears both round and not-round. And we do, I hope, succeed in partially explaining our terms "reality" and "unreality" when, even prior to a discussion of contradictory propositions, we mark out such self-contradictory entities as unreal.

Of our propositions "S_1 is P" and "S_1 is not P," at least one, we have seen,[44] is false in our sense of "falsity." We can not conclude, however, that, of our propositions "S_1 is P" and S_1 is not P," at least one is true in our sense of "truth." Our proposition: "The present King of France is bald" is true only if a bald present King of France exists; our proposition: "The present King of France is not bald" only if a not-bald present King of France exists. If, however, there is no present King of France, a bald present King of France is unreal and a not-bald present King of France unreal, hence our proposition: "The present King of France is bald" false and our proposition: "The present King of France is not bald" false. When the alleged entity S_1 is unreal, both our proposition: "S_1 is P" and our proposition: "S_1 is not P" are false. Indeed even when S_1 is real, "S_1 is P" and "S_1 is not P" may both be false. This good deed alleged to be yellow may be unreal and this good deed alleged to be not-yellow may be unreal. S_1, in short, may be real and yet, having regard to the deductions our explanation of "reality" permits us to make, S_1 P may be unreal and S_1: not-P unreal.

Similarly with our contradictory propositions: "All S is P" and "Some S is not P." Our proposition: "All centaurs are intelligent" is false in that the alleged universal 'intelligent centaur' is unreal; our proposition "Some centaurs are not intelligent" false in that the alleged universal 'unintelligent centaur' is unreal. And just as the alleged individual: 'this good deed' may be unreal both when presented as yellow and when presented as not-yellow, so the alleged universal 'good deed' may be unreal both when presented as yellow and when presented as not-yellow.

Since the word "false" is the predicate-term in "One of a given pair of propositions is false," it follows that whether or not one of a given pair of propositions is false will depend upon the meaning of "falsity." [45] And since the word "true" is the predicate-term in "One of a given pair of propositions is true," whether or not one of a given pair of propositions is true will depend upon the meaning of "truth." "In our sense of 'falsity' and with respect to propositions of ours, at least one of each pair of what are commonly called contradictory propositions is false." [46] But, except for propositions of the forms "No S is P" and "Some S is P," it does not follow from our explanation of "truth" that, with respect to propositions of ours, at least one of each pair of what are commonly called contradictory propositions is true in our sense of "truth." Within the framework of our explanations of "reality" and "truth," the law of contradiction in at least one formulation of it has been deduced as valid with respect to propositions of ours. Within the framework of our explanations of "reality" and "truth," the law of identity in at least one formulation of it has been deduced as valid with respect to propositions of ours—but only provided the subject-term represents an existent entity. But it is only within much narrower limits that the law of excluded middle in at least one formulation of it can be found to be valid within the framework of our explanations of "reality" and "truth."

Summary

If X exists in our sense of "existence," then our proposition "X exists" is true in our sense of "truth" and our proposition "X does not exist" false in our sense of "falsity." Thus the explanation of our terms "truth" and "falsity" utilizes and refers back to the explanation of our term "existence." Various types of categorical propositions are considered and the entities pointed out whose existence or non-existence in our sense of "existence" determine these propositions to be true or false as we explain our terms "truth" and "falsity."

The so-called laws of thought are statements about what must be true or must be false. But we can not say what must be true or must be false until we know what "truth" and "falsity" mean. "Truth" and "falsity," like "existence" and "non-existence," are capable of various meanings. It is only after the meanings of "truth" and "falsity" have been determined that we are in a position to consider the validity of the so-called laws of thought. When "truth" and "falsity" have the meanings we assign those terms, the law of contradiction is true, the other so-called laws of thought only qualifiedly true.

Chapter V

MORE ABOUT TRUE AND FALSE PROPOSITIONS

We have at this point agreed that various sentences are real in our sense of "reality," some of them being sentences of ours, some of them sentences of others. Those propositions of others which express no assertion of existence or of non-existence in our sense of "existence" are, to be sure, real. But, as we explain our terms "truth" and "falsity," they are neither true nor false.[1] Except for judgments or facts that may be called "true," it is to sentences expressing assertions of existence or of non-existence in our sense of "existence" that we are limiting the application of our terms "truth" and "falsity,"—to sentences expressing assertions of existence or of non-existence in our sense of "existence," whether these sentences be propositions of ours or propositions of others. It is however only in their application to *some* of these sentences that we have thus far explained our terms "truth" and "falsity." Categorical propositions occurring in this treatise, whether singular, particular or universal, whether affirmative or negative, are,—provided the predicate-term is not "true," "false," "real" or "unreal,"—true or false according as some entity or entities are real or unreal. Categorical *existential* propositions occurring in this treatise are likewise true or false according as some entity is real or unreal. And those propositions of others which are synonymous with one or more categorical existential propositions as they might be used by me are true or false according as all of the categorical existential propositions of ours to which they may be reduced are true or one of them false.

In explaining our terms "truth" and "falsity" as applied to propositions of others, little more need be said. It remains, however for us to determine the categorical existential propositions of ours, if any, to which our non-categorical propositions may be reduced. And it remains for us to determine whether any of our propositions can not be reduced to categorical existential propositions, whether any of our propositions express no assertion of existence or of non-existence in our sense of "existence," whether, consequently, any of our propositions, in accordance with our explanations of "truth" and "falsity," are neither true nor false.

Within the framework of our explanations of "truth" and "falsity" as thus far stated, it may seem that our sentence: "This proposition is true" may be true, false, or neither true nor false. For "This proposition is true" is not an explicitly existential proposition like "Socrates exists" nor, since "P" has been said not to cover the predicate-terms "true" and "false," [2] an instance of "S_1 is P." The only sentences which are neither true nor false, however, are those which are not propositions and those which express no assertions of existence or of non-existence in our sense of "existence." Our sentence: "This proposition is true" *is* what we call a "proposition";[3] it does not express an assertion of mere subsistence; it is not synonymous with: "This true proposition subsists." Rather it expresses an assertion that 'this true proposition' exists; it is, as we explain "truth," true or false according as 'this true proposition' is real or unreal.

Let us take as our alleged object: 'the sentence "This proposition is true," apparently presented as false.' What we seem to have before us is then a 'this proposition' with the characteristic of being true and with the characteristic of being false. What we seem to have before us is a subsisting 'this proposition' which appears self-contradictory, a subsisting 'this proposition' which consequently is unreal. 'This proposition' is real when presented as true but not false, unreal when presented as both true and false. And since "This proposition is true," when not presented as false, exists, "This proposition is true" is itself, let us say, a proposition which is true.

Just as our sentence: "This proposition is true" exists when presented as true and not false, so our sentence: "This proposition is false" exists when presented as false and not true. Since 'this true-false proposition' does not exist, "This proposition is

132

false" is not true. And yet, since 'this false proposition' exists, a sentence which expresses an assertion of the existence of 'this false proposition' does not express an assertion of mere subsistence and is consequently either true or false. "This proposition is false" is, it follows, false. To be sure, when the predicate-term is not "real," "unreal," "true" or "false," then, when S_1 P exists, our proposition: "S_1 is P" is true.[4] And if "This proposition is false" were to be treated as an instance of "S_1 is P," then, since 'this false proposition' exists, "This proposition is false" would be true. But "This proposition is false" is, as we have just seen, not true. And so it follows that the conditions determining the truth or falsity of a proposition of ours whose predicate-term is the word "false" are not always the conditions determining the truth or falsity of a proposition of ours whose predicate-term is neither "true" nor "false" nor "real" nor "unreal." It is some entity's existence or non-existence which determines a proposition to be true or false, in our sense of these terms, rather than neither true nor false. But in one case where an entity exists, a proposition asserting the existence of that entity is true; in another case where an entity exists, a proposition asserting the existence of that entity is false.

Our sentence: "This proposition is true" is a proposition which is true, our sentence: "This proposition is false" is a proposition which is false. But whereas our proposition: "This proposition is true" is in all instances true, our proposition: "Proposition A, which is not this proposition, is true" is, it would seem, true or false according as proposition A is true or not. And whereas our proposition: "This proposition is false" is in all instances false, our proposition: "Proposition B, which is not this proposition, is false" is, it would seem, true or false according as proposition B is false or not.

There exist, let us agree, propositions whose subject terms are propositions; there exist propositions whose subject-terms are propositions which in turn have propositions as *their* subject-terms. There exist, that is to say, what we may call the first-order proposition A, what we may call the second order proposition: "Proposition A is false," what we may call the third-order proposition: "It is true that proposition A is false." Generalizing, we may say that a proposition of the $(n+1)$th order in which the predicate-term is the word "true" is true or false according as the proposition of the nth order, which is its subject-term, and not identical with it, is true or not. And we may say that a proposition of the $(n+1)$th order in which the predicate-term is the word "false" is true or false according as the proposition of the nth order which is its subject-term, and not identical with it, is false or not. We thus elaborate the explanation of our terms "truth" and "falsity" with respect to propositions of ours of higher and higher order. But no questions concerning propositions of an allegedly infinite order are involved. For the most complex proposition whose truth or falsity is to be determined will, however complex, be a proposition definitely presented to us, a proposition which is real and of a finite order.

There is our singular proposition: "The proposition 'All men are mortal' occurring on this page is a true proposition." And there is our enumerative proposition: "Each proposition occurring on this page is true." There is our singular proposition: "The proposition 'All centaurs are animals' occurring on this page is a false proposition." And there is our enumerative proposition: "Each proposition occurring on this page is false." But, as we use it, "Each proposition occurring on this page is true" is, let us say, synonymous with "This proposition is true" and "Each remaining proposition on this page is true." And, as we use it, "Each proposition occurring on this page is false" is, let us say, synonymous with "This proposition is false" and "Each remaining proposition on this page is false." Since our proposition: "This proposition is true" is always true, our proposition "Each proposition occurring on this page is true" is true if each *remaining* proposition on this page is true. And since "This proposition is false" is always false, our proposition "Each proposition occurring on this page is false" is never true. If Lucian had been using "existence" in our sense of "existence" and if he had ended his "True History" with the statement: "Each of the propositions in this book is false," his final proposition would have been false in the sense in which we are using the terms "falsity" and "truth."

"Given any set of objects such that, if we suppose the set to have a total, it will contain members which presuppose this total, then," say Whitehead and Russell, "such a set can not have a total" and "no significant statement can be made about all its members." [5] But our statement: "Each proposition occurring on this page is false" is not without meaning in the sense in which the statement: "Eeny meeny miny mo" is without meaning. Indeed it expresses an assertion of the existence of various false propositions and, since it itself exists as a false proposition, it is a proposition which is false. It is itself, we hold, a proposition; and hence adds to the number of propositions on this page. And so if it is the last proposition on a page containing twenty others, that page, it would seem, contains twenty-one propositions and not propositions having no total at all.

If S_1 P exists, our proposition "S_1 is P" is true; whereas if 'this false proposition' exists, our proposition: "This proposition is false" is false. To this extent there is a difference between "truth" as we explain it in its application to certain propositions of the first order and "truth" as we explain it in its application to certain propositions of a higher order. It may seem to be a matter merely of the choice of words whether, as with Whitehead and Russell, the distinction is said to be between "truth of the first order" and "truth of a higher order" or whether, as with us, the distinction is said to be between the conditions under which certain propositions of the first order are true or are false, and the conditions under which certain propositions of a higher order are true or are false. No doubt some theory of types, though not Whitehead and Russell's, might distinguish as we do the conditions under which certain propositions of the first order are true or are false from the conditions under which certain propositions of a higher order are true or are false. It is to be pointed out, however, that it is not the order of a proposition alone that determines the conditions under which a proposition is true or false as we explain "truth" and "falsity." The conditions determining the truth or falsity of our second-order proposition: "This proposition is false" are, to be sure, not the conditions determining the truth or falsity of a first-order proposition of the form: S_1 is P. But the conditions determining the truth or falsity of our first-order proposition "S_1 is unreal" are likewise not the conditions determining the truth or falsity of our "S_1 is P." For our "S_1 is unreal" is true, not if an unreal S_1 exists, but if S_1 is unreal. And our "S_1 is unreal" is false, not if an unreal S_1 does not exist, but if S_1 is real. The conditions under which propositions of ours are true or false vary with the form of proposition in which assertions of existence or of non-existence are expressed. But it is always the existence or non-existence of some entity or entities —in our sense of "existence"— that determines a proposition's truth or falsity. It is not existence in one sense that characterizes entities whose existence is asserted in first-order propositions, existence in another sense that characterizes entities whose existence is asserted in second-order propositions. And it is to this extent not truth in one sense that characterizes first-order propositions, truth in another sense that characterizes second-order propositions.

There are second-order propositions whose subject-terms are first order propositions; there are propositions, that is to say, which are about propositions. And as there are propositions about propositions, so there subsist relations between relations, qualities of qualities, classes whose members are classes. Alleged situations of these various types may present us with difficulties, with apparent contradictions. Where such contradictions appear, "the appearance of contradiction," it has been held,[6] "is produced by the presence of some word which has systematic ambiguity of type, such as *truth, falsehood, function, property, class, relation, cardinal, ordinal, name, definition.*" Indeed, as these apparent contradictions may elicit similar diagnoses, so, it may be held, they call for similar solutions. And so what is said about propositions about propositions, it may be held, indicates what is to be said about alleged relations between relations, about alleged qualities of qualities, about alleged classes whose members are classes. No doubt apparent contradictions apparently presented to us in connection with alleged qualities of qualities or in connection with alleged classes whose members are classes require our attention at some point. It is however in connection with our discussion of qualities and relations that we shall consider the alleged quality of being a quality.[7] It is in connection with our discussion of universals that we shall consider the alleged universal whose instances are universals.[8] And it is in connection with our discussion of meanings that we shall consider an ambiguity in the term "name." Let us at this point limit our attention to propositions varying in form and to the conditions under which propositions varying in form are true or false as we explain our terms "truth" and "falsity."

Ever since Aristotle, many logicians hold, propositions of the subject-predicate type have occupied our attention too exclusively. It is felt that many of the sentences in which we normally express ourselves fall into the subject-predicate form only by an artificial and unnatural treatment. "King James was King Charles's son," for example, is to be symbolized, it is felt, by "A r B" rather than by "S_1 is P." Moreover, it has been pointed out, our neglect of "A r B" has led us to neglect various valid implications, as, for example, the implications which are valid when "r" is a transitive relation. We need, however, merely note these criticisms and pass on. For our task is not to catalog and discuss the implications that are valid with respect to propositions of various forms. Nor is our task to catalog the forms in which we normally express ourselves. No doubt through the existential proposition: "Anne exists with the quality of having Ruth as her sister and with the quality of having Mary as her sister," attention is directed to Anne as it is not directed to her through the relational proposition: "Ruth, Mary and Anne are sisters." But the various existential propositions of ours which are synonymous with our: "Ruth, Mary and Anne are sisters" need no pointing out. Our task at this point is to explain our terms "truth" and "falsity" in their application to propositions of ours, however these propositions may vary in form. But the conditions under which our relational propositions are true or false are, it would seem, clear. For with whatever shift in emphasis the reduction of them to existential propositions may be carried out, however inelegantly the existential propositions to which they are reduced may have to be expressed, the existential propositions with which they are synonymous are, it would seem, clear; hence the conditions under which they are true or false are clear.

Sentences of others which express no assertions of existence or of non-existence in our sense of "existence" are, we have said,[10] neither true nor false. There are writers whose term "existence" has a meaning different from that which our term "existence" has. And there are perhaps sentences—and certainly clauses—which express no assertion of existence or of non-existence in *any* sense of "existence." In the hypothetical sentence: "If A is B, C is D," the clause: "If A is B" expresses no assertion that there exists, in any sense of "existence," an A that is B. There is, for example, the hypothetical sentence: "If it rains tomorrow, the ground will be wet." And yet, as this sentence is commonly used,—whatever meaning "existence" has for its author,—this sentence's initial clause expresses doubt, rather that belief, in the occurrence of rain tomorrow. The statement however is: "If it rains tomorrow, the ground will be wet," not "If it rains tomorrow, the ground will be dry." If there is any sense of "truth," any sense of "falsity," in which the former proposition is true and the latter false, there would seem to be a corresponding sense of "existence" in which rain is wet and not dry, a corresponding sense of "existence" in which rain exists with the quality of causing the ground to be wet, not with the quality of causing the ground to be dry. Some other author's: "If A is B, C is D" may express no assertion of existence or of non-existence in our sense of "existence"; his sentence may be neither true nor false in our sense of "truth" and in our sense of "falsity." Nevertheless there would appear to be *some* entity whose existence in his sense of "existence" he is asserting, some entity which from his point of view is an existent and supports the statement: "If A is B, C is D" rather than the statement: "If A is B, C is not D." [11]

There is likewise some entity whose existence or non-existence in *our* sense of "existence" determines the truth or falsity—in *our* sense of "truth" and "falsity"—of a hypothetical proposition of *ours*. And it is by pointing out the entities whose existence or non-existence determines the truth or falsity of a hypothetical proposition of ours that we explain our terms "truth" and "falsity" in their application to that proposition of ours.

A hypothetical proposition of ours is, generally speaking, a proposition having the form: "If A is B, C is D." But "If it rains tomorrow" is synonymous with: "If rain tomorrow should exist"; [12] "If some men have six legs" synonymous with: "If the universal 'six-legged man' should exist." [13] And so with our "C is D." There is the hypothetical proposition: "If rain tomorrow should exist, then wet grounds tomorrow would exist" and the hypothetical proposition: "If 'six-legged man' should exist, then 'six-legged animal' would exist." Many of our hypothetical propositions, that is to say, may be reduced to instances of: "If entity E should exist, then entity F would exist," may be said to be true or false according as the corresponding instance of: "If E should exist, then F would exist" is true or false.

138

Our proposition: "If rain tomorrow should exist, then wet grounds tomorrow would exist" does not express an assertion that rain tomorrow will exist nor an assertion that there will be wet grounds tomorrow. Our proposition: "If 'six-legged man' should exist, then 'six-legged animal' would exist" does not express an assertion that 'six-legged man' exists nor an assertion that 'six-legged animal' exists. There are however two-legged men; and 'two-legged man' implies 'two-legged animal.' And there are six-legged insects; and 'six-legged insect' implies 'six-legged animal.' Likewise there was rain yesterday which caused wet grounds and rain a month ago which caused wet grounds. If what may be said to be analogous to rain tomorrow does not cause what is correspondingly analogous to wet grounds tomorrow, then our proposition: "If rain tomorrow should exist, then wet grounds tomorrow would exist" is false. And if what may be said to be analogous to 'six-legged man' does not imply what is correspondingly analogous to 'six-legged animal,' then our proposition: "If 'six-legged man' should exist, then 'six-legged animal' would exist" is false. E may not exist and F may not exist. But in order for our proposition: "If E should exist, F would exist" to be true in our sense of "truth," some entity in some sense analogous to E must exist in our sense of "existence"; and some entity correspondingly analogous to F must exist. Indeed, the entity or entities that may be said to resemble E must really cause the entity or entities that seem correspondingly to resemble F, must really imply the entity or entities that seem correspondingly to resemble F, or must really be synchronous and concomitant with the entity or entities that seem correspondingly to resemble F. Our proposition: "If E should exist, F would exist," that is to say, expresses an assertion that entities in some sense resembling E exist; indeed, that they exist when presented as entering into certain relational situations with entities seeming to resemble F. Unless these entities thus presented are real, our hypothetical proposition, let us say, is false. Provided these entities thus presented are real, our hypothetical proposition, let us say, may be true.

There is, moreover, not only an assertion of *existence* expressed in our proposition: "If E should exist, F would exist"; there is also an assertion of *non-existence*. There may or may not be rain tomorrow. But an alleged rain tomorrow presented as not causing, or not being concomitant with, wet grounds tomorrow is asserted not to exist. 'Six-legged man' may or may not be real. But 'six-legged man,' presented as not implying 'six-legged animal,' is asserted not to be real. Only if E presented as not causing, not implying and not being concomitant with F is *unreal,* and only if entities in some sense resembling E presented as entering into certain relational situations with entities in some sense resembling F *are* real, then and only then is our proposition: "If E should exist, F would exist" true.

"If it rains tomorrow," we have said,[14] is synonymous with "If rain tomorrow should exist"; "If some men have six legs" synonymous with "If 'six-legged man' should exist." Since, however, our proposition: "No men are immortal" has been reduced to: "Immortal men do not exist," [15] it follows that "If no men are immortal" is synonymous with: "If immortal man should not exist." There is thus not only our hypothetical proposition: "If E should exist, then F would exist"; there is our hypothetical proposition: "If E should not exist, then F would exist," our hypothetical proposition: "If E should exist and E′ not exist, then F would exist"; our hypothetical proposition: "If E should not exist, then F would not exist." There is, for example, not only our proposition: "If six-legged man should exist, then six-legged animal would exist," but also our proposition: "If 'animal' should not exist, then 'man' would not exist." And there is not only our proposition: "If rain tomorrow should exist, then wet grounds tomorrow would exist," but also our proposition: "If there should be no fire, there would be no smoke."

Our proposition: "If it should rain tomorrow, the ground would be wet" expresses an assertion that rain tomorrow not concomitant with wet grounds will not exist. And our proposition: "If there should be no fire, there would be no smoke," we may tentatively say, expresses an assertion that the absence of fire concomitant with smoke does not exist. But what is this absence of fire that is asserted not to exist when presented as concomitant with smoke? Where there is no fire, there is, let us assume, matter at a temperature below the point of combustion. It is non-combusting matter presented as concomitant with smoke that, it would appear, we are asserting to be unreal. And it is what might be alleged to exist on a planet where there are no animals that,

140

it would appear, we are asserting to be unreal when presented as concomitant with man. In order that our proposition: "If E should not exist, F would not exist" may be true, what may be alleged to exist in the absence of E must be unreal when presented as concomitant with F, must be unreal when presented as not concomitant with what is alleged to exist in the absence of F.

But when we say: "If E should not exist, F would not exist," is there anything that we are asserting *does* exist? Are we asserting that something *does* exist in the absence of E and *is* concomitant with what exists in the absence of F? Are we asserting at least that something exists which seems to resemble what might exist in the absence of E and that this entity is concomitant with an entity that seems to resemble what might exist in the absence of F? Or does our: "If E should not exist, F would not exist" merely express an assertion of non-existence, express no assertion of existence at all? With respect to that with respect to which we can speak with certainty, with respect to propositions that are expressions of mine, let us adopt the last and simplest course. Let us say that our: "If E should not exist, F would not exist" expresses no assertion not expressed in: "What is alleged to exist in the absence of E is unreal when presented as concomitant with F." Let us consequently say that our proposition: "If there should be no fire, there would be no smoke" is true or false, in our sense of "truth" and "falsity," according as non-combusting matter alleged to be concomitant with smoke is unreal or real. And let us say that our proposition: "If there should be no animals there would be no men" is true or false according as there is not, or is, a world containing men but not animals.

There is our categorical proposition: "All centaurs are animals" and there is our hypothetical proposition: "If centaurs should exist, animals would exist." Just as our proposition: "All men are mortal" is true, as we explain "truth," only if immortal men do not exist, so "All centaurs are animals" is true only if centaurs who are not animals do not exist.[16] "If centaurs should exist, animals would exist" is likewise true only if centaurs who are not animals do not exist. For our proposition: "If E should exist, F would exist" is true "only if E presented as not causing, not implying and being concomitant with F is unreal."[17] The two propositions which we are comparing, one categorical and one hypothetical, both, to be true, require the *non-existence* of centaurs who are not animals. But they differ in the entities that must *exist,* if they are to be true. In order for: "If centaurs should exist, animals would exist" to be true, there need be no centaurs, —only entities analogous to centaurs whose existence causes or implies or is concomitant with the existence of animals. But in order for: "All centaurs are animals" to be true, there must be some centaur that is an animal. Our categorical proposition: "All centaurs are animals," it follows, is not synonymous with our hypothetical proposition: "If centaurs should exist, animals would exist." For with horses, which may be said to be analogous to centaurs, being real and being animals, and with centaurs not being real and not being animals, the hypothetical proposition is true and the categorical proposition false.

"A hypothetical proposition of ours," we have said,[18] "is, generally speaking, a proposition having the form: "If A is B, C is D." But along with the assertions expressed in: "If A is B, C is D," there may be the assertions expressed in: "A is not B" as when we say: "If A were B or had been B, C would be or would have been D." And along with the assertions expressed in "If A is B, C is D" and expressed in "A is not B," there may be the assertions expressed in: "C is D." We may be asserting that C is D but that A is not B; and we may also be asserting that A being B would cause or imply C being D. We may in short assert that C is D as though—or as if—A were B.

In the writings of Vaihinger and others much importance is attached to fictions. There is the fiction: "All of the sun's mass is concentrated at the centre." And there is the fictitious or "as if" proposition: "The earth revolves about the sun in an elliptical path exactly as if all of the sun's mass were concentrated at the centre." The fiction itself—the proposition, for example: "All of the sun's mass is concentrated at the centre,"—may be a proposition that the physicist finds useful to consider. The mental attitude which has as its apparent object an alleged sun whose mass is concentrated at the centre may lead to other mental attitudes directed upon the behavior of the sun as it actually exists. But when we assert that C is D as if A were B, we are asserting that A is *not* B. We are asserting that A is not B; that C is D; that if A should be B, C would be D. We are asserting for example: "If the sun's

142

mass should be concentrated at its centre, the earth would revolve in an elliptical orbit about it." And whereas, in order that this latter proposition may be true, the sun's mass need not be concentrated at the centre, there must be something analogous to a sun whose mass is concentrated at the centre; and this analogous entity that is real must really imply, or must really be concomitant with, an entity analogous to an earth that follows an elliptical path. It is true, let us suppose, that a laboratory approximation of a body alleged to have its mass concentrated at its centre does exist, a body, for example, with a dense core. And it is true, let us suppose, that the satellite of such a body follows an elliptical path. If, then, among other assumptions we assume that the earth's orbit is indeed an ellipse, then the fictitious proposition: "The earth revolves about the earth in an elliptical path exactly as if all of the sun's mass were concentrated at the centre" is a proposition which is true; whereas the fiction: "All of the sun's mass is concentrated at the centre" is a proposition which is false.

Vaihinger distinguishes, however, between what he calls "real fictions" and what he calls "semi-fictions." "Semi-fictions," he holds,[19] "assume the unreal, real fictions the impossible." But if a real fiction is to be symbolized by: "The self-contradictory entity E exists," then the fictitious or "as if" proposition that is based upon it becomes, let us suppose: "F exists as if the self-contradictory entity E existed." "F exists as if the self-contradictory entity E existed" is, however, true,—at least this proposition as it might be used by me is true,—only if an entity in some sense analogous to the self-contradictory E is real and only if this analogous entity really causes, really implies, or is really synchronous and concomitant with, an entity analogous to F. Is there then, we may ask, a real entity that may be said to be analogous to the E that is presented as self-contradictory? If each entity presented as analogous to E appears as self-contradictory as E itself, then no entity analogous to E exists and the fictitious proposition based upon what Vaihinger calls a real fiction is false. And if a real entity may be said to approximate and resemble a self-contradictory one, if a many-sided polygon, for example, may be said to be analogous to a circle bounded by straight lines, then real fictions and semi-fictions seem to require no separate treatment. For in that case the fictions are equally false and the fictitious propositions based upon them are equally likely to be true; in that case, whether our alleged E be self-contradictory or not, there is a real entity that may be said to be analogous to it, a real entity whose participation in a particular relational situation is asserted.

There may be no circle bounded by straight lines. But if there is a many-sided polygon that may be said to be analogous to such an alleged circle, then the hypothetical proposition that begins with the clause: "If a circle were bounded by straight lines" may be true. There may be no men with six legs. But if 'two-legged man' may be said to be analogous to such an alleged 'six-legged man,' then the hypothetical proposition that begins with the clause: "If some men had six legs" may be true. It may not have rained last Tuesday. But if there have been other instances of rain all followed by wet grounds, then the hypothetical proposition: "If it had rained last Tuesday, the ground would then have been wet" may be true. My alcoholic friend may not be seeing a snake. But if people have seen snakes and have jumped, my proposition: "He is jumping as though he were seeing a snake" may be true.

But if other people have really seen snakes, how can their experiences which are real be really analogous to an alleged snake-seeing experience which is unreal? How can yesterday's rain which was real have the real quality of being analogous to an alleged but non-existent rain last Tuesday? Real entities, it would seem, can have only real qualities. Unreal entities, it would seem, can have only unreal qualities. Last Tuesday's rain is unreal no matter how it is presented. *It* is unreal; and its alleged quality of being analogous to yesterday's rain is unreal. And yesterday's rain is real only when presented with qualities that it really has. The quality of resembling an unreal entity is unreal. And the yesterday's rain that is presented as resembling an unreal rain is an unreal subsistent, a subsistent other than the subsisting yesterday's rain which is real.[20]

A real entity, we must agree, can not *really* resemble an unreal one. But unreal entities may be presented as apparent objects. And real entities, which to be sure do not really resemble them, may subsequently be selected as our objects. There are the real

144

words: "Last Tuesday's rain." And after having these real words before us, we may subsequently select as our object the real entity: yesterday's rain. There may be no entities really resembling an unreal E. But our term: "Entities resembling an unreal E" is real; and this term may suggest other terms which not only are real but which have real meanings. "If E should exist, F would exist" is a proposition of ours which is real and which may be true or may be false. A condition of its truth, we now find, is not that entities really resembling E enter into relational situations with entities really resembling F, but rather that the real entity E^1, suggested by our real phrase "entities resembling E" enter into relational situations with the real entity F^1 suggested by our real phrase: "Entities resembling F."

There is our hypothetical proposition: "If A is B, C is D"; and there is our alternative proposition: "A is B or C is D." Both in general usage and as an expression of ours, " A is B or C is D or E is F" is called true if "A is B" is a true proposition or "C is D" a true proposition or "E is F" a true proposition. And if each of the included propositions is false, then the alternative proposition which includes them is called "false." No matter how disparate the entities whose existence is asserted or denied in "A is B" and in "C is D," the alternative proposition: "A is B or C is D," it would seem, may be true. Thus, since both "Caesar crossed the Rubicon" and "No centaurs are animals" are true in our sense of "truth," our alternative proposition: "Caesar crossed the Rubicon or no centaurs are animals," let us say, is likewise true in our sense of "truth." Since our proposition: "All men are mortal" is true in our sense of "truth," our alternative proposition: "All men are mortal or Washington crossed the Hellespont" is true in our sense of "truth." And as we explain our term "falsity" in its application to alternative propositions of ours, since "The present King of France is a married man" and "This proposition is false" are both false, our alternative proposition: "The present King of France is a married man or this proposition is false" is false. Our alternative proposition is thus a proposition *about* propositions, a proposition that resembles: "At least one of the propositions on yonder page is true." In its simplest form it is what we have called a proposition of the second order rather than a first-order proposition like: "All men are mortal" or like: "If it

145

should rain tomorrow, the ground would be wet." [21]

Let us assume that we have before us a true hypothetical proposition that is, or may be reduced to, an instance of: "If E should exist, then F would exist." Among the various assertions that this proposition expresses, there is the assertion that E, presented as not concomitant with F and presented as neither causing nor implying F, does not exist.[22] Since the hypothetical proposition which we are considering is assumed to be true, the entity whose non-existence is asserted in it does not exist. And since an E presented as not concomitant with F and presented as neither causing nor implying F does not exist, it follows that an E presented as not even co-existent with F does not exist. If, that is to say, E does not exist unless it causes, implies or is concomitant with F, then E does not exist unless it co-exists with F. Either E does not exist at all or F is also an existent. Thus at least one of two propositions is true. Either "E does not exist" is true or "F exists" is true. In short, if our hypothetical proposition: "If E should exist, then F would exist" is true, then our alternative proposition: "Either E does not exist or F exists" is true.

If our hypothetical proposition: "If E should exist, then F would exist" is true, then our alternative proposition: "Either E does not exist or F exists" is true. It is not to be concluded however that if our alternative proposition: "Either E does not exist or F exists" is true, then our hypothetical proposition: "If E should exist, then F would exist" is true. Our hypothetical proposition: "If E should exist, then F would exist" expresses an assertion of existence as well as an assertion of non-existence. And even the assertion of non-existence expressed in it is not the assertion of the non-existence of an E that is alleged merely not to co-exist with F. It is an E, alleged not to enter into a particular relational situation with F, which is asserted to be unreal and which,—since our proposition is assumed to be true,—*is* unreal. E does not merely not exist without F existing; E does not exist without implying F, or without causing F, or without being synchronous and concomitant with F.[23] A Caesar who crossed the Rubicon existed; and rain yesterday existed. The two events co-exist in the sense that the one is not an existent and the other a non-existent. But Caesar's crossing the Rubicon did not cause yesterday's rain, did not imply yesterday's rain, was not synchronous with yesterday's

146

rain. As we explain our terms "truth" and "falsity" in their application to propositions of ours, our alternative proposition: "Either Caesar did not cross the Rubicon or it rained yesterday" is true; our hypothetical proposition: "If Caesar crossed the Rubicon, then it rained yesterday" is false.

"It rained yesterday" is a true proposition. There is however a difference between: "It rained yesterday" being presented as a true proposition and rain yesterday being presented as an existent entity, a difference between: "Either it rained yesterday or Caesar did not cross the Rubicon" being presented as a true proposition and 'rain yesterday or Caesar not crossing the Rubicon' being presented as an existent entity. There is no real entity: 'Rain yesterday or Caesar not crossing the Rubicon.' And the real entity 'rain yesterday' does not really imply 'rain yesterday or Caesar not crossing the Rubicon.' The implication in short is from one true proposition to another, not from the existent referred to in one proposition to the existent referred to in another. It is the true proposition P which implies the true proposition: P or Q; not the entity whose existence is asserted in P which implies some entity described as "E or F" whose existence might be said to be asserted in 'P or Q.' There are implications between propositions, that is to say, which can not be reduced to implications between the entities that seem to be referred to in these propositions. There are true hypothetical propositions *about* propositions, true hypothetical propositions of the second order, that have no true hypothetical propositions of the first order corresponding to them.

It is beyond the scope of this chapter to point out the bearing, if any, which the remarks of the last few pages have upon propositions advanced in treatises on symbolic logic. "Existence" may be assigned various meanings; "truth" may be assigned various meanings; "implication" may be assigned various meanings. And the relevance of the distinctions to which we have just alluded will vary with the meanings selected. Our primary task has been to explain our terms "truth" and "falsity" in their application to categorical propositions of ours and to alternative propositions of ours, to hypothetical propositions of the first order and to hypothetical propositions of the second order. And at this point this part of our task has, it would seem, been accomplished.

Let us however not take leave of the alternative proposition without some discussion of the dilemma, without some discussion of the situation in which we are alleged to be confronted by two equally unsatisfactory alternatives. Consider, for example, the plight of the ship's barber who has agreed to shave each man on board ship who does not shave himself and no man on board ship who *does* shave himself.[24] The barber is himself a member of the ship's personnel. If he shaves himself, he is breaking his agreement; since he has agreed to shave *no* one on board ship who shaves himself. And if he does not shave himself, he is failing to shave *each* man on board ship who does not shave himself. The barber appearing with the characteristic of shaving all non-shavers and with the characteristic of shaving only non-shavers,—like the Cretan appearing with the characteristic of making the true assertion that no Cretan ever expresses himself in a true proposition[25]—is a subsistent implicitly appearing as self-contradictory, a subsistent that is unreal. Of the two statements the barber may be supposed to have made before entering upon his duties, one is false. Either "I shall shave each man on board who does not shave himself" is false or "I shall shave no man on board who shaves himself" is false. The sentence: "Either the proposition 'I shall shave each man on board who does not shave himself' is false or the proposition 'I shall shave no man on board who shaves himself' is false" is, however, not without meaning in the sense in which the statement: "Eeeny meeny miny mo" is without meaning.[26] Our alternative proposition expresses an assertion that, of two alleged false propositions, one presented as false exists. It expresses an assertion of existence and, as we explain our term "truth," is true rather than neither true nor false.[27]

There is likewise the dilemma that may be supposed to have been presented to the court in the hypothetical case of Protagoras versus Euathlus.[28] Euathlus is supposed to have agreed to complete payment for the training he had received only after winning his first case. When his teacher Protagoras sued him for the unpaid balance and thus forced upon Euathlus his first and last case, Euathlus is imagined to have proposed to the court a dilemma. "Either I shall win this case, in which event the court will have decided that the balance is voided; or I shall lose this case, in which event I shall never have won my first case." An

148

alleged correct decision in favor of Euathlus is implicitly presented with contradictory consequences and is unreal. An alleged correct decision in favor of Protagoras is implicitly presented with contradictory consequences and is unreal. The agreement to pay after the first case no matter what the first case might be, and to pay only after the first case,—like the agreement to shave each non-shaver and no shavers,—turns out to have been an agreement that cannot be kept. Either our proposition: "Protagoras will receive payment only after Euathlus wins his first case" is false; or our proposition: "Euathlus will pay after winning his first case" is false. Unless the case of Protagoras versus Euathlus was implicitly excepted, there was no real agreement at all and judgment must be rendered on the basis that there was no agreement.

There is our alternative proposition: "A is B or C is D." [29] "A is B" may be positive or negative, singular, particular or universal. So with "C is D"; and so with any other propositions that are included in our alternative proposition. "A" may moreover be identical with "C," or "B" may be identical with "D." But however one alternative proposition of ours may differ from another, despite the multiplicity of types, nevertheless not every proposition containing the words "or" or "nor" is an instance of "A is B or C is D." "All animals are vertebrates or invertebrates," for example, is not synonymous with "All animals are vertebrates or all animals are invertebrates," but, as generally used, seems, among other assertions, to express the assertion that no animal is both non-vertebrate and non-invertebrate. And "Neither Taft nor Wilson is now President" seems, as generally used, to be synonymous with: "Taft is not now President; and Wilson is not now President." It is in short our alternative proposition that we have been discussing, not every proposition containing the word "or" or the word "nor."

When we turn to the apodeictic proposition, it is likewise not each proposition containing the word "necessary" or the word "must" that concerns us. "S must be P" or "S must exist" may simply express in more emphatic form what would be expressed in "S is P" or in "S exists"; "S can not be P" or "S can not exist" may simply express in more emphatic form what would be expressed in "S is not P" or in "S does not exist." "S must be P" or "S can not be P" may simply point to the deep conviction with

149

which "S is P" or "S is not P" is asserted. "I am thoroughly convinced that S is P" is, however, no apodeictic proposition, and "I am thoroughly convinced that S is not P" no apodeictic proposition.

Whether they be positive or negative, singular, particular or universal, existential or not explicitly existential, our categorical propositions, we have said, express assertions of existence, assertions of non-existence, or assertions of the existence of one entity and of the non-existence of another. They may each be reduced, let us say, to an instance of: "F exists," to an instance of: "F does not exist" or to an instance of: "F exists; and F^1 does not exist." Likewise each of our apodeictic propositions, let us say, expresses an assertion that some entity must exist; an assertion that some entity can not exist; or an assertion that it is necessary that one entity exist and impossible that another exist. Each apodeictic proposition of ours, that is to say, may be reduced to an instance of: "F must exist" or to an instance of: "F can not exist" or to an instance of: "F must exist; and F^1 can not exist." What, however, is asserted in our proposition: "F must exist" that is not asserted in our proposition: "F exists"? And what is asserted in our proposition: "F can not exist" that is not asserted in our proposition: "F does not exist"?

As we have explained our terms "reality" and "unreality," those subsistents are unreal which appear as self-contradictory, those subsistents unreal which appear as lacking any date, those subsistents unreal which appear with various other characteristics.[30] A distinction suggests itself between those unreal subsistents which explicitly or implicitly appear as self-contradictory and those unreal subsistents which neither explicitly nor implicitly appear as self-contradictory. Perhaps we should call subsistents appearing as self-contradictory "impossible subsistents," and should call unreal subsistents not appearing as self-contradictory "unreal subsistents" but not "impossible subsistents." We might then give "truth" and "falsity" significations from which it follows that "F can not exist" is to be called "true" if F appears self-contradictory. The sentences: "F appears self-contradictory" and "F does not appear self-contradictory," however, merely present us with subsistents. They seem to put before us an F appearing as self-contradictory or an F appearing without the characteristic of

150

being self-contradictory. They express no assertions of existence or of non-existence, are not what we call propositions and hence, as we have agreed to use the terms, "truth" and "falsity," are not true or false at all.[31] Within the statement: "F appears self-contradictory; therefore F is unreal," it is not the sentence: "F appears self-contradictory" that is true or false, but only the sentence: "F is unreal."

Moreover the alleged distinction between that which appears self-contradictory and that which does not even implicitly appear self-contradictory becomes, with further consideration, less clear-cut. There is the subsistent which appears with the characteristic of lacking any date. As we explain our term "reality," this subsistent is unreal. But if, in rejecting this subsistent, it is an alleged real entity appearing as lacking any date that we are rejecting, then it is an entity implicitly appearing as self-contradictory that we are rejecting. For the alleged real entity appearing as lacking any date implicitly appears as real and as unreal, implicitly appears with characteristics which seem to contradict one another.

The entity appearing as self-contradictory is unreal; the entity appearing as lacking any date is unreal; the entity appearing as generally discredited is unreal. But it is not as mutually exclusive groups of non-existent entities that we have presented these subsistents. The entity appearing as lacking any date may appear as generally discredited; the entity appearing as generally discredited may appear as self-contradictory. It is any entity appearing with any characteristic listed in the closing pages of Chapter Three that is unreal; and any entity listed among the Y's in the appendix to that chapter.[32] On the other hand, it is only the entity not appearing with any of these characteristics that is real, only the entity not appearing with any of these characteristics that, explicitly or implicitly, is listed among the X's in that appendix. Among the entities which are real, however, among the entities not appearing with certain characteristics and listed among the X's enumerated in the appendix to chapter three, our propositions explaining our terms "existence" and "reality" do not permit us to point to some as more real and to others as less real. As we explain our terms "existence" and "reality" there are no degrees of reality. There are not some entities which merely exist and others which have a more exclusive kind of existence to be called "necessary existence." Thus an alleged distinction between merely existing entities and necessary entities is, one might say, more repugnant to our explanation of "existence" than an alleged distinction between merely non-existing entities and impossible entities.

As we explain our term "existence," there are not existing entities and, among them, entities with a kind of existence called "necessary existence." And as we express ourselves in the proposition: "F must exist," "F must exist" does not express an assertion that F has a kind of existence not asserted in our proposition: "F exists." Our proposition: "F must exist," let us say, expresses an assertion that F exists and is implied by some entity E. Our proposition: "Some animals must exist" is synonymous with the proposition: "Some entity exists,—as, for example, the universal 'man,'—which implies that some animals exist." Our: "F must exist" expresses what might be expressed in: "Therefore F exists." For, like "Therefore F exists," it refers back to some entity whose existence has previously been asserted or whose existence has implicitly been asserted in the context. Our "F must exist" is true if F exists and is implied by the E thus referred to. Our "F must exist" is false if F does not exist or is not implied by this E. And if we are unable to determine which the alleged entity E is that is alleged to imply F, then we are unable to understand "F must exist," unable to determine whether it is true or false.

There is our hypothetical proposition: "If E should exist, then F would exist"; and there is our apodeictic proposition: "F must exist." They differ, to be sure, in that in the former the term "E" occurs within the proposition itself, whereas in the latter it is neighboring sentences that explicitly or implicitly supply the reference to E. They also differ in that, whereas our apodeictic proposition asserts the existence of some implication, our hypothetical proposition asserts the existence of some relational situation which may be one of simultaneity or of cause and effect rather then one of implication. In spite of the rain yesterday, "The grounds must have been wet" may not be a true apodeictic proposition. For yesterday's rain, it may be said, caused yesterday's wet grounds, but did not imply them. In view of various instances of rain followed by wet grounds, including yesterday's sequence,—in view furthermore of the non-existence of rain not followed by wet grounds,—the proposition: "If it should rain tomorrow, the

152

ground would be wet" is true. Nevertheless, unless there is an *implication* from rain to wet grounds, the proposition: "The grounds yesterday had to be wet" is false.[33]

Our hypothetical proposition and our apodeictic proposition differ, moreover, with respect to the assertion of the existence of F and with respect to the assertion of the existence of E. "F must exist" is true only if F exists and only if F is implied by E. And F is really implied by E only if there is a real E to imply it. If it is the existence of man that enables us to express ourselves in the true apodeictic proposition: "There must be some animals," 'man' must exist, 'animal' must exist, and 'man' must imply 'animal.' But 'man' need not exist in order for: "If there should be men, then there would be animals" to be true, any more than 'centaur' need exist in order for: "If there should be centaurs, then there would be animals" to be true. It is the existence of an entity in some sense analogous to man or in some sense analogous to centaur that is required if our hypothetical proposition is to be true. It is an entity in some sense analogous to E that must exist and that must enter into a certain relational situation with an entity in some sense analogous to F.[34]

The apodeictic proposition that we have thus far discussed is our apodeictic proposition: "F must exist," "F has to exist," "It is necessary that F exist." What about our apodeictic proposition: "F can not exist," our apodeictic proposition: "It is impossible that F exist"? We may say, to be sure, that it is only when F is unreal that our proposition "F can not exist" is true. But when F is unreal, this alleged F, with whatever characteristics it may seem to be presented to us, is unreal. An unreal F is not really implied by any entity E.[35] The unreality of F is not really implied by any entity E. The proposition: "Some entity E implies the unreality of F" is always false. If, then, in explaining our terms "truth" and "falsity" in their application to our proposition: "F can not exist," we were to say that "F can not exist" is true only when "F does not exist" is true and only when in addition "Some entity E implies the unreality of F" is true, then it would follow that our proposition "F can not exist" is never true. If F is unreal, it is some entity that is alleged to exist in the absence of F that may be real, some entity alleged to exist in the absence of F that may really be implied by E.[36] Or it is the proposition: "F is unreal"

153

that exists as a true proposition and it is the true proposition: "F is unreal" that may really be implied by E. Our proposition: "F can not exist" is true, let us say, if F is unreal and if some entity E implies what exists in the absence of F or implies the true proposition: "F does not exist." And our proposition: "F can not exist" is false, let us say, if F is real or if there is no entity E which either implies what exists in the absence of F or implies the true proposition: "F does not exist." "Men can not be immortal" is true, for example, in our sense of "truth," if what exists in the absence of immortal animals implies what exists in the absence of immortal men or if our true proposition: "No animals are immortal" implies our true proposition: "No men are immortal."

There are the apodeictic propositions: "F must exist" and "F can not exist." And there are the problematic propositions: "F may exist" and "It may be that F does not exist." There are the apodeictic propositions: "It is necessary that F exist" and "It is impossible that F exist"; and there are the problematic propositions: "It is possible that F exists" and "It is possible that F does not exist." Just as it is not all propositions containing the word "necessary" or the word "must" that are apodeictic propositions, so it is not all propositions containing the word "possible" or the word "may" that are problematic propositions.[37] The: "That may be John" which is synonymous with: "I rather think but am not sure that that is John" is not what we shall call a problematic proposition. And the: "Oranges may be seedless" which is synonymous with: "Some oranges are seedless" is no problematic proposition.

When F does not exist, there exists the true proposition: "F does not exist." And there may, in addition, be some entity which exists in the absence of F. Our proposition "F may exist" is false, let us say, if some entity E, referred to in the context in which "F may exist" occurs, really implies the true proposition: "F does not exist," or really implies what exists in the absence of F. My hat being in this room implies the true proposition: "My hat, presented as being in some other room, does not exist." Within a context which informs us that my hat is in this room, our proposition: "My hat may be in some other room" is false. If, on the other hand, there is no true proposition: "F does not exist," or if, "F does not exist" being true, there is no entity referred to in the context that really implies it, then, let us say, our proposition: "F

154

may exist" is true. If my hat *is* in this room, if, that is to say, there is no true proposition: "My hat, presented as being in this room, does not exist," then: "My hat may be in this room" is true. And "My hat may be in this room" may be true even if my hat is in fact not in this room, even if: "My hat, presented as being in this room, does not exist" is true. "My hat may be in this room" is true, provided there is no entity referred to in the context that implies the true proposition: "My hat, presented as being in this room, does not exist." "My hat may be in this room" is true, for example, if the context informs me only that my hat is not outside this house. The "F may exist" that is an expression of ours is, in short, synonymous with: "Either F exists or, if F does not exist, the proposition 'F does not exist' is not really implied by E." As we explain our term "truth" in its application to it, "F may exist" is true if F is real or if, F being unreal, the proposition "F is unreal," presented as implied by E, is unreal.

It is in an analogous manner that we explain our terms "truth" and falsity in their application to our problematic proposition: "It may be that F does not exist." Assuming that our context tells us that some men are mortal and assuming that 'mortal man' implies 'mortal animal,' then our problematic proposition: "It may be that mortal animal does not exist" or: "It is possible that no animal is mortal" is, let us say, false. Assuming, on the other hand, that our context tells us merely that some plants are mortal, and assuming that 'mortal plant' does not imply 'mortal animal,' then, even though 'mortal animal' is real, "It is possible that no animal is mortal" is, let us say, true. And if 'mortal animal' is unreal, then, no matter what the context, "It is possible that no animal is mortal" is likewise true.

"As we explain our term 'existence,' there are not existing entities and, among them, entities with a kind of existence called 'necessary existence.'[38] And as we explain our term "truth," no sentence is true which merely distinguishes those subsistents which appear self-contradictory from those subsistents which do not appear self-contradictory. If our sentence: "Whatever is, is possible" is to be regarded as a true proposition, this sentence is to be regarded as expressing, not the assertion that existent entities, in addition to being real, have a kind of existence called "possible existence," but rather the assertion that, if an entity exists, then

155

the proposition that it is possible for it to exist is true. It is in connection with propositions rather than in connection with entities, intended to be represented by the terms of a proposition, that the word "possibility" has been considered. And it is in connection with propositions rather than in connection with entities intended to be represented by the terms of a proposition that the word "necessity" has been considered. Whatever must be, it may be said, exists. But what is true is not that entities having a special kind of existence also have an existence of a more general kind. What is true, rather, is that, if the proposition: "S must exist" is true, then: "S exists" is true.

The world of existent entities has on occasion been described as something of a hierarchy, with effects pointing up to causes and with conclusions pointing up to premises until at the apex a First Cause is reached whose existence is not contingent but necessary. Contingent existents, on such a view, presuppose other existents; they presuppose, finally, an entity that presupposes nothing outside itself, an entity that has necessary existence. As we use the term "necessity," however, there is, as has been pointed out, no kind of existence to be called "necessary existence." And as we have explained our term "truth" in its application to apodeictic propositions of ours, the proposition "F must exist" is not true unless F is implied by some entity E.[39] If the alleged Being presented to us is a Being which appears with the characteristic of not being implied by anything referred to in the context, then, as we have explained our term "falsity," the proposition expressing an assertion that this Being must exist is false.

It is often a difficult matter to determine whether an entity is real or unreal. And it is often a difficult matter to determine whether a sentence placed before us is true or false or, perhaps, neither true nor false. Whatever the other difficulties, it is a prime requisite that we recognize the 'reality' and the 'truth' that are in question. We have, to be sure, not found it possible to attach to our terms "reality" and "unreality" a signification which is in accord with every author's use of these terms. And we have not found it possible to explain our terms "truth" and "falsity" in their application to categorical propositions, to hypothetical propositions, to various other propositions varying in form, in such a way as to conform with the usage of every logician. But the explanations of our terms "reality" and "truth," now completed, present *a* reality and *a* truth. They place before us the formal conditions under which an entity is real in *one* sense of "reality," the formal conditions under which a proposition is true in *one* sense of "truth." In order to determine whether or not consciousness exists, we must understand the term "consciousness" as well as the term "existence." [40] In order to determine whether or not the sentence: "Some collections are infinite" is true, we must understand the term "infinite collection" as well as the term "truth." With the 'reality' before us that our term "reality" represents and with the 'truth' before us that our term "truth" represents, we are, we hold,[41] prepared to turn to what, by contrast, may be called the less purely formal problems of metaphysics. We are, we hold, prepared to consider the extent to which entities discussed by metaphysicians are, in our sense of the word, "real"; and the extent to which propositions which assert the existence or the non-existence of these entities are, in our sense of the word, "true."

Summary

Chapter Five continues the explanation of our terms "truth" and "falsity." It asks: Is the proposition: 'This proposition is false' true or false in the sense in which we are using the terms "truth" and "falsity"? And it attempts to point out the entities whose existence or non-existence determines the truth or falsity, in our sense of "truth" and "falsity," of various types of propositions of ours not considered in Chapter Four.

The discussion of "This proposition is false" leads to comments on the theory of types. The discussion of the "as if" proposition has implications for the discussion of the problem of error in Chapter Eight.

Chapter VI

DOES THINKING EXIST?

"I was then in Germany to which country I had been attracted by the wars which are not yet at an end. And as I was returning from the coronation of the Emperor to join the army, the setting in of winter detained me in a quarter where, since I found no society to divert me, while fortunately I had also no cares or passions to trouble me, I remained the whole day shut up alone in a stove-heated room where I had complete leisure to occupy myself with my own thoughts. One of the first considerations that occurred to me was . . ."

These opening lines from Part Two of Descartes' "Discourse on Method" seem to introduce to us a situation in which there was an instance of thinking. This thinking is alleged to have occurred in Germany, in a stove-heated room, and in winter; and presumably it was about man, God and the universe. In this chapter, however, our primary interest is not in determining the existence or non-existence of Germany, of winter, or of the stove-heated room. Nor are we at this point interested in determining whether or not there exists the 'man,' the God or the universe about which Descartes may be held to have been thinking. Our present problem is to determine whether or not thinking exists. To the extent feasible, let us then at this point disregard problems concerning the existence of brains which may be held to be the vehicles of thinking; let us disregard problems concerning the existence of particular settings in which various instances of thinking may be held to occur; and let us disregard problems concerning the existence of objects towards which instances of thinking may be held to be directed.

Let us disregard vehicle, setting and object to the extent to which we can disregard them. But if we are to concentrate our discussion upon some specific instance of alleged thinking, as, for example, that suggested by the lines quoted from Descartes, we must already have passed over the thinking alleged to be alone in the world, the thinking that is held to be without vehicle, setting, or object. And if we are to discuss the existence of some specific instance of thinking in a simple and straight-forward manner, we must already have acknowledged the existence of some of the features of the setting in which that instance of thinking is alleged to have occurred. Our query must be: Granting that Descartes had a brain and was in a stove-heated room, was he thinking? For, with the reality of brain, room and thinking all in question, we should find ourselves confronted by a host of questions all clamoring at once for solution and all having to be answered before the reality of Descartes' thinking could be acknowledged.

To be sure, what we have before us when the meaning of our term "existence" has been determined is, it may seem, merely an empty canvas. The method we have agreed to employ, it may be held, imposes upon us the task of filling in this canvas bit by bit. In considering whether or not Descartes' thinking belongs on this as yet empty canvas, our method, it may be said, requires us to assume the non-existence of everything else. But such candidates for existence as a thinking alleged to be alone in the world— without vehicle, setting or object—are, we find, presented as generally discredited and are unreal. And such candidates for existence as the thinking of Descartes' that is presented as *having* a vehicle and a setting can be discussed in fewer words and in a less complicated fashion when, instead of regarding thinking, vehicle and setting as all mere subsistents, we accept the premise that vehicle and setting are real. We are the less constrained to regard vehicle, setting and thinking as all mere subsistents, we are the less reluctant to make use of the premise that vehicle and setting are real, in that Descartes' brain and the stove-heated room have already been listed as existents in the appendix to Chapter Three. As we begin this chapter, we have thus no empty canvas before us, but rather a canvas containing all of the entities previously listed as real.

Yet if this be true, our deduction ends with the appendix to Chapter Three and all the rest of this treatise is mere commentary. What then becomes of our decision to discuss particular existential problems "in the proper order"? What becomes of our decision to "be on the watch for existential problems so related that the solution of one may reasonably be expected to aid us in the solution of the other"?[1] We must, I think, distinguish between logical objection on the one hand and puzzlement and lack of concurrence on the other. The reader who has read the appendix to Chapter Three will agree that the entities there listed as real *are* real in the sense in which we have explained our term "reality." But he may feel that some of these entities are listed without due consideration or that our term "reality" has been assigned a strange and unacceptable meaning. It is in the effort to dissolve such objections that an analysis of one entity and a discussion resulting in the reaffirmation of its reality may aid in the analysis of some other entity and may be utilized in the discussion resulting in the reaffirmation of the latter's reality. Except to the extent to which the listings in the appendix to Chapter Three are too enigmatic to be understood and require elaboration, the remainder of this treatise is not needed. But it does not follow that the remaining chapters contain no reasoned arguments and that they appeal merely for psychological concurrence. A conclusion arrived at from one set of premises may again be arrived at from similar premises or from other premises. A conclusion arrived at on a second occasion may be redundant, but it is a logical conclusion nonetheless. It is then as analysis and argument rather than as rhetoric that the remainder of this treatise is presented.

Indeed it is only within the framework of some explanation of the term "truth," only after some such section as is incorporated in Chapter Four, that there is valid argument that may be recognized as valid, and true conclusions that may be recognized as true. For just as "A is A" may be true in one sense of "truth" but not in another,[2] so "A implies B" may be true in one sense of "truth" but not in another. The existential conclusions to be arrived at in the remainder of this treatise thus not only describe the entities whose existence is asserted in greater detail than was possible at the end of Chapter Three, but, in contrast to the conclusions of Chapter Three, they follow as conclusions that can be

160

recognized as validly deduced. It is not then an empty canvas that confronts us as we begin this chapter but rather a canvas which, although well-filled, requires minute criticism and re-affirmation. It is not as the painter putting on the initial daubs of oil that we approach the canvas; but rather as the painter-critic who concentrates his attention on minute sections of his work in turn, at each point regarding the rest of the work as un-questioned and making such adjustments as the section under consideration requires.

It is then with the premise that there are such entities as brains and rooms that we inquire whether thinking exists. Yet our question is not whether all subsisting instances of thinking exist. For just as: "All subsisting men exist" is false as we have explained "truth" and "falsity," so: "All subsisting instances of thinking exist" is false.[3] And "some subsisting instances of thinking exist" is true only if there are some such instances as the thinking that is alleged to have characterized Descartes as he paced up and down the stove-heated room and pondered, or seemed to ponder, the existence of man, God and the universe. We choose as our question then whether the instance of thinking that allegedly characterized Descartes was real. Granted the existence of Descartes' brain rather than the existence of brains generally, and granted the existence of Descartes' stove-heated room rather than the existence of settings of all sorts, our query is: Was Descartes thinking?

Yet, whereas we have what may be described as an individual situation as our apparent object, it is not clear at this point what element in this alleged situation is being called: "Descartes' thinking." There are various alleged entities that need to be untangled. There is the alleged public object, such as God him-self, to which Descartes' thinking may be alleged ultimately to refer. There is an alleged mental attitude which is not in the first instance content, but said to be directed upon content. And there is allegedly private content, such as Descartes' idea of God, which may be held to refer beyond itself to some such public object as God himself. But it is not the public object that we choose to call "Descartes' thinking" and not private content. The thinking whose existence we are primarily questioning in this chapter is mental attitude rather than private content. It is some such entity

161

as Descartes' alleged mental activity rather than any image or picture or object. It is, in a word, thinking rather than what is thought.

At first sight the distinction between what is alleged to be mental attitude and what is alleged to be content, whether private or public, seems clear. And yet this distinction becomes less clear-cut when we attempt to introspect and to make mental attitude a part of content. "For my part," says Hume,[4] "when I enter most intimately into what I call *myself*, I always stumble on some particular perception or other, of heat or cold, light or shade, love or hatred, pain or pleasure. I never can catch *myself* at any time without a perception, and never can observe anything but the perception." Or, as Lovejoy[5] puts it, "what I seem to discover when perception occurs is not a perceiving, but a certain complex of content which is subject to conscious change." On the other hand, there are those who hold that what we call "mental attitude" may be introspected. And there are others who hold that mental attitude is an object to be inferred, an object to be inferred even from the circumstances reported by Lovejoy and Hume. Let us not at this point exclude from the denotation of "mental attitude" the alleged mental attitude which is presented as on occasion being an object. So far as we have yet seen, it may be that, if what we call "thinking" exists, it can be apprehended by a second act of thinking. It may be that, with respect to such a second act of thinking, thinking is revealed as content of one sort or another. And since thinking may be held to be revealed in introspection or otherwise given as an object, this thinking whose existence we are to consider is not to be described as something that is never content. It is rather to be described as something that, if given as content, is given as attitude, attitude that is perhaps directed towards other content.

Indeed the possibility of thinking, if it exists, becoming content is not the only consideration that blurs our initial distinction between thinking on the one hand and the object of thought on the other. When we distinguish between thinking or mental attitude or mental activity on the one hand and object of thought or private content or what is presented as a datum on the other, we make use of such terms as "activity" and "passivity," terms which, it would seem, apply to things which move or are moved, things which attack or are attacked, rather than to such alleged entities as Descartes' thinking on the one hand and Descartes' idea of God on the other. We do very little to clarify the distinction between the mental attitude whose existence we are to consider and the idea of God whose existence we are not at this point to consider by calling the former "active" and the latter "passive." To be sure, Descartes' alleged thinking is not presented as a mental picture or image, not presented as passive in the way in which a picture or image is usually passive. But it need not be presented as manipulating its content in the way in which an active organism may be held to bring about changes in entities in its environment. The distinction between what we call "thinking" and what we call "private content" must at this point remain a bit blurred. What *we* call "mental attitude" may by some be included in what *they* would call "private content." Yet what we call "mental attitude" is presented as not a mental picture or image and it is presented as not being content except in so far as it is the object upon which it or some further mental attitude is directed.

Our problem is whether or not thinking exists. More specifically, our problem is whether or not, as Descartes paced up and down his stove-heated room, there existed a mental attitude apparently directed upon man, God and the universe. We have at this stage made it clear that we are not in this chapter concerned with the existence of the stove which is in Descartes' environment, with the existence of God, upon whom Descartes' thinking is alleged to be directed, or with the existence of a picture or description of God which may be alleged to be part of the private content of Descartes' mind. It remains for us to distinguish what we call Descartes' thinking from certain physical activities in which Descartes was engaged. Descartes, let us say, was pacing up and down the room, knitting his brows, staring past the furniture that was around him. These, to be sure, were physical activities, whereas his alleged thinking may be said to be a mental activity. But the thinking whose existence we are questioning is not at this point being presented as non-physical. Our query is as to the existence of Descartes' mental attitude, whether it be non-physical or an aspect of his total bodily reactions. The mere words "mental" and "physical" do not at this point point to mutually exclusive entities, do not at this point mark off Descartes' alleged thinking from what is roughly called his behavior.

It may be held, to be sure, that what we call Descartes' thinking is presented as subject to observation by none but Descartes himself. Whereas Descartes' behavior may be an object for others, his thinking, it may be said, is, if it exists, an object for him alone. We might well make use of this difference, it may be held, to distinguish the mental attitude whose existence we are to consider from the behavior whose existence we in this chapter assume. We may, however, say at once that Descartes' thinking, if it exists, is not an object for Descartes alone. It is Descartes' alleged thinking that you and I are now considering, an instance of thinking, consequently, that, at least implicitly, is presented as apparently an object for you and for me.[6] Indeed it is only the thinking, *not* presented as an object for Descartes alone, that is presented as free from self-contradiction; only the thinking, *not* presented as an object for Descartes alone, that may be real. Hence it is not in being an object for Descartes alone that Descartes' thinking, if it is real, differs from Descartes' behavior.

But being an object, it may be said, is one characteristic; being an object which is sensed another. And whereas Descartes' thinking and Descartes' behavior are both presented as objects for you as well as for Descartes, Descartes' thinking, it may be said, is presented as not only an object for Descartes, but as *sensed* by Descartes. However, we do not care to restrict our attention to an alleged thinking that is presented as having been sensed by Descartes; or to an alleged thinking that is presented as an entity that Descartes *might* have sensed. We do not care to exclude from our consideration the alleged instance of thinking that may be alleged *not* to have been sensed by Descartes. What we are to consider is a mental attitude of Descartes' that he may or may not have sensed, a mental attitude that he may or may not have been able to sense. And with this latitude in the entity which we are to consider, we can not distinguish Descartes' alleged thinking from his behavior by a reference to the manner in which that thinking was apprehended by Descartes.

Is there not a difference, however, between the manner in which Descartes' contemporaries apprehended his behavior and the manner in which, if they apprehended it at all, they appre-

164

hended his thinking? His behavior, it may be held, is something which they saw, his thinking something which they inferred from what they saw. We have agreed not to limit the entity under consideration to the mental attitude alleged to have been sensed by Descartes. But shall we not at least describe the entity under consideration as a mental attitude that is not sensed by others? Here however we run into the difficulty of distinguishing what is a sense-datum from what is inferred. "When looking from a window and saying I see men who pass in the street, I really do not see them, but infer that what I see are men. . . . What do I see from the window," asks Descartes,[7] "but hats and coats which may cover automatic machines? Yet I judge these to be men." Our inference however, if it be called inference, is so inseparable from our apprehension of what is sensed, that we are at once aware of men. We see two converging tracks with our experienced eyes and we *see* the distance. We look at a picture of a landscape and we see, not a two-dimensional manifold, but a scene which goes back from foreground to horizon. As Bode says,[8] "we do not first observe and then supply a context, but we observe by seeing things as existing in a context." So, if Descartes' thinking exists, the contemporary observer may be held to have seen not only Descartes' knitted brow and distant stare, but also the thinking implicit in his total behavior. When we look at Rodin's "Thinker," we seem to be aware at once of the alleged thinking; just as we seem to be aware of depth as soon as we look at a landscape painting. In both cases it is, one might say, when we attend to the artist's technique that we distinguish the sense-datum from what then appears to us to have been inferred. The thinking of Descartes' that we are to consider is presented as likely to be given to an outside observer as soon as is Descartes' knitted brow or distant stare. Whether it be physical or non-physical, Descartes' thinking, if it exists, is as an object so commingled with his other behavior that any study of his total behavior must include a study of what we call his thinking.

The distinction between total behavior and thinking is, as we choose to describe it, not so much the distinction between the immediately given and the subsequently inferred, as it is the distinction between the unanalyzed whole and an alleged selection from this whole. Given the pacing, the staring and the alleged

165

thinking which characterize Descartes, we can say that the pacing is not the entity whose existence we are to examine; and that the staring is not this entity either. We may pass from a consideration of Descartes' total behavior to a consideration of his knitted brow or distant stare. Or we may pass to a consideration of his alleged thinking. Indeed, if we accept a suggestion of Alexander's,[9] we will agree that thinking is normally presented to us as an object before the knitted brow and the distant stare. It is by separating out of Descartes' total behavior his alleged interest in man, God and the universe, it is by concentrating our attention upon one alleged element in his total behavior, that we come to have as our apparent object the alleged entity that we call Descartes' thinking. For whether Descartes' thinking is in his body or merely associated with his body, it is, if it exists, so intimately associated with his body that, in having Descartes before us as an unanalyzed whole, his alleged thinking is within, rather than outside, the entity before us.

The thinking of Descartes' that may be real may be presented as a characteristic of Descartes' body like his knitted brow or distant stare. Or the thinking of Descartes' that may be real, whereas alleged to be an element abstracted as an object from his total behavior, may be presented as an entity that is merely associated with his body, may be presented as an entity that in itself lacks position and extension. Whereas we may be led to consider Descartes' alleged thinking through having Descartes' total behavior, Descartes as an unanalyzed whole, as our apparent object, the alleged thinking that we come finally to consider is, it may be held, an entity that has no position within Descartes' body and no position anywhere else, but is rather an entity that is non-spatial and merely associated with Descartes' body.

We find no clearer exposition of the view that thinking is immaterial and non-spatial, and merely associated with the body, than in the writings of Descartes himself. Thinking is for him the sole attribute of a thinking substance. And this substance whose sole attribute is thinking—and with it the thinking that is presented to him as inhering in a substance which has no position and no extension—is real, he holds,[10] "because, on the one side, I have a clear and distinct idea of myself inasmuch as I am only a thinking and unextended thing, and as, on the other,

I possess a distinct idea of body inasmuch as it is only an extended and unthinking thing."

Now we shall not deny that an instance of thinking with no position and no extension is an apparent object. For it is such an apparent object, such a subsistent, whose claim to reality we are here attempting to evaluate. Something may, to be sure, be said with respect to its clarity and distinctness. As Arnauld pointed out,[11] we appear to apprehend a right triangle clearly and distinctly even when we do not apprehend the fact that the square on its hypotenuse equals the sum of the squares on its other sides. Nevertheless we do not conclude from this that the right triangle exists without the square on its hypotenuse being equal to the sum of the squares on its sides; and, he holds, we should not conclude that thinking is unextended, merely because we seem clearly and distinctly to apprehend it without extension. It appears however to be Descartes' more matured opinion that it is only when two *substances* are clearly and distinctly apprehended without either of them being presented with the essential qualities of the other, it is only then that we can conclude that these entities exist as they appear to us. If we could apprehend the substance 'right triangle' clearly and distinctly without apprehending the substance 'triangle the square on whose hypotenuse is equal to the sum of the squares on its sides' and if we could likewise apprehend clearly and distinctly the substance 'triangle the square on whose hypotenuse is equal to the sum of the squares on its sides' without apprehending the substance 'right triangle,' only then, Descartes would seem to hold, could we conclude that right triangles exist without this ratio obtaining between their sides and hypotenuse.

But even with this emendation, even if we limit ourselves to the cases in which two entities are presented as *substances* and each appears without the attributes of the other, how can we "conclude that the substances are really distinct one from the other from the sole fact that we can conceive the one clearly and distinctly without the other?"[12] To arrive at a valid conclusion which expresses an assertion of existence, there must be a reference to existence in our premises. The validity of Descartes' conclusion depends upon the validity of some implicit premise which ties together existence and alleged entities that are clearly and distinctly appre-

167

hended. It is an essential part of his argument that "God can carry into effect" (i.e., into existence) "all that of which we have a distinct idea." And so we find Descartes' argument for the immateriality of the soul, his argument for the inextendedness of thinking, resting upon what in a previous chapter we decided was an implicit determination of the meaning of the term "existence." [13]

It would ill become us to speak slightingly of an argument because it makes use of a proposition determining the meaning of the term "existence." For it has been our thesis that any valid existential proposition must point back to some proposition in which the term "existence" is explained. We make no reference to the 'clear and distinct' in our own explanation of "existence." And so we find Descartes' argument, culminating in the conclusion that thinking is concomitant with no extension, without relevance to our own problem. What this suggests, however, is that we turn to our own explanation of "existence" to determine the existence or non-existence, in our sense of "existence," of a thinking that is presented as non-spatial. And when we recall that, for an entity to be real in our sense of "reality," it may not be presented as lacking all position, we realize that the alleged instance of thinking which is presented as non-spatial is, in our sense of the term, "unreal." Descartes' alleged thinking as he paced up and down the stove-heated room may or may not exist. But if it exists, it is not an entity that is utterly non-spatial.

In rejecting the mental attitude which is presented as non-spatial however, perhaps we eliminate the possibility of Descartes' alleged mental attitude being real, however presented. Perhaps the alternative—an alleged mental attitude presented as being spatial, as having position—is so absurd that the unreality of non-spatial thinking involves the unreality of thinking of any sort. What is presented as mental, it may be said, is presented as quite different from what is presented as spatial. It is presented as so different, it may be said, that any instance of thinking presented as having position is implicitly presented as generally discredited. Such a spatial thinking, it may consequently be held, is just as unreal in our sense of "reality" as the non-spatial thinking which we have already eliminated.

For one thing, it may be said, there are inorganic phenomena to which scientific formulae apply; and there are organic phenomena to which these formulae do not apply with equal force. There are organic phenomena, it may be said, which are wayward and unpredictable and which point to the existence of some entity whose activities do not fall within the scope of scientific formulae. It is the waywardness and unpredictability of organic phenomena which point back, it may be held, to a mental attitude that is non-spatial and which make incredible a mental attitude that is alleged to have position with respect to the spatial entities that are its contemporaries.

So long as we focus our attention upon some alleged mental attitude presented to us and disregard the organic and inorganic phenomena that are alleged to be its contemporaries, we can not come to grips with such a doctrine. Let us then in this chapter agree that there exist organic phenomena and inorganic phenomena, and that the scientific formulae that have come to be accepted can on the whole be applied more readily and more satisfactorily to the latter than to the former. Each organism, let us agree, seems to have a structure and to develop along the lines that its nature determines for it. It seems to maintain its own course of development with a persistency which is not altogether at the mercy of the environment. The motions of inorganic bodies, on the other hand, let us agree, seem to be completely dependent upon the forces which act upon them. They seem to be such that similar actions call forth similar reactions; whereas, in the case of organisms, 'learning' takes place and the reaction to a stimulus applied a second time may not be identical with the first reaction.

With this much common ground established, let us consider the status of the scientific formulae which, we have agreed, can on the whole be applied to inorganic phenomena more readily and more satisfactorily than to organic phenomena. In so far as a formula is valid, it is, it would seem, both a generalization and a tool enabling prediction. But, both as a generalization and as a tool for prediction, it applies, it would seem, not so much to behavior as a whole as to qualities which are numbered qualities. It is not the concrete behavior of an entity that some scientific formula enables us to predict, but rather, it would seem, some particular measurable characteristic, as, for example, the number that is to characterize that entity's speed or the number of degrees that is to characterize its heat. The admission then that scientific formulae can be applied to inorganic phenomena more readily and more satifactorily than to organic phenomena turns out to be the admission that numbered qualities to which scientific formulae apply are to be found among inorganic phenomena to a greater extent than among organic phenomena. The mental attitude which we are to consider is presented as manifested in organic phenomena which are poor in numbered characteristics to which scientific formulae apply. The question is whether a mental attitude so presented may be presented as spatial without being presented as generally discredited.

Organic phenomena are to be called "wayward," it would seem, if they *have* characteristics which are numbered and to which scientific formulae are ready to be applied, and if, nevertheless, they fail to conform to these formulae. There seems, however, to be no specific scientific law ready to be applied to organic behavior that is in fact violated by the apparently teleological behavior of organisms, no specific scientific law ready to be applied to organic behavior that 'learning' violates. The disorder that is implicit in waywardness, as we have described waywardness, seems not to be a fact. And so, with waywardness described as we have described it, the mental attitude which is alleged to give rise to wayward organic phenomena comes to be presented as discredited and unreal. Just as Descartes' alleged mental attitude does not exist when presented as non-spatial, so Descartes' alleged mental attitude does not exist when presented as giving rise to organic phenomena which in our sense are wayward. The mental attitude which we are to consider is the mental attitude alleged to be manifested in organic phenomena which are poor in numbered qualities. Or it is the mental attitude alleged to be spatial and to be manifested in organic phenomena which *have* numbered qualities, qualities, however, to which, in large part, scientific formula do not apply or are not ready to be applied. But the mental attitude, alleged to contravene specific scientific formulae applicable to it, we at this point reject as discredited and unreal.

Neither the absence of numbered qualities nor the absence of scientific formulae applying to what numbered qualities there are, seems to point to an entity that is non-spatial. Before there were thermometers to measure heat, when heat was presented as

170

an unnumbered quality, heat was not generally presented as non-spatial or as the manifestation of something non-spatial. And when heat is presented as a quality that can be measured and assigned a number, and yet no scientific formula presented which is applicable to the relation between the heat of one day and the heat of another, we still do not think of heat as the manifestation of something non-spatial. For, the quality that is not numbered, we seem generally to hold, may perhaps be numbered. And the qualities which are presented without some scientific formula which applies to them need not be presented as incapable of having such a formula apply to them. The mental attitude which is presented as manifested in organic phenomena which are poor in numbered qualities is not presented as generally discredited, we find, when presented as spatial. And neither is the mental attitude which is presented as manifested in organic phenomena having numbered qualities to which, in large part, scientific formulae are not ready to be applied.

There is a distinction to be made, however, between the entity alleged to be poor in numbered qualities and the entity which, it is alleged, *cannot* have numbered qualities; a distinction to be made between the entity presented as having numbered qualities to which scientific formulae are not ready to be applied and the entity presented as having numbered qualities to which scientific formulae *cannot* be applied. We read in McDougall's "Body and Mind" that "the soul has not the essential attributes of matter, namely, extension (or the attribute of occupying space) and ponderability or mass"; for, says he,[14] "if it had these attributes it would be subject to the laws of mechanism, and it is just because we have found that mental and vital processes can not be completely described and explained in terms of mechanism that we are compelled to believe in the cooperation of some non-mechanical teleological factor." But when, as with McDougall, the phrase is "can not be described" rather than "is not described," the inference would seem to be from what is non-spatial to what is not subject-matter for scientific formulae rather than vice versa. The mental attitude which is alleged to have manifestations to which no scientific formula could ever be applied is, we find, already presented as non-spatial. It is in view of the non-spatiality with which it is implicitly presented that the mental

171

attitude, alleged to have manifestations to which no scientific formulae could be applied, is presented as discredited when also presented as spatial.

The mental attitude is unreal which is alleged to be spatial and also alleged to be non-spatial. So is the mental attitude which is alleged to be spatial and implicitly alleged to be non-spatial, the mental attitude, for example, which is alleged to be spatial and also alleged to be manifested in phenomena to which scientific formulae *cannot* be applied. Not only however is the mental attitude unreal which is alleged to be both spatial and non-spatial; "the alleged instance of thinking which is presented as non-spatial" is, we have found, likewise unreal.[15] There remains—as an entity that, so far as we have yet seen, may be real—the mental attitude which is alleged to be spatial and not alleged to be non-spatial. There remains the mental attitude which is alleged to be spatial and not alleged to be manifested in phenomena to which scientific formulae *cannot* be applied. And this mental attitude may be real whether it be presented as having or lacking manifestations which are in fact numbered, whether it be presented as having or lacking manifestations to which scientific formulae are in fact or will in fact be applied.

The mental attitude which may be real is the mental attitude which explicitly or implicitly is alleged to have position with respect to the spatial entities that are its contemporaries. The mental attitude of Descartes' which may be real is the mental attitude of his which is not merely associated with his body but is alleged to have position with respect to the phase of his brain and the phase of the stove that are its contemporaries. Position, to be sure, may be definite position, position of a sort that a point is alleged to have; or it may be indefinite position, position of a sort that an extended entity is alleged to have. Let us however dismiss at once the mental attitude which is alleged to be at a point. Let us mark out as unreal the mental attitude of Descartes' which is alleged to have *position* with respect to brain and stove, but no *extension*. We thus find ourselves considering the mental attitude which is alleged to have not only position with respect to its contemporaries but also extension. We thus find ourselves holding that, if Descartes had any mental attitude at all as he paced up and down

172

the stove-heated room, that mental attitude had, or was concomitant with, an extension.

Is however an extended mental attitude at all plausible? Is not a mental attitude or instance of thinking that is alleged to be extended presented as discredited and unreal? There are, let us agree, distinguishable mental attitudes which form an integrated whole and which can not be separated one from the other as my foot can be severed from the rest of my body. Does it however follow that "there is a great difference between mind and body, inasmuch as body is by nature always divisible and the mind is entirely indivisible"? [16] To be sure, the bolt of blue cloth or the gallon of water that is presented as extended is implicitly presented as in some sense divisible. And the mental attitude or complex of mental attitudes that is presented as extended is likewise implicitly presented as in some sense divisible. There is however a sense in which an extended substance is divisible and the quality of an extended substance likewise divisible. And there is another sense in which a quality, without regard to the substance in which it inheres, is, or is not, divisible. The gallon of water can be divided into four quarts of water, the bolt of blue cloth into small pieces of blue cloth. The blueness of the bolt of cloth is divisible in the sense that the bolt of cloth in which it inheres is divisible. And if thinking or mental attitude is a quality of an extended substance, thinking is divisible in the sense that the substance in which it inheres is divisible.

It may however well be another sense of divisibility that is suggested when we say that blue is a primary color, purple not; or when we say that some complex of mental attitudes is divisible or indivisible. The assertion that blue is a primary color is generally the assertion that blue can not be analyzed or reduced to other colors, not the assertion that bolts of blue cloth can not be separated into parts. And the assertion that thinking is indivisible may well be the assertion that thinking is not to be analyzed rather than the assertion that thinking does not inhere in an extended substance. Whether blue be alleged to be capable of analysis or not, the blueness that is alleged to be the quality of an extended and divisible substance is, I find, not presented as incredible and unreal. And whether the mental attitude of Descartes' that we are considering be alleged to be capable of analysis or not, this entity, alleged to be the quality of an extended and divisible substance, is, I find, likewise not presented as incredible and unreal.

It may, to be sure, be pointed out that whereas the segments into which a bolt of blue cloth is cut are all blue, the segments of some extended substance in which thinking is alleged to inhere are substances in which no mental attitudes inhere at all. Yet a round plate may be circular, it would seem, without any of the fragments into which it is broken being circular. And a molecule may have properties which none of its constituent atoms have. The alleged circularity of a round plate is not presented as incredible when the segments are alleged not to be circular. And the thinking that is alleged to be a quality of some extended brain or nerve-fibre is not presented as incredible when a segment of that brain or nerve-fibre is alleged not to be thinking, alleged not to have a mental attitude inhering in it as a quality.

But if thinking is extended, or the quality of an extended substance, then the extension of the substance that thinks about a gallon of water, it may be said, must be four times the extension of the substance that thinks about a quart of water. If thinking is extended at all, it may be held, the extension with which it is concomitant must be proportionate to the extension of the object upon which it is directed. Thinking about a house would then have to have the shape of a house, thinking about the moon the shape of the moon; and a mental attitude apparently directed upon an inextended object would have to be inextended, and thus be both extended and inextended at once. If the thinking that we are considering, the thinking that is alleged to be extended, had such implicit characteristics as these, it would, to be sure, be presented as discredited and unreal. But if my uncle is twice as big as yours, it does not follow that I am twice as big as you. And if my uncle is twice as big as yours and yet I not twice as big as you, it does not follow that neither you nor I are extended at all. Two entities may both be extended and yet the ratio between their extensions not be equal to the ratio between the extensions of the entities to which they are respectively related. And two thinking substances may both be extended and yet, assuming that they have objects, the ratio between their extensions not be equal to the ratio between the extensions of their respective objects. The mental attitude of Descartes' that we are considering is alleged to be concomitant with an extension; and it is alleged to be the quality of an extended substance whose extension does not depend upon the extension of the object, if any, upon which the mental attitude is apparently directed. The mental attitude that we are considering is not presented with the implicit characteristics just considered; it is not, so far as we have yet seen, presented as discredited and unreal.

In order that we might have a suitably limited framework within which to consider the reality of Descartes' alleged mental attitude, we have in this chapter agreed that Descartes' brain is real and his stove-heated room real.[17] Let us likewise agree that there is some real entity distant from Descartes' body upon which his alleged mental attitude is alleged to be directed. And let us agree that there is some real entity distant from Descartes' body that is alleged to be causally related to his alleged mental attitude. Whether or not the moon is really the object of a mental attitude of Descartes,' and whether or not the moon really brings about the mental attitude that may be alleged to be directed upon it, the moon, let us in this chapter agree, is real and really distant from Descartes' body. Yet if the moon is real and distant from Descartes' body, how can a mental attitude which is concomitant with an extension within Descartes' body be either affected by the moon or aware of it? Given a real moon that is *there* and an alleged mental attitude that is alleged to be extended and *here,* any alleged relational situation, whether of cause and effect or of subject and object, is so incomprehensible, it may be said, that the mental attitude, which is presented as extended and here, comes to be presented as incredible and unreal.

The statement that the distant moon affects a thinking substance which is extended and here would seem to be less perplexing than the statement that the distant moon affects a thinking substance which is here but at a point. And the statement that the moon affects a thinking substance which is at a point would seem to be less perplexing than the statement that it affects a thinking substance which has no position at all. The alleged influence of one extended substance upon another extended substance, distant from it, has the advantage of seeming somewhat analogous to the generally credited influence of the moon

175

upon the tides, or to the generally credited influence of the sun upon vegetation on the earth. Similarly, an alleged situation in which there is a subject-object relation between a thinking substance which is extended and a substance which, although distant, is likewise extended has the advantage of seeming somewhat analogous to the generally credited situation in which two extended substances have the relation of being *distant* from one another or in which two extended substances, although distant, are *like* one another.

We may, to be sure, wonder how any substance can influence another, distant from it. We may wonder through what media a distant entity comes to affect a substance that is characterized by a mental attitude; and to what extent the mental attitude is due to the media rather than to the distant entity itself. We may likewise wonder how the mental attitude can, figuratively speaking, reach to the distant substance and have it as an object. And we may perhaps conclude that a mental attitude can not have a distant entity as its object, that it either has no object at all or only an object that is where it itself is. These however, are questions for subsequent chapters. In this chapter our question is whether Descartes was thinking, not whether that thinking had an object, much less how thinking and the distant entity, alleged to be the cause of that thinking, come to be related. What we are considering is the alleged mental attitude of Descartes' that *seems* to be directed upon man, God and the universe; or that *seems* to be directed upon the moon. The mental attitude of Descartes' that we are considering is presented with the characteristic of seeming to be directed upon the moon, whether or not it is presented in addition as having the real moon as its object. In a later chapter the mental attitude, seeming to be directed upon the moon, that is alleged to have the real moon as its object, may be found to be presented as incredible. Or the subsistent then found to be presented as incredible may be the mental attitude, seeming to be directed upon the moon, that is alleged to be directed only upon private content; or the mental attitude, seeming to be directed upon the moon, that is alleged to have no object at all. At this point the mental attitude under consideration is presented without any claim as to what, if anything, is its real cause or what, if anything, its real object. Our subsistent is the mental attitude which pretends to be directed upon the moon. And this subsistent presented with no claim as to its real cause or real object need not, so far as we have yet seen, be presented as incredible.

Our subsistent has been Descartes' mental attitude as he paced up and down his stove-heated room and seemed to be thinking about the moon or as he "seemed to ponder the existence of man, God and the universe." [18] But it is no longer this alleged entity presented as non-spatial—which has been found to be unreal—that we have to consider; [19] nor is it this alleged entity presented as having position, but not extension.[20] Our subsistent is Descartes' mental attitude presented, not as itself an extended substance, but as the quality of an extended substance such as Descartes' body or such as the brain, the cortex or a nerve-fibre within Descartes' body. On the view which seems to remain before us for our consideration, Descartes' body, or part of his body, has such qualities as extension, weight and color, qualities which may be called "non-mental." And it is to such qualities that our attention is directed when the substance in which these qualities inhere is called "Descartes' body" or "Descartes' cortex." But the substance in which these qualities inhere is also, on the view which we are examining, the substance in which Descartes' thinking inheres as a quality. For Descartes' thinking, on this view, "is an *event* and not a thing or stuff; and it is an event adjectival to the brain." [21] In order to think of Descartes' brain or Descartes' body as a substance in which not only non-mental qualities but also thinking inheres, we must, says Sellars, "enlarge our conception of a cerebral state over that which physiology gives." [22] And to give recognition to the differing types of qualities which, on this view, this substance has inhering in it, this substance may be called, not Descartes' brain or Descartes' nerve-fibre, but rather Descartes' mind-brain or Descartes' mind-nerve-fibre. It is this mind-brain or mind-nerve-fibre which, on this view, thinks. And since this mind-brain or mind-nerve-fibre is extended, Descartes' thinking is concomitant with the quality of extension and may to this extent be said itself to be extended.

When it is alleged that there is a substance to be called Descartes' brain or Descartes' mind-brain, a substance in which thinking and extension inhere as qualities, there are various questions that may be raised with respect to substances in general and with respect to qualities in general. It may be asked what "substance" means and what "quality" means. And it may be asked how a substance can *have* qualities inhering in it, how a substance, for example, can *be* thinking or can *be* extended. To discuss such questions at this point would, however, carry us far afield. Descartes' alleged mental attitude "presented as having a vehicle and a setting can be discussed in fewer words and in a less complicated fashion when, instead of regarding thinking, vehicle and setting as all mere subsistents, we accept the premise that vehicle and setting are real."[23] And Descartes' alleged mental attitude, presented as the quality of an extended substance, can be discussed in fewer words and in a less complicated fashion when we assume that there *are* substances and that an instance of thinking and an instance of extension can, if real, each be the quality of a substance. "It is not as the painter putting on the initial daubs of oil that we approach the canvas, but rather as the painter-critic who concentrates his attention on minute sections of his work in turn, at each point regarding the rest of the work as unquestioned."[24] In our present discussion, let us then make use of the fact that certain substances are listed as real in the appendix to Chapter Three; and certain qualities. And let us reserve for subsequent chapters discussions that deal with substance in general rather than with Descartes' alleged mind-brain or mind-nerve-fibre and discussions that deal with quality in general rather than with Descartes' alleged mental attitude.

Let us in this chapter agree that Descartes' brain is a real substance and extension a real quality inhering in it. Indeed let us agree that there are some qualities of the sort that are generally called "secondary qualities." Let us agree that a certain piece of metal is a real substance which is really hot and really red. And let us agree that the electric bulb on the desk before me is really bright and incandescent. Let us further agree that on some occasion before our piece of metal was placed in a furnace, it was not yet red; and that, after I have turned the switch, the bulb is no longer incandescent. It is in some such fashion as this that the alleged mental attitude of Descartes' that remains for our consideration may be held to qualify the substance in which it inheres. Just as redness may be held to be a quality of the metal

178

which, before it was heated, was not red, and just as incandescence may be held to be a quality of the bulb which, after I turn the switch, is no longer incandescent, so Descartes' alleged thinking, on the view that remains for our consideration, is presented as a quality of an extended mind-brain or mind-nerve-fibre which in some earlier phase may not have been thinking and in some later phase may again not be thinking. So far as we have yet seen, the mental attitude of Descartes' may be unreal that is alleged to be the quality of an extended substance and alleged to be the quality of a substance which in other phases is not thinking. But if this subsistent is unreal, it is not unreal in so far as it is presented as a quality concomitant with extension or in so far as it is presented as the quality of one phase of a substance but not of another.

Descartes' alleged mental attitude is not presented as incredible in so far as it is presented as a quality concomitant with extension. For there *are* qualities concomitant with extension. But this alleged mental attitude, it may be said, is a peculiar quality, unlike redness or incandescence. And, it may be held, whereas instances of redness and of extension inhering in the same substance are plausible, alleged instances of thinking and of extension inhering in the same substance are not. Descartes' brain and its extension, it may be said, were objects for Descartes' contemporaries but not for Descartes; whereas his mental attitude was an object for him alone. With the piece of metal and its extension on the one hand and that metal's redness on the other, or with the concave side of an arc on the one hand and its convex side on the other, the situation, it may be said, is different. For, both the metal and its redness can be objects for the same observer. And "when two percipients observe different sides of the same thing, like the hasty knights in the fable, they can," as Ward says,[25] "change places and each connect the two aspects in one experience of an object."

We have in effect agreed, however, that, if Descartes' alleged mental attitude is real, it and the mind-brain in which it is alleged to inhere may be objects for the same observer. It is Descartes' alleged mind-brain that you and I are now considering and Descartes' alleged mental attitude that you and I are now discussing.[26] To this extent each of us may be said to connect a substance, its extension and its alleged thinking in one experience, just as we connect the metal, its extension and its redness in one experience, and just as each knight connects the two sides of the arc in one experience. It may still be pointed out, however, that, even if a substance, its extension and its alleged thinking are apparent objects for the same observer, the substance and its extension seem to be apprehended in one way, its alleged thinking in another. By Descartes, it may be said, his thinking is sensed, his brain and its extension inferred; by others, it may be said, Descartes' brain and its extension may be sensed, but his thinking must be inferred. But in spite of the fact that we see the metal and its redness and do not see but feel its heat, we do not seem to disbelieve that the metal is both red and hot. And when we do not feel the heat but only infer it from what we see, we likewise do not seem to disbelieve that the metal is both red and hot. Qualities are generally believed to inhere in the same substance, even when they are perceived through different senses, and even when one is sensed and the other inferred. And an instance of thinking and an instance of extension alleged to inhere in the same substance need not be presented as incredible when they are presented as being apprehended in different ways or when they are presented as one being a sense-datum, the other an object which is inferred.

The mental attitude which is alleged to be a quality inhering in a mind-brain or mind-nerve-fibre need not be presented as incredible in that mental attitude and nerve-fibre are presented as being apprehended in different ways. But such an alleged mental attitude is presented as incredible, it may be said, in that mental attitudes and nerve-fibres appear totally incommensurate with one another. "If we know so little what we mean by a 'nerve-process' that it may turn out . . . to be an emotion or a tooth-ache," then, says J. B. Pratt,[27] "we have no business to use the term 'nerve-process' at all." When, however, Descartes' thinking is presented as a quality of his nerve-process, it need not be presented as itself the nerve process. In order for a nerve-process to have the quality of thinking, the terms "thinking" and "nerve process" need be no more synonymous than the terms "redness" and "piece of metal" or the terms "incandescence" and "electric bulb." It may be held, to be sure, that "thinking nerve-fibre" is a perplexing combination of terms, that "thinking" and "nerve-fibre" joined together seem to represent no apparent object at all. It is

180

however such an apparent object, such a subsistent, that we have through several paragraphs been describing. Having eliminated as unreal Descartes' thinking appearing with the characteristic of being utterly non-spatial, Descartes' thinking appearing as having position but not extension, and Descartes' thinking appearing as itself an extended substance, the subsistent remaining for our consideration is: Descartes' mental attitude seemingly directed towards man, God and the universe, a quality of, and abstractable from, all or part of the breathing, reacting, extended substance that may be called Descartes' mind-body. Although perhaps perplexing, this subsistent, so far as we have yet seen, need not be presented as generally discredited. So far as we have yet seen, *this* alleged mental attitude of Descartes' may be real.

We have agreed that qualities exist; and substances in which they inhere. Let us further agree that, when a quality inheres in a substance, there is a sort of parallelism between them. When an electric bulb is destroyed, its incandescence disappears. And when its incandescence disappears, the electric bulb is different from what it was before, if only in that it no longer has the quality of incandescence. The view which we are considering, the view that thinking is a quality of an extended mind-brain or mind-nerve-fibre which thinks, has implicit in it the view that, as thinking changes, there is some change in the extended substance which thinks. The change in the substance may be merely the change from a phase which has a given mental attitude inhering in it to a phase which has no mental attitude or a different mental attitude inhering in it. Or there may be held to be other qualities of this substance, non-mental qualities, that change when its thinking changes. If however a change in the thinking extended substance parallels a change in its mental attitude, then a change in mental attitude need be no more dependent on a change in the substance in which it inheres than a change in that substance need be dependent on a change in its mental attitude.

We may ask how an outside stimulus causes both a change in thinking and a change in the substance which thinks. And we may ask whether thinking and certain non-mental qualities inhering in the same substance change together. But the view which we are considering involves no epiphenomenalism. On the view which we are considering, there may be changes in non-mental qualities just prior to a change in mental attitude; so that an examination of non-mental qualities may enable us to predict mental attitudes. There may likewise be a change in mental attitude just prior to changes in certain non-mental qualities; so that an examination of mental attitudes may enable us to predict non-mental qualities. But in so far as mental attitude, substance and non-mental qualities change simultaneously, they are, on the view which we are considering, presented as interdependent. "Take away the neural process," says Hodgson,[28] "and there is no sensation. Take away the sensation—it can not be done save by taking away the neural process. There is therefore," he continues, "dependence of the sensation on the concomitant neural process but not vice-versa." But if thinking and neural process are concomitant, we do not take away the neural process and *then* take away the thinking. If we take away the neural process, we take away simultaneously the thinking and whatever non-mental qualities inhere in this substance. If we take away, not the substance, but those of its non-mental qualities, if any, that occur only when its thinking occurs, we take away its thinking. Similarly, however, if we take away its thinking, we take away those of the substance's non-mental qualities that occur only when thinking occurs; and we change the substance in which both they and the thinking concomitant with them formerly inhered.

Even if we disregard those non-mental qualities inhering in the thinking substance that may be alleged to change before or after there is a change in mental attitude, even if we restrict our attention to those non-mental qualities, if any, in which a change is alleged to occur simultaneously with a change in mental attitude, we may, to be sure, find it convenient to explore what happens to non-mental qualities more intensively than we explore what happens to thinking. Let us assume that, when light disappears from an electric bulb, the bulb simultaneously ceases to have an electric current running through it. Let us assume that the quality of being lighted and the quality of being affected by an electric current are interdependent; that the occurrence of the quality of being lighted does not precede, and does not enable us to predict, a *subsequent* occurrence of the quality of being affected by an electric current; and that the occurrence of the quality of being affected by an electric current does not precede, and does

182

not enable us to predict, a *subsequent* occurrence of the quality of being lighted. We may nevertheless, it would seem, find it convenient to explore the onset and disappearance of electric currents more intensively than we explore the onset and disappearance of the quality of being lighted, a quality that is concomitant with it. Such priority, however, as under these circumstances we might give to the quality of being affected by an electric current over the quality of being lighted would be a priority in attention and would not imply that one quality is temporally prior to the other or that one quality is real and the other unreal. In a similar fashion, it would seem, priority in attention may be given to certain non-mental qualities of a thinking, extended substance rather than to the mental attitude which is alleged to vary with them. Descartes' mental attitude seemingly directed upon man, God and the universe may be presented as the quality of an extended thinking substance. And other qualities of this substance, non-mental qualities, may be presented as varying with this attitude, as being present when it is present, absent when it is absent. But these alleged other qualities may be presented as being more promising to investigate without being presented as being temporally prior to the mental attitude seemingly directed upon man, God and the universe. And they may be presented as more promising to investigate without this alleged mental attitude being presented as unreal.

Certain non-mental qualities, let us agree, offer a more fruitful field for investigation than the mental attitudes which, if they exist, are concomitant with them. These non-mental qualities along with others, which all together may be said to constitute an organism's behavior, have been the subject of much study on the part of behaviorists. Organisms have been confronted by various stimuli and the organisms' responses noted. "The desire in all such work," says Watson,[29] "is to gain an accurate knowledge of adjustments and the stimuli calling them forth. The reason for this is to learn general and particular methods by which behavior may be controlled. The goal is not the description and explanation of conscious states as such." As a result of such work, however, one may come to hold that we can disregard mental attitudes even if they exist, that information with respect to behavior alone will teach us all that we can know that might en-

183

able us to predict and control what organisms will do. If a mental attitude exists and is concomitant with some non-mental quality, a given stimulus may be said to bring about both the non-mental quality and the mental attitude; and a given response may be said to be due both to the non-mental quality and the mental attitude. But if a study of the causal relation from stimulus to mental attitude to response gives us no ability to predict and control not given us by a study of the causal relation from stimulus to non-mental quality to response, then the alleged mental attitude, it may be said, is, like LaPlace's God, an unnecessary hypothesis.

The mental attitude which is alleged to be the quality of an extended mind-brain or mind-nerve-fibre need not be presented as incredible, we have seen, when it is presented as less promising to investigate than the non-mental qualities with which it is alleged to be concomitant. But is it not presented as incredible when it is presented as unnecessary for prediction and control? We may imagine two worlds before us, only one of which is the world of real entities. In the one, an organism is stimulated; the stimuli bring about non-mental qualities in the brain; and these non-mental qualities lead the organism to make characteristic responses. In this imagined world, however, organisms are like robots; there *are* no mental attitudes. In the other, organisms behave just as they behave in the world just described. But, intervening between stimulus and response there are not only the brain's non-mental qualities, but the brain's mental attitudes, its thinking, as well. Entities, according to the dictum attributed to William of Occam, are not to be multiplied beyond what are necessary. Admitting, then, that mental attitudes, if they exist, are not needed to enable us to predict and control what organisms will do, should we not accept the world with fewer entities and reject the other? In view of its being presented as not needed, do we not find the mental attitude alleged to be an additional quality inhering in an extended brain or extended nerve-fibre presented as incredible and as generally disbelieved?

Let us first remark that, whereas one writer may hold that entities are not to be multiplied beyond what are necessary, another may hold that all entities are real that *can* be real, all entities, that is to say, that are not inconsistent with some entity

184

that *is* real. Both assertions ascribe characteristics to what is taken to be "reality." Each assertion, we hold, depends for its truth upon the signification that is assigned the term "real." As we have explained *our* term "reality," the world of real entities, so far as we have yet seen, need be neither a world with the maximum number of compossible entities nor a world with the minimum number needed for prediction and control. As an element in the explanation of our term "reality," we have, however, said that "whatever explicitly or implicitly appears as generally discredited is unreal." [30] Consequently, it remains for us to determine whether an entity may be presented as not needed for prediction and control; and yet not be presented as generally discredited.

There is a distinction to be made, let us suggest, between the entity which is proposed in order that we may organize our knowledge, in order that the facts that we know may be known to be related, or in order that we may predict and control future events, and the entity which is not proposed with the purpose of accomplishing any of these objectives. When facts are puzzling and hypotheses proposed in order that we may become aware of relations between these facts, it would seem that, on the whole, we accept the simpler hypothesis, the hypothesis which introduces and proposes fewer entities; and that we reject the more complicated hypothesis, the hypothesis which introduces and proposes a greater number of entities. When there are similar objectives and when alternative hypotheses are proposed, we likewise seem on the whole to accept the hypothesis which accounts for a large number of facts and to reject the hypothesis which accounts for a lesser number of facts. But these observations do not apply to the entity that is *not* introduced in order that we may predict and control, *not* introduced in order that we may become aware of other entities as mutually related. An alleged God may be proposed, not after miracles have been experienced and found puzzling, but as an entity that is itself experienced. The suggestion that my electric bulb is bright may be made, not to suggest a cause for the waves that travel out from the bulb,—the electric current running through the bulb may already have been accepted as such a cause, —but the suggestion may be made on the basis of other evidence, on the basis of independent belief. Whatever may be the situation with respect to entities that are proposed in order that we may become aware of other entities as mutually related, entities that are not proposed and introduced with such a purpose need not, we hold, be presented as incredible when they are alleged not to be needed in order that we may become aware of other entities as mutually related. The alleged brightness of my electric bulb need not be presented as incredible when it is alleged not to be needed in order that we may become aware of a cause of the waves travelling out from the bulb. And the mental attitude that is alleged to be a quality of an extended substance need not be presented as incredible when it is alleged not to be needed to enable us to predict and control the organism's responses.

The subsistent that seems to be before us is Descartes' mental attitude seemingly directed upon man, God and the universe, a mental attitude which is alleged to be the quality of an extended mind-brain or extended mind-nerve-fibre. It is a mental attitude which, along with such concomitant non-mental qualities as vary with it, is alleged to be a result of certain stimuli and a cause of certain responses; a mental attitude, nevertheless, which is alleged to offer a less promising field for investigation than the non-mental qualities which accompany it; and a mental attitude which is alleged not to have been proposed in order that we might be able to predict and control Descartes' responses. Such an alleged mental attitude need not be presented as incredible. And yet, since there are certain behaviorists who reject it, this alleged mental attitude is presented as being in some quarters disbelieved.

To what extent, however, do behaviorists disbelieve in the particular subsistent that we are considering? A behaviorist may assert that there are no entities which lack position altogether. He may assert that he disbelieves in an entity which is alleged not to inhere in any extended substance. He may hold that nothing exists outside what we have called "total behavior." [31] And he may sum up his position by stating that thinking *is* behavior. The statement, however, that thinking is behavior may not be inconsistent with the statement that thinking and non-mental qualities inhere in the same substance, with the statement that thinking and certain non-mental qualities which are concomitant with that thinking vary together. And the statement that there is no observable object outside total behavior may not be inconsistent with the statement that, "in having Descartes before us as an unanalyzed whole, his alleged thinking is within, rather than out-side, the entity before us."[32] There are, let us agree, behaviorists who seem to disbelieve in the subsistent that appears to be before us. There are behaviorists who find that, when they attempt to abstract thinking, mental attitude, mental activity, from Descartes' mind-brain or mind-nerve-fibre or total behavior, there is an irruption of disbelief similar to that which breaks in upon us when we attempt to abstract from this rectangular desk its alleged roundness. To a considerable extent, however, it is some other subsistent, and not the subsistent which we are considering, that seems to be the object of their disbelief. The subsistent which we are considering is presented as seemingly disbelieved by some behaviorists, but not as generally disbelieved by behaviorists.

Some behaviorists seem to disbelieve in the alleged mental attitude which we are considering. And some epistemologists who assert the existence of ideas seem likewise to disbelieve in this subsistent. Such epistemologists may agree that, in addition to Descartes' non-mental behavior, there is a real mental entity to be abstracted or to be inferred from his mind-brain or from his mind-nerve-fibre or from his total behavior. But they may hold that whatever mental entity is thus to be really abstracted or inferred is what they would call "content" or "idea," not what they would call "mental attitude" or "mental activity" or "thinking." Just, however, as the behaviorist who asserts that thinking is behavior may not disbelieve in the alleged mental attitude which we are considering, so the epistemologist who denies the existence of mental entities other than what he calls "ideas" may not disbelieve in the alleged mental attitude which we are considering. For "what *we* call 'mental attitude' may by some be included in what *they* would call 'private content.'"[33] To be sure, what we call "mental attitude" has not been presented as *private* content, as an object for Descartes alone.[34] But it has been presented as an entity that may be held to be *sensed* by Descartes alone. And whereas what we call mental attitude has been presented as think-*ing* rather than as what is thought, it has been presented as an entity that may be held to be an object "upon which it or some further mental attitude is directed."[35] The epistemologist who holds that there are no mental entities that are not pictures or images disbelieves, we may say, in what we are calling "mental

187

attitudes." But what is alleged to be an idea and not alleged to be a picture or image may be what we should call a mental attitude presented as an object for some further mental attitude.

The alleged mental attitude which we are considering is presented as seemingly disbelieved by some behaviorists, but not as generally disbelieved by behaviorists. And it is presented as seemingly disbelieved by some epistemologists who assert the existence of ideas, but not as generally disbelieved by epistemologists who assert the existence of ideas. Indeed when we turn from the opinions of behaviorists and epistemologists to the opinions of men generally, we seem to note a general belief that men are not robots and that their mental life is not made up of pictures and images. In addition to the words "idea" and "thought," there are in common use the words "thinker" and "thinking"; and the statement that there are thinkers who think would seem to express a belief in entities that are not pictures or images but are rather what we in this chapter have called mental attitudes. In any case the particular mental attitude which we have been considering, and which we are now considering, is not presented as generally discredited. And this alleged mental attitude is listed as real in the appendix to Chapter Three. As Descartes paced up and down his stove-heated room, he *was*, we conclude, thinking. He *had* a mental attitude which seemed to be directed upon man, God and the universe, and which was a quality inhering, along with extension and other non-mental qualities, in his mind-brain or mind-cortex or mind-nerve-fibre.

Summary

Positive statements about what exists in our sense of "existence" should, according to our program, be statements about individual subsistents carefully identified. In this chapter we select an alleged instance of thinking—what we call a "mental attitude"—distinguishing it from object, from mental content and from non-mental behavior.

Such an instance of thinking may be presented as spatial or as non-spatial. Presented as non-spatial it is unreal. Presented as spatial it may be real; for the arguments which have been advanced against spatial and extended thinking are unconvincing.

The entity we present is an instance of thinking that is a quality of an extended substance. Even though this entity is presented as something that need not be considered in investigations into behavior, it is not presented as generally discredited and is real.

Chapter VII

MINDS AND BODIES

We begin this chapter with the reality of one instance of think-ing established. As Descartes paced up and down his stove-heated room, he *had* a mental attitude which seemed to be directed upon man, God and the universe, a mental attitude which was a qual-ity inhering, along with extension and other non-mental quali-ties, in his mind-brain or mind-cortex or mind-nerve-fibre.[1] With-out discussions that would repeat or parallel the discussion in the preceding chapter, we shall, I am sure, be permitted to conclude that there are similar instances of thinking that are likewise real. Thinking, alleged to be a quality of Plato lecturing in the Academy, is, let us say, real in the sense in which we are using the term "reality." The thinking is likewise real that is alleged to be a quality of a mind-nerve-fibre of yours as you read this page. And the thinking is real that is alleged to be the quality of a clerk who, as he sits at his desk with a ledger before him, is engaged in tran-scribing figures to a statement which he is preparing to mail out.

But whereas there are various instances of thinking that are real, let us, on the basis of the appendix to Chapter Three, agree that there are also certain substances which do not have the qual-ity of thinking.[2] In the sense in which we have explained our terms "existence" and "reality," there is a ledger which does not think and a statement on which figures are being jotted down which likewise does not think. It is, in short, the ledger clerk who thinks, not the ledger or the statement. The mind-cortex or mind-nerve-fibre of the ledger clerk who thinks has, like the mind-nerve-fibre of Descartes', not only the quality of thinking, but also such non-mental qualities as extension, weight and color.[3] It follows that there is no motion from this mind-nerve-fibre's extension to its thinking; or from its thinking to its weight. For these qualities are qualities of the same substance. And surely entities that are alleged to be concomitant, and also alleged to enter into a relational situation in which there is motion from one to the other, are entities presented with implicitly contradictory characteristics, entities which are unreal.

But what about an alleged motion to the thinking nerve-fibre, not from that nerve-fibre's extension, but from the unthinking ledger in front of which the ledger clerk sits? And what about an alleged motion from the thinking nerve-fibre, not to that nerve-fibre's weight, but to the statement on which figures are being jotted down? Can the ledger which is not thinking affect or bring about our clerk's mental attitude? And can our clerk's mental attitude be the cause of the figures that are jotted down on the unthinking statement?

According to Descartes, mind thinks but is unextended, whereas matter is extended and unthinking. Between entities so unlike, some of his successors found interaction incredible. There is difficulty enough, some of them hold, in accepting a causal interaction between two unthinking bodies. "Those that suppose that bodies necessarily and by themselves communicate their motion to each other," says Malebranche,[4] "make but a probable supposition." But, he continues, "the mind and body are two sorts of being so opposite that those who think that the commotions of the soul necessarily follow upon the motion of the blood and animal spirits do it without the least probability." There is moreover a simple experiment which reenforces Malebranche's conviction that there is no causal relation between entities so disparate as mind and matter. My mind, he holds, can not cause my arm to be raised since it is not even aware of the means that must be used to bring about the raising. "Most men," Malebranche finds,[5] "know not so much as that they have spirits, nerves and muscles, and yet move their arms with as much and more dexterity than the most skilful anatomists. Men therefore will the moving of their arms, but," Malebranche's conclusion is, "t'is God that is able and knows how to do it."

If, however, to be a cause, an entity had to be aware of the means by which its results are effected, one billiard ball could not cause the motion of another without being aware of the laws of motion. Chemical substances would have to be chemists and bacteria bacteriologists. The word "cause" may, to be sure, be used in various senses. But there is no sense in which we shall use the word "cause," and no sense in which "cause" is commonly used, where "A causes B" implies "A is aware of the means by which A causes B." It is the thinking substance C that is alleged to be aware of the causal relation between A and B. And whereas C may be A itself or B itself, there is no self-contradictory subsistent before us when we present to ourselves a C that is completely outside the relational situation involving A and B.

An alleged causal relation flowing from ledger to mind-nerve-fibre is not presented as self-contradictory when this ledger is presented as unaware of the means by which it affects the ledger clerk's mind. Nor do we find an alleged causal relation flowing from ledger to mind-nerve-fibre presented as incredible when the mind-nerve-fibre is presented as thinking, but the ledger presented as unthinking. A causal relation between mind and matter has been held incredible in that the former thinks and is unextended whereas the latter is unthinking and extended.[6] But whereas the ledger and the mind-nerve-fibre that we are considering are presented as unlike in that one is unthinking and the other thinking, they are not presented as unlike with respect to extension or the lack of extension. It is an *extended* mind-nerve-fibre that we have found real and that is presented to us as affected by the ledger; an *extended* mind-nerve-fibre that we have found real and that is presented to us as the cause of the figures on the statement. An alleged causal relation between two entities which are presented as unlike in that one is presented as thinking and the other as unthinking is not, we find, presented as incredible when, along with this difference, both entities are presented as extended. So far as we have yet seen, the ledger may be the cause of our clerk's mental attitude; and our clerk's mental attitude may be the cause of the figures on the statement.

There *is*, let us say, a motion from the ledger to our clerk's mind-nerve-fibre, to the mind-nerve-fibre which has a mental attitude apparently directed upon the figures in this ledger. For, such an alleged motion subsists without any of the characteristics that would mark it out as unreal; and such an alleged motion is listed as real in the appendix to Chapter Three. The mind-nerve-fibre to which this motion flows is a substance with non-mental qualities and with a mental attitude as well. Hence the motion that flows from the ledger flows to the thinking, flows to the extension that is concomitant with that thinking, and flows to the substance in which thinking and extension inhere. But whereas the substance, its thinking and its extension are equally end-points of the motion that flows from the ledger, are they all to be called "results" caused by the ledger? And whereas the substance, its thinking and its extension are equally originating points for the motion that flows to the statement, are they all to be called "causes" of the figures that appear upon the statement?

There are, let us suppose, other instances of motion flowing from other ledgers to other mind-nerve-fibres. And on the basis of many instances, it may be found that there are certain limited characteristics which ledgers always have when the mind-nerve-fibres, in which motions from them terminate, are identical with our ledger clerk's. Or it may be found that, given motions from many identical ledgers, the mind-nerve-fibres to which these motions severally flow are identical in some respects but not in all respects. On the basis of many instances, it may be decided that, not the ledger, but some particular quality of the ledger, is to be called the "cause." And it may be decided that, not the mind-nerve-fibre which is a substance, but some quality of it,—some non-mental quality, some type of thinking, or both,—is to be called the "result." We may use "cause" and "result" in such a way that not every entity at the source of motion is a cause and not every entity at the terminus a result. But pending a determination that there *is* a *sine qua non* at the source and pending a determination that there *is* a constant or inevitable quality at the *terminus ad quem,* let us not attempt to distinguish among the various entities at the source or among the various entities at the *terminus ad quem.* Let us hold that our clerk's mind-nerve-fibre *and* its non-mental qualities *and* its thinking are affected by the ledger. Let us hold that our clerk's mind-nerve-fibre *and* its non-mental qualities *and* its thinking affect the statement that he is preparing to mail out.

The assertion that the ledger affects our clerk's thinking and that our clerk's thinking in turn affects the statement he makes out may be said to be an assertion that mind and matter interact. Our doctrine consequently may be held to be a denial of parallelism. Yet it is not every form of parallelism that is in conflict with the particular form of interactionism that we have propounded. Our clerk's thinking, we have held, acts, not upon the non-mental qualities which inhere in the very mind-nerve-fibre in which *it* inheres, but upon such entities as statements that are separated from it and have positions different from its position.[7] "The view that thinking is a quality of an extended mind-brain or mind-nerve fibre which thinks has implicit in it the view that, as thinking changes, there is some change in the extended substance which thinks. The change in the substance may be merely the change from a phase which has a given mental attitude inhering in it to a phase which has no mental attitude or a different mental attitude inhering in it. Or there may be held to be other qualities of this substance, non-mental qualities, that change when its thinking changes."[8] A change in thinking may thus be held to parallel a change in certain non-mental qualities that inhere with it in the same substance; nonetheless, this thinking and these non-mental qualities may be held to act upon other entities situated elsewhere.

Indeed it is not only a parallelism between thinking and non-mental qualities inhering in the same substance that is consistent with the particular form of interactionism which we have propounded. If various ledger pages are the sources of motions flowing to various mind-nerve-fibres, if for each page there is a mind-nerve-fibre that it acts upon, a mental attitude of which it is in some sense the cause, then it may be found that the series of acting ledger pages has a one-to-one correspondence with the series of resultant mental attitudes. Not, to be sure, that each element in the series of causes will, in such case, be simultaneous with its corresponding result; or that it will resemble the resulting entity that corresponds to it. But the assertion that a given non-mental entity which is a cause has a resulting mental attitude which corresponds to it, or the assertion that a given mental attitude which is a cause has a resulting non-mental entity which corresponds to it, may be said to be the assertion of a sort of parallelism. It is the assertion of that sort of parallelism that is asserted to obtain between the heat of the sun and the heat of the

194

earth when we hold that the heat of the earth varies with the heat of that phase of the sun which acts upon it.

Yet the parallelism which we have just considered, a parallelism which we have found consistent with the particular form of inter-actionism that we have propounded, is a parallelism between such entities as ledgers or statements on the one hand and mental attitudes or mind-nerve-fibres on the other. It is a parallelism between causes and results and a parallelism between external things and mental attitudes, not a parallelism between external things and private contents or ideas. We have attempted to distinguish what we call "mental attitude" from what we call "private content" or "idea." What we call "mental attitude" is "presented as not a picture or image and it is presented as not being content except in so far as it is the object upon which it or some further mental attitude is directed." [9] Corresponding to the distinction between mental attitude and idea, there is a distinction to be made between an alleged correspondence or parallelism between a series of ledger pages and a series of resultant mental attitudes on the one hand and, on the other hand, an alleged correspondence or parallelism between a series of ledger pages and a series of private ideas of ledger pages. "The order and connection of ideas," says Spinoza,[10] "is the same as the order and connection of things." The parallelism between ideas and things that this proposition is used to assert may be an alleged parallelism between a series of ledger pages and a series of mental contents, a series of private ideas of ledger pages. Such an alleged parallelism differs both from the parallelism which may obtain between the thinking and the non-mental qualities that inhere in the same mind-nerve-fibre; and from the parallelism or correspondence which may obtain between a series of external entities and a series of mental attitudes. It is a form of parallelism that does not exist unless private ideas, as distinguished from mental attitudes, exist. And whereas we have agreed that various mental attitudes exist, we have not yet agreed that there are any real instances of what we call "private contents" or "ideas."

Various substances that have mental attitudes exist. Among them there is the mind-nerve-fibre within Descartes' body as he paced up and down his stove-heated room, the mind-nerve-fibre with a mental attitude apparently directed upon man, God and

195

the universe. Among them, as Descartes paced up and down his stove-heated room, there is also, let us say, a mind-nerve-fibre of his with a mental attitude apparently directed upon the stove. Descartes, we might say, seemed not only to be thinking about man, God and the universe, but he seemed also to be aware of the stove. Let us then consider an alleged substance that includes both of these mind-nerve-fibres. Let us consider an alleged composite substance that has these extended thinking mind-nerve-fibres of Descartes' as its parts. This alleged composite substance is presented as composed of extended, thinking mind-nerve-fibres that are its parts, just as a chair may be said to be composed of seat, back and legs; and just as a French flag may be said to have three parts, one red, one white and one blue.

It may, to be sure, be said that there are no substances that are parts of other substances. It may be said that, if the chair is real, the leg of the chair, taken by itself, is unreal. Or it may be said that, if the blue strip of a French flag is real, the flag, taken as a whole, is unreal. We have however found that Descartes' alleged mental attitude "presented as having a vehicle and a setting can be discussed in fewer words and in a less complicated fashion when, instead of regarding thinking, vehicle and setting as all mere subsistents, we accept the premise that vehicle and setting are real." [11] And in the previous chapter, instead of discussing the reality of substances as such and the reality of qualities as such, we have made use of "the fact that certain substances are listed as real in the appendix to Chapter Three; and certain qualities." [12] At this point let us similarly agree that there are situations in which some composite substance is real and substances which are its parts likewise real. Let us agree, for example, that this chair is real and each of its legs real, that a given French flag is real and the blue strip which is a part of it likewise real. Let us also agree that the composite substance and the substance which is a part of it may each have qualities which are real; and that the quality which inheres in a partial substance may not be identical with the corresponding quality which inheres in the including substance. Just as a plate may be circular "without any of the fragments into which it is broken being circular," [13] so, let us agree, a chair may have a size greater than the size that is the quality of one of its legs. And whereas one of the strips that is a part of our French flag has the quality of being blue, the flag as a whole, let us say, has, not the quality of being blue, but the quality of being tri-colored. With these examples before us, the entity that we are considering, the substance that is alleged to include several of Descartes' thinking, extended mind-nerve-fibres, comes to be presented as having an extension that may be greater than the extension of one of its parts. And it comes to be presented with the quality of apparently thinking about various things rather than with the quality of having a mental attitude apparently directed upon the stove.

It is certain mind-nerve-fibres of Descartes' as he paced up and down his stove-heated room that are alleged to be parts of the including substance that we have been proposing. Let us however enlarge this alleged including substance. Let us consider an alleged substance that has among its parts, not only the mind-nerve-fibre with a mental attitude apparently directed upon man, God and the universe, and not only the mind-nerve-fibre with a mental attitude apparently directed upon the stove, but also the earlier mind-nerve-fibre of Descartes' with a mental attitude apparently directed upon some teacher standing in front of him at La Fleche, and the later mind-nerve-fibre of his with a mental attitude apparently directed upon Queen Christina. Let us in short consider a substance alleged to have duration, a substance alleged to have the substance proposed in the preceding paragraph as one of its momentary phases. This substance is presented as having the quality of thinking, but as having the quality of thinking now about one thing and now about another, rather than as having a mental attitude apparently directed upon the stove. It is likewise presented as extended in the sense that it is presented as having momentary phases which are extended. And it is further, let us say, presented as in some degree a *system* of parts rather than as a haphazard aggregation of parts. That is to say, the mind-nerve-fibre with a mental attitude apparently directed upon man, God and the universe and the mind-nerve-fibre with a mental attitude apparently directed upon the stove are presented as in some sense affecting one another, as being parts of what might be called a "natural" unit. And parts such as these that are earlier are presented as affecting certain parts that occur later. Descartes' mind-nerve-fibre with a mental attitude apparently directed upon Queen Christina, for example, is pre-sented as affected by previous mind-nerve-fibres, previous mental attitudes, of his. In short, the composite substance which we are considering is presented, not only as including parts some of which are earlier and some later, but as including parts which are in some sense held together so as to constitute a system.

Now some such entity as has just been proposed does, we conclude, exist. For, the various mind-nerve-fibres of Descartes' that have been alleged to be its parts exist. And just as certain composite substances, such as this chair and the French flag, exist along with the partial substances which they include, so some such entity as we have been considering, composed of mind-nerve-fibres of Descartes', is presented without any of the characteristics that would mark it as unreal and is indeed listed as real in the appendix to Chapter Three.

To be sure, the mind-nerve-fibre of Descartes' with a mental attitude apparently directed upon man, God and the universe is a part of several composite substances which are real. The moon and the earth, we may say, constitute a system, a composite substance, which is real. The solar system is a more extended composite substance which is real and which likewise includes the earth as one of its parts. And so with the galaxy which includes our solar system and of which the earth is again a part. In an analogous manner we may say that there is a composite substance which includes Descartes' mind-nerve-fibre with a mental attitude apparently directed upon man, God and the universe and which also includes other mind-nerve-fibres of his at various periods of his life when he seemed to be thinking about philosophical subjects; a composite substance, however, which does not include such mind-nerve-fibres of Descartes' as have mental attitudes apparently directed upon non-philosophical subjects. But there is also, we may agree, a composite substance which includes every mind-nerve-fibre which ever occurred within Descartes' body. There are in short systems within systems. There is one real composite substance composed of thinking, extended mind-nerve-fibres of Descartes' which has a greater duration and instantaneous phases with a greater extension. And there is another real composite substance composed of thinking, extended mind-nerve-fibres of Descartes' which has a lesser duration and instantaneous phases with a lesser extension. The latter may have, not the quality that one of its parts has, not the quality of having a mental attitude apparently directed upon man, God and the universe, but the quality of thinking philosophically. The former may have, not the quality that one of *its* parts has, not the quality of having a mental attitude apparently directed upon the stove, but the quality of now and then being more or less aware.

There are then various composite substances that are real, one more inclusive than another, but each having thinking, extended mind-nerve-fibres of Descartes' among its parts. There is in particular a composite substance, which on the one hand has no parts outside Descartes' body, but which on the other hand may not include every thinking extended nerve-fibre that is within his body. The mind-nerve-fibres, if any, which, although within Descartes' body, are not parts of this particular composite substance, are those which we shall say are not parts of a single "person." There are, we are told, divided personalities. And if one group of Descartes' mind-nerve-fibres holds together to form a Mr. Hyde whereas another group holds together to form a Dr. Jekyll, then it is only one of these two groups that furnishes parts for the particular composite substance which we are describing. The mind-nerve-fibres which constitute the particular composite substance that we are describing have in short a special type of coherence. The particular composite substance which they compose we call a "person." And whereas one of a person's component mind-nerve-fibres may have a mental attitude that we describe as apparently directed upon the stove or as apparently directed upon Queen Christina, the person taken as a whole has a mental quality that we may call its "personality."

There are, we have agreed, various groups of Descartes' thinking extended mind-nerve-fibres which are real. There exists the group which, taken together, we call Descartes' person. And there exists the mental quality which this composite substance has, its personality. Similarly there exists the substance that is my person and the substance that is your person, the quality that is my personality and the quality that is your personality. In this treatise we have, to be sure, discussed the existence of Descartes' person after having agreed to the existence of a particular mind-nerve-fibre of his, have discussed the existence of his personality after having agreed to the existence of his mental attitude apparently directed upon man, God and the universe. But it is not to be concluded that wholes and parts are generally presented in this order. I may first seem to be aware of a chair and may subsequently discriminate within this chair its seat, its back and its legs. Similarly I may first seem to be aware of a person as a whole, a person which has some duration as well as extension; and I may subsequently seem to be aware of some phase or of some part of this person, of some mind-nerve-fibre or mind-nerve-fibres that have a lesser duration or a lesser extension. Thus it is not to be concluded from the order in which they are presented in this treatise that mind-nerve-fibres with their mental attitudes have a greater reality than what we call "persons" with their personalities, or that the former are normally presented as apparent objects before the latter.

Indeed if we begin with a person as a whole as our apparent object, there is, it would seem, no fixed number of parts or phases to be discriminated within that person. One thinker may, figuratively speaking, break an apparent object up into fifteen parts where another breaks it up into ten parts. For, as we shall later find occasion to observe, "unity, duality and multiplicity are, it seems, relative qualities." [14] The composite substance which we call Descartes' "person" is, it will be remembered, but one substance in a series of "systems within systems." [15] The mind-nerve-fibres which are its parts have a special type of coherence.[16] There may thus be mind-nerve-fibres within Descartes' body which do not have this coherence and which consequently are not parts of his person. But with such non-coherent mind-nerve-fibres excluded, Descartes' person does not have an absolute, rather than a relative, number of parts. It has many parts or few parts, many phases or few phases, according as the person taken as a whole is discriminated into many parts or into few parts, into many phases or into few phases.

There exist various persons with their personalities, various parts of persons with their mental attitudes. We must look outside this chapter to justify the conclusion that persons and personalities, parts of persons and mental attitudes, are not only in some instances real, but in some instances real objects for thinking subjects. Assuming however that there are situations in which a subject has first an including substance as his real object and subsequently one of its partial substances as his real object, let us call the sequence an instance of "discrimination." And assuming that there are situations in which a subject has first a substance as his real object and subsequently a quality of that substance as his real object, let us call the sequence an instance of "abstraction." We are thus discriminating when we turn our attention from Descartes' person to one of his mind-nerve-fibres, abstracting when we turn our attention from his person to his personality or from a mind-nerve-fibre of his to the mental attitude which that mind-nerve-fibre has as a quality. It is not Descartes' person, but one of his mind-nerve-fibres, that has a mental attitude. And yet if we say, as we shall, that "Descartes had a mental attitude," our proposition is true in the sense in which "Caesar crossed the Rubicon" is true. "Caesar crossed the Rubicon" is true in so far as it is synonymous with our existential proposition: "Caesar-at-moment-M, having the quality of crossing the Rubicon, exists." [17] And "Descartes had a mental attitude apparently directed upon man, God and the universe" is true in so far as it is synonymous with our existential proposition: "A mind-nerve-fibre that was a part of Descartes' person, a mind-nerve-fibre with a mental attitude apparently directed upon man, God and the universe, exists."

The mind-nerve-fibres, that taken together are Descartes' person, constitute, let us repeat, but one of several systems within systems. In constituting the particular system that they *do* constitute, they exhibit a special type of coherence. But what *is* this special type of coherence? What makes Descartes' mental attitude apparently directed upon the stove and Descartes' mental attitude apparently directed upon Queen Christina qualities that inhere in parts of one person? What common characteristics, if any, do these mental attitudes have? And what holds together and unifies the partial substances in which they inhere?

What we seek is some further description of the special type of coherence that holds together mental attitudes inhering in parts of the same person. As an answer it may be suggested that, where this coherence exists, the cohering mental attitudes are all apparent objects for the same subject. Mental attitudes, however, are to be distinguished from what we call "private contents" or "ideas." [18] Hence it is one thing to suggest that certain *mental attitudes* are held together and exhibit a special type of coherence in so far as they are apparent objects for the same subject. And it is another thing to suggest that alleged private contents or ideas are held together by being apparent objects for the same subject. "I myself," says Berkeley,[19] "am not my ideas but . . . a thinking active principle that perceives, knows, wills and operates about ideas. I know that I, one and the same self, perceive both colors and sounds: that a color can not perceive a sound, nor a sound a color: that I am therefore one individual principle, distinct from color and sound; and for the same reason from all other sensible things and inert ideas." The entities however that we in this chapter have found cohering are, not an idea of color and an idea of sound, but such entities as Berkeley's mental attitude apparently directed upon a color and Berkeley's mental attitude apparently directed upon a sound. If ideas exist and are inert, they may be held to imply a thinking substance that in some figurative sense is active, an entity that is or has what we have called a mental attitude. But if it is to be held that Berkeley's mental attitude apparently directed upon a color and Berkeley's mental attitude apparently directed upon a sound require some further entity that is apparently directed upon both of these *mental attitudes,* then the observation that a color can not perceive a sound is irrelevant. Even, however, if Berkeley's arguments do not all apply when the subject-matter is altered, it may still be maintained—so far as we have yet seen—that Berkeley's mental attitude apparently directed upon a color and Berkeley's mental attitude apparently directed upon a sound are each apparent objects for the same entity, that their coherence is due to the fact that "one and the same self" is aware of them both.

There exist, let us agree, certain mental attitudes which are apparently directed upon other mental attitudes. For just as Descartes' mental attitude apparently directed upon the stove is real, so, let us say, there is a real mental attitude of yours that is apparently directed upon Descartes' mental attitude. There likewise exist, let us say, certain mental attitudes which are apparently directed upon mental attitudes of one's own. For just as my present mental attitude is real that is apparently directed upon the mental attitude inhering in one of Descartes' mind-nerve-fibres as he paced up and down his stove-heated room, so my present mental attitude is real that is apparently directed upon a mental attitude I had last night when I was looking at the moon. To go one step further, there are, let us say, certain mental attitudes which are apparently directed upon themselves. For it is such a mental attitude that one of my present mind-nerve-fibres has when I now say: "Let me think about the mental attitude which inheres in the mind-nerve-fibre of mine that is now thinking."

Your mental attitude apparently directed upon a mental attitude of Descartes' is, we hold, real; my mental attitude apparently directed upon a mental attitude that I had last night real; my mental attitude apparently directed upon itself real. We are not at this point asserting that these mental attitudes which we hold to be real do in fact *reach* to the entities that seem to be presented to them. We are not at this point asserting, that is to say, that these mental attitudes have apparent objects which are their *real* objects. Nor are we asserting that their apparent objects are percepts with respect to them. A mental attitude that Descartes had may be neither a sense datum nor a percept with respect to the mental attitude of yours that is apparently directed upon it.[20] And my present mental attitude may not be a percept with respect to itself, with respect, that is to say, to the mental attitude of mine that is apparently directed upon itself. If the sort of perceiving called "introspecting" exists, it would seem to involve a relation between a slightly later mind-nerve-fibre which introspects and a slightly earlier mind-nerve-fibre within the same body which is introspected. Assuming, however, that it is not presented as an instance of introspecting as thus described, your alleged mental attitude, presented as apparently directed upon a mental attitude of Descartes', is, we hold, real. And assuming that *it* likewise is not presented as an instance of introspecting as thus described, my mental attitude, presented as apparently directed upon itself, is also real.

Thus Descartes' mental attitude apparently directed upon the stove may have itself or another mental attitude apparently directed upon it. And Descartes' mental attitude apparently directed upon Queen Christina may have itself or another mental attitude apparently directed upon *it*. But in so far as the mental attitude apparently directed upon the stove is apparently directed upon itself, and the mental attitude apparently directed upon Queen Christina apparently directed upon *it*-self, what we seem to have before us are separated mental attitudes which need not be parts of one person. We are presented with various mental attitudes of Descartes' each aware of *it*self; not with various mental attitudes of Descartes' each belonging to *his* self.

What, then, about some one persisting entity that has each of Descartes' mental attitudes as its apparent object? Is the coherence between Descartes' mental attitude apparently directed upon the stove and Descartes' mental attitude apparently directed upon Queen Christina a coherence that points back to some persisting entity to be called Descartes' "self," some persisting entity that is aware of both of these mental attitudes? There is, to be sure, the composite substance which we call Descartes' "person." But Descartes' person, we find, has the mind-nerve-fibre with a mental attitude apparently directed upon the stove and the mind-nerve-fibre with a mental attitude apparently directed upon Queen Christina, not as its objects, but as its parts. Descartes' person, we have seen, had a mental attitude apparently directed upon man, God and the universe in the sense that such a mental attitude inhered in a mind-nerve-fibre which was one of its parts.[21] But, whereas Descartes' mental attitude apparently directed upon the stove and his mental attitude apparently directed upon Queen Christina may have been apparent objects for themselves or for other mental attitudes of his, they were not, let us agree, apparent objects for his enduring person taken as a whole. We say, to be sure, that Descartes *"had"* various mental attitudes or that various mental attitudes were *"his."* But the system which we call "Descartes' person" does not *possess* mental attitudes except in the sense in which a French flag possesses the blueness which inheres in one of its parts.[22] And Descartes' person taken as a whole was not *aware* of mental attitudes; although our language, in calling mental attitudes *"his,"* may seem to assert the existence of a "he" that is outside his attitudes.[23]

It is not the person taken as a whole which is aware of each of Descartes' mental attitudes. There is no entity outside Descartes' person, no entity, at any rate, which endures while his person endures, which either possesses, or is aware of, these mental attitudes. And there is likewise no transcendental Ego, presented as having no date at all, which possesses or is aware of them. "No knowledge can take place in us," says Kant,[24] "no conjunction or unity of one kind of knowledge with another, without that unity of consciousness which precedes all data of intuition."

204

But an empirical Ego, presented as an entity which is not the person, but presented as an entity which persists unchanged during the life of the person, is, we find, presented as generally discredited and is unreal. And a transcendental Ego, presented as having no date, is presented with a timelessness that marks it out as unreal in our sense of "reality." Except in the sense in which every object implies a subject, the coherence exhibited by mental attitudes inhering in parts of one person does not point to an entity outside these mental attitudes taken collectively. This coherence may, to be sure, be called a "unity of consciousness" or a "unity of apperception." But if neither the person taken as a whole nor any entity outside the person, if neither an empirical Ego nor a transcendental Ego, is definitely aware of each of the mental attitudes inhering in a part of the person, then it is difficult to see what the phrase "unity of apperception" adds to the phrase: "special type of coherence."

There is one sense in which "unity of apperception" may be used in which this phrase seems to represent an entity other than that represented by our phrase: "special type of coherence." There were mental attitudes of Descartes' which had other mental attitudes of his apparently directed upon them. Just as the various mental attitudes inhering in parts of Descartes' person may be said to have cohered in a system, so the mental attitudes of his which had other attitudes of his directed upon them may be said to have cohered in a more limited system of their own. But if the one system is more limited than the other, if not every mental attitude of Descartes' had another mental attitude of his apparently directed upon it, then the coherence of the more limited system is not the coherence of the more inclusive system. Each mental attitude of Descartes' that was introspected, or that had some other mental attitude of his directed upon it, has the characteristic of having been introspected or the characteristic of having had some other mental attitude of his directed upon it. And in using the term "unity of apperception," we may be referring to the characteristic which these introspected mental attitudes had in common. There *were,* however, real mental attitudes of Descartes' which were not introspected by him. There were, let us agree, real mental attitudes, inhering in parts of the system that we call Descartes' person, upon which no other mental attitudes of his were definitely directed. It is as qualities of parts of a more inclusive system that these non-introspected mental attitudes cohere; as qualities of parts of the *person*, not as qualities of parts of a system from which non-introspected mental attitudes are excluded. Their coherence is not the sort of unity of apperception that would imply that each cohering mental attitude has been introspected. Theirs is a special type of coherence exhibited by various mental attitudes of Descartes', some of which may have been introspected and some of which were not introspected. It is this special type of coherence exhibited by mental attitudes inhering in parts of a person that we seek to describe in other terms, in terms that are more informative.

What we call a special type of coherence is not commensurate with introspectedness. But is it not commensurate with introspectability? The mental attitude which I had last night when I was looking at the moon inheres in a part of my person even though I did not introspect it. But does it not inhere in a part of my person in that I *might* have introspected it? Where difficulty arises is in distinguishing non-introspected mental attitudes that might have been introspected from non-introspected mental attitudes that could *not* have been introspected. If the term "introspecting" represents the sort of perceiving which involves a relation between a slightly earlier mind-nerve-fibre that is introspected and a slightly later mind-nerve-fibre that introspects,[25] then no mental attitude of mine today—and no future mental attitude of mine—can introspect the mental attitude which I failed to introspect last night. I may assert that the mental attitude which I failed to introspect last night might have been introspected by a mental attitude occurring slightly later last night. But such an assertion adds nothing to the assertion that the mental attitude which I failed to introspect inheres in a part of my person and coheres with other mental attitudes of mine. For the belief in such a coherence is the only basis I have for the assertion that last night's mental attitude might have been introspected.

Let us then turn from the introspecting, which, if it exists, is a sort of perceiving, to the mental attitude which has another mental attitude, not necessarily as its percept, but in any case as its apparent object. It may be suggested that last night's mental attitude inhered in a part of my person in that a present mental attitude of mine may apparently be directed upon it. But Descartes' mental attitude was not yours, even though your present mental attitude is apparently directed upon that attitude of Descartes.' Last night's mental attitude inhered in a part of my person, it would seem, not in that my present mental attitude is apparently directed upon it, but in that my present mental attitude asserts it to have been *mine*. The proposition which we are to consider comes thus to be this: "Two mental attitudes cohere with what we have called a 'special type of coherence' when one of these mental attitudes believes and asserts that they so cohere." But I am not describing coherence in other terms when I say that two mental attitudes cohere when one of them asserts that they cohere. Furthermore, it would seem that my present mental attitude and last night's mental attitude may not have inhered in parts of the same person even though my present mental attitude asserts that they did. If my mind is deranged, I may believe myself to be Napoleon, may assert that his mental attitude at Waterloo inhered in a part of my person. And even if my mind is not deranged, I may seem to remember, may seem to have as an apparent object, some mental attitude which I never had.

Two mental attitudes cohere with what we have called a special type of coherence, two mental attitudes inhere in parts of the same person, not, let us say, whenever one of these mental attitudes asserts that they cohere, but whenever their alleged coherence is presented as not generally discredited and is real. To be sure, the statement: "Two mental attitudes cohere when their alleged coherence is presented as not generally discredited and is real" is no more an explanation of "coherence" than is the statement: "Two mental attitudes cohere when one of them believes and asserts that they cohere." But perhaps our search for some further general description of what we call a "special type of coherence" can fail; and our term "special type of coherence" nevertheless be understood. Taken by itself, the proposition: "Two mental attitudes cohere when one of them believes and asserts that they cohere" fails to explain "coherence." But, in addition, it is false. Taken by itself, the proposition: "Two mental attitudes cohere when their alleged coherence is presented as not generally discredited and is real" likewise fails to explain "coherence." But it is, we hold, true. And it will lead us to point to individual situations serving to distinguish the coherent from the incoherent.

Let us suppose that Napoleon had certain mental attitudes at the battle of Waterloo and that a patient at St. Elizabeth's in Washington asserts that these attitudes were his. His statement asserting the coherence of mental attitudes at Waterloo with mental attitudes at Washington seems to be generally understood. But the alleged coherence that he seems to be asserting is presented as generally discredited and is therefore unreal. I may likewise assert that a mental attitude last night when I was looking at the moon coheres with my present mental attitudes. Again the statement asserting coherence seems to be generally understood. And in this instance the alleged coherence that is asserted is not presented as generally discredited and is real. When the body has not changed fundamentally, testimony that there is coherence, coming from a mental attitude inhering in a part of that body, seems generally, though not always, to meet with general acceptance. And so there are many instances in which, when coherence has been asserted between some earlier mental attitude and some later mental attitude, and when the speaker's body has undergone no fundamental change, that alleged coherence is not presented as generally discredited and is real. As we have explained "existence" and "reality," general credence or discredence is a consideration of greater relevance than the speaker's beliefs. The Sparrow may assert, and may seem to believe, that he never had an intention to kill Cock Robin. But if coherence between such an intention and a later mental attitude of the Sparrow's is not presented as generally discredited, such an alleged coherence may very well be real.

Your mental attitude does not cohere with a mental attitude of Descartes' even though you seem to be aware of that mental attitude of Descartes'. The mental attitude of the patient at St. Elizabeth's does not cohere with Napoleon's mental attitude at Waterloo even though the patient at St. Elizabeth's seems to be aware of Napoleon at Waterloo. A contemporary of mine may be aware of what happened to some one at a distant place or in a bygone era. And if we find no normal channel through which his knowledge may have been acquired, we may be led to believe in telepathy or in some impulse, delayed in transmission, that

208

originated in some past mental attitude and is now affecting my contemporary. But such puzzling phenomena as may be due to telepathy do not, I find, lead to the general belief that two mental attitudes, distant from one another, cohere in parts of the same person. And if a contemporary of mine, without having studied Greek history or the Greek language, should think and speak as Plato did, this likewise, we hold, would not lead to the general belief that his mental attitudes and Plato's cohere in parts of one person, or to the belief that Plato's person has a phase existing now. Not only would the method of transmission not be resolved by the mere assertion of coherence, but coherence, we find, when it is alleged to hold between mental attitudes not in the same body, is presented as generally discredited and is unreal. There is no coherence of the special type which we have been discussing where there is the sort of discontinuity that there is between Descartes' body and yours or between Plato's body and the entities that exist today. In this sense there is no transmigration of souls and no person that endures subsequent to the disintegration of its body.

Is there then no force in the classic arguments for the immortality of the soul? "The compound or composite may be supposed to be naturally capable of being dissolved in like manner as of being compounded; but that which is uncompounded," we read in the *Phaedo*,[26] must be indissoluble if anything is indissoluble." To what extent, however, is a mind-nerve-fibre uncompounded or its mental attitude uncompounded, a person uncompounded or its personality uncompounded? Both the mind-nerve-fibre and the composite substance which we call a "person" have extension. Both are divisible in the sense in which a bolt of blue cloth is divisible. 'Mental attitude' and 'personality' are, to be sure, qualities. And just as it may be held that blue is a primary color, but purple not, so it may be held that 'mental attitude' is indivisible in the sense of not being analyzable into other qualities. But just as the blueness of a bolt of cloth is divisible in the sense that the bolt of cloth in which it inheres is divisible, so mental attitudes and personalities are divisible in the sense that the extended substances in which they inhere are divisible.[27] It may, to be sure, be held that mental attitudes and personalities, mind-nerve-fibres and persons, are not the only entities to be considered. Mind-

209

nerve-fibres with their mental attitudes have dates; persons with their personalities have dates. There is however, it may be held, some soul or self or ego which has no date. And what has no date, it may be argued, can not be subject to so temporal a happening as perishing. As we have explained "existence," however, there is no soul which has no date. A transcendental Ego which is presented as having no date is unreal.[28] And any soul or self which is presented as having no date is unreal. There are real mind-nerve-fibres and real mental attitudes, real persons and real personalities. And each of them has a final phase which is temporal. There is no entity which has no date, hence no entity which, in addition to having no date, is neither a mind-nerve-fibre nor a mental attitude, neither a person nor a personality.

It will be remembered that the system which we call "Descartes' person" is one of several systems within systems, and that what we call a "special type of coherence" is the coherence exhibited by mental attitudes inhering in parts of the same person.[29] There are systems, however, which are *not* persons. And the mental attitudes inhering in parts of a system that is not a person may exhibit a coherence which is not an instance of what we have called a "special type of coherence." There is "no person that endures subsequent to the disintegration of its body." [30] And no entity is real that is presented as having no date. Provided, however, that it is not presented as timeless and not presented as a person, there may, so far as we have yet seen, be some system of thinking substances which does not perish with the disintegration of a body with which it has been associated. Provided that it is not presented as timeless and not presented as a person, such a system, so far as we have yet seen, may in some sense be immortal, and may be composed of thinking substances exhibiting *some* sort of coherence.

There can be no causal relation, it may be held, between two entities one of which is thinking and the other unthinking.[31] But mental attitudes *do* exist. They point back to earlier entities which caused them; and they bring about subsequent entities which are their effects. From such premises the alleged conclusion may be drawn that mental attitudes point back only to other mental attitudes which are their causes and issue only into other mental attitudes which are their effects. Thus we are presented

210

with an alleged causal chain of mental attitudes, the last of which may be subsequent to the disintegration of a given body and the first of which may have antedated that body.[32] We are presented with a chain of thinking substances that constitutes a system, a chain of thinking substances which is not a person, but which may be held to exhibit some coherence, though not the special type of coherence which we have examined.

It is, to be sure, not true that there can be no causal relation between thinking entities and unthinking entities.[33] And if the chain of thinking substances that is presented to us is alleged to have earlier and earlier phases without any beginning, and later and later phases without any end, then this chain or system is presented with so indefinite a date that it is marked out as unreal. For a subsistent is unreal, we have said,[34] "if it appears with the characteristic of having only a very indefinite date with respect to an entity that appears real." The argument recounted in the preceding paragraph does not imply that a chain of successive mental attitudes *must* be real. And such a chain presented as everlasting, or presented as so enduring that it is presented as having only a very indefinite date, *can not* be real. Presented however as having a date that is not too indefinite, presented nevertheless as enduring subsequent to the disintegration of some body with which it has been associated, such a chain of successive mental attitudes *may* be real. The system, in which these mental attitudes, taken together, inhere, is one of the systems that "may in some sense be immortal," is one of the systems that "may be composed of thinking substances exhibiting *some* sort of coherence."[35]

Persons are not the only systems of thinking substances exhibiting some sort of coherence. The coherence characteristic of a person is not identical with the coherence exhibited by a system of thinking substances which has parts or phases in different bodies. And the coherence characteristic of a person may not be identical with the coherence exhibited by a system of thinking substances composed of all the thinking substances within my body. "There are, we are told, divided personalities,"[36] that is to say, two or more persons within one body. It may be that various cells scattered through my body have mental qualities of some sort and yet are not parts of my person. And it may be that bacteria for whom my body is host, or that leucocytes within my

211

blood-stream, have some rudimentary form of mental life. Should such alleged thinking substances be real, or should there be both a Dr. Jekyll and a Mr. Hyde within my body, the composite substance composed of all the thinking substances within my body might well have phases more extended than that composite substance which I call my "person." Each phase of the composite substance composed of all the thinking substances within my body might, that is to say, be co-extensive with my body, each phase of my *person* limited to my cortex.[37] Nevertheless there *is* a substance from which none of the thinking substances within my body are excluded. Such a substance, even though it is not a person, may be called a "system." Such a system, even though it does not exhibit a coherence of the special type that a person exhibits, may be said to be held together in some way, may be said to exhibit a coherence of some sort.

There are thinking substances which are parts of my person, some of which may be introspected and some of which are not introspected. There are, let us agree, substances within my body which have no mental attitudes. And there may be substances within my body which have mental attitudes, but which are not parts of my person. If to be conscious is to be thinking, to have mental attitudes, then it is only those substances within my body which have *no* mental attitudes that, literally speaking, constitute my "*un*conscious." If, on the other hand, we extend the denotation of "unconscious" to include whatever is not introspected, then the mental attitude of mine which I failed to introspect last night, the mental attitude of which I now seem to be aware and which I now claim coheres with other mental attitudes of mine, inheres in a part of my unconscious. The word "unconscious," it would appear, is used in various senses. Some instances of this word may refer to mental attitudes which inhere in parts of my body, but not in parts of my person. And some instances may refer to substances which shift, so to speak, from one group to another. It may be held, for example, that there are substances within my body that have successive phases; and it may be held that, with respect to a substance of this sort, there may be an earlier phase which has a mental attitude and a later phase which does not, or an earlier phase which thinks and inheres in a part of my person and a later phase which thinks but does not inhere in a part of my person. With such facts assumed, it may be the unthinking phase, of what in some other phase thinks, that is said to be a part of the unconscious. Or with such facts assumed, the entity said to be a part of the unconscious may be the phase, not a part of my person, of what in some other phase *is* a part of my person.

Let us agree that there are some substances within my body with respect to which thinking phases alternate with unthinking phases. Let us further agree that there are some substances whose phases that are parts of my person alternate with phases that are not parts of my person. Finally, let us agree that there may be phases of my *body* when there are no phases of my *person*. Let us agree, that is to say, that my person may be discontinuous, that each of the nerve-fibres, which today constitute my person, may last night have lacked mental attitudes exhibiting what we call a "special type of coherence." It may be pointed out that criminal courts seem to find relevant the defense that, when a given crime was committed, the accused was not "himself." [38] And last night when I was asleep, whereas there were thinking substances within my body, it seems plausible to hold that none of them had mental attitudes exhibiting a coherence of the special type that would have determined them to inhere in parts of my person. In short, a person alleged to be discontinuous need not be presented as generally discredited; and some allegedly discontinuous person, not presented as generally discredited, is, I find, real. [39]

Thus the thinking substances which have phases that are parts of my person bear some resemblance, we may say, to a group of bulbs on an instrument board. Just at it may be one set of these bulbs that is now shining and now another set, so my person may now have certain nerve-fibres as its parts and now others. And just as occasionally all of the lights on an instrument board may be out, so my person may be discontinuous. Just, that is to say, as there may be no lights shining, so there may on occasion be no phase of my person. Even, however, if my person is discontinuous, there is a sense in which it may be said to be "one." Even if many phases may be discriminated within it, phases between which entities that are not parts of my person intervene, nevertheless my person need not be presented as a collection of units rather than as itself a unit. A net may be said to be one even though there are interstices between the strands that compose it. And the light from a light-house may be said to have shone through the night, although intermittently.[40]

The system of thinking substances that we call my "person" is, we hold, discontinuous. But what constitutes an interruption of my person may not constitute an interruption of some other system of thinking substances exhibiting some other type of coherence. If the leucocytes within my blood-stream have some rudimentary form of mental life,[41] if they are parts of a composite substance composed of all the thinking substances within my body, then, whereas my person was interrupted last night, some more inclusive system of thinking substances may not have been. Moreover, there may be intermediate systems of thinking substances, systems more inclusive than my person but less inclusive than that which is composed of all the thinking substances within my body. We would, to be sure, be hard put to describe the coherence that characterizes each system in such a series of systems within systems. And we would be hard put to determine with which system discontinuity ends and with which more inclusive system continuity begins. The boundaries between one system and another seem too fluid to permit us to describe with accuracy the type of coherence that characterizes any one of them. The system that we call my person has however been described with a fair degree of definiteness; and so has the system that we call the substance composed of all the thinking substances within my body.

Yet whatever systems are distinguished and placed before us, it is still a problem to determine in which systems a given mental attitude is to be included and from which systems it is to be excluded. Does a given mental attitude inhere in a part of my person; or does it not? Does it exhibit, or fail to exhibit, a coherence of the sort that characterizes the particular system in which it may be alleged to be included? A mental attitude of Napoleon's at Waterloo and a mental attitude of a patient at St. Elizabeth's in Washington may be alleged to exhibit the type of coherence that would determine them to inhere in parts of the same person. But if these mental attitudes, so presented, are presented as generally discredited, then they do not have a co-

214

herence of the type ascribed to them.[42] Similarly with mental attitudes alleged to inhere in leucocytes within my blood-stream. If these leucocytes are presented as generally believed to have no mental attitudes at all, if, consequently, any type of coherence exemplified by mental attitudes is presented as generally believed not to obtain between leucocytes and other thinking substances, then these leucocytes do not think; and no coherence of any type obtains between them and substances within my body that really think. In short, for any special type of coherence to characterize a given mental attitude, that mental attitude, presented as exhibiting a coherence of that type, must be presented as not generally discredited. Just as an entity, alleged to have a mental attitude, really *has* that mental attitude only if, presented as having it, it is not presented as generally discredited, so a mental attitude, alleged to be included in a particular system, really *is* included in that system only if, presented as being included in that system, it is not presented as generally discredited.

"There are behaviorists," we have said,[43] "who find that, when they attempt to abstract thinking, mental attitude, mental activity, from Descartes' mind-brain or mind-nerve-fibre or total behavior, there is an irruption of disbelief similar to that which breaks in upon us when we attempt to abstract from this rectangular desk its alleged roundness." A Descartes who not only behaves but also thinks is presented as seemingly disbelieved by some behaviorists, but not as generally disbelieved. A Descartes who not only behaves but also thinks is not presented as generally discredited and is, we have found, real. Similarly with my dog Fido presented as having within his body substances with mental attitudes. Mental attitudes attributed to substances within Fido's body and alleged to be apparently directed upon man, God and the universe are, to be sure, presented as generally discredited; and so are alleged introspecting mental attitudes of Fido's. But alleged mental attitudes of Fido's apparently directed upon Kitty or apparently directed upon dog biscuits are not. Aside from Descartes and a few moderns, everyone, says Fechner,[44] "takes the nightingale singing in the tree and the lion roaring in the desert to be something more than acoustic machines." Thus various mental attitudes, alleged to inhere in substances that are parts of animals, seem to be presented as not generally discredited. Various mental attitudes, alleged to inhere in substances that are parts of animals, not only *may* be listed as real, but, let us assume, are listed as real.

Let us then hold that not only was Descartes' mental attitude apparently directed upon man, God and the universe real, but also Fido's mental attitude apparently directed upon Kitty. And let us hold that not only was Descartes' mental attitude apparently directed upon Queen Christina real, but also the mental attitude alleged to inhere in one of the leucocytes within my blood-stream. In holding, however, that various animals have mental attitudes, we are not precluded from holding that mental attitudes of a certain type are restricted to men. "Thinking" and "having a mental attitude" are, as we use these words, generic terms. And just as a green substance may be pea-green or emerald green, so a thinking substance may be conceiving or introspecting or feeling. It may be that none but men conceive, that none but men introspect. But whereas a mental attitude apparently directed towards man, God and the universe, which Fido is alleged to have, is, I find, presented as generally discredited and is unreal, nevertheless a mental attitude that is an instance of fearing, which some non-human animal is alleged to have is, I find, not presented as generally discredited and is real.

There are behaviorists, let us repeat, who disbelieve in the mental attitude which is alleged to inhere in one of Descartes' mind-nerve-fibres. But the alleged mental attitude of Descartes' which we finally considered was not presented as generally discredited and was, we found, real. There are, as Fechner says, "Descartes and a few moderns" who disbelieve in the mental attitude which is alleged to inhere in some part of Fido's body or in a leucocyte's. But some of these alleged mental attitudes are likewise, we find, not presented as generally discredited, and are likewise, we find, real. When, however, we turn to the thinking substance which is alleged to be embodied in, or to animate, a rolling ball or the sun or wind, we find disbelief more general. It is not only certain behaviorists, but most of us, who find that when we attempt to abstract its alleged mental attitude from a rolling ball "there is an irruption of disbelief similar to that which breaks in upon us when we attempt to abstract from this rectangular desk its alleged roundness."[45] The alleged mental attitude which we are considering, the mental attitude which is alleged to inhere in inorganic matter, is, let us say, presented as generally discredited. And any mental attitude which is alleged to inhere in inorganic matter is, let us say, unreal.

The world of real entities, as we have explained "reality," includes mental attitudes inhering in substances to be found within the bodies of animals, but no mental attitudes to be found in inorganic matter. What shall we say, however, with respect to plants? Plants live; they reproduce themselves; and, like animals, they grow through intussusception. Shall we say that, just as conceiving, introspecting and feeling are species of mental attitudes, so there is a species of mental attitude that is indistinguishable from life, from reproduction and from growth through intussusception? Or shall we say that, despite the fact that mental attitudes are of various species, there is no species of mental attitude that is implied merely by life, by reproduction, and by growth through intussusception? Aristotle, writers of the Renaissance, Leibniz and others put before us such terms as "psyche," "anima," "soul," "entelechy," "monad"—terms which frequently seem to represent 'vital principle' as well as 'mental attitude.' And if our term "mental attitude" had a similar meaning, if our term "mental attitude" were to represent a vital principle manifested wherever there is life, there would of course be some species of mental attitude, instances of which would be qualities of living plants.

As we use "mental attitude," however, "mental attitude" and "vital principle" are not synonymous. "We may pass from a consideration of Descartes' total behavior," we have said,[46] "to a consideration of his knitted brow or distant stare." "Or," we have said, "we may pass to a consideration of his alleged thinking." His thinking is distinguishable from his staring; and it is likewise distinguishable from his living. There are, to be sure, species of mental attitude that are exemplified in qualities inhering in mind-nerve-fibres of Descartes', and not exemplified in qualities inhering in a leucocyte. But those qualities inhering in a leucocyte which we call "mental attitudes" are distinguishable from the leucocyte's quality of being alive or from the leucocyte's vital principle; just as the quality that we call "Descartes' mental attitude" is distinguishable from the quality of being alive that accompanies it. As we use "mental attitude," a plant's alleged mental attitude is not presented as identical with the plant's quality of being alive. If our term "a plant's mental attitude" represents anything, it represents something comparable to an instance of feeling rather than something implied by the fact that the plant lives, reproduces, and grows through intussusception.

What then shall we say with respect to the existence or non-existence of a mental attitude, comparable to a feeling, that a plant may be alleged to have? The subsistent that I seem to be considering is presented as not a feeling, but as comparable to a feeling, as mental life of a rudimentary form, but as mental life that is not of any of the forms with which I am familiar. This alleged mental attitude appears, I find, in the undetailed manner in which 'everything' appears.[47] And it likewise appears with the characteristic of appearing in a detailed manner to no one. It is, in short, one of those subsistents, "explicitly or implicitly appearing as definite appearances for no one," which are unreal.[48] Thus the subsistent which I seem to be considering is unreal; and so are other alleged thinking plants. As we have explained "existence" and "reality," plants, consequently, do not think, do not have mental attitudes.

But if the transition from one form of life to another is gradual, how can we draw a line so that on one side there will be animals having mental attitudes of various types and on the other side plants having no mental attitudes at all? There are, we must agree, borderline cases; just as there are borderline cases between a tent and a house, between work and play, between neighboring colors in a spectrum. Such cases, however, do not force us to abandon all distinctions, do not lead us to say that whatever is a tent is a house and that whatever is a house is a tent. It may depend upon the system of classification used whether some borderline organism is a plant or an animal. Hence the denotation, and even the meaning, of the term "plant" will vary according as one system of classification is used or another. And to the extent to which the meaning of the term "plant" is unclear, so is the meaning of the proposition in which it is asserted that plants do not think. Without a drawing of lines between plants on the one side and animals on the other, the assertion that plants do not think is not, we must admit, completely definite. It does not follow, however, that the attempt to distinguish between plants and animals must be abandoned altogether, or the attempt to distinguish between organisms which may think and organisms which do not.

It still may be asked, however, why the distinction between organisms which may think, on the one hand, and organisms which do not, on the other, coincides with the distinction between animals and plants. The term "plant" may be assigned various meanings in that the line between plants and animals may be drawn at one point or at another. Yet there are not fewer organisms which think, it may be said, when "plant" has a more extensive denotation; nor are there more organisms which think, when "plant" has a narrower denotation. Now, we must agree that the proposition that only animals think is true only when "animal" and "plant" each have meanings which fall within a narrow range. Yet, within such a range of meanings, our terminology *does* seem to be a factor in determining whether or not a given borderline organism may have a mental attitude. Thinking exists only in such organisms as are not presented as generally discredited when presented as *thinking* organisms. And, with respect to certain borderline organisms, I find that mental attitudes attributed to them tend to be presented as generally discredited when these organisms are called "plants," whereas certain mental attitudes attributed to these borderline organisms are not presented as generally discredited when these organisms are called "animals."

We may grade the mental attitudes which are real, may present to ourselves an ordered series of mental attitudes, each mental attitude being of a different type. Thus we may have as an apparent object a series of mental attitudes, ordered in such a way that near one end of the series there is some instance of feeling inhering in a simple animal, near the other end an instance of conceiving inhering in some mind-nerve-fibre of a man. Such a series of mental attitudes, however, is not to be confused with a series of systems within systems. The series of mental attitudes which has as one of its initial members a feeling, as a subsequent member an instance of perceiving, and as a still later member an instance of conceiving, is not to be confused with a series of *systems* of mental attitudes which has as an earlier member a

219

substance including only those of my mind-nerve-fibres which have mental attitudes apparently directed upon philosophical subjects, as a later member the more inclusive substance which we call my "person," and as a still later member the substance including all parts of my body which have any mental attitudes at all. The one series may be alleged to have as a member, subsequent to the instance of conceiving that inheres in some mind-nerve-fibre of a man, an instance of some allegedly higher type of mental life inhering in some part of what is said to be an angel. The other series may be alleged to have as a member, subsequent to the substance including all thinking substances within my body, a substance which includes all thinking substances which are in or on the earth. But the coherence exhibited by mental attitudes inhering in parts of the composite substance which includes all thinking substances within my body is not itself an instance of conceiving. And the coherence exhibited by mental attitudes inhering in parts of the composite substance which includes all thinking substances on the earth is not itself an instance of some allegedly higher type of mental life.

There are in Fechner's writings some curious and perhaps edifying statements allegedly referring to the angel of the earth and to a heaven "filled with hosts of angels instead of with a system of dead bowling balls."[49] But if the substance composed of all the thinking substances on earth is to be called an "angel," it is an angel which feels, perceives and conceives only in so far as its parts feel, perceive and conceive; and the coherence exhibited by the mental attitudes inhering in its parts is a coherence quite different from that exhibited by mental attitudes inhering in parts of my person. It is a coherence much closer to that which characterizes the composite substance composed of all thinking substances within my body than it is to the coherence which characterizes my person.

There are mental attitudes which vary in type and systems of mental attitudes which vary in inclusiveness. We may group together mental attitudes characteristic of a certain epoch and may speak of the Romantic mind or of the spirit of Romanticism. But the coherence that relates mental attitudes of Schelling and mental attitudes of Schleiermacher is not the coherence that relates mental attitudes inhering in parts of the same person. We

220

may agree that the mental attitudes of one person are affected by the mental attitudes of those with whom he is associated. But no society, no corporation and no State, has a mental attitude of a special type which is coordinate with feeling, with perceiving and with conceiving. And no society, no corporation and no State, is characterized by a coherence of the type that we have found characterizing a person.

Summary

Is our doctrine interactionism or parallelism? The position taken is a form of interactionism in that mental attitudes, qualities of nerve-fibers, are held to affect, and to be affected by, substances in the environment. But this is not inconsistent with certain doctrines that might be called parallelist. There is a) concomitant variation between the series of mental attitudes and the series of non-mental characteristics of the nerve-fiber in which these mental attitudes inhere, b) correspondence between a series of mental attitudes and a series of external stimuli, but c) no parallelism of the sort Spinoza is often held to urge, i.e., no parallelism between mental content and objects referred to by that content.

Mental attitudes inhere in mind-nerve-fibers. A systematic series of mind-nerve-fibers constitutes a *person*. What we call "personality" inheres in a person just as a mental attitude inheres in a mind-nerve-fiber that is a part of (and "discriminated" from) that person.

What is it that holds certain mind-nerve-fibers together and makes them parts of one person? Various mental attitudes are not 'mine' because I claim they are mine or claim to be able to introspect them. Various mind-nerve-fibers constitute one person when they are generally believed to constitute one person.

The term 'the unconscious' may refer to mind-nerve-fibers which at the moment have no mental attitudes; or it may refer to *thinking* mind-nerve-fibers which are not parts of my person.

There are various grades of mental attitudes, conceiving, perceiving and so on down to the sort of mental attitude that characterizes leucocytes in the blood stream. Not to be confused with this classification is the fact that there are systems within systems of cohering mental attitudes. The system that we call a person is neither the most exclusive nor the most comprehensive. What we call a person has definite temporal limits (that is, it is not immortal). It is like the set of lit-up bulbs on an instrument board, where some bulbs are now lit up and at other times others.

Chapter VIII

THINKING, OBJECT AND IDEA

Two chapters back we directed our attention to certain mental attitudes which Descartes had, when, returning from the coronation of the Emperor, he found himself in a stove-heated room. Let us begin *this* chapter by turning back to the coronation itself. Let us take as our apparent object the ceremonies in which the Emperor and the Bishop of Mayence were among the actors and at which Descartes was an interested spectator. For our concern at this point is with the Emperor and Descartes in relation to one another; our concern is with certain relational situations within which Descartes and the Emperor may be alleged to have been terms.

For one thing, the Emperor may appear as the source of motions which flowed to Descartes, as the source of motions which affected Descartes' thinking and Descartes' behavior. Just as we have found [1] a ledger clerk's mind-nerve-fibre, its non-mental qualities and its thinking affected by the ledger from which this clerk was transcribing his figures, so Descartes' mind-nerve-fibre, its non-mental qualities and its thinking may appear as having been affected by the Emperor. With Descartes or his behavior or his thinking presented as result or as *terminus ad quem,* and with the Emperor presented as source or as cause, our apparent object may be an alleged causal relation flowing from the Emperor to Descartes. Our apparent object may be the alleged relational situation: Descartes-here-affected-by-Emperor-there or Emperor-there-affecting-Descartes here.

Instead, however, of our apparent object being what in some

sense may be called a causal relation, our apparent object may be an alleged relational situation within which one term is characterized by a response adapted to the other. If I say: "Come to dinner," then, as we use the words "adapted to," my auditor's response is, let us say, adapted to the meal that is about to be eaten. And if I hurl a ball and the dog at my feet starts after it, his response, let us say, is adapted to the ball that is about to fall to the ground some distance away. The alleged relational situation that we call "A-making-a-response-adapted-to-B" is thus distinguishable from the alleged relational situation that we call "A-affected-by-B." For, whereas it is to a future phase of the ball that my dog's response may be held to be adapted, it is the ball leaving my hand that may be said to bring about my dog's behavior. And whereas my words "Come to dinner" may be said to be the stimulus which leads my auditor to start for the table, it is to the meal about to be eaten that his response may be said to be adapted.

There is then the alleged relational situation Descartes-affected-by-the-Emperor and the alleged relational situation which we call "Descartes-making-a-response-adapted-to-the-Emperor." These alleged relational situations are presented as distinguishable from one another but not as requiring different terms. So far as we have yet seen, Descartes' response alleged to be adapted to the Emperor need not be presented as having been brought about by a neighbor's: "Here comes the Emperor!" It may be presented as having been brought about by the Emperor himself. Nor need it be one phase of the Emperor that is presented as the cause of Descartes' response, a later phase of the Emperor to which Descartes' response is presented as being adapted. To be sure, it is to a future phase of the ball that my dog's response has been presented as being adapted, to a meal *about to be* eaten that my dinner companion's response has been presented as being adapted. But if sunlight comes to me in a straight line from where the sun *was* rather than from where the sun now *is*, then, when I look at the sun, my response may be held to be adapted to a past phase of the sun rather than to the sun's present phase. As we use the expression "adapted to," A's response that is alleged to be adapted to B is presented as having a certain direction, as directed, as it were, to a certain focus. But that focus need not be presented as future rather than as present or past. Descartes' response may

224

be presented as adapted to a past phase of the Emperor, may be presented as adapted to the very phase of the Emperor that is alleged to have brought about his response. In short, Descartes-making-a-response-brought-about-by-the-Emperor and Descartes-making-a-response-adapted-to-the-Emperor are presented as distinguishable relational situations. And yet they are not presented as relational situations such that the terms of the one can not coincide with the terms of the other.

There is yet another alleged relational situation to be considered, a relational situation within which Descartes and the Emperor are again alleged to be terms. It is as a terminus of motions flowing towards him that Descartes or his mind-nerve-fibre is a term in the alleged relational situation: Descartes-affected-by-the-Emperor. And it is as an organism whose behavior has a direction that Descartes is a term in the alleged relational situation: Descartes-making-a-response-adapted-to-the-Emperor. Descartes' mind-nerve-fibre however has mental qualities as well as non-mental qualities.[2] And as an element within Descartes' total behavior there is Descartes' mental attitude.[3] Thus we may direct our attention to an alleged relational situation into which Descartes enters, not by virtue of his total behavior, but by virtue of his mental attitude. We may take as our apparent object, not the alleged relational situation: Descartes-making-a-response-adapted-to-the-Emperor, but rather the alleged relational situation: Descartes-having-a-mental-attitude-which-reaches-the-Emperor-as-its-ultimate-object.

Descartes, let us say, is making a certain response, is characterized by a certain behavior. And when we are presented with the alleged relational situation: Descartes-making-a-response-adapted-to-the-Emperor, this behavior that characterizes one term is, let us say, presented as being directed and adapted to a certain entity. Descartes or Descartes' mind-nerve-fibre is likewise alleged to have a mental attitude, a mental attitude which we may describe as seeming to be directed towards the Emperor. And when we are presented with the alleged relational situation: Descartes-having-a-mental-attitude-which-reaches-the-Emperor-as-its-ultimate-object, this mental attitude is, let us say, presented, not only as *seeming* to be directed towards the Emperor, but as *reaching* the Emperor as its ultimate object. Manifesting a certain behavior and having a mental attitude which seems to be directed towards the Emperor,—these, in short, are being presented as intrinsic qualities by virtue of which Descartes may be related to the Emperor. But our apparent object may not be a Descartes that, it is alleged, has a quality which permits him to be related to the Emperor; our apparent object may rather be a Descartes that, it is alleged, *is* related to the Emperor. Our apparent object may not be Descartes' intrinsic quality of behaving, but his alleged quality of manifesting a behavior that is adapted to the Emperor. Our apparent object may not be his intrinsic quality of having a mental attitude which seems to be directed towards the Emperor, but his alleged quality of having a mental attitude which reaches the Emperor as its ultimate object.

There subsists then the quality: Descartes' mental attitude reaching the Emperor as its ultimate object. And there subsists the relational situation: Descartes-having-a-mental-attitude-which-reaches-the-Emperor-as-its-ultimate-object or the-Emperor-reached-as-an-ultimate-object-by-Descartes'-thinking. Indeed there are several subsistents, distinguishable subsistents, each of which may seem to be represented by our expression: "The Emperor reached as an ultimate object by Descartes' thinking." The thinking Descartes, for example, may be held to have as an immediate object an idea of the Emperor, an idea which succeeds in referring beyond itself to the Emperor and which thus makes the Emperor the ultimate object of Descartes' thinking. Or the Emperor himself may be held to be, not merely the objective reached by Descartes' thinking, but also the immediate object of that thinking. The expression: "the Emperor reached as an ultimate object by Descartes' thinking" may seem to represent an allegedly unmediated relational situation within which Descartes appears as thinking subject and the Emperor himself as immediate object. Or this expression may seem to represent a relational situation within which we are presented not merely with an ultimate object and a thinking subject, but with an idea of the Emperor as well.

At this point, however, let us not differentiate between the alleged relational situation that is presented as direct and unmediated and the alleged relational situation that is presented as indirect and mediated by an idea. It may be that one of these alleged relational situations is real, the other not. But at this

226

point we choose to ask whether Emperor-reached-as-ultimate-object-by-Descartes'-thinking is real at all, however it may be particularized, whatever more definite characteristics may be ascribed to it. Also we present to ourselves the alleged relational situation: Descartes-here-affected-by-Emperor-there; and we present to ourselves the alleged relational situation: Descartes-making-a-response-adapted-to-the-Emperor. To whatever extent each of these subsistents may be in need of further differentiation, we turn first to the question whether or not in some form they are real.

Let us begin by agreeing that Descartes and the Emperor are each real. Each appears with the characteristic of being in Frankfurt in 1619; neither appears as generally discredited; and each is listed as real in the appendix to Chapter Three. Let us likewise agree that various intrinsic qualities of Descartes' are real; and various intrinsic qualities of the Emperor's. Just as we have agreed that Descartes in the stove-heated room was "knitting his brows" and "staring past the furniture that was around him," [4] so let us agree that Descartes in Frankfurt had an air of eagerness and attention. And just as we have agreed that Descartes in the stove-heated room had "a mental attitude which seemed to be directed upon man, God and the universe," [5] so let us agree that Descartes in Frankfurt had a mental attitude which seemed to be directed towards the Emperor. Whether or not Descartes manifested a behavior that was adapted to the Emperor, he *was*, let us agree, behaving. And his mind-nerve-fibre had a mental attitude which seemed to be directed towards the Emperor, whether or not that mental attitude *reached* the Emperor as its ultimate object.[6]

But whereas Descartes and the Emperor were each real, there was, it may be said, no real link between them, no real relational situation within which Descartes and the Emperor were terms. A may be real, and B may be real; but, it may be said, A-r-B is in all cases unreal. Hannibal and Napoleon, for example, may be acknowledged to be real, but not the similarity that is alleged to obtain between them. Socrates and Xanthippe may each be acknowledged to be real, but not 'being married to.'

Our primary concern at this point, it is to be pointed out, is with such alleged relational situations as Descartes-making-a-response-adapted-to-the-Emperor and Descartes-having-a-mental-attitude-which-reaches-the-Emperor-as-its-ultimate-object. Were we at this point to discuss the reality of relations in general, we should find ourselves delayed in coming to close quarters with the alleged relational situations which in this chapter are our primary concern. On the basis of the explanation of "existence" already laid down, let us then assert that, in the sense in which we use the term "reality," some alleged relational situations are real. The marriage relation in which Socrates and Xanthippe are alleged to participate as terms appears dated and placed in the Athens of the second half of the fifth century B.C. It appears neither explicitly nor implicitly as generally discredited. And it is listed among the existents enumerated in the Appendix to Chapter Three. There is, let us agree, the real relational situation: Socrates-married-to-Xanthippe and the real relational situation: Hannibal-like-Napoleon. There is likewise, let us agree, the real relational situation: Descartes-younger-than-the-Emperor and the real relational situation: Descartes-near-the-Emperor. Let us in short defer to a later chapter[7] such remarks as are to be made with respect to A-r-B. And let us in this chapter agree that, if Emperor-reached-as-an-ultimate-object-by-Descartes'-thinking is unreal, it is not its being presented as a relational situation that makes it so.

There is the real relational situation: Descartes-near-the-Emperor; and there is the real relational situation: Descartes-affected-by-the-Emperor. For, just as there is a motion flowing to a ledger-clerk's mind-nerve-fibre from the ledger in front of him,[8] so there is a motion flowing from the Emperor to Descartes. The clerk's "mind-nerve-fibre *and* its non-mental qualities *and* its thinking are affected by the ledger."[9] And Descartes, his behavior and his mental attitude are affected by the Emperor. One may, to be sure, be puzzled that, when motions terminate in Descartes, qualities should appear which are not themselves motions, but, rather, are such qualities as behaving and thinking. It may seem less puzzling for one billiard ball on receiving impulses from another to be itself set in motion than for a piece of metal on receiving heat waves to be set glowing or for Descartes on being affected by the Emperor to be set thinking and behaving. For we may see no reason for the connection between the reception of motions, waves or impulses on the one hand and the origination of glowing or thinking or behaving on the other. Such problems however lead us to seek a reason through a closer study of the structure of the entity which is heated and glows, of the entity which is affected from outside and thinks. Or we may be led to abandon such problems as specious ones. But whether we pursue these problems or abandon them, we do not, it seems, deny the glowing, the thinking or the behaving.

We have agreed that a "certain piece of metal is a real substance which is really hot and really red." [10] And we have agreed that Descartes in the stove-heated room had a mental attitude which seemed to be directed upon man, God and the universe. Our piece of metal's alleged glowing is not presented as generally discredited, even though the transformation, as it were, of heat waves into glowing is presented as puzzling. Nor is Descartes' mental attitude seemingly directed upon the Emperor presented as generally discredited, even though its occurrence just when Descartes is affected by the Emperor is presented as puzzling. Descartes *was* behaving, and his behavior *was* affected by the Emperor, whether or not his behavior was adapted to the Emperor. He had a mental attitude seemingly directed upon the Emperor and this mental attitude was affected by the Emperor, whether or not this mental attitude reached the Emperor as its ultimate object.

There is however a difference between the metal which on being affected by heat waves glows and the behavior which on being affected by in-coming motions is held to be adapted to something outside it. In the latter instance there is not only a transformation, as it were, from motion to what is not motion; the quality which arises at the *terminus ad quem* is presented as having direction also. This again however is not a respect in which thinking and behaving are presented as unique. The needle of a compass, on being affected by a magnet, is presented as having direction. And this needle, presented as related to the magnetic pole of the earth, is not presented as generally discredited even when the entity presented as impinging upon it is presented as adjacent to it. With the needle's behavior, Descartes' behavior and Descartes' mental attitude all alleged to be brought about by entities which impinge upon them, the relational situation: Needle-related-to-the-magnetic-pole-of-the-earth is, we hold, real and the alleged relational situations: Descartes-making-a-response-adapted-to-the-Emperor and Descartes-having-a-mental-attitude-which-reaches-the-Emperor-as-its-ultimate-object need not be presented as incredible and *un*real.

When a needle, however, is related to the magnetic pole of the earth, it is also related to intervening entities in the magnetic field which stretches from it to the pole. A needle which is related to the magnetic pole is, it may be admitted, real. But a needle alleged to be related to the pole and also alleged not to be similarly related to intervening entities,—such a needle, it may be said, is presented as generally discredited and is unreal. Descartes' behavior may, so far as we have yet seen, be adapted to the Emperor; but only, it may be said, if it is also adapted to the entities through which the motions originating in the Emperor have passed. It is only by going back step by step, as it were, over the path through which its behavior was affected that the needle, it may be said, comes to be related to the magnetic pole of the earth. And it would only be by going back step by step, as it were, over the path through which Descartes' mental attitude was brought about, that that mental attitude, it may be said, might come to reach the Emperor as its ultimate object.

When there exists the relational situation: A-grandson-of-C, there also exists the relational situation: A-son-of-B. And when a compass needle points in the direction of the magnetic pole of the earth, it also points in the direction of some intervening entity. But not all relational situations are similar. A butterfly may be like a butterfly ancestor, but not like the larva and caterpillar that intervene. And the sounds that come out of my telephone receiver may be like the sounds spoken into another instrument some distance away, but not like the intervening telephone wires. The alleged relational situation A-like-C need not be presented as generally discredited when A-like-intervening-B is presented as unreal. And the alleged relational situation: Descartes-having-a-mental-attitude-which-reaches-the-Emperor-as-its-ultimate-object need not, we hold, be presented as unreal when Descartes-having-a-mental-attitude-which-reaches-intervening-air-waves-as-objects is presented as unreal. So far as we have yet seen, Descartes' behavior may not only be brought about by the Emperor but also adapted to the Emperor. And it may be adapted to the Emperor even though it is not adapted to Descartes' own ears, to the ears through which the Emperor's voice has affected Descartes' behavior.

230

The Emperor, alleged to be both the cause and the ultimate object reached by Descartes' thinking, need not be presented as unreal when intervening entities are presented as nearer causes, but not nearer objects, of Descartes' thinking. Nor need the Emperor alleged to be both the cause of Descartes' behavior and the entity to which that behavior is adapted, be presented as unreal when intervening entities are presented as causes but not as entities to which Descartes' behavior is likewise adapted. But the Emperor whom we are considering, it may be said, is not presented as what is properly to be called a "cause" at all. The Emperor, or parts of the Emperor, may be at the sources of light waves and sound waves which terminate in Descartes. In this sense the Emperor may be said to affect Descartes' thinking and Descartes' behavior. But it is not "every entity at the source of motion," [11] it may be said, that is properly to be called a "cause." And for A's behavior to be adapted to B without being caused by B, this, it may be said, is incredible. When Descartes' behavior is presented as not having been caused by the Emperor, the alleged relational situation: Descartes-making-a-response-adapted-to-the-Emperor is, it may be said, presented as incredible and is unreal.

It is, it may be said, certain vibrations of the Emperor's larynx that are, properly speaking, the cause of Descartes' behavior, certain vibrations of the Emperor's larynx and certain points on the surface of the Emperor's body from which light waves of different wave-lengths emanate. Strictly speaking, it may be said, it is not the Emperor himself or the Emperor's beard or the Emperor's piety which is the "cause" of Descartes' behavior. Indeed it is not the Emperor's size and not the spatial relation between one point on the surface of the Emperor's body and another. For "the connection of anything manifold," it has been held, "can never enter into us through the senses." [12] But if none of these entities are causes of Descartes' behavior or of Descartes' thinking, how can they be entities to which his behavior is adapted or entities reached by his thinking as ultimate objects? An Emperor's piety, alleged to be the entity reached as an ultimate object by Descartes' thinking but alleged not to be the cause of Descartes' thinking, is, it may be said, incredible and unreal. And the Emperor himself, alleged to be the entity to which Descartes' behavior is adapted but alleged not to be the cause of that behavior, such an entity

231

likewise, it may be said, is incredible and unreal.

To be sure, the Emperor's piety and the Emperor himself are, if they exist, at the source from which motions flow to Descartes' thinking and to Descartes' behavior. But they may, let us in this chapter grant, not be *sine quibus non* with respect to Descartes' thinking or behavior. As we use the verb "to affect,"[13] such entities, if they exist, affected Descartes' behavior, although, in some sense of "cause," they may not have caused that behavior. But is it not possible for Descartes' behavior to be adapted to the Emperor without the Emperor having caused that behavior? Indeed is it not possible for Descartes' behavior to be adapted to the Emperor without the Emperor being at the source of motions terminating in that behavior?

It would seem that some relational situation A-r-B may be real when B is presented as not the cause of A. And it would seem that some relational situation A-r-B may be real when B is presented as not having affected A. No waves or impulses, let us agree, flowed from Confucius to Socrates. And yet when we are presented with the alleged relational situations Socrates-later-than-Confucius or Socrates-thinner-than-Confucius, we do not ask: How can Socrates have been later or thinner than Confucius when Confucius was at the source of no motions flowing to him? Some instances of A-r-B, it would appear, are not presented as generally discredited, need not be unreal, when B is presented as not having affected A.

Let us turn however to an instance of the alleged relational situation: A-like-B. If we are told that two primitive peoples in different parts of the world have identical ceremonies or speak similar languages, we look for some mutual influence or for some common ancestry. We expect to find the relational situation A-like-B supplemented by some additional relational situation in which A and B are likewise terms. Similarly, it may be said, when Descartes' behavior is alleged to be adapted to the Emperor or Descartes' mental attitude alleged to reach the Emperor as its ultimate object, we look for some additional relation uniting the Emperor to Descartes. In the absence of a causal relation of some sort, it may be said, Descartes' behavior allegedly adapted to the Emperor and Descartes' mental attitude allegedly reaching the Emperor as an ultimate object are presented as generally discredited and are unreal.

232

What, however, is the situation with respect to the two primitive peoples alleged to have similar customs? We do not, it would seem, withhold belief in the alleged similarity until some mutual influence or common ancestry has been tracked down. Indeed, assuming that after investigation any mutual influence or common ancestry has been ruled out, nevertheless the alleged fact of similarity still remains, is still an entity that need not be presented as generally discredited. "One may," we have noted,[14] "be puzzled that, when motions terminate in Descartes, qualities should appear which are not themselves motions, but, rather, are such qualities as behaving and thinking." And one may likewise be puzzled that peoples should be similar despite a lack of mutual influence or common ancestry. In the former instance, however, we do not, we have found, reject the thinking itself, do not find the behaving itself presented as discredited. Similarly we need not, in the present instance, reject the existence of a similarity. A "piece of metal's alleged glowing is not presented as generally discredited even though the transformation, as it were, of heat waves into glowing is presented as puzzling."[15] And a similarity between two peoples need not be presented as generally discredited even though such a similarity unaccompanied by mutual influence or common ancestry is likewise presented as puzzling.

Presented as unaccompanied by a causal relation, the alleged relational situation: Socrates-thinner-than-Confucius need not be unreal. Presented as unaccompanied by a causal relation, the alleged relational situation: this-primitive-people-like-that-primitive-people need not be unreal. And, so far as we have yet seen, presented as unaccompanied by a causal relation, the alleged relational situation: Descartes'-behavior-adapted-to-the-Emperor need not be unreal.[16] The Emperor is real, Descartes real and Descartes' behavior real. Descartes'-behavior-adapted-to-the-Emperor need not be presented as generally discredited. And the subsisting Descartes'-behavior-adapted-to-the-Emperor which *we* are considering *is* not presented as generally discredited. Some subsisting relational situation which we call "Descartes making a response adapted to the Emperor" is, we hold, real. The Emperor has the real quality of being that to which Descartes' response is adapted. And Descartes has the real quality of making a response adapted to the Emperor.

How is it, however, with respect to Descartes-having-a-mental-attitude-which-reaches-the-Emperor-as-its-ultimate-object? There are, to be sure, several subsistents, "each of which may seem to be represented by our expression: 'The Emperor reached as an ultimate object by Descartes' thinking.' " [17] But the Emperor is real, Descartes real, and Descartes' mental attitude seemingly directed towards the Emperor real. [18] The alleged relational situation: Descartes-having-a-mental-attitude-which-reaches-the-Emperor-as-its-ultimate-object need not be presented as generally discredited. And whereas the relational situation which we are considering—the relational situation which we call "Descartes-having-a-mental attitude-which-reaches-the-Emperor-as-its-ultimate-object"—is indefinite in that it is not definitely presented as an unmediated relation and not definitely presented as a relation that is mediated by an idea, nevertheless this relational situation is not presented as generally discredited. *Some* subsisting Descartes-having-a-mental-attitude-which-reaches-the-Emperor-as-its-ultimate-object is, we hold, real. Whether or not he be the *immediate* object, the Emperor has the real quality of being reached as an *ultimate* object by Descartes' thinking. And whatever its *immediate* object may be, the mental attitude of Descartes which seems to be directed towards the Emperor really reaches the Emperor as its *ultimate* object.

There is a real relational situation: Descartes-in-Frankfurt-having-a-mental-attitude-which-reaches-the-Emperor-as-its-ultimate-object. And there is a real relational situation: Descartes-in-Frankfurt-making-a-response-adapted-to-the-Emperor. There is a real relational situation: My-dinner-companion-making-a-response-adapted-to-the-meal-about-to-be-eaten. [19] And there is a real relational situation: Descartes-en-route-to-Frankfurt-making-a-response-adapted-to-the-ceremony-about-to-be-witnessed. There is likewise, let us say, a real relational situation: Descartes-en-route-to-Frankfurt-having-a-mental-attitude-which-reaches-as-its-ultimate-object-the-Emperor-about-to-be-witnessed-in-Frankfurt. And, taking it for granted that, in reading this chapter, you have had a thinking mind-nerve-fibre with the intrinsic quality of seeming to be directed upon the Emperor, there is, let us say, a real relational situation: Your-having-a-mental-attitude-which-reaches-the-Emperor-in-Frankfurt-as-its-ultimate-object. The Emperor has the real quality of being reached as an ultimate object by a mental atti-

234

tude belonging to Descartes at Frankfurt, the real quality of being reached as an ultimate object by a mental attitude belonging to Descartes en route to Frankfurt, and the real quality of being reached as an ultimate object by a mental attitude of yours. Some thinking mind-nerve-fibre of Descartes' en route to Frankfurt did not only have the intrinsic quality of seeming to be directed upon the Emperor; it also had the quality of reaching the Emperor as an ultimate object. And so with some thinking mind-nerve-fibre of yours as you were reading this chapter.

One of the alleged relational situations which seem to be represented by "Descartes at Frankfurt having a mental attitude which reached the Emperor as an ultimate object" is real. But is this relational situation which is real an unmediated relation; or is it a relation in which an idea of the Emperor intervenes? The Descartes en route to Frankfurt had the real quality of having a mental attitude which reached the Emperor as an ultimate object. But is this real quality of Descartes' or of Descartes' mind-nerve-fibre the quality of being aware of the Emperor as an immediate object? Or is it the quality of being aware of "an idea which succeeds in referring beyond itself to the Emperor"?[20] The Emperor has the real quality of being reached by a mental attitude which you had as you were reading this chapter. But is this real quality of the Emperor's the quality of being the entity of which you were immediately aware? Or is it the quality of being referred to by an idea of which you were aware?

Our problem at this point is whether or not an idea of the Emperor intervenes in the relational situation within which the Emperor is one term and you, or Descartes en route to Frankfurt, or Descartes *at* Frankfurt, another term. But what is it to *intervene*? Your mental attitude directed upon the Emperor at his coronation may have been preceded by a mental attitude of yours directed upon some other episode in the Emperor's life. This other episode in the Emperor's life, which was an object for a previous mental attitude of yours, is, let us agree, related to that phase of the Emperor's life in which he was being crowned. And it may deserve mention in an account of the genesis of your present mental attitude directed upon the coronation. But if this object for a previous mental attitude is no longer an object of yours, then it does not, let us say, intervene in the relational situ-

235

ation within which your present mind-nerve-fibre with its present mental attitudes is a term. Being an immediate object, being an idea, is not, in short, merely being an object for some previous mental attitude.

There is the proposition "The world exists"; and there is the proposition: "God exists." It may be held that the existence of the world implies the existence of God, that the proposition "God exists" may be deduced from other propositions. Or it may be held either that God is known intuitively or that His existence is to be accepted as a postulate, that the proposition "God exists" is not to be "deduced from other propositions which are its premises."[21] There is a distinction, that is to say, between the entity whose existence we accept, or in whose existence we believe, without proof; and the entity in whose existence we believe as the result of proof. This distinction, however, is not the distinction between an unmediated subject-object relation and a subject-object relation in which an idea intervenes. For, just as objects for previous mental attitudes of yours, in so far as they are merely objects for previous mental attitudes, need not intervene "in the relational situation within which your present mind-nerve-fibre with its present mental attitudes is a term,"[22] so, if I am really aware of God and really believing in His existence, the relation between me and the proposition "God exists" may be unmediated, whether or not some previous mental attitude of mine reached as its ultimate object the proposition: "The world exists." "I cannot demonstrate" says Thomas Reid,[23] "that two quantities which are equal to the same quantity are equal to each other; neither can I demonstrate that the tree which I perceive exists. But, by the constitution of my nature," Reid continues, "my belief is irresistibly carried along by my apprehension of the axiom"; and it is "no less irresistibly carried along by my perception of the tree." But if, contrary to Reid's opinion, there are other entities such that a belief in their existence leads to a belief in the existence of the tree, nevertheless the relational situation which exists when Reid's mental attitude reaches the tree as its ultimate object need not be mediated by an idea. And if, on the other hand, a belief in the existence of the tree is intuitive and the proposition: "This tree exists" accepted without proof, there may nevertheless be an idea of the tree which is Reid's immediate object, an idea of the

236

tree which intervenes when Reid's thinking reaches the tree as its ultimate object.

As we use "intervene," an entity does not, by being an object for a previous mental attitude, intervene in the relation between thinking subject and ultimate object. And as we use "idea," an entity is not an intervening idea when it is indistinguishable from the subject's thinking. Descartes had a mental attitude which seemed to be directed upon the Emperor. And if this mental attitude, as a mental attitude, were to be called an "idea," then of course the real relational situation: Emperor-reached-as-an-ultimate-object-by-Descartes'-thinking would imply the existence of an idea in one of its terms. If it is a type of thinking, a mental attitude, that we call a "perception," then "it is clearer than the day that we are able to see, perceive and know" ultimate objects "only by the perceptions that we have of them."[24] The relational situation, however, which is alleged to involve only the Emperor and Descartes' mental attitude is, let us say, presented as an unmediated relation, not as a relation in which an idea of the Emperor intervenes. The relation between thinking subject and ultimate object is mediated by what we call an "idea," only if some entity exists which is distinguishable from the subject's thinking and which refers beyond itself to the ultimate object.

What we call "mental attitude" may, to be sure, be called "idea" in some other terminology.[25] Hence, the relational situation which we should say is presented as "unmediated by an idea" might by others be said to be presented as "involving an idea." It is not to be concluded, however, that the question whether or not the subject-object relation is mediated by an idea resolves itself into a question as to how we are to use the term "idea." Whatever meaning is assigned the term "idea," there are several subsisting relational situations each of which may seem to be represented by our expression: "Descartes having a mental attitude which reaches the Emperor as an ultimate object." There is on the one hand the alleged relational situation within which there is alleged to be a mental picture of the Emperor. And since what we call "mental attitude" is "presented as not a mental picture or image,"[26] the relational situation which is alleged to include a mental picture presents an entity distinguishable from the mental attitude which we have found real. On the other hand, there is the relational situation alleged to include no mental picture, the relational situation in which the Emperor is alleged to be the direct object of Descartes' thinking and alleged to be referred to by no entity distinguishable from that thinking. Descartes' mental attitude is real and reaches the Emperor as its ultimate object. The question is whether the Emperor is a direct object of what is not a mental picture or whether he is referred to by an entity distinguishable from the mental attitude that has been found real.

In order for the relation between thinking subject and ultimate object to be mediated by what we call an "idea," some entity must be real, and involved in the relation, which is distinguishable from what we have described as the subject's thinking. The entity which is alleged to be an intervening idea need not be presented as differing in date or position from the thinking subject. Thinking and idea, for example, mental attitude and immediate object, may be presented as qualities inhering in the same substance. On the other hand, an entity may be called an "idea," let us say, if it is real and has a date or position different from that of the mental attitude itself. The idea of the Emperor, alleged to be distinguishable from Descartes' thinking, may be alleged to be where Descartes' thinking is or where the Emperor is; it may be alleged to have a position which is neither Descartes' nor the Emperor's; or it may be alleged to have no position at all.

To be sure, if the idea alleged to intervene is nothing but the Emperor himself, then the relation said to be mediated by an idea is the very relation that we should describe as unmediated. But what about a quality of the Emperor's presented as the intervening idea? The relational situation: Descartes-having-a-mental-attitude-which-reaches-the-Emperor-as-ultimate-object may be presented as a situation in which Descartes' immediate object is a quality of the Emperor's, a quality of the Emperor's which points to the Emperor in which that quality inheres. Just as it may be said[27] that it is a quality of the Emperor's, rather than the Emperor himself, that is the *sine qua non* of the mental attitude of Descartes' which reaches the Emperor as an ultimate object, so it may be said that it is a quality of the Emperor's which is Descartes' immediate object, a quality of the Emperor's which refers to the Emperor as ultimate object.

Let us agree that, whereas one phase of the thinking Descartes may have reached the Emperor as an ultimate object, a previous phase or a subsequent phase may have reached as an ultimate object a given quality of the Emperor's. When this quality is the ultimate object, the immediate object, it may be said, *is* the ultimate object and the subject-object relation an unmediated one. But when a mental attitude which reaches this quality is succeeded by a mental attitude which reaches the Emperor himself, then the immediate object, it may be said, although intrinsically unaltered, acquires a reference. And when this quality is abstracted[28] from its substance, this immediate object, it may be said, although intrinsically unaltered, loses its reference and becomes the ultimate object also.

But why should the relation between Emperor and thinking Descartes, in which a quality of Emperor's is alleged to intervene as immediate object, be presented as real; and the relation between them, in which it is alleged that no entity intervenes, be presented as incredible? It may be that, with respect to the causal relation flowing from the Emperor to Descartes, some quality of the Emperor's, rather than the Emperor himself, is the *sine qua non* of Descartes' mental attitude.[29] The relation between thinking subject and ultimate object is, however, distinguishable from the relation between cause and effect. The Emperor, presented as ultimate object, need not be presented as generally discredited when it is a quality of the Emperor's, rather than the Emperor himself, that is alleged to be the cause of Descartes' thinking. And a quality of the Emperor's which is alleged to be the cause of Descartes' thinking need not be presented as an intervening idea. The Emperor himself, that is to say, need not be presented as generally discredited when he is presented as not the cause, but nevertheless the immediate object, of the thinking directed upon him. Moreover, if a mental attitude may reach a quality of the Emperor's without the intervention of an idea, another mental attitude, it would seem, may likewise reach the Emperor himself without the intervention of an idea. A quality which is reached directly and a substance which is reached indirectly—this combination is not impossible. But it is not a combination that we find necessary. In order not to be presented as generally discredited, the Emperor himself, so far as we have yet seen, need not be presented as an ultimate object which is not an immediate object, need not be presented as an ultimate object with respect to which a quality of the Emperor's is an intervening idea.

The quality of the Emperor's, whose function as intervening idea we have been considering, appears as an individual quality having the position and date that inhere in the Emperor himself. It is some such entity as the Emperor's color or the Emperor's quality of being the source of certain vibrations. But there also subsist such entities as color in general, universal qualities which are held to be in some manner exemplified or instanced in the Emperor's color or in the Emperor's being the source of vibrations. And it may be held that, when Descartes' mental attitude reaches the Emperor as ultimate object, it is color in general that is the intervening idea rather than the Emperor's color, a universal rather than that quality of the Emperor's which is the cause of Descartes' thinking. The subsisting relational situation with which we are presented may be Descartes-aware-of-universal-which-refers-to-the-Emperor rather than Descartes-aware-of-a-quality-of-the-Emperor's-which-refers-to-the-Emperor. But the universal, whose function as an intervening idea we are now to consider, subsists, let us say, either as *in* its instances or as *not* in its instances. Color in general is presented as being where various colored things are, as having, along with other dates and positions, the date and position of the Emperor's color. Or color in general is presented as merely being realized in the Emperor's color, as being in itself without any dates or any positions. Yet if, when the Emperor is presented as ultimate object, it is not required that *his* color be presented as intervening idea, it would not seem to be required that the color, which is where he is and where other colored things are, be presented as intervening idea. If, in order not to be presented as generally discredited, the Emperor need not be presented as "an ultimate object with respect to which a quality of the Emperor's is an intervening idea," [30] then, in order not to be presented as generally discredited, he need not be presented as an ultimate object with respect to which a universal, alleged to be *in* its various instances, is an intervening idea.

But what shall we say with respect to the universal which is alleged merely to be realized in entities having dates and positions, the universal which in itself is alleged to be non-temporal and non-spatial? "Whatever appears as lacking a date or as having

240

no spatial position" is, we have said,[31] unreal. Hence the alleged relational situation with which we are presented is one in which a real thinking subject is alleged to be aware of an unreal immediate object and this unreal immediate object alleged to refer to a real ultimate object. But the entity which is presented as unreal *is* unreal. And the entity which *is* unreal has no real qualities, inheres in no real substance and is a term in no real relational situation. The universal which is unreal refers to no real Emperor, is the immediate object of no real mental attitude, intervenes in no real subject-object relation. The relational situation in which only an unreal universal intervenes is a relational situation in which there is no intervening idea. "*Some* subsisting Descartes-having-a-mental-attitude-which-reaches-the-Emperor-as-its-ultimate-object is, we hold, real." [32] So far as we have yet seen, this subsistent may be Descartes-aware-of-an-intervening-idea-which-refers-to-the-Emperor. But it is not Descartes-aware-of-a-non-temporal-and-non-spatial-universal-which-refers-to-the-Emperor.

The relation between thinking subject and ultimate object may, so far as we have yet seen, be a mediated relation. And it may, so far as we have yet seen, be an unmediated relation. But if Descartes is here and the Emperor there, is it not necessary that there be an intervening idea, an immediate object which is here and hence distinct from the ultimate object? The mind, it is said, does not travel out to interact with its ultimate objects in the places where they are. "We see the sun, the stars and an infinity of objects outside of us." But, as Malebranche [33] puts it, "it is not likely that the soul leaves the body and goes, so to speak, to wander through the heavens to contemplate all these objects there." Nor is there an interaction which somehow occurs both where the subject is and where his ultimate object is. "If I do not perceive the effects of the fixed stars, remaining all the while here upon the earth," then, says Montague, "I and they must interact at a distance, that is, must be in two places at once." [34]

Now, we have agreed that "Descartes, his behavior and his mental attitude are affected by the Emperor." [35] They are affected in such a way that what finally impinges on Descartes' thinking is here where his thinking is, not there where the Emperor is. But the last cause need not be the first object. That which finally impinges on Descartes' thinking and is here may be no object for

Descartes at all. It is one thing to be a cause, whether last cause or distant source. And it is another thing to be an object, whether immediate object or ultimate object. "The Emperor, alleged to be both the cause and the ultimate object reached by Descartes' thinking, need not be presented as unreal when intervening entities are presented as nearer causes, but not nearer objects, of Descartes' thinking."[36] And the Emperor need not be presented as unreal when he is alleged to be the immediate object of Descartes' thinking as well. For, if it is not incredible for intervening entities to be causes but not objects, then it is not incredible for the Emperor to be the nearest object, hence the immediate object. Whereas the thinking and its last cause are *here,* the immediate object of that thinking may, so far as we have yet seen, be *there.* The mind-nerve-fibre which is *here* may have concomitant with it no mental picture, no mental quality distinguishable from its mental attitude, no characteristic, in short, which, as we have explained our term "idea,"[37] is an idea of the Emperor.

There exists a relational situation represented by our expression: "Descartes in Frankfurt having a mental attitude which reaches the Emperor as its ultimate object," a relational situation in which the subject is here and the ultimate object there. But there also exists a relational situation represented by our expression: "Your having a mental attitude which reaches the Emperor in Frankfurt as its ultimate object,"[38] a relational situation in which the subject is now and the ultimate object then. In the instance in which the subject is here and the ultimate object there, the entity which is the ultimate object may, so far as we have yet seen, be the immediate object as well. But may the ultimate object also be the immediate object in the instance in which the subject is now and the ultimate object then? Your present mental attitude, it may be said, can not have as its immediate object the Emperor in Frankfurt who is past. "The present awareness," as Lovejoy puts it,[39] "manifestly has, and must have, a compresent content." For if your only object were the Emperor who is your ultimate object, your attention, it may be said, would be directed entirely to the past and you would not be aware of the Emperor as past with respect to your present thinking. To think of the past, it is held, is in part to think of the present with respect to which the past is past. It is, it is said, to have a contemporary immediate

242

object which refers beyond itself to an ultimate object which is past.

Now when your present mental attitude reaches the past Emperor in Frankfurt as its ultimate object, there is, to be sure, one sense in which your immediate object is present. Your immediate object is "present" in the sense that it is given or *presented* to the mental attitude directed upon it. But it is one thing to be *presented* to your present mental attitude, another thing to be *contemporaneous* with your present mental attitude. Whatever the date of your immediate object, your ultimate object, in the instance we are now considering, is past with respect to your present thinking, past with respect to Napoleon Bonaparte, future with respect to Julius Caesar. It would appear that you may be aware of the Emperor in Frankfurt as past with respect to Napoleon without being aware of him as past with respect to any present immediate object of yours. And it would likewise appear that you may be aware of this Emperor as past with respect to what is now happening without being aware of him as past with respect to a present idea. For the entities with respect to which the Emperor is dated, the entities which are objects of yours along with the past Emperor, may be the events chronicled in today's newspaper, or they may be your present mental attitudes, rather than some present idea of the Emperor. In order to think of the Emperor as past, it is, we conclude, not necessary that your immediate object be a present idea of him. Your immediate objects may, on the one hand, be contemporaneous events which are not ideas, and, on the other hand, the Emperor himself who is your ultimate object.

"When I think of my grandfather's time, I do not think *in* my grandfather's time." [40] And if your present mental attitude reaches the Emperor in Frankfurt, not only as its ultimate object but as its immediate object as well, then subject and immediate object are not contemporaneous with one another. It is, however, no more incredible for a subject to be now and its immediate object then than it is for one end of this couch to be here and the other end there. The couch taken as a whole is presented as having an indefinite rather than a punctual position. And the relational situation, within which your mental attitude is now and the Emperor who is your immediate object then, is presented as having an indefinite rather than a momentary date. It is

243

presented, that is to say, as having a date no more definite than that of an entity which has endured since 1619. The alleged relational situation which is thus presented with an indefinite date need not however be presented as unreal, need not be discarded in favor of an alleged relational situation in which subject and immediate object are presented as contemporaneous with one another.

So far as we have yet seen, the relation between subject and ultimate object need not be mediated by an idea. Indeed such a relation *can* be mediated by an idea only if the idea which is alleged to intervene is real. Now, the idea which is alleged to be the immediate object, and alleged to refer beyond itself to the ultimate object, is frequently held to be an entity which is non-spatial. Thinking itself is held to be non-spatial, incapable of entering into causal relations with extended entities. And in view of the lack of "proportion" [41] between an inextended thinking and extended ultimate objects, the immediate object of such a thinking, it may be held, must be an idea which, like thinking itself, is inextended and non-spatial. Were such an argument acceptable, we should likewise have to agree, it would seem, that there is no proportion between the inextended idea and the extended ultimate object. We should have to reject the alleged relation between inextended *idea* and extended ultimate object. And we should likewise have to reject the alleged relation between inextended *thinking* and extended ultimate object. We should in short find ourselves considering an alleged extended object presented as not referred to by an intervening idea and presented as not reached as an ultimate object by the inextended thinking said to be directed upon it.

It has been our conclusion, however, that the thinking which appears as non-spatial is unreal;[42] that thinking presented as spatial is in some instances real;[43] and that some instances of a thinking which is spatial reach the ultimate objects upon which they are directed.[44] As we use the term "reality," whatever appears as non-spatial is unreal. Hence the subsistent which appears as a non-spatial idea does not exist and does not intervene as an immediate object. In the real relational situation in which Descartes' mental attitude reaches the Emperor as its ultimate object, the immediate object may be the Emperor himself, but cannot be an alleged non-spatial idea of the Emperor. So far as we have yet seen, it is similarly possible for the immediate object to be a quality of the ultimate object or a universal which exists *in* the ultimate object. But it can be no "essence," [45] no universal, no logical entity, which appears as having no date and no position.

There subsists the intervening idea which is presented as having no position. And there subsists the intervening idea which is presented as having position, but only with respect to other ideas. An idea of the sun may be presented as having no position. Or an idea of the sun may be presented as being to the right of an ideal Venus and beyond an ideal mountain, but as lacking position with respect to Venus, the mountain and the sun which are, let us agree, real ultimate objects. An idea however which appears as having no spatial position with respect to entities which appear real, and with respect to which it appears present, is itself unreal.[46] And so alleged ideas are unreal and cannot function as immediate objects, either if they appear as non-spatial, or if, appearing as located with respect to other ideas, they appear as not in the same spatial world as real ultimate objects contemporaneous with them.

There is also to be considered the idea which is held to be an object for but a single subject. There may be held to exist: Descartes' idea of the Emperor presented only to Descartes, your idea of the Emperor presented only to you, and the Emperor who is an ultimate object both for your mental attitude and for Descartes', the Emperor, that is to say, to whom both your idea and Descartes' idea are alleged to refer. But the idea of the Emperor that is alleged to be an object for Descartes alone is a subsistent implicitly presented as an entity which you and I are now considering.[47] Descartes' idea of the Emperor subsists explicitly with the characteristic of being an object for Descartes alone and implicitly with the characteristic of being an object for others also. Descartes' alleged idea of the Emperor appears free from self-contradiction only when Descartes' alleged exclusive awareness of it is limited to an awareness of some special kind, only when, for example, Descartes' idea of the Emperor is presented as being an *immediate* object for Descartes alone, or is presented as being presented *in detail* to Descartes alone.

We turn then to the idea which is alleged to have position with respect to ultimate objects and alleged to be an object of some sort for various subjects. There is for example the idea of the moon which is alleged to be my immediate object, presented in detail to me alone, but which is alleged to be here with respect to my mental attitude and to be there with respect to the moon which is my ultimate object. The alleged idea of the moon which is presented to me in detail, but presented in some sense to you also, is presented, let us say, not only as being in my head, but as having certain intrinsic characteristics also. It is, let us say, presented as silver in color and shaped like a crescent. But along with the alleged silver crescent in my head, I find myself considering another subsistent, namely, an alleged silver crescent in the sky. And I find that what is presented as my immediate object is an alleged silver crescent in the sky rather than an alleged silver crescent in my head. The silver crescent in my head when alleged to be my immediate object is presented as disbelieved and is unreal. And the alleged silver crescent in the sky is unreal and cannot be my immediate object. Nor is there an idea of the moon in my head which is not silver and not a crescent. For whatever in my head is not silver and not a crescent appears as no object of mine in the situation in which the moon is my ultimate object. My mental attitude is real and the moon real which is its ultimate object. Descartes' mental attitude is real and the Emperor real which is *his* ultimate object. But when Descartes' mental attitude reaches the Emperor as its ultimate object, his immediate object is not his thinking itself and it is not an alleged idea that has approximately the same position as that thinking.

When a mental attitude reaches an entity outside it as its ultimate object, no idea need intervene which is distinguishable from thinking itself and distinct from the ultimate object. Indeed the immediate object *is* not an idea when that idea is held to be nonspatial, held not to be spatially related to ultimate objects contemporaneous with it, held not to be an object for other subjects, or held to be adjacent to thinking itself. It would seem that in order for the immediate object to be an idea distinct from the ultimate object, it must, in the case of non-introspective thinking, be some public object distinct from the ultimate object but related to it in some such fashion as a sign is related to that towards which it points. Either Descartes' immediate object is the Emperor himself or it is some symbol, picture, description, or what not, that refers beyond itself to the real Emperor. But if the immediate object has spatial position with respect to the real Emperor, if it is not adjacent to the thinking which has it as an object and if it is in some sense an object for all of us, then it is not plausible for the Emperor himself to be held incapable of being an immediate object. Just as the admission that a quality of the Emperor's may be an immediate object seems to carry with it the admission that the Emperor himself need not be an indirect object,[48] so does the admission that the immediate object may be a picture of the Emperor which is spatially related to the Emperor and not adjacent to Descartes' thinking. For the picture then simply takes the place of the Emperor. The unmediated subject-object relation between the thinking subject and the picture is to be classified, it would seem, with the alleged unmediated relation between subject and ultimate object rather than with the relation in which an idea is alleged to intervene.

What indeed is the function of a sign, of a description, of a picture? An arrow succeeds in being a sign pointing to some place of interest in so far as mental attitudes directed upon the arrow are followed by mental attitudes directed upon the place of interest to which the arrow refers. I may have before me a picture of the Emperor. But if my attention is not directed exclusively to colors on a flat surface in front of me, my attention turns to other objects, to the seventeenth-century individual, for example, whose picture is before me. In being aware of the Emperor or of the place of interest, the arrow or the picture may no longer be an object of mine. And if arrow and picture are no longer objects, then, as we use "intervene," they do not intervene in the relational situation within which the Emperor or the place of interest is my ultimate object. For, "being an immediate object, being an idea, is not," we have said,[49] "merely being an object for some previous mental attitude."

It may be however that, simultaneous with the mental attitude directed upon the picture, there is a mental attitude directed upon the Emperor. I may, as it were, see through the picture to the Emperor; or see around the arrow to the place of interest. But this is to see picture and Emperor together, to be aware of the relational situation picture-of-Emperor or of the relational situation: arrow-pointing-to-place-of-interest. Yet if arrow-pointing-to place-of-interest is an immediate object, it would seem that a component within that relational situation may be, and on occasion is, an immediate object also. If one of Descartes' mind-nerve-fibres has as its immediate object picture-pointing-to-the-Emperor, another of his mind-nerve-fibres may have, and at least one of them we hold *does* have, the Emperor as its immediate object.

Some relational situation is real, we have said,[50] which is represented by our expression: "Descartes in Frankfurt having a mental attitude which reaches the Emperor as its ultimate object." What we are now concluding is that the expression representing this real relational situation may be spelled out as: "Descartes in Frankfurt having a mental attitude which reaches the Emperor both as its ultimate object and as its immediate object." There exists a relational situation in which no idea intervenes, a relational situation in which the thinking Descartes is one term and the Emperor the other term. And there likewise exists an unmediated subject-object relation in which your mind-nerve-fibre is one term and the Emperor the other term. The Emperor, we hold, is not only the ultimate object, but also the immediate object, reached by a mental attitude belonging to Descartes at Frankfurt, reached by a mental attitude belonging to Descartes en route to Frankfurt, and also reached by a mental attitude of yours.

Up to this point, however, we have failed to consider the situation in which a mental attitude fails to reach an ultimate object. A straight stick may be real and in one of its phases may be half under water, half above. I may have been looking at the partially submerged stick; but my mental attitude may have failed to reach the straight stick as its object. I was, let us agree, aware of no straight stick, but seemed, rather, to be aware of a bent stick. Since, however, there was no bent stick in the water in front of me, what was the entity, it may be asked, to which my thinking mind-nerve-fibre was joined in a subject-object relation? In one of the relational situations which we have been considering, in the relational situation in which your mental attitude reached the Emperor as its ultimate object, it was the Emperor himself, we have concluded, and not an idea, that was your immediate object. But was not my immediate object an idea, we now ask,—or an entity analogous to an idea—in the situation in which my mental attitude failed to reach the straight stick in front of me, in the situation in which I seemed to be aware of a bent stick?

248

Let us begin by agreeing that the straight stick partially submerged was the source of vibrations reaching my mind-nerve-fibre and affecting my thinking. Light waves, reaching me from that part of the stick which was under water, followed a path not parallel to that followed by light waves coming from that part of the stick which was above water. Hence, it may be agreed, my mental attitude had the intrinsic quality of seeming to be directed upon a bent stick rather than the intrinsic quality of seeming to be directed upon a straight stick. Our problem, however, is not with respect to the cause of the mental attitude of mine which we are considering, but with respect to the object, if any, that this mental attitude had.

Now just as the straight stick that is real was no object for this mental attitude of mine, so there is no bent stick that is real and that was its object. There are, to be sure, bent sticks which are real, bent sticks in the forest and elsewhere. But when I was looking at the stick in the water in front of me, it was not such sticks that were my objects. Presented with the characteristic of having been my objects, that is to say, such other bent sticks are presented as discredited and are unreal. A bent stick alleged to have been in my head and to have been my object is likewise presented as discredited and is unreal. For along with the bent stick alleged to have been in my head, "I find myself considering another subsistent," [51] namely, an alleged bent stick in the water. And I find that what is presented as having been my object is an alleged bent stick in the water, not the bent stick alleged to have been in my head. I find, that is to say, that the bent stick in my head, presented with the characteristic of having been an object for the mental attitude which we are considering, is presented as disbelieved and is unreal.

My past mental attitude had as its object no bent stick in the forest and no bent stick in my head. And it had as its object no bent stick in the water and no non-spatial bent stick. There exists no bent stick in the water and no stick which is non-spatial. "And the entity which is unreal has no real qualities, inheres in no real substance and is a term in no real relational situation." [52] If I have no sister, if all my alleged sisters are unreal, then there is no real sister-brother relation in which I participate as a term. And just as there is no real relational situation joining me to an

249

imaginary sister Mary, so there is no real relational situation joining a mental attitude of mine to a bent stick that is unreal. When I was looking at the stick in the water in front of me, I was behaving and I was thinking. But since there was no bent stick in the water in front of me, my behavior was not adapted to a bent stick in front of me. And since there was no bent stick that was my object, no bent stick was either the ultimate object or the immediate object of my mental attitude. My behavior was real; but there was nothing to which it was directed and adapted. My thinking was real; but it had no object.

Now it may be agreed that my behavior can not have been adapted to a bent stick that didn't exist, that my mind-nerve-fibre cannot have been aware of a bent stick that wasn't real. But what do our words mean, we may be asked, when we say that I was thinking, but that my thinking had no object, when we say that I was aware, but not aware of anything? To be aware, it may be said, is to be aware of something. The phrase "being aware, but not aware of anything" is, it may be said, a phrase which is unintelligible.

There is, let us recall, a distinction to be made between Descartes' "intrinsic quality of having a mental attitude which seems to be directed towards the Emperor" and "his alleged quality of having a mental attitude which reaches the Emperor as its ultimate object"; and there is a distinction to be made between "Descartes' intrinsic quality of behaving" and "his alleged quality of manifesting a behavior that is adapted to the Emperor." [53] There are similar distinctions to be made when, confronted by a menacing dog, Kitty is characterized by a certain mental attitude and a certain behavior. It is by virtue of Kitty's tenseness and arched back, by virtue of her behavior, that Kitty enters as a term into the relational situation: Kitty-manifesting-a-behavior-that-is-adapted-to-the-menacing-dog. But Kitty might be tense, might have her back arched, and might fix her eyes on some spot in front of her, even if there were no dog there. Were this the situation, Kitty would, let us say, have the intrinsic quality of behaving, but not the quality of manifesting a behavior adapted to a menacing dog in front of her. She would, we may say, be "responding," but not "responding-to."

It is in a similar fashion, we hold, that a mind-nerve-fibre may

250

be aware, but not aware-of. There is an intrinsic quality which Descartes' mind-nerve-fibre has when it reaches the Emperor as both its ultimate and immediate object, an intrinsic quality which we describe as Descartes' mental attitude seemingly directed upon the Emperor. A similar intrinsic quality may have been present, we hold, on a different occasion, may have been present in a situation in which Descartes' mind-nerve-fibre failed to reach the Emperor as its object. If such a situation existed, Descartes was then aware, but not aware-of. And when I was looking at the stick in the water in front of me, I likewise was aware, but not aware-of. My mind-nerve-fibre had the intrinsic quality of having a mental attitude seemingly directed upon a bent stick, but not the quality of being joined in a relational situation to any ultimate object or to any immediate object.

Even if it is agreed however that there was an intrinsic quality which I had when I was looking at the stick in the water in front of me, it may be said to be confusing to call this quality an instance of "thinking" or an instance of "being aware" and also to describe this quality as "having a mental attitude seemingly directed upon a bent stick." There is, it may be said, no quality that the reader recognizes as being called to his attention by the term "being aware." And when, on the other hand, we describe the mental attitude as "seemingly directed upon a bent stick," we refer to an entity external to the mental attitude and thus, it may be said, belie the assertion that we are describing an intrinsic quality. In order to identify the mental attitude which we hold to be real and which we hold has no immediate object, we use the expression "seemingly directed upon a bent stick," an expression which has meaning, it may be said, only if the mental attitude *has* an immediate object.

Since it had no immediate object, it is not altogether unobjectionable, let us admit, to describe as "seemingly directed upon the Emperor" the mental attitude which Descartes had when his mind-nerve-fibre failed to reach the Emperor. And it is not altogether unobjectionable to describe as "seemingly directed upon a bent stick" the mental attitude which *I* had when, looking at the stick in the water in front of me, my mental attitude had neither a straight stick nor a bent stick as its immediate object. In the situation in which there is no menacing dog in front of Kitty, it is equally objectionable, it would seem, to describe Kitty's behavior as "seemingly adapted to a menacing dog." For if it is objectionable to use the expression "seemingly directed upon a bent stick" in connection with a situation in which I was aware but not aware-of, it is equally objectionable to use the expression "seemingly adapted to a menacing dog" in connection with a situation in which Kitty was responding, but not responding-to. In an effort to avoid any reference to this unreal menacing dog, we may, to be sure, say that Kitty was tense, that she had her back arched, and that she was staring at a spot in front of her. And in an effort to avoid any reference to a bent stick, we may describe my mental attitude as an entity that was not a mental picture and, further to identify it, may describe the non-mental behavior which accompanied it. We may perhaps point to the fact that I uttered the sounds "bent stick" or to the fact that I indicated with my fingers two lines at an angle. Yet when we attempt to avoid any reference to menacing dogs or to bent sticks in pointing to the intrinsic quality of behaving that Kitty manifested or in pointing to the intrinsic quality of being aware that *I* had, then our expressions are awkward and will in many instances fail to direct the reader's attention to the qualities we wish to describe.

Kitty's behavior was not adapted to anything. We may point to her behavior by saying that she had her back arched and was staring at a spot in front of her. But we may also point to her behavior by saying that she was behaving as though her behavior were adapted to a menacing dog. Similarly, I was aware; but my mental attitude had no ultimate object and no immediate object. We may point to the mental attitude which I had by saying that it was an instance of thinking, not a mental picture, and by saying that it was an element in a total behavior in which I indicated with my fingers two lines at an angle. But we may also point to this mental attitude of mine by saying that I was aware as though I were aware of a bent stick.

For let us recall the conditions under which the proposition is true which has the form: "C is D as though A were B." Our proposition: "C is D as though A were B" is true, we have indicated,[54] when "C is D" is true, "A is not B" true and "If A should be B, C would be D" true. There is the proposition: "Kitty has her back arched and is staring at a spot in front of her as though her behavior were adapted to a menacing dog." And this proposition is true, as we have explained our term "truth," if Kitty *has* her back arched, if her behavior is *not* adapted to a menacing dog, and if it is true that, if Kitty's behavior *should* be adapted to a menacing dog, her back *would* be arched and she *would* be staring at a spot in front of her. Advancing another step, the proposition: "If Kitty's behavior should be adapted to a menacing dog, her back would be arched and she would be staring at a spot in front of her" is an instance of: "If A should be B, C would be D." And in order that this instance of: "If A should be B, C would be D" may be true, there must be instances of behavior analogous to Kitty's arched back and there must be relational situations in some sense analogous to the alleged but unreal situation: this - Kitty's - behavior - being - adapted - to a - menacing-dog-in-front-of-her. There must, that is to say, be some other cat, or this cat on some other occasion, whose behavior *is* adapted to a menacing dog. There must be some instance of adapted behavior which, if not *really* analogous to the unreal: this-Kitty's-behavior-being-adapted-to-a-menacing-dog-in-front-of-her, is at least suggested by our real words: "Analogous to Kitty's behavior being adapted to a menacing dog in front of her." [55] Further, the cat whose behavior *is* adapted must have that adapted behavior accompanied by a back arched as Kitty's is and not *un*accompanied by a back arched as Kitty's is. [56] These conditions however are fulfilled. The propositions are true which determine the "as if" proposition before us to be true. And just as it is true that Kitty has her back arched and is staring at a spot in front of her as though her behavior were adapted to a menacing dog, so it is true that I had a mental attitude as though I were aware of a bent stick. I *had* a mental attitude. I was *not* aware of a bent stick. But other subjects have been aware of bent sticks; and in such real subject-object relational situations, the subjects have been characterized by mental attitudes which, considered as intrinsic qualities, resemble mine.

There is thus at least one sense, in which the proposition: "I had a mental attitude seemingly directed upon a bent stick" may be used, in which this proposition does not imply that there was a bent stick in front of me and does not imply that my mental attitude had an object. When "A had a mental attitude seemingly directed upon B" is used in a sense in which it is synonymous with our proposition: "A had a mental attitude as if he were aware of B," what is asserted is that A was not aware of B but that some subject A^1 had some entity B^1 as an object. Not every instance of "A had a mental attitude seemingly directed upon B" is, however, synonymous with an instance of "A had a mental attitude as if he were aware of B." For, some instances of our proposition: "Descartes had a mental attitude seemingly directed upon man, God and the universe" do not express an assertion that some other subject was aware of man, God and the universe and that Descartes was not.[57] And some instances of our proposition: "I had a mental attitude seemingly directed upon a bent stick" do not express an assertion that other subjects have been aware of bent sticks.[58] Some instances of our proposition: "A had a mental attitude seemingly directed upon B" are synonymous with: "A had a certain attitude, an intrinsic quality which the phrase 'seemingly directed upon B' may help to identify." When: "A had a mental attitude seemingly directed upon B" is used in the latter sense it substitutes for a proposition which points to intrinsic qualities alone.[59] Used in either sense, however, "I had a mental attitude seemingly directed upon a bent stick" is, we hold, true. I *had* a certain mental attitude, a mental attitude which the phrase "seemingly directed upon a bent stick" serves to identify. And in view of the fact that others *have* been aware of bent sticks, I had a mental attitude as though I were aware of a bent stick.

Others have been aware of bent sticks. But no one, let us agree, has really been aware of a unicorn. In the situation in which one seems to be aware of a unicorn, is there then no real subject-object relation analogous to that in which some other subject is really aware of a bent stick; no real subject-object relation in view of which "I had a mental attitude as though I were aware of a unicorn" may be just as true as: "I had a mental attitude as though I were aware of a bent stick"? There have been instances, let us assume, in which a horse has been dressed up with a horn; and there have been instances in which a mental attitude has had such a horse as an object. Considered as an intrinsic quality, the mental attitude which participated in such a subject-object relation resembles the mental attitude of mine which I describe by saying that it was seemingly directed upon a unicorn. Based on such facts as these, "I had a mental attitude as though I were aware of a unicorn" may, we hold, be true and "I had a mental attitude as though I were aware of a griffin" may be true. Neither the attitude seemingly directed upon a unicorn nor the attitude seemingly directed upon a griffin had an object. They can not be distinguished from one another by a reference to the objects that they respectively had. And when we attempt to distinguish between them by pointing to intrinsic qualities alone, our words may fail to identify either of these mental attitudes and may fail to call the reader's attention to the difference between them. But there is a real subject-object relation in which there is a mental attitude analogous to the one; and a real subject-object relation in which there is a mental attitude analogous to the other. There are in each case real entities which are objects for *resembling* mental attitudes; and the differences between these real objects may serve to distinguish one mental attitude which has no object from another.[60]

There is no unicorn, no griffin, no bent stick that was my object. What, then, becomes of the bent stick that was alleged to have been my object? This bent stick, to be sure, subsists. It subsists with whatever characteristics it may be alleged to have. There is a subsisting bent stick which appears as the immediate object of my thinking. There is a subsisting bent stick which appears as independent of all thinking, unaffected by the mental attitudes which are alleged to direct themselves towards it. But "when the alleged entity S_1 is unreal, both our proposition: 'S_1 is P' and our proposition: 'S_1 is not P' are false." [61] "The bent stick in yonder pool is independent of my thinking" is false; and "the bent stick in yonder pool is not independent of my thinking" is false. For these propositions resemble "the present King of France is bald" and "the present King of France is not bald." The only true propositions that can be asserted with respect to the bent stick are those in which non-existence is predicated of it. A bent stick subsists with the characteristic of being bent at an angle of 5°. And a bent stick subsists with the characteristic of being bent at an angle of 55°. The one subsists as well as the other. The one is no more real than the other.

But surely, it may be said, the bent stick which I seem to *see*, the bent stick which appears to be one inch in diameter and bent at an angle of 5°, has more reality than a purely imaginary stick, a stick which I imagine to be bent at an angle of 55°. Similarly when

I look towards the moon, a silver crescent in the sky, although un-real, has, it may be said, more substance and more reality than, for example, a black dwarf in the sky. But if all unreals are equally unreal, what can be the basis for such alleged distinctions? Since Ivanhoe was unreal, "Ivanhoe married Rowena" and "Ivanhoe married Rebecca" are both false propositions. There may, to be sure, be more instances of the real proposition: "Ivanhoe married Rowena," fewer instances of the real proposition: "Ivanhoe married Rebecca." Again, there is a real mental attitude which is as though it were directed upon a silver crescent in the sky; and a real mental attitude which is as though it were directed upon a black dwarf in the sky. But there may be more mental attitudes which, considered as intrinsic qualities, resemble the former than resemble the latter. There may be more mental attitudes which are as though they were directed upon a stick bent at an angle of 5° than there are that are as though they were directed upon a stick bent at an angle of 55°. And finally, there is the dis-tinction that may be made between an hallucinatory experience and an illusory experience. Some attitudes, which merely *seem* to be directed upon objects, are caused, or at least are affected, by entities which exist where the alleged object is alleged to be; whereas others are not. When I look at the moon, there is a round moon which brings about the mental attitude of mine which is as though it were directed upon a silver crescent in the sky. But when, sitting at my desk, I have a mental attitude which is as though it were directed upon a black dwarf in the sky, this round moon is not at the source of light waves which travel uninter-ruptedly to my mind-nerve-fibre and which thus affect my think-ing. Nevertheless, black dwarf and silver crescent, stick bent at an angle of 5° and stick bent at an angle of 55°, all are equally unreal. The mental attitudes which seemingly are directed upon them are equally without objects.

It is, we may say, only real entities that can be objects for real mental attitudes. The world of real entities is, as it were, closed off from the world of merely subsisting, unreal entities. As Par-menides held in the early days of Greek philosophy, Being is and Non-Being is not. And Being is not related to Non-Being.

Summary

Descartes is said to have witnessed the coronation of the Emperor. In this situation we distinguish three relational situations in which Descartes and the Emperor are terms, namely, a) Descartes-affected-by-the-Emperor, b) Descartes-responding-to-the-Emperor, c) Descartes-aware-of-the-Emperor. Corresponding to the relational situation: Descartes-responding-to-the-Emperor there is an intrinsic quality of Descartes', the quality of behaving or responding in a certain direction. And corresponding to the relational situation: Descartes-aware-of-the-Emperor there is Descartes' intrinsic quality of being aware as if of the Emperor. All of these entities are real. (In the main body of this chapter, we assert first the reality of the intrinsic qualities and then, after various objections are disposed of, the reality of the relational situations: Descartes-responding-to-the-Emperor and Descartes-aware-of-the-Emperor.)

But is Descartes-aware-of-the-Emperor an unmediated relational situation or one in which ideas mediate between Descartes and the Emperor? We consider various entities that may be proposed as intervening ideas and conclude that, generally speaking, there is no intervening idea. Generally speaking, the subject-object relation is an unmediated one.

How can this be so when there is the phenomenon of error? Where there is error, there is a mental attitude which is as if it had an object; but there *is* no object, hence no subject-object relation. The mental attitude is real and can be described, but it is not the term of a subject-object relation.

257

Chapter IX

PERCEPT, MEMORY AND CONCEPT

There are, we have seen, instances in which mental attitudes are affected by entities in their environment. And there are instances in which mental attitudes reach entities in their environment as their ultimate objects. While Descartes was witnessing the coronation ceremonies at Frankfurt, light and sound waves originating in the Emperor were flowing to Descartes' mind-nerve-fibres and were affecting his thinking.[1] And the thinking thus brought about reached the Emperor as its ultimate object. There was, that is to say, not only the real relational situation: Descartes-affected-by-the-Emperor, but also the real relational situation: Descartes-in-Frankfurt-having-a-mental-attitude-which-reached-the-Emperor-as-its-ultimate-object.[2] Similarly with the ledger clerk mentioned in a previous chapter, the ledger clerk concerned with figures on a ledger page in front of him. On the one hand, this clerk's mind-nerve-fibre, its non-mental qualities and its thinking were affected by the figures on the page in front of him.[3] And on the other hand, before turning to the statement which he was about to prepare, he was aware of the figures which had affected him. It is within such situations that there are what we shall call "percepts" and what we shall call "instances of perceiving." A mental attitude is an instance of perceiving, let us say, when it reaches as its object an entity which is at the source of motions flowing uninterruptedly to it and affecting it. And an entity is a percept, let us say, when it is at the source of motions flowing uninterruptedly to the mental attitude directed upon it and reaching it as an object. As we use the words "percept" and "perceiving," Descartes at Frankfurt was perceiving and the Emperor was his percept.

We have, to be sure, suggested a distinction between the entity merely at the source of motions terminating in a given mind-nerve-fibre and the entity at the source, in the absence of which the mind-nerve-fibre would not have been affected as it was. "We may use 'cause' and 'effect' in such a way that not every entity at the source of motion is a cause and not every entity at the terminus a result."[4] As *we* use the terms "percept" and "perceiving," however, no strict sense of "cause," and no strict sense of "result," is involved. An entity which is real, which is the object reached by a given mental attitude, and which is at the source of motions flowing uninterruptedly to that mental attitude, such an entity is in our terminology a "percept"—whether or not it be a *sine qua non* with respect to the mental attitude directed upon it. And a mental attitude which is real, and which reaches as its ultimate object an entity at the source of motions flowing uninterruptedly to it, is, in our terminology, an "instance of perceiving," whether the entity which it reaches as an object merely has *affected* it or, in some strict sense of "cause," has *caused* it. If the Emperor presented as a substance was real and if the Emperor was really pious, then Descartes at Frankfurt, in being aware of the Emperor or of his piety, was perceiving. The Emperor and his piety were percepts, even if it should be true that, in a strict sense of "cause," it was not the Emperor but some quality of his, and not the Emperor's piety but some *other* quality of his, that caused Descartes' thinking.[5]

Descartes at Frankfurt was aware of the Emperor in front of him. Descartes was perceiving and the Emperor was his percept. You too, we have agreed,[6] are aware of the Emperor. And yet, as we have explained our term "perceiving," your mental attitude directed upon the Emperor is not an instance of perceiving. For, whereas the Emperor was at the source of motions flowing uninterruptedly to Descartes' mental attitude, he was, let us agree, not at the source of motions flowing uninterruptedly to your mental attitude. The Emperor, it follows, was a percept with respect to one thinking mind-nerve-fibre reaching him as an ultimate object, but not a percept with respect to another mind-nerve-fibre reaching him as an ultimate object.

The Emperor was real, a percept with respect to one mind-nerve-fibre but not with respect to another. The mere fact that a given mental attitude reached the Emperor as an object does not determine whether that mental attitude was, or was not, an instance of perceiving. And the mere fact that the Emperor was real, plus the fact that he was an object for some mental attitudes which were instances of perceiving and for some mental attitudes which were not, does not determine whether a given mind-nerve-fibre was aware of him or was not aware of him. The Emperor's being real, in short, does not imply that Descartes was perceiving him or even that Descartes was aware of him. And we may express our rejection of such alleged implications by asserting that the Emperor might have been real if Descartes had not perceived him and might have been real if Descartes had not been aware of him.

The Emperor in Frankfurt, although an entity reached as an *object* by your mental attitude, is not a *percept* with respect to your mental attitude. And the other side of the moon, although reached as an object by various mental attitudes, is not a percept with respect to any of the mental attitudes reaching it as an object. Just as your mental attitude reaches the Emperor as an object but is not at the terminus of motions originating in the Emperor and flowing uninterruptedly to this mental attitude of yours, so various mental attitudes reach the other side of the moon as an object but are not at the termini of motions originating in the other side of the moon and flowing uninterruptedly to them. Nevertheless, the other side of the moon is real just as the Emperor is real. Just as the Emperor is not presented with the characteristic of lacking date or position or with the characteristic of being generally discredited, so the other side of the moon is not presented with the characteristic of lacking date or position or with the characteristic of being generally discredited. And just as the Emperor, presented without certain characteristics that would mark him out as unreal, is listed as real in the appendix to Chapter Three, so is the other side of the moon. As we have explained our term "reality," the characteristic of not being a percept with respect to any mental attitude is not a mark of unreality. An entity presented with the characteristic of not being a percept with respect to any mental attitude need not be unreal. And the other side of the moon, so presented, is, we find, real.

There is a fallen tree in the woods which is real and which is a percept of mine. And there was a prior phase of this tree, a phase in which the tree was *falling*, which, although real, was, let us agree, a percept for no one. Since one entity which is real is a percept with respect to some mental attitudes and another entity which is real a percept with respect to no mental attitudes, the mere fact that the fallen tree is real does not determine whether it was some one's percept or no one's percept. Just as the Emperor's being real "does not imply that Descartes was perceiving him,"[7] so the fallen tree's being real does not imply that the fallen tree was some one's percept. Just as in the one case we may express our rejection of an alleged implication by asserting that the Emperor might have been real if Descartes had not perceived him, so in the other case we may express our rejection of an alleged implication by asserting that the fallen tree might have been real if no one had perceived it.

Descartes however *was* perceiving the Emperor; and I, similarly, *am* perceiving the fallen tree. An Emperor presented as perceived by Descartes and presented as not perceived by Descartes is presented as self-contradictory and is unreal. And an Emperor presented as in no sense an object of consciousness is presented with a characteristic which likewise marks out the Emperor so presented as unreal.[8] Similarly with the fallen tree. The fallen tree presented as some one's percept and no one's percept is unreal; and the fallen tree presented as no one's object is unreal. Thus in a context which informs us that the Emperor was Descartes' percept, it is not possible, as we have explained the term "truth" in its application to problematic propositions, for Descartes not to have perceived the Emperor.[9] And in a context which informs us that the fallen tree was some one's percept, it is not possible for the fallen tree to have been no one's percept. In a more limited context, however, in a context which informs us merely that the Emperor was real and the fallen tree real, we may say that the Emperor may have been real, though unperceived by Descartes; and we may say that the fallen tree may be real though unperceived by anyone. But even within so limited a context, the proposition: "The Emperor may have been real, though an object for no one" is false, and the proposition: "The fallen tree may have been real, though an object for no one" is likewise false. There is a sense, we have seen, in which it may be asserted that the fallen tree might have been real if no one had perceived it. But the proposition is false in which we express the assertion that the fallen tree might have been real if no one had been *aware* of it. The fallen tree's being real, in short, does not imply that this tree was some one's percept, but it *does* imply that this tree was some one's object or, more precisely, that it did not have the characteristic of being no one's object.

The Emperor was a percept of Descartes'. And lawyer Jones, who stands before me, is a percept of mine. There was, however, some previous occasion on which I first saw lawyer Jones and was about to be introduced to him. And on that occasion, let us agree, I was at first not aware that the man before me was a lawyer or that his name was Jones. The lawyer Jones who now stands before me had, in short, a prior phase, a phase which affected my thinking and which led me to be aware, not of lawyer Jones, but of Mr. X. Let us then abstract from the lawyer Jones who stands before me his quality of being a lawyer and his quality of being named Jones. And let us seek within my present percept for some residual element to correspond to what my object was when lawyer Jones first affected my thinking. Indeed, let us seek to disregard or to neutralize not only the mental attitudes which I have directed upon lawyer Jones since that first meeting, but various other mental attitudes as well. When I first met lawyer Jones, I was aware of him as being a man. "What do I see," we have, however, found Descartes asking,[10] "but hats and coats which may cover automatic machines?" When a baby is first confronted by a man, he is, let us agree, no more aware of his percept as being a man than I was of lawyer Jones as being a lawyer named Jones. Just as my present mental attitude aware of lawyer Jones' name and profession points back not only to what I first saw but to what I later learned, so the baby's mental attitude which is aware of a man as being a man points back not only to what he was aware of when first confronted by a man but to other experiences of his as well.

It is the alleged residual element within a given percept that we shall call a "sense-datum." A sense-datum, that is to say, is, if

262

it is real, that real quality of a percept, or that real element within a percept, which corresponds to the object of some previous instance of perceiving unaffected by experience. To be sure, when today I am confronted by lawyer Jones, I do not, let us agree, first perceive a sense-datum or even a Mr. X. While I am looking at lawyer Jones, there need be no particular succession of mental attitudes, no mental attitude directed upon a sense-datum followed by a mental attitude directed upon lawyer Jones, his name and his profession. Indeed if there is any element within my percept which is to be called a "sense-datum" as we have explained that term, it may be that I today am aware of it only after a process of analysis and abstraction. When confronted by Rodin's "Thinker" or by a landscape painting, "it is, one might say, when we attend to the artist's technique that we distinguish the sense-datum from what then appears to us to have been inferred." [11] And if there is a sense-datum within the lawyer Jones who is the object of my present perceiving, it is perhaps only after reflecting upon the meaning of "sense-datum" that I today come to be aware of it. The prior instance of perceiving, to whose object the sense-datum included in my present percept corresponds, need not then be the earliest in the series of mental attitudes that I today direct upon lawyer Jones. The prior instance of perceiving to whose object a sense-datum corresponds is allegedly a mental attitude with a real object but a mental attitude unaffected by experience. And the search for such a mental attitude may lead us to think of mental attitudes much earlier in the history of the individual or in the history of the race.

A sense-datum, if real, is that element within a percept which corresponds to the object of some previous instance of perceiving unaffected by experience. But as I look at lawyer Jones, my mental attitude is an instance of perceiving, whether I am aware of a lawyer named Jones, whether I am aware of my object as Mr. X., or whether I am aware of a sense-datum that is a real quality or element in lawyer Jones. As we use the terms "percept" and "sense-datum," a sense-datum, if it is real, may be a percept; and an element in the object before me, an element not a sense-datum, may likewise be a percept. If there is a quality of the lawyer Jones who stands before me that is a sense-datum,—and if I am aware of it,—then that quality is at the source of motions which flow uninterruptedly to me and which lead me to be aware of it. But the quality of being a lawyer named Jones is likewise at the source of motions which flow uninterruptedly to me and which lead me to be aware of a lawyer named Jones. In either instance I am perceiving. For whether it be a substance or a quality, a residual element or some less elementary object, so long as the entity of which I am aware is at the source of motions flowing uninterruptedly to me and leading me to be aware of it, that entity is a percept of mine and my mental attitude an instance of perceiving.[12]

As we use the term "percept," lawyer Jones' quality of being a lawyer is a percept of mine and the Emperor's piety was a percept of Descartes'. But whereas lawyer Jones' quality of being a lawyer is at the source of motions flowing uninterruptedly to me and leading me to be aware of this quality, there may be some other quality inhering in lawyer Jones without which I would not be affected as I am. Some other quality inhering in lawyer Jones may be that without which I would not be aware of Jones as a lawyer; and some quality other than the Emperor's piety may be that without which Descartes would not have been aware of the Emperor as pious.[13] Although Jones' quality of being a lawyer affected my thinking, and although the Emperor's piety affected Descartes' thinking, there may be some strict sense of "cause" in which Jones' quality of being a lawyer does not *cause* my thinking nor the Emperor's piety Descartes' thinking.[14] As we use the term "percept," the Emperor's piety was a percept with respect to Descartes' thinking whether or not it was a sense-datum with respect to that thinking. And as we use the term "percept," the Emperor's piety was a percept with respect to Descartes' thinking, whether it merely affected that thinking or whether, in a strict sense of "cause," it was the cause of that thinking.[15]

Nevertheless, the distinction which we have sought to make between the percept which is a sense-datum and the percept which is not a sense-datum is not to be confused with the distinction which we have sought to make between the entity at the source, which merely affects the instance of perceiving directed upon it, and the entity at the source, which, in a strict sense of "cause," is the *cause* of that instance of perceiving. A mental attitude which is an instance of perceiving has been affected by its percept; it also reaches its per-

264

cept as its ultimate object. In the search for sense-data we concern ourselves with the relational situation involving mental attitude and object and are led to consider relational situations involving earlier mental attitudes and earlier objects. But in the search for entities at the source without which a given instance of perceiving would not be affected as it is, we concern ourselves with relational situations involving motions flowing to terminus from source. We are led to consider, not earlier mental attitudes with real objects but unaffected by experience, and not residual objects, but rather a group of mental attitudes, some similar and some dissimilar and a group of sources, some similar and some dissimilar. On the one hand, if any entities exist which are denoted by our term "sense-data," they are, it would seem, such vague entities as something - making - a - noise - somewhere or something - shining - somewhere. On the other hand, if there is some entity at the source in the absence of which a given mental attitude would not be affected as it is, that entity at the source may be some quality which is neither vague nor elementary; it may rather be a quality such that only a student of physics is aware of it and can describe it.

The Emperor was at the source of motions which flowed uninterruptedly to Descartes who was in front of him, at the source of motions affecting the mental attitude of Descartes' which reached him as an object. He was likewise, let us agree, at the source of motions which flowed uninterruptedly to the Bishop of Mayence who stood at the Emperor's side, at the source of motions affecting the mental attitude of the Bishop which likewise reached him as an object. Not only then was the Emperor a percept with respect to Descartes; he was also a percept with respect to the Bishop who stood at his side. He may indeed have been an *immediate* object both for Descartes' perceiving and for the Bishop's perceiving. For he was, we have held, "not only the ultimate object, but also the immediate object, reached by a mental attitude belonging to Descartes at Frankfurt."[16] And he may likewise have been, not only the ultimate object, but also the immediate object, of the mental attitude belonging to the Bishop.

But how, it may be asked, can Descartes and the Bishop have had a common immediate object?[17] Descartes and the Bishop looked at the Emperor from different positions just as when there are ten people "sitting round a dinner table," [18] they all see the table from slightly different points of view. What is it, however, that I see when I sit at one end of a rectangular table, and what is it that you see when you sit at the other end? The table is rectangular, neither narrower at your end nor narrower at mine. It is a rectangular table, not a table narrower at my end, that affects your thinking. And it is a rectangular table, not a table narrower at your end, that affects my thinking. Hence, if your apparent object is a table, presented not as rectangular but as narrower at my end, then the real table which has affected your thinking is not the object of your thinking. And if my apparent object is a table, presented not as rectangular but as narrower at your end, then the real table which has affected my thinking is not the object of *my* thinking. In such a situation you are not perceiving and I am not perceiving. In so far as you seem to be aware of a table narrower at my end, you are aware but not aware-of.[19] And in so far as I seem to be aware of a table narrower at your end, I too am aware but not aware-of.

Instead, however, of my seeming to be aware of a table narrower at your end, it may be that I am aware of a rectangular table. And instead of your seeming to be aware of a table narrower at my end, it may be that you too are aware of a rectangular table. A state of affairs in which you and I are in continual disagreement as to the shape of the table is presented as generally discredited and is unreal. What exists, let us agree, is a relational situation in which my mental attitude, having been affected by a rectangular table, is aware of a rectangular table; and a relational situation in which your mental attitude, having been affected by a rectangular table, is likewise aware of a rectangular table. A mental attitude apparently directed upon a table narrower at your end may have preceded my mental attitude reaching the rectangular table as its object. But the trapeziform table alleged to have been the object for such a preceding mental attitude is not a residual element, not a sense-datum, within the rectangular table that comes to be my object. Nor is it a quality of the rectangular table without which I would not be aware of the rectangular table. Being unreal, it "inheres in no real substance and is a term in no real relational situation." [20]

There is a situation in which my mental attitude, having been

266

affected by the rectangular table at which I sit, is without a real object, but is as though its object were a trapeziform table. And there is a situation in which my mental attitude, having been affected by a straight stick in the water in front of me, is without a real object, but is as though its object were a bent stick.[21] These mental attitudes are, let us say, "instances of pseudo-perceiving." They differ from mental attitudes which are without objects, but which are not instances of pseudo-perceiving, in that they are "affected by entities which exist where the alleged object is alleged to be." [22] The distinction, in short, to which we have already alluded, the distinction between illusory experiences on the one hand and hallucinatory experiences on the other, is the distinction between mental attitudes without objects which we call "instances of pseudo-perceiving" and mental attitudes without objects which are not what we call "instances of pseudo-perceiving."

There is motion flowing uninterruptedly from the rectangular table to the mental attitude of mine which is as though it were directed upon a trapeziform table. And there is motion flowing uninterruptedly from the Emperor at Frankfurt to that mental attitude which Descartes had when he perceived the Emperor in front of him.[23] What is the situation, however, when I listen to a symphony by Beethoven as recorded on a phonograph record; or when I see the coronation of George VI as represented in a news-reel? If I am aware of sounds as coming from the record or of colors as being on a screen, my mental attitude has as its object the sounding record, or the picture on the screen, which is at the source of motions flowing uninterruptedly to my mental attitude and affecting it. My mental attitude is an instance of perceiving and the sounding record, or the picture on the screen, is its percept.

Let us agree, however, that, while the record is being played, some mental attitude of mine is directed upon what happened in the studio when the Philadelphia orchestra was performing the symphony and recording it. And let us agree that, while looking at the news-reel, I turn my attention from the screen in front of me to certain events which occurred in Westminster Abbey. Neither the performance in Philadelphia nor the events in Westminster Abbey are, it would seem, at the source of motions flowing uninterruptedly to my present mental attitudes. Motions originating in Westminster Abbey were, as it were, held up in the film and released only when the film was run off in front of me. And motions originating in Philadelphia and finally affecting me were interrupted while, for example, my record lay in a warehouse or in my cabinet. There are, let us agree, relational situations in which I am aware of such entities as this performance in Philadelphia or this coronation in Westminster Abbey. There are indeed relational situations in which such entities as these are my *immediate* objects.[24] Such objects are however not *percepts* for the mental attitudes thus directed upon them. For they are, as in the instances given, not at the source of motions travelling *uninterruptedly* to the mental attitudes whose objects they are.

I may attend a performance by the Philadelphia orchestra. The performance may affect me through a phonograph record. Or a friend who attended the performance may describe it to me. Just as, when I listen to the record, the sounding record may be my object rather than the performance to which it refers, so when I listen to my friend, his voice or his mental attitude may be my object rather than the performance to which his words refer. But just as I may turn my attention from the record, which is here and now, to the performance which was there and then, so I may direct my mental attitude, not upon my friend, but upon the performance which he is describing. Again my object is the past performance in Philadelphia. Again, when I come to fix my attention on this object, it may be my immediate object.[25] And again my object is at the source of motions which have travelled, but have not travelled uninterruptedly, to me. For the process by which the performance affected my friend corresponds to the process by which the recording was made. And the motion, coming to me from the playing record which I hear, corresponds to the motion coming to me from the friend of mine who describes to me the performance he has attended. My friend, to be sure, is no record and no record cabinet. But in the process from ultimate object to mental attitude aware of that object, motions may, as it were, be intercepted, more or less transformed, and later released, by mind-persons as well as by records or pictures.

When I direct my attention to a performance which my friend describes to me, my experience is no doubt different from what it is when the performance takes place in my presence. To think *about* a performance is, one may say, to be aware of an object which is presented somewhat indefinitely, without its full detail. But whether I attend the performance, hear a recording of it or merely think *about* it, it is the performance which is my object. And when I pass over air waves in the one case, the record in the second, and my friend's voice and attitude in the third, when, in short, I do not direct my attention to the intermediaries through which my object has affected me, then the performance is my *immediate* object.

There are instances of perceiving, as when I am aware of the rectangular table in front of me which has affected me. There are instances of pseudo-perceiving, as when, with a rectangular table in front of me which has affected me, I seem, nevertheless, to be aware of a trapeziform table.[26] Similarly there is on the one hand the situation in which I am aware of a performance in Philadelphia which, through friend or record, has affected me; and there is on the other hand the situation in which, after listening to a friend who was pseudo-perceiving, I seem to be aware of an alleged event which did not occur. A soldier may have left the battle at Waterloo with the report that the French were victorious. Some of the sentences written by an historian may not be true. My friend may have given me what is commonly called a "false impression" of what occurred in Philadelphia. Indeed, with reporters, historians or other interpreters as intermediaries, it may be held that we are never aware of events as they actually occurred, that our mental attitudes are always analogous to instances of pseudo-perceiving rather than to instances of perceiving. But whereas the object of which I came to be aware through an interpreter may not be presented with the detail with which that object is presented when I am perceiving it, nevertheless the elements in the object which *are* presented need not, we hold, be unreal. Charles the First, let us agree, *did* die on the scaffold. And when, with many historians and ultimately an eye-witness as intermediaries, I come to be aware of Charles dying on the scaffold, then I am aware of a real object. My object, that is to say, is at the source of motions, which, although delayed in transmission and transformed by the intermediaries through whom they have passed, have affected the mental attitude of mine directed upon this real object.

"Motions may, as it were, be intercepted, more or less transformed and later released, by mind-persons as well as by records or pictures." [27] And the mind-person doing the intercepting, transforming and releasing may, it would seem, be a previous phase of the very subject who is aware of the ultimate object. It may not have been my friend, but I, who attended the performance in Philadelphia. And the mental attitude which I today direct upon this past performance may have been affected by the performance, not through my friend as intermediary, but through the attitudes which I had last night when I was attending the performance. Last night I was perceiving; today I am not. Today I seem again to be aware of last night's performance; and if my apparent object is not unreal, if it is all or part of what *did* occur, then I today am really aware of last night's performance. But last night's performance is not at the source of motions which have travelled *uninterruptedly* to the mental attitude which I have today. With respect to today's mental attitude directed upon last night's performance, those motions have been intercepted, and yet in some sense passed on, by nerve-fibres within my body which were affected last night. I *am*, let us agree, aware of last night's performance. My present mental attitude which has a real object is then in our terminology an instance of "remembering." And last night's performance, which is reached as a real object by today's mental attitude is, let us say, a "memory" with respect to this attitude.

As we use the terms "percept" and "memory," last night's performance was a percept with respect to the mental attitude which I directed upon it last night, a memory with respect to the mental attitude which I direct upon it today. Last night's moon was a percept with respect to the mental attitude of yours which was aware of it last night, with respect, that is to say, to the mental attitude of yours which was at the terminus of motions flowing uninterruptedly from moon to mental attitude. And last night's moon is a memory with respect to the mental attitude which you today direct upon last night's moon, with respect to the mental attitude where the flow of motions from moon to mental attitude has been interrupted and yet transmitted by earlier phases of your body or mind-person.

When a record is being played in my presence, I may, on the one hand, we have seen,[28] be aware of the sounding record before me rather than of the events in the studio where the record was made; or I may, on the other hand, be aware of the performance in the studio and not of the record. Descartes at Frankfurt may at one moment have been aware of the Emperor who was his percept; and he may at another moment have been aware of his own ears, of the ears through which the Emperor was affecting him. Similarly there may today be one thinking mind-nerve-fibre of yours which is aware of last night's moon and remembering it. And there may today be another thinking mind-nerve-fibre of yours which is aware of the mental attitude which you had last night when you were perceiving the moon. There are in short, let us agree, instances of remembering; but there also are instances in which mental attitudes reach as their objects prior mental attitudes of one's own, prior mental attitudes which are intermediaries in the process from memory to instance of remembering.

In being aware of the fact that the Emperor was his percept, Descartes, we may suppose, was aware of the fact that the Emperor was affecting him through air-waves and ears, through light waves and retina. To be aware of a percept *as* a percept, we may say, is to be aware of the process from percept to instance of perceiving. And to be aware of a memory *as* a memory, to be aware of the fact that a given entity is a memory with respect to a given instance of remembering, is, we may say, to be aware of the process from memory to remembering. But there are, we hold, instances of perceiving which are not accompanied by mental attitudes aware of the percept *as* a percept. And there are instances of remembering not accompanied by mental attitudes aware of the memory *as* a memory. Descartes' behavior may have been adapted to the Emperor. but not to Descartes' own ears, not "to the ears through which the Emperor's voice has affected Descartes' behavior." [29] The relational situation: Descartes-having-a-mental-attitude-which-reaches-the-Emperor-as-its-ultimate-object may be real; and the alleged relational situation: Descartes-having-a-mental-attitude-which-reaches-intervening-air-waves-as-objects unreal. And you today may be remembering last night's moon, but aware neither of the process from last night's moon to today's remembering, nor of the perceiving which occurred last night and which was an intermediary in that process. When I remember the performance which I attended last night, I say, for example: "First they played an overture, then a symphony" rather than "First I heard an overture, then I heard a symphony." My mental attitude, that is to say, is directed towards last night's performance, and not towards the mental attitudes which I had last night. It is directed towards the entity that was a percept with respect to last night's perceiving and is a memory with respect to today's remembering, but not towards the *fact* that that entity was a percept with respect to last night's perceiving and is a memory with respect to today's remembering.

Let us assume that one of my mind-nerve-fibres today is aware of the process from last night's performances to today's remembering, or is aware of the mental attitude which I had last night when I was perceiving the performance. And let us assume that subsequently another of my mind-nerve-fibres remembers the performance but is not aware of it as a memory. Then in the subject-object relation between remembering mind-nerve-fibre and memory not recognized as a memory, the performance need not be an indirect object with process or prior perceiving intervening as idea. For being an idea, we have said, is not "merely being an object for some previous mental attitude." [30] Nor does the fact that there are intermediaries in the process from memory to instance of remembering imply that there is an idea intervening in the subject-object relation involving remembering subject and memory object. "The Emperor, alleged to be both the cause and the ultimate object reached by Descartes' thinking, need not be presented as unreal when intervening entities are presented as nearer causes, but not nearer objects, of Descartes' thinking." [31] And last night's performance, presented as the *immediate* object of today's remembering, need not be presented as unreal even though last night's perceiving is presented as an intermediary in the process from performance to remembering. The process from memory to remembering need not be an intervening idea. Last night's perceiving need not be an intervening idea. And no entity which is present and not past need be an intervening idea. For it is "no more incredible for a subject to be now and its immediate object then than it is for one end of this couch to be here and the other end there." [32] Indeed last night's performance, presented as the immediate object of my present remembering, is, we hold, real; and last night's moon, presented as the immediate object of your present remembering, is, we hold, likewise real. For last night's performance and last night's moon so presented are presented neither as self-contradictory nor as incredible; and they are listed as real in the

272

appendix to Chapter Three.

It has been held, to be sure, that a given mental attitude's immediate objects must all be contemporaneous with it. If a bell is struck twice in succession, then, although I am perceiving the second stroke which is now, I can be aware of the first stroke which is past, it is said, only by being aware of a present idea referring back to that past stroke. If I am to be aware of both strokes together, if I am to compare them, or if I am to say: "The bell has struck twice," one of the objects of my present mental attitude, it has been held, must be a contemporaneous replica of the entity that was my object when I was perceiving the first stroke. I must, it is said, "reproduce" [33] the object of my former perceiving.

When, however, my present mental attitude reaches the past stroke as its ultimate object, my immediate object is not an idea "held to be non-spatial," not an idea "held not to be spatially related to ultimate objects contemporaneous with it," not an idea "held not to be an object for other subjects," and not an idea held to be adjacent to my thinking.[34] The alleged contemporaneous replica of the object of my former perceiving is unreal when it is presented with any of these characteristics and when it is also presented as primarily an *object* and hence as distinguishable from my mental attitude itself. It is my present mental attitudes which are real. And these mental attitudes have as their immediate objects, we hold, the second stroke which is present, the first stroke which is past, and the relational situation first-stroke-prior-to-second-stroke as well. The first stroke which is past enters as immediate object into subject-object relational situations with two thinking mind-nerve-fibres of mine, with my former mind-nerve-fibre with respect to which it was a percept and with my present mind-nerve-fibre with respect to which it is a memory. There are indeed respects in which my present mind-nerve-fibre, which remembers, resembles my former mind-nerve-fibre which perceived. Both mind-nerve-fibres, for example, have the same object. It is however not an *object* which is *reproduced,* but two *mind-nerve-fibres* which are *similar,* one occurring after the other in different phases of the same mind-person.

There are instances of remembering. But "there also are instances in which mental attitudes reach as their objects prior mental attitudes of one's own, prior mental attitudes which are inter-

273

mediaries in the process from memory to instance of remembering." [35] I may remember the first stroke which is past, and may be aware of the fact that it was prior to the second stroke which is present, without being aware of the process from first stroke to present remembering, and without being aware of the former perceiving of mine with respect to which the first stroke was a percept. But along with instances of being aware of a series of objects, there are instances of being aware of a series of mental attitudes, all of which are directed upon one of these objects. I may, it would seem, be aware both of my present remembering and of my past perceiving, may be aware of the fact that an earlier mental attitude directed upon a given object has preceded a later mental attitude directed upon the same object. We do not agree, however, that "without our being conscious that what we are thinking now is the same as what we thought a moment before, all reproduction in the series of representations would be in vain." [36] Not only is there no reproduction of objects, but such repetition of mental attitudes as there is does not require a mental attitude which is both contemporaneous with the second of two resembling mind-nerve-fibres and aware of the first.

This much however is true. The entity which is alleged to be my memory, and also alleged to be recognized as my memory by no one, is unreal. For to impute to the quality of being my memory the characteristic of being no one's object is to impute to that alleged quality a characteristic which, as we have explained "reality," marks out that alleged quality as unreal. [37] But to say that my memory does not exist when presented with the characteristic of being recognized as my memory by no one is somewhat different from saying that, for my memory to be real, it must have the quality of being recognized as my memory by someone. [38] And it is far different from saying that, for my memory to be real, it must be recognized as a memory by a mental attitude of mine contemporaneous with my remembering.

Last night's performance in Philadelphia may be at the source of motions travelling uninterruptedly to the mental attitude which I had when I was attending the performance. Or it may be at the source of motions, which were held up, as it were, in a record, but which affected the mental attitude which I had when I listened to this record. It may be at the source of motions which affected my

274

friend who attended the performance, and which, through him, affected the mental attitude which I had when I heard him describe the performance. Or it may be at the source of motions affecting me through a process in which some previous mental attitude of mine was an intermediary. There are real mental attitudes at the termini of motions flowing uninterruptedly from the entities of which those mental attitudes are aware. And there are real mental attitudes such that the motions, flowing to them from the objects of which they are aware, have been delayed in passing through some such intermediaries as a record, a friend's attitude, or a prior mental attitude of one's own.

What however is the situation when there are alleged to be no interrupted motions, and no *un*interrupted motions, flowing from an alleged object to a mental attitude alleged to be aware of that object? There are, let us agree, no interrupted motions, and no uninterrupted motions, flowing to you from the other side of the moon. And similarly the mental attitudes which I have today are not affected, let us agree, by the sunrise which will occur tomorrow morning. Nevertheless as you read this, you *do* have a mental attitude which seems to be directed upon the other side of the moon. And since the other side of the moon is real,[39] your mental attitude is not without a real object, but reaches as its object the other side of the moon. The other side of the moon is thus a real object with respect to a mental attitude of yours which it has not affected. And tomorrow's sunrise is, we hold, a real object with respect to a mental attitude of mine which *it* has not affected. Tomorrow's sunrise may be a percept with respect to a mental attitude that will exist tomorrow morning. It may be a memory with respect to a mental attitude that will exist still later. But with respect to the mental attitude which I have today, it is, let us say, an "inferred object." And the other side of the moon is, let us say, an "inferred object" with respect to the mental attitude which you successfully direct upon it.

Some phase of the sun today, or some prior phase of the sun, has affected me. And these phases which have affected me are related to that phase of the sun which will exist when the sun rises tomorrow. They are all, that is to say, phases of the same enduring entity; and the past phases with their acceleration lead on to the future phase. But does the fact that past phases of the sun reach out, as it were, in two directions,—on the one hand, to the present mental attitude which they affect and, on the other hand, to to-morrow's sunrise—account for the fact that my present mental atti-tude has as its object tomorrow's sunrise? The ball which I am about to throw affects the dog at my feet and is related to the ball's falling to the ground which will occur some distance away. But if we do not confuse what is usual with what is free from puzzle-ment, we may find it puzzling that my dog's behavior, unaffected by a future phase of the ball, is nevertheless "adapted to the ball that is about to fall to the ground some distance away."[40] Such be-wilderment as there may be, however, does not imply that my dog's behavior, presented as adapted to a future phase of the ball, is presented as generally discredited and is unreal. "A similarity between two peoples need not be presented as generally discredited even though such a similarity unaccompanied by mutual influence or common ancestry is . . . presented as puzzling." [41] So with my dog's behavior presented as adapted to a future phase of the ball which has not affected him. And so with my present mental atti-tude presented as reaching as its object tomorrow's sunrise. There *is,* we find, a real relational situation: my-dog's-behavior-adapted-to-the-ball-about-to-fall-to-the-ground. And there is a real rela-tional situation: my-present-mind-nerve-fibre-aware-of-tomorrow's-sunrise.

Suppose, however, that I do not throw the ball but merely pre-tend to throw it. The dog starts off. But whereas he behaves as though his behavior were adapted to a ball about to fall to the ground, his behavior is not adapted to anything.[42] Somewhat similarly, having been affected by entity A, I may merely *seem* to be aware of an entity B that is alleged to be related to it. B may be unreal, not *really* connected with A and not *really* the object of a mental attitude of mine. In short, just as there are instances of perceiving and instances of pseudo-perceiving; and just as "there is on the one hand the situation in which I am aware of a perform-ance in Philadelphia which, through friend or record, has affected me," and, "on the other hand, the situation in which, after listen-ing to a friend who was pseudo-perceiving, I seem to be aware of an alleged event which did not occur;" [43] so, let us agree, there are instances of mental attitudes which are aware of inferred ob-jects and instances of mental attitudes which merely *seem* to be aware of inferred objects.

I may, we have seen, be aware of the performance in Philadelphia and may pass over the friend or record through which this performance has affected me.[44] The performance in Philadelphia, that is to say, may be my immediate object. Similarly, tomorrow's sunrise, which is an inferred object with respect to my present mental attitude, may be my immediate object. For just as I may be aware of the performance without being aware of friend or record, so I may be aware of tomorrow's sunrise without there being a contemporaneous mental attitude of mine directed upon the past phases of the sun which have affected me. Tomorrow's sunrise may be an immediate object with respect to the mental attitude with respect to which it is an inferred object. It may be an immediate object with respect to tomorrow's mental attitude with respect to which it will be a percept. And it may be an immediate object with respect to some later mental attitude with respect to which it will be a memory.

Furthermore, just as there is a distinction to be made between the mind-nerve-fibre which perceives and the mind-nerve-fibre which is aware of a percept *as* a percept; and just as there is a distinction to be made between the mind-nerve fibre which remembers and the mind-nerve-fibre which is aware of a memory *as* a memory,[45] so there is a distinction to be made between the mind-nerve-fibre aware of an inferred object and the mind-nerve-fibre aware of its object *as* an inferred object. For just as I may be aware, not only of last night's performance, but also of the fact that I formerly perceived this performance and am now remembering it, so I may be aware, not only of tomorrow's sunrise, but also of the fact that my present mental attitude, although directed upon tomorrow's sunrise, has been affected, not by it, but by other entities related to it.

The mental attitudes which we have thus far in this chapter been classifying and discussing have all been mental attitudes directed upon individual objects or seeming to be directed upon individual objects. But what about mental attitudes alleged to be directed upon universals? Are there real instances of mental attitudes reaching universals as their objects, just as there are real instances of mental attitudes reaching what for them are inferred objects, and just as there are real instances of perceiving?

If there were no real individuals, there would be no mental attitudes reaching individuals as their objects. And if there were no real universals, there would be no mental attitudes reaching universals as their objects. That some universals exist is a proposition which calls for considerable discussion.[46] But it would carry us far beyond the limits set for this chapter to discuss this proposition at any length at this point. Just then as in previous chapters we have agreed to the existence of certain entities on the basis of their being listed as real in the appendix to Chapter Three,[47] so here let us on a similar basis agree to the existence of certain universals. The universal 'man,' presented as existing where various individual men exist, is, let us agree, a real entity; and the universal 'star,' presented as existing where various individual stars exist.

Moreover there was, let us say, a mind-nerve-fibre of Newton's which seemed to be directed upon the universal 'star,' and a mind-nerve-fibre of Aristotle's which seemed to be directed upon the universal 'man.' The mind-nerve-fibre of Newton's, which had the intrinsic quality of seeming to be directed upon 'star,' was brought about, let us suppose, not by 'star,' but by various individual stars. And it was various individual men, let us suppose, who affected Aristotle and brought about his mental attitude seemingly directed upon 'man.' But it is not incredible, we have seen, that my dog's behavior should be adapted to a future phase of a ball even when that future phase is presented as not having affected my dog's behavior.[48] And Newton's mental attitude, presented as having *reached* 'star' as its object, and also presented as not having been affected by 'star,' is not presented as generally discredited and need not be unreal. Even though my present mental attitude has not been affected by tomorrow's sunrise, it not only *seems* to be directed upon tomorrow's sunrise, but *reaches* tomorrow's sunrise as its object. So with Newton's mental attitude apparently directed upon 'star'; and so with Aristotle's mental attitude apparently directed upon 'man.' 'Star' is a real universal and 'man' a real universal. And they are, we hold, real objects with respect to certain mental attitudes directed upon them.

There was a mental attitude of Aristotle's which reached the universal 'man' as its object. And there is a mental attitude of *yours* which reaches the universal 'man' as its object. Both mental

278

attitudes are, let us say, "instances of conceiving." And the universal 'man' let us call a "concept" with respect to the mental attitude which Aristotle directed upon it and a "concept" with respect to the mental attitude which *you* direct upon it. 'Man,' that is to say, is in our terminology a "concept" with respect to several instances of conceiving, just as the Emperor at Frankfurt was a percept with respect to Descartes and a percept with respect to the Bishop of Mayence.[49]

Along with instances of perceiving, however, there also exist instances of pseudo-perceiving.[50] Just so, let us hold, there exist instances of pseudo-conceiving, mental attitudes, that is to say, which resemble instances of conceiving but which fail to reach real universals as their objects. The universal 'man' is real, but the alleged universal 'centaur' unreal. Nevertheless there are thinking mind-nerve-fibres seemingly directed upon 'centaur,' thinking mind-nerve-fibres with intrinsic qualities similar to those of mind-nerve-fibres which succeed in reaching universals as their objects.[51] Such thinking mind-nerve-fibres have no object, since their alleged object is unreal. They are instances of pseudo-conceiving which, in that they have no object, resemble instances of pseudo-perceiving and resemble "instances of mental attitudes which merely *seem* to be aware of inferred objects."[52]

"I may be aware of tomorrow's sunrise," we have said,[53] "without there being a contemporaneous mental attitude of mine directed upon the past phases of the sun which have affected me." Similarly, although your mental attitude directed upon 'man' may have been brought about by various individual men whom you have seen, or by some instance of the word "man" which you have read, your mental attitude directed upon 'man' need not be accompanied by a mental attitude directed upon the entities which have affected your thinking. 'Man' may be your immediate object just as tomorrow's sunrise may be my immediate object and the performance which I remember my immediate object.

There is some universal 'man' which is real. But an alleged universal 'man,' "presented as in no sense an object of consciousness,"[54] presented, we may say, as not a concept with respect to any mental attitude, is unreal. Similarly the universal 'man' is unreal which is presented as a concept with respect to the mental attitude which you had a moment ago and also presented as *not* a

279

concept with respect to the mental attitude which you had a moment ago. For the subsistent presented as in no sense an object is unreal and the subsistent presented with contradictory characteristics is unreal. But the universal 'man,' presented as not having been a concept with respect to any mental attitude which you had yesterday, need not be unreal. And unless it is also presented as a concept with respect to your mental attitude of a moment ago, the universal 'man,' presented as *not* a concept with respect to your mental attitude of a moment ago, need not be unreal. The fact that there is some universal 'man' which is real does not imply that any *particular* mental attitude is aware of that real 'man.' And we may express our rejection of such an alleged implication by asserting that 'man' would have been real even if you a moment ago had not conceived it.

An entity is unreal which is presented as no one's object. A universal is unreal which is presented as no one's concept. An entity need not be unreal, however, which is presented as no one's percept. And an entity need not be unreal which is presented as no one's memory. For the entity presented as no one's percept, or presented as no one's memory, need not be presented as no one's object. But just as a universal is unreal which is presented as no one's concept, so is a *percept* unreal which is presented as no one's percept and a *memory* unreal which is presented as no one's memory. Within a context which informs us that an entity is an object for some particular mental attitude or for mental attitudes of a certain type, it is not possible for that entity not to be an object for that particular mental attitude or for it not to be an object for mental attitudes of that type. Within a context however which merely informs us that a given universal is real, then, although it is not possible for that universal to be no one's concept, it *is* possible for that universal not to be a concept with respect to this or that mental attitude. And within a context which merely informs us that a given *individual* is real, then, although it is not possible for that individual to be no one's object, it *is* possible for that individual not to be a percept with respect to this or that mental attitude and not a percept at all. And it *is* possible for that individual not to be a memory with respect to this or that mental attitude and not a memory at all.

There is a sense then in which it is not this or that mental atti-

280

tude which makes its percept real or its memory real or its concept real. Not that mental attitudes which are earlier may not be at the source of motions flowing to objects of theirs which are later. Lady Macbeth may have had a mental attitude directed upon Macbeth's queen which she was to be; and this mental attitude of hers may have been effective in bringing about her future regal status. But Descartes did not create the Emperor who was his percept and his immediate object. *I* did not create last night's performance which was my memory and my immediate object. And *you* did not create the universal 'man' which was *your* concept and your immediate object.

The universal 'man,' let us agree, did not bring about your mental attitude directed upon 'man.' But how can we conclude from this that your mental attitude created 'man'? Again, there may be assumed to be elements in the Emperor which, in a strict sense of "cause," were not the cause of Descartes' mental attitude directed upon the Emperor. But how can we conclude from this that such elements in the Emperor were created by Descartes' mental attitude? There seem, however, to be instances of arguments of this sort. Secondary qualities, it may be held, are not, in a strict sense of "cause," the cause of the mental attitudes directed upon them. Therefore, it seems to have been held, these mental attitudes create the secondary qualities which are their objects. The distance between two points, it may be said, is not the cause of the mental attitude directed upon that distance. Therefore, it may be held, points have various spatial relations added to them through the action of the subjects who are aware of them. Universals, it may be said, do not bring about the instances of conceiving which are directed upon them. Therefore concepts, it may be said, are mental products.

But if 'man' exists where Socrates exists and where you exist, then Aristotle did not produce 'man' any more than he produced Socrates. And if the Emperor's qualities existed in the Emperor, then Descartes did not produce the Emperor's color or the sound of the Emperor's voice any more than he produced the Emperor's size. Similarly I do not produce the distance between two points outside me any more than I produce the points themselves. Except in so far as there are motions from certain mental attitudes which are earlier to certain objects of theirs which are later, one real object, we hold, is not more mental than another. The term "mental" may, to be sure, be used in various senses; and there is a certain sense of the term "mental" in which all real entities are mental, individuals as well as universals, secondary qualities as well as primary qualities, relational situations as well as the terms which they relate. Each real entity is mental in the sense that it is an object for a mental attitude, or, rather, in the sense that, presented as not an object, it is unreal. But it is one thing to assert that an alleged entity, presented as not an object, is unreal; and it is another thing to assert that entities are created by the mental attitudes aware of them.

But what about primeval events which occurred before there were sentient beings to be aware of them? If we imagine ourselves back at a date at which there were no sentient beings, can we not say that such primeval events did not then exist and that they with their dates first became real when sentient beings, occurring later, came to be aware of them? And can we not say that there were no instances of 'star,' that 'star' did not exist, until some one was aware of 'star'? In general, whereas it may be agreed that a given entity did not come into being following motions flowing to it from a mental attitude, is it not true, we may be asked, that that entity first came into being at the date of the first mental attitude aware of it?

Surely, however, events can not have existed both with the characteristic of having preceded all sentient beings and with the characteristic of having existed only *after* there were sentient beings. And 'star' can not exist in so far as it is presented both with the characteristic of having had instances prior to sentient beings and with the characteristic of not existing before there were sentient beings to conceive it. Events and universals, we must hold, exist with the dates which they have, not, on the whole, with the dates of the mental attitudes which are aware of them. And if we are asked to imagine ourselves back at a date at which there were no sentient beings, we are, in effect, asked to present to ourselves events occurring in a world devoid of mental attitudes, events alleged to be objects for no one. Such alleged primeval events are however unreal. For such alleged entities are, as we have seen,[55] implicitly presented with the characteristic of being objects for ourselves. What may be real, it follows, are not primeval events presented as objects for no one, but primeval events presented as objects only for later thinkers who did not create them. Indeed some alleged primeval events, so presented, do, let us agree, exist. They exist with the early dates which they are alleged to have. And they exist with the characteristic of being objects, not for thinkers contemporaneous with them, but for various mental attitudes which came after them.

Similarly with the universal 'star.' The statement that 'star' is made real by the first mental attitude aware of 'star' is, to say the least, confusing. For such a proposition may seem to express an assertion that a given subsistent called "star" is first unreal and then real. Instead, there are distinguishable subsistents to be considered. There is the subsistent 'star' which is unreal, the subsistent 'star,' presented not only as not an object for mental attitudes contemporaneous with its earliest instances, but presented also as not an object at all. And, distinguishable from it, there is the subsistent 'star' which is real, the subsistent 'star' presented, not as no one's concept, but presented as a concept with respect only to mental attitudes which were subsequent to its earliest instances. The subsistent 'star' which is unreal does not become real through the action of the first mental attitude allegedly directed upon it. Nor is the alleged primeval event which is unreal transformed into the alleged primeval event which is real. On the contrary, the date or dates with which a given subsistent is presented are elements within that subsistent, characteristics with which it is presented. If the subsistent is real, the dates with which it is presented belong to it. And if it is unreal, it never *becomes* real.

There is then some subsistent 'star' which is real and which is an object with respect to various mental attitudes directed upon it. And there are such entities as last night's performance in Philadelphia, tomorrow's sunrise and the Emperor's piety, entities which likewise are real and real objects for various mental attitudes. But what about the *mental attitude* directed upon 'star' or upon last night's performance, upon tomorrow's sunrise or upon the Emperor's piety? I may, it would seem, be aware of the mental attitude which Descartes directed upon the Emperor's piety or of the mental attitude which Newton directed upon 'star.' I may, it would seem, be aware of the mental attitude which I had last night when I was perceiving the Philadelphia orchestra's performance.[56] And I may, it would seem, be aware, not only of tomorrow's sunrise, but of the mental attitude which I have just directed upon tomorrow's sunrise. Indeed, let us agree that an introspecting mental attitude of mine exists, namely, the introspecting mental attitude which perceives the slightly earlier mental attitude directed upon tomorrow's sunrise. And let us agree that there exists the mental attitude of yours which is not an instance of perceiving, the mental attitude of yours which reaches as its object Descartes' mental attitude directed upon the Emperor's piety. For we have already agreed that certain mental attitudes exist which apparently are "directed upon other mental attitudes," [57] which, that is to say, have the intrinsic qualities which they would have if they reached other mental attitudes as their objects. And having found that "the mental attitude of Descartes' which seems to be directed towards the Emperor really reaches the Emperor as its ultimate object," [58] we find no reason to deny that the mental attitudes now being considered, not only *seem* to be directed upon other mental attitudes, but reach these other mental attitudes as their real objects.

Thus there is Descartes' mental attitude directed upon the Emperor; there is your mental attitude directed upon this mental attitude of Descartes'; and there is my mental attitude directed upon this mental attitude of yours. But such a series of thinking mind-nerve-fibres with mental attitudes directed upon other thinking mind-nerve-fibres does not, it would seem, lead us to accept the actual existence of additional thinking mind-nerve-fibres *ad infinitum.* There is, it would seem, a last term in each series of real entities, in each series composed of a mental attitude, a second person's mental attitude directed exclusively upon the first person's mental attitude, a third person's mental attitude directed exclusively upon the second person's mental attitude, and so on. For at some point in an alleged series of this sort, we are presented with an alleged mental attitude which, at least implicitly, is presented as no one's definite object. And since "subsistents explicitly or implicitly appearing as definite appearances for no one are unreal," [59] such an alleged mental attitude has no place in a series of real mental attitudes each directed upon another mental attitude. There is, let us agree, a real mental attitude of yours which is directed upon the mental attitude which Descartes directed upon the Emperor. But this series of mental attitudes directed upon other mental attitudes has, let us hold, a finite number of different members, not an infinite number of different members.

A subsistent is unreal, we have said, if it is alleged to be a definite object for no one. And a subsistent is unreal if it is presented as not an object at all. How then can there be a last in the series of mental attitudes directed upon mental attitudes? For the last in such a series, it may be said, has no mental attitude directed upon it and is consequently presented as not an object at all.

In approaching the problem thus put before us, let us recall a distinction which we made in explaining our term "reality." "A subsistent is unreal," we have said,[60] "when, explicitly or implicitly, it appears *with* the characteristic of being in no sense an object, *with* the characteristic, that is to say, of appearing to no one." A subsistent is not unreal, however, in so far as it appears *without* the characteristic of being an object; nor is it unreal in so far as it appears *without* the characteristic of being a definite object.

There subsists, for example, a bird outside my window. This bird appears neither explicitly nor implicitly *with* the characteristic of being no one's definite object. Implicitly, we may say, this bird appears with the characteristic of being my definite object. But explicitly it does not. This subsisting bird is, let us agree, real. And it exists with the characteristics with which it explicitly appears. But it does not follow from what has been said in this paragraph that there is a real mental attitude of mine directed upon this bird and that this bird which is real has the real quality of being my definite object. For it is one thing to say that an entity is unreal which implicitly appears with the characteristic of not being a definite object. And it is another thing to say that an entity which is real has the quality of being a definite object. Particularly is the distinction to be pointed out when the quality of being a definite object is a quality with which the subsistent under consideration appears only implicitly. The entity which appears explicitly or implicitly as not an object is unreal. And the entity is unreal which appears implicitly as an object and explicitly as not an object.[61] But so far as we have yet seen, the entity which is real need not *have* the quality of being a definite object, a quality with which it appears only implicitly.

So far as we have seen, the bird outside my window need not *be* a definite object; although, presented as *not* a definite object, it is unreal. And so with the mental attitude directed upon a mental attitude. A mental attitude, it would seem, may have the real quality of being directed upon another mental attitude, and yet not have the real quality of having still another mental attitude definitely directed upon *it*. A contrary position would seem to lead us to accept the existence of an infinite number of thinking mind-nerve-fibres, most of which are presented as generally discredited and as definite objects for no one. For if the bird outside my window had to be an object and, indeed, a definite object, the mental attitude whose object it is alleged to be would have to be real. And if this mental attitude in turn had to be a definite object in order to be real, the further mental attitude whose definite object *it* is alleged to be would have to be real.

Let us agree then that there are such entities as the bird outside my window and such entities as my mental attitude directed upon the mental attitude which Descartes directed upon the Emperor,— entities which are real but which do not have the quality of being definite objects. Being real, however, these entities are not presented with the characteristic of *not* being definite objects. Thus the real bird outside my window lacks the quality of being a definite object but does not appear, even implicitly, *with* the quality of *not* being a definite object. And similarly with one of the thinking mind-nerve-fibres in each series of thinking mind-nerve-fibres with mental attitudes directed upon other thinking mind-nerve-fibres. In a given series of this sort there may be no fifth member which is real, an alleged fifth member being presented as no one's definite object. In this series the fourth member may be real and may have the real quality of being the fourth member. But presented as itself no definite object, such an alleged fourth member is unreal. The fourth member is real, we may say, in so far as it is presented as the fourth member but not presented as the last member.

There exists, then, a thinking mind-nerve-fibre with a mental attitude directed exclusively upon another mental attitude, which in turn is directed exclusively upon *another* mental attitude, which in turn is directed upon an object which is *not* a mental attitude. There also exists, let us say, a thinking mind-nerve-fibre with a mental attitude directed exclusively upon *itself*. For example, I may try to direct my attention to my present thinking.[62] When I do this, my mental attitude, let us hold, not only *seems* to be directed upon itself, but *is* directed upon itself. Like the mental attitude directed upon another mental attitude, the mental attitude which is directed upon itself is an instance of a mental attitude directed upon a mental attitude. But whereas in the one instance we are called upon to distinguish the mental attitude presented, say, as the fourth member of a series from that mental attitude presented as the last member of a series, in the other instance we are not. For the mental attitude directed upon itself is presented as its own definite object and is not so readily presented as no one's definite object. Consequently, when there is a mental attitude directed upon itself,—either alone or in conjunction with a mental attitude directed upon another mental attitude,—the problem of an alleged infinite series is less troublesome. If my mental attitude directed upon your mental attitude directed upon the mental attitude which Descartes directed upon the Emperor is a definite object for itself, then this self-conscious mental attitude of mine is not only the fourth member of the series but also the last member. For in being presented as the last member it is not being presented as no one's definite object but as its own definite object.

Summary

There are various kinds of mental attitudes and various kinds of objects. This chapter attempts to develop a vocabulary that will distinguish with some precision these various kinds. It also attempts to discuss problems that arise with respect to them.

The mental attitude which is aware of an object at the source of motions flowing uninterruptedly to it I call an instance of perceiving and I call its object a percept with respect to it.

A sense-datum, if it exists, is, in our terminology, "that element within a percept which corresponds to the object of some previous instance of perceiving unaffected by experience." It is to be distinguished from another element within the percept which, if it exists, is that without which the percept would not cause the perceiving.

Some mental attitudes are instances of remembering. Their objects are memories with respect to them. A public object may be the immediate object of an instance of perceiving and also the immediate object of an instance of remembering. It may be a percept with respect to one mental attitude, a memory with respect to another. Being aware of a percept or of a memory is to be distinguished from being aware of the fact that one's object is a percept or a memory.

Finally we define conceiving as that type of mental attitude in which the object is a universal; and we call a universal in so far as it is the object of a mental attitude a "concept."

Neither percepts, memories or concepts are mental in the sense of being created by the mental attitudes which have them as objects. But a percept, memory or concept, presented as not a percept, memory or concept, or presented as no one's definite object, is unreal.

Chapter X

FEELING, BELIEVING, AND KNOWING

Descartes, we have found, was perceiving, and the Emperor was his percept.[1] You today are remembering; last night's moon is a memory of yours.[2] And I am aware of tomorrow's sunrise which is an inferred object with respect to the mental attitude which I today direct upon it.[3] Similarly, let us agree, Laöcoon standing on the walls of Troy perceived the Greeks fighting in the plains below. Later, standing beside the wooden horse, he remembered the Greeks whom he had formerly perceived. Or his mental attitude reached the Greeks who had temporarily sailed away, so that the Greeks off in their ships were an inferred object with respect to him. But whether Laöcoon was aware of the Greeks off in their ships or of the Greeks whom he had formerly perceived, there was. it may be held, an additional mental attitude which Laöcoon had. Laöcoon was afraid. Distinguishable from his remembering or from his mental attitude directed upon an inferred object, there was, it may be held, a mental attitude of his which was an instance of fearing.

Our question is whether this alleged instance of fearing, presented as a mental attitude of Laöcoon's, exists. But just as, in order to determine whether or not Descartes was thinking, we had to distinguish Descartes' mental attitude apparently directed upon man, God and the universe from other entities with which that alleged mental attitude might be confused;[4] so, in order to determine whether or not Laöcoon was fearing, we must distinguish his mental attitude alleged to be an instance of fearing from other entities whose existence at this point is not in question. Descartes, we have seen, was pacing up and down the room, knitting his

289

brows and staring past the furniture that was around him.[5] And Laöcoon standing beside the wooden horse was, let us suppose, trembling; his heart was beating more rapidly than usual and his glands secreting more freely. But just as Descartes' thinking is distinguishable from his non-mental behavior, so is Laöcoon's alleged fearing presented as distinguishable from Laöcoon's non-mental behavior. Descartes' thinking and Descartes' non-mental behavior are each abstractable from Descartes' total behavior.[6] And it is by separating out of Laöcoon's total behavior an alleged mental attitude held to accompany that mental attitude of his which was directed upon the Greeks,—it is thus that we come to have as our apparent object his alleged fearing.

The alleged instance of fearing whose existence we are to determine appears with the characteristic of being a quality of the extended substance that is Laöcoon or Laöcoon's mind-nerve-fibre, a quality distinguishable from its substance's non-mental behavior. And the alleged relational situation alleged to have as its terms the fearing Laöcoon and the feared Greek army is to be distinguished from the relational situation which has as its terms the reacting Laöcoon on the one hand and, on the other hand, the Greek army to which Laöcoon's behavior is adapted.[7] There is the relational situation: Laöcoon-affected-by-the-Greek-army-which-he-formerly-perceived. There is the relational situation: Laöcoon-making-a-response-adapted-to-the-Greeks. And there is a subject-object relational situation which is either Laöcoon-remembering-the-Greeks or Laöcoon-having-as-an-inferred-object-the-Greeks-off-in-their-ships. What is still in question is the existence of fearing in addition to remembering or being aware of an inferred object; and in addition to behaving. And what is still in question is the existence of a relational situation including Laöcoon and the Greeks, into which Laöcoon enters, not by virtue of his remembering or of his being aware of an inferred object, and not by virtue of his responding, but by virtue of his fearing.

It may be held, we have seen, that behavior exists, but that no mental attitudes exist which are distinguishable from behavior.[8] And as mental attitudes in general appear to be discredited in some quarters, so do such alleged mental attitudes as we would call "instances of fearing." Just as it may be said that thinking is behavior, so it may be said that Laöcoon's secreting glands, beating

290

heart and trembling are his fearing. It is however a rather rare form of behaviorism whose proponents disbelieve in a fearing which, while distinguishable from bodily excitation, is nevertheless alleged to be an element in total behavior. The fearing of Laöcoon's which we are considering, it is to be pointed out, is not presented as some non-spatial entity. It is presented, to be sure, with the characteristic of being distinguishable from bodily excitation, and yet with the characteristic of being an element in Laöcoon's total behavior. So presented, we find, it does not appear with the characteristic of being generally discredited. In a word, we find Laöcoon's fearing, appearing with the characteristics just described, a subsistent which is real. Laöcoon, we hold, was remembering. Laöcoon, we hold, was reacting. And Laöcoon, we also hold, was fearing. He was characterized by non-mental behavior in that he was reacting. And he was thinking, characterized by mental attitudes, in that he was fearing and remembering.

On the one hand there is Laöcoon's remembering, reacting and fearing. And on the other hand there exists the Greek army formerly on the plains of Troy and now resting in its ships out at sea. It is to some phase of the Greek army that Laöcoon is reacting. It is towards some phase of the Greek army that Laöcoon's remembering is directed. And it is in connection with his remembering the Greeks, or in connection with his mental attitude directed upon the Greeks off in their ships, that Laöcoon is fearing. His fearing is related to the Greeks. There is a real relational situation, that is to say, which includes on the one hand the Greeks who are real and on the other hand the fearing Laöcoon who is likewise real. It is a relational situation which appears with the characteristic of being somewhere outside Troy, in the extended place which includes the spot at which Laöcoon was standing and the place where the Greek ships were idling. And it is a relational situation which, appearing neither as non-spatial nor as discredited, is listed in the appendix to Chapter Three. It is a relational situation which is real just as is the relational situation whose terms are the Greeks and the reacting Laöcoon and just as is the relational situation whose terms are the Greeks and the remembering Laöcoon. There is thus a relation between Laöcoon and the Greeks into which Laöcoon enters by virtue of his reacting, a relation between Laöcoon and the Greeks into which Laöcoon enters by virtue of his remembering, and a relation between Laöcoon and the Greeks into which Laöcoon enters by virtue of his fearing.

In so far as there is a relation between Laöcoon and the Greeks into which Laöcoon enters by virtue of his reacting, the Greeks may be said to have the quality of being responded to. In so far as there is a relation between Laöcoon and the Greeks into which Laöcoon enters by virtue of his remembering, the Greeks may be said to have the quality of being a memory. And in so far as there is a relation between Laöcoon and the Greeks into which Laöcoon enters by virtue of his fearing, the Greeks may be said to have the quality of being feared. Laöcoon, we hold, is reacting, remembering, and fearing. The Greeks, we hold, are responded to, a memory, and feared. They are a memory in that vibrations emanating from them, after being held up in some phase of Laöcoon's mind-person, led to Laöcoon's remembering. They are feared in that the mental attitude directed towards them is, or is accompanied by, fearing.

Fearing is a mental attitude by virtue of which Laöcoon is related to the Greeks, remembering a mental attitude by virtue of which Laöcoon is related to the Greeks, perceiving a mental attitude by virtue of which Descartes is related to the Emperor. We have agreed however that mental attitudes exist which have other mental attitudes directed upon them.[9] There exists, we suppose, a mental attitude of Descartes' which is directed upon his thinking about the Emperor, a mental attitude of Laöcoon's which is directed upon his thinking about the Greeks, and a mental attitude of mine which is directed both upon Descartes' perceiving and upon Laöcoon's remembering. But if it is agreed that Descartes' perceiving may be an object both for Descartes and for me, and if it is agreed that Laöcoon's remembering may be an object both for Laöcoon and for me, then there appears to be no reason to deny that Laöcoon's fearing may likewise be an object. My thinking of a moment ago was real. Laöcoon, we have agreed, had a mental attitude which was an instance of fearing. And there was, we hold, a real subject-object relation between my thinking and the fearing of Laöcoon's that is my alleged object. Similarly with Laöcoon's mental attitude alleged to have been directed upon his fearing. In one phase, we may suppose, Laöcoon was perceiving the Greeks; in a later phase, we may suppose, he was introspecting his previous remembering or his previous fearing.

We find real, accordingly, instances of the mental attitude that is fearing and instances of the mental attitude that is the introspecting of fearing. Indeed we may take another step and admit the existence of mental attitudes which are directed, not upon the mental attitude that is fearing, but upon the relation between the fearing subject and the feared object. Fearing, the introspecting of fearing, the thinking that is directed upon the relation between the fearing subject and the feared object,—these mental attitudes resemble respectively remembering, the introspecting of remembering, and the thinking that is directed upon the relation between the remembering subject and its memory. To be aware of a memory as a memory is to be aware of it as related to the subject remembering it.[10] That is to say, to be aware of the quality of being a memory that an object has is to be aware of the memory object, of the remembering subject, and of the subject-object relation between them. So it is, we suggest, with the quality of being feared. In so far as Laöcoon is fearing the Greeks and is not aware of the relation between his fearing and the Greeks, he is aware of the Greeks but not of the Greeks as feared. When, on the other hand, he is aware of the Greeks as feared, he is, we hold, aware of his previous mental attitude; and he is aware of the relation between the Greeks and his fearing. When he is not introspecting but is merely fearing the Greeks, we might expect him to exclaim: "Alas! The Greeks!" But when his mental attitude is directed towards the relation between his fearing and the Greeks, we might expect him to say: "I fear the Greeks" or "the Greeks are feared by me."

There are instances of fearing and instances of the introspecting of fearing, instances of the relation between a fearing subject and a feared object and instances of the awareness of a feared object as feared. But whereas it may be agreed that fearing is distinguishable from the introspecting of fearing, and that there are real instances of both, it may be held that there are no instances of fearing that are not introspected by the fearing subject. And whereas it may be agreed that the relation between a fearing subject and a feared object is one thing and the awareness of a feared object as feared another, it may be held that there are no instances of a feared object not recognized as feared by the fearing subject. There are instances, we have agreed, of mental attitudes which are

293

not introspected.[11] But whereas there are some mental attitudes that are not introspected, it may be held that none of them are instances of fearing, it may be held that there is no consciousness instances of fearing. With respect to those mental attitudes that are without self-consciousness.

To be sure, it seems easy to pass from the state in which I am fearing an object to the state in which I am aware of my fearing. There is, we may suppose, a bodily excitation accompanying my fearing. And both this excitation and the fearing that accompanies it may be so pronounced, may compel attention to such an extent, that I become introspective and aware of my fearing. Let me suppose, however, that on my way home yesterday I saw a flash of lightning and that thereupon I directed all of my energies to the attainment of a haven. I was, we may say, conscious of the storm about me and was paying no attention to my own mental attitudes. It was after I was safe at home, we may suppose, that I became aware of the fearing that had been mine. Or it was my companion in the storm, observing my feverish activity and lack of composure, who perceived or inferred my fearing. Surely cowards are not all introspectors. On the contrary it would seem that those whom we call cowards are those who act so as to lead us to think that they fear unduly. Yesterday's fearing as I rode home in the storm appears then as not having been accompanied by introspecting. Appearing in this manner, it does not appear as generally discredited. In a word, yesterday's fearing unaccompanied by introspecting is real. Fearing exists. The introspecting of fearing exists. And the instances of the former are not all accompanied by instances of the latter.

Fearing is a mental attitude, the awareness of fearing a mental attitude directed upon a mental attitude. Among the entities that are not mental attitudes, among the entities that are external objects, there exist, we hold, the feared Greeks and the feared flash of lightning. What shall we say, however, with respect to the existence of a private object, an idea of fear, in addition to, or in place of, either mental attitude or external object? As we have already seen, it may be held that the immediate object is not the external object, but rather an idea referring beyond itself to the external object.[12] And as it may be held that the immediate object of Laöcoon's remembering is not the Greeks themselves but rather an idea of the Greeks, so it may be held that, when Laöcoon fears, his immediate object is an idea of fear. The contents of Laöcoon's mind, it may for example be held, consist of an idea of the wooden horse, an idea of the Greeks, and an idea of fear.

Either, however, the alleged idea of fear that Laöcoon has appears as an idea referring beyond itself to some public object; or it appears as a bit of content without a self-transcendent reference. Either it appears as an idea referring to a quality of the Greeks or as an idea referring to the mental attitude we call Laöcoon's fearing; or it appears simply as fear, a bit of content in Laöcoon's mind that is content and not mental attitude. We have seen, however, that public objects may be the immediate objects of the mental attitudes that are directed upon them.[13] The subject-object relation between Descartes and the Emperor is, we have agreed, direct rather than one that is mediated by an idea of the Emperor. And as there is no idea of the Emperor mediating between Descartes' thinking and the Emperor himself, so, we hold, there is no idea of fear mediating between the fearing Laöcoon and the feared Greeks and no idea of fear mediating between the introspecting Laöcoon and the fearing Laöcoon whom he introspects. An idea of fear alleged to be an immediate object and to refer beyond itself to either a quality of the Greeks or to Laöcoon's mental attitude that is fearing is, we hold, a subsistent that is unreal.

How is it, however, with respect to the idea of fear that is not alleged to refer beyond itself but is alleged merely to be Laöcoon's immediate object? Such an alleged idea of fear appears as passive content rather than as active thinking or fearing; and it appears as content that is mental rather than as non-mental behavior. If however this mental content appears as non-spatial, it is, as we use "reality," unreal. And if it appears with the characteristic of being in space, if it appears, for example, as distinguishable from non-mental behavior but as a quality of Laöcoon's mind-body or mind-neural process, the question is how this alleged passive mental content, this idea of fear that is alleged to inhere in Laöcoon, is to be distinguished from Laöcoon's fearing itself. "At first sight," we have said,[14] "the distinction between what is alleged to be mental attitude and what is alleged to be content, whether private or public, seems clear." But since the entities we call "mental attitudes" may themselves be objects, Laöcoon's alleged idea of fear can

295

hardly be distinguished from an act of fearing that Laöcoon introspects. In short, what we call Laöcoon's introspecting of fearing might in some other terminology be called Laöcoon's having an idea of fear. But since there can be fearing without the introspecting of fearing, there can be fearing without what others might call: "Having an idea of fear." An idea of fear does not exist in each situation in which there is a fearing subject and a feared object. It exists, if at all, only where there is the introspection of fearing. And where there is the introspecting of fearing, the fearing that is introspected may be called an active mental attitude or a passive idea. It is in any case a quality of the extended substance that is the thinker's mind-body or mind-neural process. And in the instance in which Laöcoon fears the Greeks, it is directed towards, or accompanies Laöcoon's remembering of, the Greeks. Since however neither "active" nor "passive" are adjectives that can appropriately be applied to it, we can only say that in our terminology nothing exists to be called an "idea of fear" rather than a mental attitude, that in our terminology Laöcoon is either fearing the feared Greeks or is introspecting his fearing, but is not aware of an "idea" of fear.

Laöcoon feared the Greeks and Cato was angry at the Carthaginians. Abelard was in love with Eloise and Victor Hugo was defiant towards Napoleon III. Kant was condescending towards Berkeley and Hitler was disgusted at modern art. All of these alleged situations resemble one another. Just as Laöcoon was remembering the Greeks and fearing them, so Cato was remembering the Carthaginians and hating them and Abelard perceiving Eloise and loving her. In each of these instances there is a subject who is perceiving, remembering, conceiving, or otherwise thinking about an object. And in each of these instances the perceiving, remembering or what not that is directed upon an object is accompanied by, or intermingled with, some such mental attitude as fearing, loving, being pleased or being disgusted. Just as we find Laöcoon's fearing real, so we find real Cato's being angry and Hitler's being disgusted. And just as we hold that the Greeks have the quality of being a feared memory with respect to Laöcoon, so we hold that Eloise has the quality of being a beloved percept with respect to Abelard. In brief, we find real many instances of a type of mental attitude that, to use a term constructed like "perceiving," "fearing" and "thinking," we shall call "feeling."[15] And we find many real instances of the subject-object relation in which the object is real, the subject real, and the subject not only aware of the object but also feeling.

However, just as an alleged object of perceiving, remembering or conceiving may not exist, so an alleged object of fearing, loving or hoping may not exist. When Descartes perceives the Emperor, Descartes' perceiving is real, the Emperor is real, and there is a real relation between the perceiving subject and his percept. But when I seem to perceive a bent stick, when the bent stick appearing as my object is unreal, then, although my mental attitude is real, there is neither a real object nor a real subject-object relation between my thinking and its alleged object.[16] Similarly, when Laöcoon remembers the Greeks and fears them, there is a real relation between the fearing, remembering Laöcoon and the Greeks who exist as his feared memory. But when I seem to fear the devil, when the devil who is alleged to be my object does not exist, there is no real relation between this non-existent devil and any mental attitude which I may have. President Roosevelt, we may say, was in October 1936 hoping for re-election. His re-election in November was real and was really related to the hoping that was his mental attitude in October. But what about his opponent, Governor Landon? It may be alleged that in October, 1936 Governor Landon was hoping for election to the presidency. But, since the alleged election of Landon in November was unreal, it can not have been related to any October hoping. Instances of hoping, fearing or loving, like instances of perceiving, remembering or conceiving, can only be related to entities which have occurred or which will occur. Governor Landon in October 1936 may have had a mental attitude just as I have a mental attitude when a bent stick appears to be my object. But the hoping that may then have been his was neither related to an object nor did it accompany a mental attitude that had an object.

There is a real mental attitude which, although it has no bent stick as its object, I describe as being apparently directed towards a bent stick. It is a mental attitude which exists and which has intrinsic characteristics such as it would have if the bent stick appearing as an object existed.[17] So too Governor Landon in October 1936 had a mental attitude which, we hold, existed. His al-

leged attitude appears neither as non-spatial nor as generally
credited; and it is listed as real in the appendix to Chapter Th
It had no real object; but it had intrinsic characteristics res
bling those of mental attitudes really hoping for, and really aw
of, events about to exist.

It is a matter of terminology whether, when the bent st
that appears as my object is unreal, we call my mental attitu
"pseudo-perceiving" or "perceiving that is without an obje
And it is a matter of terminology whether we call Gover
Landon's mental attitude "pseudo-hoping" or "hoping that
without an object." Mental attitudes, instances of thinking, t
are without real objects exist. But when we choose a term
represent some species of real mental attitude, we would se
to be at liberty either to restrict the species thus represented
mental attitudes that have real objects or to extend it so tha
includes certain real mental attitudes without objects. Exercis
this liberty, let us call only those mental attitudes which ha
real objects instances of "perceiving," "conceiving" and "reme
bering." That is to say, let us define 'perceiving,' 'conceiving' a
'remembering' so that there is no perceiving without a perce
no conceiving without a concept, and no remembering witho
a memory. But, whereas we do not call those mental attitue
which resemble perceivings but which lack objects instances
"perceiving," let us call Governor Landon's mental attitude th
has no object an instance of "hoping," just as we designate
"hoping" the mental attitude of President Roosevelt's that h
an object.

It is, we say, a terminological decision that leads us to call
mental attitude, when it is as if the bent stick appearing as
object existed, an instance, not of "perceiving," but of "pseuc
perceiving," [18] whereas we call Governor Landon's mental attitue
although it lacks an object, an instance of "hoping." But this d
ference between the manner in which we use "perceiving" and t
manner in which we use "hoping" suggests that the situation
which subjects have real objects and hope for them may not
analogous to the situation in which subjects have real objects a
perceive them. We say, to be sure, that Abelard loved Eloise a
that Laöcoon feared the Greeks just as we say that Descart
perceived the Emperor. But we also say that Abelard was in lo

298

vith Eloise, Laöcoon afraid *of* the Greeks, Cato angry *at* the Carhaginians, and President Roosevelt hoping *for* re-election. It may eem, not that Laöcoon remembered the Greeks and feared them, not that his fearing and his remembering had a common object, out that, on the occasion on which he remembered the Greeks, ne had a feeling which, in so far as it was a feeling, was without n object. The fearing of a fearing, remembering subject may oe held to be related to the feared memory just as directly as his emembering is. Or the relation between the remembering and he object may be held to be the primary subject-object relation; nd the object may be held to be feared only in that a fearing that s without an object accompanies the remembering that is directed ipon the object.

The distinction that we have just drawn is however a specious one. Upon either interpretation Laöcoon is fearing and emembering. And upon either interpretation there is a real reition between the feared object and the fearing that accompanies the remembering. There is no entity that must be real if aöcoon's fearing as such has an object and that must be unreal Laöcoon's fearing has an object only indirectly, only in so far as ne accompanying remembering has an object. And since there no ontological decision to sway us, we find no basis upon which accept one interpretation and to reject the other.

To sum up, there are some mental attitudes which have no obcts. Among these there are some which we call instances of hoping, some which we call instances of pseudo-perceiving, none which e call instances of perceiving. Other mental attitudes have obcts which are real. There are, for example, instances of perceiving, remembering, and the like. And accompanying some of them, itermingled with them or associated with them, there are inances of feeling. Fearing as well as remembering may be abracted from the thinking substance who both fears and remembers or who fears while he remembers. The feared memory is e object of his remembering. And either directly or by virtue its relation to the accompanying remembering, it may also be id to be the object of his fearing.

Fearing exists when Laöcoon remembers the Greeks and fears em. Fearing exists when my mental attitude is as if the devil ppearing as my object existed and when, in addition to seeming to be aware of the devil, I am afraid. Can I not however be afraid when there is neither an object that I am definitely aware of nor a subsistent that appears to be my object? It would seem that I can be pleased at my son's progress or at the up-turn in the stock-market. And yet it would also seem that, without the awareness of any specific object accompanying my feeling, I can be pleased or in good spirits. Hamlet, we may suppose, was displeased and troubled at his mother's infidelity. Or, to allow him a broader object, he was displeased and troubled at man's worthlessness and the world's decadence. But not even so definite an object as this is needed to make him the melancholy Dane. Some feelings, we might almost say, require the accompaniment of mental attitudes directed upon no objects at all. It would seem that I can be happy or timorous, displeased or optimistic, without being able to account for my mood, without my mood being tied up with any specific object or apparent object. Some feelings in this respect seem to resemble mental attitudes which are not feelings. The relation between being unhappy at Hamlet's mother's infidelity, being unhappy at man's worthlessness, and simply being in a melancholy mood seems to resemble the relation between perceiving a definite object, gazing into space, and the sort of contentless thinking in which, when offered a penny for our thoughts, we can not earn the proffered penny.

The mental attitude exists in which Laöcoon is fearing the Greeks. The mental attitude exists in which Governor Landon is hoping, although his election, appearing as his object, does not exist. And the mental attitude exists in which I am optimistic but unable to point out a prospective situation with which my mood is tied up. A feeling, however, can exist without being introspected. And if this is true with respect to feelings in general, it must be true with respect to the optimistic mood for which I am unable to account. In order that my optimistic mood may exist, it need not be accompanied by a mental attitude in which I am aware of my optimistic mood. On the other hand, my optimistic mood, to be real, can not appear as no object at all or as not a definite object for some subject. In general, feelings exist that are not introspected by the feeling subjects themselves. But these non-introspected feelings that are real are not presented as non-objects. They are presented neither as objects nor as non-objects; or they are presented as objects for other subjects.

Laöcoon remembered the Greeks and feared them. The leader of the Greeks within the wooden horse remembered his former companions and hoped for their success. Both in Laöcoon and in the man within the horse there was a mental attitude which was remembering the Greeks. The thinking of the two men differed in that their similar rememberings were accompanied by different feelings. There was a similar difference, we may say, between President Roosevelt's attitude towards his re-election and Governor Landon's attitude towards the re-election of President Roosevelt. Both men, we may assume, were on occasion aware of the event that was about to take place. But in the one mind the mental attitude directed towards this future event was accompanied by, or intermingled with, hoping; in the other mind accompanied by, or intermingled with, dreading.

But besides there being hoping in the one case and dreading in the other, may we not also say that there was believing in the one case and disbelieving in the other? May we not describe President Roosevelt's mental attitude as hoping for and certain of his re-election and Governor Landon's as not only dreading but also as sceptical of, or disbelieving in, the re-election of President Roosevelt? President Roosevelt's re-election in November 1936 was real; and in October Governor Landon and many others had mental attitudes directed towards it. Some of these attitudes were, let us agree, accompanied by, or intermingled with, instances of believing; and some accompanied by, or intermingled with, instances of disbelieving. Governor Landon, for example, disbelieved in the forthcoming re-election of President Roosevelt. Presented, that is to say, as a quality of the thinking mind-person whom we call Governor Landon, an instance of disbelieving existed. And this instance of disbelieving was really related to the November event upon which either it, or the mental attitude of Governor Landon's which accompanied it, was directed.

But what about an alleged believing or disbelieving directed upon an entity which is unreal? There are instances of pseudo-perceiving, we have seen, which are real but which have no objects, instances of pseudo-perceiving which are as though the objects they seem to have were real. And there are instances of hoping such that neither they nor the mental attitudes which ac-

301

company them have objects, instances of hoping such that they and the mental attitudes with which they are intermingled have "intrinsic characteristics resembling those of mental attitudes really hoping for, and really aware of, events about to exist."[19] Similarly with the instance of believing apparently directed upon an unreal object. And similarly with the instance of *dis*believing apparently directed upon an unreal object. A child who says: "I believe in Santa Claus" may be believing; but she is not aware of an object and not, strictly speaking, believing in anything. And when I say: "I disbelieve in Santa Claus," whereas my disbelieving is real, neither it nor the mental attitude accompanying it has a real object. There may, that is to say, be instances of believing, and instances of disbelieving, which are as though their alleged objects existed. But it is only real entities, we conclude, that may really be believed in, and only real entities that may really be disbelieved in.

I may disbelieve in the re-election of President Roosevelt but not in Santa Claus. I may believe in Socrates but not in Ivanhoe. But what about the entity which we have distinguished from Socrates and called: "The existence of Socrates"? And what about the alleged entity which seems to be represented by our phrase: "The existence of Ivanhoe?" Distinguishable from Socrates there is the entity which we have called a judgment or fact, namely, "existence appearing as an alleged quality of the subsistent Socrates."[20] And distinguishable from an alleged Ivanhoe there subsists an alleged *existence* of Ivanhoe. As the word "Socrates" which I utter differs from the proposition: "Socrates exists" which I assert, so, we have seen, Socrates differs from the existence of Socrates. And with Socrates being distinguishable from the existence of Socrates, believing in Socrates, it would seem to follow, differs from believing in the existence of Socrates. The wife of Socrates is not the same person as Socrates; and the father of the wife of Socrates is not the same person as the father of Socrates. Somewhat similarly, it would seem, since "the existence of Socrates" and "Socrates" represent different entities, believing in the existence of Socrates is not believing in Socrates.

But, it may be objected, not all situations in which an A is related to a B which is related to a C are analogous to the situation in which A is the father of the wife of Socrates, but not the father

Socrates. The wife of Socrates may not be the same person as
rates. But in a monogamous society where there are no extra-
rital relations, if A is the son of the wife of Socrates, A is also
son of Socrates. In such a situation being-the-son-of and being-
-wife-of are not what one might call "additive" as are being-the-
er-of and being-the-wife-of. Or consider the proposition: "A is
wife of the wife of Socrates." Since the wife of Socrates has no
e, either the reader does not understand our proposition at all;
he disregards what he takes to be a redundancy and believes
proposition to be synonymous with "A is the wife of Soc-
s." Somewhat similarly, it may be said, "A is believing in B"
"B is the existence of C" do not imply that there is a believing
he *existence* of C which is distinguishable from a believing in
Believing and existing may be held to involve each other to
an extent that believing in the existence of Socrates is not
inguishable from believing in Socrates.

he connection between belief and existence is so close, it may
aid, that to believe in an entity is to be aware of that entity as
ting. But even as "existence" is commonly used, it would seem
we can be aware of an entity as existing without believing in
An instance of believing, it would seem, is not an instance of
ely being aware, whether the alleged object of that awareness
entity presented as existing, an entity presented as not exist-
or an entity presented neither as existing nor as not existing. An
ance of believing, it would seem, is an instance of being aware
feeling; or, rather, it is a feeling which accompanies, or is
rmingled with, an instance of being aware. Thus a child may
me that Santa Claus exists; and upon hearing her words I may
a mental attitude which has as its apparent object a Santa
is presented with those vague characteristics to which "exist-
" as commonly used seems to refer. Using the word "existence"
is used in ordinary discourse, my apparent object is, in short,
existence of Santa Claus. But whereas I seem to be aware of the
ence of Santa Claus, I am not, let us agree, presented as *believ-
in Santa Claus. For my mental attitude which seems to be
cted upon the existence of Santa Claus is not presented as
g accompanied by a mental attitude which is an instance of
ving.

o be believing in an entity, let us then agree, is not to be

303

merely aware of that entity as existing. In order that there may be an instance of believing, there must be an instance of what we have called a "feeling." But assuming that we have before us an instance of the feeling that we call "believing," how are we to distinguish the believing which accompanies a mental attitude directed upon a given entity from the believing which accompanies a mental attitude directed upon the *existence* of that entity? When the word "real" has the meaning with which that word comes to us out of common speech, "seeming to have as an object a hundred real dollars" may not be "identical with seeming to have as an object a hundred imaginary dollars." [21] In the one situation, we have suggested, the alleged object appears with "some vague quality of being related to certain other things, some vague quality of being important"; in the other situation, not. Whatever difference there may be, however, seems rather intangible and elusive. Certainly then, when we compare seeming to *believe* in a hundred real dollars with seeming to *believe* in a hundred imaginary dollars, the difference is no less elusive. Indeed, when "existence" is used in the sense in which it is used in common speech, one may go so far as to say that it is all one whether I say: "I believe in a hundred dollars" or "I believe in the existence of a hundred dollars," whether I say: "I believe in Santa Claus" or "I believe in the existence of Santa Claus."

Our failure to find a noticeable difference between the signification of: "I believe in A," as this phrase is commonly used, and the signification of: "I believe in the existence of A," as commonly used, may be partially accounted for by the fact that "existence" in ordinary discourse has a meaning which is extremely vague and indefinite. But if the difference between "believing in A" and "believing in the existence of A" is less marked than the difference between "A" and "the existence of A," then our failure is not completely accounted for by pointing to the vagueness of the meaning with which "existence" is commonly used.[22] Our failure may be due in part to the juxtaposition of "existence" and "belief." As "existence" is commonly used, that is to say, the meanings of "existence" and "belief" may involve one another. "Existing," for example, may not mean merely being somehow important; it may mean being somehow important and being an object of belief. It would be unrewarding, however, to pursue with any vigor investigations as to the meaning which "existence" usually has. For, since the meaning of "existence" as commonly used is extremely vague, we are unable to determine with any accuracy what that meaning is. And to the extent to which *our* term "existence" is not involved, we are expressing ourselves in sentences to which our terms "truth" and "falsity" do not apply.[23]

Let us turn then to believing in A and believing in the existence of A, where "existence" has the meaning which has been assigned it in this treatise. To exist is to appear without the characteristic of being self-contradictory, without the characteristic of being non-spatial, etc.; and it is to be listed in the appendix to Chapter Three. There is believing in the existence of an entity when the mental attitude which accompanies an instance of believing has as its object that entity's quality of appearing without the characteristic of being self-contradictory, that entity's quality of appearing without the characteristic of being non-spatial, etc. And there is believing in A rather than in the existence of A when the mental attitude which accompanies the instance of believing has as its object A itself but not such qualities as A's freedom from self-contradiction. I am believing in the hundred dollars in my pocket when, while I am believing, I am aware of these hundred dollars but not of their being presented without the characteristic of non-spatiality. And I am believing in the *existence* of these hundred dollars when the mental attitude which accompanies my believing is directed upon those characteristics of these hundred dollars which determine these hundred dollars to be real.

But can we be believing in A without being aware of such qualities of A as A's freedom from non-spatiality? Believing occurs, it may be said, only when there are among our objects those characteristics of the entity that we are considering which determine that entity to be real. When however the terms "feeling of acceptance . . . or belief" and "feeling of . . . rejection or disbelief" were first used in this treatise,[24] our term "existence" had not yet been fully explained. Had we at that point introduced the expression: "belief in the existence of A," the reader of that expression would not have been led to think of those characteristics of A upon which belief was presented as being directed. He might have understood "belief" and he might have understood: "belief in A"; but he would not have understood: "belief in the existence of A."

What then was the reader's object when he read: "Whe[n] think of the King of England I seem to have a feeling of acc[ept]ance or assent or belief. No feeling of hesitation or of disbe[lief] seems to intervene"? [25] And what seemed to be the reader's ob[ject] when he read: "When I press my eye-ball and seem to see a sec[ond] rose in the vase on my desk, . . . I may become aware of a fee[ling] of hesitation, a feeling of dissent or rejection or disbelief?" In one instance, we hold, there was among his objects my believ[ing] directed upon the King of England; not,—using "existence" [in] our sense,—my believing directed upon the *existence* of the K[ing] of England. And in the other instance there was among his [ob]jects my disbelieving apparently directed upon a second rose, [or] a disbelieving apparently directed upon qualities which had [not] yet been pointed out, not a disbelieving apparently directed up[on] what in our sense of "existence" would be the existence of [the] second rose, provided the second rose existed. Believing in A [was] an object, but not believing in the existence of A. An instance [of] disbelieving which was as though it were directed upon B was [an] object, not an instance of disbelieving which was as though it w[as] directed upon the existence of B.

Using "existence" in our sense then, believing in A may be [an] object without believing in the existence of A being an obj[ect] also. But whereas the *observer* may be aware of a belief in A wi[th]out being aware of a belief in the existence of A, perhaps [the] *believer* may not be believing in A without also believing in the [ex]istence of A. Perhaps believing in A, although distinguishable fr[om] believing in the existence of A, does not occur without it. It w[ill] be agreed, however, that I was believing and disbelieving bef[ore] I was engaged in determining the meaning of our term "exi[st]ence." There were entities in which I was believing, that is to s[ay] when I was not yet aware of those characteristics of my object th[at] were later to be determined to constitute its existence. Similar[ly] there are instances of your believing—and instances of your d[is]believing—on occasions when you are not definitely aware of t[he] meaning of our term "existence." Situations exist, that is to s[ay] where your believing or disbelieving is directed upon certa[in] entities but not upon what, in our sense of the term "existence[,]" is the *existence* of these entities.

306

Using "existence" in our sense then, believing in an entity need
ot be accompanied by believing in the existence of that entity.
nd using "existence" in our sense, the entity which exists need
ot be an object of belief with respect to each of the thinking
ind-nerve-fibres directed upon it. An entity is unreal, to be sure,
if it is presented as generally discredited. But the entity which is
al may be presented without the characteristic of being generally
scredited and yet not presented *with* the characteristic of being
nerally believed in, or even with the characteristic of being
lieved in by some. Just as the entity presented *without* the char-
teristic of being a definite object may be real,[26] so may the
tity presented *without* the characteristic of being an object of
lief. Just as an entity may be real and yet not have any real
ental attitudes definitely directed upon it, so an entity may be
al and yet not *be* an object of general belief or an object of be-
f at all.

There are, we have agreed, instances of believing and instances
disbelieving which are directed upon such entities as the re-
ection of President Roosevelt.[27] And there are, let us agree, in-
nces of believing and instances of disbelieving which are di-
cted upon such entities as the *existence* of the re-election of
esident Roosevelt. Using "existence" in our sense of that word,
e subject who is disbelieving in the *existence* of the re-election
President Roosevelt, or disbelieving in the *existence* of the King
England, is, let us say, "erring" or "in error." And the subject
ho is believing in the *existence* of the re-election of President
osevelt, or believing in the *existence* of the King of England,
let us say, "knowing." As we choose to use the words "erring"
d "being in error," a subject is not erring when he is aware of
e existence of an existing entity but is not disbelieving. And
is not erring when he is disbelieving in an entity which is real
t not disbelieving in the existence of that entity. A subject is
error, his mental attitude is an instance of erring, when that
ental attitude is an instance of disbelieving in the existence
an existing entity. And similarly with our terms "having knowl-
ge" or "knowing." A mental attitude is not an instance of know-
g, as we choose to use the word "knowing," when, although
rected upon the existence of an existing entity, it is not an in-
nce of believing. And it is not an instance of knowing when it

307

is believing in an entity which is real, but is not believing in the existence of that entity. A subject knows,—his mental attitude is an instance of what we call "knowing"—when that mental attitude is directed upon the existence of an existing entity and is believing in that existing entity's existence.

There are, then, instances of erring, as, for example, Governor Landon's mental attitude disbelieving in the existence—in our sense of "existence"—of the re-election of President Roosevelt. And there are instances of knowing as, for example, my mental attitude believing in the existence of the King of England. But what shall we say with respect to such alleged objects as the existence of Santa Claus or the non-existence of the King of England? Just as "there is no real non-existence of Socrates," [28] so there is no real non-existence of the King of England. And just as the existence of Ivanhoe is unreal and the non-existence of Ivanhoe unreal, so is an alleged existence of Santa Claus and an alleged *non*-existence of Santa Claus. The entity that is unreal, however, is neither an object of belief nor an object of disbelief.[29] Just as the child who says: "I believe in Santa Claus" is not believing in him, so the child who says: "I believe in the existence of Santa Claus" or "I believe that Santa Claus exists" is, it follows, not believing in Santa Claus's existence. And similarly with instances of belief and instances of disbelief allegedly directed upon the non-existence of Santa Claus or upon the non-existence of the King of England. If I say: "I disbelieve in the non-existence of the King of England" or "I disbelieve in the alleged fact that the King of England does not exist," I may be disbelieving, but my disbelieving has no non-existence of the King of England as its object. And if I say: "I believe in the non-existence of Santa Claus" or "I believe that there is no Santa Claus," I may be believing, but my believing is not directed upon the non-existence of Santa Claus which, we have seen, is unreal.

Shall we say, then, that there is no erring when some one says: "I believe that Santa Claus exists," no knowing when I say: "I believe in the alleged fact that Santa Claus does not exist"? These are situations, to be sure, in which there is believing, but believing not directed upon the existence of an existing entity. And yet they are situations to which the terms "knowledge" and "error" as commonly used would seem to be applicable. Let us then at-

308

tempt to use our terms "knowing" and "erring" so that some instances of believing or of disbelieving may be called instances of "knowing" or instances of "erring," even though they are not directed upon the existence of existing entities.

We attempted to apply the distinction between "truth" and "falsity," it will be recalled, to facts or judgments. But then, finding no real judgments to be called "false," we returned to a discussion of true propositions and false propositions.[30] Our present situation is somewhat similar. We have introduced our terms "knowing" and "erring" by considering the situation in which a judgment or alleged judgment is apparently the object of belief or of disbelief. But finding no false judgments to be believed in or disbelieved in, we turn to the situation in which believing or disbelieving is directed upon propositions or upon the truth or falsity of propositions. Just as we chose to explain our terms "truth" and "falsity" so that truth or falsity may be the quality not only of a real judgment but also of a real proposition, so let us choose to explain our terms "knowing" and "erring" so that a mental attitude which is believing or disbelieving may be knowing or erring, not only when it is directed upon a real judgment, but also when it is directed upon the truth or falsity of a real proposition.

The qualities of an individual substance, let us assume, have the date and position of the substance in which they inhere. The quality which we call "the existence of Socrates" was, like Socrates himself, in Athens. The truth of some true proposition which I am reading is, like that proposition itself, on the page in front of me. My believing may be directed towards the Socrates who was in Athens, towards the existence of this Socrates, towards the proposition "Socrates exists" which is on the page in front of me, or towards the truth of this true proposition. We have chosen to call my believing an instance of "knowing" when it is directed towards the existence of Socrates. But let us also call my believing an instance of knowing when it is directed towards the truth of the true proposition: "Socrates exists" which is on the page in front of me. Let us call my believing an instance of knowing, that is to say, not only when it is directed towards the existence of an existing entity, but also when it is directed towards the truth of a true proposition. And let us call my disbelieving an instance of "erring," not only when that in which I disbelieve is the existence of an existing entity, but also when that in which I disbelieve is the truth of true proposition.

As we explain our term "knowing," I am knowing when I a believing in the existence of Socrates. And I am again knowin when I am believing in the truth of some proposition: "Socrat exists" which I find before me. But whereas I am knowing whe I am believing in the truth of "Santa Claus does not exist," I a not knowing when I seem to be believing in the non-existence Santa Claus. And whereas I am knowing, let us say, when I a believing in the falsity of "Santa Claus exists," I am not knowin when I seem to be disbelieving in the existence of Santa Clau

Similarly, as we explain our term "erring," I am erring when am disbelieving in the existence of Socrates. And I am again errin when I am disbelieving in the truth of some sentence readin "Socrates exists." On the other hand, I am erring when I am di believing in the truth of "Santa Claus does not exist," but n when I seem to be disbelieving in the non-existence of Santa Clau And I am erring when I am disbelieving in the falsity of "San Claus exists," but not when I seem to be believing in the existen of Santa Claus. In short, what we call "knowing" is believing i the existence of an existing entity, in the truth of a true propos tion, or in the falsity of a false proposition. And what we ca "error" is disbelief directed towards such entities. Finally, whe what I seem to be believing in or disbelieving in is neither th existence of an existing entity nor the truth of a true propositio nor the falsity of a false proposition, then, let us say, I am neith knowing nor erring.

However, "what I find least to my taste," we have already foun Leibniz saying *a propos* Locke's discussion of truth, "is that yo seek truth in words." [31] And if one finds it distasteful to assig "truth" a meaning from which it follows that a sentence on th page is one entity that is true, and an identical sentence on anoth page another entity that is true, one may well find it distastefu to assign "knowledge" a meaning from which it follows that th truth of the sentence on this page is one object of knowledg and the truth of the identical sentence on another page anoth object of knowledge. But just as the non-existence of Santa Clau being unreal, can not be true and can not pass its truth on t various identical sentences each reading: "Santa Claus does no

310

t," so this non-existence of Santa Claus can not be my object of
wledge either when I am believing in the truth of a sentence
this page reading: "Santa Claus does not exist," or when I
believing in the truth of a sentence on another page reading:
ita Claus does not exist." Even though we may be assigning
owledge" a meaning at variance with the meaning which
owledge" usually has, we choose then to assign "knowledge"
eaning from which it follows that the truth of this sentence
the truth of that sentence may be separate objects of knowl-
: and not entities reflecting an alleged object of knowledge to
h they are alleged both to be related.

, believing in the truth of some sentence reading: "Santa
is does not exist," I come to believe in the truth of a second
ence reading: "Santa Claus does not exist," then, as we use
term "knowledge," I have come to have a second object of
wledge. As "knowledge" is commonly used, to be sure, a man
ld not be said to increase his knowledge when he comes to
:ve in the truth of a second proposition identical with one in
se truth he already believes. Even as "knowledge" is commonly
, however, there seems to be a distinction between having
tional objects of knowledge and having more knowledge or
ng greater knowledge. As "knowledge" is commonly used, the
ker who has the greater knowledge, who is the more erudite,
)t he who has the greater number of objects of knowledge, but
ho has the greater number of *important* objects of knowledge.
:cts of knowledge, that is to say, may be weighted and not
:ly added together as equal units. And similarly when "knowl-
" has the meaning which we are assigning it. Although I have
: to have an additional object of knowledge when I have come
elieve in the truth of a second proposition reading: "Santa
is does not exist," I may be said not to have increased my
vledge. Just as, when "knowledge" has the meaning which it
lly has, the thinker who knows how clothing is dyed knows
: than he who knows that his tie is blue, so, when "knowledge"
he meaning which we are assigning it, the thinker who believes
ie truth of one important proposition may be said to know
: than he who believes in the truth of several identical but
iportant propositions.

here is the fact in which I am now believing, the true proposition in whose truth I am now believing, the false proposition in whose falsity I am now believing. And there is the object of knowledge of which I was formerly aware and of which I can, when I choose, again be aware. There is what, according to Locke,[32] "may be called habitual knowledge." There is the object of knowledge such that I "can on a given occasion think of it." [33] Thus there is a distinction to be made when "knowledge" has its usual meaning. And there is a similar distinction to be made when "knowledge" has the meaning which we are assigning it. For it is one thing to be believing in the existence of an existing entity, in the truth of a true proposition, or in the falsity of a false proposition. And it is another thing to be *able* to be believing in the existence of this entity or in the truth or falsity of this proposition.

There are some respects, however, in which "knowing," as we use it, is not the "knowing" of ordinary usage. The English verb "to know," as commonly used, is in some instances synonymous with "kennen" or "connaître." But in so far as you are acquainted with your next-door neighbor, you are not knowing him, in our sense of "knowing," nor do you have the quality of being able to know him. The mental attitude which you have, or are able to have, is a mental attitude directed upon your neighbor rather than upon your neighbor's existence. You have spoken to him, he is one of your memories, or you are one of his memories. But it is not the fact that he exists that is your object and the object in which you are believing; and it is not the fact that he exists with the quality of living next door. In so far as you are acquainted with your neighbor, you do, to be sure, have an object. But you are not believing in a fact or judgment, in the truth of a true proposition, or in the falsity of a false proposition.

But what about the situation in which there *is* believing in the existence of an existing entity, in the truth of a true proposition, or in the falsity of a false proposition? I may be believing in the existence of the Shah of Persia and you may be believing in the existence of your neighbor and in the fact that he lives next door. As we have explained our term "knowing," I am knowing and you are knowing. But whereas you are aware of your neighbor's age, physiognomy and disposition, the Shah of Persia is not presented to me with a similar wealth of detail. Whereas the entity in whose existence you believe is an entity of which you are definitely

312

aware, the entity in whose existence I believe is an entity of which I am aware only indefinitely. There are those, it is to be pointed out, who discuss what they call "knowledge of acquaintance." [34] But in so far as you are believing in the *existence* of your neighbor or in the *fact* that he lives next door, and in so far as I am believing in the *existence* of the Shah of Persia, the mental attitudes of each of us are instances of what we call "knowing," not instances of what we call "being acquainted with." We are each knowing, although in the one situation the entity whose existence is believed in is a definite object, in the other an indefinite object.

It is an entity that is presented to me only indefinitely when I am believing in the existence of the Shah of Persia. It is an entity that is presented to me only indefinitely when I say that I know *that* there is a Shah of Persia but not *who* the Shah of Persia is. And it is an entity that is presented to me only indefinitely when I say that I know *that* alcohol is but not *what* it is. Nevertheless, even though the name of the Shah of Persia is not an object of mine, when I am believing in the *existence* of the Shah of Persia, I am knowing in our sense of "knowing." And even though the chemical formula for alcohol is not an object of mine, I am again knowing when I am believing in the existence of alcohol.

Indeed, as we explain "knowing," when I say that I do not know such and such a fact, I may well be knowing the fact of which I claim to be ignorant. The fact of which I claim to be ignorant, that is to say, may be a fact in which I believe, although not presented with the detail that would make my mental attitude directed upon it an important instance of knowing. Thus I may say that I do not know who was the tenth President of the United States. But my mental attitude need not be without an object; and I may indeed be knowing. What is presented to me, let us assume, is some President of the United States, but not his name. I may be knowing that there *was* a tenth President and that he held office at some date near the middle of the nineteenth century. The tenth President however is not presented to me with the definiteness with which your neighbor is presented to you. I am knowing that there *was* a tenth President; but my object of knowledge is not presented with the definiteness with which your object of knowledge is presented when you are believing in the existence

313

of your neighbor.

There are, we have agreed, instances of what we call "knowing."[35] And there are, let us agree, instances of mental attitudes which reach instances of knowing as their objects. Just as "Descartes' perceiving may be an object both for Descartes and for me" and just as Laöcoon's fearing may be an object both for Laöcoon and for me,[36] so an instance of knowing may be an object both for the knower and for some other subject. Indeed the subject who is aware of a given instance of knowing may be believing in the existence of this instance of knowing. He may in a word be knowing that this mental attitude is an instance of knowing.

A knower may be knowing; and he may be knowing that he is knowing. But is it possible for one to know *without* knowing that he knows? "Whereas it may be agreed that fearing is distinguishable from the introspecting of fearing, and that there are real instances of both, it may be held that there are no instances of fearing that are not introspected by the fearing subject."[37] And whereas it may be agreed that there are instances of knowing and instances of knowing that one is knowing, it may be held that there are no instances of knowing unaccompanied by instances of knowing that one is knowing. If, in order to know, I had to know that I know, then in order to know that I know, I would, it seems, have to know that I know that I know; and so on, *ad infinitum*.[38] An alleged infinite regress of this sort, however, need not trouble us. "There are instances, we have agreed, of mental attitudes which are not introspected."[39] And there are, let us agree, instances of knowing which are not objects for the knowing subject. In order that my knowing may be real, this alleged knowing of mine can not be presented with the characteristic of being no one's definite object. But it need not be presented with the characteristic of being the object of a contemporaneous mental attitude of mine. Much less need it be presented with the characteristic of being the object of a contemporaneous mental attitude of mine which is believing in its existence. Just as I may be perceiving, remembering or fearing, without being aware of my perceiving, of my remembering, or of my fearing, so I may be knowing, without knowing that I am knowing. I may be knowing in our sense of "knowing" without knowing that I am knowing; and I may be knowing in our sense of "knowing" without being aware of the

314

meaning which our term "knowing" has. I may be believing in the existence of some entity, that is to say, and yet not be believing in the existence of the believing mental attitude of mine which is directed upon the existence of that entity. And I may be believing in the existence of some entity, without being definitely aware of the fact that, as we explain our term "knowing," a mental attitude is an instance of knowing if it is believing in the existence of an existing entity, in the truth of a true proposition, or in the falsity of a false proposition.

As we are using the terms "existence," "truth," and "knowledge," certain entities exist or are real and certain alleged entities are unreal; real judgments are true and real propositions true or false; and certain mental attitudes which are believing or disbelieving are knowing or erring. We chose to introduce our term "truth" after explaining our term "existence" and have chosen to introduce our term "knowledge" after explaining our terms "existence" and "truth." Indeed in explaining our term "truth" we have presupposed an understanding of our term "existence"; and in explaining our term "knowledge" we have presupposed an understanding of our terms "existence" and "truth." We have, for example, suggested that our proposition: "Socrates exists" is true, in our sense of "truth," if Socrates exists in our sense of "existence." [40] And we have suggested that my mental attitude believing in the truth of the proposition: "Socrates exists" is an instance of knowing, in our sense of "knowing," if "Socrates exists" is true in our sense of "truth." [41]

There are those however who hold that truth is prior to reality,[42] those who, if they believed that their terms "truth" and "existence" required explanation, would choose to explain their term "existence" by referring back to what they call "truth." And there may be those who somewhat similarly would prefer to explain "truth" or "existence" by referring back to what they call "knowledge." One may choose to say that an entity exists if it has been determined that the proposition in which the assertion of its existence has been expressed is true. And one may choose to say that, given a mental attitude or state of mind which is an instance of knowledge, the object in which that mental attitude believes or to which that state of mind refers is real, and the proposition in which that belief is expressed true. There were no logical reasons

315

which compelled us "to begin with a discussion of 'reality' and to explain 'truth' in terms of reality." [43] And there are no logical reasons which compel us, on the one hand, to presuppose an understanding of our terms "existence" and "truth" when we explain our term "knowledge" and which, on the other hand, prevented us from presupposing an understanding of our term "knowledge" when we explained our terms "existence" and "truth." Just however as something analogous to the appendix to our third chapter, some enumeration of propositions or judgments which are true, would be called for as a partial explanation of our term "truth," were we to explain, first "truth," and then "reality"; [44] so, we hold, there would be called for, as a partial explanation of our term "knowledge," some enumeration of the mental attitudes which are knowing, were we to explain, first "knowing," and then "existence" and "truth."

As we use the terms "existence," "truth" and "knowledge," their meanings are interrelated. And as "existence," "truth" and "knowledge" are generally used, their meanings seem likewise to be interrelated. We have chosen to explain, first our term "existence," then our term "truth," then our term "knowledge." But whatever distinguishes what we call "real" from what we call "unreal" comes into play in distinguishing what we call "true" from what we call "false," and comes into play in distinguishing what we call "knowledge" from what we call "error." So it may be with respect to some other writers when it is a matter of distinguishing what they call "real" from what they call "unreal," what they call "true" from what they call "false," what they call "knowledge" from what they call "error." Indeed, when some distinction is held to depend on the presence or absence of A, it may be difficult to tell whether the presence or absence of A is being held primarily to distinguish the real from the unreal and only indirectly to distinguish the true from the false and knowledge from error; whether the presence or absence of A is being held primarily to distinguish the true from the false and only indirectly to distinguish the real from the unreal and knowledge from error; or whether it is being held primarily to distinguish knowledge from error and only indirectly to distinguish the real from the unreal and the true from the false.

Thus one may point to the clear and distinct on the one hand, to the obscure or confused on the other. Or one may point to the coherent on the one hand, to the incoherent on the other. It may be intelligible entities that are held to be presented as clear and distinct, sensible entities that are held to be presented as obscure or confused. The distinction between the clear and distinct and the obscure or confused may thus be held to be applicable to the universe of subsistents which we dichotomize into the real and the unreal.[45] Primary qualities to which numbers apply, it may for example be said, are real; whatever appears as merely sensible, it may be said, is unreal.[46] And similarly with the distinction between the coherent and the incoherent. Whatever coheres with the entities of which we are usually aware, it may be said, is real. And whatever appears as not coherent with the entities of which we are usually aware may be said to be unreal.[47] Propositions may then be said to be true in so far as they refer to entities which are clear and distinct or to entities which cohere with other real entities in the world of existents. And mental attitudes may be said to be instances of knowing in so far as the alleged object of knowledge, being clear and distinct, or cohering with other objects, is real.

But these distinctions—between the clear and distinct and the obscure or confused and between the coherent and the incoherent —may be held to have their primary use in distinguishing the true from the false. It may be alleged passive ideas, alleged private mental contents, which are held to be clear and distinct or obscure or confused. It may be *propositions* which are held to be consistent or inconsistent with one another. Or it may be alleged entities called "judgments." Entities may then be said to be real in so far as the ideas alleged to refer to them are clear and distinct, or in so far as the ideas alleged to refer to them cohere with other ideas in a coherent system of mental contents. Or entities may be said to be real in so far as the judgments alleged to refer to them, being coherent, or being clear and distinct, are true.

Finally, as we have already noted, "one may choose to say that, given a mental attitude . . . which is an instance of knowledge, the object in which that mental attitude believes . . . is real, and the proposition in which that belief is expressed true." [48] One may say, for example, that the feeling of certainty which is intermingled with certain mental attitudes is a mark of their clarity. One may say that mental attitudes which are clear and distinct, in the sense

317

that they are intermingled with mental attitudes which are not only instances of believing but instances of being certain, are mental attitudes which are instances of knowing. And one may subsequently say that the objects of thinking mind-nerve-fibres which are thus undisturbed by doubt are objects which are real.

When we began to assign a meaning to our term "existence," various alternative meanings were before us from which to make our selection. And whereas there were no logical grounds which forced us to adopt one universal negative existential proposition and to reject another, there were, we found, "grounds of expediency" [49] which permitted us to prefer one universal negative existential proposition to another. Similarly when we began to assign a meaning to our term "truth" and when we began to assign a meaning to our term "knowledge." We might have chosen to explain "truth" without referring back to what we call "existence." And we might have chosen to explain "knowledge" without referring back to existence and truth.

Having chosen, however, to explain "truth" in terms of reality, and "knowledge" in terms of reality and truth, certain alternative explanations could no longer be adopted. If the distinction between what we call "true" and what we call "false" was to apply only to entities which are real in our sense of "reality," we could not explain our terms "truth" and "falsity" so that truth and falsity characterize alleged judgments alleged to have their "habitat in a world of objective but disembodied entities." [50] Nor could we explain our terms "truth" and "falsity" so that alleged private ideas are true or false. For ideas, alleged to be immediate objects, do not exist, in our sense of "existence," when they are presented as non-spatial, as not spatially related to contemporaneous ultimate objects, as not objects for more than one subject, or as adjacent to thinking itself.[51]

Explaining our term "existence" as we have, nevertheless, we might still have chosen to introduce the term "truth" by saying that real propositions are true if they are members of a large system of real propositions, members of a system none of the members of which contradict one another. We might have chosen to introduce the term "knowledge" by saying that real mental attitudes are instances of knowing if they cohere with other real mental attitudes in parts of the same mind-person. Or we might

318

have chosen to introduce the term "knowledge" by saying that real mental attitudes are instances of knowing if they are intermingled with instances of the feeling of being certain.

It is on what we have called "grounds of expediency" that we turn away from certainty and coherence in explaining our terms "truth" and "knowledge." For it would not be in accord with ordinary usage to assign "knowledge" a signification from which it would follow that there is no knowing without being certain, no being certain without knowing. As we have chosen to explain our term "knowledge," and, it seems, as "knowledge" is commonly used, there may be knowing without there being a feeling of being certain and there may be a feeling of being certain without the alleged object being real or true. Nor does *"coherence"* seem to have a meaning that is readily understood. To say merely that real propositions are true in so far as they cohere would not be to be pointing out certain propositions which do not appear self-contradictory as definitely true and certain propositions which do not appear self-contradictory as definitely false. And to say merely that real mental attitudes are instances of knowing in so far as they cohere would not be to be pointing out certain mental attitudes which inhere in parts of my mind-person as instances of knowing and certain mental attitudes which inhere in parts of my mind-person as instances of erring. What indeed is coherence? We have chosen to use the term "coherence" in connection with mental attitudes inhering in thinking substances which are interrelated and form a system. We have chosen to use this term, for example, in connection with mental attitudes which inhere in parts of one mind-person.[52] And using "coherence" in this sense, we find that not all cohering mental attitudes are instances of what is commonly called "knowing." We find that mental attitudes which are instances of what seems commonly to be called "erring," and mental attitudes which are instances of what seems commonly to be called "knowing," cohere in parts of the same mind-person. And so we choose not to assign our term "knowing" a meaning from which it would follow that mental attitudes are instances of knowing in so far as they cohere in our sense of "coherence"; we choose rather to explain our term "knowing" by saying that mental attitudes are instances of knowing if they are instances of believing in the existence of existent entities, in the truth of true propositions or in the falsity of false propositions.

There is another set of proposals that calls for comment in connection with our discussion of the meanings to be assigned "knowledge" and "truth." In some of the writings of William James it is suggested that the knowing subject has a private idea which corresponds to the public object of knowledge. And it is suggested that, in some later experience, the subject, acting upon his belief, finds his private idea merging with the public object. It is as though I in America had a picture of Vesuvius, carried it with me to Naples, and there found my picture becoming Vesuvius itself. But since private ideas are unreal, there is no real relational situation having as its terms the private idea which I am alleged to have while in America and the Vesuvius which is alleged to be a public object in Italy. What is real in addition to Vesuvius, when I in America think about Vesuvius, is some mind-nerve-fibre within my body with what we call a "mental attitude" and with what others may call an "idea." And when I arrive in Naples and look at Vesuvius there is likewise some quality of my body's, or of my mind-nerve-fibre's, by virtue of which Vesuvius is *my* object rather than some one's else. The thinking which is within my body in America, and Vesuvius in Italy, can hardly be regarded as earlier and later phases of the same enduring entity. What are more readily regarded as inhering in parts of the same enduring entity are my thinking while I am in America and my looking or perceiving when I am in Naples.

The proposal which we are examining, it is also to be pointed out, seems to attribute an unquestioned validity to the experience which I have when I look at Vesuvius from Naples. This experience is regarded, it would seem, as involving knowledge or truth or reality *par excellence*. And the mental attitude which I have in America is called "knowing," or the idea which I have in America is called "true," in so far as it matches up with the experience which I am to have in Naples. But although my object seems to be in front of me when I am in Naples, I may, we hold, be pseudo-perceiving and not perceiving. As we use the term "reality" and as this term is commonly used, the entity which is presented as being before one, and presented as being presented with the definiteness with which percepts are presented, need not be real. If while in

Naples I take smoke from some other source to be smoke from Vesuvius, then the mental attitude which I have in America, and which matches up with the mental attitude which I am to have in Naples, would not commonly be called an instance of knowing. Hence if the pragmatist is to assign "truth" and "knowledge" meanings not completely out of accord with common usage, he must, it would seem, say that a mental attitude is an instance of knowing or an idea true, not if it matches up with a mental attitude or idea which *seems* to be directed upon, or *seems* to correspond with, an ultimate object which is perceived; he must say that a mental attitude is an instance of knowing, or an idea true, if it matches up with a mental attitude which is *really* perceiving. He must, it would seem, distinguish perceiving from pseudo-perceiving, real percepts from alleged percepts. As a part of the explanation which explains his term "knowledge," he is thus called on, it would seem, to distinguish the real from the unreal; hence, to explain his term "real." But if he were to explain his term "real," he might, we suggest, find it unnecessary to refer to a comparison of earlier experiences with later experiences in explaining either his term "truth" or his term "knowledge."

A thinker may be said to know if, acting on his belief, he will later perceive and know. Or a thinker may be said to know if, acting on his belief, he will later keep out of trouble. I may be said to be in error if, acting on my belief, I am led into a situation in which I am puzzled and forced to revise my beliefs. Or I may be said to be in error if, acting on my belief, I make responses which are inappropriate, enter into situations in which I do not prosper. The term "knowing" may be explained by referring to a relational situation involving, on the one hand, the knowing subject and, on the other hand, a later situation in which that subject finds himself, a later situation characterized by mental stability or happiness or by biological adjustment and success. And the term "erring" may be explained by referring to a relational situation involving, on the one hand, the erring subject and, on the other hand, a later situation in which there is mental puzzlement or unhappiness or biological maladjustment and failure.

But if I see a missile coming towards me and try unsuccessfully to avoid it, my maladjustment would not commonly be said to mark my earlier mental attitudes directed upon the missile as erroneous. And mental puzzlement, it would seem, points back to curiosity and doubt as frequently as it points back to what is commonly called "error." Which, moreover, is the previous mental attitude that is being marked out as an instance of knowing or erring? A situation in which there is adjustment and success or maladjustment and failure points back to a series of successive mental attitudes in the previous history of the adjusted or maladjusted subject. And so the terms "knowing" and "erring" are not assigned definite meanings unless the explanations, through which it is sought to explain these terms, enable us to determine which mental attitude in the previous history of the adjusted individual is being marked out as an instance of what is being called "knowing" and which mental attitude in the previous history of the maladjusted individual is being marked out as an instance of what is being called "erring."

We choose then not to explain our terms "knowing" and "erring" by comparing some earlier mental attitude with some later situation in which the knowing or erring subject is to find himself. But why, we ask, have such explanations been attempted? They may be traced back, it would seem, to a desire not to leave unexamined the alleged correspondence between alleged ideas and real ultimate objects, the relation between mental attitudes which are instances of knowing and the real objects of knowledge upon which these mental attitudes are directed. But whatever "correspondence" may mean, if we are to understand "correspondence with reality," we must, we hold, understand "reality," must be able to distinguish the real from the unreal. And if we are to understand: "being directed upon what are really objects of knowledge," we must again be able to distinguish the real from the unreal. With our term "reality" explained as we have explained it, we have, we hold, made it clear what it is with which instances of knowing and true propositions must match or correspond or be related. Using "existence" in our sense, there exist, to be sure, no ideas which are non-spatial or which are intra-cranial, but not mental attitudes. Hence there is no correspondence between such ideas and ultimate objects. There may however be said to be a correspondence between reality and what we call "truth," a correspondence which is *not* indefinite and has *not* been left unexamined.

As we explain our term "truth," truth corresponds with reality in

322

the definite sense that propositions are true or false according as certain entities represented, or alleged to be represented, by the terms of those propositions are real or unreal.[53] And as we explain our term "knowledge," mental attitudes which are instances of knowing match up with reality and truth in the definite sense that the subject who knows is believing in the existence of existing entities, in the truth of true propositions or in the falsity of false propositions. With the propositions which explain our term "reality" as a foundation, we have, we hold, assigned our terms "truth" and "knowledge" meanings which are rather definite and precise. Being in a position to determine whether the alleged object of knowledge is real or unreal, true or false, we are in a position to determine whether the subject alleged to be believing or disbelieving in that alleged object of knowledge is knowing or erring. Thus in order that "knowing" and "erring" may be assigned definite meanings, we need not assign them meanings which involve a comparison between the mental attitudes of the knowing subject and later situations in which that subject is to find himself. In so far as the meanings of our terms "knowing" and "erring" enable us to distinguish knowing from erring, there is no occasion, we hold, to assign these terms alternative meanings in an effort to be in a position to distinguish knowledge from error.

Summary

Along with mental attitudes which are instances of perceiving, remembering and conceiving, there are mental attitudes which are instances of what we call "feeling." Among them are instances of fearing, of being in love, of being disgusted. These instances of feeling can exist without the subject who feels being aware of them. But he *can* be aware of them, in which case the situation resembles that in which a subject is aware of the fact that he is perceiving.

Where there is error, the subject has a mental attitude but no object. Somewhat similarly, when one fears or hopes for something that has no reality, the feeling exists but it has no object.

Just as instances of fearing, of hating and of hoping are instances of feeling, so are instances of believing. Believing in an entity is distinguished from believing in the existence of that entity. This leads to a definition defining knowledge and error. Knowing is believing in the existence of an existing entity, in the truth of a true proposition or in the falsity of a false proposition. Being in error is disbelieving in the existence of an existing entity, in the truth of a true proposition or in the falsity of a false proposition.

Knowing *that* a thing is is often distinguished from knowing *what* a thing is. As we define knowing, these entities are also to be distinguished, but perhaps differently.

At this point our terms "reality," "truth" and "knowledge" have all been explained. These terms are so interrelated, both in our terminology and as generally used, that what are put forward as criteria of existence may be put forward as criteria of truth or criteria of knowledge. Hence it is appropriate at this point to discuss these alleged criteria in relation to all three. Included is a discussion of pragmatism.

Chapter XI

SPATIAL RELATIONS AMONG CONTEMPORANEOUS
ENTITIES

Let us consider what is alleged to be a baseball diamond, or, rather, what is alleged to be an instantaneous phase of a baseball diamond. There appears, let us say, a phase of the pitcher which is presented as in the pitcher's box having just hurled the ball. There appears, let us say, a phase of the batter which is presented as at the plate about to swing at the ball. And there appears, let us say, a phase of the catcher which is presented as behind the plate prepared to catch the ball. Among our subsistents there are thus instantaneous phases of pitcher, batter and catcher which are alleged to be substances. But among our subsistents there is also the quality of being contemporaneous with a phase of the batter, a quality which is alleged to inhere in the phase of the pitcher which we are considering and another instance of which is likewise alleged to inhere in the phase of the catcher which we are considering. Also there is among our subsistents a quality which is alleged to inhere in the pitcher, the quality, namely, of being out-there-in-front with respect to the batter; and there is the quality of being a short distance behind with respect to the batter, a quality alleged to inhere in the catcher.

We began Chapter Six of this treatise by asking whether Descartes, as he paced up and down his stove-heated room, was really thinking. And we begin this chapter by asking whether the phase of the pitcher which we are considering was really out-there-in-front with respect to a phase of the batter contemporaneous with him; and by asking whether the phase of the catcher which we are considering was really a short distance behind. Let us recall, however, that while we were asking whether or not Descartes was thinking, we agreed to take it for granted that Descartes *had* a body and that there *was* a stove-heated room. Otherwise, we held,[1] "we should find ourselves confronted by a host of questions all clamoring at once for solution and all having to be answered before the reality of Descartes' thinking could be acknowledged."

Similarly let us at this point take it for granted that the phases of pitcher, batter and catcher which we are considering are real substances and really contemporaneous, or present, with respect to one another. It may, to be sure, be questioned whether alleged substances can be real and can have real qualities inhering in them. And it may be questioned whether alleged instantaneous phases of substances can themselves be real substances and can, without reference to bodies from which they are measured, be really contemporaneous with one another. But to consider such questions at this point would complicate the subject-matter of this chapter and would delay us in coming to close quarters with such alleged entities as our pitcher's being out-there-in-front with respect to a contemporaneous phase of the batter. Just as "such candidates for existence as the thinking of Descartes' that is presented as *having* a vehicle and a setting can be discussed in fewer words and in a less complicated fashion when, instead of regarding thinking, vehicle and setting as all mere subsistents, we accept the premise that vehicle and setting are real,"[2] so such candidates for existence as our pitcher's alleged quality of being out-there-in-front with respect to a contemporaneous phase of the batter can be discussed in fewer words and in a less complicated fashion when we take it for granted that a given instantaneous phase of the pitcher is a real substance and take it for granted that it has the real quality of being contemporaneous with a real instantaneous phase of the batter. Instantaneous phases of pitcher, batter and catcher, presented as substances—and simultaneity with a phase of the batter, presented as a quality of our phase of the pitcher and as a quality of our phase of the catcher—these entities are all presented without any of the characteristics that would mark them out as unreal; and they are all listed as real in the appendix to Chapter Three. At this point, then, we hold that our instantaneous phase of the pitcher is real and really contemporaneous, or present, with respect to a phase of the batter. And we ask whether this instantaneous phase of the pitcher is also out-there-in-front with respect to this phase of the batter. Our instantaneous phase of the catcher is, we hold, real and really contemporaneous, or present, with respect to a phase of the batter. But is it also a-short-distance-behind with respect to this phase of the batter?

Now we may say at once that our phase of the pitcher, presented as having some *other* position with respect to the contemporaneous batter, is presented as generally discredited and is unreal. And we may say that our phase of the pitcher presented as having *no* position with respect to the contemporaneous batter is likewise unreal. For as we have explained our term "reality," that subsistent is unreal "which appears as lacking position with respect to an entity that appears real and with respect to which it also appears present."[3] But whereas our phase of the pitcher is unreal if it is presented as having no position with respect to the contemporaneous batter, the phase of the pitcher which is real need not be a phase which is presented as *having* position with respect to the contemporaneous batter. The phase of the pitcher which is real may be a phase of the pitcher presented without the characteristic of having position with respect to the batter and without the characteristic of having no position with respect to the batter. The phase of the pitcher which is real, that is to say, may have neither the real quality of having no position with respect to the contemporaneous batter nor the real quality of being out-there-in-front with respect to him. For upon examination the pitcher's alleged quality of being out-there-in-front with respect to the contemporaneous batter may reveal itself as unreal; just as the pitcher's alleged quality of having no position with respect to this batter is unreal.

Let us suppose that the pitcher is out-there-in-front with respect to the contemporaneous batter; and let us suppose that he is at the source of motions which later reach some spectator in the grandstand, leading that spectator to be aware of the pitcher. Now, whereas the pitcher and his alleged quality of being out-there-in-front with respect to the batter may be at the source of motions leading to the spectator's mental attitude, neither the pitcher as a substance nor his alleged quality of being out-there-in-front with respect to the batter, it may be said, are, in a strict sense of "cause," *causes* of the spectator's mental attitude.[4] The pitcher's alleged quality of being out-there-in-front with respect to the batter, that is to say, may not be an element at the source such that, without it, the spectator would not have the mental attitudes he has. Moreover, the pitcher's alleged quality of being out-there-in-front with respect to the batter has, it may be said, no special channel open to it whereby it brings about the spectator's mental attitudes. The spectator, it may be pointed out, may hear the pitcher's voice, see the pitcher's gestures or his white uniform; but there is no line of communication, it may be said, through which the pitcher's alleged quality of being-out-there-in-front with respect to the batter could affect the spectator's thinking. There is no more a line of communication, it may be said, to the spectator from the pitcher's alleged quality of being out-there-in-front than there is to me from the alleged man on my ceiling. Just as the mental attitude of mine, apparently directed upon the man on my ceiling, is an instance of thinking that is without a real object rather than an instance of perceiving, so, it may be said, is the spectator's mental attitude apparently directed upon the pitcher's quality of being out-there-in-front with respect to the batter. Just as there is no real man on my ceiling, so, it may be said, the pitcher has no real quality of being out-there-in-front with respect to the batter.

As we have explained our term "reality," however, a subsistent may be real when it is presented as at the source of motions leading to a given mental attitude, but presented as not a *sine qua non* with respect to that mental attitude. And a subsistent may likewise be real when it is presented as an entity such that there is no special channel through which it affects the mental attitude apparently directed upon it. As we have explained our term "reality," an entity is unreal if it is presented as generally discredited. Thus the man on my ceiling, presented as having no special channel through which to affect the mental attitude of mine apparently directed upon him, since we also find this alleged man presented as generally discredited, is unreal. But there also subsists an other-side-of-the-moon which is presented as having no special channel through which to affect the mental attitude of yours apparently directed upon it. And this other-side-of-the-moon is not presented as generally discredited and is, we hold, real. The other side of the moon is real, even though it is an inferred object with respect to the mental attitude which you direct upon it.[5] The Emperor's piety was real even though it should be true that, in a strict sense of "cause," it was not the Emperor's piety, but some other quality of the Emperor's, that caused Descartes' thinking.[6] And the pitcher's alleged quality of being out-there-in-front with respect to the batter may be real, even though it has no special channel through which to affect the spectator apparently aware of it.

But let us consider the pitcher's alleged quality of being out-there-in-front, not as being at the source of motions which affect a spectator in the grandstand, but as at the source of motions which affect the batter. It is, let us agree, a phase of the pitcher which is slightly past which is at the source of motions leading to the present batter's mental attitudes. If then the present batter seems to be aware of the *present* pitcher as being out-there-in-front with respect to him, his object, if real, is an inferred object and not an object which is at the source of motions affecting him. In seeming to be aware of the phase of the pitcher contemporaneous with him as being out-there-in-front with respect to him, the batter's alleged object may, to be sure, be real. For just as tomorrow's sunrise is real even though it is an inferred object for the mental attitude which I today direct upon it,[7] so the present phase of the pitcher may really have the quality of being out-there-in-front with respect to the present batter, even though it is presented as an inferred object with respect to the present batter's thinking.

But how does the present batter come to be aware of the present pitcher as being out-there-in-front with respect to him? He is, to be sure, affected by a past phase of the pitcher. But the past pitcher's quality of being out-there-in-front, it may be said, is not an entity from which the present pitcher's quality of being out-there-in-front can be inferred. On the contrary, it may be said, the past pitcher's quality of being out-there-in-front must itself be inferred from the fact that the present phase of the pitcher is out-there-in-front. Primarily, it may be held, I have position only with respect to present entities. I have position with respect to some past entity only by having position with respect to some present entity which is in the very place in which that past entity was.[8] Thus the spatial relation seems in the first instance to be a relation involving terms having identical dates, the causal relation one involving terms having different dates. If we are to conclude that a past phase of the pitcher has not only affected the present batter but was also out-there-in-front with respect to him, we must already, it appears, have accepted the fact that the present phase of the pitcher is out-there-in-front. On the other hand, the present batter infers the present pitcher's quality of being out-there-in-front with respect to him, only, it would seem, as a consequence of being affected by the past pitcher's quality of being out-there-in-front. It is puzzling "that my dog's behavior, unaffected by a future phase of the ball"[9] that I throw, is nevertheless "adapted to the ball that is about to fall to the ground some distance away."[10] It is puzzling that my mental attitude reaches tomorrow's sunrise as its object when the entity which has affected it is a past phase of the sun.[11] And it is puzzling that the batter is aware of the present pitcher's quality of being out-there-in-front with respect to him when, to accept the fact that the past pitcher who has affected him is out-there-in-front, he must already, it would seem, have accepted the fact that the present pitcher is out-there-in-front. "Such bewilderment as there may be, however, does not imply that my dog's behavior, presented as adapted to a future phase of the ball, is presented as generally discredited and is unreal"; it does not imply that my mental attitude is not really aware of tomorrow's sunrise; and it does not imply that the present batter has no real object when he seems to be aware of the present pitcher as being out-there-in-front with respect to him.

So far as we have yet seen, the pitcher's alleged quality of being out-there-in-front with respect to a contemporaneous phase of the batter need not be unreal. But no entity is real, we have said, which "appears with the characteristic of having only a very indefinite position with respect to an entity which appears real and with respect to which it appears present."[12] There subsists, for example, the phase of the Cosmos which is alleged to be present with respect to the batter. This subsistent appears with the characteristic of having only a very indefinite position with respect to the real and allegedly contemporaneous batter. Hence both this Cosmos and its alleged position are unreal. But being out-there-in-front, although not so definite a position as being over

330

there where a certain spot is, is not, we hold, an indefinite position. Being out-there-in-front with respect to the batter who appears real and with respect to whom the pitcher is present—this alleged quality of the pitcher appears neither indefinite in position nor self-contradictory, neither generally discredited nor undatable. It is, we find, enumerated in our list of real entities. In brief, the pitcher who is real has the real quality of being out-there-in-front with respect to the batter with respect to whom he is present. Similarly, keeping to the baseball players already mentioned, the catcher is a short distance behind with respect to the batter with respect to whom he is present and the pitcher out-there-in-front with respect to the catcher with respect to whom *he* is present.

Consider now the path from pitcher's mound to home plate. It is, let us agree, a real substance. It is present with respect to the catcher. And it appears with the characteristic of being-out-there-in-front with respect to the catcher with respect to whom it is present. To be sure, the position with which it appears with respect to the catcher is less definite than the position with which the pitcher appears with respect to the catcher. The one, we might say, appears away out in front, the other more or less out in front. But if we call the pitcher who has no punctual position real, if we call the pitcher and his position with respect to the catcher real, we may, it would seem, call the path real and *its* position with respect to the catcher. And as the position of the path with respect to the catcher is real, so is the position of the distance between pitcher and batter. For as we use the term "distance," a distance is a certain line or path with the emphasis on the *termini*. The baseball diamond as a whole has a less definite position with respect to the catcher with respect to whom it is present than has the pitcher. And the distance between pitcher and batter has a less definite position than its *termini*. But the difference in definiteness is one of degree. If only points were real, neither pitcher nor distance nor diamond would be real. But if entities may be real provided only that their alleged positions are not too indefinite, distances may be real along with their termini and baseball diamonds along with the entities alleged to be included within them. Distances and baseball diamonds may be real; and they may have real positions with respect to the catcher contemporaneous with them.

Assuming then that the catcher appears real and that pitcher, path and diamond all appear 'out-in-front' and present with respect to him, pitcher, path and diamond may all be real despite the difference in the degree of definiteness with which they are located with respect to the catcher. But if the catcher is presented as unreal, if pitcher, path or diamond appears out in front only with respect to unreal entities—with respect, for example, to the catcher of some juvenile romance or with respect to the private idea of a catcher which some subject is alleged to have—then it is not true that pitcher, path and diamond may all be real. For, as we have determined the significations of our terms "real" and "unreal," those entities are unreal which appear as having no position with respect to an entity which appears real.[13] And if there *is* some entity which appears real, and if pitcher, path or diamond appear as having no position with respect to it but only with respect to private ideas or characters in fiction, then the pitchers and diamonds that thus appear are unreal. If, however, we are considering a situation in which the catcher appears real and pitcher, path and diamond all appear out-in-front with respect to him, then, our conclusion is, the indefiniteness with which the diamond is located does not bar it from reality.

But what about the entity which appears more definitely located than the diamond, the path, or even the pitcher? What about the position which may be alleged to inhere in the pitcher's center of gravity? Unlike pitcher, path or diamond, the position of such a center of gravity with respect to the catcher with whom it appears present subsists as a definite position, a punctual position. Yet neither this center of gravity which subsists as a substance, a point, nor its definite position which subsists as a quality of that substance, appears as a source from which motions flow to the mental attitudes apparently directed upon them. A point, that is to say, appears as a limit never reached by division, an entity that I never succeed in seeing. Yet even if we do not dissect the pitcher to place his center of gravity before us and even if this center of gravity and its definite punctual position do not appear as sources from which motions flow to the mental attitudes apparently directed upon them, nevertheless both this center of gravity and its position with respect to the catcher may, we hold, be real. For the pitcher's center of gravity which appears as having a definite position with respect to the catcher does not appear as having no position; it does not appear as non-temporal; and it does not appear as generally discredited. In short, both it and its punctual position with respect to the catcher appear without any of the characteristics which would mark them as unreal. They are, we find, real.

The pitcher's center of gravity appearing as a point, a definitely located substance, is a subsistent which we find real. We may of course use the word "point" to represent a group of volumes within volumes, a group of alleged percepts rather than a limit which is not itself a percept. And we may call "the pitcher's center of gravity" a collection of parts of the pitcher's body that are within parts of the pitcher's body. When "points, straight lines and areas are all defined as series of converging volumes," points may be real; and familiar geometrical propositions using the word "point" may be true.[14] But "point" need not be assigned a signification of this sort to represent a real entity. Some individual substances having definite positions with respect to real contemporaneous entities are real. And when such substances are called "points," some alleged points are real and their punctual positions real.

Just as the pitcher's center of gravity and its definite position with respect to the real contemporaneous catcher are, we hold, real, so are the North Pole and *its* position. And just as these points and their positions are real, so are the equator and *its* position. A phase of the equator appears present and below the horizon; but the position with which it appears is an indefinite one, since the part of the equator that lies in Ecuador is in a somewhat different direction from the part of it that lies in Sumatra. Its position is below the horizon and more or less distant just as the path from pitcher to batter is out there in front, not due north, and is more or less distant, not an exact distance away. Neither the equator nor any part of it appears as an entity that is seen. And yet just as the North Pole, a substance with a definite position, is real, so is the equator, a substance without breadth, a substance that is a line. For, like the pitcher, the path, and the pitcher's center of gravity, the present phase of the equator appears spatial, free from self-contradiction, not generally discredited, and is enumerated in our list of real entities.

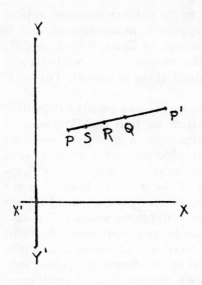

Some alleged points with their definite positions are real, the pitcher with his less definite position is real, and some lines with *their* positions are real. In the diagram on this page, there is an invisible point O, a substance with a definite position, within the region in which the two broad marks XX' and YY' cross each other; and there is a real line without thickness or breadth within the broad, visible and undulating mark PP'. This line is not non-spatial. It has roughly the same position with respect to O that the printed mark PP' has, only a more definite position. It is perhaps without color or weight, but appears neither self-contradictory nor generally discredited. It is real as the equator is real and its position with respect to the contemporaneous phase of O real as the position of the equator with respect to the contemporaneous phase of the catcher is real.

There is a real point P, a real point P', and a real point Q that lies between them. Their positions with respect to O are definite positions, whereas the position of the line PP' is indefinite. Yet they are parts of PP' in that their positions are included within that of the line on which they are. Q is a real point between P and P', R a real point between P and Q, S a real point between P and R. Within each dot that we make on the undulating mark PP' there is a substance with a definite position with respect to O, there is a point, that is to say, whose position is included within that of the breadth-less line PP'. But since the dot that we make is not the point but merely indicates the point's position, the number of real points on the line PP' may not be limited to the number of dots that we make.

If we ask ourselves how many points, not dots, there are on the line PP', the answer that is most likely to occur to us is that the number is infinite. It is, however, not easy to explain "infinite number" satisfactorily. If the number of points on our line is infinite, then not all of these points are points that we shall discover. Yet some finite numbers, it may be held, elude enumeration also; the points on our line, it may be held, are finite in number, and yet so many that not all of them will ever be discovered. It is not the existence of points that will not be discovered that implies the existence of an infinite number of points, but the existence of points that can not be discovered during any finite duration, however long it may last. The number of points on our line is infinite if, and only if, it would require an infinite duration to discover them all. But when we describe an infinite collection as one that would require an infinite duration for an enumeration of its members, we have merely substituted "infinite duration" for "infinite number" as a term to be explained.

We may mark out a point S in the segment PQ and then a point R in the whole line PP'; and if PP' contains an infinite number of points, we may continue to mark out points in segment and whole line, alternately, as long as we please. But the number of points on PP' may be finite and yet so large a number that in view of the shortness of life and our failure to persevere, we will be able to mark out points in segment and whole line, alternately, as long as we please. If the number of points on the whole line is to be infinite rather than a very large finite number, no failure in the attempt to find corresponding points in whole line and segment could occur, it must be held, until after the lapse of an infinite duration. At the end of any *finite* duration, the infinitist must hold, there exist real but undiscovered points both in whole line and in segment. But this observation, like the observation in the preceding paragraph, carries us no further than from 'infinite number' to 'infinite duration.' And if we say that the whole line contains an infinite number of points when its segment contains an infinite number, the circularity of our explanation is even more apparent.

If the whole line contains an infinite number of points, the segment likewise contains an infinite number. When we say this, or when we say that an infinite collection is one that would require an infinite duration for an enumeration of its members, we give "infinite number," it would seem, the signification which it usually has, but a signification that is not made entirely clear. On the other hand, if we say that a line contains an infinite number of points when a segment of it contains as many points as the whole line, the signification we assign "infinite number," although not circular, may not be the signification which "infinite number" usually has. There is a point Q on the line PP' which is not included in the segment PR; whereas every real point included in PR is likewise included in PP'. Whether the number of points included in PP' be termed "infinite" in number or "finite" in number, there are more points in the whole line than in its segment. If, in order that the number of points on PP' might be termed "infinite," it were necessary for PR to contain as many points as PP', then the number of real points on PP' could not be infinite and "infinite collection" would appear to have a signification from which it would follow that no infinite collections exist. A collection of points on a segment, appearing with the characteristic of being as many as the collection of points on the whole line,—such a subsisting collection appears self-contradictory and is unreal. If "infinite collection" is used to represent such an alleged collection, infinite collections are non-existent.

If "infinite collection" signifies a collection such that it would require an infinite duration before the subject matter blocked an attempt to discover additional points alternately in whole line and segment and before the undiscovered real points in whole line and segment were exhausted, infinite collections may, so far as we have yet seen, exist; but the signification of "infinite collection" is not entirely clear. If, on the other hand, "infinite collection" signifies a collection such that there are as many points on a segment as on a whole line of which the segment is a part, then infinite collections do not exist; and "infinite collection," although apparently given a more readily understood signification, represents nothing real.

We are offered, it may appear, a compromise between these two significations when we are told that "infinite collection" signifies a collection such that there is a one-to-one correspondence between the points on the whole line and the points on the segment. If the points on the segment were as many as the points on the whole line, there would, we may agree, be correspondence. But if the whole line contains each point on the segment and additional points besides, "correspondence," if it refers to anything real, refers to the failure of the subject matter to block the discovery of points in whole line and segment alternately and to the existence of an inexhaustible number of points in each. But to say that there is an infinite collection when there is correspondence in this sense of "correspondence" is to give "infinite collection" a signification which is identical with, and no clearer than, the signification which we give it when we say that a collection is infinite only if it would require an infinite duration before the subject matter blocked the discovery of additional points alternately in whole line and segment and only if any shorter duration left us with existing undiscovered points in each. Unless we use "infinite collection" to refer to something that does not exist, we can do no better, it would seem, than explain "infinite collection" in propositions which involve a certain circularity. For, the attempt to avoid circularity seems to end merely in ambiguity and evasion.

If the line PP′ contains an infinite number of points, an infinite number of real substances having definite positions with respect to the contemporaneous point O, then each segment of it likewise contains an infinite number. If PP′ contains an infinite number of points, an infinite duration would be required before the subject-matter blocked the attempt to discover additional points either in the whole line or in any of its segments. But conjoined with the requirement that an infinite duration would be needed before blocking occurred is the requirement that the end of any finite duration leave us with real but undiscovered points. Now it is possible to hold—and we shall ourselves hold—that at the end of no finite duration is there blocking and at the end of some finite duration no undiscovered points. There are, it would seem, two questions. First: could the subject matter ever block the attempt to discover additional points? And second: Is there some finite duration at the expiration of which there are no real undiscovered points? Only if both questions are truly answered in the negative does the line PP′ contain what we shall term an "infinite number" of points.

A point, we must repeat, is not a dot, but an alleged substance appearing to have a definite position with respect to the contemporaneous point of reference O. Real dots between S and R are definitely marked out as real only if some alleged entities appearing between S and R, appearing to be made by ink, and appearing

337

without the characteristic of being generally discredited, are listed among the group of entities enumerated at the end of Chapter Three. Real points, on the other hand, exist between S and R if some alleged entities appearing between S and R, appearing as definitely located objects, appearing as not visible, and appearing without the characteristic of being generally discredited, are so listed. An alleged dot between S and R appears generally discredited and is unreal. But an alleged point between S and R appears without the characteristic of being generally discredited and is real. Whether an alleged point is presented to us with the characteristic of being one millimeter or one thousandth of a millimeter from S, it does not appear, either explicitly or implicitly, with the characteristic of being generally discredited. In the search for additional points, there is no finite duration such that at the end of it the further alleged points with which we would meet would all appear with the characteristic of being generally discredited. For since the process of finding additional points is not an overt physical process but a process whereby we present to ourselves additional alleged objects, points about to be presented, like those already presented, appear without the characteristic of being generally discredited. In order for there to be no real point between S and R there must be no subsisting point between S and R, or the subsisting point between S and R must be unreal. If however there is no subsisting point between S and R, there is no frustration possible, nothing but the sort of puzzlement with which we would approach the task of finding a point between S and S. And, on the other hand, if a point between S and R subsists, it appears, whether real or not, without the characteristic of being generally discredited.

In order that a subsistent may be real, it must appear without the characteristic of being generally discredited. But it must also appear without the characteristic of being no definite object for any subject. Between Q and R points subsist in so far as we consider such points as possible existents. Whatever points subsist between Q and R appear without the characteristic of being generally discredited. But the points that subsist between Q and R may subsist with the characteristic of not being definite objects for any subject. No one, let me suppose, happens to be aware of any subsisting point between Q and R as being a definite number

338

of millimeters nearer to Q than to R, or as being joined to O by a line which makes an angle of a definite number of degrees with XX'. Each subsisting point between Q and R, let me suppose, appears implicitly with the characteristic of not being a definite object for any subject. Then, as we use the term "existence," no subsisting point between Q and R is real. It is not that there are no subsisting points between Q and R; and it is not that the points subsisting between Q and R subsist with the characteristic of being generally discredited. There are no real points between Q and R in that each subsisting point between Q and R appears implicitly with the characteristic of not being a definite object for any subject.

There are no points between Q and R that appear without the characteristic of being only indefinite objects, no points between Q and R which are real. There are six or sixty-six or some other finite number of real points on the whole line PP'. All other subsisting points between P and P' appear implicitly with the characteristic of not being definite objects for any subject and consequently are unreal. The number of real points on PP' is limited to those that appear without the characteristic of being only indefinite objects. And it is only a finite number that thus appears.

At the expiration of some finite duration, our conclusion is, all of the real points on PP' will have been enumerated. For, at the expiration of some finite duration, all alleged points remaining unenumerated will be such as appear with the characteristic of being only indefinite objects. To say just how many real points there are on PP' is thus to make a prediction. To say that there are no more than sixty-six points on PP' is to predict that no sixty-seventh point will be a definite object for any subject, or, rather, that no sixty-seventh point appearing without the characteristic of being no one's definite object will be listed as real. It is difficult to predict how many points on PP' will be definite objects and real just as it is difficult to predict how many readers will read this sentence. In both cases, however, the total is a number which is finite, a number which can be reached by enumeration in a finite duration. In the two cases, moreover, there are similar circumstances which account for the fact that the number is no larger than it is. Potential readers do not fail to be included among actual readers because they are thwarted but because they have not chosen to read. And subsisting points are only indefinite objects and unreal, not because the subject-matter at the expiration of a finite duration frustrates or would frustrate the searcher after additional points, but because at the expiration of a finite duration no desire to find additional points will remain.

"The meaning of 'existence,'" we said in the first chapter of this treatise,[15] "may be regarded as having two components," one corresponding to the law of contradiction, the other to Leibniz's principle of sufficient reason. An infinite collection which contains as many members as some part of itself appears self-contradictory and is ruled out of existence by that element in our explanation of "existence" which marks out self-contradictory subsistents as unreal. But an infinite collection which would require an infinite duration for its enumeration, which at the expiration of any finite duration has an infinite number of undiscovered members, need not appear self-contradictory. It is unreal because of one of the various elements in our explanation of "existence" which together take the place of Leibniz's principle of sufficient reason. "It is not essential to the existence of a collection," says Russell,[16] "or even to knowledge and reasoning concerning it, that we should be able to pass its terms in review one by one." But what is essential to existence depends upon the signification of "existence." And as we use "existence," nothing exists that appears with the characteristic of being a definite object for no one.

The pitcher's center of gravity is real and its position real with respect to the contemporaneous point of reference: O. A finite number of points on the line PP' is real, and the positions of these points with respect to O likewise real. So with the North Pole and its position, the center of the sun and its position, the center of Sirius and its position. There is a finite number of real points, a finite number of real points whose positions with respect to the contemporaneous phase of O are real. The point nearest to O whose position with respect to O is real is the nearest alleged point that does not appear as merely an indefinite object and is listed as real, the nearest point, one might say, whose distance and direction from O are specifically mentioned. And the point farthest from O of all real points is likewise the farthest of all those whose distances from O are not merely indefinite objects. One may of course imagine with Lucretius a man standing in this allegedly most distant point and hurling a dart outward.[17] But if through some such fancy a more distant point comes to be a definite object, and, appearing as a definite object, is listed as real, we have simply misjudged the position of the farthest definite object. There is, we may agree, no point so distant that one would be frustrated in an attempt to hurl a dart beyond it. But there is a distant point—and it is the most distant point that is real— which happens to be a point such that no one having it as a definite object will imagine a dart hurled beyond it. It is a point of which we can say, in effect, that no more distant point is or will be a definite object and real.

There is no real point between Q and R, no real point between the point that is the most distant but one and the point a dart's throw beyond that is the most distant of all. Points between Q and R subsist; points beyond the most distant of all real points subsist. They subsist in that the preceding sentence intends to refer to them. But they appear with the characteristic of being only indefinite objects. Q and R are next to one another, not in the sense that the subject-matter will frustrate any attempt to present to ourselves intermediate points, but in the sense that intermediate points will appear as indefinite objects and will not be listed among the entities enumerated as real.

When we say that, for a subsisting entity to be real, it may not appear with the characteristic of being only an indefinite object, we rule out of existence, it would appear, all subsisting points between Q and R. Why then, the question suggests itself, lay down the additional requirement that real entities be listed in the appendix to Chapter Three? If no alleged point appearing as a definite object appears as generally discredited, why not explain "existence" so that each point appearing as a definite object is real, whether listed or not? We have agreed, to be sure, that the world of existents, both as we are to use "existence" and as "existence" is generally used, is a world not to be populated at will.[18] In order not to be required to call "real" the entity that merely *appears* to be a definite object, merely *appears* to be spatial, temporal, and so on, we have agreed to determine as real only those entities that we enumerate. But whereas one may hold that there is a

341

subsisting man on my ceiling who *appears* to be an object of belief, *appears* to be causally related to other entities, but who
nevertheless is unreal, what is the significance of the corresponding assertion that there is a subsisting point which appears as a
definite object and an object not generally discredited, but which
nevertheless is unreal?

A singular existential proposition is required, we may answer,
to distinguish the man on my ceiling who *is* an object of belief
from the subsisting man on my ceiling who merely *appears* with
the characteristic of being an object of belief. And similarly a
singular existential proposition is required to distinguish the
point which *is* a definite object from the alleged point which
merely *appears* with the characteristic of being a definite object.
It is to eliminate the alleged point that merely claims to be a
definite object that we must definitely determine as real only such
points as are individually enumerated as existents.

What distinguishes subsisting points, lines and spaces from
subsistents in general is this:—With respect to subsistents in general which do not appear self-contradictory, non-spatial or generally discredited, those are real which are listed as X's, those unreal
which are listed as Y's; and the ontological status of those which
are neither X's nor Y's is left undetermined. But among subsisting
points, lines and spaces there are no Y's. No points, lines or spaces
not appearing as self-contradictory, non-spatial or generally discredited and not appearing as not definite objects are available to
be specifically listed as unreal. And so there are only those points,
lines, spaces subsisting without self-contradictoriness, etc. which
are real and those whose ontological status is left undetermined.

There is then a finite number of points which are real, a finite
number of points whose definite positions with respect to the
contemporaneous point O are real. Similarly there is, let us agree,
a finite number of lines which are real together with their indefinite positions with respect to the contemporaneous point O, a
finite number of planes, a finite number of volumes. The line PP'
has as many segments as are definite objects. There exist as many
spherical figures as, let us say, lines or segments of lines are presented as being diameters of. The most distant spherical figure
is some such figure as that which has as a diameter the line joining the most distant real point to the real point that is most dis-

342

tant but one. The smallest spherical figure has as diameter a line such that no point subsisting between its extremities will itself appear as a definite object and be listed as real. It is not that the subject-matter frustrates or would frustrate an attempt to present to ourselves as definite objects points subsisting between the smallest diameter's extremities in the way in which the subject-matter might frustrate an attempt to separate off some part of an atom or small material particle. It is that the attempt will not be made.

As, in consonance with the conclusions of the last few paragraphs, there is a most distant spherical figure and a smallest spherical figure, so there is a longest line and a smallest segment of a line. No line extends beyond the most distant point on it that is a definite object and real. And yet each line is extensible in that we are not blocked in the attempt to present to ourselves as definite objects more distant points lying along it. If a curve has an asymptote, there is a point on the curve that is closer to the asymptote than any other point on it that will be a definite object and real. And yet curve and asymptote approach indefinitely in that the attempt to find smaller and smaller distances between them never stops through frustration, always through lack of perseverance. As we use "infinite," nothing infinite exists and nothing infinitesimal. For as we use "infinite," an infinite collection implies not only the absence of frustration after any finite duration, which we accept, but also the existence after every finite duration of real undiscovered entities, which we deny.

In order, however, that a point, a line, or a spherical figure may exist and have position with respect to the contemporaneous point O, there must exist, it may be said, a larger spherical figure in which it is included and adjacent figures by which it is bounded. Just as the State of Wyoming is included in the United States and bounded by neighboring states, so each real entity having position, it may be said, has real parts of space around it and a real all-inclusive Space including it. "A limit of extension," it has been said,[19] "must be relative to extension beyond." "We must look upon every limited space," says Kant,[20] "as conditioned also, so far as it presupposes another space as the condition of its limit." To be sure, with respect to any real entity having position, we are never frustrated in the attempt to present to ourselves alleged parts of space surrounding it and an alleged Space including it. If the alleged parts of space surrounding it appear as definite objects and are listed, they are real. And if an all-inclusive Space were presented as a definitely located object and listed, it too would be real. But there are real entities having position such that no alleged parts of space surrounding them appear as definite objects and are listed as real. And since an all-inclusive Space appears as having only an indefinite position, any alleged all-inclusive Space is unreal. Bounding figures, more inclusive figures, appear without the characteristic of being generally discredited. But in so far as they appear as indefinite objects, they do not follow as definite objects the more circumscribed figures that would otherwise imply them.

Some figures do not have, and therefore do not imply, real figures beyond them. Some figures do not have, and therefore do not imply, real points and real included figures within them. Where a figure is real and a figure within it real, where a segment of a line is real and a point within it real, the implication from one to the other is no one-way street. Belief in the existence of the included point precedes belief in the existence of the line as readily as it follows it. And as we can make no true universal propositions with respect to logical priority, so we can make no true universal propositions with respect to psychological priority. In one subject a mental attitude directed towards the point marked by the dot Q may precede a mental attitude directed towards the line marked by the undulating scratch PP′; in another subject a mental attitude directed towards PP′ precedes a mental attitude directed towards Q. Q is real and PP′ real; and we may pass from a mental attitude directed upon either of these objects to a mental attitude directed upon the other. Geometrical propositions require the existence of no all-inclusive Space. They depend for their truth upon the existence of the lines and figures to which they refer. And if there is a problem with respect to the universality and alleged necessity of true geometrical propositions, that problem is not resolved by reference to an all-inclusive Space.[21]

If we ask ourselves how we come to know so many true universal propositions concerning lines and figures, it would seem that our inquiry must be in two directions. There is a question how, whatever the subject-matter, a limited number of individual propositions lead us to accept a universal proposition; there is, in a word, the problem of induction or generalization. And there is a question as to what the unique characteristics of lines and figures are—simplicity, for example—that facilitate generalization when lines and figures constitute the subject-matter. But an all-inclusive Space, even if it existed, could not account for our mathematical knowledge any more than the mere presence of a catalyst accounts for a chemical reaction. A certain chemical reaction takes place only in the presence of a catalyst. But how? Similarly, an all-inclusive Space, if it existed, might be held to be present whenever mathematical generalization took place. But such an assertion would still leave us asking how this all-inclusive Space enters into, and facilitates, our mathematical generalizations.

PP' is a real line; Q, R, S, and a finite number of other entities real points that are included within it. PP' has a rather indefinite position with respect to the contemporaneous phase of O; P, S, R, Q, P' have each, taken individually, a definite position with respect to O. Taken collectively, however, the points included within PP' *are* the line PP'. For, taken collectively, the collection has no more definite position with respect to O than has PP'. And yet, just as an army may be strong and yet called a "collection" of individuals, individuals who, taken individually, are weak; so the line, called a "collection" of points, may have length, a quality which each point composing it, taken individually, lacks. Thus what, taken individually, are points may, taken collectively, be a line, a plane, a space; and what, taken individually, are three-dimensional figures or spaces, may, taken collectively, be a more inclusive space.[22] The individuals which are real have positions with respect to the contemporaneous point O which are real; and the collections which are real have less definite positions with respect to the contemporaneous point O which likewise are real.

Among the spaces, the closed three-dimensional figures, which are real and whose positions with respect to the contemporaneous phase of our baseball catcher are real, there is the space within the periphery of the pitcher's body as well as the space within some distant spherical figure. The distant spherical figure is, let us assume, real appearing as an empty space, unreal appearing as material. The space within the periphery of the pitcher's body is real as a space and real as a body. But although the space within the periphery of the pitcher's body is a real substance and the pitcher's body a real substance, nevertheless, as we shall later agree to use "one" and "two," the collection of these substances is one and not two. Just as Socrates is real appearing as a Greek and also appearing as a philosopher, so there are some substances which are real appearing as spaces and also appearing as material bodies. Just as a man may be both Greek and philosophical and thus both a Greek and a philosopher, so an entity may be both three-dimensional and material and thus both a space and a body. A body, in short, is not *in* a space so much as it *is* a space. Real spaces may be, some of them material, some of them non-material, and some of them partly material and partly non-material. Those spaces which are material may also be called three-dimensional bodies just as those Greeks who are philosophical may also be called Greek philosophers.

Whether or not there are non-material spaces depends of course upon the significations we assign "material" and "body." If mere three-dimensionality plus the ability to transmit energy do not suffice to make a substance a "body," there may be non-material spaces, the most distant body may not be so distant as the most distant space, the largest body may be smaller than the largest real space; and the number of real bodies less than the number of real three-dimensional figures or spaces. Alleged *bodies* beyond some great distance may be unreal, not for the reason for which some alleged spaces may be unreal, not because they appear as not definite objects, but because, presented as material, they appear as generally discredited. And frustration, which never puts an end to our efforts to think of larger or of smaller spaces, may well put an end to our efforts to find larger bodies appearing as relatively homogeneous that are not discredited and our efforts to find smaller and smaller bodies that are qualitatively distinguishable from the entities around them.

We find then that real points, real lines, real spaces are unlimited in number but not *infinite* in number. Real body-spaces that are homogeneous and distinguishable from the entities around them are likewise not infinite in number; and when "body" is used in such a way that not every space is a body, they, unlike real points, real lines and real spaces, are not even *un-limited* in number. But what about real spaces, if there be any such, that are not body-spaces, not material bodies? If 'body' is defined in such a way that empty spaces—three-dimensional figures having volume but containing no matter—are not self-contradictory and do in fact exist, then it would seem that these existing empty spaces are scattered about and related to one another in much the way in which we customarily think of stars and other material bodies as being scattered about and interrelated. For it is not each such existing empty space that would then have other existing empty spaces contiguous to it. Not that each such alleged contiguous empty space appears with the characteristic of being generally discredited; and not that one is frustrated in the attempt to become aware of such an alleged contiguous empty space. It is simply that "there are real entities having position such that no alleged parts of space surrounding them appear as definite objects and are listed as real."[23] And in so far as alleged empty spaces, alleged to be contiguous to *real* empty spaces, are presented as definite objects for no one, these alleged empty spaces do not exist and the empty spaces which *are* real have no real empty spaces contiguous to them. Bodies, in short, are discrete rather than all contiguous; and if 'body' is defined so that not all spaces are bodies, then empty spaces are discrete also.

No collection, neither the collection of all empty spaces nor the collection of all points with definite positions with respect to the contemporaneous point O nor the collection of all grains of sand contemporaneous with O, is infinite in number. But is each of these collections *finite* in number? Taken as an extended, indefinitely located collection rather than as a group of individual units, all empty spaces, taken collectively, is presented with the characteristic of being so indefinitely located that, as we explain our term "reality," it is unreal. The collection of all grains of sand contemporaneous with O, taken collectively, is, however, presented without the characteristic of having so indefinite a location that it must be unreal. If the earth may be real and the surface of the earth real, then the sand on the earth's surface, taken collectively, may be real. But how many granular parts, how many grains of sand, does it contain? There is no particular number, it would seem, that anyone is aware of as being the number of particles making up the sand on the earth's surface. And since such an alleged number is presented as no one's definite object, the sand on the earth's surface *has* no definite number of parts. The grains of sand, taken as a collection of individual grains, is unnumbered or numberless. And yet, taken as individuals, there are only so many grains of sand as are individual objects. There may be fifty or a thousand or ten thousand individual grains of sand which are real. But the sand on the earth's surface, taken as a collection of individual grains, is without number. There is, to be sure, "a finite number of points which are real, a finite number of points whose definite positions with respect to the contemporaneous point O are real."[24] These, however, are all points that are objects as individuals, or, rather, points that are not presented as no one's definite objects. Points taken collectively, on the other hand, may be presented as forming so extended, so indefinitely-located, a collection that the collection is not only without number—as is the collection of grains of sand—but is unreal altogether.

There is, let us agree, a point on the line OX which, measured from a certain reference body, is π inches from O. There is, let us likewise agree, a point on the line OX which, similarly measured, is 3.14159 inches from O. Corresponding to real decimals greater than 3.14159 and less than π, there are intermediate points, one of which is, we hold, the nearest, of all points exemplifying decimals, to the point π inches from O. There is, let us agree, the number π; but no *decimal* exemplified by the distance from O to the point π inches from O. There *is* a decimal exemplified by the distance from O to the point nearest, of all points exemplifying decimals, to the point π inches from O. The decimal which is less than π may be as large as we please. But alleged decimals larger than we do in fact make explicit, alleged points so close to the point π inches from O that they appear as definite objects for no one, are, we hold, unreal. What then is the decimal exemplified—not by the point π inches from O; for there is no such decimal—but by the point nearest to the latter point of all points exemplifying decimals? What, to put it arithmetically, is the largest decimal less than π? It is, we may say, a decimal with a great number, but a finite number, of digits. Presented as a decimal whose last digit is a particular number, odd or even, it is presented as some one's definite object. But its last digit, whether odd or even, is presented as no definite object of mine. Just as facts known by paleontologists are real even though I am not aware of them in any detail,[25] so the last digit in the largest decimal less than π is real and is odd or is even, even though it is not presented to me as definitely odd or as definitely even.

The alleged number presented as the largest decimal less than π differs from the alleged number presented as characterizing the sand on the earth's surface, taken as a collection of individual grains. In each case what is presented is an alleged number presented as no definite object of mine. But the latter alleged number is presented as no one's definite object and is unreal, whereas the former alleged number is not so presented and is real.

We turn now to the number of pennies in a bowl full of pennies that I see in some store window. I, let us agree, do not know how many pennies are in the bowl. But the number alleged to characterize this collection of pennies, taken individually, is not presented as no one's definite object. Just as the number presented as the largest decimal less than π may be real even though presented as no definite object of mine, so may the number be real which, presented as no definite object of mine, is alleged to characterize the collection of pennies in the bowl before me. I do not know whether the largest decimal less than π has a last digit which is odd or even and I do not know whether the number of pennies in the bowl is odd or even. There is nevertheless a difference between these two situations. For whoever is definitely aware of the largest real decimal less than π is definitely aware of no larger decimal less than π, merely because he has not chosen to prolong the process of determining larger decimals; whereas he who is definitely aware of the number characterizing the collection of pennies taken individually is definitely aware of no larger number characterizing this collection, because there are no more pennies to count. In both situations the largest number that is real and applicable to the collection being numbered is finite and is presented as no definite object of mine—although not presented as no one's definite object. But in the one situation one would be frustrated in the attempt to find real applicable numbers beyond the last; whereas in the other situation the last number that is real and applicable merely indicates the end of our perseverance.

In the past few paragraphs we have been discussing collections to which finite numbers are applicable, finite numbers, however, which are presented as not definite objects of mine. There are, let us agree, collections to which finite numbers are applicable where these finite numbers *are* definite objects of mine. Thus counting each chair in this room as one, the number of chairs in this room is, let us agree, four, and is presented to me as four.

There is the number of chairs in this room which is four. There is the number of positive integers up to four which is four. A fifth chair in this room is unreal in that it appears generally discredited. A fifth integer no greater than four is unreal in that it appears self-contradictory as well. Between the chair in this room nearest to me and the chair in this room furthest from me there is a finite number of other chairs. Between one and four there is a finite number of other positive integers and a finite number of decimals. But whereas the search for intermediate chairs or for intermediate positive integers may be brought to an end by frustration, whereas, that is to say, one may reach the point where alleged additional intermediate chairs appear generally discredited and alleged additional intermediate integers appear self-contradictory as well, the number of intermediate decimals, although finite, is unlimited. One may find intermediate decimals, but not intermediate chairs or intermediate integers, as long as one pleases.

And yet there are respects in which the collection of real chairs, the collection of integers up to four and the collection of decimals from zero to four resemble one another and differ from other finite collections whose characteristics we have still to point out. Not only is the collection of decimals from zero to four as well as the collection of chairs in this room finite in number, and not only are these collections such that their end-terms have definitely determined characteristics; they have in common the fact that between members of the collection there are real entities not members of the collection. Thus between 3.14 and 3.15 there is the real entity π which is not a decimal between zero and four; and between the chair nearest to me and the chair next nearest to me there is a table which is not a member of the collection of chairs in this room.

And so we are led to consider the last type of collection that we shall mention, the collection, namely, in which no real entities that are not themselves members of the collection interpose themselves between entities that *are* members. In contrast to the collection of chairs in this room and in contrast to the collection of decimals from zero to four, the collection of all numbers from zero to four and the collection of all numbers without limitation are collections of this latter type. They are collections which we may call "continua." And yet whereas we are never frustrated in the attempt to find new members between members of a continuum and never find real non-members between members, the members which compose a continuum, we should like to emphasize, are, like the members of every real numbered collection, finite in number.

Some points, some lines, some three-dimensional figures or spaces, exist; they are finite in number. Some, if not all, of the spaces which exist are body-spaces or material bodies. Points, lines, spaces and bodies alike have each a real position with respect to the phase of the point O with respect to which they each are present. And each of them has a real position with respect to a finite number of other real and contemporaneous entities—points, bodies, or what not—that may function as points of reference.

The point P', the baseball pitcher, the sun, have each of them the real quality: position with respect to the phase of the batter with respect to whom they are present. And they have each of them the real quality: position with respect to the phase of the point P with respect to which they are present. Position with respect to P inheres in P' along with position with respect to the batter. And since in describing these qualities inhering in P' we refer in the one instance to P and in the other instance to the batter, position with respect to P and position with respect to the batter may be said to be relative qualities inhering in P'. There are occasions of course when we describe the position that an entity has with respect to some other entity without any explicit mention of the point of reference. I may say that an entity is far away and the context may make it clear that I am asserting this entity to be far away from where I now am. Or I may attribute to some point on the earth's surface the quality of being seventy-five degrees west and forty degrees north without bothering to make it explicit that I am discussing this point's position with respect to the intersection of the equator and the meridian of Greenwich. There are thus positions that entities have that may be described without explicit mention of the point of reference. "Position" may be synonymous with "position with respect to P." And in so far as the quality which P′ has may be called "position" where "position" is synonymous with "position with respect to P," this quality may be called a pseudo-absolute quality as well as a relative quality.

If I talk about "the position of P′" and no point of reference is implied, then "the position of P′," if it is not merely a collection of words, refers, or means to refer, to an alleged absolute quality of P′. As we use "the position of P′" however, either there is a point of reference implied and my expression represents a pseudo-absolute quality, or my expression is merely a collection of words. P′ has no absolute quality represented by my expression: "the position of P′," for my expression: "the position of P′" puts before me no subsisting quality alleged to be absolute whose reality or unreality might be considered. But, from the fact that P′ has no absolute quality represented by my expression: "the position of P′," we can not conclude that P′ does not have an absolute quality somehow connected with the relative quality that it really has, the relative quality represented by my expression: "the position of P′ with respect to P." P′ has position with respect to P and P position with respect to P′. If either P or P′ appeared as nonspatial, neither P nor P′ could appear without contradiction as having position with respect to the other. If either Peter or Paul appeared as lacking height, Peter could not without contradiction appear as taller than Paul nor Paul as shorter than Peter. We may then present to ourselves an alleged absolute quality in P′ that we may call "spatiality," a quality that may be alleged to make it possible for P′ to have position with respect to various points of reference. This alleged spatiality is not position with respect to some unmentioned point of reference, some center of the universe, for example; for what we call "spatiality" is alleged to be absolute, whereas a position with respect to some unmentioned point of reference would be merely pseudo-absolute. Spatiality, it turns out, is nothing but the possibility of having position with respect to various entities.[26] Vague, however, as a spatiality of this sort is, the alleged spatiality of P′ appears without the characteristic of being no definite object and without the characteristic of being generally discredited. I find in short that P′ has the absolute quality that I call "spatiality," but no absolute quality represented by my expression: "the position of P'." P' has the absolute quality 'spatiality' and the pseudo-absolute quality 'position' which is merely position with respect to some implied point of reference. Similarly, Peter has the absolute quality 'height' and the pseudo-absolute quality 'tallness' which is merely tallness with respect to some implied standard.

P' has position with respect to P, we hold, and Peter tallness with respect to Paul. But just as "P' has position" and "Peter is taller than" are incomplete expressions, so "P' has position with respect to P" and "Peter is taller than Paul" may be held to be incomplete expressions. Peter is taller than Paul, it may be said, from the point of view of a man equally distant from both, not from the point of view of an eye so close to Paul that the angle subtended by the distant Peter is less than that subtended by Paul. And P' has one position with respect to P, it may be said, when the distance between them is measured from an entity at rest with respect to them. another position with respect to P when the distance between them is measured from an entity in motion. The length of the line PP' may, we must agree, be assigned various numbers. To number a quantitative entity is to correlate it with some external unit quantity. To measure a given length is to engage in a process involving motion and hence involving spatio-temporal entities other than the length that is to be measured. We use an incomplete expression, we may agree, when, without any point of reference being implied, we say that PP' is "one inch in length." PP' may be one inch long with respect to the contemporaneous point O that is at rest with respect to it, less than one inch long with respect to the contemporaneous phase of the sun that is in motion with respect to it. There is no absolute quality represented by my expression: "one inch long"; there are the relative qualities represented by: "one inch long as measured from O" and by: "less than one inch long as measured from the sun." And in so far as the context or common usage makes it clear that the point of reference is some such contemporaneous entity as O that is at rest with respect to PP', PP' has the pseudo-absolute quality of being one inch long and the proposition: "PP' is one inch long" is neither incomplete nor ambiguous, but true. Being one inch long is a real pseudo-absolute quality of PP' in so far as "being one inch long" is synonymous with "being one inch long as measured from O"; just as position is a real pseudo-absolute quality of P′ in so far as "position" is synonymous with "position with respect to P." But with no point of reference implied, my expression "being one inch long," like my expression "position," does not represent a quality that is absolute and real.

P′ however has the absolute quality of spatiality which may be said to be the possibility of having position with respect to various entities. Peter has the absolute quality of height without which he would not be taller than one entity and shorter than another. And PP′ may appear with the absolute quality of extension or length. It is this length that we think of as being assigned one number or another, as being correlated with one entity or another, in a word, as being measured. The alleged quality of length or extension that PP′ has is not the quality of being one-inch long, but the possibility of being one inch long with respect to O and of being less than one inch long with respect to the sun. Allegedly it is what is measured, what is correlated with spatio-temporal entities other than PP′. To be sure, this alleged absolute length or extension of PP′, that, as absolute, has no number, is vague. But it appears without the characteristic of being generally discredited and is, I hold, real. PP′ has absolute length, P′ position with respect to P, P position with respect to P′. Absolute length and relative position exist within the same situation, the situation, namely, which includes P, P′, and PP′. As absolute length, in so far as it is absolute, does not involve a reference to entities outside PP′, so relative position does not involve a reference to entities outside P, P′ and PP′. "P′ has position with respect to P" is true, does not first become true by being changed into "P′ has position with respect to P a measured from O." It is for the purpose of giving a number to P″s position with respect to P or for the purpose of giving a number to the length of PP′ that reference to some such entity as O is required if ambiguity is to be avoided. To hold, on the contrary, that "P″s position with respect to P" is ambiguous and must be changed into "P″s position with respect to P as measured from O" may well lead us to hold that "P″s position with respect to P as measured from O" must give way to "P″s position with respect to P as measured from O from the point of view of A"; it may well lead us to hold that no propositions referring to position are unambiguous and true. And to deny to PP′ an absolute quality of length may well lead us to hold that new points of reference without limit must be brought into consideration before "PP′'s length as measured from O" is freed from ambiguity.

What is true with respect to the line PP′ will also be true with respect to a line connecting P with O. Just as PP′ is one inch long as measured from one spatio-temporal entity and less than one inch long as measured from another, so the number assigned the length of OP is relative to the spatio-temporal entity from which this length is measured. But PP′, we have said, has absolute length, vague as length that is not numbered length may seem; and P′ has position with respect to P that is not relative to any point of reference outside PP′. Just so, OP has absolute length and P position with respect to O that is not relative to entities outside O P.

To say that P is three inches away from O is to say that OP is three inches long. And since "O P is three inches long" is an incomplete expression, since O P is three inches long as measured from some entity outside O P, P is three inches away from O only relatively, only as measured from some entity or other. The position that P has with respect to O, the position that involves no reference to entities other than P and O, is consequently not a numbered position. Just as the spatiality that P has is merely what makes it possible for P to have one position with respect to P′ and another position with respect to O, so the position that P has with respect to O is merely what makes it possible for P to be three inches away from O as measured from one entity and less than three inches away from O as measured from another entity.

It is with this sense of "position" in mind that we hold to the conclusions arrived at in the earlier paragraphs of this chapter. The real position that we asserted that P has with respect to O and the real position that we asserted the pitcher has with respect to the batter, these are not numbered positions but rather positions that have the possibility of being numbered differently from different points of reference. P has a definite position with respect to O and the pitcher's center of gravity a definite position with respect to the batter, not in the sense that these positions carry with them unique definite numbers with respect to their respective points of reference, but rather in the sense that they have the possibility of being given various definite numbers varying with the spatio-temporal entity from which their relations to their points of reference are measured. Similarly, the path from pitcher's box to home plate has an indefinite position with respect to the catcher, is more or less out-in-front, in the sense that the spatial relation it sustains to the catcher has the possibility of being given various number ranges, all of them indefinite.

The path from pitcher's box to home plate and the line PP′ each have extension; whereas the point P and the pitcher's center of gravity are not extended. But how can a large extended entity affect the mental attitude which comes to be directed upon it? And how can an inextended entity, a point, affect the mental attitude which comes to be directed upon *it*? One may perhaps accept as free from puzzlement the situation in which one billiard ball impinging upon another is in some sense the cause of the second ball's motion. And the situation may be held to be analogous when some minutely extended entity is at the source of motions leading to the mental attitude which is said to perceive it. Thus one may agree that there are minute percepts, such as atoms or electrons, which, after the fashion of billiard balls, initiate impulses affecting the sense-organs and resulting in instances of perceiving. But that entities of greater size or that entities with no size at all, should bring about instances of perceiving, this, it may be held, is not only bewildering but incredible. There is no entity outside the perceiving subject himself, it may be said, which is the cause of the mental attitude directed upon a large extended object. For "the connection of anything manifold," it may be held with Kant,[27] "can never enter into us through the senses." And similarly with the mental attitude allegedly directed upon inextended objects. My mental attitude allegedly directed upon a point, it may be said, points back to no external entity as its cause. Hence mental attitudes allegedly directed upon entities not big enough to be sources of material motion are, it may be said, examples of mental over-simplification and distortion. And mental attitudes allegedly directed upon large objects are to be accounted for, it may be said, by referring to a faculty of mental synthesis or imagination.

Now we may agree that some extended entities are not percepts with respect to the mental attitudes directed upon them. And we may agree that points are *never* percepts. Nevertheless it does not follow that points are unreal and unperceived extended entities unreal. To be puzzled as to how my dog's behavior happens to be adapted to a future phase of the ball which I am about to hurl does not imply that his behavior is *not* adapted to that future phase of the ball. To be puzzled as to how my mental attitude happens to be directed upon tomorrow's sunrise does not imply that my mental attitude is *not* directed upon tomorrow's sunrise.[28] And to be puzzled as to how I happen to be aware of a point, on the one hand, or of a large unperceived extended entity on the other, does not imply that these alleged objects of mine are unreal or that I am not really aware of them. The pitcher's center of gravity, discussed earlier in this chapter, is, we have found, real.[29] My mental attitude, seemingly directed upon this pitcher's center of gravity, is, we hold, real. And my mental attitude reaches as its object this center of gravity upon which it seems to be directed. Thus my mental attitude reaches a point as its real object, even though the processes leading up to this mental attitude of mine are obscure. And so with the mental attitude of mine directed upon a real entity too large to be perceived.

To be sure, the mental attitude which is not an instance of perceiving, and not caused by the object upon which it is directed, may have some cause other than its object. But if a given mental attitude is not at the terminus of motions leading to it from the entity upon which it seems to be directed, we can not conclude that it is at the terminus of motions leading to it from some other definite entity in the absence of which this mental attitude would not have occurred. Much less can we conclude that the mental attitude, not at the terminus of motions leading to it from the entity upon which it seems to be directed, has a *mental* cause; that it is affected by some *mental* faculty of synthesis or imagination which is responsible for synthesis on the one hand and for over-simplification on the other. Moreover, the bewilderment which we may experience at being unable to give a detailed account of the genesis of the mental attitude directed upon an unperceived entity,—this bewilderment is not assuaged by our being referred to an alleged mental faculty of synthesis or imagination. For such an alleged faculty is presented, not as the source of motions leading to the mental attitudes whose origin puzzles us, but as having no existence apart from these very mental attitudes themselves.

The conclusion which we have reached in this chapter is that some extended entities are real and some inextended entities real. Extension is a real quality of some minute entities and it is a real quality of the line PP', of the baseball diamond, of various entities which may be too big to be perceived by the mental attitudes directed upon them. There exists a finite number of extended entities just as there exists a finite number of points, lines, spaces and bodies. Each real extended entity, whether it be a line or a space, material or immaterial, has absolute spatiality and relative position, position, that is to say, that is relative to a finite number of contemporaneous points of reference. And each real extended entity, similarly, has absolute length and relative measured length, measured length, that is to say, that is relative to the spatio-temporal status of the contemporaneous entity from which it is measured.

In this chapter we have derived directly from our propositions explaining our term "reality" the existence of certain entities contemporaneous with one another, the existence, that is to say, of entities having the quality of being present with respect to certain other entities. Moreover, we have in this chapter discussed spatial relations only in so far as they are alleged to hold among contemporaneous entities. It will require another chapter to discuss temporal relations as such; and still another to discuss such spatial relations as are held to obtain between entities temporally related, but not present with respect to one another.

Summary

Certain entities have position with respect to other entities contemporaneous with them. These positions may be definite (the position that a point has with respect to some contemporaneous entity) or indefinite (the position that an extended entity has); but it may not be too indefinite. Some points are real and some lines real. There is a finite number of points on a line; for alleged points in excess of this finite number appear with the characteristic of not being definite objects for any subject.

There is a finite number of bodies and a finite number of three-dimensional volumes or spaces which may not be bodies. Not all bodies are contiguous and not all empty spaces.

Position is a quality which is relative in that an entity has one position with respect to its contemporary P, another position with respect to its contemporary P'. But what we call the quality of "spatiality" is not relative. Spatiality is the quality of an entity without which it could not have one position with respect to one entity and another position with respect to another. Just as there is a distinction between spatiality and position, so there is a distinction between extension or length, which is absolute, and numbered extension or length, which is relative.

The awareness of extended entities does not presuppose that the mind's object in such a situation is a mental construction.

Chapter XII

DATE, DURATION AND INTERVAL

We began the preceding chapter by presenting to ourselves a baseball batter, a pitcher appearing as out-there-in-front with respect to him, and a catcher appearing as a short distance behind him.[1] Let us begin our investigation of temporal relations in an analogous manner, by presenting to ourselves Napoleon Bonaparte, Louis IX (called St. Louis,) appearing as having preceded him, and Napoleon III appearing as being subsequent to him. Pitcher, batter and catcher all appeared as substances. So do St. Louis, Napoleon and Napoleon III. Out-there-in-front with respect to the batter and a short-distance-behind with respect to the batter appeared as qualities of pitcher and catcher respectively. Similarly, before-Napoleon is presented, let us say, as a quality inhering in St. Louis, after-Napoleon as a quality inhering in Napoleon III. As in the preceding chapter let us derive directly from the propositions which explain our term "existence" the existence of the *substances* that particularly concern us; and the existence of certain qualities inhering in these substances. St. Louis, Napoleon and Napoleon III, let us thus agree, are real substances; and there are real qualities inhering in St. Louis and in Napoleon III. Our question is whether, among the real qualities inhering in Louis IX there is the real quality of being prior to Napoleon Bonaparte, whether among the real qualities inhering in Napoleon III there is the real quality of being subsequent to Napoleon Bonaparte.

In the preceding chapter, it will be recalled, we took it for granted that the pitcher, alleged to be out-there-in-front with respect to the batter, was not only a real substance having qualities, but also that he had the particular quality of being present with respect to the batter.[2] In investigating St. Louis's alleged quality of being prior to Napoleon, shall we not then complete the analogy by taking it for granted that St. Louis is 'here' with respect to Napoleon? Since we chose to restrict our discussion of spatial relations to the discussion of spatial relations among entities which are 'now' with respect to one another, should we not similarly choose to restrict our discussion of temporal relations to the discussion of temporal relations among entities which are 'here' with respect to one another?

The substances which are presented to us, let us say, are not St. Louis taken as a whole, Napoleon taken as a whole, and Napoleon III taken as a whole. Rather, the substances which we take to be real are, let us say, a phase of King Louis IX when he was in Paris and indeed in Notre Dame cathedral, a phase of Napoleon Bonaparte when *he* was in Notre Dame, and a phase of Napoleon III when *he* was in Notre Dame. But when our objects are St. Louis in Notre Dame, Napoleon in Notre Dame and Napoleon III in Notre Dame, does it follow that these objects of ours are presented as 'here' with respect to one another? If the sun and not Notre Dame is taken to be at rest, the position which St. Louis in Notre Dame had with respect to the phase of the sun contemporaneous with him is, it may be said, not identical with the position which Napoleon in Notre Dame had with respect to the phase of the sun contemporaneous with *him*. St. Louis, that is to say, may be said to have been much farther away from the sun contemporaneous with him than Napoleon was from the sun contemporaneous with *him*. And taking a given position with respect to successive phases of the sun as our enduring point of reference, Napoleon may have been 'here' and King Louis IX 'there.' Being 'here' with respect to Napoleon in Notre Dame, it may thus be said, is a quality that inheres in St. Louis from one point of view but not from another. St. Louis, it may be said, is *here* with respect to Napoleon relative to an enduring *Notre Dame* which is at rest, but is *there* with respect to Napoleon relative to an enduring *sun* which is at rest.

Let us then not take it for granted that the St. Louis, whose alleged priority to Napoleon we wish to investigate, has the real quality of being 'here' with respect to Napoleon. For if we were to

361

take it for granted that St. Louis has the quality of being 'here' with respect to Napoleon whatever the enduring point of reference, we should be assuming as real an alleged quality of St. Louis's which, it would appear, is unreal. And to accept as a premise the alleged fact that St. Louis had the quality of being 'here' with respect to Napoleon relative to an enduring Notre Dame which was at rest, would be to presuppose the existence of enduring entities and to presuppose an understanding of our terms "duration" and "at rest." At this point, then, we choose not to take it for granted, either that there is some absolute sense of "being here" in which St. Louis was 'here' with respect to Napoleon; or that St. Louis had the real quality of being 'here' with respect to Napoleon relative to an enduring Notre Dame which was at rest.

Thus to some extent the premises with which we enter upon our discussion of temporal relations differ from those with which we entered upon our discussion of spatial relations. In discussing the existence of the pitcher's alleged quality of being out-there-in-front with respect to the batter, we took it for granted, not only that pitcher and batter were real, but also that the pitcher was really present with respect to the batter. But in discussing the existence of St. Louis's alleged quality of being prior to Napoleon, we take it for granted that St. Louis and Napoleon were real, but not that St. Louis was really 'here' with respect to Napoleon. St. Louis, Napoleon Bonaparte and Napoleon III were all, let us agree, in Notre Dame. But in asking whether, with respect to Napoleon, St. Louis was before or Napoleon III after, let us not assume that they were all 'here' with respect to one another.

The pitcher, we have seen, was out-there-in-front with respect to the phase of the batter contemporaneous with him. But to attribute to a substance position with respect to another substance *not* contemporaneous with it is, it would seem, to refer, explicitly or implicitly, to a third entity, to an enduring point of reference which is at rest and which has phases, one contemporaneous with one of the substances being compared and one contemporaneous with the other. But if, explicitly or implicitly, we are referring to an enduring point of reference when we attribute to a given substance the quality of being 'here' with respect to an entity not contemporaneous with it, is there not, similarly, a reference to some third entity when we attribute to a given substance the quality of being 'now' with respect to a substance which is not 'here' with respect to it?

Early in the last chapter we agreed that the phase of the pitcher being considered was 'now,' or present, with respect to the phase of the batter being considered. But perhaps it was no more to be taken for granted that the pitcher alleged to be out-there-in-front was absolutely 'now' with respect to the batter than it is to be taken for granted that St. Louis, alleged to be prior, was absolutely 'here' with respect to Napoleon. If in assuming that St. Louis is absolutely 'here' with respect to Napoleon we would be taking for granted a quality of St. Louis's which we hold is unreal, perhaps in assuming that the pitcher was absolutely 'now' with respect to the batter, we took for granted a quality of the pitcher's which he did not have. Perhaps the pitcher was contemporaneous with the batter from a certain point of view, when dates are measured in a certain manner, and was not contemporaneous with the batter from another point of view, when dates are measured in another manner.

We found in the preceding chapter, however, that there are instances of the quality 'spatiality,' an absolute quality; and instances of the quality 'position,' which is a relative quality. Similarly there are instances of the quality of having length which are instances of an absolute quality and instances of the quality of being one-inch long which are instances of a relative quality.[3] But if some line PP′ has, on the one hand, the absolute quality of having length and, on the other hand, the relative quality of being one-inch long as measured from O, may it not be that some entity A has, on the one hand, a quality of simultaneity with B which is *not* relative to C and, on the other hand, the quality of being no seconds earlier, and no seconds later, than B—as measured from C? That is to say, may there not be a sense of "simultaneity" in which the assertion that A is simultaneous with B is not synonymous with the assertion that A is no seconds earlier and no seconds later than 3 as measured from C? What we are attempting to present is a sense of "simultaneity" such that a given instantaneous phase of A may be held to be simultaneous with a given instantaneous phase of B, even though it is agreed that it is an earlier phase of A which is found to be no seconds earlier and no seconds later than B as measured from a body moving in one direction; and even

363

though it is agreed that it is a later phase of A which is found to be no seconds earlier and no seconds later than B as measured from a body moving in another direction. In short, what is being presented is A's alleged quality of co-existing with B as distinguished from A's quality of having been found by measurement to have a date identical with B's.

A co-existence of this sort, an unmeasured simultaneity, may, it seems, be presented without being presented as incomplete. We seem on occasion to consider simultaneity without considering measurements, just as we seem on occasion to consider redness without considering wave-lengths, and just as we seem on occasion to consider heat without considering mercury-filled thermometers. Such an unmeasured simultaneity, presented as an absolute quality, subsists. And there are instances of it which are, we find, real. Presented as a quality of some entity A, that is to say, unmeasured simultaneity with B is presented, we find, without any of the characteristics which would mark it out as unreal in our sense of "reality"; and, so presented, it is listed as real in the appendix to Chapter Three. Thus the phase of the pitcher and the phase of the batter which we considered at the beginning of the previous chapter *were,* we hold, simultaneous with one another. In taking it for granted that the pitcher, alleged to be out-there-in-front, was present with respect to the batter, we were not taking for granted an alleged quality of the pitcher's which he did not have.[4]

In this chapter, we have said, we do not take it for granted that St. Louis in Notre Dame was 'here' with respect to Napoleon in Notre Dame. St. Louis was real and Napoleon real. But did St. Louis have the real quality of being before-Napoleon?

Napoleon, let us assume, had a mental attitude which reached St. Louis as its object. And this mental attitude may have been at the terminus of motions originating in St. Louis. There may have been motions, that is to say, "which, although delayed in transmission and transformed by the intermediaries" through whom they passed, originated in St. Louis and terminated in Napoleon's mental attitude directed upon St. Louis.[5] But St. Louis as a substance is to be distinguished from his alleged quality of being prior to Napoleon. It is St. Louis's alleged quality of being prior to Napoleon, let us remember, that at this point concerns us. And this alleged quality of St. Louis's, it may be said, can hardly be believed to have initiated motions which resulted in Napoleon's mental attitude directed upon it.

Just as the pitcher's alleged quality of being out-there-in-front with respect to the batter has no special channel through which to affect the spectator apparently aware of it, so, it may be said, St. Louis's alleged quality of being prior to Napoleon has no special channel open to it through which to affect Napoleon. But whereas "the man on my ceiling, presented as having no special channel through which to affect the mental attitude of mine apparently directed upon him" is, we have seen, unreal, the other-side-of-the-moon, "presented as having no special channel through which to affect the mental attitude of yours apparently directed upon it," is real.[6] The entity, that is to say, which is presented as having no special channel through which to affect the mental attitude apparently directed upon it, need not be presented as generally discredited and need not be unreal. So far as we have yet seen, the quality of being prior to Napoleon which is alleged to inhere in King Louis IX may be real even though it is not a *sine qua non* with respect to Napoleon's mental attitude apparently directed upon it and even though it is presented as having no special channel open to it through which to bring about that mental attitude of Napoleon's. We may be puzzled as to how Napoleon could come to be aware of St. Louis as past with respect to him. But it does not follow that Napoleon had no mental attitude apparently aware of St. Louis as past. And it does not follow that St. Louis's alleged quality of being past with respect to Napoleon was unreal.

It is with a thirteenth century date that Louis IX is alleged to have existed. But could St. Louis in the thirteenth century have had the quality of being prior to a Napoleon who did not yet exist? It may be said that it was not until the fourteenth century that St. Louis acquired the quality of being prior to fourteenth century events, not until the fifteenth century that he acquired the quality of being prior to fifteenth century events, and so on. In the thirteenth century, it may be said, St. Louis's alleged quality of being prior to Napoleon was unreal. But what *was* the situation in the thirteenth century? No one was aware of Napoleon as the victor at Marengo or as a prisoner at St. Helena. If he was an object at all for thirteenth century mental attitudes, he was an object only in so far as thirteenth century mental attitudes may have been directed upon some unnamed future person who might be a ruler and a soldier. But St. Louis's alleged quality of being prior to Napoleon, presented as not an object, or as not a *definite* object, for mental attitudes contemporaneous with it, need not be unreal. It may have been real, though an object only for mental attitudes occurring centuries later. And if it *is* real, its thirteenth century date belongs to it. To be aware, apparently, of Louis IX as now *lacking* the quality of being prior to Napoleon and of Louis IX as now *having* the quality of being prior to Napoleon is, as we have seen,[7] to exchange one subsistent for another.

So far as we have yet seen, the quality of being prior to Napoleon, alleged to inhere in the thirteenth century Louis IX, need not be unreal. Indeed the subsisting quality of being prior to Napoleon, which *we* are considering, is, we find, real. It is presented without the characteristic of lacking position or date; it is presented without the characteristic of being generally discredited; and, so presented, it is listed as real in the Appendix to Chapter Three. Similarly with the quality of being subsequent to Napoleon, an entity presented as a quality of Napoleon III. Neither Napoleon III nor his alleged quality of being after-Napoleon were percepts of Napoleon's. Neither Napoleon III nor his alleged quality of being after-Napoleon had special channels open to them through which to affect the mental attitudes which Napoleon may have directed upon them. But just as St. Louis's alleged quality of being before-Napoleon is presented without any of the characteristics which would mark it out as unreal in our sense of "reality," so is Napoleon the Third's alleged quality of being after-Napoleon. Just as St. Louis had the real quality of being before Napoleon, so Napoleon III had the real quality of being after-Napoleon.

With respect to today's events, to be sure, King Louis IX, Napoleon Bonaparte and Napoleon III are all, let us agree, past. But what is past, it may be said, no longer *is*. If we may say that "existence" as commonly used is predicated only of that which is somehow important,[8] only of that which in some fashion must be reckoned with, then the tendency of many languages to identify "existence" with "present existence" points perhaps to the fact that what is past need no longer be combatted or propitiated by living men. But using "existence" in the sense in which we are using it, the proposition: "St. Louis is dead" does not imply the proposition: "St. Louis is unreal." An entity which is presented as past with respect to today's events need not be presented with any of the characteristics which would mark it out as unreal. As we use "existence" and "reality," an entity presented as past may be real just as may an entity presented as present.

Similarly with an entity presented as future. Just as, using "existence" in some sense other than that in which we are using this term, an event which is alleged to have occurred last year no longer exists, so, using "existence" in some sense other than that in which we are using it, an event, which, it is alleged, will occur next year, may be said to have only potential existence, may be said to be unrealized rather than real. As we use "existence" and "reality," however, to have potential existence is not to be non-existent; to be as yet unrealized is not to be unreal. In our sense of "reality," to be sure, an entity is unreal if it appears with the characteristic of being generally discredited. And, it may be agreed, no event, which, it is alleged, will occur next year, is so firmly believed in by today's thinkers as are Napoleon Bonaparte and today's sunrise. The inauguration of Lincoln as President in 1861 appears, let us say, with the characteristic of being generally believed in, whereas the inauguration of a President of the United States in 1961 appears with the characteristic of being less firmly believed in. Our government may be overthrown; there may be no inauguration in 1961. There may be some cosmic catastrophe; and there may be no sunrise tomorrow. Nevertheless the inauguration in 1961 appears without the characteristic of being generally discredited. Or, rather, there is *a* subsisting inauguration in 1961 which, appearing without the characteristic of being generally discredited, is listed as real in the appendix to Chapter Three.

The inauguration of 1961 is real; and it has, we hold, the real quality of being subsequent to certain real events of today. But if certain alleged future events are real, if, for example, there *will* be an inauguration in 1961, then, it may be said, there is an inevitability with respect to future events which rules out chance and accident. "What will be, will be" is a tautological proposition. But it is frequently understood as an assertion that we can not affect the course of history, that future events are already determined. And in holding that certain future events are real, we may be held to be committed to the doctrine that future events are determined by present events, to the doctrine that there is a compulsion issuing out of the past and present which makes the future inevitable.

Let us recall however our discussion of the necessary proposition: "F must exist." "F must exist" is true, we have said,[9] if F exists and if there is in the context some proposition: "E exists" which implies the existence of F. If E implies the existence of F, then F must exist and it is not possible for F not to exist. If the inauguration of 1961 exists, then it is not possible for there not to be an inauguration in 1961. An implication from one proposition to another is however to be distinguished from an alleged compulsion linking prior physical events with subsequent physical events. It is some proposition: "E exists" which implies that there will be an inauguration in 1961, not some prior physical event which makes the 1961 inauguration inevitable. Moreover, whether or not "There must be an inauguration in 1961" is true depends upon the instance of : "E exists" that occurs in the context. If we start with the premise that the 1961 inauguration is real, then it is not possible for there to be no inauguration in 1961. If we start with the premise that I today am really aware of a 1961 inauguration, then, since a real subject-object relational situation implies real terms,[10] it is again impossible for there to be no inauguration in 1961. But if what is given is merely the fact that I seem to be aware of a 1961 inauguration, if it is left undetermined whether my real mental attitude has a real object or whether it is merely "as though"[11] I were aware of a 1961 inauguration, then our premises do not imply the 1961 inauguration and it is possible for there to be no inauguration in 1961.

Certain future events are real; and certain future events are real objects for today's mental attitudes. On the other hand, just as I may seem to be aware of a griffin or of a centaur, so I may seem to be aware of an inauguration in 1961 or may seem to be aware of myself as falling down the stairs five minutes hence. In the latter instance, the mental attitude which is as though it were directed towards an accident on the stairs may itself bring about

368

the caution that avoids the accident. In short, certain future entities are real and necessarily so in so far as assertions that they will occur are accepted as premises. But this implies neither that what is to be flows inexorably out of what is; nor that present mental attitudes are impotent. Indeed it would seem that determinists and indeterminists alike must accept the doctrine that certain future entities are real. If there is no present King of France, it is not true that the present King of France is bald and it is not true that the present King of France is not bald.[12] If all alleged future entities are unreal, they are neither determined by what has gone before nor do they spring up without being determined by what has gone before. If they are unreal, nothing can truly be said about them—other than that they do not exist—or about the manner in which they are related to the events that precede them. If one is to hold that no future entities are real, one can be neither a determinist nor an indeterminist; one must hold that "the future is simply nothing at all." [13]

We hold then that Napoleon Bonaparte is real, has the real quality of being 'after' with respect to St. Louis, the real quality of being 'before' with respect to today's mental attitudes and the real quality of being 'before' with respect to the inauguration of 1961. Similarly we hold that the inauguration of 1961 is real, that it has the real quality of being 'after' with respect to Napoleon, the real quality of being 'after' with respect to today's mental attitudes and the real quality of being 'before' with respect to the inauguration of 1965. To be sure, there are some respects in which the inauguration of 1961 which is in the future differs from the inauguration of 1861 which is in the past. When I today am aware of the inauguration of 1861, I know that it was Lincoln who was being inducted into office. I may know what the weather was and what Lnicoln said on that occasion. In short, the object towards which my mental attitude is directed is presented with a wealth of detail. Not so the inauguration of 1961. I am aware of the inauguration of 1961 neither as the inauguration of a Democrat nor as the inauguration of a Republican, neither as occurring in fair weather nor in foul. My object is vague. And if perchance my object is not vague, if, for example, the President-elect to be inducted into office in 1961 is presented to me as John Stevenson, a Democrat from Indianapolis, my mental attitude directed towards such a subsistent is accompanied by a feeling of incredulity. Real entities appearing as future appear in the main with few characteristics, appear in the main as indefinite objects. But they need not appear as entities that no one has or will have as definite objects. "When I think of paleontology," we have said,[14] "I think of nothing definite." "But my subsistent takes on the characteristic of appearing with more details to paleontologists." So it is with the inauguration of 1961. Although this future entity towards which my present mental attitude is directed is bare of details, it appears with the characteristic of being a more definite object for other subjects with respect to whom it will not be future. Subsistents which appear with the characteristic of being only indefinite objects for all of the mental attitudes which are or will be directed towards them are unreal. But in so far as future entities appear with the characteristic of being indefinite objects for certain subjects only, they need not be unreal.

Indeed the distinction to which we have pointed between future entities and past entities is not so much a distinction between what is future with respect to today's mental attitudes and what is past with respect to today's mental attitudes as it is a distinction between what is future and what is past with respect to the particular mental attitude which happens to be aware of it. The real Napoleon is presented with some detail to us; but to St. Louis he can only have appeared as an indefinite object, as he who would rule France at the beginning of the nineteenth century.[15] Indefiniteness is not so much a characteristic of real entities which are future with respect to *us* as it is a characteristic with which entities appear to mental attitudes which precede them.

Last chapter's catcher has the real quality of being a short distance behind with respect to the batter;[16] Napoleon III and the inauguration of 1961 have each the real quality of being 'after' with respect to Napoleon Bonaparte. Last chapter's pitcher has the real quality of being out there in front with respect to the batter; and St. Louis has the real quality of being past or 'before' with respect to Napoleon. But along with the pitcher, the baseball diamond too has the real quality of being out there in front with respect to the catcher. The position which the baseball diamond has with respect to the catcher is less definite than that which the pitcher has. Yet the indefinite position with which the baseball diamond appears is not so indefinite as to require us to call the subsisting baseball diamond and its subsisting position with respect to the catcher unreal.[17]

So it is with the Middle Ages in France and its date with respect to Napoleon. As contrasted with a subsisting St. Louis, the subsisting Middle Ages in France is presented to us as having a less definite date with respect to Napoleon. It is presented merely as some centuries past with respect to him. Yet such a date with respect to Napoleon is not so indefinite a date as to require us to call the subsisting Middle Ages in France which appears with such a date, unreal. On the other hand, that which appears merely as having occurred once upon a time, that which appears as being presented to no one with a more definite date than "once upon a time," is unreal. And that which is presented as everlasting is, considered as a single object, likewise unreal. These last-named entities are unreal along with the entity which appears supra-temporal, out of time, and along with the entity which appears dated with respect to private ideas or fictional objects only, the entity which we have described as one that "explicitly or implicitly appears as undated with respect to some other entity while appearing explicitly or implicitly with the claim that that other entity is nevertheless real." [18]

The pitcher's center of gravity, the pitcher, the baseball diamond, the Cosmos:—this series has its analog in the last moment of St. Louis's life, St. Louis, the Middle Ages in France, the world of all temporal events. The Cosmos and the world of all temporal events are unreal. The last moment of St. Louis's life is still to be discussed. But the pitcher and the baseball diamond are real, together with their more or less indefinite positions with respect to the catcher. And St. Louis and the Middle Ages in France are real, together with their more or less indefinite dates with respect to Napoleon. The pitcher and the baseball diamond, having indefinite positions with respect to the catcher, have extension. And St. Louis and the Middle Ages in France, having indefinite dates with respect to Napoleon, have, let us agree, duration.

Now date, like position, is relative. If I use the expression: "the date of St. Louis" or "the date of the Middle Ages," and if it is agreed that I am not referring to the dates that these entities may be alleged to have with respect to Napoleon or with respect to Christ or with respect to any other point of reference, then my expression: "the date of St. Louis" puts before me no subsisting quality alleged to be absolute whose reality or unreality might be considered. But just as in the preceding chapter we found the point P′ to have the absolute quality of spatiality which we described as "the possibility of having position with respect to various entities," [19] so we hold that St. Louis and the Middle Ages have each the real absolute quality of temporality. St. Louis and the Middle Ages have temporality absolutely, not temporality with respect to Napoleon and temporality with respect to the inauguration of 1961. Similarly duration, which we have found to be a real quality of St. Louis and of the Middle Ages, is an absolute quality. St. Louis and the Middle Ages have duration absolutely, not duration with respect to Napoleon and duration with respect to some phase of the planet Jupiter.

To be sure, if we have clocks at hand to measure the 'length of time' that an entity endures, the number of seconds that our clocks tell off to us will depend upon the speed with which we and our clocks are moving with respect to the entity whose duration we are measuring. Napoleon may have a duration of fifty-two years with respect to an observer at rest with respect to him, a duration of a different number of years with respect to an observer on Sirius. Measured duration, duration numbered by seconds or years, is relative. It presupposes motion between the enduring entity whose duration is being measured and one or another of the spatio-temporal entities outside it from which it might be measured. Yet this measured duration which is relative points back to the quality of duration which we find not relative. If Napoleon lacked the quality of temporality, if he were nontemporal, we could not without contradicting ourselves attribute to him either the quality of being earlier than Napoleon III or the quality of being later than St. Louis. And if he lacked the quality of duration—the unmeasured or pre-measured duration that we hold to be absolute—we could not without contradicting ourselves attribute to him either the quality of enduring fifty-two years as measured by one observer or the quality of enduring through a different number of years as measured by another. If he did not endure, his duration would not be there for various observers to measure.

Napoleon, St. Louis and the Middle Ages have each of them duration. That is to say, the duration which I present to myself as a quality of each of them does not appear undated with respect to real entities, does not appear lacking position with respect to its contemporaries, does not appear generally discredited, and is listed as real in the appendix to Chapter Three. Like unnumbered length or extension,[20] this unnumbered duration is vague. It does not have the one number that comes from measuring duration from some preferred point of view, that comes from measuring duration, for example, from some entity at rest with respect to it. In itself it is unnumbered, being equally receptive to various numbers. So it is with temporality. Temporality is not the date that an entity has with respect to some preferred point of reference, not date for example with respect to an event at the beginning of the Christian era. It is not date with respect to some implied point of reference, but rather the possibility of being dated with respect to various points of reference.

But let us come back to duration. If Napoleon has, as we hold, the real quality of duration, how, we may ask, do we become aware of it? Events in his early life may have been witnessed and ultimately relayed to my present mental attitude. Although these events are past with respect to me, a chain may be traced from them to me and they may be both the ultimate causes and the immediate—though non-present—objects of my present mental attitude. Similarly his last words at St. Helena may have initiated disturbances in the air and these waves may be traced in one form or another to the present mental attitude of mine which is directed towards Napoleon's last days. But how can the enduring Napoleon who began in Corsica and ended at St. Helena be the cause of a mental attitude of mine? How can a single impulse start from the enduring Napoleon and bring about a present mental attitude directed towards an enduring entity? Even extension can be held to be a percept with greater plausibility. For we can imagine a wave-front advancing from an extended object and being foreshortened more and more as it approaches the eye. But in the case of Napoleon we would have to imagine a single front formed by impulses started at different dates, a sort of wheeling column whose earlier and later elements by the time that I become aware of the enduring Napoleon have developed simultaneity with one another. We may agree that this is not a satisfactory account of the genesis of the awareness of duration. But what then are the alternatives offered us?

It may be held that, corresponding to the earlier and later phases of an enduring entity, there result in the first instance earlier and later ideas. But to be aware of the enduring entity as a whole, as enduring, the acts of apprehension which have been successive must be replaced by a mental state existing at a given date which refers equally to the earlier and to the later phases of the enduring object. Hence, it may be held, the earlier idea is reproduced at a later moment when the later idea is present; and it may be held that some web of connection is then spun between the ideas, now simultaneously held, to correspond to the object's duration, to correspond, that is to say, to the connection in the object between its earlier and later phases.[21] It has been our doctrine, however, that private ideas do not exist, and, hence, cannot be reproduced. Mental attitudes may be repeated. An early phase of an enduring entity may be a percept with respect to one mental attitude and a memory with respect to a later mental attitude belonging to the same mind-person. The successive mental attitudes of the same mind-person may have the early phase of the enduring entity as their common object, their common direct object. But the early phase of the enduring entity does not change its dates, nor does it become mental, by becoming the object of the second mental attitude. Making these changes to bring the doctrine we are discussing into alignment with our own epistemological views, we may agree to the possibility of a subject having a mental attitude directed towards a later phase of the enduring object and simultaneously a mental attitude which, like some previous mental attitude of his, is directed towards an earlier phase of the enduring object. Yet if this be all, the subject is not aware of the enduring entity itself, not aware of earlier and later phases as phases of one enduring entity. The problem of accounting for the awareness of the object's duration is still unsolved.

It may be held that the awareness of the connection in the object is initiated in the mind itself. But this is mere acknowledgement of failure to discover processes travelling from object to subject without discovering intra-cerebral processes to substitute

374

for them. Nor does failure to discover processes travelling from object to subject prove the alleged object to be unreal. For whether or not the alleged object is real, whether or not, in this case, the alleged enduring object really endures, depends upon such considerations as whether or not the alleged enduring object appears with the characteristic of being generally discredited. An entity, such as tomorrow's sun or the inauguration of 1961, may be real and may be the real object of my present mental attitude, even though there *is* no process travelling from future object to present mental attitude.[22] How much less proof of unreality there is then in the fact that we can not *find* processes travelling from alleged object to present mental attitude! We hold then that Napoleon, the Middle Ages in France, and the man who will be inaugurated President in 1961, each of them has the real quality of duration. And we hold that the reality of the quality of duration that each of these entities has is not affected by the unsatisfactory outcome of our efforts to find processes, initiated by the enduring object as a whole, that bring about the mental attitudes directed upon this enduring object's duration.

Napoleon, we hold, had duration. There was, let us agree, an early phase of his life which was spent in Corsica and a late phase of his life which was spent on St. Helena. These phases, like Napoleon taken as a unitary substance, have, we hold, duration. Just as we use the word "part" to point to a substance 'discriminated' from a more extended substance that includes it, so we use the word "phase" to point to a substance discriminated from a more enduring substance that includes it.[23] Like Napoleon taken as a whole, Napoleon on St. Helena is a substance, has duration, and is dated with respect to various points of reference. It has, to be sure, a lesser duration than the Napoleon from whom it is discriminated as a phase; and the date which it has with respect to Napoleon III, or with respect to today's events, is not so indefinite. But Napoleon-on-St. Helena is a real enduring substance. Assuming now that each real substance has some qualities, it would appear that a certain set of qualities inheres in Napoleon on St. Helena, that another set of qualities inheres in Napoleon taken as a whole, and that still another set inheres in Napoleon's boyhood. According to Schopenhauer,[24] we may "define time as the possibility of opposite states in one and the same thing." Yet it is not Napoleon taken as a unitary substance who was both powerful and powerless. Strictly speaking, it was not Caesar, but Caesar at moment M, who crossed the Rubicon.[25] Similarly it was Napoleon on St. Helena who was powerless, Napoleon in some earlier phase who had tremendous power. As a French flag is not red, not white and not blue but, rather, tricolored, so Napoleon taken as a whole was not powerful and not powerless but, rather, has the quality of having been powerful and powerless in turn. That is to say, different phases of Napoleon have different qualities just as different parts of a French flag have different colors. Substances do not have contradictory qualities in so far as they have duration and have phases; any more than they have contradictory qualities in so far as they have extension and have parts.

Along with Napoleon's boyhood, Napoleon while First Consul, and Napoleon on St. Helena, substances which are real, let us consider an alleged phase of Napoleon which is presented as being Napoleon at the instant at which exactly half of his life had been lived. Napoleon on St. Helena, we have remarked, has a lesser duration than Napoleon as a whole; but it has the quality of duration. The entity however which presents itself as Napoleon at the instant at which exactly half of his life had been lived appears as an instantaneous phase, as a phase without duration. As the baseball pitcher's center of gravity appears as having position with respect to the batter but no extension, so this instantaneous phase of Napoleon appears as having a date with respect to today's events but no duration. The pitcher's center of gravity is no percept. The point is a limit that is never reached by division.[26] Similarly we may agree that nothing happens at an instant. The camera's shutter is not shut as soon as it is opened. The most minute impulse that reaches us, we may agree, has its origin, not in an instantaneous phase of the object, but in an emitting part whose action 'takes some time.' Yet none of these observations, if true, imply that an alleged instantaneous phase is unreal. The instantaneous phase of Napoleon that I present to myself does not appear undated with respect to real entities, does not appear lacking position with respect to its contemporaries, does not appear generally discredited. Like the point on the line PP′ or like the pitcher's center of gravity, it is, we hold, real.

376

But whereas there is an instantaneous phase of Napoleon and an instantaneous phase of the Duke of Wellington contemporaneous with it, there is no 'instant.' An instantaneous phase, not of Napoleon and not of the Duke of Wellington, but of the cosmos, subsists with too indefinite a position with respect to its contemporaries. There is perhaps a set of real instantaneous phases contemporaneous with one another; and there may be a universal which has these instantaneous phases as its instances. But these instantaneous phases, taken together, form no real individual to be called an "instant." Similarly with things and phases of things which endure. There is a set of contemporaneous substances:— Napoleon in 1812, the Duke of Wellington in 1812, and the like— which are alike with respect to duration. There may be a universal substance which has these individual substances as its instances; there may, that is to say, be the universal substance: 'Thing enduring through 1812.' Similarly there may be a universal quality which has the durations of various individual substances as its instances; there may, that is to say, be the universal quality: 'enduring through 1812.' But there is no real individual substance that we put before us by taking Napoleon in 1812, the Duke of Wellington in 1812, and so on, collectively. There is no year 1812 and no real entity which is the quality of such an alleged collective individual substance.

Let us suppose that I return home after having been away on a short trip. The phase of my life during which I am away on the trip has *its* duration; and the phase of my home while I am absent has *its* duration. It may be that, when these two enduring entities are measured from some spatio-temporal entity outside them, their durations will be assigned different numbers. But let us direct our attention to the unnumbered or prenumbered quality of duration that this phase of my life has and to the unnumbered or prenumbered quality of duration that this phase of my home has. It may be said that the phases of the two entities are alike with respect to the unnumbered quality of duration that each of them has. But there is nevertheless no duration beginning when I leave home and ending when I return that is not the duration of some substance. "A distance," we have said,[27] "is a certain line or path with the emphasis on the *termini*"; and an interval, we may say, is the phase of a certain substance with the

377

emphasis on its beginning and end. As there is no distance that is not, so to speak, imbedded in some path, so there is no interval that is not, so to speak, imbedded in the phase of some substance. Now, when we do not specify "distance by automobile road" or "distance by water," the distance between P and P' is imbedded, so to speak, in the straight line PP'. But when we refer to the interval between my departure from home and my return, are we referring to the interval that is a phase of my home or to the interval that is a phase of my life? "Interval" we conclude, differs from "distance" in this respect. Whereas "distance between P and P'," as contrasted with "distance between P and P' by route A," refers to single path, "interval between P and P'" that is not similarly specified is either ambiguous or points to a universal whose instances are phases of substances that are alike in that they have identical unnumbered durations.

Enduring from my departure from home to my return, there are phases of two substances, and hence two intervals, that we have found real. Perhaps there is a phase of a third or of a fourth substance which begins when I leave home and ends when I return. But we must remember that no entity is definitely to be called "real" unless it is presented without the characteristic of being an indefinite object and unless it is enumerated in the appendix to Chapter Three. Napoleon is real, and the instantaneous phase of Napoleon at which exactly half of his life had been lived; the Middle Ages are real, and the inauguration of 1961. But since it is only singular or particular affirmative existential propositions which are both true and informative, the reality of a whole world of temporal entities can not be validated in a single proposition. The Middle Ages in France, Napoleon's boyhood and the inauguration of 1961, all have duration and all have dates with respect to various entities such as the birth of Christ or my present mental attitude. But no alleged event of the year 1,000, no duration that may be attributed to such an event and no date that such an alleged event may seem to have with respect to Napoleon or to you, is to be accepted as real until that event, that duration or those dates are shown to be free from the characteristics that would mark them out as unreal, and until they are pointed out as real in the propositions in which real entities are enumerated. What we have found real up to this point, in short, are a few instantaneous phases, a few substances having duration, a few intervals. And although we may take it for granted that there are many enduring entities like Napoleon and like the inauguration of 1961, we have thus far no basis for concluding that their durations are contiguous and that, taken together, they completely fill an alleged Time-continuum.

In the preceding chapter we pointed to the distinction between material spaces and non-material spaces. Some distant spherical figure may be real; and yet we may so define 'body' and 'matter' that this spherical substance is not a body, is not material.[28] We may present to ourselves something equal in size and shape to the sun, something that at each moment is in the same direction as the sun, but twice as distant. If, now, we may agree that there is no 'matter' where this substance is, what we have before us is a non-material substance of definite size and shape whose successive phases, like the successive phases of the sun itself, lie in different directions with respect to the observer at a given point on the earth's surface. What we have before us is a substance alleged to have the quality of duration, a substance alleged to differ from the sun in its distance from us and in the fact that it is not a body. This alleged substance presented as immaterial is, let us agree, real. For no instantaneous phase of it appears lacking in position with respect to contemporaneous real entities; its various enduring phases, like the corresponding enduring phases of the sun, appear dated with respect to various real entities; and, presented as immaterial, it is listed as real in the appendix to Chapter Three. Along, then, with the Middle Ages in France, Napoleon and the inauguration of 1961, there are various enduring entities that are non-material, various enduring entities whose instantaneous phases are all empty spaces. Yet even when we consider real enduring entities that are non-material along with real enduring entities that are material, we have no basis for asserting that the set of entities with real durations, in addition to overlapping, completely fills an alleged Time-continuum.

It may be held, however, that each enduring substance, whether material or immaterial, implies some other substance preceding it. Just as, when we follow the State of Wyoming to its boundaries, we do not stop but become aware of neighboring States that bound it,[29] so it may be held that the awareness of each entity having a certain duration, whether material or immaterial, leads us on to the awareness of some predecessor. But if the alleged predecessor subsists as no one's definite object, it and its alleged prior date are unreal. Just as, "with respect to any real entity having position, we are never frustrated in the attempt to present ourselves alleged parts of space surrounding it," so it may be that we are never frustrated in the attempt to present to ourselves alleged predecessor substances having prior dates with respect to Napoleon or with respect to the birth of Christ. But with respect to those enduring substances where alleged prior substances appear as no one's definite objects, there exists no prior substance, whether material or immaterial, and no duration or prior date as a real quality of it. Even empty time, to put it colloquially, is no continuum.

When we limit our attention to material substances, the doctrine that every real entity implies a predecessor receives support from the dictum that every event has a cause. For if every material substance points back to a preceding material substance which brought it into being, there is an unbroken series of real material substances and hence an unbroken series of more and more remote dates. If, however, there are substances, material or immaterial, where alleged predecessor substances appear as no one's definite objects, then there are events which we fail to trace back to causes. Alleged entities, appearing as no one's definite objects, are not real and not causes. The material substances, that might otherwise be regarded as their consequents, have no real material substances preceding them and no real causes.

We are never frustrated when we attempt to put before ourselves more and more distant points. There is a point which is the farthest away of all real points, the point, namely, which is farthest away of all definite objects.[30] In a similar fashion we can present to ourselves, as fairly definitely-dated objects, substances of a million years ago, a trillion years ago, and so on. To be real, however, an entity must not only be presented without the characteristic of lacking definite dates; it must also be presented without the characteristic of lacking position with respect to real contemporaries. The substances consequently that are the most remote in time of all real substances are those, not presented as lacking in spatial relations with their contemporaries, that are the most remote in time of all definite objects. Assuming however that our objects are not limited to bodies, we can place before ourselves set after set of spatially related contemporaries, one prior to another. The earliest set that we thus place before ourselves includes the earliest of all substances; the dates that its several members have are the earliest of all dates.

What shall we say, however, with respect to the series of earlier and earlier substances—or phases of substances—that are bodies? We may present to ourselves phases of the sun at various past dates, one phase earlier than the other. But we may come to some alleged phase of the sun which is not really a phase of the sun and not really a body. Although we will not be frustrated when we search for earlier and earlier substances, we may reach a point where the entities presented to us, appearing as material, are all presented as generally discredited. The earliest body, it follows, may have a later date than the earliest substance. For the date of the earliest body depends, not merely upon the extent to which we persevere in presenting to ourselves earlier and earlier definite objects, but upon the qualities which we insist on substances having before we will agree to call them "bodies." If we follow Descartes in calling each extended entity a "body," the earliest substance is a body. But if "body" has a more limited denotation, there may be early phases of empty spaces which have only other empty spaces contemporaneous with them; there may be early phases of empty spaces which are real and which precede each body that is real.

Our discussion of the last few paragraphs concerns the past. We have asked whether each event points back to a cause which must have preceded it, how far the series of earlier and earlier substances extends, how far the series of earlier and earlier bodies. "The world's having a beginning," it has however been said,[31] does not "derogate from the infinity of its duration *a parte post*." An event, it may be felt, implies that a series of preceding causes is given and real, but does not imply the existence of an equally definite series of later consequents.[32] As we use the term "reality," however, the inauguration of a President of the United States in 1961 is, we have found, real.[33] And since the inauguration of 1961 is real along with the inauguration of 1861, since certain future events, certain present events and certain past events are equally real, then causal relations, if there *are* any, may flow from present events to future events as well as they may flow from past events to present events. Whatever be the sense of "cause" in which the inauguration of 1861 was caused or affected by the election of 1860, it is in this sense of "cause" that the inauguration of 1961 will be caused or affected by the election of 1960. Whatever compulsion or lack of compulsion flowed from the election of 1860 to the inauguration of 1861, a similar compulsion or lack of compulsion will flow from the election of 1960 to the inauguration of 1961.

Moreover, the conditions determining the truth or falsity of the proposition: "There may be no inauguration in 1961" are analogous to the conditions determining the truth or falsity of the proposition: "There may have been no inauguration in 1861." "There may be no inauguration in 1961" is true only if there are no propositions in the context which imply a 1961 inauguration. And "There may have been no inauguration in 1861" is true only if there are no propositions in the context which imply an 1861 inauguration. To be sure, the inauguration of 1961 is not so firmly believed in by today's thinkers as is the inauguration of 1861.[34] Hence an instance of "There may be no inauguration in 1961," occurring today, may occur in a context in which there is no proposition implying a 1961 inauguration; whereas an instance of "There may have been no inauguration in 1861," occurring today, is likely to occur in a context in which there *is* a proposition implying an 1861 inauguration. But if we start with the premise that certain future events are real and certain past events real, it is just as impossible for these future events to be unreal as it is for these past events to be unreal. And if certain alleged future events are real, as we hold that they are, the alleged relational situations into which they enter with preceding events that have affected them are just as real as the relational situations into which past events entered with *their* predecessors.

There are however past events with respect to which prior events, alleged to have affected them, or alleged merely to have preceded them, appear as no one's definite objects. There are, that is to say, past events which *had* no predecessors.[35] Just so, there are real future events such that alleged subsequent events, alleged to have been affected by them, or alleged merely to have

382

followed them, appear as no one's definite objects and are unreal. And just as there is an end both to the series of earlier and earlier material substances that are real and to the series of earlier and earlier *im*material substances that are real, so there is an end both to the series of later and later material substances that are real and to the series of later and later immaterial substances that are real.

We hold then that there were substances contemporaneous with one another,—possibly immaterial,—which were the earliest real substances, and whose dates with respect to various points of reference are the earliest of all real dates. We hold that there was a first real body which,—assuming "body" to have a more limited denotation than "substance"—may have been later than the first substances and may have had only empty spaces contemporaneous with it. We hold that, beginning with the earliest body, there have been, are, and will be, various enduring bodies and various instantaneous phases of bodies; also various enduring substances which may not be bodies, and various instantaneous phases of such substances. And, finally, we hold that there will be a last body, or bodies, and, possibly subsequently, substances contemporaneous with one another that will be the last substances.

But how full of material substances is the alleged interval between the earliest material substance and the latest material substance? And how full of substances, material or immaterial, is the alleged interval between the earliest of all substances, material or immaterial, and the latest of all substances? Let us imagine a day of none but immaterial substances, alleged to intervene between a set of enduring bodies preceding it and a set of enduring bodies following it. On the hypothesis that there has been a day of empty time, a day on which no events occurred and no bodies existed, preceding bodies could not have been at the source of motions travelling continuously through *bodies* and finally affecting us who are subsequent to this allegedly immaterial day. But an immaterial day is not, by hypothesis, a nonexisting day. And impulses, alleged to have their source in bodies preceding it, may be held to have travelled through this day's nonmaterial substances just as motions originating in the sun may be held to have reached us across empty spaces. Indeed even if it were held that there *were* no motions reaching us across this day from bodies that had preceded it, it would not follow that these alleged earlier bodies were unreal or that we could not be aware of them. For tomorrow's sunrise is real and a real object for my present mental attitude, a situation in which there is likewise alleged to be no set of impulses travelling from object to mental attitude. Our conclusion, to be sure, is not that there *was* an immaterial day intervening between the earliest material substances and the latest material substances. But it would seem that the hypothesis which we have been considering is not inconsistent with any of the propositions that have been laid down in this chapter.

Indeed let us go one step farther. Let us suppose that, between the bodies which precede and the bodies which follow, there not only are no material substances but no immaterial substances either. What we are suggesting is as if bodies and immaterial substances existed through January 15, 1940, and as if no subsequent bodies and no subsequent immaterial substances began until January 17, 1940. Whereas on the hypothesis previously considered alleged intervening bodies were assumed to be unreal, on this hypothesis alleged intervening substances, presented as immaterial, are likewise assumed to be unreal. Yet this hypothesis, like the preceding one, is not inconsistent with any of the propositions that have been laid down in this chapter.

If no substance, material or immaterial, existed with a January 16th date, then, to be sure, there would be no substance enduring from earlier than January 16th to later than January 16th. And since what we call an "interval" is imbedded in the phase of some enduring substance,[36] there would be no interval between the events of January 15, 1940, and the events of today. If there were no line OP, there would be no number to assign P's position with respect to O. And without an interval between the events of January 15, 1940, and the events of today, there would be no number to assign the date that an event of January 15, 1940, has with respect to us. But P may have position, albeit an unnumbered position, with respect to O, without there being a line OP. And an event having neither material nor immaterial entities as immediate successors may have a date, albeit an unnumbered date, with respect to today's events.

Thus there exists a series of enduring bodies whose durations

384

need not be contiguous. And there may exist an additional series of immaterial enduring substances, whose durations, so far as we have seen, likewise need not be continuous. But, whether an enduring substance be material or immaterial, whether it have material substances contiguous with it, immaterial substances contiguous with it, or no substances at all contiguous with it, how many instantaneous phases, we now ask, does it include?

As an example of an enduring substance which may be immaterial, we have pointed to what is equal in size and shape to the sun, a substance that at each moment is in the same direction as the sun, but twice as distant.[37] Within today's phase of this substance—which we shall assume to be immaterial—we can place before ourselves as definite objects the instantaneous phase of this substance as it was at three o'clock, the instantaneous phase at four o'clock, the instantaneous phase at three thirty o'clock, and so on. These instantaneous phases do not appear lacking in position with respect to entities contemporaneous with them; for, even if there are no instantaneous phases of bodies contemporaneous with them, there may be other empty spaces. Nor do they appear generally discredited; for, whereas we may doubt the measurability of their dates, the bit of empty space that has an unmeasured and perhaps immeasurable date with respect to me is no more incredible than the point between the extremities of the line PP′ that has an as yet unmeasured distance from me.[38] There exists, then, a number of these instantaneous phases that do not appear as no one's definite objects and that are listed in the appendix to Chapter Three; just as there exists a number of points on a given line. But since there are only so many that, appearing without the characteristic of being no one's definite objects, are listed as real, alleged instantaneous phases in excess of this number, appearing as no one's definite objects, are unreal.

An enduring immaterial substance includes then at most a finite number of instantaneous phases. And an enduring substance that is a body, Napoleon, for example, or today's phase of the Capitol at Washington, likewise includes at most a finite number of instantaneous phases. In the one case as in the other, there are only so many instantaneous phases that appear as definite objects for some subject. In the one case as in the other, additional alleged instantaneous phases appearing as no one's definite objects are unreal. But whereas the number of instantaneous phases that an immaterial substance has is limited only by the limits to our perseverance, whereas we are never frustrated in our efforts to place before ourselves additional instantaneous phases of immaterial substances that are real, the situation may be different with respect to substances that are bodies. It is possible, so far as we have yet seen, that Napoleon or the Capitol at Washington exists now and again, but not as a continuous body. Material substances may be intermittent like the light of a lighthouse or firefly. If so, if at four o'clock, for example, the Capitol has ceased as a body and has not yet reappeared, then an alleged four o'clock phase of the Capitol is no real phase of a material substance. If bodies are intermittent, our discovery of additional real instantaneous phases of bodies will be limited not only by the limits to our perseverance but by the subject matter itself. Certain alleged instantaneous phases of bodies will be unreal, not because they appear as no one's definite objects, but because they are believed to be phases of non-bodies rather than of bodies.

The hypothesis that enduring bodies do not endure continuously but are interrupted by phases which are not phases of bodies is analogous to the hypothesis that extended bodies are not continuous but include empty spaces within them. One may hold that an atom has a certain extended position and may nevertheless hold that there are empty spaces within it. The atom taken as a whole might then well be described as partly material and partly immaterial and the empty space within it as an immaterial part of an including substance that is partly material and partly immaterial. Similarly with respect to the duration of the Capitol at Washington. If there is no four o'clock phase which is material, let us not say that the duration of the Capitol is not continuous, but let us rather describe the Capitol as an enduring substance which in some of its phases is material and in some of its phases immaterial.

It may be observed that greater plausibility attaches to the doctrine that the extended atom includes empty spaces within it than attaches to the analogous doctrine that the enduring Capitol includes phases which are immaterial. We become aware of positions within the extended atom at which we find no mass, no qualities that would make these positions the positions of bodies.

386

We find extension and date; hence these positions are positions of substances. But if we define 'body' so that only substances with certain additional qualities are bodies, then these positions may well be the positions of immaterial substances. Whether or not the enduring Capitol has an immaterial phase at, let us say, four o'clock will similarly depend in part upon the signification we assign the term "body." Each phase of the enduring Capitol or of an enduring atom will be extended and dated and will consequently be a substance. But if additional qualities are required of bodies, if by definition, for example, we restrict the denotation of "body" to instances of jumping from one electronic orbit to another, then there may be dates at which no such jumping is occurring, dates belonging to phases which are immaterial substances.

Subject to such differences as have been pointed out, the situation with respect to enduring substances and enduring bodies is analogous, we hold, to the situation with respect to extended substances and extended bodies. Subject to such differences as have been pointed out, the situation with respect to date, duration and interval is, on the whole, analogous to the situation with respect to position, extension and distance. There are, to be sure, alleged differences in addition to those which we have pointed out. When we measure distances and compare them in size, we frequently make use of the method of superposition. We take a standard distance, as, for example, that between the ends of a yardstick; and we place this distance, first over one of the distances to be measured, and then over the other. When we are dealing with intervals, however, it is held that a similar method can not be followed. We can not retain the interval between two strokes of a clock in order to have the terms of this interval coincide in date with the terms of a subsequent interval. "In the measuring of extension," says Locke,[39] "there is nothing more required but the application of the standard or measure we make use of to the thing of whose extension we would be informed." "But in the measuring of duration," he continues, "this can not be done; because no two different parts of succession can be put together to measure one another."

In the process of finding the length of the yard-long object on my left equal to the length of the yard-long object on my right, I compare the former with the length of the yardstick placed over it.

387

I find this in turn equal to the length of the yardstick in a subsequent phase when it has been moved into a different position, and this in turn equal to the length of the object on my right over which a still later phase of the yardstick comes to rest. Similarly instead of comparing directly the duration that my clock has between two o'clock and three o'clock with the duration that it has between three o'clock and four o'clock, I can make use of some hour-long duration that begins shortly after two o'clock and ends shortly after three o'clock. No matter how many hour-long durations I interpolate, there are no two of them that can be seen to be equal in duration. But similarly no matter how often I stop my yardstick in its transit from the object on my left to that on my right, I can not see that its length when in one position is equal to the length it had just previously when it was in another position.

To be sure, the object on my left and the object on my right *are* equal in length only relatively, only with respect to certain spatio-temporal entities. And the duration of my clock between two o'clock and three o'clock likewise equals the duration of this clock between three o'clock and four o'clock as measured from certain spatio-temporal entities and not from others. For whether it is lengths or durations that we are measuring and to which we are assigning numbers, the process involves spatio-temporal entities outside those whose lengths or durations are being measured.[40]

Another allegation is that what is to the left of me and what is to the right of me can change places whereas what is past and what is future can not. But if a_1 was to the left of me and b_1 to the right of me, it is later phases of a and b that have different positions. It is a_2 that is now to the right of me and it is b_2 that is now to the left of me. Similarly however d_2 that is future with respect to me can have a phase d_1 that preceded me and c_1 that is past can have a future phase c_2.

Let us suppose however that I am considered not merely as a point of reference but as a thinking, experiencing subject. I am free to become aware of what is on my left before I become aware of what is on my right or to become aware of what is on my right before I become aware of what is on my left. But, it has been felt, my awareness of earlier events precedes and can not follow my awareness of subsequent events.

Real subject-object relations, however, exist between subjects and objects that are not contemporaneous with one another as well as between subjects and objects that are present with respect to one another.[41] One mental attitude may be directed upon the inauguration of 1961 that is future with respect to it; and a subsequent mental attitude may be directed upon the inauguration of 1861 that is past with respect to it. The temporal order obtaining among objects may be the reverse of the temporal order obtaining among the mental attitudes directed upon these objects. To some extent this is true even when we limit our attention to instances of perceiving. For I may perceive one of today's events and may later have as my percept a past phase of a distant star. Thus, we conclude that, only when we limit our attention to instances of perceiving and only when in addition we put other limitations upon our objects, only then do we find spatial entities reversible in a way in which temporal entities are not.[42]

The inauguration of 1861 that is past, an event that is present, and the inauguration of 1961 that is future may all three be immediate objects for mental attitudes that are contemporaneous with one another. If this were not true, if in thinking at a given moment about both the inauguration of 1861 and the inauguration of 1961 my immediate objects had to be present, one might well wonder how these objects would be distinguished from one another. They would differ, it might be answered, in that they would refer to different dates. Yet such a difference, it might be felt, would not suffice. It might be held that the two immediate objects, both present, would have to differ in some characteristics which are completely given in the present and yet which represent the temporal qualities of the non-present ultimate objects. It may be to some such reasoning as this that we owe the doctrine that ultimate objects having different dates are represented by immediate objects having different positions. "In order to make even internal changes afterwards conceivable to ourselves," says Kant,[43] "we must make time, as the form of the internal sense, figuratively comprehensible to ourselves by means of a line, and the internal change by means of the drawing of this line (motion): in other words, the successive existence of ourselves in different states by means of an external intuition." Or, let us suppose that

389

we have to do with sheep which have passed before us one by one. "If we picture to ourselves each of the sheep in the flock in succession and separately, we shall never have to do with more than a single sheep." [44] If we are at this moment to think of the fifty sheep that passed us in succession, it may be felt that we must have fifty present images. And, Bergson holds, these images can be recognized as fifty only if they are spatially external to one another.

Even however if we should agree that immediate objects must carry their differences with them and can not merely refer to ultimate objects that differ among themselves, we should not agree that immediate objects can not differ in date and so must differ in position. Immediate objects, we hold, *do* differ in date. I need not put dots on a sheet of paper to distinguish the inauguration of 1861 from the inauguration of 1961; nor need I draw a line to be aware of the interval in Napoleon's life between his birth and his death. This is not to say that dots and figures and diagrams can not be of service in thinking about objects that differ among themselves in date. They can be of service in thinking about objects that differ in various ways. In particular, just as they can be of service in thinking about objects that differ among themselves in date, so they can be of service in thinking about objects that differ among themselves in position. For just as with points on a line in front of me I can visualize and retain a picture of successive events in the history of a clock or of a person or of a nation, so a map enables me to visualize and to retain a picture of the relative positions of various places, and a figure on a flat surface enables me to visualize and to retain a picture of a three-dimensional object. A map is of as much service in representing the distance between New York and Chicago as a set of dots is in representing the successive strokes of a clock. It is not then that spatially distinct entities as such tend to substitute themselves as objects of our thinking for temporally distinct entities, but that such differences in position as can be included within the extension of a limited surface are useful representations, representing now temporal differences, now spatial differences, now differences of other sorts.

There are, as we have seen, various respects in which temporal relations are not entirely analogous to spatial relations. In comparing durations there is no process available to us that is exactly equivalent to the process of superposition.[45] There may be several intervals between events having different dates, whereas the straight line PP′ indicates *the* distance between P and P′.[46] And there is no series of successive events that can be of the help that maps and diagrams can be. If there were and if the analogy between spatial relations and temporal relations were complete, such differences in position as can be included within the extension of a limited surface could of course continue to be used to represent temporal differences. Spatial relations could be substituted for temporal relations; but there would be nothing to be gained from the substitution.

Despite such differences as have been pointed out, the difference, for example, that makes substitution helpful, we hold that relations between entities having different dates are, on the whole, analogous to relations between contemporaneous entities having different positions. But it is to spatial relations between *contemporaneous* entities that we hold temporal relations on the whole to be analogous. Spatial relations between *non-contemporaneous* entities are a different matter. It will only be after we shall have undertaken to enlarge the significations of "here" and "there" that we shall be in a position to understand an assertion that attributes a spatial relation to Napoleon III to what is contemporaneous but 'there' with respect to Napoleon Bonaparte. Without such an enlargement of the significations of "here" and "there," spatial relations between non-contemporaneous entities can not be determined to be analogous to temporal relations of any sort.

Summary

Certain entities are dated with respect to other entities. In asserting this, we do not limit our assertion to situations in which the entity that is the point of reference is in the same place as the entity that has a date with respect to it.

As we use "existence," entities presented as past with respect to present-day entities may be real and entities presented as future. But future events are generally not definite objects with respect to mental attitudes that precede them. The assertion that some future events are real does not imply that we can not affect our surroundings, that what will be will be. (Except to the extent that "What will be will be" is tautological.)

Analogous to the quality of extension, there is the quality of duration. But since duration is the quality of some enduring substance, there may be as many durations from a given initial event to a given final event as there are substances persisting from the one event to the other.

Just as there may be empty three-dimensional volumes or spaces, so there may be enduring entities which are not bodies. But enduring entities which are real, whether they be bodies or not, need not follow one another without interruption. There is an earliest body and an earliest enduring entity which is not a body; also there will be a last body or bodies and last enduring entities which are not bodies.

On the whole, temporal relations are analogous to spatial relations between contemporaries. But there are several respects in which the analogy breaks down or is alleged to break down. Various alleged differences are discussed towards the end of the chapter.

392

Chapter XIII

SPATIAL RELATIONS AMONG
NON-CONTEMPORANEOUS ENTITIES;
MOTION

It is often felt that we could picture to ourselves the spatio-temporal relations obtaining among existing entities if we could visualize four lines drawn through a given point at right angles to one another, if, instead of a three-dimensional box, we could visualize a four-dimensional super-box wherein four co-ordinates would be required to determine the position of one point with respect to another. But the discussions of the two preceding chapters suggest an alternative representation, a representation equally crude, but quite different. Let us imagine a box into which a number of paper-thin plates are put. Each plate standing on its end represents a set of instantaneous entities contemporaneous with one another. To be sure, since substances are here and there but not at positions which are presented as not definite objects, each plate turns out to resemble the heavens wherein we can see stars wherever we look hard enough, but where we never look hard enough to find just one continuous star. Indeed the plate is nothing apart from its contents just as the heavens are nothing apart from heavenly bodies (and heavenly non-bodies). Like the plate, the set of contemporaneous entities has its limits. But unlike the fixed circumference of most plates, the limits of our plate resemble the limits of a man's field of vision. By turning to right or left, new objects are brought within his field of vision. But his field of vision never stretches off to infinity.

There are a great many plates in our box. There is a plate

393

made up of all real entities, material and immaterial, that were contemporaneous with Napoleon at the first instantaneous phase of his life. And there is a plate made up of all real entities, material and immaterial, that were contemporaneous with Napoleon at the last instantaneous phase of his life. Our box is never so full that there is no room for additional plates. Additional plates can always be inserted between any two plates already in the box and additional plates can be inserted without limit at each end. Nevertheless there is a last plate to be inserted; there is not an infinite number of plates behind a given plate nor in front of it.

If now we imagine a line perpendicular to the parallel plates, a line that pierces a given plate at a given point, then we may ask how we determine the point at which this line pierces some second plate. If Napoleon's birth is 'here' with respect to some point of reference contemporaneous with his birth, which of the events contemporaneous with his death is 'here' with respect to that earlier point of reference? Does our line piercing plate after plate always pass through some event in Napoleon's life and is consequently Napoleon dying at St. Helena here? Or does our line pass through successive phases in the history of Ajaccio so that Ajaccio in 1821 is 'here' and not the dying Napoleon contemporaneous with it? Among contemporaneous entities position is a quality which is relative.[1] An entity may be 'here' with respect to one of its contemporaries and 'there' with respect to another. But when the entity that is to be called 'here' or 'there' is not a contemporary, its here-ness or there-ness, it would seem, is relative, not to some instantaneous point of reference, but rather to some enduring point of reference. It is the enduring Napoleon with his various instantaneous phases that is the point of reference, so that Ajaccio in 1769 is 'here,' Moscow in 1812 'here' and St. Helena in 1821 'here.' Or it is the enduring Ajaccio with its various instantaneous phases that is the point of reference, so that Ajaccio in 1769 is 'here,' but Moscow in 1812 and St. Helena in 1821 'there.' Without such an enduring point of reference being given or implied, my expression: "the position of the dying Napoleon with respect to the birth of Napoleon" puts before me no definite subsisting quality whose reality or unreality might be considered.[2] It is the position of the dying Napoleon with respect to the birth of Napoleon, taking the enduring Napoleon as the point of reference,—it is this that is real or unreal; or it is the position of the dying Napoleon with respect to the birth of Napoleon, taking the enduring Ajaccio as the point of reference.

The pitcher really has position, really is 'out in front' with respect to the batter who is present with respect to him.[3] Similarly the dying Napoleon has a real position with respect to the phase of Ajaccio that is his contemporary, with respect, that is to say, to Ajaccio in 1821. But the alleged position of the death of Napoleon with respect to what happened in Ajaccio in 1769 appears to involve two relational situations taken together. It is presented to us as involving the temporal relation between the birth of Napoleon and the 1821 event that happens to be regarded as a later phase of the same enduring entity; plus the spatial relation between this 1821 event, which comes from projecting the birth of Napoleon into 1821, and the death of Napoleon which is its contemporary.

In order that the death of Napoleon may really have position with respect to what happened in Ajaccio in 1769, not only must the two relational situations just referred to both be real, but the combination must be real. It is of course possible to restrict the denotation of "relation" to what we may call uncombined relations. If, for example, we restrict our attention to blood relatives, my brother is a relation of mine, but my brother-in-law is not. As we use the term "relation," however, three-termed relational situations may be called "relations" as well as two-termed relational situations. And as we use the term "reality," both two-termed and three-termed relational situations may be real. I am, let us agree, related to my brother-in-law. For the relational situation involving my wife and myself and the relational situation involving my wife and her brother compose a three-termed relational situation which itself is real. Similarly, let us hold, Napoleon's death may have position with respect to his birth. That is to say, the spatial relation between two 1821 events and the temporal relation between the 1769 and the 1821 phases of an enduring entity compose a three-termed relational situation which may itself be real.[4] In order for this three-termed relational situation to be real, the two-termed relational situations which compose it must, it would seem, be real; and the three-termed relational situation which includes them must not appear with characteristics that would mark it out as unreal. In order that there may be a real three-termed relational situation within which the dying Napoleon has position with respect to the birth of Napoleon, this alleged relational situation can not appear as having no date with respect to an entity that appears real, can not appear as having no position with respect to an entity that appears real and with respect to which it appears present, can not appear as generally discredited.[5]

But these, we hold, are conditions which are met. And so we go on to find listed as real the position which the dying Napoleon is alleged to have with respect to the birth of Napoleon relative to an enduring Napoleon; and the position which the dying Napoleon is alleged to have with respect to the birth of Napoleon relative to an enduring Ajaccio. Relative to an enduring Napoleon, the dying Napoleon is here with respect to his birth. And relative to an enduring Ajaccio, the dying Napoleon has a position with respect to the birth of Napoleon, a position, namely, identical with that which St. Helena in 1821 has with respect to Ajaccio in 1821. The plates in our box, it would seem, move back and forth at our will in their planes. If our perpendicular line pierces our 1769 plate at the birth of Napoleon at Ajaccio, we can, it would seem, move our 1821 plate in its plane at will so as to have the perpendicular pierce it at Ajaccio, at St. Helena, or at any other point.

Relative to an enduring Ajaccio, St. Helena in 1821 has a certain position with respect to the birth of Napoleon, a position identical with that which St. Helena in 1821 has with respect to Ajaccio in 1821. But with respect to the birth of Napoleon in 1769, the 1769 phase of St. Helena had a similar position. That is to say, if a 1821 measuring stick stretching from Ajaccio to St. Helena could be carried back to 1769, it might be found to fit exactly the distance between the 1769 phases of Ajaccio and St Helena.[6] We have before us then the position that St. Helena in 1821 has with respect to the birth of Napoleon, a position which involves a spatial relation between two 1821 events conjoined with a temporal relation; and we have before us the position that St. Helena in 1769 has with respect to the birth of Napoleon, a position which involves a spatial relation between two 1769 events. One position characterizes St. Helena in 1821, the other characterizes St. Helena in 1769. But when we say that the two positions are similar, we bring into consideration the enduring St. Helena and not merely instantaneous phases of it. Relative to an enduring Ajaccio, it is the enduring St. Helena that has two instantaneous phases with similar positions with respect to a given event.

Relative to an enduring Ajaccio, the enduring St. Helena has two phases, namely, an 1821 phase and a 1769 phase, with similar positions with respect to the birth of Napoleon. But the enduring St. Helena has additional phases with similar positions with respect to the birth of Napoleon. Relative to an enduring Ajaccio, the positions with respect to Napoleon's birth that belong to St. Helena in 1769, to St. Helena in 1803, to St. Helena in 1812 and to St. Helena in 1821 are all similar, indeed, we may say, identical. The St. Helena that endures from 1769 to the death of Napoleon has, we have seen,[7] only a finite number of instantaneous phases. But if the number of real instantaneous phases that it includes is limited only by our failure to make alleged additional phases definite objects, and if no instantaneous phase that is real has a dissimilar position with respect to the birth of Napoleon, then, relative to the enduring Ajaccio, the St. Helena that endures from 1769 to the death of Napoleon is, let us say, "at rest." Using "at rest" in this sense, the enduring St. Helena is indeed at rest relative to the enduring Ajaccio. For, whereas we have recognized the possibility of bodies being intermittent, we should, if intermittence really characterized Ajaccio and St. Helena, call these substances enduring substances which in some of their phases are material and in some of their phases immaterial.[8] There are no two successive phases of either Ajaccio or of St. Helena such that we will be balked in our efforts to find another real phase (which may turn out to be material or immaterial) between them. And there is no phase of St. Helena which *is* real—whether it be material or immaterial—that lacks position with respect either to the phase of Ajaccio contemporaneous with it or with respect to the 1769 phase of Ajaccio; no phase, indeed, whose position with respect to the birth of Napoleon is dissimilar to the positions with respect to this event of other phases of St. Helena. The instantaneous phases which the enduring St. Helena includes have

397

all of them similar positions with respect to a given event. Taken by themselves, however, these instantaneous phases are not at rest. They are at rest only in the sense that they are instantaneous phases of a resting enduring entity; and even in this sense they are at rest relative to the enduring Ajaccio and not relative to some instantaneous phase of Ajaccio.

We turn now from the enduring Ajaccio as our point of reference to the enduring Napoleon or, rather, to the enduring September 1815 phase of Napoleon. St. Helena at the end of the month has a position with respect to Napoleon-at-the-beginning-of-the-month identical with that which it has with respect to Napoleon-at-the-end-of-the-month. For the position which the September thirtieth phase of St. Helena has with respect to the September first phase of Napoleon involves the spatial relation between the two September thirtieth contemporaries plus an interval in the life of Napoleon. But these positions that St. Helena at the end of the month has with respect to both phases of Napoleon differ from the position that St. Helena at the beginning of the month had with respect to the phase of Napoleon that was its contemporary. During the month Napoleon was on board the "Northumberland" and he was continually approaching St. Helena or, taking Napoleon as our point of reference, St. Helena was continually approaching *him*. If a measuring stick, that on September thirtieth stretched from St. Helena to the "Northumberland," could be applied to the distance that on September first separated St. Helena from the "Northumberland," there would be much open water that it would not span.[9] Relative to the enduring Napoleon, St. Helena, as we have seen, has as many real instantaneous phases as we choose to make definite objects; although some of them may turn out to be immaterial.[10] So it is, we have seen, with respect to the enduring Ajaccio; and so it is with respect to Napoleon during September, 1815. Just as there is no real phase of St. Helena that lacks position with respect either to the phase of Ajaccio contemporaneous with it or with respect to the 1769 phase of Ajaccio, so there is no real phase of St. Helena during September 1815 that lacks position with respect either to the phase of Napoleon contemporaneous with it or with respect to the September first phase of Napoleon. But whereas, relative to an enduring Ajaccio, no two instantaneous phases of St. Helena

398

have dissimilar positions with respect to the birth of Napoleon, relative to Napoleon during September 1815 no two instantaneous phases of St. Helena have *similar* positions with respect to the September first phase of Napoleon. The enduring St. Helena we called "at rest" with respect to the enduring Ajaccio; the enduring St. Helena we call "in motion" with respect to the enduring Napoleon of September, 1815. It is the enduring St. Helena which, as we use "rest" and "motion," is at rest with respect to one enduring point of reference and in motion with respect to another. It is the enduring St. Helena, that is to say, whose real instantaneous phases have, in the one case, all of them similar, and, in the other case, all of them dissimilar, positions with respect to a given event.[11] "Rest" and "motion," in short, are terms that we use to point to qualities of enduring entities, to qualities that enduring entities have relative to one enduring point of reference or another. And just as an instantaneous phase is at rest only in the sense that it is an instantaneous phase of an enduring entity at rest, so an instantaneous phase is in motion only in the sense that it is an instantaneous phase of an enduring entity in motion.

Let us suppose that an object rests in one position, then in a slightly different position. Relative to a given enduring point of reference, the initial phase of our object has a certain position and a second phase has a similar position. A third phase, however, has, let us suppose, a dissimilar position, and a fourth phase has a position similar to that of the third phase. Taken as a whole, our enduring object is neither what we call "at rest" nor what we call "in motion." For the positions that its various instantaneous phases have are neither all of them similar nor all of them dissimilar. The enduring phase of our object which endures from its first instantaneous phase to the second is, it would seem, at rest. But, we ask, is the enduring phase of it which endures from the second instantaneous phase to the third in motion? If efforts to present to ourselves phases of our object later than the second and earlier than the third could meet with frustration, our object would be neither at rest nor in motion. And if our efforts to present to ourselves such intermediate phases did not meet with frustration, if intermediate phases were real, then the motion or rest of the enduring phase under discussion would depend upon the type of position that these intermediate phases were found to have.

Let us suppose, however, that no intermediate phases are sought and that as a consequence the third instantaneous phase of our object is the first real instantaneous phase subsequent to the second. One phase of our object has then a given position; the next real phase a dissimilar position. As we are explaining our term "motion," such a state of affairs is one in which there is an object in motion; for, included within the enduring phase of our object that endures from what we have called the second instantaneous phase to the third, there are as many instantaneous phases as we choose to seek and no two instantaneous phases with similar positions.

In the sense in which we are using the term "motion," there are, let us agree, real instances of entities in motion. In this sense of the term "motion," the September 1815 phase of St. Helena, let us agree, was in motion with respect to Napoleon; and today's phase of the sun is in motion with respect to the Capitol at Washington. They and a finite number of other enduring entities are really in motion with respect to enduring points of reference outside them.

Indeed, as we are using the term "motion," real instances of motion need not be limited to enduring substances whose included phases are all material. If the Capitol at Washington is intermittent and includes immaterial as well as material phases, it may still be in motion relative to a given enduring entity outside it. For we may regard instantaneous phases while it is immaterial as phases of the Capitol; and we may find the positions of these phases dissimilar to each other and dissimilar to the positions of other phases of the Capitol. Indeed substances whose phases are all immaterial may really be in motion, as we are using the term "motion." There may be a bit of empty space that is a definite object, an entity that is regarded as the same substance as a later bit of empty space elsewhere. We may think of a bit of empty space in the same direction as the sun, but twice as distant;[12] we may never be frustrated in our attempts to present to ourselves additional instantaneous phases of this enduring immaterial substance; and we may find no two such instantaneous phases with similar positions. But it is at most only a finite num-

400

ber of bits of empty space that we *do* make definite objects; hence at most only a finite number of enduring bits of empty space that can be found to be in motion.

It may also be pointed out that, as we are explaining "rest" and "motion," an enduring entity is neither at rest nor in motion with respect to an enduring point of reference which lacks instantaneous phases corresponding to some of its own. The enduring September 1815 phase of St. Helena is in motion relative to the September 1815 phase of Napoleon. But that phase of St. Helena which endures through the nineteenth century is not. For an 1850 phase of St. Helena finds no instantaneous phase included within the Napoleon of September 1815 with respect to which to have position. It has no position with respect to a given event in Napoleon's life that might be found similar or dissimilar to the position that some earlier instantaneous phase of St. Helena has.

With our terminology thus explained and with these observations behind us, let us consider the situations brought to our attention by Zeno's well-known arguments. "You must traverse the half of any given distance," says Zeno,[13] "before you traverse the whole, and the half of that again before you can traverse it." Relative to the starting point, that phase of our runner in which he begins his journey is 'here,' that phase in which he reaches his goal 'there.' Let us agree that there are intermediate instantaneous phases and that no two of them have similar positions with respect to the starting point. But how many intermediate instantaneous phases and successive positions are there? And how does the runner live to the next phase and advance to the next position if there are always prior phases to be lived through and nearer positions to be traversed? The infinitist will hold that our runner enduring from the beginning of his journey to its end, enduring with a limited duration, lives, nevertheless, through an infinite number of instantaneous phases. To be aware of each of these instantaneous phases, our runner would require an infinite duration. But to live through them without making each one a definite object is no more self-contradictory than it is for a two-inch line to include an infinite number of points. As we use the term "existence," an infinite number of instantaneous phases does not exist. But our rejection of the infinist view has been due, not to any intrinsic self-contradiction involved in that view, but to one of those elements in our explanation of "existence" that, taken together, correspond to the principle of sufficient reason.[14] So far as we have yet seen, there is no self-contradiction involved in holding that the runner lives through an infinite number of instantaneous phases and that, correspondingly, he has successively an infinite number of positions. It is simply that the assertion of such a view does not describe what exists in our sense of "existence."

But even if our runner had an infinite number of instantaneous phases, no two of them would be simultaneous. There would, it would seem, be one such that only the initial phase preceded it and such that all others, infinite in number, followed it. In short, there would, we hold, be an instantaneous phase of our runner immediately following his initial phase. Since, by hypothesis, it would require an infinite duration to discover all of the instantaneous phases included within the duration of his journey, no finite duration would suffice to present to us this instantaneous phase that would be immediately subsequent to our runner's initial phase. There would, to be sure, be an infinite number of real instantaneous phases included within each finite duration. But the duration between our runner's initial phase and his next instantaneous phase would not be finite, but, we may say, infinitesimal. The infinitist hypothesis in the form in which we find it most nearly acceptable has thus implications in two directions, implications however which are not irreconcilable, the one with the other. It seems on the one hand to imply that there is an infinite number of instantaneous phases included within any phase of our runner having a finite duration. And it seems on the other hand to imply that there is no instantaneous phase at all within that phase of the runner which endures from the initial phase to the immediately following phase. Our runner would endure up to this immediately following phase without having endured through any intermediate instantaneous phase.

An infinitist view can thus be developed which, whereas it is untrue, is not intrinsically self-contradictory. Similarly one need not be involved in self-contradiction when one holds that our runner lives through a finite number of instantaneous phases, a number so great that we do not in fact make each of these phases a definite object; and when one holds that our runner has successively a correspondingly great number of positions, some of which

402

are not presented to us as definite objects. The initial phase of the runner, on this view, is immediately followed by an instantaneous phase that occurs after a finite interval, but so soon afterwards that we do not present it to ourselves as a definite object; and this immediately following phase has a position with respect to the starting point, so close that we likewise do not present it to ourselves as a definite object. On the view which we are now examining, however, it would require, not an infinite duration, but a greater finite duration than we do in fact have at our disposal to present to ourselves that phase of our runner which immediately follows the initial one. With a duration at our disposal greater than this would require, we should find, it may be held, no prior intermediate phases and possibly no positions nearer the starting point. For in dealing with finite intervals between adjacent instantaneous phases, in dealing, that is to say, with what might be called atomic or elementary finite durations, the subject-matter, it might be held, would balk our efforts at sub-division in a manner in which it does not do so when we are dealing with greater durations and in a manner, in consequence, for which our experiences will never prepare us. We can, to be sure, refer in words to an intermediate phase within the atomic or elementary finite duration which itself will never be presented to us. But whereas, on the view which we are examining, the elementary finite duration which will never be presented to us is real, our verbal expressions apparently referring to an intermediate phase within this duration do *not* refer to anything real.

It is not self-contradictory, it would seem, to hold that the alleged elementary finite duration which will never be presented to us is real; and to hold that the alleged instantaneous phase within it, which likewise will never be presented to us as a definite object, is unreal. But such assertions imply a signification of "existence" different from our own. As we have chosen to use "existence," a subsistent appearing as no one's definite object is unreal.[15] The alleged elementary finite duration that, it is held, will never be presented to us as a definite object is unreal; and so is the alleged instantaneous phase within this duration. So likewise are the infinitesimal durations and the positions infinitely close to the runner's starting point which it would allegedly require an infinite duration to present to ourselves as definite objects. It is our doctrine,—deduced, we hold, from our propositions explaining "existence,"—that the first real instantaneous phase of our runner to follow his initial phase is one that is not presented as no one's definite object, one that is in effect presented as a definite object for some one. The interval intervening between the initial phase and this next instantaneous phase has a finite duration, a duration, however, the determination of which is more a matter of psychology than of physics. For the duration of this interval is determined by the persistence with which subjects present to themselves as definite objects instantaneous phases of the runner closer and closer to his initial phase. It is as enduring as the most persistent seeker of next phases permits it to be.

The subject-matter, we hold, will never block us in our attempts to present to ourselves real instantaneous phases of the runner closer and closer to his initial phase. But there is an end to persistence and, with it, an end to the series of closer and closer instantaneous phases. There is the initial phase of our runner when he is at the starting point; then no instantaneous phase of him and no position occupied by him until the next real instantaneous phase when, taking the earth to be at rest, his position is different. There are as many instantaneous phases of our runner as we choose to seek, and yet no two of them with similar positions. Hence, as we have explained "motion," our runner is in motion.[16] It is however the enduring runner who is in motion, or some enduring phase of him that includes at least two instantaneous phases. "An instantaneous phase is in motion only in the sense that it is an instantaneous phase of an enduring entity in motion." [17]

It may be objected, however, that our view just outlined, along with the infinitist and finitist views that we have rejected, reduces motion to a touching of positions. "What the cinematograph does," says Bergson,[18] "is to take a series of snap-shots of the passing regiment and to throw these instantaneous views on the screen so that they replace each other very rapidly." On the infinitist view which we examined, two successive snapshots are separated by an interval having an infinitesimal duration. For the finitist who holds that the never-to-be-discovered instants are finite in number, two successive snap-shots are separated by an interval having a finite, though perhaps an unattainably small,

404

duration. And on our view they are separated by an interval which is as enduring as the most persistent seeker of snap-shots permits it to be. Yet all three views, it may be said, present to us a series of snap-shots rather than motion itself. There is, says Bergson,[19] "more in the transition than the series of states, that is to say, the possible cuts—more in the movement than the series of positions, that is to say, the possible stops."

Now it can hardly be maintained that the term "motion" can not be assigned the meaning which we assign it. Our runner *does* have a series of successive instantaneous phases. Each of these phases *does* have a different position with respect to his starting point. And the term "motion" may be assigned a meaning from which it follows that the enduring runner having these instantaneous phases is in motion with respect to his starting point. What may be maintained, however, is that the meaning which we have assigned our term "motion" is not identical with the meaning which the term "motion" commonly has. In addition to the motion that touches—which we have found real,—there is to be considered, it may be held, an alleged motion that flows.

In order to put an alleged motion that flows before us, let us go back to the box of plates with which we began this chapter. In addition to the paper-thin plates, each of which represented a set of instantaneous entities contemporaneous with each other, let us suppose our box to have inserted in it plates which are not paper-thin but thick. Entities exist which have duration but which nevertheless are, roughly speaking, contemporaneous with one another. Thus, roughly speaking, the enduring Descartes and the enduring Hobbes were contemporaries, the 1812 phase of Napoleon and the 1812 phase of Wellington contemporaries, Gladstone and Disraeli contemporaries. A plate having some thickness may accordingly be used to represent a set of entities each of which has some duration but each of which is in an indefinite sense contemporaneous with all other members of the set. The fact that various points on a two-inch line are real does not keep the extended line which includes them from being real. The fact that the legs of a chair are real does not keep the chair taken as a whole which has a somewhat similar position, but a less definitely located position, from being real. And, reverting to our metaphor of a box of plates, our paper-thin plates do not hinder the insertion among them of plates having some thickness, of plates of which they themselves may be regarded as cross-sections.

There exist, let us agree, pairs of entities each having some duration where one is in an indefinite sense contemporaneous with the other. And with respect to such a pair of entities, one, it may be said, is not only contemporaneous with respect to the other, but 'moving' with respect to the other. One may, that is to say, use the term "motion" to point to an alleged quality which one entity has with respect to another enduring entity in an indefinite sense contemporaneous with it. During a brief period on a summer's afternoon I may, for example, be sitting on my porch and a dog chasing a squirrel in my garden. There are phases of me, of dog and of squirrel, each having some duration, but all in an indefinite sense contemporaneous with one another. Now without attending to the instantaneous phases which each of these enduring phases include, we may say that the dog is in motion with respect to me, and the squirrel also. Instead of using the term "motion" to point to a quality which an enduring entity has by virtue of the different positions which its successive instantaneous phases have, "motion" may be used to point to an unanalyzed quality which briefly enduring phases have with respect to other briefly enduring phases which are in an indefinite sense contemporaneous with them.

There are, let us agree, instances of motion, when "motion" is used in this second sense. There is a motion which flows as well as a motion which touches. It may well be that, wherever there is an instance of a motion which flows, there is an instance of a motion which touches. It may well be that wherever there is a *perceptible* motion, such as characterizes the phase of the dog running in my garden, there exists a succession of instantaneous phases, each with a different position. The entity however which is presented as having a motion which flows, and not presented with a motion which touches, is not presented *with* the instantaneous phases which it may well have. Indeed, in so far as an entity is merely presented as having a motion which *flows*, its motion can not be numbered. For it is only by considering initial instantaneous phases, final instantaneous phases, and the distances traversed in the intervals between them, that numbers can be

406

assigned to the speeds of moving objects. It is the motion which touches that can be numbered. And it is in connection with a motion which touches that the problems treated by Zeno arise. We evade these problems, and we also cut ourselves off from the possibility of assigning numbers to motion, when we limit our attention to the motion which flows. To do this however is to close our eyes to something that is real and that calls for discussion. When "motion" is used to point to a motion which flows, it points to something real. But when "motion" is used as we have for the most part used it in this chapter, when it is used to point to a motion which touches, it likewise points to something real. It is thus no pseudo-problem with which we deal when we ask how a runner can reach the end of his journey or, indeed, begin it. And it is not giving an answer not relevant to reality when it is stated that the runner has as many instantaneous phases as we choose to seek and passes through no positions that are presented as not definite objects.

Our runner *does* have a series of instantaneous phases, *does* touch a series of positions. In living from the initial phase to the next real instantaneous phase, he no more has to live through alleged intermediate instantaneous phases or to touch alleged intermediate positions than a man at the most distant of all real positions would have to hurl a javelin beyond it. If the javelin were hurled and its resting place presented as a definite object, he would not be at the most distant of all real positions.[20] And if an intermediate instantaneous phase is definitely presented to us as one that the runner has lived through, what we have taken to be the 'next' real instantaneous phase is not the next. By hypothesis, the runner's next instantaneous phase is the very next that will be presented as a definite object. Any nearer instantaneous phase that he may be alleged to have lived through is presented as no one's definite object, is unreal, and can not truly be said to be one that he has lived through.

The situation which Zeno describes in the "Stadium" may be transferred to the stage of a theatre. Let us imagine three individuals side by side at the rear of a theatre stage, hidden from our view by three other individuals who place themselves alongside one another in front of them. We must now introduce three additional individuals who place themselves side by side at the front of the stage and who conceal those in the second row as these conceal those in the rear. The individuals in the second row now each move a pace to the left, so that the middle member of this group comes to be directly in front of the left end member of the back row. And the individuals in the front row each move a pace to the right so that the middle member of this group comes to be directly in front of the right end member of the back row. Whereas the one on the left in the front row was in front of the one on the left in the back row, now, having moved to the right, he is in front of the middle member of the rear group. But, whereas he was in front of the left end member of the second row, now, since the members of the second row have also been moving, he is in front of the right end member of the second row.

Suppose now that our individuals are mere points and that they are separated from their neighbors by distances in which no points intervene. Suppose further that there are no instantaneous phases of any of our nine objects between the phases in which they have their initial positions and the phases in which they have the positions that they have when the motions that have been described have been completed. In one instantaneous phase the left end member of the front row is in front of the left end member of the second row; and in its very next instantaneous phase it is in front of the right end member of the second row. No intervening instantaneous phase of it exists in which it might be in front of the middle member of the second row. By hypothesis we do not fix our attention upon our member of the front row in the act of passing the middle member of the second row. And if, contrary to our hypothesis, we do fix our attention upon this intervening phase of it and do present it to ourselves as a definite object, then it *has* an intervening phase in which it is in front of the middle member of the second row; and the instantaneous phase in which it is in front of the right end member of the second row is not its next.

If it *has* the intervening phase, either this intervening phase is presented to us neither as having nor as lacking position with respect to some member of the row in the rear. Or, if its relation to some member of the rear row is presented as a definite object, the rear row contains more than three real members and, contrary to our original hypothesis, the members of this row first presented to us are not separated from their neighbors by distances in which no points intervene. In destroying our hypothesis, we merely show ourselves to have misjudged the number of points or instantaneous phases that are to be definite objects.

The "Achilles and the tortoise" calls, we hold, for a similar treatment. Prior to catching the tortoise there are as many instantaneous phases of Achilles as we choose to present to ourselves as definite objects; and, contemporaneous with each of them, an instantaneous phase of the tortoise ahead of him. There is however a final stage which Achilles begins by being behind the tortoise and ends by being abreast of him. There is no instantaneous phase of Achilles at which he has a position similar to that from which the tortoise begins the final stage; just as in the "Stadium" there is no instantaneous phase of our member of the front row in which he is passing the middle member of the second row. The alleged instantaneous phase of Achilles in which he might have such a position is, by hypothesis, presented as no one's definite object. For, by hypothesis, the instantaneous phase from which he begins the final stage of the chase, the instantaneous phase which has a tortoise in advance contemporaneous with it, is Achilles' very last instantaneous phase, preceding the final one, that will be a definite object and real.

There are, it follows, more points on the path than Achilles will touch. Nevertheless the enduring Achilles is in motion with respect to the enduring tortoise and with respect to the enduring path. For in order that there may be motion, as we have explained our term "motion," it is not necessary that each instantaneous phase of the enduring point of reference have a phase of the moving object contemporaneous with it. It is necessary that the number of the moving object's instantaneous phases be limited only by our failure to make alleged additional phases definite objects.[21] And it is necessary that no two instantaneous phases of our moving object, no two phases that we do make definite objects, lack position or have similar positions. These conditions are fulfilled—and the enduring Achilles is in motion, as we have explained "motion"—even though there be points on the path that he does not touch. Similarly the runner whom we considered a few pages back is in motion, the runner whose first instantaneous phase after leaving his starting point has a position dissimilar to that of his initial phase.[22] He is in motion whether or not points intervene between the starting point and the position he next occupies.

We turn now to figure 1 in which O_1O_2 is an enduring point of reference, P_1P_2 an enduring point that is in motion with respect to it. P_1 has a position with respect to its contemporary O_1 and, relative to the enduring O_1O_2, P_2 has a dissimilar position with respect to O_1, the position, namely, that it has with respect to O_2, the instantaneous phase of O_1O_2 that is its contemporary.[23] The enduring P_1P_2, taken as a single enduring object, has no single punctual position with respect to O_1O_2. But if P_1P_2 is to be real and O_1O_2 real, the former can not be presented to us as lacking position with respect to the O_1O_2 that in an indefinite sense is its contemporary. Although my dog is running, a phase of him having duration is nevertheless out there where my garden is.[24] And although P_1P_2 is in motion, it is nevertheless above and to the left with respect to the enduring O_1O_2.

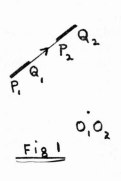

Fig 1

Let us however consider, not the moving enduring point P_1P_2, but the moving enduring extended entity $P_1Q_1–P_2Q_2$. The instantaneous phase P_1Q_1 has a position, though not a punctual position, with respect to the O_1 that is its contemporary. And relative to an enduring O_1O_2, the later instantaneous phase P_2Q_2 has a dissimilar position which likewise is not punctual. The enduring entity $P_1Q_1–P_2Q_2$ has a duration similar to that of the enduring entity P_1P_2 and its position with respect to the enduring entity O_1O_2 is only slightly less definite. It too, that is to say, is above and to the left. But unlike P_1, P_1Q_1 has length. What it has, and what the instantaneous phase P_2Q_2 likewise has, is, it will be recalled,[25] an unnumbered or pre-numbered length that is absolute and a numbered length that is relative to spatio-temporal entities outside it. But the enduring $P_1Q_1–P_2Q_2$ has, we shall say, taken as a whole, no length at all. The instantaneous phases P_1Q_1 and P_2Q_2 are in motion, we have said,[26] only in the sense that they are instantaneous phases of the enduring moving entity $P_1Q_1–P_2Q_2$. And, on the other hand, the enduring entity

410

P_1Q_1—P_2Q_2 has length only in the sense that it includes instantaneous phases that have length, instantaneous phases such as P_1Q_1 and P_2Q_2.

Let us suppose that, in measuring the length of PQ, we move a measuring stick along it, starting at P and counting the times our stick is applied before the stick reaches Q. We begin measuring by placing one end of our stick over P_1. But when our stick covers Q, it covers a phase of Q that is not contemporaneous with P_1; it covers a later phase of Q that we may call Q_2. If P Q is in motion with respect to the enduring point O, if P_1Q_1 and P_2Q_2 have such positions as are shown in the figure on page 410, our measuring carries us from P_1 to Q_2. But P_1Q_2, not being an instantaneous entity, has in itself no length. Even if P Q is at rest with respect to O, even if Q_1 and Q_2 have similar positions with respect to O_1, we complete our measuring by having our stick over Q_2, not over Q_1. Measurement, in short 'takes time.' [27] In measuring we are dealing in the first instance, not with P_1Q_1 or with P_2Q_2, not with instantaneous phases that have length, but with the enduring P_1Q_2 that in itself has no length.

Measurement 'takes time'; and it also involves motion with respect to the entity being measured. The measuring stick is moved along P Q. Or, if measurements are recorded at the enduring point of reference O_1O_2, there are particles or waves that move from phases of P and Q to later phases of O. Nevertheless the numbers that our measuring puts before us are applied to the instantaneous entity P_1Q_1. We may be presented with one set of numbers to apply to P_1Q_1 in so far as P_1Q_1 is regarded as an instantaneous phase of an entity at rest with respect to our enduring point of reference, with another set of numbers to apply to P_1Q_1 in so far as P_1Q_1 is regarded as an instantaneous phase of an entity in motion with respect to our enduring point of reference. But it is still only instantaneous phases that have length.[28]

To sum up, P_1Q_1 has unnumbered length as an absolute quality. But the application of numbers to this length involves a reference to spatio-temporal entities outside P_1Q_1. P_1Q_1 is one inch long, not absolutely, but as measured from O, making use of information obtained from P_1Q_2. P_1Q_2, on the other hand, has no length to which numbers may really be applied. For, the numbers with which we are presented when we measure P_1Q_2

apply, not to P_1Q_2 but to instantaneous phases that do have length.

What $P_1 Q_1$ has, and what $P_2 Q_2$ likewise has, is "an unnumbered or pre-numbered length that is absolute and a numbered length that is relative to spatio-temporal entities outside it." [29] What $P_1 P_2$ has, and what $P_1 Q_1 - P_2 Q_2$ has, is similarly an unnumbered or pre-numbered *duration* that is absolute and a numbered duration that is relative to other entities.[30] In the process of assigning numbers to the duration of $P_1 P_2$, or to the duration of $P_1 Q_1 - P_2 Q_2$, we make use of clocks or we make use of light or electrical waves or we make use of both. What we find is that the numbers to be assigned to $P_1 P_2$'s duration vary with the relative motion of the entity from which that duration is measured. But it is again to be pointed out that we have already jumped into a world of both spatial and temporal relations when we first begin numbering either lengths or durations.

P_1 has position with respect to its contemporary O_1, St. Helena in 1821 position with respect to its contemporary: Ajaccio in 1821. To use numbers, however, in describing the position that P_1 has with respect to O_1, to say, for example, that P_1 is one centimeter north of O_1, is to assign a number to the length of O_1P_1. Similarly to say that St. Helena in 1821 has a position three thousand miles from Ajaccio in 1821 is to assign a number to a distance, to the length of a path. Since the numbered length that a line or path has varies with the spatio-temporal entities from which that length is measured, the numbered position that P_1 has with respect to O_1, or that St. Helena in 1821 has with respect to Ajaccio in 1821, likewise varies. But just as we have held that there is an unnumbered length that $O_1 P_1$ has that is not relative to spatio-temporal entities outside $O_1 P_1$, so we hold that P_1 has an unnumbered position with respect to O_1 that is not relative to other entities.[31]

St. Helena in 1821 has an unnumbered position with respect to Ajaccio in 1821 that may be measured from various entities and may hence be assigned various numbers. But the position that St. Helena in 1821 has with respect to Ajaccio in 1769 is, we have seen, relative to some enduring point of reference.[32] Depending upon the enduring point of reference we choose, the Ajaccio in 1769, with respect to which St. Helena in 1821 may be claimed to have position, may be projected into 1821 in various ways. If Napoleon is

412

our enduring point of reference, our phrase: "the position that St. Helena in 1821 has with respect to Ajaccio in 1769" points to the position that St. Helena in 1821 has with respect to itself. And if Ajaccio or St. Helena is our enduring point of reference, our phrase: "the position that St. Helena in 1821 has with respect to Ajaccio in 1769" points to the position that St. Helena in 1821 has with respect to Ajaccio in 1821. With respect to Ajaccio in 1821, St. Helena in 1821 is "there"; it has an unnumbered position that may be assigned various numbers. With respect to St. Helena in 1821, St. Helena in 1821 is here; it has an unnumbered position that may or may not be assigned various numbers.

"The position of St. Helena in 1821 with respect to Ajaccio in 1769" is however relative and incomplete, whereas it is merely the *numbered* position of St. Helena in 1821 with respect to Ajaccio in 1821 that is relative and incomplete. With respect to Ajaccio in 1821, St. Helena in 1821 has an unnumbered position that may be assigned various numbers. But my phrase: "the position that St. Helena in 1821 has with respect to Ajaccio in 1769" may refer to the unnumbered position that St. Helena in 1821 has with respect to Ajaccio in 1821 or to the unnumbered position that St. Helena in 1821 has with respect to St. Helena in 1821 or to the unnumbered position that St. Helena in 1821 has with respect to some other contemporary. In one case we know what we are talking about but not how it is going to be measured. In the other case we do not know what we are talking about until the enduring point of reference has been made explicit.

With respect to Ajaccio in 1821, St. Helena in 1821 has an unnumbered position which may be assigned various numbers. Similarly with respect to the birth of Napoleon, the death of Napoleon has an unnumbered *date* which may be assigned various numbers. Indeed, since Napoleon might not be the only enduring entity beginning in Ajaccio in 1769 and ending in St. Helena in 1821, there may be several durations and several intervals;[33] the event of 1821 may have with respect to the event of 1769 several unnumbered dates, each of them capable of being assigned various numbers. Neglecting this possibility, however, and directing our attention to the duration of Napoleon, we have agreed that this duration will have one number assigned to it if measured from an entity at rest with respect to Napoleon, another number if measured from an entity at rest with respect to the surface of the earth.[34] However we measure, nevertheless, it is the same Napoleon who endures; it is an unequivocal duration of his that is being numbered.

We talk about speeds of ten miles per hour or three centimeters per second. The numbers that we thus assign to the motions of moving entities are quotients derived by dividing the numbers of numbered lengths by the numbers of numbered durations. Since the application of numbers to both lengths and durations brings into consideration spatio-temporal entities from which measurements are made, the determination of speeds, the application of numbers to the motions of moving entities, also brings such spatio-temporal entities into consideration. Moreover, since the lengths involved indicate distances between non-contemporaries, the determination of speeds brings into consideration an enduring point of reference as well. It is with respect to an enduring light-house and not with respect to an enduring star that a given ship has a speed of ten miles per hour. And it is with respect to that enduring light-house, as measured from it and not as measured from another ship, that it has that definite speed.

There is no speed, it has been asserted, that is greater than the speed of light. No matter what entity we choose as our enduring point of reference and no matter what entity we make our measurements from, numbers in excess of a certain maximum, we are told, will not be found applicable to speeds. It may be that such a result follows from the assumptions we make in assigning numbers to lengths and to durations and hence in determining speeds,—that is, in assigning numbers to the motions of moving entities. But there may be moving entities that are bodies and moving entities that are not bodies. "We may think of a bit of empty space in the same direction as the sun but twice as distant; we may never be frustrated in our attempts to present to ourselves additional instantaneous phases of this enduring immaterial substance; and we may find no two such instantaneous phases with similar positions." [35] We may, similarly, present to ourselves a substance in motion which yesterday had an instantaneous phase in common with Arcturus, which today is a bit of empty space moving in the direction of the North Star and which tomorrow will have an instantaneous phase in common with Polaris. Such

414

a substance which is now material and now immaterial is in motion with respect to the earth. If it, as contrasted with the material entities it from time to time passes through, is the source of no vibrations reaching us, perhaps its speed can not be measured. But with respect to the earth it is in motion, whether or not it has a measurable speed. Its motion, whether measurable or not, belongs outside the scope of any dictum as to maximum speeds.

We have had occasion to distinguish motions that touch from motions that flow.[36] In so far as we divide the numbers of numbered lengths by the numbers of numbered durations and thus talk about speeds of ten miles per hour or three centimeters per second, we are assigning numbers to motions that touch. That is to say, we are regarding an entity in motion as one that has a series of different positions at successive instantaneous phases. If however there is a motion that flows, then, as flowing, it would seem, no dissection into successive positions and instantaneous phases is permissible and no numbering possible.

A line, we have said,[37] "may have length, a quality which each point composing it, taken individually, lacks." Similarly an entity in motion, whether it be motion that flows or motion that touches, may have qualities that instantaneous phases of that entity do not have. An entity in motion has duration, whereas the individual instantaneous phases that, taken together, *are* that entity in motion do not have duration.[38] Just as we have suggested that percepts may be restricted to entities that are neither inextended nor greatly extended,[39] so it may be suggested that only entities having some small duration, enduring through some "specious present," may be percepts. If however we agree that instantaneous phases, taken individually, are not percepts, it does not follow that certain collections of instantaneous phases, taken collectively, and together constituting an entity in motion, can not be percepts. The flying arrow is in motion with respect to the observer on the earth; and certain not too long enduring phases of this arrow may be percepts with respect to this observer. He may, as we say, *see* the arrow in motion with respect to the earth, *see* the tree at rest with respect to the earth. But if this be true, the enduring phase of the moving arrow and the enduring phase of the resting tree that are percepts, and the instantaneous phases of arrow and tree that are not percepts, are equally real.

A ship, let us suppose, is gliding down a river; and a phase of the moving ship that has duration, not an instantaneous phase, is a percept with respect to the observer on the bank. While the ship moving down-stream is real and a percept, we may imagine a subsisting ship that has remained upstream, a subsisting ship that claims to be at rest. But in contrast to the moving ship that was a percept, the alleged ship that was at rest and that is alleged still to be at rest upstream appears with the characteristic of being generally discredited. Let us suppose, however, that I am looking at a house, first at the attic, then at the ground floor, then at the basement.[40] It is first the attic at rest that is my percept, finally the basement at rest. While I am looking at the basement, I may imagine that the upper stories, now unseen, have vanished or have moved and been transformed into the basement that I see. But since my percept was an attic at rest, an alleged attic in motion, or that has since vanished, is presented to me with the characteristic of being generally discredited. Upstream now empty of ship and attic still at the top of the house and at rest are not so presented. Upstream now empty of ship and attic still at the top of the house are not percepts, but they are real. Ship still upstream and attic no longer at the top of the house are likewise presented as not percepts. But since they are not inferred from the entities that previously were percepts, since, on the contrary, they appear generally discredited, they are unreal.

Although the phase of the attic that is a percept is prior to the phase of the basement that is a later percept, there is an unseen phase of the basement contemporaneous with the seen phase of the attic; and an unseen phase of the attic contemporaneous with the seen phase of the basement. Entities perceived successively may be phases of entities that have phases contemporaneous with one another. Indeed the very phases that are perceived successively may be contemporaneous with one another. The phase of the sun that is a percept for a present mental attitude of mine may be contemporaneous with a phase of the tree that was a percept for a mental attitude of mine some eight minutes ago. And, similarly, mental attitudes that are simultaneous may have objects that are not contemporaneous with one another. For, physicists and astronomers have taught us to distinguish simultaneity among per-

416

ceivings from simultaneity among percepts. They have brought it about, that is to say, that objects of simultaneous perceivings, presented as simultaneous with one another, appear in certain instances as generally discredited.[41]

The ship that was upstream is a moving ship and an enduring ship that in one of its phases was upstream and now, in a later phase, is downstream. There is also a certain section of the river—let us call it: "upstream"—that is enduring and at rest. Simultaneous with the phase of the ship that is down-stream, there is a phase of 'upstream' that is empty of ship. But previously there was a phase of 'upstream' that was not empty of ship. Both ship and 'upstream' have duration and various instantaneous phases; and one of the instantaneous phases of 'upstream' was also an instantaneous phase of ship. Just as two lines may intersect one another at a point so that this point is on both of them, so an enduring entity at rest and another enduring entity in motion may have an instantaneous phase in common. The enduring entity that we are calling "upstream" has one instantaneous phase that is also an instantaneous phase of ship; it has a later instantaneous phase that is air and water; and it might even have some phase that is immaterial altogether. If, nevertheless, 'upstream,' taken as an enduring entity that in some of its phases is material and in some of its phases possibly immaterial, is not presented as no one's definite object, 'upstream' may very well be real.

There are, we hold, entities such as 'upstream' that are real, enduring entities at rest that we shall call "places." As we use the term "place," "an enduring entity at rest" and its "place" are expressions representing the same substance. In so far as material entities are at rest, they and their places are not separate substances. And in so far as the material substances with which we concern ourselves are all in motion, the relation between a place, which in many of its phases may be immaterial, and a moving enduring entity, which on some occasion occupies it, is similar to the relation between two intersecting lines. As we have explained "motion" and "place," it may be added, an enduring entity at rest, a "place," need not be an entity most of whose phases are immaterial; nor need an entity in motion be one most or all of whose phases are material. A bit of normally empty space in the same direction as the sun but twice as distant may be in motion;[42] some resting body that it moves through may be the place of one of its phases.

It is of course relative to one enduring point of reference that a given enduring entity is at rest and relative to another enduring point of reference that it is in motion. Hence what are places with respect to one enduring point of reference may not be places with respect to another. It is within the framework of a given enduring point of reference that enduring entities A, B, C, etc., are places. Given this point of reference, the enduring entities A, B, C, etc. that are places are finite in number; and their instantaneous phases that are contemporaneous with one another need not be contiguous. Whether we deal with the collection of all empty spaces, the collection of all body-spaces, or the collection of all spaces, material and immaterial alike, we are dealing with a collection which is discrete and which has a finite number of members.[43]

Let us turn now to the consideration of a wheel with, let us say, twelve spokes which we suppose to be revolving in a clockwise direction with respect to a given enduring point of reference. With respect to this given point of reference there is a place which extends from the hub to where the number "eleven" would appear on a clock, a place from the hub to where the number "twelve" would appear on a clock, and a place from the hub to where the number "one" would appear on a clock. Likewise there is a spoke which now has an instantaneous phase in common with the place which points to "twelve" and is about to have an instantaneous phase in common with the place which points to "one"; and a spoke behind it which now points to "eleven" and is about to point to "twelve."

If the speed with which one spoke revolves is increased or retarded, the other spokes seem to be similarly affected. But since a pre-established harmony seems incredible, it is reasonable to conclude that through motions within the wheel the acceleration is carried from spoke to spoke and hence to conclude that the different spokes do not alter their speeds simultaneously. If however the rate of revolution is constant, one spoke ceases pointing to eleven exactly when the spoke ahead of it ceases pointing to twelve. By what may seem to be a remarkable coincidence all twelve spokes vacate their places simultaneously, or, to use the terms which we have just explained, cease having phases in common with the places with which they have just had them in common. What is a place, however, and what is in motion is, we have said, relative to the enduring point of reference. The enduring point of reference may be so chosen that the wheel is at rest and the spokes themselves places. Hence the coincidence whereby spokes vacate their places simultaneously is, using a different point of reference, the coincidence whereby spokes are at rest with respect to one another, the coincidence whereby the spatial relations obtaining among one set of instantaneous phases turn out to be similar to the spatial relations obtaining among a previous set of instantaneous phases. Whatever would be a satisfactory answer to the question why the spatial relations between New York in 1942 and Washington in 1942 are similar to those between New York in 1932 and the Washington that was its contemporary would be a satisfactory answer to the question why the spokes of a revolving wheel vacate their places simultaneously.

It has sometimes been assumed that a group of substances can not vacate their places simultaneously and, with this premise, it has been argued that some places void of matter are necessary. "If there were not void," writes Lucretius,[44] "by no means could things move; for that which is the office of body, to offend and hinder, would at every moment be present to all things; nothing therefore could advance, since nothing could give the example of yielding place." To reject the premise and hence the necessity of empty places is however not to hold that there are no places with phases which are immaterial. The spoke which has just pointed to eleven may move into a next place whose preceding phase was immaterial. The next place with which it is to have an instantaneous phase in common may just previously have been material or may just previously have been immaterial. And it may be contiguous or not-contiguous to the place which the spoke has just vacated. For, if an alleged contiguous place is presented as no one's definite object, it is unreal and the next real place is one that is not contiguous. Indeed if one were to suppose that the 'next' place is contiguous and previously immaterial, one might still be asked to explain the simultaneous movement of different substances. For in that case the "void" would have to move simultaneously with the spoke behind it. And although this

419

"void" would not be thought of as having as its function to "offend and hinder," it would nevertheless have either to move simultaneously with the spoke behind it or to "give the example of yielding place."

A place, we have said,[45] is an enduring entity at rest, an enduring entity that may be material or immaterial or in one phase material and in a subsequent phase immaterial. In previous chapters we have used the term "space." [46] Among a group of entities contemporaneous with each other, there are points and lines and baseball players and volumes and spheres and bodies and perhaps empty spaces. We have used the term "space" to refer to any volume, a volume that might be filled with matter or be void of matter or be partly material and partly immaterial. It appears then that in our terminology a space is an instantaneous phase of a place. In so far as a body is at rest and hence a place, its instantaneous phases are material spaces; and insofar as there is a place through which bodies and vacua move, its instantaneous phases are now material spaces and now empty spaces.

Our language presents us with the two terms "space" and "place" to which we have chosen to assign different significations. But our language does not present to us an analogous pair of temporal terms. There is only the term: "time"; and even that we have not felt urged to explain or to make use of in this or the preceding chapters. Even though we have in many respects found temporal relations analogous to spatial relations among contemporaries, our treatment of the terms: "space," "place" and "time" is a parting reminder of the differences between spatial relations, temporal relations, and spatial relations among non-contemporaries.

Summary

When two entities are not contemporaneous, the position that one has with respect to the other depends upon what entity is considered to be at rest during the interval from one to the other.

We define rest and motion as a preliminary to discussing Zeno's paradoxes. Whereas neither the finitist nor the infinitist arrives at self-contradictory conclusions, our explanation of "existence" implies that a body in motion touches only a finite number of positions.

Besides motion as we have defined it, there is a motion that flows. The latter exists too, but is not useful when we want to apply numbers.

When we measure motion (motion that touches) we make use of certain assumptions. This may account for certain results such as the fact that the speed of light is a maximum. But when we do not limit our subject matter to moving *bodies,* the speed of light is not a maximum.

Chapter XIV

UNITY AND SUBSTANCE

We have compared entities in their spatial and temporal relations to entities on a series of plates in a box. The entities contemporaneous with Napoleon at the first instantaneous phase of his life we have represented by one plate, the entities contemporaneous with Napoleon at the last instantaneous phase of his life by another plate.[1] The plate, as first introduced, stood for a set of instantaneous entities contemporaneous with one another. But to this was added the fantasy of plates having some thickness, plates whose members have some duration but are nevertheless in an indefinite sense contemporaneous with one another.[2] Whether a plate have some thickness or be without it, whether our set of contemporaneous entities be a set of instantaneous entities or a set of enduring entities that are in only an indefinite sense contemporaneous with one another, our plate is nothing apart from its members and its members, finite in number, are not everywhere contiguous to one another.[3] We are presented with a set of entities, in one sense or another contemporaneous with one another, that are, as it were, spread out before us. And we have said that these entities, some of them material and some of them perhaps immaterial, some of them spaces that are bodies and some of them perhaps empty spaces, are both discrete and finite.

One might say that, being presented with an extended manifold, we concentrate our attention here and there, and that only the objects of such a concentrated attention, only the entities presented as not merely indefinite objects, are real. Since, however, the extended manifold, alleged to be presented to us before we concentrate our attention, is without a definite position and is presented as no one's definite object, there can be no true proposition discussing its alleged priority to the more definitely located entities within it. It is simply that various contemporaneous entities within the alleged but non-existent manifold are real and are objects of a concentrated attention.

My desk is real; it is an object of my concentrated attention; it is, we shall say, "one." The man in my garden is likewise real and an object of my concentrated attention; he, too, we shall say, is "one." If the man's background and the desk's background were real, we could say that man and desk are severally selected as objects of concentrated attention from their respective backgrounds. But we can in any case say that, in our sense of "many," there are as many objects as are severally objects of a concentrated attention. Man and desk, that is to say, are to be called "two." And even if the man comes inside to sit on the desk, even if I am presented with a real man and a real desk that are contiguous, man and desk are still to be called "two," assuming that each is the object of a concentrated attention.

But whereas I may be aware of the desk and also aware of the man sitting on it, some other subject may be aware simply of the composite: 'man-on-desk.' With respect to his mental attitudes, 'man-on-desk' may, it seems, be one, whereas, with respect to mine, man and desk are two. As we use "one," "two" and "many," unity, duality and multiplicity are, it seems, relative qualities. Man-on-desk, it seems, is both two with respect to my mental attitudes and one with respect to those of some other subject—just as Socrates was both young with respect to Parmenides and old with respect to Plato.

In several previous chapters we have had to pass over objections that might be raised against the existence of alleged qualities in order to devote ourselves to the determination of the existence of the specific instances of qualities then up for consideration. Without having delayed to discuss the arguments that might lead to the conclusion that no qualities are real, we concluded directly from our propositions explaining "existence" that the incandescence of the electric bulb before me is real[4] and that the baseball pitcher is really present with respect to the batter.[5] So here let us agree that man-on-desk is real and let us assume that no arguments will be brought forward against the existence of qualities as such that will prevent man-on-desk from having the real quality of being 'two with respect to my mental attitudes' and the real quality of being 'one with respect to your mental attitudes.'

When I am presented with a man-on-desk as my apparent object that is alleged to be one absolutely or two absolutely, no feeling of belief accompanies my mental attitude, but rather one of dismay and incredulity. No man-on-desk that is absolutely one or absolutely two is listed among the real entities enumerated in the appendix to Chapter Three. Both man-on-desk that is absolutely one and man-on-desk that is absolutely two are unreal entities in the sense in which we are using "reality." When, on the other hand, my apparent object is a man-on-desk alleged to be one with respect to you and two with respect to me, my mental attitude is accompanied by a feeling of belief. My object is presented to me as not generally discredited. It is listed as real; and my mental attitude alleged to be directed upon it is a mental attitude that enters into a real subject-object relational situation with a real object. Assuming, that is to say, that some qualities are real, man-on-desk has the real quality of being two with respect to me' and the real quality of being one with respect to you.

In considering the problem of error, however, we considered the straight stick partly immersed in water, in connection with which a subject may seem to be aware of a bent stick.[6] The stick that is alleged to be absolutely bent, like the man-on-desk that is alleged to be absolutely one, we held to be unreal. But whereas the man-on-desk that is alleged to be absolutely two we likewise hold to be unreal, the stick that is alleged to be absolutely straight we held to be real. So far there is no great difficulty. For whereas, when I seem to be presented with a man-on-desk that is alleged to be absolutely two or a place alleged to be absolutely near, I have a feeling of puzzlement and my alleged object is unreal, the alleged absolutely straight stick that is presented to me appears as not generally discredited and is real.

But if the man-on-desk has the real quality of being two with respect to me and one with respect to you, why should not the stick have the real quality of being straight with respect to me and bent with respect to you? In a certain sense, to be sure, the alleged qualities of being straight with respect to me and bent with respect to you do really inhere in the stick.

The stick affects my mental attitude which is really directed upon a straight stick and affects your mental attitude, which, although without an object, is as if it were directed upon a bent stick. To say that the stick is straight with respect to me or bent with respect to you may merely be to refer to the qualities that the straight stick has as a source of motions flowing to one of these mental attitudes or the other. In a similar sense man-on-desk is two with respect to me and one with respect to you. For man-on-desk is at the source of motions flowing to my mental attitude which has man and desk as each the object of a concentrated attention; and it is at the source of motions flowing to your mental attitude which has man-on-desk as a single object of concentrated attention.

But man-on-desk is two with respect to me and one with respect to you in another and seemingly simpler sense. Man-on-desk, not as cause but simply as object, is two as I am aware of it and one as you are aware of it. The stick as object is straight as I am aware of it; that is to say, I am aware of a straight stick. But the stick as object is not bent as you are aware of it. For the stick is not really bent and a bent stick is not really the object of your mental attitude, which, we have asserted, has no object.

We have pointed to man and desk that we choose to call "one" with respect to a given mental attitude and "two" with respect to another mental attitude. And we have found that these designations apply to real qualities, that man-on-desk is really one with respect to one mental attitude and really two with respect to another. But in going beyond this individual instance of what is really one and this individual instance of what is really two, in attempting to explain our terms "unity," "duality" and "multiplicity" generally, we have indicated no more than that, if a group of alleged objects is presented as the object of a single instance of concentrated attention, we shall call it "one," whereas if presented as having various of its parts severally the objects of a concentrated attention we shall call it "many,"—no more than that, to the extent to which a group of objects is really the object of an instance of concentrated attention, it is really one in our sense of "unity," whereas, to the extent to which its parts are severally real objects of a concentrated attention, it is really many in our sense of "multiplicity." But such explanations may well leave the reader

425

unsatisfied. For we are saying very little, if anything, more than that an entity is one in so far as it is the object of one thinking mind-nerve-fibre, many in so far as the subject's thinking mind-nerve-fibres directed upon it are many. We fall back upon and leave unexplained the terms "one" and "many" as applied to a subject's mental attitudes or, rather, as applied to the mind-nerve fibres in which those mental attitudes inhere. We have no more been able to avoid circularity in our attempts to explain our terms "unity," "duality" and "multiplicty" than in our attempt to explain our term "infinity." [7] And yet, just as with "infinity," our propositions through which we attempt to explain our terms "unity," "duality" and multiplicity" are not without implications. They imply that an object or group of objects is not one, two, or many absolutely, that its number is not to be determined by considering it apart from the relational situations into which it enters. And they imply further that, as we use "unity," "duality" and "multiplicity," the number of a thing or group of things is in some sense dependent upon mental attitudes.

To determine the extent and the limits of this dependency, let us once more compare the duality that the man-on-desk has with respect to my mental attitude with the straightness that the stick partly immersed in water has. For it is only to the extent to which duality is dependent upon mental attitudes and straightness not similarly dependent that duality has peculiarities flowing from our propositions explaining "number." If there were no subjects at all, there would be no man-on-desk that is two; but there would likewise be no stick that is straight. That is to say, if we present to ourselves a man-on-desk alleged to be both two and no one's object, our alleged datum is unreal, having the contradictory characteristics of being no one's object and at the same time of being two as some one's object. And a straight stick alleged to be no one's object is likewise unreal, being presented as no one's object and at the same time implicitly as being the subject-matter of our present discussion. Whatever is presented as being in no sense an object of consciousness is unreal; to this extent each entity that is real is dependent upon there being mental attitudes.[8] But real entities as such do not require the existence of John Brown's mental attitudes or William James's. They require, to put it perhaps too simply, that there be mental attitudes

426

in general, whereas unity and duality require specified instances of mental attitudes. For unless *I* am aware of the man-on-desk, man-on-desk is not two with respect to *me*; and unless William James is aware of the man-on-desk, man-on-desk is not two with respect to *him*.

As we use "duality," the only duality that man-on-desk has is duality with respect to particular mind-persons. However, whether it be straightness or duality, whether the dependence be on mental attitudes in general or on particular instances of mental attitudes, dependence does not imply causation or creation. Mental attitudes do not bring the straightness of the stick into being and *my* mental attitudes do not bring the duality of the man-on-desk into being. Straight sticks in the primeval forests presented as objects for no contemporary, but only for subsequent, mental attitudes are real.[9] And some past instance of man-on-desk, presented as an object for my present mental attitudes, is really two with respect to me. It is the stick, and not my mental attitude, that is straight; the man-on-desk, and not *just* my mental attitude, that is two. Mental attitudes do not 'put' the straightness in the stick or the duality in the man-on-desk; although, if there were no mental attitudes, the stick would not be straight, and if I had no mental attitudes, the man-on-desk would not be two with respect to me.

Man on desk, we hold, is really two with respect to me. For the man-on-desk is real; I have mental attitudes really directed upon it; and these attitudes are focussed separately upon its component parts, namely, upon man and upon desk. Let us suppose however that I am presented with Sir Walter Scott and the author of Waverley alleged to be separate individuals. Let us suppose the alleged couple: Sir Walter Scott and the author of Waverley; and let us suppose mental attitudes of mine said to be focussed upon the component parts of this couple, upon Scott and upon the author of Waverley. Scott, we may agree, is real and the author of Waverley real. But the position of the one is the position of the other. If my apparent object is a Scott and an author of Waverley alleged to be outside one another, my apparent object is unreal and can not really be two with respect to me. Scott, the author of Waverley, can be two with respect to me only if I focus my attention separately upon such entities, for example, as Scott's head and the rest of Scott's body. But a pair of intersecting circles, even though they have a common segment, can, let us say, be two with respect to me. For the overlapping components are both real and in perceiving the total object before me my attention may be concentrated separately upon each of them. Without mental attitudes, however, that are focussed separately upon what in some sense are parts, there is no multiplicity in the object, in our sense of "multiplicity." Scott is real and the author of Waverley real; and when they are not presented to me as outside one another, there is no error. But when I focus my attention separately upon Scott and upon the author of Waverley, my object is not two with respect to me. My object has two names, is the object of two mental attitudes, but, failing a discrimination of parts, there is no duality with respect to me, in our sense of "duality."

Up to this point we have in this chapter been considering "a set of entities, in one sense or another contemporaneous with one another, that are, as it were, spread out before us." [10] But there is date as well as position, duration as well as extension, and the discrimination of phases as well as the discrimination of parts. Its left half and its right half are parts of the desk and Napoleon's boyhood and Napoleon's manhood are phases of Napoleon. With respect to the subject for whom the desk as a whole is an object of concentrated attention, the desk is one. Similarly let us say that, with respect to the subject for whom Napoleon as a whole is an object of concentrated attention, Napoleon is one. On the other hand, the desk's left half and its right half being severally objects of my concentrated attention, the desk is two with respect to me. And Napoleon's boyhood and Napoleon's manhood being severally objects of my concentrated attention, Napoleon, let us say, is likewise two with respect to me. In order however for Napoleon in the one case or Napoleon's boyhood in the other to be one with respect to me, there must, let us say, be no instantaneous phase of my object in which I discriminate parts, no instantaneous phase that is two with respect to me. As we use "one," that is to say, that is one which has none of its instantaneous phases discriminated into parts and which with its entire duration is a single object of concentrated attention. A spatio-temporal unit is an enduring entity in which there is no discrimination of phases and which is built up, as it were, of instantaneous phases

428

in which there is no discrimination of parts. We have already had occasion to point out that temporal relations are not entirely analogous to spatial relations.[11] Our propositions explaining "unity" exhibit accordingly the temporal unity of an enduring entity as superimposed, at it were, on the spatial unity of its instantaneous phases.

In this connection let us consider a trip on a train leaving Washington at three o'clock and arriving at New York at seven; and a trip on a train leaving New York at three o'clock and arriving at Washington at seven. The duration of the one journey is similar to that of the other and the locale is in each case the New York—Washington line. In so far as a duration of four hours and the New York—Washington line are a single object for my thinking, the trains are not two with respect to me. It is difficult to see how they can properly be called "two" in any sense of duality in which spatial and temporal characteristics occur on the same level in our propositions explaining "duality." But at four o'clock the traveler who has left New York is near Trenton and the traveler who has left Washington near Baltimore. Traveler near Trenton plus traveler near Baltimore do not form an object in which there is no discrimination of parts. And this being the case, the journeys, in the sense in which we are using the terms "unity," "duality" and "multiplicity," are not one with respect to me.

Spatial and temporal characteristics seem not to have an equal bearing on the significations of "one," "two" and "many," as those terms are commonly used. Indeed common usage seems to go so far as to say that whereas one entity can not be at one time in two places, one entity can at two times be in one place. As we are explaining "unity" and "duality," in so far as there are two simultaneous positions, in so far, that is to say, as there is discrimination of simultaneous parts, the object is two and not one. But we have chosen also to apply the term "two" where there is discrimination of phases. If I was at home yesterday, am away today and will again be at home tomorrow, then in so far as these various phases of my life are severally the objects of a concentrated attention, yesterday's phase and tomorrow's phase are in our terminology likewise two and not one. As an enduring whole enduring from yesterday through tomorrow, I do not exist

429

"at two times" any more than an instantaneous phase of an extended entity exists in two positions when there is no discrimination of parts.

Let us suppose that my desk is four feet long and touches no other furniture. The airy space adjacent to it is real in so far as it is some one's definite object. But I am neglecting what is beyond and around my desk. The four-foot desk is an object of my concentrated attention and is one with respect to me. But now, let us suppose, I shift my attention two feet to the side. One-half of my desk has come to be neglected background. My attention is directed towards two feet of desk and two feet of airy space. The two feet of desk and the two feet of airy space are not however severally the objects of my concentrated attention. Mine, on the contrary, is, we suppose, a single object four feet long. It is one with respect to me, although with respect to mental attitudes where there is discrimination of parts it is part desk and part airy space. My hybrid object is real and it follows from our propositions explaining "unity" that it is really one with respect to me. To explain "unity" in terms of spatial characteristics is to imply that a real four-foot hybrid object such as we have just described is one, just as is a real four-foot desk. To hold that any extended object in which there is no discrimination of parts is one is to imply that there are what might be called artificial units as well as what might be called natural units. Not only is an instantaneous phase of the desk one with respect to me; so also are instantaneous phases of the four feet of desk and air.

In explaining our term "unity," moreover, we have referred to temporal characteristics as well as to spatial characteristics. And in the process of taking together various successive instantaneous phases as a single object, in the process of placing before ourselves an enduring entity that is the object of a single concentrated attention, there are new opportunities for the occurrence of artificial units. Yesterday's phase of my life when I was at home, today's phase when I am away and tomorrow's phase when I shall again be at home are, taken together, what may be called a "natural" enduring unit. But in so far as I have as a single object of my concentrated attention a bit of empty space the size of the sun but twice as distant, whose successive phases are in different directions just as those of the sun are, this enduring empty space that is moving with respect to me is also *one* with respect to me.[12] An enduring place may likewise be one with respect to me though it be successively the place of a series of moving objects.[13] And finally there is the four-foot object that is constantly in front of me as I move my head, the object that is now a four-foot desk, now part desk and part airy space, and now all airy space.

Let us suppose that a rocket is shot into the air which explodes into a thousand fragments. With respect to one subject, the unexploded rocket and one of its fragments may be a single enduring object, an entity from which in the middle of its history other entities are, as it were, excreted. With respect to another subject, it may be the unexploded rocket and a different fragment that constitute a single object. And for a third the unexploded rocket and its fragments may be many, the entity taken as one being considered to have had its final phase at the moment of explosion. Unexploded rocket and fragment may be one with respect to you and two with respect to me; and unexploded rocket and fragment may be one with respect to you whereas unexploded rocket together with a different fragment constitute a single object with respect to me.

I may have as a single enduring object a piece of worsted as it forms part of a ball of worsted and a later phase of this worsted when it has been woven into a stocking. Or I may have as my enduring object a stocking that is now mostly silk and that later will be mostly worsted. "If anyone wants an instance of the value of our ordinary notions, he may find it perhaps," Bradley says,[14] "in Sir John Cutler's silk stockings. They were darned with worsted until no particle of the silk was left in them; and no one could agree whether they were the same old stockings or were new ones." What is the "same," let us say, is what is one. And as what is one with respect to you may be two with respect to me, what is the same with respect to you may not be the same with respect to me. In so far as 'silk stocking becoming worsted' is a single enduring object, a phase of the stocking in which it is mostly silk and a later phase in which it is mostly worsted are successive phases of the same entity. But in so far as 'worsted formerly in ball and now in stocking' is a single enduring object, a phase of the stocking in which it is silk and a later phase in which it is worsted are not successive phases of the same entity.

431

What is the same, we say, is what is one. Scott is the same as the author of Waverley. That is, Scott given without discrimination of parts and the author of Waverley, given without discrimination of parts, are one, although having two names. And with respect to certain mental attitudes, Sir John Cutler's stockings are the same. That is to say, there is one persisting object although in one of its phases it is mostly constituted of one material and in another of its phases of a second material.

Two hundred years ago, let us suppose, a comet appeared in the sky. It was observed, written up, and forgotten. One hundred years ago there was a similar apparition. Again some astronomer observed and described what he saw. Today there is another appearance of comet. Some one happens upon the article of two hundred years ago and also upon the article of one hundred years ago. From them he is able to infer that the three appearances are appearances of one comet; and he is able to discover the orbit of this comet which returns each hundred years. His hypothesis is that there is one enduring comet of which the three observed phenomena are short-lived phases. The observer of two hundred years ago was not in error in so far as he was aware only of a short-lived entity. This short-lived entity was one; it was what we now call one phase. Nor was the astronomer of one hundred years ago in error, having as his object a similarly short-lived entity, although with a different date. But there is also a longer-lived enduring comet which is real and, with respect to certain present mental attitudes, one. With such present mental attitudes in mind, the three short-lived phases are successive phases of the *same* entity. What has been discovered is what might be called a 'natural' unit. But if some one, without discovering the orbit, had taken the three successive appearances of comet together as a single object, then unless there were some assertion of continuity of matter in interim positions which the comet did not in fact have, there would likewise be a real unit, although an artificial one.

What is now comet, now empty space and now comet again may be one object, but not one comet. To a large extent such artificial units as we have suggested are eliminated when we discuss, not one entity or one object, but one comet or one desk or one mind-person. There is not "one comet" where there are

432

intermediate phases that are not phases of a comet; there is not 'one desk' where there are intermediate phases that are not phases of a desk. The object that is now desk, now part desk and part airy space, and finally all airy space may be one object; but it is not one desk. Limitating my attention to an extended manifold of simultaneous entities, my desk may be two with respect to me. My attention may be concentrated severally upon its right half and upon its left half. But whereas in this case I have two objects, I am not aware of two desks. To be one comet is to be not only one, but an entity each of whose phases is a phase of a comet. And to be two desks is to be not only two, but an entity discriminated into two parts each of which is a desk.

Just as the right half of my desk may be one object but not one desk, so let us say that an instantaneous phase of my desk, although one object, is not to be called "one desk." What is to be called "one desk," let us say, is an enduring entity, beginning when the desk is made and ending when it is broken up. And just as, when my attention is concentrated severally upon its right half and its left half, my objects are two but not two desks, so let us say that, when my attention is concentrated severally upon today's phase of the desk and upon tomorrow's phase, my objects similarly are two but not two desks.

Various phases of the enduring entity that alone is one desk are qualitatively similar. Without this similarity the enduring whole would not be one desk. There is mutual coherence running through successive phases of Descartes' mind-person. Without this coherence the enduring whole would not be one mind-person.[15] But if we can suppose an immaterial phase of the Capitol at Washington intervening between material phases of the Capitol, then not all of the successive phases of the enduring Capitol are qualitatively similar. Even in this instance however we should call the duration of the Capitol continuous, describing the Capitol as an enduring substance which in some of its phases is material and in some of its phases immaterial.[16] What is called one desk or one mind-person or one Capitol appears to have a continuous duration and some phases that are qualitatively similar, but need not have all phases qualitatively similar. What is one, on the other hand, need not have any phases qualitatively similar; an enduring entity is one merely by being a single object of concentrated attention.

To explain "unity" in terms of spatial and temporal character-istics is, we have said,[17] to imply that there may be what might be called artificial units as well as what might be called natural units. To be sure, what is now desk, what is now part desk and part airy space, and what is now all airy space are not successive phases of the same desk. But since the object in this instance is one, although not one desk, they are successive phases of the same enduring entity. Would it not accord better with common usage, however, to explain "unity" so that there are no artificial units; so that such an entity as we have just been considering will not only not be one desk, but not one at all? "It is always necessary," says Leibniz, "that besides the difference of time and place there be an internal principle of distinction." "Although time and place serve us in distinguishing things," he holds,[18] "it is rather by the things that one place or one time must be distinguished from another, for in themselves they are perfectly alike." The notion of individuality, Leibniz implies, is prior to the notions of time and space. We must not rely on spatial and temporal characteristics, it may be held, in explaining "unity" and "indi-viduality," since time and space are merely frameworks to relate individuals and to hold them together.

To be sure, we have made little use of "time" in this treatise;[19] and 'Space,' an alleged omnipresent entity without definite posi-tion, we have found to be unreal.[20] Here and there there are spaces which are bodies and spaces which perhaps are immaterial. We may arbitrarily select a definite extension and make the space in which it inheres an object of concentrated attention. Or we may concentrate our attention upon some entity that appears to be internally homogeneous and to be distinct from its neighbors. As we use "unity" any entity is 'one' that is real and an object of concentrated attention. But perhaps it would accord better with common usage to apply the term "unity"—or, at any rate, the term "individuality"—only where there is internal homogeneity, an entity set apart from its neighbors.

The desk, one may say, is internally homogeneous, being all wood; whereas the entity which is part desk and part air is com-posed of different materials. A distinction of this sort, however, can not be applied to all objects. The solar system is one; and it

434

is what would seem to be a "natural" unit. Nevertheless it is not internally homogeneous, comprising, as it does, sun, planets, meteors and vast empty spaces between. Indeed the wood of this desk turns out to be equally devoid of internal homogeneity. For it is composed of separated molecules which are themselves miniature solar systems. To find entities which are, so to speak, all of one piece, we must search within the molecule, within the atom, within the electron. If only entities having an internal homogeneity are called "units," there are no artificial units; but many objects generally called "individual" objects also fail to be units.

If this desk, this stone, this man are to be called "units," we can not explain "unity" in terms of internal homogeneity. But, it may be said, there is in each "natural" unit a more or less permanent organization of parts. Unless a desk is violently severed in two, the parts move together retaining their ties and relations with one another and the desk retaining its form or pattern. On the one hand, however, a liquid which is evaporating and out of which a precipitate is forming does not retain its volume and internal organization. And on the other hand, the hybrid entity which is part desk and part air may be regarded as an enduring entity retaining its dual composition and shape.

"Physical points," says Leibniz, "are only indivisible in appearance; mathematical points are so in reality, but they are merely modalities." "Only metaphysical points or those of substance (constituted by forms or souls) are," he holds,[21] "exact and real." These true units "possess a certain vitality and a kind of perception; and mathematical points are their points of view to express the universe." Since a true unit is associated with each mathematical point, it follows that, for Leibniz, an extended "body is an aggregate of substances and not, properly speaking, one substance."[22] But if this is the case, unity has disappeared as a concept applicable to this desk and that chair. We have consequently a use of the term "unity" which is out of accord with customary usage, according to which this desk is "one" and this desk and that chair "two."

To be sure, true units, for Leibniz, are not all of the same order. There are simple immaterial units, simple monads; and there are units which are souls, dominant monads. "Each important . . . monad which forms the center of a compound substance (as, for example, of an animal) . . . is surrounded by a mass composed of an infinity of other monads which constitute the body proper of this central monad."[23] A dominant monad is associated not merely with a mathematical point, but indirectly with an extended mass. And so we are presented with a secondary use of "unity," in which not all monads associated with mathematical points are called "units," but only monads associated indirectly with extended masses. But if there is to be a secondary use of "unity" in which unity does not characterize all monads and their mathematical points, then which are the extended entities that are units in this secondary sense and which are the extended entities that are not? Is there, for example, a central monad dominating all those associated with the mathematical points within this desk; and no central monad dominating those associated with the mathematical points in the hybrid object that is part wood and part air? "Body," Leibniz holds,[24] "is not a substance." "It is a collection of several substances, like a pond full of fish or a flock of sheep; . . . it is what is called *unum per accidens*, in a word, a phenomenon." "A true substance, such as an animal," he continues, "is composed of an immaterial soul and an organized body; and it is the compound of these two which is called *unum per se*." But if we are looking for suggestions as to how to apply "unity" and "multiplicity" to entities that are not living organisms, we look in Leibniz's writings in vain for criteria by which to distinguish the desk from the entity that is part desk and part air.

A natural unit, it has been suggested,[25] is one in which there is a more or less permanent organization of parts, one whose parts move together retaining their ties and mutual relations. Such a unit, it may be held, is more than a unit; it is an individual, an individual indeed in more than the literal sense of being undivided. "Individuality," to quote Bosanquet,[26] "is essentially a positive conception." The unit which is an individual "is individual primarily because his own content is stable and self-contained."[27] The pattern and internal organization which such a unit maintains give it character, give it what in speaking of a person we are wont to call "individuality." Living organisms, it would appear, are outstanding examples of such units. The parts of such an organism are closely interrelated so that the health or

436

disease of one part more or less affects the functioning of all. And the organism itself has a structure and a balance which all of the parts assist in maintaining.

According to the passage which we have quoted from Bosanquet, however, an individual is not only an entity whose content is stable; it is an entity that is "self-contained." Not only are the parts closely interrelated; they also have the characteristic of being independent of entities outside the individual of which they are parts. The individual, as Bosanquet explains "individual," is a world "self-complete."[28] And in view of this requirement of self-completeness, the living organisms which at first sight seem to be individuals do not quite fill the bill. We do not find an entity that is self-contained until we envisage the world as a whole. And so we find that, using "individual" in this sense, there is apparently but one individual: the Universe, the All-inclusive, or God. A similarly monistic picture is put before us by Spinoza in the propositions in which he undertakes to define 'substance.' What he describes as a substance and what we should prefer him to describe as an individual or unit is an entity that enters into no causal relations with entities outside itself; and it is an entity that is not limited or restricted by other entities of the same order. It follows that what he calls a substance and what we should prefer to have him call a unit or individual can not, he holds, be finite[29] and can not be divided into parts which are individuals.[30] For him as for Bosanquet there is but one entity, generally called God, to which the terms "substance," "individual" and "one" properly apply.

As we are using the terms "existence" and "reality," however, "an everlasting subsistent, taken collectively, is unreal in so far as it appears, explicitly or implicitly, with the characteristic of having only a very indefinite date with respect to an entity that appears real." And "an instantaneous but unlimited Space, as distinguished from limited portions of it, is unreal in so far as it appears, explicitly or implicitly, with the characteristic of having only a very indefinite position with respect to an entity which appears real and with respect to which it appears present."[31] "No subsistents are real that explicitly or implicitly appear as lacking all spatial position"; and "no subsistents are real that explicitly or implicitly appear as utterly undated."[32] It follows that, as we

437

use the terms "existence" and "reality," the alleged all-inclusive Whole is non-existent. If then we were to use the term "unity" in such a way that it applied only to an all-inclusive whole, we would be using the term in such a way that it would apply to nothing real and we would be giving the term "unity" a signification from which it would follow that there are no units or individuals.

But are there real units when certain finite entities not self-complete are called "units"? In so far as my object is the desk in front of me and nothing but this desk, my alleged object, it may be said, is not real. For the desk, it may be said, is made of wood which came from distant trees. It reflects the light of the sun and is referred to in various passages in this treatise. I do not really know the desk to be a real object, it may be said, unless I am aware of trees and sun and treatise. No entity taken out of its context, it may be said, is real; and its context is the universe. If then we explain "unity" so that certain finite entities which are not complete in themselves are units, we too, it may be said, give "unity" a signification from which it follows that there are no real units.

As we are using "existence" and "reality," however, this desk is real; and when I am aware of it but not definitely aware of each of the relational situations into which it enters with external entities, my mental attitude is really directed upon an existent object. In explaining "unity" in such a way that certain finite entities are units, we are not then giving "unity" a signification from which it follows that there are no units. Certain finite entities are real, and certain of these finite entities are units. Those, namely, are units, as we use the term "unity," which are severally the objects of a concentrated attention. There are real natural units and real artificial units. But despite our examination of Leibniz and others, we have found no way to distinguish clearly between them.

In the terminology of various monistic philosophers, only that which is self-complete is a unit or individual; and only that which is self-complete is a substance. In our terminology this desk and Napoleon and the hybrid entity which is part desk and part air are, with respect to certain mental attitudes, units. And in our terminology this desk and Napoleon and the hybrid entity which

438

is part desk and part air are, let us say, substances. An entity is a unit in so far as it is an object of concentrated attention. But what is the signification of "substance" from which it is to follow, in our terminology as in the terminologies of various other writers, that what is one is also a substance?

An instantaneous phase of this desk has a left half and a right half; but it also, we may say, is large, heavy, and made of mahogany. Whereas its left half and its right half are parts having more definite positions than the desk as a whole, its size, its weight and its being made of mahogany are presented, not as parts having more definite positions, but as being where the desk is, as having the same indefinite position as the desk as a whole. There is what may be called an *extensive* taking together when, after being presented severally with the desk's left half and its right half, we present to ourselves the less definitely located desk as a whole. On the other hand, let us suggest, there is what may be called an *intensive* taking together when after being presented severally with the desk's size, its weight and its being made of mahogany, we present to ourselves the desk constituted by these qualities or in which they may be said to inhere. Reversing the order in which these alleged objects appear, there is, we have said,[33] discrimination when a mental attitude directed upon the desk is followed by mental attitudes directed upon its parts; and there is abstraction when that mental attitude is followed by mental attitudes, if there be any such, that are really directed upon its size, its weight, or its being made of mahogany.

An instantaneous phase of this desk is one, an individual; and it is real. It is an individual substance. Its size, its weight and its being made of mahogany are, if real, qualities, qualities of an individual substance. The individual substance, one might say, is an unanalyzed whole which comprises a full set of concomitant qualities, every thing real concomitant with a given position together with that position itself. Any selection from this unanalyzed whole, whatever is concomitant with other entities and does not claim to include them and their position, is, if real, a quality of that individual substance.

Its size, if real, is a quality of this desk. Its weight, alleged to be concomitant with it, is a quality of this desk. And its size and weight taken together, but abstracted from the desk as a whole and not implicitly including, for example, its being made of mahogany and its position, is likewise, if real, a quality of this desk. I may have a mental attitude which appears to be directed upon the desk's size and another mental attitude which appears to be directed upon its weight; whereas you may have a mental attitude which appears to be directed upon its size and weight taken together. Nevertheless let us not say that this size and this weight are two qualities with respect to me but one quality with respect to you. "Without mental attitudes that are focussed separately upon what in some sense are parts, there is no multiplicity in the object in our sense of 'multiplicity.'"[34] When I focus my attention separately upon Scott and upon the author of Waverley, my object is not two with respect to me. My object has two names, is the object of two mental attitudes, but, failing a discrimination of parts, it is not two with respect to me, in our sense of "duality." Similarly, since it is abstraction and not discrimination that puts the size of this desk and the weight of this desk before me as distinct objects, this size and this weight, if real, are not in our terminology "two" with respect to me. When, without discrimination of parts, I am aware of Scott and the author of Waverley, my mental attitudes may be two but my object is one substance. When I seem to be aware of the size of this desk and also of its weight, my mental attitudes may be two, but my objects, if real, are one quality, if, indeed, number is to be applied to such objects at all.

To be sure, we may picture what are alleged to be concomitant qualities as being laid out side by side. By a sort of *suppositio substantialis,* we may suppose them to form an extended manifold, a group having several members. If they *were* such separated individuals, the size of this desk and the weight of this desk might be two. But presented as concomitant, the desk in which they inhere is one and "number," as we have explained it, may not be applicable to its qualities at all.

An instantaneous phase of this desk is one with respect to me for whom it is a single object of concentrated attention. It is two with respect to you who discriminate between its right half and its left half. The size of the whole desk is, if real, a quality of the desk as a whole, the size of its right half a quality of its right half. It is you for whom the right half is one, who abstract from the right half of the desk the alleged size of this right half. And

440

it is I for whom the desk as a whole is one who abstract from the desk as a whole the size of the whole desk. A quality, it would appear, has as its substance an entity that is one with respect to the mental attitude that is directed upon this quality and its substance. This desk and Napoleon and the hybrid entity which is part desk and part air are each substances. And with respect to certain mental attitudes, this desk and Napoleon and the hybrid entity which is part desk and part air are each units. Each entity that is a substance, it would appear, is a unit with respect to the mental attitudes which are aware of it as a substance having qualities.

This desk is one with respect to me, an individual substance alleged to have qualities. Or, rather, it is an instantaneous phase of this desk that is one with respect to me, an instantaneous phase within which I do not discriminate parts. But unity, duality and multiplicity are terms that apply to the enduring desk as well as to an instantaneous phase of it. An enduring entity is *one* "which has none of its instantaneous phases discriminated into parts and which with its entire duration is a single object of concentrated attention." [35] The enduring desk, Napoleon and this caterpillar-butterfly are each one with respect to me. And they are each substances from which qualities may be alleged to be abstracted. Just as the size of the whole desk is, if real, a quality of the desk as a whole and the size of its right half a quality of its right half, so the size of an instantaneous phase is, if real, a quality of that instantaneous phase and the size of the enduring desk a quality of the enduring desk. The enduring desk may be said to be made of mahogany, the enduring Napoleon French and the enduring caterpillar-butterfly alive. But the enduring desk, the enduring Napoleon and the enduring caterpillar-butterfly that are each one with respect to me may each be two or many with respect to you. You may discriminate between today's phase of this desk and tomorrow's phase, between Napoleon before Waterloo and Napoleon after Waterloo, between the phase in which this caterpillar-butterfly is a caterpillar and the phase in which it is a butterfly. The caterpillar may be one with respect to you and the butterfly one. From the one may be abstracted the alleged quality of being able to crawl, from the other the alleged quality of being able to fly. The caterpillar-butterfly, the caterpillar and the

441

butterfly are each, if they are real, what we are calling individual substances. And being alive, being able to crawl and being able to fly are respectively, if they are real, what we are calling qualities of these individual substances.

"In all changes in the world," it has been said,[36] "the substance remains and only the accidents change." Such a proposition however implies significations of "substance" and "accident" or "quality" out of accord with the significations we are assigning these terms. To be presented as what we are calling the quality of an enduring substance is to be presented as having the duration or as being the duration of that substance. Its ability to fly, its color and its more definitely dated duration, taken together, constitute, if real, not the less definitely dated caterpillar-butterfly but the substance that is the butterfly phase of it. In our terminology, in short, a substance can neither antedate nor outlive any of the qualities that inhere in it. If qualities are real, there is at the most a substance which remains—with its qualities,—while one phase (a substance) with its qualities is succeeded by a later phase (a substance) with *its* qualities.[37]

As we have explained "quality," the size of the desk is, if real, a quality; the heaviness of the desk, if real, a quality; and its being made of mahogany, if real, a quality. But there are those who hold that none of these entities which we call qualities are real. Abstraction, it may be said, is falsification. The alleged qualities which, through abstraction, follow the desk as our apparent objects are, it may be said, mere pseudo-objects which are unreal. "If the real as it appears is X=a b c d e f g h, then our judgment," says Bradley,[38] "is nothing but X=a or X=b. But a b by itself has never been given and is not what appears. It was *in* the fact and we have taken it out. . . . We have separated, divided, abridged, dissected, we have mutilated the given."

To be sure, the size of the desk by itself, presented, that is to say, as having no concomitants which together with it constitute a substance, is not an existent entity. Indeed, one might say that if it did exist, it would be, not what we are calling a quality, but rather what we are calling a substance. But the size of the desk that is presented as being a quality is implicitly presented as having concomitants. It is presented with a position, the position of the desk, and with a date, the date of the desk. The desk has

442

not been physically dissected. But this unanalyzed whole comprising a full set of concomitant entities has, after abstraction, been followed as our object by what appears as not a full set of concomitant entities but rather a selection from it, in a word, by a quality. The size of the desk, which is distinguishable from the desk but not physically separable from it, is presented with none of the characteristics that would mark it out as unreal and it is listed among the real entities enumerated in the appendix to Chapter Three. There are, in short, some qualities which are real. And there are some substances which are real. The size of the desk is a real quality. And the desk from which it has been abstracted, the desk appearing as an unanalyzed whole comprising a full set of concomitant qualities, is a real substance. For it too is presented with none of the characteristics that would mark it out as unreal and it too is listed among the entities we call "real." It is a different desk, appearing as having no qualities, that is unreal; and a different size of the desk, appearing as having no substance in which to inhere.

Just as some may hold that abstraction is falsification, so some may hold that discrimination is falsification. The statement that the size of the desk does not exist apart from the desk has as its analogue the statement that the left half of the desk which is presented to us as a part has not actually been cut off from the desk of which it is a part. Like the size of the desk that is presented as having no concomitants, the left half of the desk, presented as having no contiguous right half, is an unreal entity. But the size of the desk, presented as *having* concomitants,—concomitants which, to be sure, are not at the moment equally definite objects for me,—is a real quality. Similarly the left half of the desk, presented as joined to other parts which at the moment happen not to be definite objects of mine, is a real part. When I am aware of the left half of the desk "but not definitely aware of each of the relational situations into which it enters with external entities," [39] my mental attitude is directed upon an existent object; just as when my mental attitude is directed upon the desk as a whole. Discrimination, we thus hold, need not result in falsification and abstraction need not result in falsification. Both the desk as a whole and the left half of the desk, presented as substances, are, we find, real. And, presented as qualities, the size of the whole desk is real and also the size of the desk's left half.

So far as we have yet seen, some substances may be real and some qualities real. But what about the manner in which we come to be aware of individual substances and the manner in which we come to be aware of qualities? According to Locke,[40] "though the qualities that affect our senses are, in the things themselves, so united and blended that there is no separation, no distance, between them; yet it is plain the ideas they produce in the mind enter by the senses single and unmixed." There is a special channel passing through the eyes through which the color of the rose brings about a mental attitude directed upon the rose's color, a special channel passing through the nose through which the fragrance of the rose brings about a mental attitude directed upon the rose's fragrance. There is however, it may be pointed out, no special channel through which the rose as a substance brings about the mental attitude allegedly directed upon the rose as a whole. And this being the case, the rose itself, it may be held, is not a percept and, indeed, not real at all. One may hold that various qualities are real being percepts, the mental attitudes directed upon them being instances of perceiving. But one may hold that the mental attitude directed upon an alleged substance, not being directed upon that mental attitude's cause, is without a real object.

As we have explained our terms "existence" and "reality," however, not all entities are unreal which fail to be the causes of the mental attitudes directed upon them. Just as tomorrow's phase of the sun is real in our sense of "reality" and just as the other side of the moon is real, so the rose alleged to be in front of me might be real even though it were not the cause of the mental attitude which I direct upon it. Some individual substances might be real even if it were not they but only their qualities that were causes of the mental attitudes directed upon them.

But is it true that no individual substance causes the mental attitude apparently directed upon it? There are, it would seem, several senses in which an entity may be said to cause the mental attitude apparently directed upon it. An entity may be at the source of motions flowing to that mental attitude. It may be at the source of motions which travel through a special channel and through no other channel. Or it may be an entity such that, if it did

444

not exist, there would be no resultant mental attitude apparently directed upon it. Now if to be a cause is merely to be at the source of motions leading to the entity that is called the "result," then the rose is, it would seem, the cause of the mental attitude which I direct upon it; just as the redness of the rose is the cause of the mental attitude which I direct upon *it* and the fragrance of the rose the cause of the mental attitude which I direct upon *it*. For, the vibrations which come to my eye and lead me to be aware of the rose's redness may also lead me to be aware of the rose itself. Rose and redness may be the common source of vibrations which lead me to be aware now of rose and now of redness. Rose and fragrance may be the common source of other vibrations which lead me to be aware now of rose and now of fragrance. As we have explained our terms "percept" and "instance of perceiving," when I am seeing, my mental attitude directed towards the rose is as much an instance of perceiving as my mental attitude directed towards the rose's redness; and when I am smelling, my mental attitude directed towards the rose is as much an instance of perceiving as my mental attitude directed towards the rose's fragrance.[41] The rose, we hold, *is* a percept, *is* at the source of motions flowing to the mental attitude of mine that is directed upon it, whether or not it is at the source of motions which travel through a special channel and through no other channel, and whether or not it is an entity such that, if it did not exist, there would be no resultant mental attitude apparently directed upon it.

The "desk appearing as an unanalyzed whole comprising a full set of concomitant qualities is," we have found,[42] "a real substance," being "presented with none of the characteristics which would mark it out as unreal" and being listed among the entities we call "real." The rose, similarly presented as an unanalyzed whole comprising a full set of concomitant qualities, we shall likewise call "real." But the rose in front of me which is real is, let us agree, not at the source of motions which travel through a special channel and through no other channel. I may see the rose as well as its redness, may smell the rose as well as its fragrance. Whereas its color and its fragrance have special paths open to them to bring about mental attitudes directed upon themselves, the rose has, it would seem, not one path but many, each path leading to an awareness of a quality being also a path through

445

which there may be brought about a mental attitude directed upon the substance in which that quality inheres.

In seeing, we hold then, I may become aware of a real rose as well as of its real redness; in smelling, of a real rose as well as of its real fragrance. But, we will be asked, is not redness *all* that you see, fragrance *all* that you smell? The real rose, we will be told, is no more to be seen than its fragrance, no more to be smelt than its redness. If I had olfactory nerves but no eyes, I might be affected by the rose's fragrance, but, it may be said, neither by the rose's redness nor by the rose as a substance. And if I had eyes but no olfactory nerves, I might be affected by the rose's redness but neither by the rose nor its fragrance. It is the fragrance alone, it may be said, that is the *sine qua non* of my smelling, the redness alone that is the *sine qua non* of my seeing.

But whatever may be the *sine qua non* of my mental attitude directed upon the rose's redness or the *sine qua non* of my mental attitude directed upon the rose's fragrance, it does not follow that without eyes I should not be aware of the rose as a substance. There is some sense of the term "percept" in which, having olfactory nerves but no eyes, the rose's fragrance would be a percept of mine but not its redness, some sense of the term "percept" in which, having eyes but no olfactory nerves, the rose's redness would be a percept of mine but not its fragrance. But it does not follow that in this sense of the term "percept" the rose as a substance would be no percept of mine. It may well be that without eyes I would, in this sense of "perceiving," perceive the rose as well as its fragrance, but not its redness, that without olfactory nerves I would in this sense of "perceiving" perceive the rose as well as its redness, but not its fragrance. We may not see the rose's fragrance, one may thus say, but we see the rose as well as its redness. We may not smell the rose's color, but we smell the rose as well as its fragrance.

In certain senses of the term "cause," the mental attitude directed towards an individual substance may be caused by the substance as well as by that substance's qualities. But what does this mental attitude have as its *object?* "Take away the sensations of softness, moisture, redness, tartness, and," says Berkeley,[43] "you take away the cherry, since it is not a being distinct from sensations." A cherry, he explains, "is nothing but a congeries of sensible impressions or ideas perceived by various senses which ideas are united into one thing (or have one name given them) by the mind, because they are observed to attend each other." Turning our attention to the cherry rather than to an alleged idea of a cherry, the substance that is the object of my mental attitude may be held to be nothing but a group of qualities which retain their mutual distinctions. Or it may be held to be a vague something underlying and supporting its qualities. We "signify nothing by the word substance," says Locke,[44] "but only an uncertain supposition of we know not what (i.e., of something whereof we have no particular, distinct, positive idea), which we take to be the *substratum* or support of those ideas we do know." But the individual substance as we have described it is neither a group of qualities appearing with their mutual distinctions nor an entity distinct from its qualities and supporting them. It is the qualities themselves appearing as an unanalyzed whole.

Moreover the individual substance, as we have explained it, is no more an epiphenomenon unnecessarily added to a group of qualities than qualities are epiphenomena unnecessarily added to a world of interacting substances. In explaining the term "individual substance," we have, to be sure, referred back to qualities, referring to an intensive taking together of the desk's size, its weight and its being made of mahogany. But we have likewise explained "quality" by referring to the totality of concomitant entities, the substance, from which through abstraction the entities we call its qualities come to be before us as objects.[45] Some substances exist and some qualities exist. To explain the term "substance," as we use it, is to call attention to that which we call "quality." And to explain the term "quality," as we use it, is to call attention to that which we call "substance." Not only are there both substances and qualities; "substance" and "quality" are correlative terms. The distinction between substance and quality is brought to mind whichever of the two terms we undertake to explain.

This desk is large. This desk is heavy. This desk is made of mahogany. This desk is an individual substance; and a certain size and a certain weight are qualities of it, qualities which inhere *in* it. A quality, it may consequently be said, is *in* its substance, whereas the substance, in contrast to its qualities, may be said to be *in* itself. This, it would seem, is but a clumsy way of saying that each quality is the quality of some substance whereas a substance is not the quality of any substance. One may however add to the assertion that a quality is *in* its substance the assertion that a quality must be *conceived* through its substance; and one may hold that a substance is not only *in* itself but conceived through itself. "We can clearly conceive substance," says Descartes,[46] "without the mode which we say differs from it, while we can not reciprocally have a perception of this mode without perceiving the substance." If, for example, "a stone is moved," says Descartes, "and along with that is square, we are able to conceive the square figure without knowing that it is moved, and, reciprocally, we may be aware that it is moved without knowing that it is square; but we can not have a conception of this movement and figure unless we have a conception of the substance of the stone." To quote Malebranche, "since the modification of a substance is only the substance itself determined in a particular way, it is evident that the idea of a modification necessarily involves the idea of the substance of which it is a modification."[47] All, he holds, "that can be conceived by itself and without the thought of anything else, all . . . that can be conceived by itself as existing independently of every other thing and without the idea which we have of it representing any other thing is," he writes, "assuredly a being or a substance."

There is a distinction however between a mental attitude that is simply directed towards a quality and a mental attitude that recognizes as a quality the entity towards which it is directed. Having abstracted from a stone its square shape, I can be aware of this squareness without fully or explicitly retaining the mental attitude directed towards the substance from which the squareness was abstracted. But to be aware of the squareness of the stone as a quality is to be aware of the relation between stone and squareness, that is to say, of the processes of intensive taking together or abstraction through which one follows the other as my object.[48] Similarly there is a distinction between a mental attitude directed towards a substance and a mental attitude that recognizes as a substance the entity towards which it is directed. After being presented severally with the stone's motion, squareness, size and weight, I may, when presented with the stone itself, no longer retain the mental attitudes directed towards its various qualities. But to be aware of the stone as a substance is to be aware of the stone as having qualities. A quality, as distinguished from a quality *recognized* as a quality, can be as self-contained an object as a substance. And a substance *recognized* as a substance involves a mental attitude directed upon qualities just as a quality recognized as a quality involves a mental attitude directed upon its substance.

Like Descartes and Malebranche, Spinoza understands substance "to be that which is in itself and is conceived through itself." "I mean," he adds,[49] "that the conception of which does not depend on the conception of another thing from which it must be formed." But it is not merely the figure of the stone that, according to Spinoza, must be conceived through the stone. Whenever there are two entities that stand to one another in the relation of cause and effect, the effect, he holds, must be conceived through the cause. "If a substance can be produced from anything else, the knowledge of it should depend on the knowledge of its cause" and consequently, according to his definition, "it would not be a substance."[50] Accordingly, since he holds that all mundane entities are produced by God, it follows that no mundane entity is a substance, that God, in Spinoza's terminology, must be the only substance. To be sure, Descartes had similarly felt that all created entities are dependent upon God. "When we conceive of substance," he had said,[51] "we merely conceive an existent thing which requires nothing but itself in order to exist." "To speak truth," he had however added, "nothing but God answers to this description as being that which is absolutely self-sustaining. . . . That is why the word substance does not pertain *univoce* to God and to other things."

It will be recalled that we have already in this chapter encountered the thesis that "there is but one entity, generally called God, to which the terms 'substance,' 'individual' and 'one' properly apply." [52] It was our conclusion that, as we use the term "existence" and "reality," an alleged all-inclusive Whole is non-existent. If we were to use the term "unity" in such a way that it applies only to an all-inclusive whole, we would be giving the term "unity" a signification from which it would follow that there are no units or individuals. And if we were to use the term "substance" in such a way that it applies only to an all-inclusive whole, we would be giving the term "substance" a signification from which it would follow that there are no substances. When I am aware of an individual substance such as this desk, but not definitely aware of each of the relational situations into which it enters with external entities, my mental attitude, we have held,[53] is really directed upon an existent object. I am aware of a real substance even though I am not at the same time definitely aware either of its causes or of the qualities that might be abstracted from it.

Socrates, Napoleon and John Smith are each individual substances. Although we have not yet discussed universals at length, we may assume that 'man' is a universal substance of which Socrates, Napoleon and John Smith are instances; and that mortality is a universal quality among whose instances are the mortality of Socrates, the mortality of Napoleon and the mortality of John Smith. "Socrates is a man" is true and "Socrates is mortal" true. There are true propositions, that is to say, in which the subject term represents an individual substance and the predicate term either a universal substance or a quality. But, it has been said, there is no value of X for which "X is Socrates" is true. "First substances," says Aristotle,[54] "furnish no predicates." Or, as Coffee[55] puts it, "the concrete individual thing itself, the 'hoc aliquid,' . . . the individual this (or substantia prima) can never be properly the predicate of any subject in the logical order."

Individual substance, it may consequently be suggested, may be distinguished from the quality of an individual substance or from quality in general in a manner different from that in which we have distinguished them. Whereas we have described the individual substance as an unanalyzed whole which comprises a full set of concomitant entities and have described the quality of an individual substance as any selection from this totality,[56] individual substance might have been described, it may be held, as that which is always a subject and never a predicate; and the quality of an individual substance might have been described as that which is normally a predicate. Kant frequently describes substance as "something that can exist as a subject only, but never as a mere predicate."[57] To be sure, as an empirical object, a substance, according to Kant, is characterized by the fact that it is permanent as well as by the fact that it is never a predicate. But "substance," he says, "if we leave out the sensuous condition of permanence,

450

would mean nothing but a something that may be conceived as a subject without being the predicate of anything else." [58] In short, "the bare rational concept of substance," according to Kant, "contains nothing beyond the thought that a thing should be represented as a subject in itself, without becoming in turn a predicate of anything else."

Is it true, however, that there are no true propositions in which the predicate term represents an individual substance? As we have explained "truth," "Socrates is Socrates" is true and "Napoleon is not Socrates" true.[59] There are, that is to say, some true propositions in which the predicate term represents the individual substance Socrates. Such propositions are, no doubt, rather the exception. For most values of X, "X is Socrates" is, it may be granted, a false proposition.

It is however one thing to hold that for most values of X, "X is Socrates" is a false proposition; and quite a different thing to hold that this characteristic of Socrates and of other individual substances points to a manner in which individual substances may be distinguished from their qualities. We shall assume that the distinction between individual and universal applies to qualities as well as to substances. Just as 'man,' if real, is a universal substance of which Socrates, Napoleon and John Smith are instances, so mortality, if real, is a universal quality having among its instances the mortality of Socrates, the mortality of Napoleon and the mortality of John Smith. There is the real individual substance: Socrates; and the real quality of that individual substance: the mortality of Socrates. And just as it is not true that Napoleon is Socrates, or all men Socrates, or all mortals Socrates, so it is not true that Napoleon has the mortality which inheres only in Socrates, or that the universal quality 'mortality' is that instance of mortality which is a quality of Socrates. To the extent to which "X is Socrates" is false, there are analogous values of X for which "X is the mortality of Socrates" is likewise false. And corresponding to the exceptional cases in which "X is Socrates" is true, there are analogous cases in which "X is the mortality of Socrates" is true. In short it is the quality of an individual substance as well as the individual substance itself that for the most part is not represented by the predicate term of a true proposition. As we have explained "truth," it is not the substance that is never a predicate,

451

but the individual—the individual substance and the quality of the individual substance—that, with certain exceptions, is not represented by the predicate term of a true proposition.

We are assuming, we have said, that mortality, if real, is a universal quality of which the mortality of Socrates, the mortality of Napoleon and the mortality of John Smith are instances. It may be thought to follow that mortality, if real, is in our terminology many, the mortality of Socrates one and the mortality of Napoleon one. We may defer—for consideration in our chapter on universals —the question whether the universal 'mortality' is in our terminology to be called "many." But does it accord with our explanations of "unity" and "duality" to describe the mortality of Socrates as one, the mortality of Napoleon as one and the mortality of Socrates together with the mortality of Napoleon as two? The mortality of Socrates may be an object of concentrated attention and the mortality of Napoleon another object of concentrated attention. In directing my attention to the mortality of Socrates and to the mortality of Napoleon I have two objects; just as I have two objects, when I attend severally to the man who sits on a desk and to the desk on which he sits. But whereas the man and desk, which with respect to my mental attitudes are two, may with respect to the mental attitudes of another be one,[60] I can not visualize the mortality of Socrates and the mortality of Napoleon forming a composite object that with respect to any mental attitude is one. Nor, if the mortality of Socrates is one and the size of Socrates one, is the mortality of Socrates together with the size of Socrates two. "Without mental attitudes that are focused separately upon what in some sense are parts, there is no multiplicity in the object in our sense of multiplicity." [61] The mortality of Socrates and the size of Socrates are certainly not two. And we are on firmer ground when we say that the universal quality "mortality" has as its instances the qualities of many individual substances than when we say that its instances are many individual qualities.

With respect to the man and desk that are severally objects of my concentrated attention, not only are my mental attitudes two but man-on-desk, we found, has the real quality of being two with respect to me.[62] Being two with respect to me exists where the man-on-desk is, where the size of this composite object is, where its weight is. The man-on-desk's duality with respect to me is presented as no totality of concomitant entities, but rather as a selection from it, in short, as a quality. Thus quality, as we employ the term, includes quantity; and it includes date and position as well. The date of this man-on-desk is, in our terminology, one of that substance's qualities; the position of this man-on-desk another of its qualities. Indeed, if we eliminate substance from the list of predicables given in Aristotle's table of categories, the remaining concepts are all of them included in that to which we give the name "quality." A quality, in our terminology, is any selection from among the concomitant entities which, taken together, form an individual substance. It includes that which formerly was more generally termed "attribute" and that which was termed "accident."

By a sort of *suppositio substantialis,* we have suggested,[63] we may picture what are in fact concomitant qualities as being laid out side by side. "Red"' and "green" are adjectives representing qualities. Redness is not a totality of concomitant entities but is in each of its instances a selection from a totality of concomitant entities, that is to say, a selection from a red thing. Yet when we say that red and green are complementary colors, the words "red" and "green" function as substantives.[64] In a similar manner we frequently treat "one" and "two" as though they were substances. "Red," "redness" and "red thing," these words, we suggest, are analogous to "two," "duality" and "couple" respectively. And when we say that two and one are three, we are treating duality, unity and triplicity as though they were substances just as, when we say that red and green are complementary colors, we are treating in this fashion redness and greenness. There are however no substances, we hold, which primarily rather than secondarily are to be called "one" or "two" or "numbers," and there are no substances which primarily rather than secondarily are to be called red or green or colors. There are, it seems, red things and green things, individuals and couples, and there are the qualities of these things: redness and greenness, unity and duality.

What does our statement mean when we say that red and green are complementary colors? This red beet and that green leaf are not complementary. We seem to be talking about some red thing that is primarily red and some green thing that is primarily green. We seem to be talking about some insignificant object colored red which for the moment we regard as having no important quality other than its redness or some pigment colored green which for the moment we regard as having no important quality other than its greenness. Similarly when we say that two and two are four, we seem to have in mind some couple, such as a couple of dots, which for the moment we regard as having no important quality other than its duality. It is red and green, hypostatized into these, so to speak, one-qualitied substances, that may be said to be complementary; and two and two, hypostatized into these, so to speak, one-qualitied couples, that we speak of as being four.

We shall continue to use "individual substance" to refer to a totality of concomitant entities, to an unanalyzed whole which comprises a full set of concomitant qualities. And we shall continue to term any selection from this unanalyzed whole, whatever is concomitant with other entities and does not claim to include them, a "quality" of an individual substance. There are, we have found, certain individual substances, in this sense of "substance," which are real. This rose and this cherry, this desk and the left half of this desk, presented as individual substances, are all of them real. Likewise we have found real certain entities presented as what we term qualities of individual substances. To be sure, we have not yet discussed the arguments that may be put forward against the existence of various types of alleged qualities.[65] But we have marked out as real the incandescence of this bulb, the presentness that a certain phase of a baseball pitcher has with respect to his catcher, the size of this desk and the mortality of Socrates.

So far as we have yet seen, there may be certain types of alleged qualities that are never real. There may be no secondary qualities, for example, no entity that is green, no entity that is pea green, no entity that is emerald green. It is to be pointed out however that if anything is green and pea-green or green and emerald green, then, as we use "quality," its pea-greenness or emerald greenness is as much a quality of the individual substance as is its greenness. Since *any* selection from the unanalyzed whole that is an individual substance is what we call a "quality," there are in our terminology no qualities of qualities. The greater precision that results when, after thinking of an entity as green, we think of it as pea-green does not, in our terminology, come from abstracting its pea-greenness from its greenness. An entity's being pea-green, if real, is, we

454

shall say, abstracted from the individual substance itself. If this rose is a very pale red, its very pale redness is a quality of the rose and not of its redness; and if this desk is four feet long, its being four feet long is a quality of the desk and not of its length.

One substance, let us suppose, is green and pea-green, another substance green and emerald green. Greenness, if real, is a universal quality having instances in both substances; emerald greenness, if real, a universal quality having an instance in only one of them. We are deferring the question whether universals having many instances are to be called "many." [66] But we may anticipate that neither greenness nor emerald greenness will be found to be "one." It is not one emerald greenness that is instanced in one of the individual substances before us, not one greenness that is instanced in two of the individual substances before us. And since it is what is one that we have agreed to call the "same" as itself, it is not the same greenness or the same color that exists in two green objects. Indeed if both objects were emerald green as well as green, they would not, in our terminology, be of the "same" color. If two desks are not only long, but each four feet long, they are not of the "same" size. And you and I being two and no species of disease being one, you and I do not in any case suffer from the "same" disease.

What is the same is what is one. What is called by different names may be, with respect to certain mental attitudes, one and the same object. Two mental attitudes may be directed upon the same substance. And two successive phases may be phases of what, with respect to some mental attitude, is the same enduring thing. But genera are not made up of species that are each "one." And two individual substances—substances, that is to say, that are severally distinguished from their backgrounds and severally the objects of a concentrated attention—are not the same, no matter how specific the universals that are instanced in each of them.

How then shall we describe the relation between two substances each of which is emerald green and the relation between two desks each of which is four feet long? Perhaps we should say that the two substances are in the one case identical in color, in the other case identical in size. What we shall call "identity" requires a repetition of qualities. But although green which is instanced in this pea-green object is again instanced in that emerald

455

green object, the two objects which are both green are not, we shall say, identical. What is required, to put it colloquially, is a green in this object identical with the green in that. What is required is that there be no shade of green, no universal that is a species of color, which has an instance in one but not in the other. If there be two substances such that no species of color is instanced in one but not in the other, then they, we shall say, are identical in color with respect to the mental attitudes for which they are two. And if there be two substances such that no species of size is instanced in one but not in the other, then they, we shall say, are identical in size with respect to the mental attitudes for which *they* are two. However, in so far as an object is one, it is the same as itself, but not in our terminology identical with itself.

Two objects may be identical in color. Two desks may be identical in size. But is it possible for two substances to be identical in all respects? Two model T Fords may be identical in many respects, but since one is on my left and the other on my right, the quality of being on my left is instanced in one of them but not in the other. In general, entities that have different positions differ from one another in the qualities that they have relative to other spatial entities. And similarly with respect to temporal qualities. My model T Ford came off the assembly line after yours and the quality of having had a phase at a certain given moment is instanced in yours but not in mine. Indeed, differences in spatial and temporal qualities will themselves, it may seem, always involve slight differences in other qualities. With respect to two leaves grown in succession on the same tree, the fact that one is earlier points, we may grant, to its having been nurtured by a richer soil and is bound up with its being slightly different in texture from its successor. And if two peas are in a pod, one, being less shaded, is, we may grant, more developed by the sunlight which it receives than its fellow. But whereas it is plausible on the basis of such instances to grant that spatial and temporal differences always involve differences in other qualities, let us recall that, as we have explained "existence," no entity is real that is presented as no one's definite object. Whereas there are two leaves which, along with their difference in dates, differ in texture, there may be two other leaves which, although they differ in date, exhibit no other quality specifically attributed to one but not to the other. Although we might be tempted to agree in general that spatial and temporal differences involve differences in other qualities, there may be two leaves differing in date such that any definite non-spatial and non-temporal quality alleged to inhere in one but not in the other is presented to us as no one's definite object. And there may be a second pod containing two peas such that, with respect to them too, any definite non-spatial and non-temporal quality alleged to inhere in one but not in the other is presented as no one's definite object.

There are, we hold, no two individual substances that are identical in *all* respects, no two individual substances with respect to which there is not some species of date or position that has an instance in one but not in the other. But when temporal and spatial qualities are excepted, when we agree to call two substances "identical" provided there is no quality not based on its date or position that has an instance in one but not in the other, then, we hold, some pairs of identical substances do exist. These two Chesterfield cigarettes from the same pack are identical. There are identical nuts and identical valves. And John and Henry are identical twins. With respect to each such pair, no specific quality not based on date or position is normally presented to me as having an instance in one but not in the other. When I *am* presented with such a quality that is alleged to be some one's definite object, the entity presented to me appears generally discredited and is unreal. And, on the contrary, when I am presented with a John alleged to have no quality not based on date or position that is not an instance of a universal quality having a corresponding instance in Henry, then the entity presented to me appears not generally discredited and is real.

When qualities based on date or position are excepted, there are, we hold, some individual substances that are identical with one another. This conclusion differs from that of Leibniz who held that there were no two entities indistinguishable from one another. It was from the premise that God does nothing without a reason that Leibniz arrived at the conclusion that, apart from their numerical diversity, two entities must differ in at least some of their internal characteristics. Had God placed one substance here and an identical substance there, Leibniz argued, God would have acted irrationally since He might just as well have transposed them.[67] Thus from a metaphysical proposition Leibniz derived his doctrine of the identity of indiscernibles. He held this to be a great triumph of metaphysics. He held this doctrine to be an outstanding example of a truth concerning experiential objects that might be discovered without going beyond the realm of metaphysics.

There are however no rabbits to be pulled out of a hat. Metaphysical propositions determine the content of the world of existence only when what we are to call "existence" has in some sense previously been imbedded in our metaphysical propositions. The proposition that the world is the result of a rational plan is, as we see it, not so much a metaphysical conclusion about to be applied to the world of experience as it is a premise containing within itself a partial determination of the signification of "existence." One may to be sure doubt whether, when one decides to call what is irrational "unreal," it follows that what are alleged to be identicals are unreal. The problem of finding a reason why one entity is placed here and an identical entity there is more hopeless when we limit our attention to instantaneous entities contemporaneous with one another than when the alleged identical objects each have their histories and perhaps non-identical phases. If, for example, there is a reason for one to grow and for the other to decline, there will be a reason for some phase of the one to be identical in size with some phase of the other. But if irrationals are to be called "unreal" and if identicals are irrational, then identicals are unreal because of the signification the author has chosen to assign the term "reality" and not because of any knowledge about identity or rationality that we have gathered from non-experiential and non-terminological sources. Similarly if, as we hold, some alleged identicals are to be called "real," the premises which lead to this conclusion are in large part our propositions explaining the significations which in this treatise are assigned the terms "existence" and "reality."

Summary

What is the object of concentrated attention is "one." What is one with respect to one subject may be two or may be many with respect to another. But to say that the number that an object (or number of objects) has is relative to the subject is not to say that the subject puts duality or multiplicity or unity into the object.

In our terminology what is the same is what is one. Hence what is the same is relative to the subject just as what is one is.

Since a subject may concentrate his attention on any segment of his environment, our use of "one" does not distinguish natural units from artificial ones.

Where there is no discrimination of parts an entity is one and where there is no abstraction of qualities an entity is a substance. Each entity that is a substance is a unit with respect to the mental attitudes aware of it as a substance having qualities.

When change takes place, a substance does not change its qualities. Rather one phase (a substance) with its qualities is succeeded by a later phase (a substance) with *its* qualities.

How do we become aware of a substance when it is only its qualities that affect our senses? The substance, we reply, is only its qualities taken together and may be said to be sensed along with each of its qualities.

A substance is not to be distinguished from a quality by saying that the latter is conceived through a substance whereas the former is conceived through itself. Nor is a substance to be defined as that which is never a predicate.

We distinguish identity from sameness. What is the same is one. But identity requires a repetition of qualities in different substances. Two substances can not be identical in all respects, but when temporal and spatial qualities are left out of consideration, they may be.

459

Chapter XV

THE QUALITIES AND RELATIONS OF AN INDIVIDUAL SUBSTANCE

The desk in my study, we have said, is presented to me as large, heavy and made of mahogany. A rose in my garden, we may likewise say, appears red, full-grown, fragrant and beautiful. The desk we have determined to be an individual substance which is real. The rose, let us similarly decide, is an individual substance which also is real. How is it, however, with respect to the alleged size and heaviness of this desk and the alleged fragrance, beauty and redness of this rose? Whereas we have determined directly from our propositions explaining "reality" that certain alleged qualities of individual substances are real, we have not examined in detail all the arguments that may lead to the conclusion that alleged qualities are unreal, that this desk is not really large or heavy or made of mahogany, this rose not really beautiful or not really red.

Today this rose appears red; but when it was a bud it appeared green. This piece of litmus paper appears red; but after dipping it in an alkaline solution it will appear blue. Colors in short are not everlasting and immutable qualities. And there are some individual substances, such as the water in this glass, that seem to have no color at all. It has been said, however, that a substance "either has a quality or has not got it. And, if it has it, it can not have it only sometimes, and merely in this or that relation."[1] Since some substances are admitted to be colorless, it may be held that no substances are really colored. And since some earlier phase of this rose appeared green, it may be held that this rose is not really red. We have agreed, to be sure, that no substance antedates a quality that inheres in it.[2] If one phase of this rose is green and a later phase red, it is not the enduring rose that is red, but the later phase of it. But this later phase of the rose, which is a substance, need not lack the quality of redness because some other substance, such as an earlier phase of the rose, appears green. Nor need it lack the quality of redness because the water in the glass appears colorless. One substance may be colorless, a rosebud green, and, so far as we have yet seen, this rose, or, rather, a certain phase of it, really red.

But, it will be pointed out, it is not merely that the phase of the rose which is alleged to be red follows another phase which appears green. The very phase that is alleged to be red appears brown or of some other color to the observer who is color-blind. This liquid which tastes sweet to one drinker tastes bitter to another. And the same water at a given moment may, as Locke puts it,[3] "produce the idea of cold by one hand and of heat by the other." Red and brown, sweet and bitter, hot and cold are, we may agree, contradictory characteristics. And since, as we have explained "existence," self-contradictory entities do not exist, the rose that is held to be red and brown, the liquid that is held to be sweet and bitter, and the water that is held to be hot and cold, do not exist. It may be, however, that the water is hot and not cold, the liquid sweet and not bitter, the rose red and not brown. He who seems to be aware of a brown rose may simply be in error. The rose may be really red and may cause in one observer a mental attitude directed upon the real cause of that mental attitude and in another observer a mental attitude which, whereas it is as if it were directed upon a brown rose, has in fact no real object at all. The observation that the rose appears brown to one and red to another may imply, in short, not that the rose can not be either red or brown, but that there are instances of error.

Yet, whereas it seems possible that the mental attitude directed upon a red rose has a real object and that the mental attitude apparently directed upon a brown rose has none, we may, by directing our attention to the manner in which these two mental attitudes are caused, be led to the conclusion that it is not the rose itself which is red any more than it is the rose itself which is brown. The rose is a source of vibrations which impinge upon the optic nerve and retina. It is the condition of nerve and retina,

461

it is sometimes said, which determines whether we seem to see red or brown. Indeed, "if we receive a blow in the eye hard enough to cause the vibration to reach the retina, we see myriads of sparks which are yet not outside our eye."[4] We may consequently disregard the rose outside, it is sometimes felt, and look exclusively to the visual apparatus within the body to account for the colors which we seem to see. Similarly it is the nerve-endings within the body, it is said, which determine whether water feels hot or cold, the condition of the ear which determines whether a bell sounds harsh or musical or seems soundless altogether.

Important, however, as the body is for the perceiving of color or heat or sound, it is not to substances within the body that we normally attribute this color or heat or sound. It is the rose and not the optic nerve or retina that is generally said to be red, the water and not the nerve endings in the hand that is generally said to be hot, the bell and not the ear that is generally said to be musical. Redness as a quality of the optic nerve or retina is a subsistent presented as generally discredited, a subsistent consequently which is unreal. If the redness that is attributed to the rose is real at all, its habitat, we conclude, is not within the body of the observer.

Given a certain condition of optic nerve and retina, there may be a mental attitude apparently directed upon a brown rose; given another condition of optic nerve and retina, there may be a mental attitude directed upon a red rose. The rose remaining unchanged, the apparent objects seemingly presented to the observer will vary with the condition of the observer's optic nerve and retina. They will also vary, it has frequently been pointed out, with changes in the light or through the interposition of microscope or of colored spectacles. "He who observes a green color in a pulverized mixture," says Leibniz,[5] "his eye being presently assisted, no longer perceives a green color but a mixture of yellow and blue." In general, "a microscope often discovers colors in an object different from those perceived by the unassisted sight."[6] So do yellow spectacles; for he who wears them will have presented to him a large group of apparently yellow objects. It is thus something in the situation surrounding rose and observer that is red, it may be said, rather than either the rose itself or the

462

visual apparatus of the observer. How great an influence is exercised by entities other than the source and the observer is shown by the fact that "all other circumstances remaining the same, change but the situation of some objects, and they shall present different colors to the eye." [7] An actress may be wearing what we normally take to be a white dress. And yet when a blue spotlight is thrown on her, she will seem to be dressed in blue. Finally, it may be pointed out, on a dark night we see no colors. The grass is not seen to be green nor this rose seen to be red. And so color, it has been said, even though it "exists as color in the absence of the eye" "does not exist as color in the absence of light." [8]

Just, however, as redness presented as a quality of the optic nerve or retina is a subsistent presented as generally discredited and hence unreal, so are redness and greenness presented as qualities of the microscope. It is not the microscope that is red and green and the pulverized mixture not red and green. To be sure, the spectacles may be yellow and the spotlight blue. But it does not follow that there is no color in the objects that are seen through the yellow spectacles or in the dress on which the blue spotlight is turned. Important, in short, as various elements in the environment are, we can not conclude that color inheres always and exclusively in something outside object and observer and that the objects that appear colored are not so.

But whereas we reject the thesis that the redness commonly said to be in the rose is not in the rose but exclusively in something outside the rose, perhaps this redness is in the rose only in relation to entities outside it. Perhaps the rose considered by itself is neither red nor brown, the actress's dress considered by itself neither white nor blue, the water considered by itself neither hot nor cold. Just as when no point of reference is implied, my expression: "the position of P'" is a mere collection of words[9] and represents no real quality of P', so it may be held that without a certain type of observer or environment being implied, the expression: "the redness of the rose" is likewise a mere collection of words representing no real quality of the rose. The rose, it may be held, is red with respect to the normal observer or yellow with respect to the observer with the yellow spectacles or black with respect to a dark night, but not black absolutely or yellow absolutely or red absolutely. Just as position with respect to P

463

really inheres in P′, so it may be said yellowness with respect to the observer with yellow glasses really inheres in the rose and blackness on a dark night. But when no reference to sunlight or to a non-color-blind observer is expressed or implied, the expression: "the redness of the rose," it may be said, presents no subsistent to be believed or disbelieved but merely elicits a mental attitude which is incredulous and dismayed.

Is it true however that the rose is yellow with respect to the observer with yellow glasses? Just as the stick which is straight may be at the source of motions leading to a mental attitude which, although without an object, is as if it were directed upon a bent stick,[10] so the rose may be at the source of motions leading to a mental attitude which is as if it were directed upon a yellow rose. Stick and rose may each bring about diverse mental attitudes. But the subsistents that are the apparent objects of these mental attitudes are not equally respected. The bent stick and the yellow rose are presented to me as generally discredited. The straight stick and the red rose are presented to me as not generally discredited and are listed as real entities in the appendix to Chapter Three. On a dark night, in the absence of light, the rose may be the cause of a mental attitude which is as if it were directed upon a black rose; under a blue spot-light the actress's dress may bring about a mental attitude which is as if it were directed upon a blue dress. But whereas, having in view these causal relations, the rose may be said to be black with respect to a dark night and the dress blue with respect to a blue spot-light, it does not follow that the rose is red and the dress white only relatively, only relative to a certain type of observer and environment. Instead of eliciting puzzlement and dismay, the expressions: "red rose" and "white dress" may put before me objects sufficiently precise to be accepted or rejected. They may, and, we hold, do, put before me apparent objects which are not presented as generally discredited but are, on the contrary, real.

The actress's dress is less frequently seen under a blue spot-light than under a white light or in the sunlight. A brown rose is less frequently an apparent object for a color-blind observer than a red rose is an apparent object for a normal observer. It may be merely on the basis of the relative frequency with which various objects are presented that one alleged object comes to be presented as generally discredited and another not. Or it may be that the blue dress is presented as discredited and the red rose not, because the apparatus for absorbing waves of certain lengths and reflecting others is held to be in the rose itself in the one case, but in the other case in the spotlight rather than in the dress. Yet, whatever the basis for the distinction, the dress, we hold, is absolutely white and not merely white with respect to a white spotlight or with respect to sunlight; and the rose, we hold, is absolutely red and not merely red with respect to an observer with normal vision. Even the observer who sees the dress under a blue spotlight may at the same time seem to be aware of a white dress, a white dress presented as not generally discredited. That is to say, he may believe that the dress is white just as when I look at the sky I may believe the moon to be round and not a silver crescent. Similarly, when I walk in my garden on a dark night, it may be a red rose that is presented to me as not generally discredited, not a rose that at nightfall changed its color from red to black.

The rose, we thus hold, is absolutely red and not merely relatively so. The redness commonly attributed to the rose is, we hold, in the rose and not in the environment or in the optic nerve or retina of the observer. The rose's redness is real and at the source of motions which flow through a special channel—through retina and optic nerve—to bring about the mental attitude which, when I see red, is directed upon this redness. But what about the alleged redness of the rose when it is night and I do not see red? And what about the color of an object alleged to be infrared or ultraviolet? What about an alleged color, that is to say, which no one sees?

In order than an entity may be real in our sense of "reality," it will be recalled, that entity must be one that is not presented as no one's definite object. During the day, let us agree, I have seen red, have had redness as a definite object. And when I am confronted by a red rose at night, the redness of which I am aware, but which I do not see, is, it would seem, not presented to me as not a definite object. Similarly an alleged infrared color may be presented without the characteristic of being no one's definite object and may consequently be real, if, for example, it is believed that some organism, equipped with some type of visual apparatus

465

not found in man, is able to see infrared and have it as a definite object. But if it is held that no sort of organism is equipped to perceive infrared, if infrared is presented as no one's definite object, then, although certain entities may emit or reflect light rays longer than those associated with red, they are not infrared in color; their alleged infraredness is unreal.

The rose, we hold, is red absolutely, not red relative to a percipient who seems to be aware of a red rose and black relative to a percipient who seems to be aware of a black rose. It does not follow, however, that the water in this basin, which feels hot to one hand and cold to another, is absolutely hot or absolutely cold. Hot and cold seem rather indefinite characterizations, like large and small, far and near. How big, we are likely to wonder, is 'large'; how close is 'near'; how hot is 'hot'? When I am presented with an allegedly hot object, no definite object to be accepted or rejected is before me, but, rather, my mental attitude is one that is perplexed and thwarted. It is only when the water in this basin is presented as cold with respect to my hand or as hot with respect to melting ice that my object is sufficiently definite to be accepted or rejected and to be presented as not generally discredited. Unless hot and cold refer respectively to certain ranges on a temperature scale, hot and cold, it would appear, are relative qualities, not qualities that inhere absolutely in the entities to which they are attributed. Whereas then this rose is black with respect to a dark night, only in the sense that the rose may bring about a mental attitude which has a black rose as its apparent object, this water is hot with respect to melting ice in the sense that being hotter than melting ice is a real quality of the water. And whereas this rose is red absolutely, this water is cold absolutely only if it is understood, for example, that cold water is water which registers between 32° and 40° Fahrenheit.

Even on a dark night this rose, we hold, is red. Even under a blue spot-light, the actress's dress, we hold, is white. What shall we say, however, about the sound of a bell struck in a vacuum? That sounds "inhere not in the sonorous bodies," says Berkeley's[11] Philonous, "is plain from hence: because a bell struck in the exhausted receiver of an air-pump sends forth no sound. The air, therefore," he concludes, "must be thought the subject of sound." Just, however, as redness attributed to the sunlight rather than to the rose is presented to me as a subsistent generally discredited, so is loudness attributed to the air rather than to the bell. Red sunlight and loud air are both presented as generally discredited and both are subsistents which are unreal. But if the air isn't loud, perhaps the bell struck in a vacuum isn't, either. The bell, we may agree, has a certain structure which gives it a capacity for sound. It would seem that we refer to this sound-making apparatus when, while the bell is still unstruck, we speak of its *tone*. But it is only when the bell is struck that it sounds. And it may further be only when it is struck in a certain medium that it sounds. Even if I am deaf, the bell, struck in a proper medium, sounds. For the bell struck in a proper medium is presented to the deaf man as generally believed to be sounding. But whereas the bell is not loud when unstruck and *is* loud despite auditory defects in certain observers, what is the situation when the proper medium is absent? Is the bell struck in a vacuum loud like the bell presented to a deaf man as being struck in the air; or not loud like the bell not struck at all? It would seem that whereas the bell struck in a vacuum is believed to have the structure which gives it a capacity for sound, presented as actually sounding it is presented as generally discredited. It is the bell immersed in air that when struck is loud, the bell immersed in water that when struck is dull, the bell struck in a vacuum that has no sound at all. The bell, in short, is not loud absolutely; not even the bell that is struck. The struck bell is loud with respect to one medium, not loud with respect to another or with respect to no medium at all.

Color, heat and sound have frequently been called "secondary qualities." Let *us* likewise call them "secondary qualities." Let us use our term: "secondary quality" to represent a quality which has a special path open to it through which it brings about in some percipients a mental attitude directed upon it or upon the substance in which it inheres. The redness of this rose is, if real, a secondary quality since it has open to it such a special path passing through light waves and optic nerve, the loudness of this bell a secondary quality with a path passing through air waves and ear, the heat of the water in this basin a secondary quality with a path passing through nerve-endings below the surface of the fingers. And since we hold this rose to be red and this bell struck in the air to be loud, we hold some instances of secondary qualities to be real. The world of existents however, it will be remembered, can only be populated piecemeal. We have not concluded that all alleged secondary qualities exist. And even those secondary qualities that we *have* found existing:—the redness of this rose, the hotness of the water in this basin with respect to my hand, the loudness of this bell struck in the air, even these we have not found alike. This rose, we have found, is absolutely red; but the water in this basin is not absolutely hot or this bell absolutely loud. What is a real quality of the bell is loudness in a medium of air and what is a real quality of the water is coldness with respect to my hand and hotness with respect to melting ice. But whether absolute qualities or relative ones, redness, loudness when struck in air and hotness with respect to melting ice are qualities of the rose, bell and water respectively. And he who is apparently aware of black rose, or of bell not loud when struck in air, or of water cold with respect to melting ice, has a mental attitude without a real object.

I extend my hand towards a burning log and I become aware of hotness with respect to surrounding objects, a hotness which I attribute to the log. I extend my hand much further and become aware of pain which I attribute to my finger. Since in the one situation as in the other a disturbance proceeds from nerve ending to cortex, it follows that if pain is really a quality in my finger it is as much a secondary quality of it,—as we have explained "secondary quality,"—as heat is of the log. Indeed the mental attitude allegedly directed upon heat has so much in common with the mental attitude allegedly directed upon pain that it has on occasion been held that heat and pain are but one object, that "the intense heat immediately perceived is nothing distinct from a particular sort of pain." [12] Surely, however, "pain in my finger" and "hotness in the log" are not expressions which are synonymous. Pain in my finger and hotness in the log are distinguishable subsistents, one of which may be real and the other unreal. Agreeing however that they are distinguishable, what justification is there, it may be asked, since the processes through which we seemingly become aware of these subsistents are so similar, for a man to hold "that the idea of warmth which was produced in him by the fire is actually in the fire and his idea of pain which the same fire produced in him the same way is not in the fire?" [13] It is of course

468

common experience that, when my finger is sufficiently close to the fire, my attention is likely to be diverted from the fire to which I attribute hotness to the finger to which I attribute pain. It is likewise common experience that when I have withdrawn from the fire my mental attitude apparently directed upon a pain in my finger may continue and my mental attitude apparently directed upon the fire may not. In short, I *do* attribute hotness to the fire and *do* attribute pain to my finger. Pain presented as a quality of the fire is a subsistent presented as generally discredited, a subsistent which is unreal; whereas pain presented as a quality of my finger is a subsistent not presented as generally discredited, a subsistent, consequently, which may, so far as we have yet seen, be real.

But, it may be said, it is only the pain in *my* finger that is a percept of mine and only the pain in my finger which has a special channel open to it through which to bring about mental attitudes of mine. An alleged pain in *your* finger, it may be said —and we may agree,—does not affect nerve endings close to the surface of my body, does not initiate a neural disturbance which leads thence to my cortex. It does not follow, however, that the alleged pain in your finger is not a percept of mine. And it does not follow that the alleged pain in your finger, if real, is not a secondary quality as we have explained "secondary quality." A secondary quality, we have said, is one "which has a special path open to it through which it brings about in *some* percipients a mental attitude directed upon it or upon the substance in which it inheres." [14] Hence the alleged pain in your finger, if real, is a secondary quality inhering in your finger if, for example, it has a special path open to it through which to bring about mental attitudes of *yours*. The alleged pain in your finger may, so far as we have yet seen, be a secondary quality inhering in your finger; and it may, so far as we have yet seen, be a percept of mine. When I look at your finger, it is not only the color of your finger that is at the source of the vibrations which result in my mental attitude. The vibrations come from the finger which is a substance with all of its qualities inhering in it. If then your finger is really paining, really sore, this pain is also at the source of these vibrations. And since the object which is reached by a given mental attitude and "which is at the source of motions flowing uninter-

469

ruptedly to that mental attitude"[15] is in our terminology a "percept," this pain is, if real, a percept of mine.

The word "pain" is, to be sure, a noun and may be held to represent a substance rather than a quality. The entity which we are considering however is not presented as being in your finger in the way in which a chair is in a room but rather in the way in which redness is in the rose. Although we shall continue to call this entity a "pain," some ambiguity might be avoided by calling it an instance of "soreness." What we are considering is a soreness alleged to be in your sore finger as redness is alleged to be in a red rose. Your finger, we are suggesting, has soreness or pain inhering in it. This soreness or pain is a secondary quality of your finger's in so far as it has a special channel open to it through which there is brought about a mental attitude of yours directed upon this soreness or pain. And this soreness or pain, presented as a secondary quality inhering in your finger, is a percept of mine in so far as it is at the source of motions flowing uninterruptedly to the mental attitude of mine which has it as an object.

The sound of the bell does not affect the deaf man through the processes peculiar to sound nor does the pain in your finger affect me through the processes peculiar to pain. Since with respect to each of these objects there is some mental attitude directed upon the object which is brought about through the special paths open to that object, the alleged pain in your finger is, if real, an instance of what we are calling a secondary quality and the alleged loudness of the bell an instance of a secondary quality. Let us suppose however, that there is *no* mental attitude directed upon the alleged pain in your finger that is brought about through the processes peculiarly open to pain and no mental attitude directed upon the alleged loudness of the bell that is brought about through the processes peculiarly open to sound. Let us suppose, for example, that you are under an anesthetic so that the stimulation of your nerve-endings does not carry through to your cortex; and let us suppose that no one is sufficiently close for his ear to be affected by the air waves set in motion by the bell.

If the alleged pain in your finger or the alleged sound of the bell that is unheard is presented as no one's object or even as no one's definite object, it is, we hold, unreal. The bell that no one hears may of course be some one's object, as indeed, it is ours as we read this

470

sentence. But can its loudness be said to be a definite object for a mental attitude that is direceted upon it, but does not hear it? The signification of "definite object," like the signification of "existence" is something to be made relatively precise only through considering its application to particular entities. Let us say that the man who is sufficiently sensitive and sympathetic and has a mental attitude directed upon the alleged pain in your finger has a definite object. And let us say that the sound of the bell that no one hears is a definite object for the man commonly said to have strong auditory imagery and imagination who has this sound as his alleged object. When the unfelt pain and the unheard sound are presented to us as objects for such thinkers, they are not presented as definite objects for no one and need not be unreal. In short, the pain in your finger that you do not feel may be real and the tree that falls in the wilderness may fall with a loud noise. But since the pain in your finger that you do not feel does not use the processes peculiarly open to pain to bring about mental attitudes directed upon itself either in you or in your sympathizer, this pain is not a secondary quality of your finger. Similarly, since no one hears the noise of the falling tree, not even the man with strong auditory imagery who has it as a definite object, this noise, although a real quality of the falling tree, is not a secondary quality of it.

In a previous chapter we pointed out various mental attitudes which are directed upon objects and which are accompanied by, or are in part, feelings. Laöcoon, we have said,[16] was remembering the Greeks and also fearing them, Cato "remembering the Carthaginians and hating them and Abelard perceiving Eloise and loving her." Certain instances of loving, fearing, hating, being angry, disgusted or pleased, presented as mental attitudes, we found real and agreed to call "feelings." There is such a feeling, let us suggest, that accompanies or is a part of your mental attitude directed upon the pain in your finger and that accompanies or is a part of my mental attitude directed upon the pain in *my* finger. I do not perceive the pain in my finger dispassionately. On the contrary, my attitude directed upon my finger is tinged with emotion: I am aching [17] as well as perceiving. The pain in my finger through processes peculiarly open to it brings about my mental attitude directed upon this pain. The pain is thus a secondary

471

quality of my finger. But my mental attitude brought about by this pain is also in part a feeling. And so, let us say, the pain is, or may be, a tertiary quality of my finger. What we call tertiary qualities, in short, are related to feelings. Since you are aching when you perceive the pain in your finger, pain is a tertiary quality of your finger just as another instance of pain is a tertiary quality of my finger. To be sure, no aching accompanies your mental attitude directed upon the pain in my finger nor my mental attitude directed upon the pain in yours. In order that an entity may be a tertiary quality, let us say, not every mental attitude directed upon it need be accompanied by feeling. An entity is a tertiary quality of an object, let us say, when certain suitable and appropriate mental attitudes directed upon it are in part, or are accompanied by, feelings.

The pain in your finger we have already determined to be real. The aching that is a part of your mental attitude directed upon it is as real as Laöcoon's fearing or Abelard's loving. Hence there exists at least one instance of what, as a matter of terminology, we have chosen to call "tertiary qualities." We are not introducing the expression "tertiary quality," however, merely to discuss instances of pain which in their status as secondary qualities have already been found to be real. We introduce it as appropriate to a discussion of the alleged perilousness of a mountain path that some suitable traveler may be said to approach with caution, the alleged horrible condition of Dachau prisoners that suitable observers may be said to think of with horror, the alleged beauty of Cezanne's "Mont Ste. Victoire" that a suitable observer may be held to perceive with an esthetic emotion.

Just as pain is a quality of the finger, so the perilousness that we are considering is, it is alleged, in the mountain path; a horrible condition, it is alleged, a quality of Dachau prisoners; beauty, it is alleged, a quality of the "Mont Ste. Victoire." Just as some mental attitude directed upon the pain in the finger is accompanied by, or is in part, an instance of aching, so there is, it is alleged, a mental attitude directed upon the alleged perilousness of the mountain path that is accompanied by a feeling of caution; a mental attitude directed upon the prisoners' alleged horrible condition that is accompanied by a feeling of abhorring; a mental attitude directed upon the alleged beauty of the "Mont Ste. Victoire" that

472

is accompanied by an esthetic emotion. But whereas it is through a special path—from nerve-ending to cortex—that the pain brings about one of the mental attitudes whose object it is, no such special path, it would appear, lies open to the perilousness of the mountain path, the horrible condition of the Dachau prisoners or the beauty of the Mont Ste. Victoire. Perilousness, horribleness and beauty, that is to say, are not presented to us as secondary qualities that through special paths brings about mental attitudes of which they are objects, if, indeed, they are presented to us as percepts at all. In view of their alleged lack of perceptibility, it may be held that this perilousness, horribleness and beauty are unreal. But as we have frequently had occasion to point out, entities need not be presented as percepts in order to exist in our sense of "existence." Even if a substance's alleged beauty is presented to me as not at the source of motions leading to any of the mental attitudes directed upon it, it need not be presented with any of the characteristics that would mark it out as unreal. Even if the beauty of the Mont Ste. Victoire is not a percept, it may be as real as the other side of the moon which is no percept or tomorrow's phase of the sun which is likewise no percept with respect to my present thinking.

Just however as it may be questioned whether the pain in your finger is not after all in some sense a cause of my mental attitude directed upon it, so it may be questioned whether the alleged beauty of the Mont Ste. Victoire is not, if real, in some sense a cause of my mental attitude directed upon *it*. When I look at the picture which is a substance, the impulses which bring about my mental attitude originate where the substance is, which is also where its qualities are. My mental attitude directed towards the picture's color scheme may be said to be caused by the color scheme; my mental attitude directed towards the picture itself may be said to be caused by the substance which is then my object; and my mental attitude directed towards the picture's alleged beauty may, if this beauty is real, be said to be caused by the picture's beauty.

The alleged beauty of the "Mont Ste. Victoire" is, to be sure, no secondary quality of the substance in which it inheres. It also differs from certain other alleged qualities of the picture in that it appears less tangible, less easily described. We can point to the picture's color, its size, its rectangular shape and can imagine specific changes in the picture that would change these qualities. Yet we would be hard put to make another person aware of the alleged beauty of the picture or to determine just what alterations would cause the loss of its alleged beauty. Even so, it does not follow that this alleged beauty is presented as no one's definite object or presented as generally discredited. Just as the loudness of the bell is presented to the deaf man as a definite object for the mental attitudes of others,[18] so the alleged beauty of the "Mont Ste. Victoire" may be presented as being a definite object for connoisseurs. He who does not feel it need not discredit the picture's beauty. On the contrary, he may have this alleged quality of the picture presented to him as one that is not generally discredited. It is such an alleged quality, so presented, that we are considering. And it is this subsistent, this alleged tertiary quality of the "Mont Ste. Victoire," that, as we are using "reality," we find real.

Not only then is redness a quality of this rose and pain a quality of my finger, not only is this bell loud in a medium of air and the water in this basin cold with respect to my hand and hot with respect to melting ice; but Cezanne's "Mont Ste. Victoire" is really beautiful and the condition of the Dachau prisoners really horrible. Just however as this rose is red absolutely, but the water in this basin hot only relatively, so certain tertiary qualities may inhere in their substances absolutely and others only relatively. The mountain path, for example, may be perilous for a motorist at night, but not perilous for a pedestrian at noon. But with certain qualifications we hold that perilousness is a real quality, a real *tertiary* quality, inhering in the mountain path as beauty is a real tertiary quality inhering in the "Mont Ste. Victoire." The beauty of the Mont Ste. Victoire is presented to me as apprehended with an aesthetic emotion by suitable observers. So presented, it is a real quality of Cezanne's picture. The perilousness of the mountain path with respect to a motorist at night is presented to me as apprehended by suitable observers with a feeling of caution. So presented, it likewise is a real quality of the mountain path.

The beauty of the Mont Ste. Victoire is presented to me as apprehended with feeling by suitable observers. The alleged beauty of a substance that is presented to me as not apprehended with feeling at all is, however, no tertiary quality and, further, is not what I should term "beauty" at all. As I use the term "beauty," beauty can be apprehended without feeling, but not presented as *always* apprehended without feeling. For the term "beauty" presents to me no alleged quality of the object that I can identify and discuss except in so far as I can relate it to a particular feeling, namely, the aesthetic emotion, that accompanies some of the mental attitudes directed upon it. The noise of the tree that falls unheard in the wilderness may be a definite object for some one with strong auditory imagery and imagination. Such a noise, we have said,[19] may be a real quality of the tree, albeit not a secondary quality. The beauty of the primeval forests that had no observers may be apprehended with feeling by some imaginative aesthete of our own day. In such a case, beauty may be a real quality of those forests, a real tertiary quality. But if all mental attitudes said to be directed upon this alleged beauty are held to be unaccompanied by an aesthetic emotion, then no specific quality of the primeval forests is presented to me whose existence or non-existence I can discuss.

Without instances of feeling on the part of some suitable observers, there are no tertiary qualities. But if this is so, it may be said, tertiary qualities are products of mind and not really in the substances to which they are attributed. Nothing up to this point in our discussion of tertiary qualities, however, warrants the conclusion that mental attitudes put beauty into objects in the way in which mental attitudes bring about marks on a piece of paper. To be sure, in painting his picture Cezanne brought into being the "Mont Ste. Victoire" along with all of its qualities, beauty included. But the mental attitude accompanied by an esthetic emotion that is directed towards the beauty of the setting sun is the source of no activity that proceeds to the setting sun and adds beauty to it. The beauty of the setting sun does not follow the feeling directed upon it in the way in which marks on paper follow the decision to write. The primeval forests *were* beautiful even if it is only some imaginative aesthete of our own day who contemplates them with an aesthetic emotion. On the other hand, without mental attitudes at all, nothing would be real. Without instances of remembering there would be no memories, without instances of perceiving no percepts, and without instances of feeling no tertiary qualities. To express ourselves more properly, the entity presented to us as no one's object is self-contradictory and unreal; and the tertiary quality presented to us as never contemplated with feeling is likewise self-contradictory and unreal. There is, in short, a sense in which tertiary qualities are dependent on mind; but it is only the sense in which all existents are dependent on mental attitudes and the sense in which special types of existents are dependent on the corresponding types of mental attitudes that have them as their objects.

Some instances of tertiary qualities, we hold, are real. Some instances of secondary qualities, we have found, are likewise real. *A fortiori* let us agree that there exist some instances of size, of weight and of motion. Let us agree, that is to say, that there exist instances of qualities that can be numbered, in a word, instances of primary qualities. Let us hold that the screaming, onrushing locomotive is not only loud and dangerous to those in its path, but also moving with respect to the earth at sixty miles an hour. And let us hold that the rose in my garden is not only red and beautiful, but also has a weight of one ounce. For, as the alleged loudness of the locomotive subsists as some one's definite object, so does its alleged motion. And as the alleged beauty of the rose subsists as not generally discredited, so does its alleged weight.

In our discussion of secondary qualities we have already met with the observation that the same water at the same time may "produce the idea of cold by one hand and of heat by the other." [20] But, asks Berkeley,[21] "why may we not as well argue that figure and extension are not patterns or resemblances of qualities existing in matter; because to the same eye at different stations, or eyes of a different texture at the same station, they appear various and can not therefore be the images of anything settled and determinate without the mind?" "Let any one," he says,[22] "consider those arguments which are thought manifestly to prove that colors and tastes exist only in the mind, and he shall find they may with equal force be brought to prove the same thing of extension, figure and motion." The converse, however, is also true. If the fact that a rose is presented to one mental attitude as red and to another as brown does not imply that the rose has no color at all, then the fact that a coin is presented to one mental attitude as elliptical and to another as circular does not imply that the coin has no shape at all. "It does not . . . follow," says Leibniz,[23] "that what does not always appear the same is not a quality of the object." "The observation

476

that the rose appears brown to one and red to another may imply . . . not that the rose can not be either red or brown, but that there are instances of error." [24] And the observation that the coin appears elliptical to one and circular to another simply points to a similar conclusion.

It may be held that the circularity which causes one mental attitude directed upon a circular coin and another mental attitude, which, although without an object, appears to be directed upon an elliptical coin, is not the circularity which is a geometrical object and which can be numbered. The former, it may be said, is a percept, a secondary quality; the latter a non-sensible object presented to our reason, hence a primary quality. Just however as we hold that there is a point on the surface of the earth that we call the North Pole and a line that we call the equator, so we hold that there is a circle close to the edge of this coin which is a real circle. [25] There are indeed no real points, lines or circles that do not lie within the world of real entities, that do not, for example, have position with respect to contemporaneous phases of the North Pole and the equator. This coin which has position with respect to my body has circularity; and no contemporaneous entity which lacks position with respect to my body *does* have it. If then there is any circularity that can be numbered, it is the sort of circularity that is a quality of this coin. Likewise, however, if there is any circularity that can be perceived, it is the sort of circularity that is a quality of this coin. For it is the coin with *all* of its qualities that is the source of the processes which lead to my eye and cause me to perceive it. Hence, if the coin has a circularity which can be numbered, a circularity which is a primary quality, this primary quality that it has is likewise the source of the processes that lead to my eye; and my mental attitude directed upon this numberable circularity is likewise an instance of perceiving. Thus we hold circularity to be a real quality of the coin that can be both perceived and numbered. Just as we hold that the pain in my finger is both a secondary quality and a tertiary quality of my finger, so we hold that the circularity of this coin is both a primary quality and a secondary quality of the coin.

Not only does this coin have a circularity which can be measured and numbered; but this red rose has a structure which permits it to reflect light waves that can be measured and numbered and this pink rose a structure which permits it to reflect light waves that can be measured and assigned a different number. "We conceive the diversity existing between white, blue, red, etc.," says Descartes,[26] "as being like the differences between figures. The same argument applies to all cases; for it is certain," he continues, "that the infinitude of figures suffices to express all the differences in sensible things." If, then, "we had but faculties acute enough to perceive the severally-modified extensions and motions" of the minute bodies of which our objects are composed, the knowledge of these primary qualities would explain "the nature of colors, sounds, tastes, smells and all other ideas we have." [27] Since there is a primary quality for every secondary quality allegedly presented to us, perhaps these primary qualities are alone real and secondary qualities mere epiphenomena that do not really inhere in the substances that are presented to us.

The question is whether this rose has merely a structure which permits it to reflect light waves that can be measured and numbered, a primary quality; or whether it also is red. On either hypothesis we can, we assume, adequately account for our mental attitudes apparently directed upon redness. On either hypothesis light waves which are not red proceed from the rose to me and bring about a mental attitude which likewise is not red. On either hypothesis the mental attitude which is not red is apparently directed upon redness. On the one hypothesis the alleged redness of the rose, which is not needed to account for our mental attitude directed upon it, is nevertheless real. On the other, the alleged redness is unreal and the mental attitude apparently directed upon it is not an instance of perceiving but a mental attitude without an object. On the one hypothesis the rose is red despite the fact that the light waves and mental attitude directed upon it are not red. On the other hypothesis the rose is not red despite the fact that it appears so. Neither hypothesis appears self-contradictory. It is through the application of our propositions explaining "existence" that we must decide whether the rose is without color or whether, in addition to its structure, its qualities that can be numbered, it also is red. But this is a decision that we have already made. The redness of this rose is presented to us as some one's definite object and as not generally discredited; and, so presented, it is, we have said,[28] real.

Some secondary qualities in short exist alongside primary qualities. There exist some instances of primary qualities, some instances of secondary qualities, and some instances of tertiary qualities as well.

Primary qualities we have chosen to describe as numberable, secondary qualities as sensible,[29] tertiary qualities as apprehended with feeling. The circularity of this coin is sensible as well as numberable, the pain in my finger apprehended with feeling as well as sensible. As a real quality may be both numberable and sensible, or both apprehended with feeling and sensible, so, we hold, a real quality may be neither sensible nor numberable nor apprehended with feeling. Marshal Ney may be said to have been brave, Aeneas pious, Lincoln kindly and Leibniz learned; but neither bravery, piety, kindliness nor learning has a special process open to it through which to bring about a mental attitude directed upon itself. These qualities, if they exist, are not secondary qualities. Nor are they either primary or tertiary qualities. For the bravery of Marshal Ney is not presented to us as measurable and numberable nor the erudition of Leibniz as apprehended by suitable observers with feeling. They are however presented to us as qualities to be abstracted from real substances, as entities that are definite objects for various mental attitudes, as entities that are not generally discredited. Marshal Ney, we hold, was really brave, Lincoln really kindly and Leibniz really learned. Some instances exist, that is to say, of qualities that are neither primary, secondary nor tertiary qualities.

Lincoln was tall, sad and kindly. Being a substance, did he have the quality of being a substance, the quality of substantiality?[30] And having various qualities, did he have the quality of having various qualities? If any instance of substantiality exists, it is neither numberable, sensible nor apprehended with feeling. But, as we have just seen, a quality need be neither a primary, secondary nor tertiary quality to be real. An alleged instance of substantiality is real if it is presented to us as a quality, presented without any of the characteristics that would mark it out as unreal and if, so presented, it is listed as real in the appendix to Chapter Three. It may be questioned however whether the alleged quality of substantiality is presented to us as a quality and not as *not* a quality, whether the alleged quality of having qualities is not at the same time presented to us as something that does not follow its substance as an object of our thinking, as something, in short, which is not abstracted from its substance. Abstraction, it may seem, puts before us the substance's redness and not something different from it to be called the substance's having the quality of being red. But whereas a mental attitude directed upon a substance may be followed by a mental attitude directed upon its redness, it may also be followed by a mental attitude directed upon the possibility that the substance affords us of thinking first of it and then of its redness. It is its being fit subject matter for abstraction that we call a substance's alleged quality of substantiality. And this being presented to us as something different from the redness or kindliness that the substance has and as something that may follow the substance as an object of our thinking, this alleged quality of substantiality is, we hold, real.

If I write the word "substantial," this word on paper is itself a substance and has the quality of substantiality. If I write in black ink the word "black," the word I have written is black; and if I write "short," the word I have written is short. Several words representing qualities are substances which have the qualities they represent. We may distinguish such words from others by calling them "autological." A mental attitude directed upon the word "substantial" may be followed by a mental attitude directed upon its substantiality; a mental attitude directed upon the word "short" by a mental attitude directed upon its brevity. In what sense, however, is a mental attitude directed upon the word "short" followed by a mental attitude directed upon its autologicality? I find myself unable to pursue much further the very interesting problem posed by Weyl with respect to autologicality and its opposite: heterologicality.[31] Weyl proposes that all adjectives that are not autological be called heterological. And he poses the problem whether the adjective "heterological" is itself heterological or not. If we hold that "heterological" is heterological, he points out, then just as "short," being short, is autological, so "heterological," being heterological, is autological; and if we hold that "heterological" is not heterological, then, just as "long," not being long, is heterological, so "heterological," not being heterological, *is* heterological. I however am hardly able to present to myself autologicality and heterologicality as qualities to be abstracted

480

from *any* substances,[32] much less from the words "autological" and "heterological." And without definite subsistents to consider, I can neither hold that autologicality and heterologicality are real nor determine how the dilemma which, if real, they might pose for us, might be resolved.

"Short," "black," "substantial," these are adjectives that represent qualities. "Brevity," "blackness" and "substantiality" are nouns that similarly represent qualities. "This story is short" appears synonymous with: "This story has brevity"; "This cat is black" synonymous with: "This cat has blackness"; "This desk is substantial" synonymous with: "This desk has substantiality." It appears to be a matter of the idiom of the language in which we write whether we say "I am hungry" or, with the French, "j'ai faim." "Brevity," "substantiality" and "blackness" are, in short, abstract nouns, that is, nouns representing qualities that may be presented to us through abstraction.[33] And if our conclusions with respect to pain are accepted, the word "pain" is likewise an abstract noun. To be sure, we speak of "a pain" as though "pain" were a concrete noun representing a substance. But we also speak of "a sound" or "a color." "A color," it would seem, generally represents a species of the universal quality: 'color,' as, for example, blackness; "a sound" an instance of the universal quality 'sound,' as, for example, the sound of an individual explosion. In line with such analogies let us suggest that we use "a pain" to represent an instance of the universal quality 'pain,' that, for us[34] at least, "I have a pain in my finger" is synonymous with: "My finger is paining (or painful) with an individual instance of the quality: pain."

If this leaf's color is to be represented by an adjective, we say that this leaf is colored; if by an abstract noun, say that this leaf has color. But this leaf is not merely colored, but green; and not merely green, but emerald green. Making use of abstract nouns, it not only has color, but has *a* color; not only has greenness, but has a certain shade of greenness. We have already pointed out, however, that "if anything is green and pea-green or green and emerald green, . . . its pea-greenness or emerald greenness is as much a quality of the individual substance as its greenness."[35] It is not the color of the leaf which has the quality of being green or emerald green, but the leaf itself which is colored,

481

which is green, and which is emerald green. But whereas this leaf is colored, green and emerald green, color is not *one* of its qualities, greenness a second and emerald greenness a third. "Without mental attitudes that are focussed separately upon what in some sense are parts, there is no multiplicity in the object in our sense of multiplicity."[36] Its color, its greenness and its emerald greenness are not *parts* of this leaf. On the contrary, they are concomitant with one another, co-extensive with the leaf from which they are abstracted. But whereas in our terminology number does not apply to the qualities that inhere in an individual substance, we can call the phase of a subject who has a mental attitude directed towards the leaf's color "one," the phase of a subject who has a mental attitude directed towards the leaf's greenness "one," and the phase of a subject who has a mental attitude directed towards the leaf's emerald greenness "one." We can therefore ask how many such phases there are that are directed towards different qualities of this leaf; even though we can not ask how many qualities this leaf has and get as a correct answer "three" or "fifteen" or "an infinite number."

There exists a phase of a subject who has a mental attitude directed toward this leaf's color; for, along with other characteristics, such a phase is presented as some one's definite object. There likewise exists a phase of a subject who has a mental attitude directed towards this leaf's greenness and a phase of a subject who has a mental attitude directed towards this leaf's emerald greenness. But there is only a finite number of such phases with mental attitudes allegedly directed upon different qualities that are presented as some one's definite object. The number of phases having mental attitudes really directed upon different qualities of this leaf is not infinite. The only qualities of this leaf that are real are its color, its greenness, its emerald greenness and such other alleged qualities as are not presented as not definite objects and might be specifically mentioned. The group of its real qualities has no number at all. And the group of phases of subjects having mental attitudes directed towards different qualities of this leaf is not infinite in number. It has a number, but a number to be determined in the manner in which we determine the number of readers that this book will have or the number of points on a given line.[37]

482

This rose, we have said,[38] is red, Cezanne's "Mont Ste. Victoire" beautiful,[39] the stick partly immersed in water straight. These instances of redness, beauty and straightness are, we hold, absolute qualities of the substances in which they inhere. On the other hand, there inheres in the water in this basin the quality of being hot with respect to melting ice; there inheres in the mountain path the quality of being perilous with respect to the motorist at night; there inheres in Peter the quality of being older than Paul. The expressions representing these last named qualities each include words which by themselves represent other substances. "Melting ice" represents a substance other than that in which hotness with respect to melting ice inheres. "Paul" represents a substance other than the Peter who is his senior. Leibniz holds that "relative terms indicate *expressly* the relation they contain."[40] But let us designate as relative qualities not only the hotness with respect to melting ice that inheres in this basin of water and not only the quality of being older than Paul that inheres in Peter, but also certain qualities represented by expressions that do not expressly include words representing other substances. "I may say that an entity is far away and the context may make it clear that I am asserting this entity to be far away from where I now am."[41] Let us call the real quality that this entity has of being far away from where I now am a relative quality even though it is represented by the expression: "far away" and not by the fuller and more explicit expression: "far away from where I now am." In short a relative quality is represented by an expression which either explicitly, or tacitly and by implication, includes words representing a substance other than that in which the quality inheres. My automobile has the relative quality of being in motion with respect to the surface of the earth even though I point to this quality by saying: "My automobile is moving" and do not take the trouble to say: "My automobile is moving with respect to the surface of the earth."

It is the quality and not the expression representing it that we call a relative quality. A relative quality may be represented by an expression including words representing some second substance. Or, as we have just seen, it may be represented by an expression in which such words are merely implied. In the latter case the quality which is relative may also be called a pseudo-absolute quality.[42] But what about the expression? Does the expression which includes words representing a second substance always represent a relative quality? We must remember that if an alleged quality is unreal, it is neither a relative quality nor an absolute quality and no expression can truly be said to represent it. Since Peter is older, not younger, than Paul, the expression: "younger than Paul" represents no relative quality inhering in Peter. And since yonder stick is not bent, since this alleged bent stick does not exist, the expression: "thinking about yonder bent stick" represents no relative quality inhering in me.[43]

Similarly the expression which seems to represent a quality and which includes no words representing another substance need not represent an *absolute* quality. As we have just seen, words representing another substance may be implied so that the expression represents a relative quality. More than this, the expression may put before us nothing that is real and hence may not represent a quality at all. If Peter is said to be "older" and there is nothing in the context to point out the person whose senior he is alleged to be, the expression "older" leaves us puzzled with no alleged quality of Peter's before us to be accepted or rejected. On the other hand, if Peter is said to be circular, there is a subsisting quality of Peter's presented to us, but presented as generally discredited and hence unreal. Neither olderness nor circularity really inheres in Peter; neither "olderness" nor "circularity" represents an absolute quality of Peter's, although in the one case a subsistent is allegedly presented to us and rejected and in the other case no subsistent presented to us at all.

"An actress may be wearing what we normally take to be a white dress. And yet when a blue spotlight is thrown on her, she will seem to be dressed in blue."[44] When we are presented with the statement that the dress is white, it may be held that we are puzzled and have no definite subsistent before us; just as when we are presented with the statement that Peter is older. It may be held that there are no absolute qualities, that expressions which include no words representing other substances either imply such words or represent nothing real. It is true that the dress's whiteness results from bleaching, that the dress appears white only in certain lights, that it would not be seen to be white unless there were light rays and retinas. But a mental attitude directed upon

484

the dress's whiteness need not be directed upon the history and causes of this whiteness. The statement that the dress is white puts before me a subsisting quality that is not outside the dress. I am not puzzled but have a definite object which, being real, is an absolute quality of the dress. Similarly the statement that the dress is blue puts before me a subsistent which is allegedly a quality of the dress, not a quality of the total situation. But, being unreal, blueness is not an absolute quality of the dress.

The relative qualities of a substance, we have said, are represented by expressions which explicitly or implicitly include words representing other substances. In the case of Peter's being older than Paul, the other substance Paul is as definitely located as Peter. But in the case of a basin of water that is hot with respect to melting ice, it is any or all instances of melting ice that constitute the second substance. Peter is tall for a man, tall with respect to an average man; a mountain high with respect to neighboring mountains. Finally the second substance is quite indefinitely located when we say that a proposition is true in your sense of the word "truth," not true in my sense of that word.

Let us, however, concentrate our attention upon certain instances in which the second substance is as definitely located as the substance in which the relative quality inheres. Peter is old with respect to Paul. This chair is near with respect to this table. Alexander was a rider with respect to his mount Bucephalus. Each of these instances puts before us an enlarged substance or relational situation which includes as its parts both the second substance and the substance in which the relative quality inheres. Rider-on-horse includes Bucephalus as well as Alexander. Chair-near-table includes table as well as chair, Peter-older-than-Paul Paul as well as Peter. Just as an instantaneous phase of Bucephalus's hoof is more definitely located than an instantaneous phase of Bucephalus, so an instantaneous phase of Bucephalus is more definitely located than an instantaneous phase of Alexander-mounted-on-Bucephalus. Paul is presented to us as approximately three feet away, Peter-older-than-Paul as from three to five feet away, that is, as having the more extended position that belongs to both boys taken together. Neither Alexander-mounted-on-Bucephalus nor chair-near-table nor Peter-older-than-Paul is, however, presented to us with so indefinite a location as to be unreal. Some

485

relational situations, substances such as Alexander-mounted-on-Bucephalus, this-chair-near-this-table and Peter-older-than-Paul, are, we may agree, real.

Moreover the relational situation or substance AB may have a quality which implies, or is implied by, a quality relative to B that inheres in A and a quality relative to A that inheres in B. If, for example, A B is dense or compact, its part A may well have the quality of being near with respect to B and its part B the quality of being near with respect to A. And if A B has the quality of being homogeneous, A may well have the quality of being like B and B the quality of being like A.

We have thus before us the substance A with the quality that it has relative to B, the substance B with the quality that it has relative to A, and the substance AB with its quality—such as compactness or homogeneity—that may imply A's quality relative to B or B's quality relative to A. But these are all substances or qualities. Is there then nothing real that is represented by the term "relation" that is neither a substance nor a quality? Chair-near-table or Peter-older-than-Paul is frequently symbolized by A-r-B rather than by AB. Is there then nothing real represented by "-r-"? In addition to the compactness that is a quality of A B and the nearness with respect to B that is a quality of A, is there, in short, no nearness that is *between* A and B?

It is not every real A and every real B that together form a relational situation AB that is real. The alleged relational situation: Hannibal-like-Napoleon, the substance, that is to say, that is alleged to have Hannibal and Napoleon among its parts, is presented with a quite indefinite date. Alexander-on-Bucephalus, chair-near-table and Peter-older-than-Paul are selected instances, real instances, of what might be symbolized by AB. A few paragraphs back we decided to concentrate our attention upon situations in which B is as definitely located as A. We have since selected instances where A and B are neither temporally remote nor have their contemporaneous phases widely separated from each other. And now if we are to place before ourselves real entities *between* A and B, real entities to be represented by the r of A-r-B, we must be still more selective.

Let us consider, for example, the relational situation: dog-chained-to-post. The dog has the quality of being chained to the post. The post, we might say, has the quality of being chained to the dog. And dog-chained-to-post is a substance of which dog and post are parts. But the chain is also a part of dog-chained-to-post. It is a real instance of the r of A-r-B. Again, let me draw a one-inch line between two points. Point A has the quality of being one inch from B, point B the quality of being one inch from A. But the one-inch line is also a real substance having the quality of length. And it is this line with its length which is *between* A and B and which constitutes the distance between them. Even in these instances however, chain and line are substances. We have presented nothing to ourselves that is between A and B and at the same time neither a substance nor a quality.

The two bottles of milk on my doorstep, one a quart bottle and one a pint bottle, taken together constitute a real instance of the relational situation: B-less-than-A. But the part of this composite substance B-less-than-A that is neither B nor A, the part that is the air between the two milk bottles, can hardly be said to be the habitat of less-ness. A less-ness that is seemingly presented to me as between A and B seems to be presented as generally discredited and is unreal; and a less-ness that seems to be presented with no position at all is likewise unreal. Greater-than-B is a quality of A and less-than-A a quality of B. But, says Bertrand Russell,[45] these are not simply adjectives of their terms:—they are analysable respectively into *less* and *A*, *greater* and *B*. Hence, he concludes, "the abstract relations *less* and *greater* remain necessary," so that "the relational form of proposition must be admitted as ultimate." In holding however that the phrase: "less than A" represents a real quality of the substance B, we are not required to hold that the word "less," taken by itself, represents a real entity. Otherwise, in holding that the word "father" represents a real substance, we should be required to hold that the syllable "fath" represents something real. Our conclusion then is that there are substances, instances of A, which have real qualities relative to B; that in some of these instances there are real relational situations, the composite substances AB or A-r-B; and that in some of *these* instances, as in dog-chained-to-post or A-one-inch-from-B, there is a real substance between A and B that may be called the link or relation between them. But there are real relational situations where there is no real link; and real relative

487

qualities where there is no real relational situation.[46]

Dog-chained-to-post is an instance of a real relational situation within which the relating component, the chain, is real. On the other hand, the two bottles of milk on my doorstep, one a quart bottle and one a pint bottle, constitute an instance of a real relational situation: B-less-than-A, within which the alleged relating component, the 'less-ness,' is unreal. The two lines that I draw on a sheet of paper, one three inches long and the other one inch long, likewise constitute an instance of a real relational situation: 'B less than A' within which the alleged relating component, the 'less-ness' is unreal. But if with respect to these two last-mentioned relational situations there is no real less-ness in the one resembling a 'less-ness' in the other, what have these relational situations in common and how can we speak of both of them as instances of the universal relational situation: B-less-than-A? The terms of the one do not resemble the terms of the other, a quart bottle of milk not resembling a three-inch line nor a pint bottle of milk a one-inch-line. But just as homogeneity is likely to be a quality of the relational situation: A-like-B and homogeneity a quality of the relational situation: C-like-D,[47] and just as density is likely to be a quality of A-near-B and a quality of C-near-D, so there is a quality of pint-bottle-less-than-quart-bottle that resembles a quality of one-inch-line-less-than-three-inch-line. Each of these relational situations, that is to say, has the quality of having two components within it, one less than the other. And it is in accordance with these similar characteristics that the two relational situations are each instances of a universal relational situation that we describe as 'B-less-than-A.'

The substance B has the quality of being less than A. The substance A has the quality of being greater than B. And the substance B-less-than-A has the quality of having two components within it, one less than the other. The quality of having two components within it, one less that the other, does not inhere in A and B each. "If so, we should have an accident in two subjects with one leg in one and the other in the other, which," according to Leibniz,[48] "is contrary to the notion of accidents." It is the relational situation as a whole,—the B-less-than-A that is less definitely located than either A or B,—of which the quality of having two components within it, one less than the other, is a real

488

quality. And it is because this quality can be abstracted from it that the relational situation: B-less-than-A, which we have found real, is a substance.

The relational situation: 'pint bottle of milk less than quart bottle of milk' is less definitely located than either the pint bottle of milk or the quart bottle of milk which are its component terms. Similarly Brutus killing Caesar is more extended, less definitely located than Brutus in the act of killing or Caesar being killed. But Brutus committing suicide is no less definitely located than Brutus the killer or Brutus the victim. In so far as I have one mental attitude directed upon Brutus the killer and another mental attitude directed upon Brutus the victim, Brutus killing Brutus, like Brutus killing Caesar, may be called a relational situation. Since, however, Brutus the killer and Brutus the victim are not parts of a larger whole with respect to the mental attitudes directed upon them, since Brutus the killer is the same as Brutus the victim, Brutus killing Brutus has but a single term. And so, in calling Brutus killing Brutus a "relational situation," we are using "relational situation" in such a way that the relational situation need not be less definitely located than either of its terms but may, on the contrary, be the same as its single term.

Let us further call John giving a book to Mary a "relational situation" and Plato telling Aristotle about Socrates. My attention may be focussed separately upon John, the book and Mary in the one case; and upon Plato, Aristotle and Socrates in the other. But along with the mental attitudes focussed upon the three terms, there is a mental attitude directed upon the more extended whole which includes John, book and Mary and a mental attitude directed upon the more enduring whole which includes Socrates, Plato and Aristotle. John giving a book to Mary and Plato telling Aristotle about Socrates are, we hold, real entities which, with respect to certain mental attitudes, are individual substances. And despite their three terms, they are real entities which we shall call relational situations.

Brutus committing suicide, that is, Brutus killing Brutus, is a real relational situation; Peter older than Paul is a real relational situation; and Plato telling Aristotle about Socrates is a real relational situation. Except in such instances as Brutus committing suicide, the relational situation is less definitely located or more enduring than any of its terms. And so it may be held that the relational situation is not a percept, but, on the contrary, a mental construct. A and B taken by themselves, it may be held, may each bring about the mental attitudes of which they are the objects, but not the connection that is between A and B or the more extended or more enduring relational situation that includes both A and B. "The connection of anything manifold," says Kant,[49] "can never enter into us through the senses, and can not be contained therefore already in the pure form of sensuous intuition." It never lies "in the objects and can not be borrowed from them by perception."[50] But unless A and B are definitely located points, not only is the relational situation extended,— and the connection between them, if real—but the terms are extended as well. The problem which Kant poses, it would appear, does not point back to the distinction between connecting links or relational situations on the one hand and, on the other hand, the terms within the relational situations or between which the connecting links lie. Rather, it would seem, his conclusion requires as a premise a proposition as to the size, or lack of it, that an entity must have in order to be the source of vibrations leading to a mental attitude directed upon its cause. But this is a subject which we have already discussed. If all causal action is linear in type analogous to the action of one billiard ball upon another, then the only entities that are perceived are of minute size, neither punctual nor greatly extended.[51] But if an extended wave front starting from an extended source can converge upon our sense organs, then entities of appreciable size may also be regarded as percepts.[52]

However, whether entities of appreciable size be percepts or not, whether, for example, the chain that connects the dog to the post or the relational situation: dog-chained-to-post be a percept or not, the entity that is our object need not be unreal. For, as we are using the term "reality," it is not the entity presented as not a percept that is unreal, but the entity presented as generally discredited or presented as lacking date or position. Dog-chained-to-post is, we hold, real; and Plato telling Aristotle about Socrates. The relational situation including Socrates, Plato and Aristotle is no percept of mine. And yet it is no product of my present mental attitude. Presented as a definite object for no

490

one or as in no sense an object for my present mental attitude, it would be unreal. But being presented as not a percept of mine, an entity with duration indefinitely dated several centuries before Christ, the instantaneous phases of which are located in Athens, and being listed in the appendix to Chapter Three, the relational situation including Socrates, Plato and Aristotle is real.

Dog-chained-to-post is, we hold, a real relational situation; and Plato telling Aristotle about Socrates. This pint bottle of milk less than this quart bottle of milk is a real relational situation; and Peter older than Paul. But these are all relational situations, instances of A r B, where the letters A and B represent individual substances such as Plato, Peter, the dog and the quart bottle of milk on my doorstep. What shall we say however with respect to such alleged relational situations as are suggested by 'being hot is preferable to being cold' or 'being courageous similar to being bold'? It is a substance A that is hot or courageous, a substance B that is cold or bold. As we have agreed to use the word "quality," it is A that is hot or very hot. Very hotness, that is to say, is a quality of A, not of A's hotness.[53] And similarly, if 'preferable to cold' is a quality, it too is a quality of some substance A rather than of A's hotness. Whereas Peter has the quality of being older than Paul, we can not in our terminology say that Peter's age has the quality of being greater than Paul's, or Peter's heat the quality of being preferable to Paul's coldness. If A were not hot, A would not be very hot. A's quality of hotness, we may say, is fundamental to A's quality of very hotness. Similarly if Peter did not have age and Paul age, Peter would not have the quality of being older than Paul. Peter's age and Paul's age may therefore be described as the "fundamenta relationis" in the relational situation: 'Peter older than Paul'; Peter's temperature and Paul's temperature as the "fundamenta relationis" in the relational situation: 'hot Peter preferable to cold Paul.' But it is Peter hotter than Paul that is the relational situation, not something different from it to be called 'Peter's heat preferable to Paul's cold.'

'Hot Peter preferable to cold Paul' is an individual relational situation. Assuming that such universals exist, it is an instance of the universal relational situation: hot things preferable to cold things. But if we say that heat is preferable to cold, we are not likely to be asserting that with respect to each pair of substances differing in temperature, the hot member is preferable to the cold one. We are likely to be asserting that the hot member is preferable to the cold one, all other things being equal, or all qualities other than temperature being disregarded. 'Hot thing preferable to cold thing, all other qualities being disregarded' is perhaps a real universal relational situation. 'Heat preferable to cold' is, it would seem, a simpler and less explicit expression representing this very situation the terms of which are substances. For I find no other relational situation differing from it in which the terms are only qualities.

There are, we hold, relational situations, the terms of which are substances; no relational situations differing from them, the terms of which are qualities of these substances. Peter's age, by itself, does not in our terminology enter as a term into a relational situation with Paul's age. And Peter's age, by itself, does not in our terminology enter as a term into a relational situation with the substance Peter in which it inheres. Peter's age can be abstracted from the substance Peter. But abstractability can hardly be called a connecting link between Peter and his age analogous to the chain that is a connecting link between the dog and the post. And Peter's-age-abstractable-from-Peter is not in our terminology a relational situation as dog-chained-to-post is.

There is the relational situation: dog-chained-to-post within which dog and post are the terms. And there is the relational situation: dog-fastened-to-chain within which dog and chain are the terms. But we can not indefinitely continue the process of regarding the connecting link of one relational situation as a term in a new relational situation. We soon find ourselves presented with a relational situation in which, as in the relational situation: B-less-than-A, the alleged connecting link, taken by itself, is unreal. There is no real 'less-ness' that is a connecting link or relating component within the relational situation: B-less-than-A.[54] And there is no real 'fastened-to' that is a connecting link or relating component within the relational situation: 'dog-fastened to chain.' Again, Peter and Peter's age are not in our terminology the terms of a relational situation: Peter's age abstractable from Peter; much less Peter and abstractability the terms of a relational situation: Peter subject-matter for abstract-

492

ability. In short there is no infinite series of relational situations: A-R-B, A-R'-R, A-R''-R'; and no infinite series of relational situations: substance related to quality, substance related to the relation between substance and quality, substance related to the relation between substance on the one hand and the relation between substance and quality on the other.

There is the real relational situation: Peter older than Paul; the real relational situation: Peter owner of the dog Fido; the real relational situation: Peter son of Caius. Into how many real relational situations, we may ask, does Peter enter as a term? Each material substance, we are told, is the source of radiations which travel outward without ceasing so that each body to some extent affects every other body, either heating it or cooling it, either attracting it or repelling it. There is no real entity, we are told, that Peter is neither near to nor far from, neither earlier than nor later than, neither like nor unlike. And so it may seem that there is no real substance that does not join with Peter in entering into a real relational situation. In order that an entity may be real however, it may not be presented, we must remember, as having only a very indefinite position or as having only a very indefinite date. 'Peter far from Sirius,' let us say, is presented with so indefinite a position as to be an alleged relational situation that is unreal, 'Peter descendant of the first organism on this planet' presented with so indefinite a date as to be an alleged relational situation that likewise is unreal. Peter may have the quality of being far from Sirius; for that quality, abstractable from Peter, is presented with the rather definite position that belongs to Peter. But there is no substance so greatly extended as to include both Peter and Sirius within it as parts, no relational situation: Peter-far-from-Sirius that in our sense of "reality" is real.

In order that an entity may be real, moreover, not only may it not be presented as having only an indefinite date nor as having only an indefinite position; it also may not be presented as no one's definite object. I may compare Peter with the Lama of Tibet, with the winner of the Kentucky Derby, with the piece of chicken on my dinner plate. But there remain many other substances S where Peter-related-to-S is unreal. For whereas in writing: "Peter-related-to-S," 'Peter-related-to-S' is presented as in some sense an object of my present mental attitude, it appears that no one will specifically compare Peter to S, and 'Peter-related-to-S' is accordingly presented to me as no one's definite object. It is thus only a finite number of S's with which Peter will be actually compared, a finite number of S's with respect to which 'Peter-related-to-S' is not presented as no one's definite object.

There is, it follows, only a finite number of real relational situations into which Peter enters as a term. Peter-far-from-Sirius is not one of them. And yet far-from-Sirius might well be a real quality of the substance: Peter.[55] If number were applicable to Peter's qualities, the number of Peter's real qualities might well be greater than the number of real relational situations into which Peter enters as a term. But as we are using "number," the group of Peter's real qualities has no number at all.[56] There is a finite number of phases of subjects having mental attitudes directed towards different qualities of Peter's, a finite number of subjects having mental attitudes directed towards Peter's quality relative to this and towards Peter's quality relative to that. And there is perhaps a smaller number of relational situations into which Peter enters as a term, a smaller number of substances: 'Peter-related-to-this' and 'Peter-related-to-that.'

'Peter-far-from-Sirius' is, we have said, an alleged relational situation that is unreal. What shall we say with respect to the alleged relational situation: 'Peter-unrelated-to-Sirius' and with respect to the alleged quality of Peter's: unrelated-to-Sirius? Since 'Peter-unrelated-to-Sirius' is an alleged relational situation within which Peter and Sirius are terms, and since there is no substance so greatly extended as to include both Peter and Sirius within it, 'Peter unrelated to Sirius' is an alleged relational situation which is unreal. On the other hand, 'unrelated-to-Sirius' is an alleged relative quality of Peter's that is presented with a sufficiently definite position to be real. But if Peter has the real quality of being far from Sirius, his alleged quality of being unrelated to Sirius is likely to be presented as generally discredited. It is thus because of one characteristic that 'unrelated-to-Sirius' fails to be a real quality of Peter's and because of a different characteristic that 'Peter-unrelated-to-Sirius' fails to be a real relational situation. There is, it would seem, no entity with respect to which Peter has the real quality of being unrelated to it. For if A is a real substance and Peter is presented as having the quality of being unrelated to it, *ipso facto* Peter is presented as having the quality of being related to A. And if A is not a substance or not real, Peter can not be related to it, can not enter into the sort of relational situation with it of which 'Peter-unrelated-to-A' would be an instance. Peter can not be related to a non-existent A any more than I can be a cousin of a non-existent person or my mental attitude directed upon a non-existent object.

Peter has the relative quality of being older than Paul, the relative quality of being the owner of the dog Fido, the relative quality of being the son of Caius. What happens to Peter's quality of being a dog-owner, we may ask, when Fido dies? And what happens to Caius's quality of being a father, if Peter dies? "Caius whom I consider today as a father ceases to be so tomorrow," says Locke,[57] "only by the death of his son, without any alteration made in himself." There is an alteration, however, in the sense that today's phase of Caius has the relative quality of being a father with respect to Peter, tomorrow's phase of Caius the quality of not being a father. Relative qualities, like qualities in general, are no more enduring and no less enduring than the substances in which they inhere. Just as it is not the caterpillar-butterfly taken as an enduring whole that crawls or that flies, but one phase that crawls and another phase that flies; so it is not Caius as a whole that is a father or not a father, but one phase of Caius that has the relative quality of being a father and another phase of Caius that has the quality of not being a father.[58] Caius taken as a whole does not discard one quality and take on another. But there is alteration in the sense that one phase of a substance with its qualities is succeeded by another phase of that substance with *its* qualities.

It may be felt that the Caius who is not a father differs from the preceding phase of Caius who *is* a father less than the butterfly that flies differs from the preceding phase: caterpillar that crawls. A succession of phases differing only in relative qualities may be less noticeable and may seem less notable than a succession of phases differing in qualities which are not relative. But if, as we hold, relative qualities are real qualities of the substances or phases of substances in which they inhere, we must agree with Leibniz's statement,[59] properly interpreted, when he says: "Nor does any one become a widower in India by the death of his wife in Europe without a real change happening in him. For every predicate is

495

truly contained in the nature of the subject."

"A succession of phases differing only in relative qualities," we have said, "may be less noticeable and may seem less notable than a succession of phases differing in qualities which are not relative." But this brings us back to a question that we have already to some extent examined, the question whether there *are* both absolute qualities and relative qualities.[60] A distinction between relative qualities on the one hand and qualities which are not relative on the other, it may be held, can not be maintained. Caius, it may be said, is not only a father with respect to Peter and a husband with respect to Anna, but the color that he has is relative to the sunlight and his height relative to some standard length with which he is compared. "When I analyze matter," says Kant,[61] "I have nothing that is absolutely, but only what is relatively, internal; and this consists itself of relations." We have already agreed, however, that some actress's dress is absolutely white and not merely white with respect to a white spotlight or sunlight; and that a rose is absolutely red and not merely red with respect to a non-color-blind observer.[62] A real quality that is relative, it is to be remembered, is one that is presented to us through an expression which either explicitly or tacitly contains words referring to some substance other than that in which the relative quality inheres. And a quality is real and not relative when an expression without such words is not puzzling, but, on the contrary, puts before us an alleged quality that has none of the characteristics that would mark it out as unreal.[63]

It is true, to be sure, that thinking is not static. A mental attitude directed upon the whiteness of a dress may be followed by a mental attitude directed upon a white spotlight or the sun; just as a mental attitude directed upon Caius's fatherhood may be followed by a mental attitude directed upon Peter. But for a quality to be absolute, it is not necessary that a mental attitude be directed upon it and rest there. If this were the requirement, there would perhaps be no qualities really "internal," no qualities that do not lead on to mental attitudes directed upon relations. But as we are using the expression "relative quality," the question is not what we think of next, but whether an expression that neither explicitly nor tacitly contains words representing other substances is merely puzzling. or puts before us something that is fairly definite and is real.

It is one thing to have a mental attitude directed upon the dress's whiteness which is real. It is another thing subsequently to have a mental attitude directed upon the sun in whose light we see the dress to be white, or upon the bleaching process through which it became white. Unless we go on to think about the sun and the bleaching process, we do not know all about the dress and its whiteness. Our knowledge is fragmentary. And knowledge that is fragmentary is sometimes held to be no knowledge at all.[64] "When I take in my judgment one fragment of the whole," says Bradley,[65] "it certainly does not exist by itself." As we are using "existence," however, the whiteness of the actress's dress exists. And as we are using "truth," "the actress's dress is white" is a true proposition. We are not using "existence" in such a way that there is but one all-inclusive real entity. And we are not using "truth" in such a way that there is but one all-embracing Truth. There are many true propositions, many individual substances. And abstractable from a number of these individual substances, there are various real qualities, some of them relative and some of them absolute.

Summary

We define a secondary quality as one which has a special path open to it through which it brings about in some percipients a mental attitude directed upon it or upon the substance in which it inheres. Such secondary qualities have been held to be unreal in that they appear inconstant qualities of the substances in which they inhere; in that whether or not one is aware of them depends on the condition of our nerve endings, on the condition of the medium through which they have affected us, etc. Our conclusion, however, is that some alleged secondary qualities exist and inhere in the public objects in which they appear to inhere. Whereas, however, a certain rose is red absolutely, a certain bell is loud with respect to one medium, not loud with respect to another.

Pain is a secondary quality which inheres in, for example, my finger. It is also a tertiary quality, that is, a quality such that, when

497

certain suitable and appropriate mental attitudes are directed upon it, these attitudes are accompanied by feelings. Pain is not the only tertiary quality which has real instances. Just as a rose may be red, so a sunset may be beautiful. The rose does not become red by being thought of, nor does the thinking make the sunset beautiful. (But there is, of course, the oft-mentioned fact that the beauty of the sunset thought of as no one's object is self-contradictory and unreal.)

Primary qualities are also real in certain instances; also qualities which are neither primary, secondary or tertiary.

Some qualities are absolute, others relative. This leads to a discussion of A-r-B, which we call a "relational situation." Many instances of A-r-B are real, but only in some of these cases is "r" taken by itself real.

Chapter XVI

UNIVERSAL SUBSTANCE AND UNIVERSAL QUALITY

"What is Man that Thou art mindful of him? And the son of man that Thou visitest him? For Thou hast made him a little lower than the angels and hast crowned him with glory and honor."[1] It is this 'Man' that concerns us in this chapter rather than Socrates or Napoleon. Our attention, that is to say, is here directed towards such alleged universals as 'star,' 'tree,' and 'circle' rather than towards Sirius, the Washington elm at Cambridge, Mass., or the circle on page 31 of my copy of James' Psychology.

There are various alleged Napoleons that may be presented to us. There is a subsisting Napoleon who wrote the "Critique of Pure Reason" and a Napoleon who is alleged to have built the Taj Mahal; as well as the Napoleon who was defeated at Waterloo and died at St. Helena. Similarly, universals may be presented to us in various ways. They may, for example, be presented to us as occurring somewhere; or they may be presented to us as utterly non-spatial. They may be presented to us as having some date or dates; or they may be presented as utterly timeless.

"People often assert that man is mortal." And yet, continues Bertrand Russell,[2] "we should be surprised to find in the *Times* such a notice as the following: 'Died at his residence of Camelot, Gladstone Road, Upper Tooting, on the 18th of June, 19—, Man, eldest son of Death and Sin.'" Whereas Socrates is often presented to us as occurring in the fifth century before Christ and Napoleon as occurring some eighteen hundred years after Christ, 'man,' it is suggested, is presented to us as having no date. And whereas Socrates is often presented to us as in Greece and Napoleon as in France, 'man,' let us suppose, is presented to us as having no spatial position. Universals such as 'man,' 'tree,' 'star' and 'circle,' that is to say, may be alleged to be neither now nor then, neither here nor there. The spatial and temporal qualities which characterize individuals may be held to be inapplicable to universals, which, it may be said, are non-temporal and non-spatial altogether.

As we have explained "existence," however, whatever is presented to us as utterly non-temporal or utterly non-spatial does not exist.[3] There is no 'man' that is neither before Christ nor after Christ, no 'tree' that is neither in Greece nor in France nor anywhere else, no 'circle' that is neither near nor far from the phase of the North Pole that may be alleged to be its contemporary. Universals that are presented to us as utterly non-spatial, it follows, are alleged universals, subsisting universals, that can not be real.

It may be said, however, that the group of propositions that make up what is roughly called "science" is full of words representing these utterly non-spatial universals. Science, it may be said, concerns itself with such non-spatial universals as the number two, man, hydrogen, the atom. Science, it may be said, is something indubitable that must be accepted. What it presupposes or implies, namely, non-spatial and non-temporal universals, must therefore, it may be concluded, likewise be indubitable and real. Just as it may be argued that experience is real, that in experience we find causes and effects, hence that the relation of cause and effect implicit in experience is real; so one may begin by accepting the existence of science and conclude from it the existence of the non-spatial universals that may be alleged to be implicit in it.

We have, however, rejected the doctrine that, because experience is real, the causal relation is real. We have held, that is to say, that experience and the causal relation are equally dependent for their reality upon the signification given the term "real."[4] Similarly with what some may call "science" and the non-spatial universals that may be alleged to be implicit in it. Science is not real except for some particular determination of the signification of "reality." It affords no basis for a conclusion as to the reality of non-spatial universals apart from such a signification, apart from a signification that may be applied with equal directness to the alleged non-spatial universals themselves. Whatever, then, may be

500

the status of science, whatever indeed the precise signification of "science," alleged non-spatial universals are unreal in the sense in which we have chosen to use the terms "existence" and "reality."

It does not follow that 'science,' in all senses of that term, or even that science, in a commonly accepted sense of that term, is unreal. But it does follow that an allegedly non-spatial 'atom' which is unreal can not truly be said to combine with other atoms; it does follow that an allegedly non-temporal circle which is unreal can not truly be said to be the locus of points equidistant from the center. If A is unreal, "A is B" is false and "A is not B" false, "A implies B" false and "A implies non-B" false.[5] Since neither non-spatial nor non-temporal universals exist, there can be no true propositions whose subject-terms represent such alleged universals,[6] no body of true mathematical or scientific propositions in which the mutual relations and implications of such universals are laid down.

We have placed before ourselves alleged universals which are non-temporal and alleged universals which are non-spatial. And we have found that, when universals are alleged to have such characteristics, they are unreal. Let us therefore turn to other subsisting universals, to universals that are not alleged to be non-temporal or non-spatial, but are alleged in some sense to have positions and dates. Let us, in particular, turn to 'man' presented to us, not as non-temporal or non-spatial, but presented to us as having the dates and positions that Socrates and Hannibal and Napoleon have. Let us in short turn from the universal that is alleged to be outside its instances to the universal that is alleged to be *in* its instances.

Socrates is a man, Hannibal a man, Napoleon a man. Together with millions of others, they constitute what may be called "mankind." But whereas Socrates lived in the fifth century before Christ and Napoleon some eighteen hundred years after Christ, there is attributed to mankind taken collectively only the indefinite date of occurring in the later geological eras of the earth's history. The Washington elm stood in Cambridge, Mass., but the position of trees taken collectively can only be described in some such sentence as: "Trees cover a large part of the earth's surface." There is, in short, each tree and trees taken collectively, each man and mankind. Just, however, as neither Socrates nor Napoleon nor the Washington elm is generally presented to us as a universal, so neither trees taken collectively nor mankind is generally presented to us as a universal. Trees taken collectively is, if real, an individual substance with a single but indefinite position with respect to the North Pole, a single but indefinite date with respect to the birth of Christ. Similarly, "mankind" normally represents an individual substance and is the expression of a single mental attitude. For when we are aware of the various parts of mankind, of various men, we are not likely to describe our object as "mankind" but as "men."

Socrates is presented to us as having date and position; but Socrates so presented is an individual rather than a universal. Mankind is presented to us as having date and position; but it too is an individual rather than a universal. In our attempt to present to ourselves a subsisting universal that is not alleged to be non-temporal or non-spatial, we are led to consider not the individual substance Socrates and not the individual substance mankind, but rather: men. In so far as the universal which we are to call 'man' points to men taken individually, this alleged universal is presented to us neither as non-temporal nor as non-spatial. On the contrary, it is presented to us as having many dates and many positions. 'Man,' so presented, has the quality of occurring in the fifth century before Christ (in its instance: Socrates), some eighteen hundred years after Christ (in its instance: Napoleon), with as many dates as there are men. Similarly 'man' so presented occurs in Tokyo, in New York, in the African jungle, has every position that belongs to an individual man.

But if, in order to present to ourselves a universal which is neither non-temporal nor non-spatial, we must turn to an alleged universal which has each of the dates and positions of its various instances, if the alleged universal that we are to call 'man' is in effect the plurality of individual men, then, it is said, 'man' will be many as men are many. "Nothing," we read,[7] "can occur at the same time, as an integral whole, in many entities if it is to be one and the same thing." Surely, "universal" intends to point to something that is in some sense one. But if the universal "is one and yet, being one, is in each one of the many . . . one and the same thing will exist as a whole at the same time in many

502

separate individuals and will therefore be in a state of separation from itself." Consequently, says Parmenides,[8] "the universals themselves will be divisible and things which participate in them will have a part of them only and not the whole idea existing in each of them."

How, then, we ask ourselves, can 'man' be presented to us as something that is neither non-temporal nor non-spatial but, on the contrary, has many dates and positions; and yet be presented to us as something that is not many as its instances are many? There are indeed many men. And yet, let me suggest, it is possible to consider this plurality of men without attending to their number or to their various dates and positions. My desk is large and heavy and made of mahogany. Yet I can, and do on occasion, disregard its size and its quality of being made of mahogany. Through abstraction I come to be aware of its heaviness, not of the desk in which that heaviness inheres, not of the qualities other than heaviness that the desk has.[9] Somewhat similarly, let me suggest, beginning with a plurality of men as my object, I can disregard the fact that one man occurred in Greece in the fifth century before Christ and another in France some eighteen hundred years after Christ. I can disregard the number of men and have as my object what we propose to call "the universal: 'man.'" The entity which we are proposing to call "the universal 'man'" is, one might say, many as it occurs in nature. There is plurality in the world to which it refers just as there is no heaviness existing alone, but, on the contrary, a large heavy mahogany desk from which heaviness is abstracted. But in so far as the heaviness of my desk is my sole object, I am not aware of the desk in which it inheres; my object is not a substance. Similarly, in so far as the entity which we are presenting as the universal 'man' is my object, I am not aware of the many men who are instances of 'man' and my object is not many.

But if the 'man' that we are proposing is not, as my object, many, neither is it, accurately speaking, to be called "one." When my attention is directed towards 'man,' my attention is not dispersed as it is when I think separately of John and of Harry. There is, one might say, a single mental attitude which to some extent justifies the use of the word: "universal." But if there is a single mental attitude directed towards 'man' and a single men-

503

tal attitude directed towards 'animal,' nevertheless we can not, consistent with the explanations of "number" previously given, say that 'man' and 'animal' are two. There is no world of 'man' plus 'animal' that can be divided into 'man' on one side and 'animal' on the other. 'Man' is not a *part* of man-plus-animal. And "without mental attitudes that are focussed separately upon what in some sense are parts, there is no multiplicity in the object in our sense of 'multiplicity.'"[10]

Again, I may have a mental attitude directed upon a desk and another mental attitude directed upon the man sitting on it; whereas some other subject may be aware simply of the composite: man-on-desk. Man-on-desk, that is to say, may be one with respect to his mental attitudes, two with respect to mine.[11] There is, however, no similar sense in which the subsisting 'man' that we are considering is two. For if in this connection someone's objects are two, his attention is being directed towards two men or two groups of men and not towards part of 'man.' Yet if 'man' and 'animal' are not two, and if 'man' is not one with respect to one subject and two with respect to another, then it serves no useful purpose to call 'man' one, 'circle' one and 'tree' one. Just as we have chosen not to call the size of my desk and the weight of my desk "two,"[12] and just as we have chosen not to apply number to qualities, so let us choose not to apply number to the alleged universals that we are considering.

The 'man' that we are presenting to ourselves is then neither one nor many. Mankind, all men taken collectively, is normally one. There are phases of mankind, such as mankind in the fifth century before Christ. And with respect to this phase of mankind, with respect to all men in the fifth century before Christ taken *collectively,* Socrates is a *part.* But the plurality of men taken *individually* do not have individual men as their parts. They do not have the one indefinite position that belongs to mankind, but rather the many positions, the more definite positions, that belong to individual men. In so far as they are many, they are not a whole and have members rather than parts. Now the universal 'man' that we are considering is, as it were, imbedded in these many men rather than in the one mankind. Like the plurality of men taken individually, this universal 'man' is not a whole and has instances rather than parts. But unlike them, it is not many; for the 'man' that

504

we are suggesting comes before us through disregarding the number of its instances. It is not many like the plurality of men taken individually; nor one like mankind.

The alleged universal 'man' that we are presenting is then presented as neither one nor many, presented not as non-temporal or non-spatial, but presented without the dates or positions that belong to its instances. "As we use the term 'existence,'" we have said,[13] "an entity is not unreal in so far as it appears without a given characteristic." An entity need not be presented to us with its date or dates, with its position or positions, in order to be real. The alleged universal that claims to be non-spatial or non-temporal is, as we have seen, unreal.[14] But the alleged universal that appears without its dates or positions, the 'man' that is presented to us without the claim that it has one instance in Greece in the fifth century before Christ and another in France some eighteen hundred years after Christ, this alleged universal may, so far as we have yet seen, be an existent entity.

The 'man' that we are considering is not presented to us with the characteristic of being non-temporal or non-spatial. Nor does it appear generally discredited or with any of the other characteristics that would mark it out as unreal. It can be,[15] and is, enumerated among the existent entities listed in the appendix to Chapter Three. It is, we conclude, an existent entity. And as there is a real 'man' that, putting it briefly, is in its instances but presented without them, so there is a real 'star,' a real 'atom,' a real 'circle.'

The individual man Socrates is a substance, the individual star Sirius a substance, the circle on page 31 of my copy of James' "Psychology" a substance. "The individual substance," we have said,[16] "is an unanalyzed whole which comprises a full set of concomitant qualities, everything real concomitant with a given position together with that position itself." The universals 'man,' 'star' and 'circle' that we have just found real are obviously not individual substances. "A given position" inheres, not primarily in 'man,' but in Socrates. But along with the term "individual substance," let us make use of the term "universal substance." An entity is a universal substance, let us say, when it is such a universal as the 'man' that we have described and when each of its instances is an unanalyzed whole which comprises a full set

505

of concomitant qualities, when each of its instances, in short, is an individual substance.

But if 'man,' 'star' and 'circle' are universal substances, universals, that is to say, whose instances are individual substances, what about 'beauty,' 'greenness,' 'size' and 'acceleration'? Just as we can present to ourselves the plurality of men taken individually, but disregarding their dates, positions and number, so we can present to ourselves the greenness of this leaf, the greenness of that tree, the greenness of many other things that are green, taken individually; and yet we can have an alleged object that leaves out the dates, positions and number of these things that are green. We can present to ourselves an alleged universal 'green' that corresponds to the alleged universal 'man' already found real, an alleged universal 'green' that, putting it briefly, is likewise in its instances but presented without them. Among its alleged instances, however, are the greenness of this leaf rather than this leaf which is an individual substance, the greenness of that tree rather than that tree which is green. Like 'man,' such an alleged universal 'green' is, we find, real. It is, let us say, a universal quality, a universal, that is to say, each of whose instances is the quality of an individual substance.

There is the universal substance 'man' whose instances are individual men. And there is the universal substance 'green thing' whose instances are the various individual substances that are green. On the other hand there is the universal quality 'green' whose instances are the greenness of this leaf, the greenness of that tree, the greenness of various other green things. And there is the universal quality 'human nature' which has among its instances, not Socrates, but the human nature of Socrates, not the individual substance John Smith, but the human nature of John Smith.

Let us, however, look more closely at the universal substance 'man' and the universal quality 'human nature.' When we are aware of the universal substance 'man,' ours is an object from which we have dropped the dates and positions of Socrates, Plato, and so on; an object where we are disregarding the number of individual men. But, it may seem, Socrates without his date or position is in effect no longer a substance, is in effect the human nature of Socrates. What we are calling the universal substance

506

'man' is, it may seem, the human nature of Socrates, the human nature of Plato and so on, disregarding the number of substances in which such a human nature inheres. The universal substance 'man,' it may seem, is indistinguishable from what we are calling the universal quality 'human nature.'

But Socrates without his date and position is not indistinguishable from the human nature of Socrates. And this green leaf without its date and position is not the greenness of this leaf. Besides being here and now and green, this leaf is an oak leaf, has a hole in it, has weight. It is this leaf with various qualities that is an instance of 'green thing,' whereas it is only the greenness of this leaf that is an instance of the universal quality 'green.' It is Socrates who is a Greek and a philosopher and ugly who is an instance of 'man,' whereas it is only the human nature of Socrates that is an instance of the universal quality 'human nature.' In the one case we are considering a quality 'human nature,' which is repeated in each man. In the other we are considering, not a common characteristic, but rather men with their various dissimilarities; we are considering men, some of whom are ugly and some of whom are not ugly, some of whom are philosophers and some not philosophers.

There is another distinction to be pointed out. Socrates has not only the quality of being a philosopher and the quality of being ugly, but also the quality of substantiality. Our attention, that is to say, may be directed first towards Socrates and then, by abstraction, towards his ugliness; or it may be directed first towards Socrates and then, by abstraction, towards the possibility that Socrates affords us of thinking first of him and then of a quality of his.[17] Substantiality is, we have held, a quality of Socrates; and it is a quality of Napoleon and a quality of John Smith. When we disregard the dates, positions and number of individual men, when we have before us the universal 'man' that we are proposing, we need not be disregarding the substantiality of various men. On the other hand, the human nature of Socrates does not have the quality of substantiality, being itself a quality. Unlike the universal 'man,' the universal 'human nature' has as its instances entities from which the quality of substantiality is excluded. 'Man' and 'green thing' in short, are universals whose instances have substantiality; 'human nature' and 'greenness' uni-

507

versals whose instances lack substantiality.

Although distinguishable from a universal quality, a universal substance is not a substance in the same sense as an individual substance. We have described an individual substance as "a totality of concomitant entities," "an unanalyzed whole which comprises a full set of concomitant qualities."[18] Clearly, the universal 'man' and the universal 'green thing' which we have found real are not, as our objects, all-inclusive totalities. For if we are to be aware of them as universals, we are to disregard their dates and positions and the number of their instances. We are to disregard, that is to say, certain qualities of their instances. There are not, it follows, two entities, both substances in the same sense, where this green leaf is,—namely, this individual green leaf and the universal: green thing. Nevertheless the universal 'green thing' and the universal 'man,' as we describe them, in some respects resemble individual substances. Just as its greenness may be abstracted from this green leaf and the human nature of Socrates from Socrates, so greenness may be abstracted from green thing and the universal quality 'human nature' from 'man.' That is to say, our attention may be directed first towards 'man,' then towards the universal quality: human nature; first towards 'right triangle,' then towards the universal quality of having the squares on two sides equal to the square on the third.

There are then certain universal substances which are to be distinguished from individual substances. And there are certain universal qualities, universals whose instances are qualities of individual substances. 'Man,' alleged to be in its instances but presented to us without them, is a universal substance which is real.[19] And greenness, alleged to be in its instances but presented to us without them, is a universal quality which is real. We must remember, however, that we have found no way to populate the world of reality on a wholesale basis.[20] We can not conclude, therefore, that all alleged universals are real, or even that all alleged universals are real which are alleged to be in their instances but presented to us without them. We can say that all universals alleged not to be in their instances, alleged to be nontemporal or non-spatial, are unreal. And we can say that certain universals, alleged to be in their instances but presented to us without them, are real. Among them there are the universal

508

qualities: 'greenness' and 'human nature,' and the universal substances: 'green thing,' 'man' and 'triangle.'

There is the universal 'greenness' and the universal 'man' and the universal 'triangle.' And there is a mental attitude of mine, let us agree, which is directed upon 'greenness' and a mental attitude of yours which is directed upon 'triangle.' Just as, when I look at this table, my mental attitude is an instance of perceiving and the table a percept with respect to it; just as, when today I am aware of last night's moon, my mental attitude is an instance of remembering and last night's moon a memory with respect to it;[21] so, when my mental attitude is directed upon 'greenness,' that attitude is an instance of conceiving and the universal 'greenness' is a concept with respect to it.[22] The quality of being a percept is a relative and not an absolute quality of the table's, the quality of being a memory a relative and not an absolute quality of last night's moon. For the expression: "a percept (or memory) with respect to my present mental attitude" contains words representing my mental attitude, representing, that is to say, a substance other than that which is asserted to be a percept or memory.[23] Last night's moon is a memory with respect to my present mental attitude, a percept and not a memory with respect to the mental attitude that was mine last night. Without an explicit or implicit reference to some particular mental attitude, "last night's moon is a memory" is consequently an incomplete and puzzling expression; and any alleged absolute quality of being a memory is unreal. Similarly let us describe the expression "concept" as incomplete. 'Greenness' is a concept with respect to my present mental attitude, 'triangle' a concept with respect to your present mental attitude. But the word "concept," as we use it, implies a reference, let us say, to some particular mental attitude that is conceiving.

Indeed, not only the word "concept," but also the word "universal," implies some reference to mental attitudes. There are many men. And these many men form the universal 'man' when I consider them "without attending to their number or to their various dates and positions."[24] It is only in so far as they are presented to conscious subjects in a certain way that the plurality of men are 'man.' To say that universals exist, it follows, is to imply that there are instances of mental attitudes that con-

509

ceive and are directed upon them. Nevertheless, we make a distinction between the terms: "concept" and "universal." To say that 'man' is a universal is, we hold, to imply that there are some, not necessarily specified, instances of conceiving. But 'man' is a concept with respect to some given instance of conceiving, as, for example, with respect to the present mental attitude of mine that is directed upon the universal 'man.' The distinction that we make between concept and universal thus resembles that between "older" and "father." 'Man' is a concept with respect to particular mental attitudes just as I am older with respect to particular individuals who are my juniors. "Man is a universal," on the other hand, resembles: "I am a father." For me to be a father, there must be some one who is my child. But in order for the statement that I am a father to be accepted, it is not necessary to know just who or how many my children are. "'Man' is a universal" similarly implies that there is some mental attitude that conceives. But whereas man is a concept only with respect to some particular mental attitude, man is a universal so long as there is any mental attitude at all directed upon the plurality of men but disregarding their dates, positions and number.

The 'man' that is presented as no object of mine is no concept with respect to me. And the 'man' that is presented as no object for anyone is no universal and does not exist. To this extent, universals depend for their existence upon mental attitudes that conceive; and concepts for *their* existence upon instances of conceiving that are directed upon them. But mental attitudes do not make 'man' a universal; nor does my present mental attitude bring into existence the 'man' that is a concept with respect to it. 'Man' has many dates; and some of these may well precede the first mental attitude directed upon 'man.' 'Man' is a concept with respect to my present mental attitude. And yet many men, many of the dates that belong to 'man,' preceded the present mental attitude of mine with respect to which 'man' is a concept. Similarly 'man' has many positions. 'Man' occurs in Tokyo, in New York, and in the African jungle.[25] It does not occur within my brain but rather in the world of objects which includes individual substances and their qualities, secondary qualities and tertiary qualities, percepts and memories. None of these entities would exist if there were no mental attitudes. To put it more accurately, all of these entities, presented as objects for no mental attitudes, are self-contradictory and unreal. But, not presented as non-objects, there are, we have found, some existing entities within each of these groups. It is only in exceptional cases that these existing entities are brought into being by the mental attitudes that are directed upon them. Conversely, it is only in certain classes that these existing entities are causes of the mental attitudes whose objects they are. The universal 'man' is no percept of mine, is not the cause of the mental attitude directed upon it. But entities that are not percepts are no less real, no *more* mental, than entities that are.

There is a mental attitude of mine directed upon 'man' and a subsequent mental attitude of mine directed upon Socrates. There is a mental attitude of yours directed upon Socrates and a subsequent mental attitude of yours directed upon 'man.' To think, first of individuals, then of a universal of which these individuals are instances, is, let us say, to generalize; to think, first of a universal, then of individuals that are instances of this universal, to individualize. But whereas one sequence of mental attitudes may be an example of generalization and another sequence of mental attitudes an example of individualization, it may be held that the mental attitude directed upon an individual and the mental attitude directed upon a universal are not of equal importance and value.

Without instances of conceiving there could, of course, be no awareness of general truths, no science. But it does not follow that there could be no awareness of individuals or that individuals could not exist. Without instances of conceiving, individuals, it would appear, would nevertheless exist and be objects for conscious subjects; but very little would be known about them.[26] On the other hand, without instances of mental attitudes directed upon individuals, there could *be* no universals and no instances of conceiving. For, the universal that we have found real has many dates and positions, many individuals that are its instances. In the absence of mental attitudes directed upon individuals, individuals would be unreal. In the absence of individuals to serve as instances, there would be no universals.[27] And without universals there could be no mental attitudes really directed upon

511

universals, no instances, that is to say, of conceiving.

To say, however, that the existence of conceiving presupposes the existence of individuals and of mental attitudes directed upon them is not to say that each instance of conceiving must have been preceded by some instance of the universal that is conceived. Just as I may be aware of an individual that is not the cause of the mental attitude of mine directed upon it, just as, for example, I may be aware of tomorrow's sun,[28] so Leonardo da Vinci could be aware of the universal 'flying machine' without his mental attitude being caused either by this universal itself or by some instance of 'flying machine.' To be sure, unless there were a flying machine at some date, the alleged universal 'flying machine' would be unreal and no real mental attitude could really have it as its object. But whereas the mental attitude apparently directed upon a universal that has no instances past, present or even future, is no real instance of conceiving, there is nothing incredible about the mental attitude directed upon a universal all of whose instances are future with respect to the mental attitude that conceives it. A mental attitude allegedly directed upon such a universal may, we hold, be real and a real instance of conceiving. And so may a mental attitude allegedly directed upon a universal all of whose instances antedate the mental attitude directed upon it. A mental attitude directed towards a given universal may, in short, be prior to the first instance of that universal, subsequent to the last instance of that universal, or subsequent to the first, but prior to the last, of the many dates that that universal has.

We may compare the date of the mental attitude that conceives with the dates of the universal that is its object. And we may compare the date of the mental attitude that conceives with the date of the earliest mental attitude of the same mind-person directed upon an individual instance of the universal conceived. There is not only the date of da Vinci's attitude directed towards 'flying machine' and the dates of 'flying machine,' not only the date of my mental attitude directed towards 'man' and the dates of 'man'; there is also the date of my mental attitude directed towards 'man' and the date of my earliest mental attitude directed towards some individual man, the date of my mental attitude directed towards 'star of the fifth magnitude' and the date of my earliest mental attitude directed towards an instance of such a star. "Without instances of mental attitudes directed upon individuals," we have said,[29] "there could be no universals and no instances of conceiving." It does not follow, however, that, in order for an instance of conceiving to be real, there must be an *earlier* mental attitude directed upon individual instances of the universal conceived. Much less does it follow that there must be such an earlier mental attitude belonging to the same mind-person. If 'star of the fifth magnitude' is to be a real universal, some individual star of that magnitude must be real and must be someone's object; but the mental attitude directed upon such an individual star need not be mine and need not antedate my conceiving the universal of which it is an instance. I may have conceived 'star of the fifth magnitude' before I directed my attention to any individual instance of such a star. Some one may have been aware of 'flying machine' before any subject had a mental attitude directed towards any individual flying machine. And, of course, my first mental attitude directed towards 'man' may have followed many mental attitudes of mine directed towards individual men. Whether we consider the sequence of mental attitudes of one conscious subject or consider the mental development of the human race, instances of conceiving need not be preceded by mental attitudes directed upon individuals; nor need instances of mental attitudes directed upon individuals be preceded by instances of conceiving.

When a mental attitude directed upon individuals is followed by a mental attitude directed upon a universal of which these individuals are instances, this sequence of mental attitudes is, we have said,[30] an example of generalization. To think first of Socrates and of Plato, and then of 'man,' or to think first of Fido and of Sport and then of 'dog,' is to generalize. In order, however, that I may think first of Socrates and of Plato and then of 'man,' it is not sufficient that I abstract from Socrates his human nature and from Plato *his* human nature. From the individual substance Socrates I can abstract only some such individual quality as the human nature of Socrates and from Plato some such individual quality as the human nature of Plato. When the process of abstraction has been completed, consequently, I have before me qualities of individual substances, not the universal quality:

513

'human nature,' much less the universal substance: 'man.' For abstraction, as we have described it, is the process whereby we think first of a substance and then of a quality inhering in that substance. It is a process, or series of mental attitudes, wherein we pass from the consideration of an individual substance to the consideration of a quality of that individual substance; or pass from the consideration of a universal substance to the consideration of a universal quality. But where there is merely abstraction as we have described "abstraction," universals do not follow individuals as objects of our mental attitudes.

Whereas, however, generalization is one process and abstraction another, there is at times to be sure an element in generalization that is not altogether unlike abstraction. The universal 'man,' as we have described it and found it real, is the plurality of men presented to us without their positions, dates and number. When I think of Socrates and Plato and then have before me a Socrates and a Plato whose dates and positions are being disregarded, I am on the way, one might say, to conceiving. I am not yet conceiving; for Socrates without his date and position and Plato without *his* date and position do not constitute the plurality of men without their dates, positions and number. In dropping dates and positions from the Socrates and Plato who were my objects, the sequence of my mental attitudes resembles the sequence when I think first of Socrates and then of a quality of his. But this sequence, which is a sort of abstraction, is at most but an element in generalization. For to end with a mental attitude that is directed upon the universal 'man,' my object must be not merely Socrates and Plato presented without their dates and positions, but the plurality of men presented without their dates, positions and number. Neither abstraction nor the process which we have found akin to abstraction is sufficient for "the isolation of universals from the individuals of which they are predicated."[31] Conceiving requires a further alteration of the object. And unless the series of mental attitudes ends with conceiving, ends, that is to say, with a mental attitude directed upon a universal, the series fails to constitute an instance of what we have called generalization.

Abstraction, then, is a characteristic of one series of mental attitudes, generalization a characteristic of another. To think first

514

of Socrates, then of his human nature, or to think first of 'man,' then of the universal quality 'human nature': these are instances of abstraction. But to think first of Socrates and Plato, then of man, or to think first of the human nature of Socrates and that of Plato, then of the universal quality 'human nature': these are instances of generalization. I may think first of Socrates, then of his human nature and that of Plato, then of the universal 'human nature' or the universal 'man.' Abstraction, that is to say, may be followed by generalization. Or I may think first of Socrates and Plato, then of man, then of the human nature that characterizes man. I may generalize first and abstract afterwards.

As we have seen, I may think first of Socrates, then of man. Or I may think first of man, then of Socrates, as when I say: "Man is mortal; therefore Socrates is mortal." Indeed, I may think of man and of Socrates simultaneously. That is to say, a mental attitude directed upon a universal may be accompanied by a mental attitude directed upon an individual that is an instance of that universal. Just as Laöcoon may have remembered the Greeks and feared them,[32] just as one may be aware of a pain and also be aching,[33] so I may be both conceiving 'man' and perceiving or remembering some instance of man. While I am developing some characteristic of triangles generally, I may have some individual scalene triangle before me. I may be concerning myself with the universal 'triangle,' I may, that is to say, be conceiving 'triangle'; and I may simultaneously be perceiving a certain scalene triangle. In such a situation, however, the mental attitude which is perceiving is distinguishable from the mental attitude which is directed upon a universal. Just as fearing may be distinguished from the perceiving or remembering that may accompany it, so conceiving may be distinguished from the mental attitude directed upon an individual that may be an element in the mental life of the same phase of the same conscious subject.

There are instances of mental attitudes which are conceiving; and there are instances of mental attitudes which are directed upon individuals. There are universals which are real and are *in* the individuals that are their instances. And there are individuals which are real and are instances of these universals. There is the universal 'man' which has many dates and positions, though presented to us without them; the universal 'man' upon which several mental attitudes are directed. And there is your mental attitude and my mental attitude which are each directed upon this public object, upon this universal 'man.'

Let us, however, turn aside from the 'man' that we have found real, the 'man' who is a public object immanent in its instances. And let us likewise turn aside from the mental attitudes which are instances of thinking rather than mental content, instances of conceiving rather than concepts that are conceived. Let us present to ourselves an alleged idea of 'man' which appears as object or content rather than as thinking or mental attitude, an alleged idea of 'man' which appears as spatially distinct from the Socrates and Napoleon who are instances of the public object: 'man.' For just as it may be held that, when I think of Socrates, my immediate object is a private idea of Socrates rather than Socrates himself, so it may be held that, when I think of 'man,' my immediate object is a private idea rather than the 'man' which, as a public object immanent in its instances, we have in this chapter found real.

When there is a book bound with a blue cover in front of me, my immediate object, it may be held, is a bit of mental content which corresponds in all particulars to the book outside me, a picture or image which is blue as the book itself is blue. A book bound in red, it may similarly be held, causes me to have as my immediate object an image which is red; and a book bound in green an image which is green. But, it is said, there is not only this blue book and that green book, not only my private idea corresponding to this blue book and my private idea corresponding to that green book. There are occasions on which I think of books in general, of the universal 'book.' And on such occasions, Locke holds, my immediate object is a "general idea."[34] This alleged general idea may be held to correspond to 'book' in very much the way in which the idea or image of an individual book is alleged to correspond to the book it represents. But since some books are bound in blue and some in green, some thick and some thin, the general idea corresponding to the universal 'book' may be presented to us as indeterminate in color, size and shape, may be presented to us as lacking much of the definiteness characteristic of individuals, but an image nevertheless.

It may be held, on the other hand, that there is no image of book and no image of color "which is neither red nor blue nor white nor any other determinate color." [35] Locke, it may be said, was correct in holding that, when I think of 'book,' my immediate object is a private object, an idea, just as it is when I am aware of an individual book. But this private object, this "general idea" of book, may be presented to us as an image which has all the definiteness characteristic of an individual. The general idea of triangle may be held to correspond to some individual scalene triangle before me, but to "stand for and represent all rectilinear triangles whatsoever." [36]

Again, it may be held that the general idea, which is alleged to be my immediate object when I think of 'book,' is neither an image indeterminate in content nor an individualized image with a variable and general reference. It may be held to be no image at all, but rather a plan for the formation of individualized images. The awareness of universals, according to Kant,[37] involves "the representation of a method of representing rather than the image itself." "The concept of dog," he holds,[38] means a rule according to which my imagination can always draw a general outline of the figure of a four-footed animal without being restricted to any particular figure."

Yet whether my immediate object when I am aware of 'book' be held to be an individualized image, an indeterminate image or a plan for the formation of images, the alleged general idea that is presented to us as a private object only is unreal. Whether the ultimate object be an individual or a universal, "the immediate object need not be an idea distinguishable from thinking itself and spatially distinct from the ultimate object." Nor *can* the immediate object be an idea, if ideas are "held to be non-spatial," or held to be not spatially and temporally related to ultimate objects, held not to be known at all by more than a single subject, or, in the case of non-introspective thinking, held to be spatially "adjacent to thinking itself." [39] When I am aware of 'man,' my immediate object is not a private image which is neither white nor black nor yellow. My immediate object may well be the universal 'man' which is in its instances, some of which are Caucasian, some Mongolian, and some Negro. When I am aware of 'triangle,' my immediate object is not a private image which has the characteristics of an individual scalene triangle; nor is my ultimate

517

object an individual scalene triangle which is a public object. To be sure, the universal 'triangle,' which is a public object and which exists wherever a scalene triangle or a right triangle or an obtuse triangle exists, may in a certain sense be an indirect object of my thinking. It may be an indirect object in the sense that my mental attitude directed upon 'triangle' may have been preceded by a mental attitude directed upon the individual scalene triangle which, along with 'triangle,' is a public object. The immediate object may, in other words, differ from the ultimate object; but only when the immediate object is, as it were, a public sign pointing to the ultimate object, an instance, for example, the awareness of which is followed by a mental attitude directed upon the universal of which it *is* an instance.

It is, we hold, the universal and not the general idea (which is unreal) which is *in* its instances. And it is the mental attitude and not the general idea which may be *ante rem* or *post rem.*[40] Likewise, it is not images corresponding to Peter, James, Mary and Jane that are followed by a general idea of 'man' whose content is "what is common to them all." [41] It is one subject's mental attitudes directed upon Peter, James, Mary and Jane that are followed by a mental attitude of his directed upon the universal 'man.' Conversely, where individualization rather than generalization takes place, it is a mental attitude directed towards a universal that is followed by mental attitudes directed towards instances of that universal. It has been held, for example, that "before we began to see or hear or perceive in any way, we must have had a knowledge of absolute equality or we could not have referred to that standard the equals which are derived from the senses." [42] If so, it is a mental attitude directed upon equality that precedes mental attitudes directed upon instances of equality, not a "general idea" of equality that precedes images of equals. It has been our conclusion, to be sure, that there are both instances of generalization and instances of individualization. "Whether we consider the sequence of mental attitudes of one conscious subject or consider the mental development of the human race, instances of conceiving need not be preceded by mental attitudes directed upon individuals; nor need instances of mental attitudes directed upon individuals be preceded by instances of conceiving." [43]

In certain instances of individualization, the mental attitude that is directed upon a universal may be said to facilitate the mental attitude that is to follow it, the mental attitude that is to be directed upon an instance of that universal. My mental attitude directed upon 'dog,' that is to say, may make it "natural" or "easy" for me subsequently to think of Fido or Sport. But the mental attitude directed upon a universal, the instance of conceiving, has an object of its own. It is not a mere potentiality to be actualized in mental attitudes directed upon individuals. The mental attitude directed upon dog, for example, has for its object dogs presented without their dates, positions and number. It is not something without an object that is to be followed by mental attitudes directed upon various dogs. Much less is it "the representation of a method of representing." [44] For, being a mental attitude and not a general idea, it is an instance of mental activity rather than content, and hence, not a representation at all.[45]

There is the real universal 'man' which has many dates and positions, but is presented without them. And there are 'greenness,' 'dog,' 'beauty' and 'triangle' which likewise have various dates and positions, and which likewise are real. Let us say, however, that there is no universal 'perfection' which is real; and no universal: 'immortal man.' For whereas "an entity need not be presented to us with its date or dates, with its position or positions, in order to be real," [46] the universal that appears to have "no one date and no several dates, no one position and no several positions, such a universal is unreal." [47] The perfection that is presented to me as occurring nowhere is unreal; and so is the immortal man that is presented to me as having never occurred. 'Immortal man,' to be sure, may be presented to me as having one of its instances in the cave where Barbarossa sleeps; 'angel' may be presented to me as having various instances in the upper clouds and various other instances on the point of a needle. But if all its alleged instances are presented as generally discredited, let us agree to list the universal that is so presented as unreal rather than as real. As we are using the terms "existence" and "reality," no alleged universal is real, let us say, unless it has instances which are real.

'Man' is real; and you and I each have mental attitudes which are really directed upon this real universal. But if 'perfection' and 'angel' are unreal, you can not really be aware of 'angel' and I can not really be aware of 'perfection.' There is a mental attitude of yours which is real and which is as if it were directed upon 'angel'; a mental attitude of mine which is real and which is as if it were directed upon 'perfection.' These mental attitudes which lack real objects resemble other mental attitudes which do have objects. They resemble mental attitudes which are conceiving real universals. But since their alleged objects are not really universals, not really concepts with respect to them, your mental attitude apparently directed upon angel and my mental attitude apparently directed upon perfection are, let us say, not real instances of conceiving but real instances of pseudo-conceiving.[48]

Each universal that is real has instances which are real. The alleged universal that has no real instances is no real universal. And the alleged universal that has but one real instance is likewise no real universal. There is, let us agree, but one sun, one mankind, one Napoleon. It is true that the Napoleon who was born at Ajaccio and died at St. Helena may be two or many with respect to some subject who has as separate objects various phases of Napoleon's life. But whereas with respect to him Napoleon is many, he is many phases rather than many Napoleons. Similarly, the term "mankind," we have said[49] "normally represents an individual substance and expresses a single mental attitude. For when we are aware of the various parts of mankind, of various men, we are not likely to describe our object as 'mankind' but as 'men.'" The man who was born in Ajaccio and died at St. Helena is then, let us say, but one Napoleon; and at no other era has there been or will there be another. For our present purposes the sun is one, though on other occasions it may be regarded as having many parts; and there is no other heavenly body, no other star, that is to be called a "sun." And so with mankind. But if Napoleon, mankind and the sun are each one, they are each individuals rather than universals. There is no entity that we shall call a universal, let us say, that appears to have its sole instance in Napoleon, or its sole instance in mankind, or its sole instance in the sun.

When I am aware of the universal 'man,' my mental attitude is directed towards the plurality of men, but their dates, positions and number are being disregarded. "When I think of Socrates and Plato and then have before me a Socrates and a Plato whose dates and positions are being disregarded," "I am not yet conceiving." [50] And I am likewise not conceiving when I think of the individual substance Napoleon, but disregard his date and position and the unity that he has with respect to me. Napoleon appearing without date, position and unity is an object that may be described as "a substance that is Napoleonic," "*a* Napoleon." But since Napoleon is one, my object is in our terminology no universal and my mental attitude directed upon it not an instance of conceiving.

As we use the term "universal," then, there is no universal 'angel' and no universal: Napoleon; no universal 'perfection' and no universal: 'being married to Xanthippe.' But whereas the universal that is real has neither a solitary instance nor no instance at all, neither does the universal that is real have an infinite number of instances. Entities that are not real are not real instances of any universal. And the collections of entities that are real are all finite in number. [51]

On the one hand, there is the universal 'man' which is real; on the other hand, there are Socrates, Plato, Callias and a finite number of other individuals who are real and who are real instances of the universal 'man.' In order that the 'man' that we are considering may be real, this 'man' may not be presented as no one's definite object. In order that the Callias that we are considering may be a real individual, this Callias may not be presented as no one's definite object. And in order that Callias may be a man, Callias may not be presented as an individual that no one thinks of as a man. It does not follow that no individual is a man who is not definitely thought of as a man, that there are only as many men as are specifically pointed to as men. But the Callias who is presented as no one's definite object is no real individual and the Callias who is presented as an individual that no one thinks of definitely as a man is no instance of the universal 'man.'

The real instances of 'man' are Socrates, Plato, Callias and a finite number of others. But what if there had been no Callias? To what extent would 'man' be different if one of its existing past, present or future instances were non-existent? We can apparently present to ourselves an alleged 'man' that has n-1 instances instead of the n instances that 'man' actually has. And we can say that such an alleged 'man' differs from the 'man' that is real in that it has a lesser number of instances. But since in thinking of 'man' our object is the plurality of men disregarding their dates, positions and number, and in thinking of a 'man' with n-1 instances our alleged object is an only slightly different number of men whose dates, positions and number are likewise disregarded, the two mental attitudes are quite similar. One is an instance of conceiving, the other an instance of pseudo-conceiving. One is directed upon an object with n instances, the other upon an alleged object with n-1 instances. But there is otherwise little to distinguish them.

Socrates is one of many individuals who are instances of 'man.' And Socrates is an individual who is an instance of various universals. Socrates, that is to say, is not only an instance of 'man,' but an instance of the universal 'Greek,' an instance of the universal 'animal,' an instance of the universal 'thing having weight.' 'Man' is not presented to me as an entity that is no one's definite object; it is a real universal. And 'thing having weight' is not presented to me as an entity that is no one's definite object; it too is a real universal. Just, however, as the Callias who is presented as an individual that no one thinks of definitely as a man is no instance of the universal 'man,' so the Socrates who is presented as an individual that no one thinks of definitely as a thing having weight is no instance of the universal: 'thing having weight.' It is only a finite number of individuals who are presented to me and yet not presented with the characteristic of not being definitely thought of as men. And so it is only a finite number of individuals who are real instances of 'man.' Similarly it is only certain universals that are presented to me and yet not presented in such a way that Socrates seems not to be definitely thought of as an instance of them. And so it is only certain universals—not an infinite number of universals—of which Socrates is a real instance.

Socrates is an instance of 'man,' an instance of 'animal,' an instance of 'thing having weight.' Since however we have agreed not to call 'man' "one," 'animal' "one," or 'man' and 'animal' "two," [52] the universals of which Socrates is a real instance can not in our terminology be called many in number or even finite in number. 'Man' differs from 'animal,' and 'animal' differs from 'thing having weight.' But 'man' plus 'animal' plus 'thing having weight,'—the various universals, indeed, of which Socrates is an instance, taken together—do not form a collection to which in our terminology any finite number applies. Much less of course, in view of the

522

discussion of the preceding paragraph, are they infinite in number.

'Man' differs from 'animal' and 'animal' differs from 'thing having weight.' What shall we say however with respect to the universal 'triangle' and the universal 'trilateral'? Each individual substance that is a trilateral is, let us assume, a triangle; and each triangle a trilateral. The plurality of triangles presented to us without their dates, positions and number is not different from the plurality of trilaterals presented to us without their dates, positions and number. The universal 'triangle,' let us hold, does not differ from the universal 'trilateral.' There are however the universal substances 'triangle' and 'trilateral' on the one hand; and, on the other hand, the universal qualities 'triangularity' and 'trilaterality.' Trilaterality is, let us assume, a quality of each individual substance that has the quality of triangularity; triangularity a quality of each individual substance that has the quality of trilaterality. Nevertheless the triangularity of an individual substance that is triangular is distinguishable from that substance's trilaterality. Correspondingly the universal quality 'triangularity' differs from the universal quality: 'trilaterality.' For whereas 'triangularity' has among its instances the triangularity of this triangle and the triangularity of that triangle, 'trilaterality' has among *its* instances the trilaterality of this triangle and the trilaterality of that.[53]

The very substance, in short, that is an instance of the universal substance 'triangle' is an instance of the universal substance 'trilateral'; whereas each instance of the universal quality 'triangularity' is distinguishable from the corresponding instance of the universal quality 'trilaterality.' If you have a mental attitude directed upon 'triangularity' and I a mental attitude directed upon 'trilaterality,' your object, we hold, is distinguishable from mine. But, we hold, if your mental attitude is directed upon 'triangle' and mine upon 'trilateral,' your mental attitude and mine are directed upon a common object. For when the various substances that are both triangular and trilateral are presented to us without their dates, position and number, we disregard their trilaterality no more than their triangularity in thinking of the universal substance 'triangle'; and we disregard their triangularity no more than their trilaterality in thinking of the universal substance 'trilateral.'

It is the individual substance, and not some particular quality of this individual substance, that is an instance of various universal substances. It is Socrates, who has animality and human nature and heaviness, who is an instance of the universal substance: 'animal.' And it is this same Socrates who has animality and human nature and heaviness who is an instance of the universal: 'thing having weight.' Whatever is an instance of 'thing having weight' has, let us assume, heaviness. Whatever is an instance of 'animal' has, let us assume, animality. But except as we select for special attention a particular universal of which Socrates is an instance, his animality is no more an essential quality of Socrates than his heaviness. If Socrates is to be an animal, one may say, he must have animality. If he is to be a thing having weight, one may say, he must have heaviness. But in so far as we consider Socrates as an individual substance and not as an instance of a given universal that we select out of the various universals of which he is an instance, his animality is no more essential to him than his human nature. Indeed, since it is only in relation to some universal that an alleged essential quality seems to be free from puzzlement, it is only in connection with universals and their definitions that we choose to use the term "essence." [54]

Socrates has his quality of animality and is an instance of the universal substance 'animal.' Socrates has his quality of heaviness and is an instance of the universal substance 'thing having weight.' However, Socrates also has the quality of having fought at Poteidaia and the quality of being an object of my present thinking. And so we may present to ourselves the alleged universal substance: 'combatant at Poteidaia' of which Socrates may be alleged to be an instance; and the alleged universal: 'object of my present thinking' of which Socrates may likewise be alleged to be an instance.

There are, we have said,[55] many men; and yet "it is possible to consider this plurality of men without attending to their number or to their various dates and positions." Those who were combatants at Poteidaia, we may agree, were likewise many; and the objects of my present thinking many. Just as it is possible to consider the plurality of men without attending to their number or to their various dates and positions, so it is possible to consider the plurality of combatants at Poteidaia without attending to their number or to their dates or positions; and to consider the plurality of objects of my present thinking without attending to *their* number, dates or positions. Just, then, as we have found that 'man' is a real universal, so let us agree that 'combatant at Poteidaia' is a real universal and 'object of my present thinking' a real universal.

In discussing the relative qualities of an individual substance, we found that "a succession of phases differing only in relative qualities may be less noticeable and may seem less notable than a succession of phases differing in qualities which are not relative." [56] Somewhat similarly, the universal 'combatant at Poteidaia,' which corresponds to Socrates' quality of having fought at Poteidaia, may seem a less 'natural,' a less homogeneous, universal than 'man.' And 'object of my present thinking,' which corresponds to a relative quality inhering in Socrates,—the quality, namely, of being an object with respect to my present thinking,—may seem less homogeneous than 'animal,' less homogeneous than the universal corresponding to the absolute quality of animality. His being an object of my present thinking is, however, just as real a quality of Socrates as his animality, his having fought at Poteidaia just as real a quality of his as his human nature. What is required in order that an alleged universal may be real is not that its instances resemble one another in important features, but that it *have* many instances which are presented without their dates, positions and number; and that, so presented, it meet the requirements laid down in our propositions explaining "reality."

Corresponding then to the quality that Socrates has of having fought at Poteidaia, there is the real universal: 'combatant at Poteidaia.' And corresponding to the quality that Socrates has of being an object with respect to my present thinking, there is the real universal: 'object of my present thinking.' Indeed, Socrates has the quality of being represented by the word "Socrates"; and various horses and cocks have each the quality of being named "Socrates." 'Thing named Socrates' is an alleged universal whose instances have a designation in common. But if the things named Socrates are presented to us without their dates, positions and number, 'thing named Socrates' may well be a real universal and each thing named Socrates may not only have its quality of being named Socrates but also the characteristic of being an instance of the universal substance: 'thing named Socrates.'

Things named Socrates may each be an instance of the universal: 'thing named Socrates.' Things called men may each be an instance of the universal: 'thing called man.' But the instances of 'thing called man' are, let us assume, instances of 'man.' Then, just as the universal 'triangle,' we hold,[57] does not differ from the universal 'trilateral,' so 'thing called man' does not differ from 'man.' Various instances of 'thing named Socrates' have each the relative quality of being named "Socrates," whereas various instances of 'thing called man'—or 'man'—have each the absolute quality of human nature. The universal: 'thing called man' may thus be more homogeneous, more fertile as a concept, than 'thing named Socrates.' One may hazard the opinion that universals are more or less homogeneous, more or less fertile as concepts, according as they correspond to absolute or to relative qualities in their instances; and according as the words representing them are precise or ambiguous. But universals represented by words that are ambiguous may be real and have real instances as well as universals represented by words that are not ambiguous; universals corresponding to relative qualities in their instances may be real and have real instances as well as universals corresponding to absolute qualities in their instances.

'Thing called man,' which, we hold, is not to be distinguished from 'man,' is a real universal. 'Animal,' we hold, is a real universal; and 'substance' a real universal. Let us assume that whatever is a man is an animal, that whatever has human nature has animality. And let us assume that whatever is a dog is an animal, that whatever has the quality of being a dog has animality. Let us assume, in short, that 'man' and 'dog' are included in 'animal' and that 'animal' is included in 'substance.'

It is obvious that 'man' and 'dog' are not instances of 'animal' as Socrates and Plato are instances of 'man.' It is Socrates and Plato and Fido and Sport who are instances of 'animal,' not 'man' and 'dog' which are themselves universals. The species 'man' is included in the genus 'animal,' it may be said, in that various instances of 'man' are instances of 'animal' and in that the alleged universal 'man but not animal' has no real instances and is no real universal. Somewhat similarly the universal quality 'brown' is included in the universal quality 'colored,' it may be said, in that various individual substances that are brown are likewise colored and in that the alleged universal: 'brown but uncolored' has no real instances and is unreal.

But if 'man' is a species and 'animal' a genus that includes 'man,' what shall we say with respect to the alleged syllogism: "Man is an animal; animal is a genus; therefore man is a genus"? Socrates who is an instance of man is likewise an instance of the genus 'animal,' indeed an instance of various universals in which 'man' is included. And there is no instance of man, we must agree, that is not an instance of some genus. 'Man but not genus,' that is to say, is an alleged universal that is unreal. "Man is a genus," when "genus" is used as we have suggested, is, we must conclude, a true proposition. To be sure, we avoid this conclusion when we treat with 'man,' 'dog' and 'animal' as though they were individual substances that might be numbered as Socrates, Plato and Callias may be numbered; when we treat with them as though they must lie outside one another as Socrates and Plato are outside one another. We seem then to think of 'dog' as one species and of 'man' as a second species which, since it *is* a species, can not also be placed in the separate compartment reserved for genera. But this personification and numbering of universals is something which we have rejected. Hence if "Man is a genus" is not to be true, we must find some meaning for the term "genus" such that it is not the universal itself which is a genus, but rather the term referring to that universal or the mental attitude directed upon it.

Whitehead and Russell put before us the alleged entity described as the class of all classes not members of themselves.[58] The question to be resolved is whether this entity, if it exists, is or is not a member of itself. To suppose this entity to be a member of itself is to suppose it to be one of the group of classes not members of themselves, hence not a member of itself. And yet if it is not a member of itself, then, it is said, it qualifies as one of the classes to be subsumed under the entity we are considering and consequently *is* a member of itself.

If, however, a class is thought of as many and not as a collective entity like mankind, if it is presented to us as either a multiplicity or a universal but not as an individual, then, not being an individual, it is no instance of a universal. A universal may be said to be subsumed under another or included within another. Indeed we may use "subsume" in such a way that a universal no more extensive than another may be said to be subsumed under the other, in such a way that a universal, being coextensive with itself, is said to be subsumed under itself. But such subsumption is hardly membership. The alleged fact, that is to say, that the class of all classes not members of themselves qualifies as one of the classes to be subsumed under itself, this alleged fact does not warrant the conclusion that this class is a *member* of itself. On the other hand, to suppose that the class of all classes is a member of itself is, it would seem, to suppose that, being coextensive with itself, it may be subsumed under itself. But this characteristic seems not to conflict with the characteristic of not being an instance of itself.

At any rate when we turn from classes, however 'class' may be defined, to what we have described as universals, it is our position that no universal is an instance of itself. On the other hand, if the terms "inclusion" or "subsumption" are applied, not only to the situation where we are comparing 'animal' with 'man,' but also to the situation where we are comparing 'animal' with itself, then each real universal may be held to be included or subsumed under itself. Among the universals which are real, there is the universal 'universal' which includes other universals and which, being co-extensive with itself, may be said to include itself also. 'Universal' however is no instance of itself; nor are any of the universals included in it instances of themselves. The fact that the universal 'universal' may be subsumed under itself does not imply that it is an instance of itself; nor does its not being an instance of itself imply that it is not subsumed under itself.

The alleged syllogism: "Man is an animal; animal is a genus; therefore man is a genus" concludes, we hold, with what, in one sense of "genus," is the true proposition: "Man is a genus." And the alleged syllogism: "Socrates is a man; man is a universal; therefore Socrates is a universal" concludes, we hold, with what, taken literally, is the true proposition: "Socrates is a universal." For since Socrates is an instance of various universals, there *is* a universal where Socrates is. He *is* a universal just as he is a philosopher, a man and a substance.[59] From the fact, however, that

528

both alleged syllogisms lead to what seem to be true conclusions, it does not follow that "man is a genus" and "Socrates is a universal" resemble one another in all important characteristics. Both may be misleading in that the one may seem to express the belief that 'man' is not a species, the other the belief that Socrates is not an individual. Both seem to be false when there is apparently presented to us a fictitious world in which individuals, species and genera are all held to be numberable entities lying outside one another in separate compartments. They differ however in that, whereas it is Socrates who is an instance of the universal 'universal,' it is not 'man,' but the individual substances who *are* men, who are instances of the universal 'genus.'

Socrates is an instance of 'man,' but 'man' not an instance of 'animal,' 'animal' not an instance of 'universal.' Can we then proceed from 'universal' to 'animal' to 'man' and finally to Socrates? Or does our thinking, unless it is to change its character, stop short of the end-term in the series, the individual substance? I think of man, I think of white man, I think of white man with a beard. But no matter how persistent I am in passing from a mental attitude directed upon an including universal to one directed upon an included universal, there is always, it may be said, another universal that presents itself, never the substance that is an individual. And no matter how specific the universal *quality* that I take as my object, there is always, it may be said, a more specific universal quality to be thought of, rather than the quality of Socrateity, the quality of an individual substance that inheres only in Socrates.

Let us recall the distinction made early in this treatise between the unlimited world of alleged subsistents and the more limited world of existing entities.[60] In the world of subsistents there appear many white men with beards, many white philosophers with beards, many white philosophers with beards who were condemned to die by drinking hemlock. I can pass from a mental attitude apparently directed upon an including universal to one apparently directed upon an included universal and never be at a loss to find, or to seem to find, another subsistent that appears to be a universal. And so with alleged universal qualities. No alleged quality is so specific that it can not appear to occur in various subsisting individual substances, that it can not appear as a subsisting universal quality.

In order, however, that an alleged subsisting universal may be a real universal, it may not be presented as having no real instances or, indeed, as having but a single instance.[61] 'Bearded white philosopher condemned to die by drinking hemlock' is an alleged universal that is presented as having but one instance. And 'bearded white *American* philosopher condemned to die by drinking hemlock' is presented as having "no one date and no several dates, no one position and no several positions." When I seem to be aware of 'bearded white American philosopher condemned to die by drinking hemlock,' my alleged object is unreal; and, whereas my mental attitude is real, it really has no object.[62] When my apparent object is 'bearded white philosopher condemned to die by drinking hemlock,' presented as a universal in the sense in which we have explained "universal," that too is unreal. When, however, my apparent object is 'bearded white philosopher condemned to die by drinking hemlock,' not presented as a universal, my apparent object is an existing entity that is an individual substance; and my mental attitude, although not an instance of conceiving, has an object, Socrates, upon which it is really directed.

There is a sense to be sure in which thinking changes its character when a mental attitude directed upon 'bearded white philosopher' is followed by a mental attitude directed upon 'bearded white philosopher condemned to die by drinking hemlock.' For the former mental attitude is an instance of conceiving, the latter not. It is, however, incorrect, we hold, to regard concepts as ideas that may be elaborated without regard to the world of existents and to think of mental attitudes directed upon individuals as alone concerned with existents. We do not spin out concepts at will and then leap over to a concern with existence when we finally direct our attention to an individual. The 'man,' 'white man,' 'bearded white man' and 'bearded white philosopher' that are my concepts—they also are existents. And whereas I may divide and divide, may time and again pass from a mental attitude directed upon an including universal to one directed upon an included universal, nevertheless, if my alleged object is to be real and my mental attitude a real instance of conceiving, I can not continue to a stage where my alleged object no longer has a plurality of instances.

530

But whereas there is a sense in which thinking changes its character when a mental attitude directed upon 'bearded white philosopher' is followed by a mental attitude directed upon 'bearded white philosopher condemned to die by drinking hemlock,' there is also a sense in which no leap is required to pass from an instance of conceiving to a mental attitude directed upon an individual. If a letter is addressed to an individual living at 4568 Spuyten Duyvil Parkway, New York 63, the clerk in the central New York Post Office, who passes, we may suppose, from the concept: 'inhabitant of New York' to the concept: 'inhabitant of the area served by substation 63,' is no less concerned with the world of existence than the maid at the Spuyten Duyvil Parkway address who puts the letter into the addressee's hands. Her mental process, it would seem, in passing from a consideration of the universal: 'resident in this house' to a consideration of the individual to whom the letter is addressed may well be, by and large,[63] a continuation of the mental process whereby the clerk in the central post office passes from including universal to included universal.

Socrates is an instance of 'bearded white philosopher' and an instance of 'man'; and 'bearded white philosopher' is included in 'man.' Similarly Socrates-married-to-Xanthippe, the relational situation which comprises both Socrates and Xanthippe, is an instance of 'married couple' and an instance of 'couple,' and 'married couple' included in 'couple.' But what about Socrates-related-to-'man'? Is Socrates-an-instance-of-'man' an individual relational situation which is an instance of individual-man-related-to-'man' and an instance of 'individual-related-to-universal'? And is 'individual-man-related-to-man' included in 'individual-related-to-universal'?

There is Peter who is older than Paul; and there is a given basin of water that is hot with respect to "any or all instances of melting ice." [64] It was, however, only in connection with such entities as Peter - older - than - Paul, this - chair - near - this - table, Alexander-mounted - on - Bucephalus,—situations "in which the second substance is as definitely located as the substance in which the relative quality inheres,"—that we discussed what we have called the "relational situation." It is possible to present to ourselves the group of entities composed of this basin of water and various instances of melting ice; and one might choose to call such a group a "rela-

531

tional situation" along with Peter-older-than-Paul, this-chair-near-this-table, Alexander-mounted-on-Bucephalus. It is likewise possible to present to ourselves a group composed of Socrates and the many men who are instances of 'man'; and to call this the relational situation: Socrates-related-to-'man.' "Socrates-related-to-man" would then be another designation for what we have described as the individual substance: mankind. Even, however, if Socrates-related-to-'man' is to be called a relational situation, it is to be remembered that "there are real relational situations where there is no real link." [65] "There is no real 'lessness' that is a connecting link or relating component within the relational situation: B-less-than-A." [66] And there is similarly no real relatedness *between* Socrates and man, no real 'relatedness' within the substance: mankind. There is the relational situation: Socrates-teacher-of-Plato; and Socrates has the quality of being a teacher of Plato. But there is no teacher-of that is between Socrates and Plato. Similarly, there is the substance 'mankind' which one may also choose to call the relational situation: Socrates-related-to-'man.' And Socrates has the quality, if it may be called a "quality," of being an instance of 'man.' But there is no real relatedness within 'Socrates-related-to-man,' no real relatedness between Socrates and man. Much less is there a real relatedness between Socrates on the one hand and the relation between Socrates and man on the other.

To be sure, the human nature of Socrates may be abstracted from Socrates and the universal quality 'human nature' may be abstracted from the universal substance 'man.' [67] It does not follow however that 'entity from which human nature may be abstracted' is a universal distinguishable from 'man,' a universal which includes Socrates, Plato and 'man' or which has Socrates, Plato and 'man' among its instances. There is Socrates, there is Plato, and there is 'man'; and there is the human nature of Socrates, the human nature of Plato, and the human nature of 'man.' There is however no real universal distinguishable from 'man' to be called " 'man' plus individual men." There is no series of real relational situations: Peter's-age-abstractable-from-Peter, Peter-subject-matter-for-abstractability, and so on; [68] no series of real links, the first within Socrates-related-to-'man,' the second within Socrates-related-to-the-relation-between-Socrates-and-'man,' and so on; and there is

532

no series of *distinguishable* universals: 'man,' 'man plus individual men,' 'man plus man-plus-individual-men.'

There is, we have said,[69] the universal: 'inhabitant of New York,' the universal: 'inhabitant of the area served by sub-station 63,' the universal: 'resident of 4568 Spuyten Duyvil Parkway,' and the individual at that address for whom a given letter is intended. 'Inhabitant of New York' is, however, a universal only in that it has a plurality of instances but is presented to some subject without them. And 'resident of 4568 Spuyten Duyvil Parkway' is a universal only in that, whereas there are several residents, the maid who handles the mail, or some one else, has 'resident of 4568 Spuyten Duyvil Parkway' presented to her without her being presented with the names, dates, positions and number of the individual residents. There is, to be sure, no universal which has the individual to whom the letter is addressed as its sole instance. But even the individual can be presented without his date, his position and his unity. He is no concept with respect to me. But the mental attitude which I direct upon him can resemble an instance of conceiving as does the mental attitude that is directed upon the substance that is Napoleonic, upon the entity that may be described as "*a* Napoleon." [70]

On the other hand, when my object is an individual, that individual need not appear without his date, his position and his unity. The individual may be presented to me as there and now and one. And the residents of 4568 Spuyten Duyvil Parkway, who are, let us say, six, may be presented to me as six, and with their various names. 'Resident of 4568 Spuyten Duyvil Parkway' is a universal in that, having a plurality of instances, it is presented to some one without its various dates, positions or number. It is a concept with respect to some one, hence a universal; but not a concept with respect to the mental attitude of mine which is directed upon each of the individuals who are its instances.

Thus both the individual and the universal may be presented to different sorts of mental attitudes. There is the individual which is presented with date and position, the individual which is on occasion a percept. And there is the individual, the same individual, which is the object of certain mental attitudes that resemble instances of conceiving. Likewise there is the universal which is a concept with respect to certain mental attitudes, but not a concept with respect to others; the universal whose various dates, positions and number are disregarded by some of the mental attitudes directed upon it, but not disregarded by others.

Whereas, however, 'resident of 4568 Spuyten Duyvil Parkway' is, it may be agreed, a universal which is a concept with respect to certain mental attitudes and not a concept with respect to other mental attitudes directed upon it, it may be questioned whether 'man,' which is a concept with respect to certain mental attitudes, is ever presented with the dates, position and number of its various instances. The residents of 4568 Spuyten Duyvil Parkway are six, whereas the number of men is, we may say, a large number, but one such that we do not know whether it is odd or even. And whereas each of the six residents may be fairly definite objects for the maid who is acquainted with each of them, no one, it may be agreed, has a similar acquaintance with each man; no mental attitude has each man as a similarly definite object.

I may however be aware of each man, even though the various individuals that make up the collection that constitutes my object are, for the most part, presented without detail. I may be aware of a collection of individuals each of whom *has* a date and a position but a date and a position that is not definitely presented to me. But to be aware of men as many is not, we hold, to conceive. No doubt my mental attitude directed upon 'man' without conceiving it, my mental attitude that is directed upon men or upon each man, is not exactly like the mental attitude of the maid who is aware of the six residents without conceiving the universal of which they are instances. Just as the collection of pennies in a bowl differs from the collection of chairs in this room, although each is finite in number;[71] so, although the maid's mental attitude differs from mine, each, we hold, is directed upon the instances of a universal and is not conceiving. 'Man,' we conclude, like 'resident of 4568 Spuyten Duyvil Parkway,' is an object for some mental attitudes that conceive and for some that do not.

There is the maid's mental attitude directed upon the six residents as individuals; and there is my mental attitude directed upon men as many. There is the enumerative proposition: "Each resident of 4568 Spuyten Duyvil Parkway is over 40"; and there is the enumerative proposition: "Each man is mortal." [72] Each resident is a definite object for the maid. She can enumerate: Mr.

Allen on the first floor, Mr. Brown on the second, and so on. But you, we shall assume, have no acquaintance with any of the residents of 4568 Spuyten Duyvil Parkway. With respect to your mental attitude, the residents of 4568 Spuyten Duyvil Parkway are indefinite objects; but each resident is presented to you, let us say, with the characteristic of being a definite object for the maid. When we have before us the enumerative proposition: "Each man is mortal," however, not only are many of the men upon whom our mental attitudes are directed indefinite objects with respect to us, but no mental attitudes are definitely presented to us to which these various men appear to be definite objects. That is to say, we are not presented with X, one of the men who are our objects, as a definite object for A, or with Y as a definite object for B. If X and Y are presented as being definite objects for no one, X and Y, to be sure, are unreal. But X and Y, presented without the characteristic of being definite objects for no one, may well be real and each a man who is mortal.

The enumerative proposition: "Each man is mortal" may well be true; each man may really be mortal. But how can I know that each man is mortal, how, that is to say, do I come to believe in the truth of the true proposition: "Each man is mortal," when many men are presented to me as mere X's, neither they being my definite objects nor any mental attitudes being definitely presented to me that *have* them as definite objects? We can only repeat what is, we hold, a fact. There are real entities in whose existence I believe, although they are only vaguely and indefinitely objects for the awareness that I direct upon them. There are entities that do not appear as definite objects for no one, entities which are real, but which are not definite objects for my thinking. I know that they exist; but I do not have them as definite objects when I believe in their existence.[73]

There is the enumerative proposition: "Each A is B" which is true, in the sense in which we have explained "truth," if A_1 is B, if A_2 is B, if each instance of A is a B.[74] And there is the universal proposition: "All S is P," which is true "when S P is real and S: not-P unreal." [75] "Each man is mortal" is true in that existence belongs to the mortal Socrates, to the mortal Plato, to the mortal Aristotle, to each real man subsisting as mortal. And "All men are mortal" is true in that 'mortal man' exists, but not 'immortal man.'

535

To ask how I come to know that each man is mortal may well be to ask how I come to believe in the existence of entities not presented to me as definite objects, in the existence of the mortality of some individual X when neither X nor the mortality of X is definitely presented to me. On the other hand, to ask how I come to know that all men are mortal is to ask how my mental attitude apparently directed upon the alleged existence of some universal—in this instance, 'immortal man'—comes to be accompanied by a feeling of disbelief.

There is the true proposition: "All men are mortal" and the true proposition: "All extended entities are extended," the alleged universal: 'immortal man' and the alleged universal: 'unextended extended entity.' There is little question as to how my mental attitude apparently directed upon the alleged existence of 'unextended extended entity' comes to be accompanied by a feeling of disbelief. For 'unextended extended entity' seems to be presented as self-contradictory and hence as unreal. But it is not only the entity presented as self-contradictory that is unreal in the sense in which we have explained the terms "existence" and "reality." "The signification of 'existence,'" we have said,[76] may be regarded as having two components, one corresponding to the law of contradiction, the other to Leibniz's principle of sufficient reason." And so it is not only 'unextended extended entity' which is unreal, but also 'immortal man'; not only, to use Kantian language, the analytic proposition: "All extended entities are extended" which is true and believed to be true, but also the synthetic proposition: "All men are mortal." For whereas 'unextended extended entity' is unreal and the apparent awareness of it accompanied by disbelief (in that 'unextended extended entity' is presented as self-contradictory), 'immortal man' is just as unreal and the apparent awareness of it likewise accompanied by disbelief (in that 'immortal man' is presented as generally discredited).

To be sure, the proposition with which Kant concerns himself is described, not so much as the synthetic proposition which is universal, but rather as the synthetic proposition which is *a priori.* It is knowledge in the absence of experience, in the absence of mental attitudes which are instances of perceiving, that gives rise, it would appear, to misgivings. Such misgivings, however, are not limited to, or even primarily concerned with, synthetic propositions which are universal. The question based on such misgivings as to how I may know that all men are mortal resolves itself, it would seem, into the question as to how I may know that some individual yet alive, or as yet unborn, will die. It is the question as to how I come to believe in the mortality of some individual X whose death or mortality no one has perceived. Just however as we have not said that, in order to be real in the sense in which we have explained "reality," an entity may not be presented as an indefinite object of mine—although it may not be presented as no one's definite object,—so we have not said that it may not be presented as no one's percept. Much less have we said that it must be presented as the percept of some subject who is past or present, but not future, with respect to me. It is, it would seem, as a result of attaching existence primarily, or perhaps exclusively, to percepts that doubts arise with respect to the mortality of individuals not yet dead. It is, it would seem, the use of the term "existence" in a sense different from that in which we are using it that leads us to question the validity of synthetic propositions *a priori*. It is, in short, not some characteristic of the human mind, but rather the use of the term "existence" in a certain way—in a way which does not demand that the existent be a percept or a definite object for each subject to whom it is presented;—it is this that makes synthetic propositions *a priori* possible.

Summary

'Man,' presented as lacking date and position, is unreal. Mankind, presented as a collective, is an individual and not a universal. 'Men,' presented as many, is likewise no universal. The 'man' that we call a universal and find real has many instances, but is presented without them.

There is the universal substance 'man' and the universal quality 'greenness.' There is the individual substance Socrates and the individual quality: the greenness of this leaf. We may think of individual substances, universal substances, universal qualities and individual qualities in various sequences. I may think first of Socrates, then of the individual quality: the human nature of Socrates, then of the universal quality: human nature, then of

537

the universal substance 'man' in which the universal quality 'human nature' inheres. Or I may think first of Socrates, then of 'man,' then of the universal quality 'human nature,' etc.

When a subject conceives,—that is, is aware of a universal,—there is no 'idea' which is his immediate object. Hence, Locke's, Berkeley's and Kant's descriptions of what is before us when we think about universals are all incorrect. Apropos of realism, nominalism and conceptualism, the universal (which is a public object) is *in* its instances, whereas it is the mental attitude and not a general idea which is either *ante rem* or *post rem*.

Some universals correspond to absolute qualities in their instances. Some are subsumed under or included within others. This leads to a discussion of: the class of all classes not members of themselves and of: Man is an animal, animal is a genus, therefore man is a genus.

Other problems considered concern the relation of the universal to the individual, the alleged universal which is presented as having a single instance, the universal all of whose instances are definite objects.

Chapter XVII

MEANING, EXPLANATION, DEFINITION

Now that we have found real certain individuals and certain universals, certain qualities and certain substances, let us once more turn our attention to the words which seem to represent these qualities and substances, these individuals and universals. Let us examine words and the sentences that we call "propositions" in relation to the mental attitudes of which they are the expressions and in relation to the individuals and universals which they seem to represent.

Various mental attitudes, we have found,[1] exist; and some of them lead the organisms, whose mental attitudes they are, to do things or to say things or to make things. Without determining just what is involved in being a cause, there is some sense of the word "cause," we have concluded,[2] in which a clerk's mental attitude is the cause of the statement that he makes out, the mental attitude of a shipbuilder the cause of the ocean liner that is subsequently constructed. Statement and ocean liner are, let us say, "expressions" of the mental attitudes which caused them. Let us not say however that a sneeze is an expression, or the sounds uttered by a man who is asleep. As we use the term "expression," an expression is the direct or indirect result of a mental attitude that coheres with other mental attitudes to characterize a unitized mind-person.[3]

A given mental attitude, to be sure, may result in a series of things. My present mental attitude is the cause of the action of my hand in writing which results in the words to be found in my manuscript, which, in turn, is causally related to the printed words in the book before you. Writing hand, manuscript word and printed word are all expressions with respect to a certain mental attitude of mine. On the other hand, a given expression may point back to two or more mental attitudes that were its causes. An actor's performance may be the expression not only of a mental attitude of his own, but of a mental attitude of the director and of a mental attitude of the playwright. Certain entities that we call expressions exist: the ocean liner, the actor's performance, the printed words before you. And each entity that *is* an expression is an expression relative to one or more mental attitudes that in some sense caused it.

My mental attitude may be an instance of fearing; and my fearing may cause my knees to shake. My shaking knees are then an expression of my fearing. But while I am thus fearing, let us suppose, I am not thinking about the impression that my shaking knees will create, am not desiring the beholder of my shaking knees to think about a specific object. There are however other mental attitudes resulting in expressions where the situation is otherwise. Some mental attitude which expresses itself in the word "Socrates" is, we suggest, accompanied by the desire that the reader of "Socrates" think of the Athenian philosopher. And a given mental attitude that results in a sign-post with an arrow on it is, we suggest, accompanied by the desire that the beholder think of an object in the direction in which the arrow points. Under such circumstances arrow and "Socrates" are, let us say, not only expressions, but representative expressions.[4] And the entity that the beholder is desired to have as his object is, let us say, the meaning represented by the representative expression.

Laöcoon, aware of the Greeks off in their ships, was also fearing.[5] And I, uttering the word "Socrates," am also desiring. What I desire—the object of my desiring or of a further mental attitude accompanying my desiring—is an auditor of my word "Socrates" who will think of the Athenian philosopher. My word "Socrates" exists and the Athenian philosopher exists. And since my word "Socrates" is caused by a mental attitude that is accompanied by a desire that the auditor think of the Athenian philosopher, Socrates exists as a meaning that is represented by my representative expression.

We shall not however limit the denotation of "meaning" to that situation in which the desire is for an auditor or beholder other than the creator of the expression himself. When I jot a note on a memorandum pad with the intention of referring to it later, that note is a representative expression and the matter that I desire to have as my object at that later date is my expression's meaning. Indeed we shall call an entity a "meaning" when no definite auditor or beholder of the expression is desired, when the expression, one might say, is "for whom it may concern." Moreover the desire for even so indefinite an auditor or beholder, let us say, need not be a desire of which the creator of the expression is aware. Just as there are instances of fearing that are not introspected,[6] so there are instances of desiring that are not introspected. I may desire whoever happens to read my word "Socrates" to think of the Athenian philosopher; and yet not have this desire of mine as my present object. But if the desire is real, to be recognized as an instance of desiring by some other subject or by the creator of the expression at some later date, the expression may well be what we call a "representative expression" and the object that some auditor or beholder is desired to have may well be what we call that expression's "meaning."

It should be pointed out, however, that, introspected or not, the desire that is involved in the relation between representative expression and meaning is a desire that auditor or beholder be aware of an object. The auditor or beholder of an expression may be affected by it in various ways. He may have a mental attitude which is an instance of feeling; he may become aware of the object that we call the "meaning"; he may be characterized by non-mental behavior of various forms. I may hold out a piece of sugar to induce a horse to approach me; but if my interest is solely in what the horse is to do, not in what he is to think, then my gesture is no representative expression. It is in short not the desire for a response that is involved in the relation between representative expression and meaning, but the desire for a mental attitude directed upon an object; not a desire for non-mental behavior directed towards some entity other than the stimulus itself, but a desire for that element in total behavior that we call awareness of an object.[7]

It is my mental attitude which causes or creates the representative expression "Socrates"; it is the representative expression "Socrates" in turn which means or represents the Athenian philosopher. In our terminology it is not my mental attitude, but the expression created by that mental attitude, which represents or means the Athenian philosopher. And it is not Socrates himself who *has* a meaning, but rather the word "Socrates" with respect to which Socrates *is* the meaning. Socrates may be important, some fact concerning him may be significant; but it is the word "Socrates" that has a signification, that represents a meaning. Only entities represented by representative expressions are what we call "meanings." Only entities that are expressions represent meanings. A cloud is sometimes said to imply rain, sometimes said to be a sign of rain. But as we use the term "meaning," a cloud does not mean rain. For, assuming that no mental attitude creates the cloud, the cloud is no expression, much less a representative expression with rain as its meaning.

My word "Socrates" exists with the Athenian philosopher as its meaning. My word "lion" exists with the real universal 'lion' as its meaning. But what about the word "Ivanhoe" that I utter; or the word "centaur"? The alleged individual Ivanhoe is unreal and the alleged universal 'centaur' likewise unreal. Ivanhoe is not really tall and fair, not really a medieval knight, not really related to any word "Ivanhoe" that I utter. The non-existent Ivanhoe, in short, is no meaning and the non-existent centaur no meaning. And since Ivanhoe and centaur are unreal, my word "Ivanhoe" can not really be related to Ivanhoe and my word "centaur" can not really be related to centaur. To be related only to an unreal entity is not to be related at all.[8] And since my word "Ivanhoe" is not related to Ivanhoe, does not represent Ivanhoe, it is no representative expression. Where there is no husband, there is no wife. Representative expression and meaning likewise are correlatives. Where, it follows, there is no meaning to be represented, there is no representative expression to represent that meaning. My word "Ivanhoe" and my word "centaur" are, to be sure, real. They are expressions in which mental attitudes of mine express themselves. But they are not representative expressions, not expressions which represent or *have* meanings.

"Centaur" has no meaning; "abracadabra" has no meaning; some sounds uttered by a man in his sleep have no meaning. It is apparent, however, that different characteristics characterize various entities that, as we use "meaning," are classed together

542

as having, or representing, no meanings. Certain sounds uttered by a man in his sleep result, we assume, from no "mental attitude that coheres with other mental attitudes to characterize a unitized mind-person." [9] They then are not expressions at all. And whereas "abracadabra" is an expression, it results from a mental attitude that is not accompanied by a desire that the auditor think of an object. The magician who utters "abracadabra," that is to say, desires his auditor to have a feeling of puzzlement or awe, not a mental attitude that is or resembles thinking about an object. On the other hand, he who writes "Ivanhoe" or "centaur" desires a mental attitude on the part of the reader that may be compared with the mental attitude desired when he writes "Socrates" or "lion." Since 'centaur' does not exist, no reader, to be sure, can really be aware of 'centaur.' And since a reader really aware of centaur will not exist, the creator of the expression "centaur" can not really desire such a reader. There is however the mental attitude which is "as if" it were directed towards a centaur. [10] And there is desiring which is "as if" the desired object were a reader aware of a centaur. [11] "Centaur" and "Ivanhoe" are not representative expressions in that they have no meanings to represent. But they are expressions in that they result from mental attitudes. And they resemble expressions which *are* representative in that the mental attitudes that cause them are accompanied, not by a desire for a reader aware of a definite object, but by a desire which is as if it were for a reader aware of a definite object.

My word "Socrates" is related both to the mental attitude of mine which expresses itself in it and to the Athenian philosopher who is meant or represented by it. But my word "Ivanhoe" enters into only the one relational situation, that which relates it to the mental attitude which is expressed in it. We found ourselves confronted by a similar situation, it will be recalled, in comparing the proposition: "Socrates exists" with the proposition: "Ivanhoe exists." Whereas both "Socrates exists" and "Ivanhoe exists" have what in a previous chapter we described as a "subjective reference," [12] only the former of these two propositions refers to an objective fact or judgment whose truth or falsity may be regarded as establishing the proposition's truth or falsity. "Socrates exists" may be said to be true in that the objective judgment: 'the existence of Socrates' is true. But in order to call "Ivanhoe exists" false and "Ivanhoe does not exist" true, we found ourselves applying the terms "truth" and "falsity" directly to these propositions themselves.[13]

Somewhat similarly, the expressions "Socrates" and "lion" may be described by referring to the meanings which they represent. But to keep within the world of real entities in describing "centaur" and "Ivanhoe," we must content ourselves with a reference to the mental attitudes which cause these expressions. The mental attitude which expresses itself in "centaur" is accompanied, we may say, by a desiring which is as if a reader aware of a centaur were desired. And the mental attitude which expresses itself in "Ivanhoe" is accompanied, we may say, by a desiring which is as if a reader aware of Ivanhoe were desired. The desiring which is as if a reader aware of centaur were desired differs intrinsically from the desiring which is as if a reader aware of Ivanhoe were desired; just as a mental attitude which is as if it were aware of a griffin differs intrinsically from a mental attitude which is as if it were aware of a unicorn.[14] "Centaur" and "Ivanhoe" differ from one another, it follows, not in having different meanings,—for neither of these expressions represents a meaning,—but in resulting from intrinsically different mental attitudes.

The word "Ivanhoe," we say, represents no meaning. And yet the sentence: "Ivanhoe exists" is false, we have indicated, in that the entity that "Ivanhoe" intends to represent does not exist.[15] What, however, is an intention to represent when there is no meaning? What justification have we for calling "Ivanhoe exists" false on the basis of the non-existence of Ivanhoe, when there is no real relation between the word "Ivanhoe" that occurs in our sentence and the alleged medieval knight? In the process of explaining "truth" and "falsity" we seem to assume a relational situation that we later reject. Indeed, a similar criticism seems to apply to our discussion of "existence." We present to ourselves various subsistents, some real and some unreal, in order to mark out some to be called "existent" and some to be called "non-existent." And yet, since we subsequently conclude that no mental attitudes can really have non-existent entities as their objects, those subsistents which are unreal can not really have been presented to us in the first place. We can not, it would seem, be aware of the unreal or assert true propositions which refer to the unreal.

544

And yet to distinguish between the real and the unreal, it would seem that the unreal must in some sense be presented to us.

The word "Ivanhoe," let us reaffirm, represents no meaning. It is, however, the expression of a mental attitude accompanied by a desiring as if a reader aware of Ivanhoe were desired. It is, one might say, a pseudo-representative expression rather than a representative expression. And its pseudo-representative character, its intention to represent, stems entirely from its relation to the mental attitude expressed in it. One mental attitude with its intrinsic characteristics results in a pseudo-representative expression. Another mental attitude with *its* intrinsic characteristics results in an expression that is really representative. One mental attitude with its intrinsic characteristics is an instance of perceiving. Another mental attitude with *its* intrinsic characteristics is an instance of pseudo-perceiving. To keep entirely within the world of reality, our distinctions must be between one mental attitude and another. But what we call the intrinsic qualities of mental attitudes can only be described by using words that seem to take us into the world of alleged objects. Some of these words represent no meanings. Some of the sentences that we use, such as "Ivanhoe subsists," are not what we call "propositions," are neither true nor false.[16] But words which have no meanings and sentences which are not propositions enable us to identify mental attitudes which are only *as if* they had objects, mental attitudes which express themselves in merely pseudo-representative expressions. When we write: "Ivanhoe is presented to us as a subsistent; Socrates is presented to us as a subsistent," our sentence is neither true nor false. But our sentence enables us to identify a mental attitude which is subsequently said to have a real object and a mental attitude which is subsequently said not to have a real object. When we write the words: "Socrates," "Ivanhoe," one of our words represents no meaning. But our words enable us to identify two mental attitudes, one of which expresses itself in an expression that is subsequently called "representative," the other in an expression that is subsequently called "pseudo-representative." Finally, the proposition: "Ivanhoe exists" is called false, although it refers to no objective judgment and contains the word "Ivanhoe" that has no meaning. We are enabled to call this proposition false in that it identifies a mental attitude which has no object, a mental attitude which is as if it were aware of a judgment: the existence of Ivanhoe. In short, the real dichotomy is a dichotomy of real mental attitudes. But we use words which are not representative expressions, and we seem to refer to alleged subsistents which are unreal, in order to identify the class of mental attitudes to be dichotomized.

"Ivanhoe" represents no meaning; "Apollo" represents no meaning; "King of France in 1948" represents no meaning. Instead, however, of holding that such expressions derive their pseudo-representative character from the mental attitudes that are expressed in them, it has been held that such expressions can be replaced by other expressions that *are* representative. Whereas "King of France in 1948" represents no meaning, points to nothing, "King of France," it may be said, points to various earlier Kings, as, for example, Francis I and Louis XIV; and "King in 1948," it may be said, points to such Kings as Haakon of Norway and George VI of Great Britain. It seems clear, however, that "King of France in 1948" points neither to Francis I nor to George VI nor to any real combination of the two. "King of France in 1948," that is to say, is not compounded of "King of France" and "King in 1948." Hence we find no meaning for "King of France in 1948" by finding meanings for two other expressions which neither individually nor collectively can substitute for it.

It is through a more complicated procedure that Whitehead and Russell attempt to eliminate non-representative expressions. The word "Apollo," they too assert, represents no meaning. It is their suggestion that we first replace this word with the expression: "the object having the properties enumerated in the Classical Dictionary"; [17] and that this latter expression in turn be replaced by a group of sentences, one of which, "X has the property P," is said to be or to represent a propositional function. An expression claiming to represent a propositional function, it may be said, is an expression containing an "X" or a blank that can be filled in with various values. In order, however, that I may be able to consider the propositional function represented by "X has the property P," I must be able, it would seem, to think of various values of X as having the property P,—among them, various values of X that do not in fact have the property P. But the entity alleged to have the property P which does not in fact have the property P, this entity is as unreal as the alleged god Apollo. And the expression: "value of X that does not satisfy the propositional function: 'X has the property P'," this expression represents a meaning no more than does the word "Apollo." We do not eliminate mental attitudes that seem to be aware of unreal objects—mental attitudes which, we hold, *have* no objects—by turning from an alleged Apollo to alleged propositional functions. And so Whitehead and Russell succeed at most in substituting one non-representative expression for another.

"Apollo" represents no meaning and "the King of France in 1948" represents no meaning. Whitehead and Russell however go further. They assert that the expression: "the author of Waverley" also represents no meaning. Instead of considering "the author of Waverley," they suggest that we turn our attention to "X wrote Waverley" and to the individual known as Sir Walter Scott, to the value of X, that is to say, that satisfies "X wrote Waverley." But "Sir Walter Scott" represents either an individual of whom I have merely heard or read; or it represents an individual whom I may point out as "that entity over there." The individual of whom I have heard or read is, however, just the sort of object for me that the author of Waverley is. If it were true—which it is not—that "the author of Waverley" represents no meaning, it would be true that "the individual of whom I have heard or read" represents no meaning. And whereas George IV may on some occasion have pointed to Sir Walter Scott as "that entity over there," when *I* use the expression "that entity over there" or when you use the expression "that entity over there," there is no Sir Walter Scott that the expression represents. It would seem to follow, on the doctrine which we are discussing, that representative expressions which will substitute for "the author of Waverley" are found only when those expressions are expressions of mental attitudes for whom Scott was a percept. There is, however, no need, we hold, to seek a substitute for "the author of Waverley." "Sir Walter Scott," we hold, represents a meaning; "the author of Waverley" represents a meaning; "the individual of whom I have heard or read" represents a meaning. Indeed it is only the expression that *has* a meaning that can be replaced by another representative expression. For, in making the substitution, the replaced expression is assigned whatever meaning the substituting expression may represent.

"Apollo" represents no meaning and "the individual with properties enumerated in a certain section of the Classical Dictionary" represents no meaning. On the other hand, "Sir Walter Scott" represents a meaning and "the author of Waverley" represents a meaning. Indeed, the expression: "Sir Walter Scott" and the expression: "the author of Waverley" represent the *same* meaning. For whether I write "Sir Walter Scott" or "the author of Waverley," it is the same nineteenth century author that I desire my reader to have as his object. To be sure, the quality of having written Waverley differs from the quality of being named Sir Walter Scott. The expression: "having written Waverley" and the expression: "named Sir Walter Scott" represent distinguishable qualities. "Sir Walter Scott" and "the author of Waverley" are, however, expressions which represent a *substance*. And they represent the *same* substance, a substance which—whichever expression be used to represent it—has the quality of having written Waverley and also the quality of being named Sir Walter Scott. "If you have a mental attitude directed upon 'triangularity' and I a mental attitude directed upon 'trilaterality,' your object," we have held,[18] "is distinguishable from mine." But, we have also held, "if your mental attitude is directed upon 'triangle' and mine upon 'trilateral,' your mental attitude and mine are directed upon a common object." Just as "Sir Walter Scott" and "the author of Waverley" represent the same individual substance, so the expressions "triangle" and "trilateral" represent a common universal substance. And just as "having written Waverley" and "named Sir Walter Scott" represent distinguishable qualities of an individual substance, so the expressions "triangularity" and "trilaterality" represent distinguishable universal qualities.

Surely, however, my mental attitude when I write: "Sir Walter Scott" may not be identical with the mental attitude which expresses itself in: "the author of Waverley." Nor is the mental attitude expected in the reader for whom I write "Scott is the author of Waverley" the mental attitude expected in the reader for whom I write "Scott is Scott." "Scott" and "the author of Waverley" point ultimately, it may be agreed, to the same individual; "triangle" and "trilateral" to a common universal in the world of spatio-temporal objects. But between the expression and the spatio-temporal entity to which it ultimately points, there is, it has been held, an intermediate entity which is not itself in the world of spatio-temporal objects. "Scott" and "the author of Waverley," differ, it may be said, in that they point to different non-spatial entities, to different "objectives" which have Sir Walter Scott as their common point of application. And "trilateral" and "triangle," it has been held, have different non-temporal meanings; although, through these meanings, they ultimately point to a common spatio-temporal object.[19]

The alleged non-spatial and non-temporal meaning or 'objective' with which we are thus presented is, however, a subsistent which, as we use the term "existence," does not exist. The entity that is presented as lacking date and position is in our terminology unreal.[20] No real universal and no real individual is really related to it; no real expression really represents it. The meanings that representative expressions represent, we continue to hold, are such spatio-temporal entities as the individual Scott and the universal 'triangle.' And the differences between such expressions as "Scott" and "the author of Waverley" and between such expressions as "trilateral" and "triangle" point, not to different objectives which have a common reference, but rather to differences between the mental attitudes that express themselves in these expressions and to differences between the mental attitudes induced by these expressions in their readers. When I write: "the author of Waverley," I and my reader may be aware of Scott and also of his quality of having written Waverley. When I write: "Sir Walter Scott," I and my reader may be aware of Scott and also of his name. But whether I write: "Sir Walter Scott" or "the author of Waverley," it is of the substance in which various qualities inhere that I desire my reader to be aware. Hence, whether I write: "Sir Walter Scott" or "the author of Waverley," it is the *substance* that my expression represents.

It has been held, we have seen, that expressions do not directly represent spatio-temporal entities, but, rather, represent non-spatial "objectives" which in turn apply to entities in the spatio-temporal world. It has likewise been held that expressions do not directly represent spatio-temporal entities but, rather, represent private ideas having no position with respect to public objects. My word "Socrates," that is to say, may be held not to represent directly the Athenian philosopher, but, rather, my private idea of this Athenian philosopher. And your word "Socrates" may be held to represent *your* private idea of this Athenian philosopher. That "which words are the marks of," says Locke,[21] "are the ideas of the speaker; nor can any one," he holds, "apply them, as marks, immediately to anything else but the ideas that he himself hath." Entities, however, that are alleged to be non-spatial are unreal. And entities that are alleged not to be known at all by more than a single subject are unreal.[22] Just as an alleged non-spatial 'objective' is unreal and can not be represented by my word "triangle," so an alleged non-spatial private idea of Socrates is unreal and can not be represented by my word "Socrates." Just as it is the universal triangle and not some non-spatial objective that my word "triangle" means, so it is the Athenian philosopher and not some private idea that my word "Socrates" means. For what is it that, in our terminology, a representative expression means? It means the entity of which the creator of the expression desires a beholder to be aware.[23] Surely when I write the word "Socrates," the entity which I desire the beholder to have as his object is not an alleged private idea of mine, an alleged idea that not only does not exist, but by hypothesis can never be presented to another subject. It is not so hopeless a desire that accompanies my writing, but rather the desire that the beholder have as his object the Athenian philosopher himself.

What we call an "idea" appears as object or content rather than as thinking or mental attitude.[24] My alleged private idea of Socrates, which is unreal, is to be distinguished from the mental attitude which I really have, the mental attitude which has Socrates as its object. Whereas, then, my alleged idea of Socrates, being unreal, can not be represented by any expression, it does not follow that a mental attitude of mine can not be represented by my expression: "my mental attitude directed upon Socrates." There are indeed instances of representative expressions which represent the very mental attitudes whose expressions they are. For when I write: "the mental attitude which created this expression," the creator of the expression and the meaning of the expression are the same mental attitude. There are situations, that is to say, in which the creator of an expression desires the beholder to turn his attention from the expression to the expression's creator. But a desire of this sort

550

does not characterize every mental attitude that expresses itself in an expression. When I write the word "Socrates," for example, my desire is for a reader aware of Socrates, not for a reader aware of that mental attitude of mine which results in my writing the word: "Socrates." When Descartes was aware of the Emperor, he may not simultaneously have been aware of his own thinking.[25] When I am aware of Socrates I need not be aware of my mental attitude directed upon Socrates. And when, on writing the word "Socrates," I desire my reader to be aware of the Athenian philosopher, I need not also be desiring him to be aware of my mental attitude directed upon the Athenian philosopher.

There are, we have said, instances of representative expressions which represent mental attitudes. There are likewise instances of representative expressions which represent expressions. Just as my expression: "my mental attitude directed upon Socrates" represents a mental attitude, so my expression: "the first sentence in this treatise" represents an expression. When I write: "the mental attitude which created this expression," the creator of the expression and the meaning of the expression are the same mental attitude. And when I write: "these words," I desire the reader of "these words" to have as his object: "these words." My expression in this instance represents itself, is its own meaning; as, in an instance of suicide, the murderer is his own victim.[26]

The expression: "these words" is the meaning represented by this expression: "these words." The number 111,777 is the meaning represented by the expression: "the least integer not nameable in fewer than nineteen syllables."[27] But the expression: "the least integer not nameable in fewer than nineteen syllables" contains eighteen syllables. Using words of a certain type—words such as "one," "seven," "eleven"—nineteen syllables are required to represent 111,777. Using words without limitation as to type, an expression containing eighteen syllables will suffice.[28] What Whitehead and Russell, who call attention to this characteristic of 111,777, set out to show is that no significant statement can be made about a totality of names.[29] But no conclusion as to the meaninglessness of "all animals" can be drawn from the fact that Socrates is an animal when "animal" denotes men as well as brutes, but not an animal when "animal" denotes only brutes. And no conclusion as to the meaninglessness of "all names" or of "all representative expressions" can be drawn from the fact that a word is used now in one sense, a narrower sense, and now in another sense, a broader sense.

Let us suppose, however, that we assert of a certain entity, not that it has no name of a certain type, but that it has no name at all. A given entity, let it be said, is represented by no representative expression at all. But "represented by no representative expression" is itself an expression, an expression which in some sense represents this entity. "Nameless," it would seem, is itself the name of whatever is said to be nameless. Now the entity that is alleged to be represented by no representative expression seems to resemble the entity that appears as in no sense an object of consciousness. Just as the entity which is presented as in no sense an object of consciousness appears implicitly with the characteristic of being in some sense an object and hence as self-contradictory and unreal;[30] so the entity which is presented as represented by no representative expression appears implicitly with the characteristic of being represented by: "represented by no representative expression" and hence appears as self-contradictory and unreal. The entity which appears as represented by no representative expression is a subsistent which is unreal. And the proposition in which some quality is attributed to this entity, like the proposition: "the present King of France is bald," and like the proposition: "all centaurs are white," is false.[31] Our conclusion is that the expression: "entity A which is represented by no representative expression" is meaningless, not in the sense in which "abracadabra" is meaningless, but rather in the sense in which "centaur" is meaningless.[32] And our conclusion is that "entity A is represented by no representative expression" is not beyond truth and falsity, but a proposition which is false.

My word "Socrates" exists with the Athenian philosopher as its meaning. My word "man" exists with the universal 'man' as its meaning.[33] The individual Socrates represented by my word "Socrates" is, however, an instance of the universal that is represented by my word "man." And so we are presented, not only with a relational situation including on the one hand the individual Socrates and on the other hand my word "Socrates," but we are also presented with a relational situation including on the one hand the individual Socrates and on the other hand my word "man." A general word, such as "man," may be said to *denote* the individuals who are instances of the universal that is its meaning. A general word such as "man," it follows, may be held on the one hand to enter into a relational situation with the universal which it means, on the other hand into a relational situation with the individual instances of that universal, with the individuals which it denotes. Since, however, the universal is in fact the individuals that are its instances thought of in a certain way,[34] the relational situation which includes a general word and the universal that it means is in fact the relational situation which includes that general word and the individuals that it denotes. It is not to be concluded, however, that whatever relational situation exists is to be described as one involving a general word and its denotation rather than described as one involving a general word and its meaning. The general word that is real is not merely a name for the individuals that it denotes; it also *means* the universal which it represents.

My word "Socrates" represents the Athenian philosopher in that I who utter this word desire my auditor to be aware of the Athenian philosopher.[35] Similarly some instance of the general word "man" represents the universal 'man' in that the mental attitude causing the expression is accompanied by the desire that the beholder of the expression think of 'man.' When some one hearing my word "Socrates" is in fact led to have the Athenian philosopher as his object, that auditor, let us say, *understands* my word "Socrates." And when some beholder of the instance of "man" that represents 'man' is in fact led to have 'man' as his object, that beholder, let us say, *understands* the expression that he has beheld. As we use the word: "understanding," there is understanding when a mental attitude directed upon a representative expression is followed by a mental attitude directed upon that expression's meaning.[36] Upon being presented with a given expression, it is one thing, it may be pointed out, to become aware of the meaning represented by that expression; and it is another thing to become aware of the mental attitude of the creator of the expression. To understand the word: "Socrates," I must become aware of the Athenian philosopher; I need not become aware of the thinking, the desiring, that characterized the writer of the word "Socrates." The writer has indeed desired me to think of Socrates. To call his word "Socrates" a representative expression is to imply that there has been such a desire. And to be aware of the fact that his word *is* a representative expression is to be aware of his desiring as well as of his word "Socrates" and its meaning. But it is one thing to become aware of a meaning and another thing to become aware of the author's purpose in creating the expression. It is one thing to understand a representative expression and another thing to become aware of the representative character of a representative expression.[37]

One individual writes the word "Socrates" desiring the reader of his expression to become aware of the Athenian philosopher. Another individual—who may of course be the same mind-person in a later phase—reads the expression, becomes aware of the Athenian philosopher and hence, in our terminology, understands this instance of the word: "Socrates." He who reads the expression, however, may become aware of Socrates, of Xenophon and of Xanthippe; whereas the writer of the expression may have been aware of Socrates, of Plato and of Alcibiades. The reader's awareness of additional objects is, however, no bar to what we are describing as "understanding." Nor are those mental attitudes of the writer relevant that happen to accompany his desire that the reader think of his expression's meaning. He who reads "the author of Waverley" may become aware of Sir Walter Scott and also of his quality of having written Waverley;[38] whereas the creator of the expression may have been aware of additional qualities. So long, however, as the writer desires a mental attitude directed upon the individual substance known as Sir Walter Scott, and so long as the reader comes to have such a mental attitude, the reader, in our terminology, understands the writer's expression.

Understanding exists, we hold, in instances in which entities in addition to the meaning are objects for the writer but not for the reader, or are objects for the reader but not for the creator of the expression. Understanding also exists, let us hold, in instances in which the meaning of the expression is a definite object for one, but only a rather indefinite object for the other. Some future reader of my expression: "the presidential inauguration of 1961" may be aware of that inauguration much more definitely than I am.[39] The reader of the expression: "a certain individual whose name I do not care to mention" may come to have as a very indefinite object the individual that the expression means. There is, however, understanding, as we explain "understanding," provided the reader has in not too indefinite a fashion as an object, whether more definitely or less definitely, the entity that the creator of the expression desires the reader of his expression to have. The understanding that we are describing is, it may be mentioned, the understanding by an individual beholder of an individual expression presented to him. Whether or not my expression "Socrates" is generally understood, there is an instance of understanding if a reader reading this word comes to have the Athenian philosopher as his object. And whether or not all instances of the word "Socrates" are understood—whatever, indeed the mental attitude that the writer of some other instance of the word "Socrates" may desire in the reader of his expression,—there is understanding of my word "Socrates" provided the reader comes to have as his object the entity that *my* expression means. Instances of understanding, thus described, exist. For example, the first instance of the word "Socrates" that exists on page 540 has the Athenian philosopher as its meaning. And I, in now re-reading that word, am led to have the Athenian philosopher as my object. My present mental attitude, that is to say, has as its object the entity that the earlier mental attitude, the creator of the word "Socrates," desired the reader of his expression to have. My present mental attitude is thus a real instance of what we are calling "understanding."

There are, we hold, instances of understanding. But there are also instances of misunderstanding. There are instances, that is to say, where the beholder of an expression has as his object, not entity A, but entity B, whereas the creator of the expression desired the beholder to have as his object entity A. There are likewise instances of lack of understanding, among them situations in which the beholder is unable to identify the entity that the author's expression means. If, for example, I assert that cats bark, the reader may be unable to determine whether my word "cat" means what is usually called "cat," in which case my assertion would be false, or whether my word "cat" means what is usually called "dog," in which case my assertion would be true.

It is not in all instances obvious what entity the author's expression means. And it is not in all instances obvious whether the reader understands or does not understand. There are occasions on which it is difficult to determine which is the entity that the beholder has as his object and which the entity A that the author's expression means. A given entity may seem to be believed by the author to be the entity that he desires the beholder of his expression to have as an object; but a different entity may seem to others to be the entity that he desires the beholder to have as an object.[40] And likewise with the beholder. A given entity may seem to the beholder to be his object; and a different entity may seem to others to be his object.

There is, to be sure, no way to assure understanding. But our discussion of what is real may aid us in determining what the author's expression really means and what entity is really the beholder's object. As we have explained "existence," the author may be mistaken as to what he desires and the beholder mistaken as to what is his object. If an entity, alleged to be the meaning of an author's expression, appears as generally believed not to be the meaning of his expression, then that entity does not exist as the meaning of his expression. If not only other instances of "cat," but also my word "cat," is generally believed not to represent what is commonly called "dog," then, whatever my belief as to what my word "cat" means, it does not mean 'dog.' And similarly with respect to the beholder. If an entity, seeming to the beholder to be his object, appears as generally believed not to be his object, then that entity does not exist as his object. What is approximately true in accordance with our explanations of "existence" and "reality" is that the author's expression means what it is generally believed to mean and that the beholder's object is the entity that is generally believed to be his object. What is approximately true is that there is understanding when the entity generally believed to be the beholder's object is the entity which the author's expression is generally believed to mean. Otherwise not.

It would seem then that, when I who am color-blind, write "red," and when you on seeing this word think of 'red,' you understand my expression even though my expression be presented to me as representing something else.[41] And it would seem that, when you read my word "Socrates" and are generally believed to be aware of the Athenian philosopher, you understand my expression even though some other entity seems to you to be your object. What is, however, perhaps more likely is that the writer is aware of the meaning of his own expression but mistaken as to the entity that the reader has as his object. And what is likewise not unusual is the situation in which the reader believes himself aware of the entity that is indeed his object but is mistaken as to the meaning of the author's expression. There is in the latter instance misunderstanding on the part of the reader. But the author who is mistaken as to the object before his reader is not misunderstanding. For it is not mental attitudes that are understood or misunderstood, but only expressions. There is misunderstanding on the part of our author, consequently, only when the reader replies, only when the reader in turn expresses himself in an expression which is misunderstood.

There is misunderstanding when an author's expression means entity A and when the reader of that expression comes to have as his object the different entity B. An assertion which is made with respect to A may consequently be misinterpreted as an assertion with respect to B. The reader may believe with respect to B what the author believes with respect to A. And so he may concur in a statement containing the expression "A" without there being what is commonly called "real" agreement. Similarly the reader may disbelieve with respect to B what the author believes with respect to A. And he may thus reject a statement containing the expression "A" without there being what is commonly called "real" disagreement.

Shall we, however, call such agreements and disagreements as stem from misunderstanding "verbal"; and other agreements and disagreements "real"? Agreements or disagreements that stem from misunderstanding point back to differing mental attitudes with respect to expressions and their meanings, to differing mental attitudes which nevertheless are real. On the other hand, disagreements with respect to some alleged fact concerning an agreed-upon meaning are not to be resolved or even clarified without some reference to words and their meanings. For the determination of what is a fact depends upon the sense in which we are to use the term "existence." We may agree that both your expression "A" and my expression "A" mean A and not B. But to determine whether or not A is large or a man or a universal, to deter-

557

mine whether our similar, or which of our dissimilar, attitudes towards this alleged fact is correct, we must concern ourselves with words, particularly with the meaning of the word "existence." Agreements or disagreements with respect to some alleged fact concerning an agreed-upon meaning are not then absolutely non-verbal; although there is no dispute with respect to the meanings of the words overtly presented. And agreements and disagreements that stem from misunderstanding, although verbal, are real.[42]

There are instances of understanding, instances of lack of understanding, instances of misunderstanding. There can of course be no understanding where there is no real meaning to be the beholder's object. For, the pseudo-representative expression that represents no real meaning represents nothing that can ever be a real object for any beholder. But where there is a real meaning, lack of understanding, or even misunderstanding, may be succeeded by understanding. A given auditor or reader, that is to say, who, on beholding a meaningful expression, fails to understand it, may in some later phase have a mental attitude which, on beholding this expression, is led to have as an object the expression's meaning. Lack of understanding, and even misunderstanding, may give way to understanding, particularly, let us point out, through the instrumentality of what we shall call an "explanation."

We call that expression an "explanation" which results in the understanding of some prior representative expression. A given representative expression may, to be sure, lead its beholder to think at once of its meaning. It may, that is to say, be what is commonly called "self-explanatory." But there are also situations, we assume, in which some beholder is not at once aware of the meaning represented by the expression he beholds, situations in which he becomes aware of this meaning only after being presented with some later expression which we term an "explanation." An explanation is thus an expression; it is an explanation of some prior representative expression; and it is an explanation with respect to the beholder—or beholders—whom it causes to understand that prior expression. Thus the final word of the preceding paragraph, the instance of the word "explanation" that occurs there, is an expression. And the present paragraph contains an explanation of it, an explanation of it to those readers who as a result of reading this paragraph become aware of the entity which that instance of the word "explanation" represents.

Both the English word "man" and the French word "homme" represent the universal substance 'man.' To pass from a mental attitude directed upon the word "homme" to a mental attitude directed upon the word "man" is one thing; to pass from a mental attitude directed upon either or both of these words to a mental attitude directed upon the universal 'man' is another. Unless some assertion of the equivalence of two expressions results in a mental attitude directed upon their common meaning, translation has taken place, but what has been put forward is no explanation. Nor has what we term an "explanation" been put forward when the expression that results from an attempt to explain fails to bring about, on the part of *any* beholder, a mental attitude directed upon the prior expression's meaning. To be an explanation, an expression must explain to some one. But with respect to a given representative expression to be explained, one expression may be a more satisfactory explanation than another. One expression, that is to say, may be an explanation with respect to more beholders than another, And one expression may result in the prior expression's meaning being a rather definite object, the other in it being a rather indefinite object. The expression that results from an attempt to explain may thus be a satisfactory explanation, an unsatisfactory or limited explanation, or no explanation at all.

It depends upon the information and vocabulary at the disposal of the beholder whether or not an expression resulting from an attempt to explain will or will not be an explanation that is satisfactory.[43] The proposition: "Xanthippe was the wife of Socrates" will, for example, be a satisfactory explanation of the expression "Xanthippe" with respect to those who understand "Socrates," but will be no explanation of "Xanthippe" with respect to those who do not. Nevertheless, when we attempt to explain a representative expression, certain exhortations may help us avoid expressions which will either be unsatisfactory explanations or no explanations at all. We are advised not to attempt both to explain "A" through the expression "B" and "B" through the expression "A." We are advised not to attempt to explain a word by means of an expression containing a word with the same root, not to attempt to explain "pentagonal," for example, by means of an expression containing the word "pentagon." And we are advised to avoid negative words, advised not to attempt to explain the expression: "real property," for example, by the proposition: "Real property is what can not be transferred from place to place."[44] The propositions in which such counsel is formulated have, to be sure, been said to be rules "in which the requirements of a good definition have been embodied."[45] But in our terminology they do not concern definitions—which are neither good nor bad—but explanations. In our terminology they are not rules of definition, but exhortations that, when we are engaged in an attempt to explain, may lead us to shun expressions which are either unsatisfactory explanations or no explanations at all.

Instances of words are not the only representative expressions that may be explained. Some gesture that I make desiring the beholder to be aware of an object may not at once be understood. But through another gesture, or through the use of words, the meaning of my former gesture may come to be the beholder's object. Similarly, propositions are not the only expressions that may serve to explain prior representative expressions. Some instance of the word "Xanthippe," for example, may be explained, not by an expression which is a proposition, but by some expression not involving the use of words. That is to say, some instance of the word "Xanthippe" that was contemporaneous with its meaning may have been explained by pointing to the individual whom this word represented. Yet we shall continue to use as examples of representative expressions to be explained such words as "Xanthippe" and "explanation" and as examples of explanations such propositions as: "Xanthippe was the wife of Socrates"[46] and "an explanation is an expression which results in the understanding of some prior representative expression."[47]

The word "Xanthippe" is a representative expression that represents an individual, the words "explanation" and "existence" representative expressions that represent universals. "Xanthippe" may be explained by the singular proposition: "Xanthippe was the wife of Socrates," "explanation" by the universal proposition: "An explanation is an expression which results in the understanding of some prior representative expression." But it is not always

560

a single universal proposition that is the explanation of a word representing a universal. There may be some auditors to whom the general word "cat" will be explained by calling attention to this Maltese cat and to that Persian cat. We may describe in general terms the signification we are about to attach to a given word. Or we may describe the signification we are about to attach to a given word by pointing out some of the individuals that we are going to use this word to denote. It is in part by enumerating entities listed in the appendix to Chapter Three that we explain our expression: "existence." [48] And so whereas, with respect to some reader, the explanation of an instance of the general word "explanation" may be a universal proposition, the explanation of an instance of the general word "existence" may, with respect to some reader, be a group of singular propositions taken together.

"Xanthippe was the wife of Socrates" is a proposition which with respect to some reader is an explanation. "Xanthippe was Xanthippe" is a proposition which is not. "An explanation is an expression which results in the understanding of some prior representative expression" is a proposition which with respect to some reader is an explanation. "An explanation is an explanation" is a proposition which is not. Yet all four of these propositions are propositions which are true. And so are various instances of "Man is an animal," of "Socrates was an Athenian philosopher," of "Man is a rational animal."

Many propositions are true; only some of them are explanations. Many propositions are true; only some of them are what we shall call "definitions." A definition, let us say, is a true proposition which is an affirmative universal categorical proposition whose subject-term and predicate-term represent commensurate universals. "A centaur is an animal, half horse and half man" is no definition in that it is not true. "Xanthippe was the wife of Socrates" is no definition in that it is not a universal proposition. "Man is an animal" is no definition in that subject-term and predicate-term do not represent commensurate universals.[49] But various instances of: "Man is a rational animal" are definitions. And so are instances of: "An explanation is an expression which results in the understanding of some prior representative expression." The former, let us say, define the universal 'man'; the latter, the universal 'explanation.' In our terminology, that is to say, a proposition which is a definition defines the universal represented by its subject-term.

Certain propositions exist in our sense of "existence" and are what we have agreed to call "definitions." Among them there is the proposition occurring in the preceding paragraph of your copy of this book which defines 'man' and the proposition occurring in the preceding paragraph of your copy of this book which defines 'explanation.' The proposition which defines the universal 'explanation' may however also be an explanation of some instance of the word "explanation." The same proposition, that is to say, may be both a definition and an explanation. But it is an individual word that is explained, the individual expression which, by means of the explanation, the reader comes to understand. And it is a universal, the universal represented by the subject-term, that the proposition which is a definition defines. The universal which a definition defines may, to be sure, be some such universal as the word "into." But if: "Into" is an English preposition of four letters representing 'motion towards' is a proposition which is a definition, if "into" and 'an English preposition of four letters representing 'motion towards' are commensurate universals, it is the universal which occurs wherever the word "into" occurs that is defined. That is to say, this proposition, if a definition, does not define its own subject-term but the universal of which its subject-term is an instance. On the other hand, the proposition: "Into" is an English preposition of four letters representing 'motion towards' may lead one reader to understand some instance of "into," may lead another reader to understand some instance of "towards," may, with respect to a third reader who already understands, be no explanation at all. Insofar as it is an explanation of "into," it explains, not the universal "into," but instances of "into" that the reader has already beheld.

As we have explained "explanation," some instance of the word "Xanthippe" may be explained.[50] But Xanthippe herself, being no universal, can not be defined. As we have explained "explanation," some instance of the word "cat" may be explained "by calling attention to this Maltese cat and to that Persian cat."[51] But unless all instances of 'cat' can be enumerated, unless the individual cats enumerated in the predicate are commensurate with the universal 'cat,' 'cat' can not be defined by a proposition listing instances of 'cat.' Furthermore, a proposition which results from an attempt to explain may be "a satisfactory explanation, an unsatisfactory or limited explanation, or no explanation at all."[52] It may be an explanation with respect to one reader, not an explanation with respect to another. But it is not relative to this or that reader that "Man is a rational animal" is or is not a definition. It is not with respect to one reader that a proposition is a satisfactory definition, with respect to another reader that it is an unsatisfactory definition. It is not so much that "a definition should be adequate, that is, the subject defined and the predicate defining should be equivalent or of the same extension."[53] Rather, subject-term and predicate-term *must* represent commensurate universals if the proposition is to be a definition at all. And if it is a definition, our explanation of "definition" makes no distinction between satisfactory definitions and unsatisfactory definitions, between good definitions and bad definitions. Our distinction is between propositions which are definitions and propositions which are not.

Our proposition is a definition when we say: "Man is a rational animal." Our proposition is a definition when we say: "An explanation is an expression which results in the understanding of some prior representative expression." But as we have explained "definition," "a man is a man" is a definition also; and so is "an explanation is an explanation." 'Man' is commensurate with 'man'; and 'man' is commensurate with 'rational animal.' Indeed the universal 'man' does not differ from the universal 'rational animal.' For the plurality of men presented to us without their dates, positions and number is not different from the plurality of rational animals presented to us without their dates, positions and number.[54] The mental attitude which is directed upon 'rational animal' may be accompanied by mental attitudes directed upon qualities of 'rational animal,' may be accompanied by mental attitudes directed upon the universal quality 'rationality' and upon the universal quality 'animality.' In so far, however, as one mental attitude is directed, not upon 'rationality' or 'animality,' but upon 'rational animal,' and another mental attitude directed upon 'man,' both mental attitudes have a common object. A definition, we have said, "defines the universal represented by its subject-term."[55] But when it is a universal *substance* that is represented by both subject-term and predicate-term, the entity defined is represented by the predicate-term also.

Just as my mental attitude as a whole when I write "Sir Walter Scott" may not be identical with the mental attitude which expresses itself in "the author of Waverley" and just as the mental attitude to be expected in the reader for whom I write: "Scott is the author of Waverley" may not be the mental attitude to be expected in the reader for whom I write: "Scott is Scott," [56] so the mental attitudes as a whole expressed or called forth by: "A man is a rational animal" may not be the mental attitudes expressed or called forth by: "A man is a man." As in the instance of "A man is a man," a definition's subject-term and predicate-term may be identical. [57] In other instances subject-term and predicate-term may be non-identical synonyms which express or call forth identical mental attitudes. [58] And in still other instances subject-term and predicate-term may express or call forth mental attitudes which as a whole are not identical but which nevertheless have a universal substance as their common object.

Indeed a subject-term and predicate-term that call forth non-identical mental attitudes on the part of one reader may call forth identical mental attitudes on the part of another. And a given reader who is characterized by non-identical mental attitudes at one reading may be characterized by identical mental attitudes at a later reading. Thus the expression: "rational animal" may at one reading lead me to be aware, not only of 'man,' but of 'rationality' and 'animality'; and at a later reading, after "Man is a rational animal" has become familiar to me, may lead me to be aware only of 'man.' On the other hand the expression "man" may at one reading lead me to be aware only of 'man'; and at a later reading, after 'man' has beeen analyzed, may lead me to be aware, not only of 'man,' but of 'rationality' and 'animality.' But whatever my mental attitudes as a whole, whatever additional entities may be my objects, [59] "man" and "rational animal" have a universal substance as their common meaning and "A man is a man" and "Man is a rational animal" are both definitions.

The universal substance 'triangle,' we have said, [60] does not differ from the universal substance 'trilateral.' Hence the proposition: "A triangle is a trilateral" is a definition whose subject-term and predicate-term represent a common meaning, a definition where

564

the universal defined is represented by the subject-term and by the predicate-term also. But the universal quality 'triangularity,' we have said,[61] although commensurate with 'trilaterality,' differs from it. "Triangularity is trilaterality" is, let us assume, a true affirmative universal categorical proposition whose subject-term and predicate-term represent commensurate universals. It is, let us say, a definition. But since the universal quality represented by its subject-term differs from the universal quality represented by its predicate-term, there would seem to be a distinction between defining 'triangularity' and defining 'trilaterality.' A definition, we have said,[62] "defines the universal represented by its subject-term." It is, it would seem, when the universal defined is a universal *substance* that the universal defined is always represented by the predicate-term as well.

As we have explained "definition," "man is a rational animal" is a definition even if with respect to some readers "man" and "rational animal" call forth non-identical mental attitudes. And as we have explained "definition," "triangularity is trilaterality" is a definition even if it should be true that "triangularity" and "trilaterality" never call forth identical mental attitudes. To be a definition, that is to say, a proposition need not have a subject-term and a predicate-term that call forth identical mental attitudes. The term "red" may not call forth the mental attitude that is called forth by "giving out vibrations with a long wave-length." "Being conscious" may not call forth the mental attitude that "behaving" calls forth. But if the universal quality 'red' is commensurate with the quality of giving out vibrations with a long wave-length, 'red' may be defined by a proposition whose predicate-term refers to wave-lengths. And if some type of behaving is commensurate with the universal quality 'being conscious,' some variant of "consciousness is behavior" may be a proposition that is a definition. This variant of "consciousness is behavior" may not be an explanation leading to an understanding of the word "consciousness"; but as we explain "definition," it may be a definition nevertheless.

Whereas "man" and "rational animal" represent a common meaning, 'triangularity,' we have said, is a universal quality that differs from 'trilaterality.' "Man is a rational animal," a definition defining a universal substance, defines what is represented by "man" and what is represented by "rational animal" as well. But "triangularity is trilaterality," a definition defining a universal quality, defines a quality different from 'trilaterality,' a quality represented by the subject-term alone. But, despite our instance of "triangularity is trilaterality," we can not conclude that each definition defining a universal quality defines what is represented by its subject-term alone. There is the definition: "Triangularity is triangularity" just as there is the definition: "A man is a man"; the definition: "Redness is redness" just as there is the definition: "An explanation is an explanation." Not each definition defining a universal quality resembles our instance of: "Triangularity is trilaterality" in defining a quality that is represented by the subject-term alone. Not each definition defining a universal quality resembles our instance of "triangularity is trilaterality" in having a subject-term and a predicate-term that call forth non-identical mental attitudes.

Whether it be a universal substance or a universal quality that is defined, a definition's subject-term and predicate-term may be identical. Whether it be a universal substance or a universal quality that is defined, "subject-term and predicate-term may be non-identical synonyms which express or call forth identical mental attitudes."[63] And whether it be a universal substance or a universal quality that is defined, the predicate-term may put forward an analysis of the universal which the subject-term represents. There is not only the analysis of 'man' expressed in: "Man is a rational animal," but the analysis of the quality 'orange' expressed in: "Orange is red and yellow." There are in short some definitions defining a universal quality where the quality defined is represented by subject-term and predicate-term alike; some definitions defining a universal quality where the quality defined differs from that represented by the predicate-term.

We put forward an analysis of 'man' when we say that man is a rational animal, an analysis of 'orange' when we say that orange is red and yellow. The terms "man" and "rational animal" may not call forth identical mental attitudes. The terms "orange" and "red and yellow" may not call forth identical mental attitudes. But in order for "Man is a rational animal" to be a definition, 'man' and 'rational animal' must be commensurate and indeed the common meaning of subject-term and predicate-term. And in order for "Orange is red and yellow" to be a definition, 'orange' and 'red and yellow' must be commensurate, though they need not be indistinguishable from one another. To be commensurate, however, 'animality' and 'rationality' must be real as well as 'man'; 'red' and 'yellow' real as well as 'orange.' It is by discussing the reality of universals and their commensurateness that we show a proposition to be a definition or not, not by discussing the identity or non-identity of mental attitudes.

There is to be sure a distinction to be made between "An extended entity is an entity which occupies space" and "Orange is red and yellow." With respect to the former of these two definitions, "extended entity" and "entity which occupies space" not only represent a common meaning, but call forth, we suppose, identical mental attitudes. With respect to the latter of these two definitions, "orange" and "red and yellow," although they represent commensurate universals, call forth on the part of some reader, we suppose, non-identical mental attitudes. An alleged extended entity which does *not* occupy space, being presented as an entity which both occupies space and does not occupy space is, like an alleged round square, presented as a self-contradictory entity. But if "orange" calls forth one mental attitude and "red and yellow" another, an alleged entity which is orange and not red and yellow is not so explicitly self-contradictory. "Veracious Cretan," we have said,[64] "does not enlarge itself to become mendacious Cretan as readily as round square enlarges itself to become round, not-round, self-contradictory square." "There are intermediate subsistents to be presented and these intermediate subsistents may not spontaneously offer themselves for discussion." So 'orange but not red and yellow' enlarges itself to become 'orange, not red and yellow, and self-contradictory' only after the analysis of orange into red and yellow has been accepted. But 'orange and not red and yellow' which may be only implicitly self-contradictory is unreal just as is the more explicitly self-contradictory 'extended entity which does not occupy space.' And the proposition: "Orange is red and yellow" is a definition just as is: "An extended entity is an entity which occupies space."

There is the difference which has been pointed out between the two definitions just discussed. And there is a similar difference in certain instances in which the propositions compared are not definitions. Instead of: "An extended entity is an entity which occupies space," we may consider: "An extended entity is an entity"; and instead of: "Orange is red and yellow," we may consider: "What is orange has yellow in it." Just as 'extended entity which does not occupy space' is more explicitly self-contradictory than 'orange but not red and yellow,' so 'extended entity which is not an entity' is more explicitly self-contradictory than 'orange without yellow in it.' We may, if we choose, overlook the distinction between what is explicitly self-contradictory and what is implicitly self-contradictory. We may call those propositions "analytic," the contradictories of which seem to put before us alleged entities that are explicitly self-contradictory. We may likewise call those propositions "analytic," the contradictories of which seem to put before us alleged entities that are only implicitly self-contradictory. And we may call propositions "analytic" which, it would appear, fall within the latter class, propositions, namely, which present an informative analysis of a universal. On the one hand, however, if no line is drawn, the analytic merges into the synthetic. And on the other hand, if a line *is* drawn, the proposition which presents an analysis of a concept and is informative would seem to be not analytic, but synthetic.[65]

'Triangle' is a real universal; 'plane figure bounded by three straight lines' a real universal; 'rectilinear figure whose interior angles total 180°' a real universal. They are, let us assume, commensurate universals. Then, as we have explained "definition," "A triangle is a plane figure bounded by three straight lines" is a definition; and "A triangle is a rectilinear figure whose interior angles total 180°" is a definition also. It has of course been said that being a plane figure and being bounded by three straight lines together constitute the *essence* of 'triangle,' whereas having interior angles totalling 180° is merely a property. "A triangle is a plane figure bounded by three straight lines," it has been said, puts the universal 'triangle' before us more clearly than does: "A triangle is a rectilinear figure whose interior angles total 180°." It is more suitable as a premise, has, one may say, greater deductive power. And it indicates how a triangle is created, thus removing doubts as to whether a triangle is 'possible' in the sense of being free from self-contradiction. But however the universal quality: 'being a plane figure' and the universal quality: 'being

568

bounded by three straight lines' may differ from the universal quality: 'having interior angles totalling 180°', the proposition: "A triangle is a plane figure bounded by three straight lines" is, in our terminology, a definition; and the proposition: "A triangle is a rectilinear figure whose interior angles total 180°" is a definition also.

When we turn our attention from definitions defining such mathematical entities as 'triangle,' 'circle' and 'parabola' to definitions defining such universals as 'cat,' 'oxygen' and 'red,' we may find it less useful to call one universal quality a "property" and another universal quality an element in the "essence" of what is being defined. We may decide to call that combination the "essence" that is represented by the predicate term of the definition in which the universal to be defined is first put before us, the definition in which the term representing that universal is explained. We may explain "essence" so that the essence of a given non-mathematical universal varies from author to author. Or we may abandon the distinction between essence and property entirely.

Whatever the justification and whatever the difficulties in distinguishing between essence and property, and however broad or however limited the field of universals to which this distinction may fruitfully be applied, the entity to be called an element in the essence, like the entity to be called a property, is, we hold, a universal. There are some writers indeed who seem to treat "essence" and "universal" as synonymous terms. "By 'essence'" says Santayana,[66] "I understand a universal . . . which may be given immediately, whether to sense or to thought." It is always such an essence, always an entity that we call a "universal," that, according to some writers, is the immediate object of a mental attitude. The individual which exists, it may be said, is apprehended only indirectly, only through the individualization in it of the universal or essence which is our immediate object. To quote again from Santayana:[67] "Transitiveness in knowledge has two stages or leaps: the leap of intuition from the state of the living organism to the consciousness of some essence; and the leap of faith and of action, from the symbol actually given in sense or in thought to some ulterior existing object."

If however it is held that only individuals exist and that universals called "essences" do not exist, then these alleged essences may

569

be classed with the alleged objectives discussed earlier in this chapter. "No real individual is really related," we have found, to an unreal objective.[68] There is similarly no real leap to an existing individual from a non-existent essence. And no real mental attitude really has a non-existent essence as its object. On the other hand, if some universal called an "essence" is real, and if some individual which is an instance of that universal is real, then that individual must itself be an object. For, "in the absence of mental attitudes directed upon individuals, individuals would be unreal."[69] If 'being bounded by three straight lines' is a universal quality which is real, then there must be some instance of 'being bounded by three straight lines,' some existing individual triangle that is bounded by three straight lines. And this individual triangle, which does not exist if presented as no one's object, may be a direct object as well as an indirect object. Indeed when one entity is a direct object and another entity to which it refers an indirect object, there may well be a subsequent mental attitude with respect to which the referent is a direct object.[70] If with respect to *one* mental attitude 'being bounded by three straight lines' is a direct object and the individual triangle which is bounded by three straight lines an indirect object, there may well be a *subsequent* mental attitude with respect to which the individual triangle and some quality of that individual triangle are direct objects.

'Being a plane figure' is, we hold, a universal which exists. 'Being a plane figure bounded by three straight lines' is a universal which exists. To call such universals "essences" and to separate the world of essences from the world of existents is, we hold, to make an incorrect dichotomy. 'Being a plane figure bounded by three straight lines' is, let us agree, an essence; but it is a universal that exists as well. To be sure, a distinction is sometimes made between knowing *that* a thing is and knowing *what* it is.[71] And the definition: "A triangle is a plane figure bounded by three straight lines" may be held to tell us *what* a triangle is, but not *that* it is. As we explain "truth," however, this proposition is true only if 'triangle' exists; and as we explain "definition," this proposition is a definition only if 'triangle,' not only exists, but is commensurate with 'plane figure bounded by three straight lines.' The proposition which is a definition, that is to say, is an assertion that a given universal exists and an assertion that some universal exists

570

with which it is commensurate. The proposition, on the other hand, whose subject-term is alleged to represent an entity which does not exist, does not tell us *what* this entity is any more than it tells us *that* this entity is. If the alleged universal 'pegasus' is unreal, there is no what-ness, no essence, that pegasus has. If there is no pegasus and no flying horse, 'pegasus' is not commensurate with 'flying horse' and "A pegasus is a flying horse," being a false proposition, is no definition at all.

What is to be admitted, to be sure, is that the expressions: "pegasus" and "flying horse," although they represent no meanings and hence can not be understood, may bring about mental attitudes which, although they have no object, may both be as though they were directed upon 'flying horse.' And what is also to be admitted is that when "truth" is assigned a meaning different from that which we have assigned to that term, then an affirmative universal proposition may be true without the universal represented by the subject-term being an existent. When we come across a land-owner's sign: "All trespassers will be punished," we do not believe the land-owner to be asserting that there will be trespassers.[72] And "truth" may be assigned a meaning according to which "A triangle is a plane figure bounded by three straight lines" may be true without there being any triangles. But as we have explained "truth" and "falsity," "A triangle is a plane figure bounded by three straight lines" would be false if there were no triangle; and it would not be a definition.

A definition's subject-term and predicate-term represent entities which are real and commensurate. And with respect to the reader who does not know these entities to be real or commensurate, a definition may be informative. A definition, we have said, defines a universal. And it is information with respect to this universal that the definition conveys, when, as a definition, it is informative. But what about an explanation? A definition defines a universal whereas an explanation leads to the understanding of an expression.[73] Obviously what we call an "explanation" conveys information with respect to the expression that it explains; and, approaching the relation between expression and meaning from the other end, it informs the reader that the entity that is the meaning has the characteristic of being represented by the expression being explained. Other than this, however, an explanation, it may seem, can convey no information. Other than this, it may be held, the proposition that we call an "explanation" can tell the reader nothing with respect to the entities represented by the terms of the proposition.

Let us not forget, however, that the same proposition "may be both a definition and an explanation." [74] A universal may be defined in a proposition through which an expression is explained. And an expression may be explained through a proposition in which a universal is defined. Since a definition may be informative, the proposition which is both an explanation and a definition may be informative. The explanation that is also a definition, that is to say, may give the reader information about the universal that is represented by the expression being explained. There is, for example, the proposition through which my expression "definition" is explained, the proposition: "A definition is a true universal affirmative categorical proposition whose subject-term and predicate term represent commensurate universals." Through it the reader may be informed not only as to what my word "definition" represents but as to the characteristics of the universal that I call "definition." The reader, that is to say, is not only enabled to identify the universal represented by the expression, but is presented with an analysis of that universal, an analysis that he may find informative.

There are perhaps explanations which merely identify the universal represented, but which convey no information with respect to that universal other than information as to its name. There are perhaps occasions when an author introduces a new term and explains it merely to have the opportunity to express what he has to say in fewer words, [75] occasions when the explanation merely substitutes a simple expression for a complex one and calls attention to their common meaning. [76] But it would seem to be the desire to engage in analysis rather than the desire for brevity that generally motivates the introduction of new terms. [77] And it would seem to be an analysis of the entity represented rather than the substitution of one expression for another that is generally presented in the explanation.

An explanation which is a definition may present an analysis, may be informative. And so may an explanation which is not a definition. Just as some instance of the word "cat" may be explained by calling attention to this Maltese cat and that Persian cat rather than through an explanation *defining* 'cat,' [78] so, to the reader properly prepared, "Orange has yellow in it" may explain "orange" instead of "Orange is red and yellow." But if "Orange has yellow in it" is ever an explanation of "orange," it too may convey information about 'orange' itself as well as about the word "orange." The explanation that is not a definition may present a partial analysis of the universal represented by the term to be explained. Or the explanation that is not a definition may call attention to the relational situation including a universal and some of its instances. Some proposition which is an explanation of "cat", but not a definition, asserts that this Maltese cat and that Persian cat are instances of the universal 'cat.' And some proposition which is an explanation of "Xanthippe" but not a definition— since Xanthippe herself can not be defined [79]—asserts that Xanthippe was the wife of Socrates. Whether or not it be a definition, and whether the term explained represent a universal or an individual, the proposition that is an explanation in many instances conveys information with respect to the entity represented by the expression explained.

But if many propositions which convey information about meanings are explanations, are there any propositions conveying information about things, rather than about words, that are not explanations? If it is a proposition conveying information about 'man' that is an explanation of the word "man," is not every proposition conveying information about 'man' an explanation of "man"? And if we explain the expression "explanation" by saying: "An explanation is an expression which results in the understanding of some prior representative expression," do we not further explain this expression when we say: "Some explanations are definitions; some not"?

An explanation, it will be recalled, results in understanding. And understanding exists, we have held,[80] when "the reader has in not too indefinite a fashion as an object, whether more definitely or less definitely, the entity that the creator of the expression desires the reader of his expression to have." If I already understand your word "man," your proposition: "Man is a rational animal," although a definition and although perhaps giving me new information, is no explanation with respect to me. And if, through my proposition: "An explanation is an expression which results in understanding," you understand my word "explanation," then my later propositions: "Some explanations are definitions; some not" is no explanation with respect to you. A proposition, in short, is an explanation of a given term only with respect to that reader who otherwise would not have that term's meaning either as a definite object or as a rather indefinite object.

'The author of Waverley' is, let us agree, a more definite object than 'a certain nineteenth-century author'; 'Scott, the author of Waverley' a more definite object, an object more fully presented, than 'the author of Waverley.' But I may understand the expression: "the author of Waverley" without knowing that Waverley was written by Scott, may understand the expression "Scott" without knowing that Scott wrote Waverley. In the former case the proposition: "Scott was the author of Waverley," although it gives me new information and results in the 'author of Waverley' being a more definite object of mine, is no explanation with respect to me of the term: "author of Waverley." In the latter case, this proposition, although it gives me new information and results in Scott being a more definite object of mine, is no explanation with respect to me of the term: "Scott." It may be objected, to be sure, that when you merely mention the new term "psang," I at once understand it, having as my object the indefinite something that your expression must mean. And it must be admitted that we have indicated no precise line to distinguish between the meaning on the one hand which, although a rather indefinite object, is represented by a term which is understood, and, on the other hand, the meaning which is so indefinite an object that the term representing it is not understood. The distinction however may perhaps be indicated by a reference to the meaning represented by "existence." The word "existence," occurring out of context and accompanied by no information as to the author, is, we hold, a word not understood. On the other hand, our proposition: "Whatever is presented as non-spatial does not exist," taken together with other propositions in Chapter Three, may well be an explanation of our term "existence," may result, that is to say, in the understanding of our term "existence." But if this is so, if the reader of: "Whatever is presented as non-spatial does not exist" has the universal represented by our term "existence" as a fairly definite object, then the later proposition:

574

"Objectives do not exist" [81] is, with respect to him, no explanation of "existence." "Objectives do not exist" may convey new information; it may result in the universal represented by our term "existence" being a more definite object. But it is not a proposition that is an explanation.

"Whether or not it be a definition, and whether the term explained represent a universal or an individual, the proposition which is an explanation," we have said,[82] "in many instances conveys information with respect to the entity represented by the expression explained." Whatever other information the explanation does or does not convey, it informs the reader that the entity represented by the expression being explained has the characteristic of being represented by that particular expression. But the proposition through which an author gives the reader information as to characteristics that an entity really has is, it would seem, always a true proposition. And the proposition through which an author informs the reader that entity A is to be represented by his expression "A" is, it would seem, always a true proposition. Indeed, since an author would seem to be at liberty to introduce a new term and to use it to represent any meaning he pleases, it may appear that an explanation can never be a proposition that is false.

Let us bear in mind however that an explanation need not be a simple proposition, need not, indeed, be a proposition at all. An explanation may not merely lead some beholder to understand the expression to be explained, may not merely inform the beholder as to characteristics that the meaning of that expression really has. The author may include as an element in the explanation itself some statement which is false. He may, that is to say, successfully lead the beholder to be aware of his expression's meaning and may nevertheless in addition attribute to the meaning characteristics which it does not have.

Moreover there are expressions resulting from an attempt to explain which are not explanations at all. The proposition: "Ivanhoe was a medieval knight" is no explanation of "Ivanhoe," the proposition: "A pegasus is a flying horse" no explanation of "pegasus." It is only where there is a real meaning that the expression representing that meaning can be explained.[83] Hence the proposition resulting from an attempt to explain is not in all instances an explanation and not in all instances a proposition which is true. We

575

can, in short, not accept each purported explanation as a statement which is true or even as a statement in which a given meaning is really revealed as having the characteristic of being represented by the author's expression.

It is only the term that has a real meaning that can be explained. It is only under the condition that it have a real meaning that the term "existence" can be explained. We determine 'pegasus' to be unreal and with this behind us determine that "A pegasus is a flying horse" is a proposition that is both no explanation and false. We determine Xanthippe to be real and with this behind us determine that "Xanthippe was the wife of Socrates" is true and, with respect to some reader, an explanation. But there is no analogous procedure to follow when it is our term "existence" that is to be explained. We do not ask whether existence exists before laying down as a partial determination of the signification of our term "existence" the proposition: "Entity A exists." For the proposition: "Entity A exists" itself partially determines the denotation of "existence," determines, that is to say, that something is real. Whereas then "A pegasus is a flying horse," put forward as an alleged explanation of "pegasus," may be false, and "Ivanhoe was a medieval knight," put forward as an alleged explanation of "Ivanhoe" false, "Whatever is presented as non-spatial does not exist" and "The present King of England apparently presented to me exists," put forward as partial explanations of my term "existence" are propositions depending on no prior propositions for their truth.[84]

Summary

When I utter the word "Socrates," this word is an *expression* of a mental attitude of mine. Socrates himself is this word's *meaning*. Someone hearing my word "Socrates" who as a consequence becomes aware of the Athenian philosopher, *understands* my expression. Misunderstandings are said to be real or verbal, but there is no sharp line between the two.

An expression which results in the understanding of some prior representative expression we call an *explanation*. A *definition*, in our terminology, is a true affirmative universal categorical proposi-

576

tion whose subject-term and predicate-term represent commensurate universals. It defines the universal represented by its subject-term, not, usually, a word. What pretends to be an explanation may be a satisfactory explanation, an unsatisfactory or limited explanation, or no explanation at all. But what pretends to be a definition either is or isn't a definition. There are not good and bad definitions.

Other distinctions discussed are: denotation vs. connotation, analytic vs. synthetic, property vs. essence.

Why should this chapter come here? Since definitions are held to define universals, a discussion of definitions had to be deferred until after the term "universal" had been explained. Moreover—and, I might say, more *especially*—our reversion at this point to the relation between words and things indicates our continuing concern with this subject and with the problem: what to do with the unreal. Except for the development and use of what we call the existential method, nothing is more central in this treatise than the thesis that what is real cannot really be related to the unreal. This thesis comes up in our discussions of the problematic proposition, of the problem of error, and again here when we consider the meaning, or lack of meaning, of "Ivanhoe" and "centaur."

NOTE

The Chapters planned for the remainder of this treatise have not been developed. What follows are brief statements of some of the problems that seem to me to call for discussion, together with tentative opinions addressed to these problems. Had these remaining chapters been developed, closer study would no doubt have revealed other problems and would have modified some of the opinions that the following pages express.

Chapter XVIII

MATHEMATICAL CONCEPTS: TO WHAT EXTENT ARE THEY REAL?

As we have explained our term "existence," no entity is real which is presented as timeless or as non-spatial. There are other senses of "existence" which likewise imply that what is presented as timeless or as non-spatial is unreal. To others as well as to us, therefore, such alleged entities as numbers, angles and mathematical formulae pose a problem. Since these entities are frequently presented as having their being and their validity in a world distinct from that in which spatio-temporal objects lie, we seem to be presented with an unpleasant alternative. Either numbers and perfect circles do not exist and mathematical formulae are false; or mathematical expressions do not represent the entities they are frequently taken to represent. We can "save the appearances," can find those mathematical entities real which are commonly called "real" and can find those mathematical propositions true which are commonly called "true" only by discarding the explanation of our term "existence" which has previously been laid down; or by giving "number," "line," "circle" and other mathematical expressions meanings different from those which these expressions frequently—and perhaps usually—have.

It is our task in this chapter to "save the appearances," not by discarding or modifying the meaning of our term "existence," but by considering how certain commonly accepted mathematical expressions may be used so that they may represent entities which are real in our previously determined sense of "reality" and so that certain commonly accepted mathematical propositions may be true in our previously determined sense of "truth." Not even that.

For there may be several senses in which "circle" may be used, each sense resulting in some circles being real in our sense of "reality" and each sense resulting in some propositions, in which "circle" is the subject-term, being true in our sense of "truth." Rather, the task to which we address ourselves in this chapter is to consider specific rather elementary mathematical expressions and with respect to each of them to propose *a* sense—regardless of alternatives—in which it may be used so that it may represent an entity which is real in our sense of "reality."

Let us begin with the term "two." As we have explained our term "existence," some instance of man-on-horse exists and this real substance has the real quality of duality with respect to my mental attitudes which are directed separately upon the man and upon the horse. There are in short couples and there is a quality called "duality" which couples have. Each unit which is a part of a composite entity called a couple has various qualities. But there exist some couples such that the couple has no important quality other than its duality. If for example I put two dots adjacent to one another on a piece of paper, each dot has the quality of being made of ink and one may be large, the other small. But the only quality of the composite entity before me on which my attention is focused may be its duality, its quality of being comprised of two units. For me the composite entity before me is only an instance of a thing with duality. It is duality hypostatized into a substance. And the substance all of whose qualities other than duality are disregarded, the substance which is duality primarily, duality hypostatized into a substance, is, let us say, an instance of the universal which we shall call "two." [1]

With "two" explained in this manner, there are, let us agree, instances of the universal 'two.' An instance of 'two' exists in the composite object made up of two ink dots on the paper before me. And an instance of 'two' exists in the composite object made up of two dots on the upper face of a six-sided die which lies on this table. Similarly there are instances of the universal 'three' and instances of the universal 'five.' The composite object made up of two dots on the upper face of a die is an instance of 'two'; the composite object made up of three dots on the upper face of an adjacent die is an instance of 'three'; and the composite object made up of the dots on the upper faces of both dice taken together is an instance of 'five.' This instance of 'two' plus this instance of 'three' is co-extensive with an instance of 'five.'

As we are proposing that "two," "three" and "five" be used, however, to assert that two and three are five is to imply that each instance of two taken together with an instance of three is an instance of five. "Two plus three equals five" is a universal proposition. And since not all instances of 'two' adjacent to instances of 'three' have been perceived, "two plus three equals five" can be true only if we can know certain facts that have not been perceived. Tomorrow's sun is however an entity which, we have held, is real, "the sun will rise tomorrow" a proposition which is true. Due to the simplicity of our objects, due to our conviction that no disturbing factors could intervene, we may be said to know that a future instance of 'two' adjacent to an instance of 'three' will be an instance of 'five' with greater certainty than we know that the sun will rise tomorrow. But neither the future instance of 'two' and 'three' that is presented as an instance of 'five' nor the alleged sunrise of tomorrow morning, neither of these entities is presented as generally discredited. "The sun will rise tomorrow" is, we hold, a proposition which is true and when "two," "three" and "five" are used in the senses which we have proposed, "two plus three equals five" is a proposition which is true.

When all qualities of a couple are disregarded other than that couple's duality, the couple is an instance of what we call "two." Somewhat similarly, I may erase two dots which I have put upon a blackboard, then concentrate my attention upon the blackboard's quality of having no dots on it. Just as an entity whose only important quality is its duality is an instance of 'two,' so an entity whose only important quality is its blankness is, let us say, an instance of "zero." And just as "two plus three equals five" is a universal proposition which is true, so "three minus three equals zero" is a universal proposition which is true.

There is an instance of 'zero,' of 'two,' or of 'five' where there is a substance whose only important quality is its blankness, its duality or its quintuplicity. But turning from numbers to lines, we do not propose that that substance be called a "line" whose only important quality is its length. For the entity which we choose to call a "line" has qualities other than length, qualities which are not disregarded when this line is considered. What we call a line has position as well as length; it may be curved or straight; and it may parallel or intersect other lines.

A line, let us say following Euclid, is a substance with length but no breadth. If it is agreed that only substances with breadth and thickness, as well as length, can affect minds and bring about mental attitudes directed upon these substances, then what we call "lines" can not be percepts. It does not follow however that what we call "lines" are unreal. On the contrary, we have found the equator real; there is a real line without breadth which we call the "edge" of my ruler; and there is a real line within the ribbon of ink that I draw from one dot to another.

When line is defined as a substance with length but no breadth, some lines exist. When plane is defined as a substance with length and breadth but no thickness, some planes exist. And when point is defined as a substance having position with respect to various entities but lacking length, breadth and thickness, some points exist. For there is a point within the period marking the end of the preceding sentence. And there is a plane which is approximated by the top of this flat desk.

With certain lines, planes and points established as real, we find it possible to find additional instances of numbers. The line which is two inches long may be regarded as an instance of 'two'; this line extended an additional inch an instance of 'three'; this line restricted to its initial point an instance of 'zero.' Indeed if our line is extended in both directions from its initial point, we can find sections of it that are instances of fractions, of negative numbers, of irrational numbers. Further, by drawing a perpendicular through the initial point, by having before us a plane with a Y-axis as well as an X-axis, we can find lines drawn from the origin to various points that will be instances of complex numbers. By means of Argand's diagram, it has been said,[2] "an objective existence can be assigned to these imaginary beings." "In other words," we read, "a concrete interpretation has been found for these imaginary beings, an interpretation similar to that which identifies negative numbers with a change in sense." As we suggest that "3 minus 2i" be used, however, a line on Argand's diagram does not represent some non-spatial '3 minus 2i'; a line on Argand's diagram, a line which has a date and a position with respect to other real entities, is itself an *instance* of '3 minus 2i.' If there

581

were no such lines, there would be no true mathematical propositions in which the expression "3 minus 2i" appears.

It may be said, to be sure, that there were true propositions containing expressions representing complex numbers before Argand drew his diagram. When expressions representing complex numbers have the meanings which we are proposing and when "truth" is used in our sense of "truth," this proposition continues to be true. A universal may be real and may be a real object of mine even though each of that universal's instances is future with respect to me. Similarly mathematicians prior to Argand were really aware of i and asserted true propositions containing the expression "i" even though no instance of i was a definite object of theirs. But if neither Argand nor any subsequent mathematician had drawn a diagram containing an instance of i, i would not be real and no proposition containing the term "i," whether asserted by predecessor or successor of Argand's, would be true.

There are various real universals such as 'two,' 'zero,' 'minus two' and 'six i.' But what about the universal to be called: "number"? Socrates and Fido, we have agreed, are instances of the universal 'animal,' not 'man' and 'dog' which are themselves universals. Similarly it is not 'two' and 'six i,' let us say, which are instances of 'number,' but each instance of 'two' and each instance of 'six i.' Since there are instances of its various species, there are instances of the genus 'number.' The expression "a" represents a real entity in so far as it represents any real instance of a universal that is a number, the expression "a plus b" a real entity in so far as it represents any composite object made up of one instance of a universal that is a number taken together with another instance of a universal that is a number.

Chapter XIX

MASS, FORCE AND ENERGY

Our statement that non-spatial and non-temporal entities are unreal, in our sense of "reality," poses the problem of defining 'two,' 'line' and 'circle,' as we use the mathematical expressions representing these entities. There is no similar motivation leading us to redefine, or, to use Carnap's term, to "explicate,"—the universals discussed by physicists. But the philosophers of the seventeenth century were concerned not only with metaphysics but also with mechanics. And some of those at the beginning of the nineteenth century felt that the development of a philosophy of nature was an integral part of the philosopher's task. Schelling's philosophy of nature has fallen into disrepute. I am not sufficiently acquainted with the writings of the romanticists to know whether or not there are any important contributions to the physical sciences to be gleaned from the philosophies of nature of these philosophers. But it would seem that the sort of attack that has in this treatise been made on such terms as "universal," "identity" and "definition" might be made with some profit on such terms as "mass," "force" and "energy."

Chapter XX

THE EFFICIENT CAUSE

In previous sections of this treatise we have referred to causal relations obtaining between one entity and another, to one entity affecting another. We have not clearly distinguished the various relational situations that in some sense of our term "cause" may be called "causal" situations. But we have indicated that in order for one entity "A" to be the cause of another entity "B," in our sense of "cause," there must, at the least, be motion of some sort flowing from A to B. Without distinguishing at this point between various senses of "cause" where there is this common denominator, this motion from one entity to another, let us consider what can be learned from our previous discussion of 'motion.'

Motion is relative. Relative to one enduring entity taken to be at rest, an instantaneous phase of A which is earlier is *there* and an instantaneous phase of B, which is later, *here*. Our enduring entity at rest may however be so chosen that the instantaneous phase of A which is earlier and the instantaneous phase of B which is later are in the same place, may be so chosen that there is no motion from A to B and hence A not the cause of B.

Moreover, we do not generally call A the cause of B when A and B are successive phases of the same substance. Whether the enduring point of reference be so chosen that the successive phases of a given substance are in the same place or in different places, the earlier phase, let us say, is not the cause of any later phase of the same substance.

Schopenhauer suggests the question: "Shall we apply the term 'cause' to situations where action is reciprocal, where A affects B and B A"? Does night cause day and day night? Without using

584

day and night as examples, let us consider two enduring substances a and b each including successive phases so that a_1 is contemporaneous with b_1, a_2 with b_2 and a_3 with b_3. In such a situation motion may flow from a_1 to b_2 and from b_2 to a_3 so that whereas a, taken as an enduring entity, may not be the cause of b taken as an enduring entity, a_1 may, so far as we have yet limited the meaning of "cause," be the cause of b_2 and b_2 the cause of a_3.

Somewhat similarly Kant calls attention to the situation in which a ball lies on a table and the table is depressed where the ball lies on it. The ball and the depression both occur, it may be said, now. And since the ball causes the depression rather than the depression the ball, we have an instance, it may be said, of a cause being simultaneous with its effect. Again, however, successive phases of the ball are to be distinguished and successive phases of the depressed table. The ball already lying on the table is not the cause of the depression simultaneous with it, but the ball when it first impinges upon the table the cause of the subsequent depression.

Up to this point we have considered only *individual* relational situations, only situations in which motion flows from individual A to individual B. But there may be many A's at the source of similar motions, many B's at the termini of similar motions. So long as we consider only the individual situation, A is no more the cause of B than are C and D that lie along the path traversed by the motion from A to B; and A is no more the cause of B than E and F that lie along the path traversed by some other motion arriving at B. Similarly, so long as we consider only the individual situation, whatever is at B is the effect, the color of the table as well as its depressed condition, the table itself as well as a given quality of the table's.

Let us first turn our attention to the terminus of motions,—to B. If we consider, not only the phase of B in which motions from A are terminated, but also preceding phases of B, we may find that the phase in which motions from A are terminated has certain qualities dissimilar to the qualities of preceding phases of B. Hence, using "cause" in a narrower sense, we may come to call these qualities which appear when motions arrive from A the "result," not B itself and not those qualities which characterized B both before and after motions were received from A. Similarly when we consider a group of individual B's, each receiving motions. If a white table is depressed after a ball is placed on it and a black table depressed after a ball is placed on *it,* we may, using "cause" in a narrower sense, come to call the depressed condition of B the result, not the color of B. And if a substance, after being placed near a fire, is characterized by a higher temperature, whether it be a man's hand or a piece of metal, we may come to call the greater heat that then characterizes this substance the "effect" rather than the substance itself. But if the substance in which motions are terminated has qualities which do not occur separately, we have no basis on which to call a given quality the "effect" and the concomitant quality "not the effect." If, for example, thinking does not occur without behavior nor behavior without thinking, then, even in the narrower sense of "cause" which we are attempting to develop, behavior is not the effect to the exclusion of thinking nor thinking the effect to the exclusion of behavior. Similarly, if redness does not occur without the quality of emitting long rays, B's quality of emitting long rays is no more and no less the effect than is B's redness.

We turn now to the entity or entities at the source of motions which travel to B, B or some quality of B being, in our narrower sense of "cause," the effect. In some individual situation in which A is at the source of motions to B, E is also at the source of motions traveling to B. If however there are other situations in which there are motions from A but none from E, then, when the result is similar to that in our original individual situation, E, in our narrower sense of "cause," is not the cause. But what about the situation in which motions from A are followed by the result at B only when these motions pass through a certain medium or take place in a certain environment? I do not hear a bell ringing if I am deaf or if the bell is struck in a vacuum. And a pistol aimed at me and fired will not kill me in certain cases in which I am protected by some intervening substance. If I am not killed, the firing of the pistol is not the cause of my death. And yet we do not choose to use "cause" in such a sense that, when there are instances of A not followed by B, those instances of A followed by instances of B are not to be called causes of the ensuing B's. Before "cause" has the meaning that we choose it, as used in our narrower sense, to have, other propositions must be added to our explanation.

A further problem arises from the fact that motions from A pass through C and D on their way to B. And yet in many instances we choose to call A the "cause," not C or D.

This and other problems arise in our efforts to give a precise meaning to "cause" used in a narrow sense, in a sense in which not every source of motion is a cause and not every entity at the terminus a result. Quite apart from them is the problem of generalization. We perceive only certain instances of motion from A to B. And yet we go beyond individual causal situations when we assert that it is A that causes B. What convinces us that instances of A yet to be experienced will cause instances of B? This however is not a problem peculiar to 'cause.' It is the general problem of generalization, the problem of knowing facts which are not percepts.

'Cause' has been held to involve 'necessary connection.' But as we have explained "necessity," it is only *propositions* which are necessarily true. There are instances of the true proposition: "A causes B" and there are instances of the true proposition: "A must cause B." Unless there is some proposition in the context which implies that "A causes B," "A causes B" may be true but "A must cause B" will be false. In such a case, that is to say, the concept 'necessity,' as we use it, does not apply.

What about quantitative relations between A and B? What about the situation in which B is a function of A so that the quantity of B varies with the quantity of A? It may be said that without some reference to quantity in a discussion of cause, 'cause' is a useless concept. It may be held consequently that we should abandon discussions of 'cause' and turn our attention instead to 'correlation.' Quantity however may be discussed in connection with cause. Correlation between A and B may be an incident in connection with a causal relation as well as an element in connection with other relations. Where we have found correlation between the quantity of A and the quantity of B, we may not have determined whether A is prior to B or B prior to A; and we may not have come to close quarters with the processes, if there are any, through which B comes to be accompanied by, or preceded by, or followed by, A. But this does not imply that there are no such processes or that the temporal relations between A and B can not be more precisely determined.

On the one hand, we may be held to be neglecting the quantitative relations between A and B. On the other, we may be held to be neglecting the animistic element in the causal relation. We are treating A and B and the motion from one to the other from the observer's point of view, neglecting the feeling of effort or strain that is said to be inherent in being an actor and in being acted upon. In so far as there *is* a feeling in being an actor or in being acted upon, we take no account of it in explaining our term "cause."

Chapter XXI

POSSIBILITY AND POTENTIALITY

In our discussion of modal propositions in Chapter Five, we explained our expressions: "S must be P" and "S may be P." It is in accordance with the explanations given in that section that "necessity" and "possibility" are generally used in this treatise. There are, however, some sections of this treatise in which "necessity" and "possibility" are used in senses which may not be the sense set forth in Chapter Five. Our task in the present chapter is to examine these other uses that we have made of "possibility" and "necessity"; and also to disentangle some of the senses in which "possibility" and "necessity" are commonly used.

The entity which is real, we have said, is not presented as non-spatial, not presented as generally discredited, and so on; and it is not presented as self-contradictory. The former requirements, we have suggested, furnish us with what may be called a Law of Sufficient Reason; the latter with a Law of Contradiction. It may seem accordingly that the entity presented as non-spatial but not self-contradictory might be called "possible" but not "real," in contrast to the entity presented as self-contradictory which might be called "impossible." When, however, our explanation of "existence" is behind us, the entity presented as non-spatial *can not* be real. Our propositions explaining "existence," that is to say, imply that the entity presented as non-spatial is unreal. Indeed, with respect to any entity that is unreal, our propositions explaining "existence" imply that it is unreal. Thus what might be called a Law of Sufficient Reason merges into a Law of Contradiction and there are no entities which are possible but unreal.

If F is a non-existent entity, it is only in a context in which

589

"existence" has been partially, but not fully, explained that the proposition: "It is possible that entity F exists" may be true. Similarly, if F is a non-existent entity, it is only in a context in which the existence of specific entities E_1, E_2, E_3 is asserted—not in a context in which the existence of all existing entities is asserted—that "F may exist" may be true. Generally speaking, the more extensive the context and the more fully "existence" has been explained, the fewer the instances in which "F may exist" may be true.

If "existence" has been partially, but not fully, explained, "F may exist" may be true. And if "existence" has not been explained at all, "F may exist," one may say, *is* true, whatever the entity represented by "F." It is on some such basis as this that we justify our use of "possible entity" in the initial chapters of this treatise where "possible entity" is synonymous with "subsistent." Even so, it is not in accordance with our use of "possibility" to imply that entities have characteristics inhering in them which make these entities possible entities. Before "existence" has been explained, all subsistents are possible entities in the sense that, with respect to any subsistent F, the proposition: "F may exist" is in such a context—or, rather in such a lack of context—true.

If E implies that F does not exist and the existence of E is asserted in the context, "F may exist" is false. If E implies that F does not exist and the existence of E is *not* asserted in the context, "F may exist" is true. But what is it to be asserted in the context? There is the situation in which "E exists" occurs in the context. There is the situation in which "E exists" does not occur in the context. And there is the intermediate situation in which what occurs in the context is not "E exists" but some proposition which may be held to imply that E exists. "E exists" may be in the context implicitly, not explicitly. Or one reader may find "E exists" implicit in the context, another reader not. To the extent to which the occurrence of "E exists" in the context is in dispute, the applicability of our term "possibility" is in dispute. To the extent to which it can not be determined whether or not the existence of E is asserted in the context, to that extent it can not be determined whether "F may exist" is true or false.

There are the propositions: "F may exist," "It is possible for S to be P," "S may be P." And there are the propositions: "A can do B," "A can become B." The former group of propositions refer to what we call "possibility," the latter to what we call "potentiality." An acorn can turn into an oak. A bridge can bear a given weight. A boy can jump a given distance. A compressed spring has potential energy. In each of these instances, potentiality seems to exist in relation to some future event; and yet, one may say, in relation to a future event which may not occur. The acorn is potentially an oak, even though it never takes root; the spring has potential energy, even though it is never released. If this use of "potential" is to be validated, if some such sentence as: "The acorn, though falling on barren ground, is potentially an oak" is to be true, we must determine the meaning of "potentiality" so as to distinguish between the acorn which though potentially an oak never becomes one and the stone which likewise never becomes an oak and is not one potentially.

Chapter XXII

INFERENCE AND IMPLICATION

We shall use the term "inference" to refer to a three-term relational situation, the term "implication" to refer to a two-term relational situation. In our terminology, that is to say, entity A implies entity B, whereas it is subject C who infers B from A.

Does C infer B from A because of the fact that A implies B? Or does A imply B in that suitable subjects infer B from A? If implication is prior to inference, then it is a brute and unanalyzable fact that A implies B. In any dispute as to whether or not A implies B we have only such bases for resolving the dispute as we would have in a dispute as to whether or not it is now raining. On the other hand, if A implies B in that subjects infer B from A, implication, which is a relational situation involving A and B, would seem to develop into a three-term relational situation involving mental attitudes.

Let us explain our term "implication" in terms presupposing an understanding of "inference." In discussing tertiary qualities we referred to "suitable observers." Let us say that if suitable observers infer B from A, then A implies B. Just, however, as beauty is a quality of a beautiful object, not a quality of the mental attitude of the suitable observer, so, let us say, it is the relational situation including A and B which is an instance of implication, not the relational situation whose terms are mental attitudes of the observer. If there were no suitable observers with mental attitudes accompanied by feelings, there would be no tertiary qualities. Similarly if there were no suitable observers inferring B from A, A would not imply B. But the implication

592

from A to B is not put into the relational situation A-r-B by the subject who infers B from A any more than the tertiary quality is put into the substance in which it inheres by the subject who feels when he is aware of that substance's tertiary quality.

What is it, then, to infer B from A? When subject C infers B from A, C's belief in A's existence or in the truth of the proposition: "A exists" is followed by his belief in B's existence or in the truth of the proposition: "B exists." But a mere sequence of believing mental attitudes is not sufficient to constitute what we call "inference." If I believe that it is raining and subsequently believe that Caesar crossed the Rubicon, it does not follow, let us say, that I infer Caesar's crossing the Rubicon from today's rain. In order for me to infer B from A, my mental attitude believing in A's existence must not only be followed by, but must lead to, must cause, my mental attitude believing in B's existence. To say that one of my mental attitudes leads to, or causes, another of my mental attitudes is to assert that there is a motion from one believing mind-nerve-fibre to another, analogous to the motion whereby one billiard ball affects another. Such a motion is not, we hold, non-existent. But what grounds have we for asserting that the mental attitude believing in A's existence causes the mental attitude believing in B's existence and does not cause the mental attitude believing in the existence of some other entity B'? What grounds have we, that is to say, for asserting that I infer from today's rain the fact that when I go out I will get wet and do not infer from today's rain the fact—of which I am likewise subsequently aware—that Caesar crossed the Rubicon? The assertion that I infer B from A and do not infer B' from A seems to be just as unsubstantiated as the assertion that A implies B and does not imply B'. In explaining "implication" in terms which presuppose an understanding of "inference," we seem to appeal to a brute and unanalyzable fact just as in explaining "inference" in terms which presuppose an understanding of "implication."

Nevertheless, let us continue to say that A implies B when suitable observers—or, rather, suitable thinkers—infer B from A. Some thinker may infer B from A without A implying B. For our thinker may not be a "suitable" thinker. But in line with our doctrine that real entities are not related to unreals, one does not infer B from A unless B and A both exist. There is, one may say, *pseudo*-inference when a thinking mind-nerve-fibre believing in A's existence leads to a thinking mind-nerve-fibre which is as if it were believing in B's existence.

Suitable thinkers may infer B from A and suitable thinkers may infer A from B. In certain relational situations including an A and a B, A, that is to say, may imply B and B may imply A. In such situations we seem to have a choice as to whether A's existence is to be asserted first and B's existence set forth as an implication following from A's existence; or vice versa. But there are considerations to guide us, the considerations that distinguish real definitions from nominal definitions.[1] It is these considerations, in fact, which lead us to explain "inference" before explaining "implication." For whereas we have found that there is, either way, a reliance upon an unanalyzed fact, an explanation of "inference" puts the subject-matter before us in a way in which that subject-matter can be more readily developed.

From the fact that a gun lies in a certain position it is inferred by suitable observers that the dead man killed himself and from the facts that all men are mortal and Socrates a man it is inferred by suitable observers that Socrates is mortal. As we use "implication," the position of the gun implies suicide and the premises of a syllogism imply the conclusion. There are implications in the field of logic, implications from mathematical facts to other mathematical facts, and there are implications which are not in the fields of logic or mathematics.[2] Implications in the fields of mathematics and logic seem, however, to be quite different from implications which are not in these fields. From the fact that the sun has risen each day I infer that the sun will rise tomorrow; but my belief is not as firm as in the fact that X^2 being 4, $X = \pm 2$. How shall we account for this difference?

My belief in the truth of "$X^2 = 4$" leads to my belief in the truth of "$X = \pm 2$." And in a context in which the existence of all existing entities is asserted, my belief in the fact that the gun is in a given position leads to my belief in the fact that the dead man killed himself. But an extensive context is required. Where the context does not go beyond the one fact which is alleged to imply the second, belief in A may not cause belief in B. In a

594

meager context "It is possible that the sun will not rise tomorrow" is true and "It is possible that the dead man did not kill himself" true. Implications in the fields of mathematics and logic are unique, it would seem, in that the cause of the belief in B rests solely in the belief in A, not in the belief in A provided it is accompanied by beliefs in other facts presented in the context.

Chapter XXIII

PURPOSE

I had an article on "Purpose" in the Journal of Philosophy in
1920 or 1921. That article, brought into line with the theses developed in this treatise, would be the basis for this chapter.

It may be that our discussion of 'meaning' may also serve as a
guide. Just as only expressions have meaning, so, we may hold, only
expressions have purpose. The mental attitude which brings about
an expression which is a representation is a mental attitude which
is accompanied by a certain kind of desiring. The mental attitude
which brings about an expression which is purposeful is, we may
hold, a mental attitude which is accompanied by a different, but
equally describable, kind of desiring.

Chapter XXIV

CHANCE AND PROBABILITY

Consider the statement: "If two dice are thrown, the chances are eleven out of thirty-six that a six will turn up." In making such a statement, am I asserting that the belief and disbelief with which I look forward to a six on the next throw of the dice are in the ratio of eleven to twenty-five, that my mental attitude consists of eleven parts of belief to twenty-five parts of disbelief? Clearly the extent to which subjects believe, disbelieve, or are in doubt, is not subject to mathematical measurement.

Is it then that our statement expresses the assertion that out of any set of thirty-six throws, a six will turn up on eleven of these throws? This interpretation must also be rejected. The assertion, it seems, is that under *standard* conditions, under *ideal* conditions, a six turns up in eleven cases out of thirty-six.

What then are these *standard* conditions, these *ideal* conditions? At golf there is a standard man, an ideal man, who plays par golf. And in throwing dice there is a standard situation, an ideal situation, in which each combination turns up in turn. Our statement thus becomes: "If two dice are thrown, then under standard conditions a six turns up in eleven cases out of thirty-six." When we explain "chance" in such a way that this last statement is synonymous with our original statement, our propositions including the term "chance" may in certain instances be true.

Standard conditions are conditions under which a specific series of events takes place. It is not a situation in which other things are equal. For if all other things are equal—the twist with which the dice are thrown, the angle from which they are thrown, etc. —then each die would always land on the same face. Statements containing the term "chance" are likely to be used when certain elements in the situation under discussion are not known or not fully known. When this is the case and we[1] use the term "chance," the unknown factors, we suggest, are not supposed to be always the same, but are supposed to follow a pattern which we call "standard conditions."

There is the concept 'chance' and the related concept 'probability.' We apply the term "probability," let me suggest, when chance is superimposed on experience. If I have drawn twelve counters from a bag and have found nine of them white and three black, the probability is greater that the next counter I draw will be white than that it will be black; and the probability is small that it will be neither white nor black. Probability occurs in so far as there are chance variations from a pattern established by experience.

Chapter XXV

THE CONTENT OF REALITY

The Appendix to Chaper Three lists—by implication—each entity that is real. Here at the end of the treatise it is intended to characterize the entities that are real in more general terms. There are substances and there are qualities. There are individuals and there are universals. What is intended, in short, is a description and enumeration of some of the salient features of what make up the world of existing entities—as we use "existence."

Also this chapter may be an appropriate place to discuss once more our existential method, directing that discussion to the ontological argument. A discussion of that argument brings out the peculiar status which "existence" has.

NOTES TO CHAPTER ONE

1. Descartes: Discourse on Method, Part 1.
2. Kant: Critique of Pure Reason, Preface to the Second Edition, pp. XIV, XV.
3. Descartes: Rules for the Direction of the Mind, Rule 5.
4. Ibid., Rule 4.
5. Bacon: Novum Organum, Bk. 1, Aph. 61. Cf. also Descartes: Discourse on Method, Part 1.
6. Cf., for example, Novum Organum, Bk. 1, Aph. 19-22.
7. Leonardo da Vinci: Notebooks, Translation by McCurdy, London, 1906, p. 54, MS. of the Library of the Institute of France, G 96 v.
8. Hobbes: Leviathan, Pt. 1, ch. 4.
9. Hobbes: De Corpore, Pt. 1, ch. 6, § 17.
10. Ibid., Pt. 4, ch. 25, § 1.
11. Descartes: Meditation 2.
12. Descartes: Discourse on Method, Pt. 2.
13. Locke: Essay concerning Human Understanding, Bk. 3, ch. 9, § 21.
14. Ibid., Bk. 1, ch. 1, § 4.
15. Kant: Critique of Pure Reason, 2nd ed., p. xxx.
16. Ibid., 2nd ed., p. xiii.
17. John Dewey: Essays in Experimental Logic, p. 8, note, which points back to T. H. Green: Prolegomena to Ethics, § 23.
18. Cf. Aristotle: Posterior Analytics, Bk. 2, ch. 1.
19. There is a further reference to synonymity on pp. 114 et seq.
20. Cf. Brentano: Psychologie vom empirische Standpunkte, 1874, v. 1, p. 283 and Royce: The World and the Individual, v. 1, pp. 274-6. The reader is also referred to the author's dissertation: The Meaning of the Terms "Existence" and "Reality," pp. 7-10, where certain considerations are adduced which are not here mentioned.
21. p. 9.
22. p. 6.

23. p. 6.

24. pp. 5-6.

25. p. 15.

26. p. 7.

27. p 7.

28. Cf. Fritz Medicus: Bemerkungen zum Problem der Existenz Mathematischer Gegenstände, Kant-Studien, 1914, p. 1.

29. Cf. B. Russell: Introduction to Mathematical Philosophy, p. 169.

30. Despite the use of "existentialism" to describe the doctrines of Sartre and of Kierkegaard before him, I find no term as satisfactory as "existential" to describe a method based upon a re-examination of the meaning of "existence."

31. p. 15.

32. Descartes: Discourse on Method, Pt. 4. Cf. also Meditation 1.

33. Descartes: Meditation 2.

34. Descartes: Principles of Philosophy, Author's Letter.

35. Descartes: Meditation 5.

36. p. 9.

37. Hobbes: De Corpore, Pt. 1, ch. 3, § 9.

38. Leibniz: Second Letter to Clarke; Duncan: The Philosophical Works of Leibniz, 1908, p. 330.

39. p. 24.

40. Kant: Critique of Pure Reason, 1st ed., p. 6.

41. Kant: Prolegomena to any future Metaphysics, § 2. b, c. Cf. also Critique of Pure Reason, 1st ed., p. 151.

42. For a discussion of the extent to which unreal entities are self-contradictory, see p. 589. For remarks on the distinction between analytic and synthetic, see p. 568.

43. Kant: Critique of Pure Reason, 2nd ed., Introduction. (Mueller, p. 720) Contrast Leibniz on 2+2=4, New Essays, Bk. 4, ch. 7, § 10.

44. Kant: Critique of Pure Reason, 1st ed., p. 112.

45. Ibid., p. 194.

46. Cf. Laas: Kants Analogien der Erfahrung.

47. Kant: Critique of Pure Reason, 1st ed., p. 217.

48. Ibid., p. 395.

49. Ibid., p. 421.

50. E.g., Pistorius. Cf. B. Erdman: Kriticismus, p. 107; N. K. Smith: Commentary, p. 323.

51. Kant: Critique of Pure Reason, 1st ed., Preface.

52. Ibid., 2nd ed., translation by Müller, p. 801.

53. Ibid., 1st ed., p. 236.

54. Kant: Prolegomena, § 13, note iii.

55. Kant: Critique of Pure Reason, 1st ed., p. 276. See also p. 30.
56. pp. 14-15.
57. Descartes: Principles of Philosophy, Author's Letter.

NOTES TO CHAPTER TWO

1. pp. 7, 8.
2. p. 27.
3. p. 19.
4. p. 92.
5. Aristotle: Phys. iii, 4; 203 b 7.
6. Herbert Spencer: Principles of Psychology, 2nd ed., 1877, § 467. See also § 59.
7. Cf. for example, Phaedo: 65, 74; Republic: 525.
8. St. Augustine: City of God, Bk. 2, sec. 2.
9. Ibid., Bk. 2, sec. 29.
10. St. Anselm: Proslogium, ch. 22.
11. pp. 73-76.
12. Diogenes Laertius: Lives of the Philosophers. Translation by Yonge, p. 435.
13. Bacon: Plan of the Instauration. Edition by J. M. Robertson, 1905, p. 250.
14. Ibid., p. 256.
15. Berkeley: Principles of Human Knowledge, Pt. 1, sec. 33.
16. Kant: Critique of Pure Reason, 1st ed., p. 376.
17. Ibid., p. 225.
18. Plato: Parmenides, 141, 152.
19. Hobbes: The Third Set of Objections to Descartes' Meditations, Objection Fourteenth. Descartes: Oeuvres, ed. by Adam and Tannery, vol. 9, p. 150.
20. Crusius: Entwurf der Notwendigen Vernunft-Wahrheiten, 1753, sec. 46.
21. Ibid., sec. 57. See also sec. 59.
22. p. 79 et seq.
23. Wolff: Ontologia, § 493.
24. Langley: Leibniz's New Essays, etc., 1916, p. 718. Gerhardt, vol. 7, p. 320.
25. Duncan: Philosophical Works of Leibniz, 2nd ed., p. 48. Animadversions on Descartes' Principles of Philosophy—on Article 4.
26. Leibniz: New Essays on the Human Understanding, Bk. 4, ch. 4, sec. 4.

27. p. 29.
28. pp. 48-9.

NOTES TO CHAPTER THREE

1. It is the partial explanation of "reality" as set forth in the above paragraph that invalidates—for us—the Anselmian ontological argument. Assuming that existence is an element in perfection, a perfect subsistent appears as existing. But if explicitly or implicitly it also appears as non-existent, it is not to be listed as real.

2. p. 42.

3. The emphasis is on the "we," and our resolve is to be expressed in singular propositions. If we were to lay down the universal proposition: "No subsistents are real which resemble one which develops contradictoriness," the 'King of England residing in Buckingham Palace' who develops contradictoriness would carry with him into the world of unreality all Kings of England living in Buckingham Palace.

4. p. 42.

5. Berkeley: The First Dialogue between Hylas and Philonous. Ed. by Frazer, v. 1, p. 411.

6. Berkeley: Principles of Human Knowledge, Pt. 1, sec. 23.

7. Perry: Present Philosophical Tendencies. p. 129.

8. Ibid., p. 130.

9. Ibid., p. 131.

10. It is a subsistent but, as will appear later, not a real object for any subject.

11. p. 71.

12. Spaulding: The New Rationalism, p. 381.

13. p. 70.

14. p. 41.

15. p. 48.

16. p. 76.

17. pp. 78-9.

18. p. 71.

19. p. 79.

NOTES TO CHAPTER FOUR

1. Cf. p. 540 et seq.

2. Cf. p. 307.

3. p. 95.

4. Locke says, I think incorrectly, that "the common use of language

. . . permits not any two abstract words . . . to be affirmed one of another." Essay: Bk. 3, Ch. 8, sec. 1.

5. Monist, 1919, p. 195.
6. G. E. Moore: The Nature of Judgment, Mind, no. 30, p. 180.
7. p. 132.
8. p. 101.
9. Rickert: Der Gegenstand der Erkenntnis, 1st ed., sec. 14, p. 63. 2nd ed., ch. 3, sec. 5, p. 116.
10. James: Pragmatism, p. 228.
11. Descartes: Meditations, III.
12. p. 101.
13. Leibniz: New Essays, Bk. 4, ch. 5, § 2.
14. p. 95.
15. p. 97.
16. p. 80.
17. p. 70.
18. p. 70.
19. p. 47.
20. p. 36.
21. p. 68.
22. p. 98.
23. p. 100.
24. p. 113.
25. Cf. Lotze: Logik, Bk. 1, ch. 2.
26. Cf. Lotze: Logik, Bk. 1, ch. 2, §§ 59, 60. Also Bradley: Logic, pp. 22-25.
27. p. 442 et seq; p. 501 et seq.
28. p. 117.
29. p. 9.
30. p. 9.
31. p. 121.
32. Cf. Bertrand Russell.
33. p. 121.
34. p. 111.
35. Coffee: Science of Logic, vol. 1, p. 189.
36. Hobbes: De Corpore, Bk. 1, ch. 3, § 7.
37. p. 122.
38. p. 123.
39. pp. 119-120.
40. p. 116.
41. p. 69.
42. p. 101.

43. p. 103.
44. p. 127.
45. p. 126.
46. p. 127.

NOTES TO CHAPTER FIVE

1. pp. 113-4.
2. pp. 121-2.
3. p. 100.
4. p. 117.
5. Whitehead & Russell: Principia Mathematica, 2nd ed., 1925, p. 37.
6. Ibid., p. 64.
7. p. 479.
8. p. 527.
9. p. 551.
10. p. 113.
11. p. 10.
12. p. 117.
13. p. 120.
14. p. 138.
15. p. 121.
16. p. 122.
17. p. 140.
18. p. 138.
19. H. Vaihinger: The Philosophy of As If; translation by Ogden, 1924, p. 80.
20. A similar discussion occurs at pp. 251-2.
21. p. 133.
22. pp. 139, 140.
23. p. 139.
24. Cf. B. Russell: Monist, 1919, p. 355.
25. p. 72.
26. pp. 134, 135.
27. p. 100.
28. Diogenes Laertius: The Lives and Opinions of Eminent Philosophers. Translation by Yonge, 1853, p. 399.
29. p. 145.
30. pp. 90-1.
31. p. 100.
32. pp. 91-2.
33. "Implication" is used here in a narrow sense, in a sense in which

there are implications in the fields of mathematics and logic, but not from one physical event to another. See p. 595.

34. p. 139.
35. p. 144.
36. pp. 140-1.
37. p. 149.
38. p. 152.
39. p. 152.
40. pp. 7, 20.
41. pp. 19, 20.

NOTES TO CHAPTER SIX

1. p. 20.
2. p. 126.
3. p. 111.
4. Hume: Treatise, Bk. 1, ch. 4, sec. 6.
5. A. O. Lovejoy: On the Existence of Ideas, J. H. U. Circular, 1914, p. 218.
6. p. 75.
7. Descartes: Meditations, 2.
8. B. H. Bode: Consciousness as Behavior: Journal of Philosophy, 1918, p. 452.
9. S. Alexander: Space, Time and Deity, v. 2, p. 32 et seq.
10. Descartes: Meditations, 6.
11. Fourth Set of Objections to Descartes' Meditations.
12. Descartes: Principles of Philosophy, Pt. 1, Prin. 60.
13. p. 24.
14. Wm. McDougall: Body and Mind, 5th ed., 1920, p. 364.
15. p. 168.
16. Descartes: Meditations, 6.
17. p. 159.
18. p. 161.
19. p. 168.
20. p. 172.
21. R. W. Sellars: The Philosophy of Physical Realism, 1932, p. 408. Sellars, however, may not intend the words in quotation marks to be predicated of thinking as we have described it.
22. Ibid., p. 421.
23. p. 159.
24. p. 161.

25. Ward: Naturalism and Agnosticism, vol. 2, p. 19.

26. p. 164.

27. J. B. Pratt: The Present Status of the Mind-Body Problem; Philosophical Review, v. 45, p. 147.

28. Shadworth H. Hodgson's Review of Flournay's Metaphysique et Psychologie, "Brain," 1894, v. 17, p. 108.

29. J. B. Watson: Behavior, p. 11.

30. p. 89.

31. p. 165.

32. p. 166.

33. p. 163.

34. p. 164.

35. p. 163.

NOTES TO CHAPTER SEVEN

1. p. 186.

2. See moreover, p. 216.

3. p. 177.

4. Malebranche: Search after Truth, vol. 2, Bk. 5, ch. 1.

5. Ibid., Bk, 6, Pt. 2, ch. 3.

6. p. 191.

7. pp. 191-2.

8. p. 181.

9. p. 163.

10. Spinoza: Ethics, Bk. 2, Prop. 7.

11. p. 159.

12. p. 178.

13. p. 174.

14. p. 423.

15. p. 198.

16. p. 199.

17. pp. 117-8.

18. pp. 162-3.

19. Berkeley: Third Dialogue between Hylas and Philonous, Frazer, v. 1, p. 450.

20. p. 164.

21. p. 201.

22. p. 196.

23. The statement that the person taken as a whole is not aware of mental attitudes does not imply that the person taken as a whole is not an object for mental attitudes.

24. Kant: Critique of Pure Reason, 1st ed., p. 107.

25. p. 203.

26. Plato: Phaedo, 78.

27. p. 173.

28. p. 205.

29. p. 199.

30. p. 209.

31. p. 191.

32. Cf. Paulsen: Introduction to Philosophy, 2nd American ed. Trans. by Thilley, p. 100.

33. p. 192.

34. p. 86.

35. p. 210.

36. p. 199.

37. "Every theory," says Lotze, (Microcosmus, Bk. 3, ch. 2) "must search out a seat for the soul." But the seat of the soul varies with that substance, composed of thinking substances, which is taken to be the soul.

38. Hamlet, Act 5, scene 2: "If Hamlet from himself be taken away, and when he's not himself does wrong Laërtes, then Hamlet does it not; Hamlet denies it."

39. Cf. Locke's Essay: Bk. 2, ch. 1, sec. 10.

40. p. 386.

41. pp. 211-2.

42. p. 208.

43. p. 187.

44. Fechner: Ueber die Seelenfrage, 1861, p. 5.

45. p. 187.

46. p. 166.

47. p. 77.

48. p. 79.

49. Fechner: Ueber die Seelenfrage, 1861, p. 189.

NOTES TO CHAPTER EIGHT

1. p. 193.

2. p. 177.

3. p. 166.

4. p. 163.

5. p. 188.

6. pp. 225-6.

7. p. 485 et seq.

8. pp. 192-3.

9. p. 193.

10. p. 178.

11. p. 193.

12. Kant: Critique of Pure Reason, 2nd ed., Of the Deduction of the Pure Concepts of the Understanding, 2nd sec. § 15.

13. p. 193.

14. p. 228.

15. p. 229.

16. pp. 229, 230.

17. p. 226.

18. p. 227.

19. Cf. p. 224.

20. p. 226.

21. p. 11.

22. pp. 235-6.

23. Thomas Reid: "An Inquiry into the Human Mind," ch. 6, sec. 20.

24. Antoine Arnauld: "Des Vrais et des Fausses Idées," ch. 6.

25. p. 163.

26. p. 163.

27. p. 231.

28. p. 201.

29. p. 231.

30. p. 240.

31. p. 80.

32. p. 234.

33. Malebranche: Recherche de la Verité, Bk. 3, Pt. 2, ch. 1.

34. W. P. Montague: Two Recent Views of the Problem of Realism. Journal of Philosophy, 1904, p. 295.

35. p. 228.

36. p. 231.

37. pp. 237-8.

38. p. 234.

39. A. O. Lovejoy: The Revolt against Dualism, p. 17.

40. Lovejoy: On Some Novelties of the New Realism. Journal of Philosophy, 1913, p. 42.

41. Malebranche: Recherche de la Verité, Bk. 3, Pt. 2, ch. 1.

42. p. 168.

43. p. 190.

44. p. 234.

45. Cf.: "Essays in Critical Realism," where the term "essence" is, I think unfortunately, used to represent either such entities as the Emperor's piety (Cf. pp. 237-8), piety in general, or some non-spatial universal (Cf. p. 569).

46. p. 81.

47. Cf. p. 75.

48. p. 239.

49. p. 236.

50. p. 234.

51. p. 246.

52. p. 241.

53. p. 226.

54. p. 142.

55. pp. 144-5.

56. pp. 139, 140.

57. E.g., p. 176.

58. p. 247.

59. Cf. p. 176.

60. Cf.: Proc. Aris. Soc., 1917, p. 117; G. E. Moore: The Conception of Reality, p. 215.

61. p. 128.

NOTES TO CHAPTER NINE

1. p. 228.

2. p. 234.

3. p. 193.

4. p. 193.

5. p. 232.

6. p. 234.

7. p. 260.

8. p. 75.

9. pp. 154-5.

10. Descartes: Meditations, 2. Quoted above, p. 165.

11. p. 165.

12. p. 258.

13. p. 232.

14. p. 193.

15. p. 259.

16. p. 248.

17. Cf. James: Essays in Radical Empiricism, p. 123.

18. Bertrand Russell: The Problems of Philosophy, 31.

19. pp. 250-1.
20. pp. 241, 249.
21. p. 253.
22. p. 256.
23. pp. 258-9.
24. pp. 247-8.
25. p. 248.
26. p. 266.
27. p. 268.
28. p. 267.
29. p. 230.
30. pp. 236, 247.
31. pp. 231, 242.
32. p. 243.
33. Kant: Critique of Pure Reason, 1st ed., p. 102.
34. p. 246.
35. p. 271.
36. Kant: Critique of Pure Reason, 1st ed., p. 103.
37. p. 75.
38. Cf. p. 81.
39. p. 260.
40. p. 224.
41. p. 233.
42. pp. 250-2.
43. p. 269.
44. pp. 267-8.
45. p. 271.
46. pp. 501-5.
47. E.g., p. 178.
48. p. 276.
49. p. 265.
50. p. 267.
51. Cf. pp. 254-5.
52. pp. 276-7.
53. p. 277.
54. p. 261.
55. p. 75.
56. p. 271.
57. p. 202.
58. p. 234.
59. p. 79.
60. p. 80.

61. p. 75.
62. pp. 202-3.

NOTES TO CHAPTER TEN

1. pp. 258-9.
2. p. 270.
3. p. 275.
4. p. 161 et seq.
5. p. 163.
6. pp. 165-6.
7. pp. 224-5.
8. pp. 184-6.
9. pp. 202-3.
10. p. 271.
11. pp. 205-6.
12. p. 235 et seq.
13. pp. 247-8.
14. p. 162.
15. A feeling, as we describe it, is a mental attitude such as fearing, hating, hoping, etc. It should not be confused with the perceiving of surfaces by means of the sense of touch. What we call "feelings" correspond roughly with what in the seventeenth and eighteenth centuries were called "the passions of the soul." I should prefer to reserve the term "emotions" for those situations in which feeling is accompanied by overt behavior.
16. pp. 249, 250.
17. p. 251.
18. pp. 266-7.
19. p. 298.
20. p. 108.
21. p. 17.
22. p. 7.
23. p. 113.
24. p. 89.
25. p. 89.
26. p. 285.
27. p. 301.
28. p. 109.
29. pp. 301-2.
30. p. 110.
31. Leibniz: New Essays, Bk. 4, ch. 5, § 2. Quoted above, p. 106.

32. Locke: Essay, Bk. 4, ch. 1, sec. 8.

33. Leibniz: What is Idea? Langley, 1916, p. 716; Gerhardt, vol. 7, p. 263.

34. Bertrand Russell: Our Knowledge of the External World, p. 145. See also Russell's: Mysticism and Logic, p. 214; Proceedings of the Aristotelian Society, 1910-11; Sellars: Critical Realism, p. 257; James: The Meaning of Truth, 1909, p. 11.

35. p. 307.

36. p. 292.

37. p. 293.

38. Cf. Spinoza: On the Emendation of the Understanding, §§ 30-35.

39. pp. 293-4.

40. p. 100.

41. pp. 309, 310.

42. p. 101.

43. p. 103.

44. p. 105.

45. p. 68.

46. p. 52.

47. pp. 59-60.

48. p. 315.

49. p. 49.

50. p. 107.

51. p. 246.

52. p. 199 et seq.

53. p. 125.

NOTES TO CHAPTER ELEVEN

1. p. 159.

2. p. 159.

3. p. 84.

4. pp. 193, 231-2, 259, 264.

5. p. 275.

6. p. 259.

7. p. 275.

8. p. 83.

9. p. 276.

10. p. 224.

11. pp. 275-6.

12. p. 86.

13. pp. 91-2.

14. C. D. Broad: Scientific Thought, p. 45.

15. p. 26.

16. Russell: Our Knowledge of the External World as a Field for Scientific Method in Philosophy. Open Court, 1914, p. 181.

17. Lucretius: On the Nature of Things, Bk. 1, line 968.

18. p. 37.

19. Bradley: Appearance and Reality, 2nd ed., revised, 1902, p. 291.

20. Kant: Critique of Pure Reason, 1st ed., p. 413.

21. Ibid., p. 24.

22. I use "space" without a capital "S" and "three-dimensional figure" as synonymous. Whatever has volume is a space.

23. p. 344.

24. p. 342.

25. p. 78.

26. Spatiality is the possibility of position with respect to various entities in the sense that an entity presented as non-spatial and yet as having position with respect to various entities is implicitly presented as self-contradictory. See other references to self-contradiction and possibility on pp. 150-1, 589-90.

27. Kant: Critique of Pure Reason, 2nd ed., Of the Deduction of the Pure Concepts of the Understanding, 2nd sec., § 18. Cf. p. 231.

28. p. 276.

29. pp. 332-3.

NOTES TO CHAPTER TWELVE

1. p. 325.

2. p. 325.

3. p. 354.

4. p. 363.

5. p. 269.

6. p. 328.

7. pp. 282-3.

8. p. 17.

9. p. 152.

10. pp. 249, 250.

11. p. 252.

12. p. 128.

13. C. D. Broad: Scientific Thought, 1927, p 66.

14. p. 78.

15. pp. 365-6.

16. p. 331.
17. p. 331.
18. p. 81.
19. p. 352.
20. p. 354.
21. pp. 271-2.
22. p. 275.
23. pp. 196-8.
24. Schopenhauer: On the Fourfold Root, etc., § 18.
25. p. 117.
26. p. 332.
27. p. 331.
28. p. 346.
29. p. 343.
30. p. 341.
31. Leibniz: Fifth Paper to Clarke, § 74.
32. Kant: Critique of Pure Reason, 1st ed., p. 410.
33. p. 367.
34. p. 367.
35. p. 380.
36. pp. 377-8.
37. p. 379.
38. p. 338.
39. Locke: Essay; Bk. 2, ch. 14, sec. 18.
40. pp. 353, 363-4.
41. pp. 234-5, 275.
42. Cf. Flammarion, Lumen, Eng. tr., London, 1897, p. 93.
43. Kant: Critique of Pure Reason. Tr. by Müller, p. 784. The reason Kant gives for this conclusion need not be considered in this discussion. For if the objects of my thinking are present momentary data, they lack permanence whether they have position or not.
44. Bergson: Time and Free Will. Tr. by Pogson, p. 77. Cf. also Ravaisson: Essai sur l'habitude; Revue de Metaphysique et de Morale, 1894, p. 11. Quoted by Lovejoy in "Mind," 1913, p. 469.
45. p. 387.
46. p. 378.

NOTES TO CHAPTER THIRTEEN

1. p. 351.
2. p. 352.
3. p. 331.

4. p. 489.
5. pp. 91-2.
6. p. 361.
7. p. 385.
8. p. 386.
9. p. 396.
10. p. 397.
11. Our explanation of "motion" would seem to require some correction if we are to call "in motion" that entity which returns periodically to the same place. But with respect to the use that we are to make of the term "motion," this is a trifling point.
12. p. 379.
13. Aristotle: Topics, Θ 8, 160 b 8.
14. p. 340.
15. p. 79.
16. p. 399.
17. p. 399.
18. Bergson: Creative Evolution; tr. by Mitchell, p. 305.
19. Ibid., p. 314.
20. p. 341.
21. p. 400.
22. p. 404.
23. p. 398.
24. p. 406.
25. p. 354.
26. p. 399.
27. p. 376.
28. p. 410.
29. p. 410.
30. p. 372.
31. p. 355.
32. pp. 394-5.
33. pp. 377-8.
34. p. 388.
35. p. 400.
36. p. 406.
37. p. 345.
38. p. 399.
39. p. 356.
40. The contrast, though not the use of it, is taken from Kant: Critique of Pure Reason, 1st ed., p. 192. Cf. also Lovejoy: On Kant's Reply to Hume, Archiv für Geschichte der Philosophie, 1906, Bk. 19,

617

Heft 3, p. 395.

41. Cf. p. 389.
42. p. 400.
43. p. 347.
44. Lucretius: On the Nature of Things, Bk. 1, line 334.
45. p. 417.
46. p. 345.

NOTES TO CHAPTER FOURTEEN

1. pp. 393-4.
2. p. 405.
3. p. 347.
4. p. 178.
5. p. 326.
6. p. 248 et seq.
7. pp. 333-7.
8. p. 73 et seq.
9. pp. 282-3.
10. p. 422.
11. pp. 390-1.
12. p. 379.
13. pp. 417-8, 420.
14. F. H. Bradley: Appearance and Reality, 2nd ed., p. 63.
15. p. 199 et seq.
16. p. 386.
17. p. 430.
18. Leibniz: New Essays, Bk. 2, ch. 27.
19. p. 420.
20. p. 330.
21. Leibniz: A New System, § 11; Duncan, p. 82.
22. Leibniz: Letter to Arnauld, 1690; Duncan, p. 39.
23. Leibniz: Principles of Nature and of Grace, 1714, § 3. Duncan, p. 299.
24. Leibniz: On the Doctrine of Malebranche, § 3; Duncan, p. 325.
25. p. 435.
26. Bosanquet: The Principle of Individuality and of Value, 1912, p. 68.
27. Ibid., p. 70.
28. Ibid., p. 68, margin.
29. Spinoza: Ethics, Pt. 1, Prop. 8.
30. Ibid., Pt. 1, Prop. 12, Proof; and Prop. 13, Corollary.

31. p. 86.
32. p. 80.
33. Cf. p. 200.
34. p. 428.
35. p. 428.
36. Kant: Critique of Pure Reason, 1st ed., p. 184.
37. pp. 375-6.
38. Bradley: Principles of Logic, Bk. 1, ch. 2, § 62.
39. p. 438.
40. Locke: Essay on Human Understanding, Bk. 2, ch, 2, sec. 1.
41. p. 259.
42. p. 443.
43. Berkeley: Third Dialogue between Hylas and Philonous, Frazer, vol. 1, p. 469.
44. Locke: Essay, Bk. 1, ch. 4, § 18.
45. p. 439.
46. Descartes: Principles of Philosophy, Pt. 1, Prin. 52.
47. Malebranche: Dialogues on Metaphysics and on Religion, Dialogue 1. Trans. by Ginsberg, 1923, p. 73.
48. p. 439.
49. Spinoza: Ethics, Part 1, Def. 3.
50. Ibid., Part 1, Prop. 6—Another Proof.
51. Descartes: Principles of Philosophy, Pt. 1, Prin. 51.
52. p. 437.
53. p. 438.
54. Aristotle: Cat. v, 3a, 36.
55. Coffee: Science of Logic, v. 1, p. 139.
56. p. 439.
57. Kant: Critique of Pure Reason, 2nd ed., Of the Deduction of the Pure Concepts of the Understanding, 2nd sec., Müller, § 23, p. 756. Cf. also Müller, p. 782.
58. Kant: Critique of Pure Reason, 1st ed., p. 147, Cf. also p. 242.
59. pp. 125-6.
60. p. 423.
61. pp. 428, 440.
62. p. 427.
63. p. 440.
64. p. 99.
65. p. 460 et seq.
66. p. 452.
67. p. 26.

NOTES TO CHAPTER FIFTEEN

1. Bradley: Appearance and Reality, ch. 1.
2. pp. 441-2.
3. Locke: Essay, Bk. 2, ch. 8, sec. 21.
4. Descartes: Principles of Philosophy, Pt. 4, Prin. 198.
5. Leibniz: Animadversions on Descartes' Principles of Philosophy, 1692.
6. Berkeley: First Dialogue between Hylas and Philonous, Frazer, vol. 1, p. 394.
7. Ibid., vol. 1, p. 395.
8. S. Alexander: Space, Time and Deity, vol. 2, p. 58.
9. p. 352.
10. p. 248 et seq.
11. Berkeley: First Dialogue between Hylas and Philonous, Frazer, v. 1, p. 390.
12. Ibid., p. 385.
13. Locke: Essay on Human Understanding, Bk. 2, ch. 8, sec. 16.
14. p. 467.
15. p. 259.
16. p. 296.
17. "Aching" is not a completely satisfactory word to represent the violently unhappy mental state to which I refer. Its virtue is that it ends in "ing," thus suggesting mental activity rather than passive content.
18. p. 467.
19. p. 471.
20. Locke: Essay, Bk. 2, ch. 8, sec. 21. Quoted above, p. 461.
21. Berkeley: Principles of Human Knowledge, Pt. 1, § 14.
22. Ibid., Pt. 1, § 15.
23. Leibniz: New Essays, Bk. 2, ch. 8, sec. 21.
24. p. 461.
25. p. 333.
26. Descartes: Rules for the Direction of the Understanding, Rule 12.
27. Locke: Essay, Bk. 2, ch. 21, sec. 73.
28. p. 464.
29. That is, as having special paths open to them through which to bring about mental attitudes directed upon themselves.
30. Cf. McTaggert: The Nature of Existence, ch. 6, § 67. See also ch. 5, § 62, note.

31. F. P. Ramsay: The Foundations of Mathematics, p. 27.
32. Cf. p. 439.
33. There is a reference to abstract nouns on p. 99.
34. Cf. p. 470.
35. p. 454.
36. pp. 428, 440, 452.
37. pp. 339, 340.
38. p. 464.
39. p. 474.
40. Leibniz: New Essays, Bk. 2, ch. 25, sec. 10.
41. p. 351.
42. p. 352.
43. pp. 249, 250.
44. p. 463.
45. Russell: On the Notion of Order, Mind, N.S., vol. 10, 1901, p. 39.
46. In various sections of this treatise we have discussed some relation between two entities. The emphasis, however, has not been on the "between." Rather, the expression: "the relation between A and B" has represented some relational situation including A and B and not an alleged link, has represented A-r-B and not just r.
47. p. 486.
48. Leibniz: Fifth Paper to Clarke, § 47.
49. Kant: Critique of Pure Reason, 2nd ed. Trans. by Müller, p. 744.
50. Ibid., p. 747.
51. p. 356.
52. p. 373.
53. pp. 454, 481-2.
54. p. 488.
55. p. 493.
56. p. 482.
57. Locke: Essay, Bk. 2, ch. 25, sec. 5.
58. pp. 441-2.
59. Leibniz: On the Method of Distinguishing Real from Imaginary Phenomena, Gerhardt, vol. 7, p. 322.
60. pp. 484-5.
61. Kant: Critique of Pure Reason, 1st ed., p. 277.
62. pp. 464-5.
63. pp. 484-5.
64. p. 438.
65. Bradley: Principles of Logic, Bk. 1, ch. 2, § 67.

NOTES TO CHAPTER SIXTEEN

1. Psalm 8, 4-5.
2. B. Russell: Principles of Mathematics, vol. 1, p. 53.
3. p. 80.
4. pp. 29, 64.
5. p. 128.
6. There is of course the exceptional case: "Universal A is unreal." Cf. p. 135.
7. Nisolius: Anti-Barbarus, Bk. 3, ch. 8. Trans. by Haureau: Histoire de la Philosophie Scholastique, 1872, v. 1, p. 329.
8. Plato: Parmenides, 131.
9. pp. 439, 442-3.
10. p. 428.
11. p. 423.
12. p. 440.
13. p. 81.
14. p. 500.
15. pp. 46-7.
16. p. 439.
17. pp. 479, 480.
18. p. 454.
19. p. 505.
21. p. 270.
20. pp. 40-1.
22. pp. 278-9.
23. p. 483.
24. p. 503.
25. p. 502.
26. Cf. Aristotle: Metaphysics. 13, 9; Kant: Critique of Pure Reason, 1st ed., p. 654; Bradley: The Principles of Logic, 2nd ed., 1922, vol. 1, Bk. 1, ch. 2, § 78.
27. p. 519.
28. p. 275.
29. p. 511.
30. p. 511.
31. Abelard: De Intellectibus. Appendix to vol. 3 of the Fragments, ed. by Cousin. Trans. by De Remusat: Abelard, vol. 1, p. 495. Quoted by Haureau: Histoire de la Philosophie Scholastique, 1872, vol. 1, p. 381.
32. pp. 291-2.

33. p. 471.
34. Locke: Essay, Bk. 3, ch. 3, sec. 6.
35. Berkeley: Principles of Human Knowledge. Introduction, § 8.
36. Ibid., Introduction, § 15.
37. Kant: Critique of Pure Reason, 1st ed., p. 140.
38. Ibid., p. 141.
39. p. 246.
40. p. 512.
41. Locke: Essay, Bk. 3, ch. 6, sec. 32.
42. Plato: Phaedo, 75. Cf. also: Meno, 85-6.
43. p. 513.
44. p. 517.
45. That is, it is no *re*presentation. It is a presentation or object in introspection, for example, or in such discussions as we are here engaged in.
46. p. 505.
47. p. 84.
48. p. 279.
49. p. 502.
50. p. 514.
51. p. 346 et seq.
52. pp. 503-4.
53. Cf. p. 506.
54. pp. 568-570.
55. p. 503.
56. p. 495.
57. p. 523.
58. Whitehead and Russell: Principia Mathematica, vol. 1, p. 60.
59. Cf. B. Russell: The Principles of Mathematics, vol. 1, p. 31.
60. p. 68.
61. pp. 519-520.
62. pp. 249, 250.
63. See, however, p. 533.
64. p. 485.
65. p. 487.
66. p. 492.
67. Cf. Plato: Parmenides, 132, 133.
68. pp. 492-3.
69. p. 531.
70. pp. 520-1.
71. pp. 349, 350.
72. p. 124.

73. pp. 312-3.
74. p. 124.
75. pp. 122-3.
76. p. 340.

NOTES TO CHAPTER SEVENTEEN

1. p. 190.
2. p. 192-3.
3. p. 199.
4. Cf. A. Meinong: Uber Annahmen; Zeitschrift für Psychologie und Physiologie des Sinnesorgane, Erganzungsband 2, p. 20.
5. p. 291.
6. pp. 293-4.
7. pp. 165-6, 289, 290.
8. pp. 241, 249.
9. p. 539.
10. p. 252 et seq.
11. Cf. pp. 296-7.
12. p. 107.
13. pp. 109, 110.
14. p. 254-5.
15. pp. 100, 101.
16. p. 98.
17. Whitehead and Russell: Principia Mathematica, v. 1, p. 31.
18. p. 523.
19. Cf. quotation in Ogden and Richards: The Meaning of Meaning, 1923, p. 421; Husserl: Logische Untersuchungen, II, pp. 47, 389. Other references in Parkhurst: Recent Logical Realism.
20. p. 80.
21. Locke: Essay, Bk. 3, ch. 2, sec. 2.
22. p. 245.
23. p. 540.
24. pp. 162, 237.
25. pp. 205-6.
26. p. 489.
27. Whitehead and Russell: Principia Mathematica, vol. 1, p. 64.
28. Cf. p. 136.
29. Whitehead and Russell: Principia Mathematica, vol. 1, p. 63.
30. p. 75.
31. Cf. pp. 128-9.
32. p. 543.

33. p. 542.

34. p. 503.

35. p. 540.

36. Cf. Hobbes: Leviathan, Pt. 1, ch. 4. Ed. by Molesworth, v. 3, p. 28.

37. The distinction is analogous to that between a mental attitude directed upon a memory and a mental attitude aware of a memory as a memory. Cf. pp. 271, 293.

38. p. 549.

39. pp. 369, 370.

40. Cf. Ogden and Richards: The Meaning of Meaning, 1923, p. 336.

41. Cf. Malebranche: The Search after Truth, Bk. 1, ch. 13.

42. If Mrs. Jones is a wife *in name only*, she lacks some of the qualities that characterize wives and hence is not really a wife. But like wives, she has the quality of being called "Mrs." The quality by virtue of which she resembles wives is a quality that concerns nomenclature, but it is a real quality none the less.

43. Cf. W. E. Johnson: Logic, v. 1, p. 105.

44. Joseph: An Introduction to Logic. 2nd Ed., 1916, p. 114.

45. Ibid., p. 111.

46. p. 559.

47. p. 558.

48. p. 92.

49. p. 35.

50. pp. 559, 560.

51. p. 561.

52. p. 559.

53. Hamilton: Lectures on Metaphysics and Logic, New York, 1884, vol. 2, p. 344.

54. p. 523.

55. p. 562.

56. p. 548.

57. An identical proposition such as: "A man is a man" is a definition which is tautological. But there are tautological propositions which are not definitions, such as: "Bald men are bald" and "Existing men exist."

58. Cf. p. 114.

59. p. 554.

60. p. 523.

61. p. 523.

62. p. 562.

63. p. 564.

64. p. 72.

65. Cf. p. 28. The distinction between analytic and synthetic is also alluded to on p. 536.

66. Essays in Critical Realism, p. 168, note.

67. Ibid., p. 183.

68. p. 549.

69. p. 511.

70. Cf. p. 247.

71. p. 313.

72. p. 122.

73. p. 562.

74. p. 562.

75. Hobbes: De Corpore, Pt. 1, ch. 6, § 15.

76. Cf. Whitehead and Russell: Principia Mathematica, vol. 1, pp. 11, 12; Ogden and Richards: The Meaning of Meaning, 1923, p. 209.

77. Another motive is to distinguish between universals which may be confused. In this treatise, for example, identity and sameness, explanation and definition are distinguished—partly through the explanations of the expressions assigned to represent them.

78. p. 561.

79. p. 562.

80. p. 555.

81. p. 549.

82. p. 573.

83. p. 542.

84. p. 19.

NOTES TO CHAPTER EIGHTEEN

1. p. 453.

2. Dantzig: Number or the Language of Science, p. 190.

NOTES TO CHAPTER TWENTY-TWO

1. pp. 568-9.

2. On pp. 152-3, however, the latter are held not to be implications at all. That is to say, there are passages in which I say A implies B only when belief in A, despite the lack of an extensive context, causes the belief in B.

NOTES TO CHAPTER TWENTY-FOUR

1. It is *our* use of "chance" that we are setting forth. It would appear that, as generally used, "chance" has neither of the meanings that we first considered and rejected. But as we proceed towards a precise use of "chance" that we find acceptable, it is only of our own use of "chance" that we can speak with assurance.

INDEX OF TERMS EXPLAINED

631

632